Out of Print in Hardcover
Was 29⁹⁵
In Paper only @ 17⁹⁵
, 9⁹⁵
(X)

D0821375

Clarence King

CLARENCE KING

A BIOGRAPHY
Revised and Enlarged Edition

Thurman Wilkins
With the help of
Caroline Lawson Hinkley

University of New Mexico Press • Albuquerque

Library of Congress Cataloging-in-Publication Data

Wilkins, Thurman.
    Clarence King : a biography / Thurman Wilkins
with the help of Caroline Hinkley. — Rev. and enlarged ed.
        p.   cm.
    Bibliography: p.
    Includes index.
    ISBN 0-8263-1096-6.   ISBN 0-8263-1085-0 (pbk.)
    1. King, Clarence, 1842–1901. 2. Geologists—United
States—Biography.   I. Hinkley, Caroline.   II. Title.
QE22.K5W5 1988
550'.92'4—dc19
[B]   88-14408
                                                                  CIP

© 1988 by Thurman Wilkins. All rights reserved. Originally
published and © 1958, The Macmillan Co. LC# 58-6965/4R85.
Revised and expanded edition published by the University of New
Mexico Press by arrangement with the author, 1988.

To the memory of
Vernon Loggins
Professor Emeritus of English
Columbia University

Contents

Preface to the Second Edition   ix
1   Enter Clarence King   1
2   The Wind's Will   15
3   The Yale Years   30
4   Shasta, Here We Come   40
5   Rooftop of the West   57
6   End of Apprenticeship   75
7   Along the Fortieth Parallel   99
8   From Washoe to the Rockies   119
9   *Mountaineering . . .*   139
10   King of Diamonds   167
11   The Pass Beyond Youth   186
12   *Systematic Geology*   206
13   Cattle Baron   230
14   Establishment of the U.S. Geological Survey   253
15   Director of Geology   271
16   Treasures of the Sierra Madre   293
17   European Interlude   312
18   Silver Clouds and Darker Linings   336
19   Panic   365
20   Ebb Tide   390
Epilogue   412
Selected Bibliography   415
Notes   443
Index   487
Illustrations following pages 90 and 242

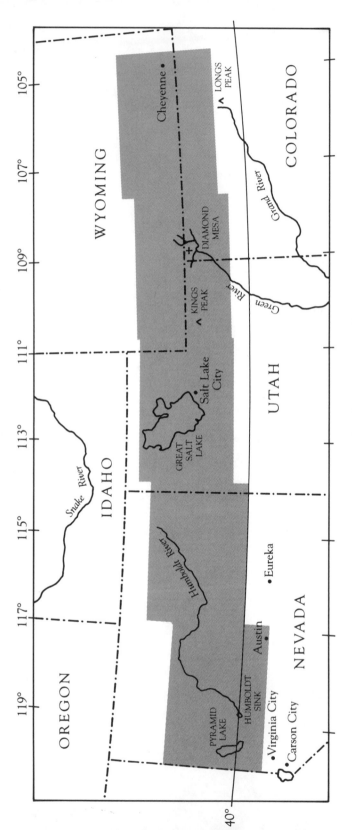

Map 1. Area covered by the Fortieth Parallel Survey.

Preface to the Second Edition

"King ought to have written his own life," Henry Adams once remarked to S. F. Emmons, the geologist, who had finished a memoir of their mutual friend,

> and the world has lost a book of capital interest in losing it; but the world may go hang, for all it can get now. We know what it has lost, and I am glad you have made a memorandum of it, to complete the record. Yet it makes me wonder at geology when I think that this is all that remains of the most remarkable man of our time. One of Walcott's Siberian trilobites has left about as much. King would have put it all easily into one short Hic jacet Echinognathus Rex, and would have stuffed it into your Survey rocks for fun. Only he would not have felt sore about it, as we do.

Certainly the friends of Clarence King had a right to feel "sore about it"; what they had seen in King's young manhood had promised to leave a deep impression on American civilization. Yet King's destiny, as they had also seen, had led only to tragic frustrations.

We agree with Adams—King should have told his story himself. He would have told it debonairly, as he did in his narratives of youthful adventure in California. His Mountaineering in the Sierra Nevada gives us absorbing accounts of climbs in the Range of Light, climbs which helped to fill wide blanks on the map of California; of his role in the saga of Mount Whitney, apex of the range and of the country; of his finding fossils that determined the age of the Mother Lode's gold-bearing slates; of the survey he ran of the first official boundaries of Yosemite; and of his subsequent sighting of actual glaciers on the flanks of Mount Shasta. The book had interest for both America and Europe, and it prompted Howells to prophesy that King's "work cannot be ignored by the historian of our literature and his name is secure of the remembrance . . . which he sometimes seemed whimsically to deprecate."
I for one was captivated by the charm of Mountaineering when I read it years ago, but I was disappointed to find that no other volume like it had come

from King's pen; that, except for a short sketch on a visit to Spain, he had given us nothing else of his autobiography.

My regret grew, the more I considered King's life, to learn that he had left no personal chronicle of the Fortieth Parallel Survey, no reminiscences of his voyage to the Sandwich Islands or his holidays among the "old-gold girls," no chapter on his bizarre brush with the so-called "Arizona diamond fields," no recollections of cattle ranching on the High Plains, no inside history of his launching the United States Geological Survey or of his work on precious metals for the tenth census, no recapitulation of his geological theories which had proved so stimulating to his colleagues, no memories of his role as expert witness in some of the fabulous mining litigation of the day, or of his ups and downs as manager-promoter of large operations for gold and silver in the Far West and Mexico. One can only speculate on what King might have told us of his journeys into Mexico, or of his two-year tour of Europe, or of his voyages to the Caribbean, including his stay with Adams at Dos Bocas, Cuba.

But upon King's death the full story of his complex career was lost, and the world could go hang, as Henry Adams lamented, for all that it could get now. What follows is a conscientious attempt to piece together what remains of the story, from details gleaned from King's own papers, from letters, diaries, field books, reminiscences, and memoirs of his associates, from government archives and official documents, from contemporary newspapers and periodicals, from court records, and now and then from the work of scholars. Now and then, also, use has been made of the memories of living persons who, having once known Clarence King, have remained in a measure under his spell.

Prefaced by the foregoing remarks, the first edition of this book was published in July 1958. Shortly thereafter Warner Berthoff noted in the *New England Quarterly* that there had been

a ready public for a biography of Clarence King—and a mental hazard for the writer attempting it—ever since *The Education of Henry Adams* put out its tantalizing intimations of the interest and possible symbolism of King's career. The rare promise, the precocity of actual accomplishment, the legendary charm and energy, the ominous unfulfillment and diminuendo—Adams outlined this drama, decreed its intensity, and insinuated an interpretation: that here was a representative American for a whole era of our history.

Professor Berthoff then ventured the opinion that the first edition of this book had run the hazard successfully and deserved to find its public.

It is my hope that the public that was suggested may still be present, and I dare believe that, after thirty years, the time has come for a new edition of *Clarence King* to take advantage of intervening scholarship and certain manuscript materials that I missed the first time around. That a new edition will now be published is due largely to the insistence of Caroline Lawson Hinkley that "*Clarence King* be brought back into print." It was she, moreover, who suggested that the idea be submitted to the University of New Mexico Press, and it is only proper that her further help be given credit on the title page.

My revisions have required no major surgery on the text. I have corrected some minor errors of fact and polished the style in a number of places. I have eliminated certain excess details, rearranged the sequence of a few passages, and reconsidered several points in the development of the narrative. No doubt the most significant difference lies in the addition of numerous details, amounting to nearly thirty-five thousand words, for whatever enhancement they may provide the text. The fresh materials that I have drawn upon include nearly two hundred letters by Clarence King, most of which are found in the Massachusetts Historical Society, the Huntington Library, and Brown University Library, and which were not available to me during my original researches.

In the years of research that preceded the first edition I incurred many unrepayable obligations, only a few of which I specifically acknowledged in the original preface. It gives me pleasure now to reaffirm those debts, especially the ones to the late Leslie E. Bliss, the late Cornelius Kelley, the late Eleanor and Marian Hague, Sherrod East, the late Dow Parkes, the late Francis P. Farquhar, William Culp Darrah, Professors Lewis Leary, David Donald, William A. Owens, Charles H. Behre, Jr., and the late Professors Richard Chase, Elliott V. K. Dobbie and—above all—Vernon Loggins. To the foregoing names I should like to add those of the late Marjorie Hope Nicolson and the late Henry Nash Smith, whose sagacious advice went unacknowledged in the prior preface owing to undue diffidence on my part.

Needless to say, my researches for the preparation of this second edition have incurred further obligations. Let me first of all express my gratitude to Clifford M. Nelson of the U.S. Geological Survey for his judicious suggestions after a critical rereading of the first edition and an examination of selected pages of my revised manuscript. His favors include his providing me generously with needed data, photographs, and various crucial research materials. A basic debt must also be acknowledged to Susan Dissette and Frances Ledbetter for arranging numerous interlibrary loans, without which my researches would have been in trouble. In addition, I should like to thank Timothy Wheeler for his help—as well as Linda Sack, Deanne Hall, Christi Stewart-Brown, Jennie Rathbun, Charles Vandersee, Viola Winner, John D. Cushing, Kathy Griffin, James H. Hutson, Jennifer B. Lee, Katherine Phillips, and Daniel H. Woodward. I should like, furthermore, to acknowledge the assistance of Peter Blodgett, Jon Stefansson, Brita Mack, Elizabeth H. Knight, Roxane Coombs, Susan W. Glenn, Annegret Ogden, Ann Nelson, Emmett D. Chisum, Donald J. Orth, Lew Thompson, Robin McElheny, Ross Urquhart, and Louis L. Tucker. I am also grateful to my former wife Sophie Wilkins and her husband Karl Shapiro for the practical encouragement of accommodations while I researched in New York City. My gratitude extends especially to Kay and Richard O'Grady for many favors and amenities, including transportation when it was most urgently needed.

Investigations for both editions of Clarence King required that I draw on the resources of numerous libraries. My research base for the first edition was the Columbia University Library; for the second edition it has been the Bandon Public Library, for whose services I am profoundly grateful. All the institutions whose aid was specifically acknowledged in my original preface have once again responded to my queries. Hence a second round of thanks to the Columbia University Library, the Huntington Library, the National Archives, the Library of Congress, the Bancroft Library, the New York Public Library, the Yale University Library, the Houghton and Baker Libraries at Harvard, as well as the Library of the Museum of Comparative Zoology. I must add, however, that the intensive review of notes made necessary by my revisions has impressed me anew with the debt I owe to several other libraries and manuscript depositories not specified in my 1958 acknowledgments. It is only fitting that I list them now for belated thanks: The Brown University Library, including the John Hay Library, the Milton S. Eisenhower Library of the Johns Hopkins University, the Cooper Union Library, the New-York Historical Society, the New York State Library, The Denver Public Library, the State Historical Society of Colorado, the San Francisco Public Library, The California State Library, the California Historical Society, the Library of the American Museum of Natural History, the Rutherford B. Hayes Presidential Center, the Connecticut State Library, the Peabody Museum at Yale, the Archives of the Smithsonian Institution, the Library of the Century Association, and the Princeton University Library. Researches for the revised edition have also placed me under obligation to the University of Colorado Library and the Massachusetts Historical Society, the Library of the U.S. Geological Survey, the U.S. Board on Geographical Names, the Boston Public Library, the University of California Library at Berkeley, the University of Oregon Library, the Oregon State Library, the Southwestern Oregon Community College Library, the Wyoming State Archives & Historical Department, and the American Heritage Center of the University of Wyoming, the Library of the Massachusetts Institute of Technology, and the Archives of the American Academy and Institute of Arts and Letters. Lastly, I cannot close these acknowledgments without noting and expressing my heartfelt thanks for the unfailing consideration of my editors, David V. Holtby and Barbara Guth at the University of New Mexico Press.

Bandon, Oregon

1

Enter Clarence King

Dawn of a late October day in 1871 had broken over southern Wyoming, and the air held a threat of snow as a young man rode his mule out on a badlands terrace a day's march from Black Buttes Station. He wore buckskin trousers. A heavy coat emphasized the stockiness of his physique, for though he was shorter than the average, only five-feet six-inches tall, his body was muscular and well-developed. A beard covered his jaws and chin, a close-cropped beard, light brown, but streaked with yellower shades. Sun and wind had darkened the natural ruddiness of his complexion, but outdoor life had failed to coarsen his youthful appearance. Clarence King, United States Geologist, looked younger than his twenty-nine years.

He felt tired and worn, however. Autumn had settled over the mountain country with extraordinary bitterness, and at the end of a hard season in the field its rigors had left King all but exhausted. Rheumatic pains ran through his back and shoulders, reminders of the deep snows, the winds, and the cold that had nearly trapped his survey party in the uplands of the Uinta. The ache had grown through days of hunger, days of eating only broiled venison and the cook's "hot rocks," for the party's fare was running low.

The rest of the company followed close behind. King could hear them coming down the gulley from their one-night camp near a patch of snow—the escort soldiers and the packers shouting at the mules, and the mules grunting under creaking packs, while the *clip-clop* of hoofs echoed through the weirdly weathered terrain.

Suddenly a movement at the edge of the terrace attracted King's attention—something dark moving slowly in the distance. He peered through his field glasses; the thing took shape, a bear rising on its hind legs with its squarish head held high, its mouth hanging open as in a grin. The early light gave its underparts a yellowish tinge which shaded to ashy brown at the sides. It was a huge grizzly, King decided; perhaps

1

a thousand pounder. He drew his single-shot Ballard. The grizzly wheeled, then bounded away on all fours along the edge of the bluff. King shouted to his men and spurred his own mount forward, but the bear loped on at tremendous speed, and managed to keep beyond the range of effective shots.

Suddenly the grizzly scrambled down the bluff, through a draw impassable for mules and horses. It gained several hundred yards before King and those of his men who had joined the hunt could reach the plain below. They chased the bear across a gray sweep of sagebrush until it disappeared amidst a labyrinth of dunes; they followed its gigantic tracks for an hour through the loose sand. Then its trail led back to the badlands, where the bluffs rose like walled cities of the East.

There was no way of riding safely into that tangle of gullies. Because no shrubbery grew there tough enough to serve as hitching posts, they tied the bridles of the animals together to keep them from straying. King took the lead, his rifle ready, and the hunters scrambled up one gulch and down the next, and around sharp corners. Now and then they passed low cavelike channels worn through juttings of shale— short cuts through which the bear had sometimes passed. They came on one such hole about midmorning—a long cave with an arch so low that the bear had grazed his back on rushing into it and left a wisp of hair pinched tightly in a seam.

The old fellow was still inside; no tracks emerged from the other end of the channel. King paused, wondering what to do; he had an abiding respect for grizzly bears. He had seen one kill a steer in California, as he would relate to Theodore Roosevelt; had seen it break the pasture rails which barred its way, overtake its victim in half a dozen bounds, and shatter several ribs from the steer's backbone with a single swipe of its paw.

King listened, caught the sound of the grizzly's breathing and judged that it lay some distance from the mouth of the cave. It would do no good to fire inside at random; so he had his men bring all the dry sedge they could gather, and build a fire at the mouth of the lair. They waited there with rifles ready. But though the smudge made their own eyes stream with tears, the grizzly refused to be smoked out. Delay made King impatient. He kicked the ashes aside and thrust his head inside the hole. In a moment he could see a faint glimmer through the smoke and darkness: the grizzly's eyes? He drew back, his decision made.

"Keep the far end covered," he said to one of the men.

He tied a reata around one of his legs so that he could be dragged from the den in case of trouble. He squirmed back into the hole, leaned on one elbow, shouldered his rifle, and waited for his eyes to readjust themselves to the gloom. He could not distinguish the grizzly's shape, only a glint again, the glint of the bear's eyes; and, aiming at that, he squeezed the trigger. The rifle cracked. Then King came sailing out of the hole, at the rope's end, with one of the escort heaving with all his might. In his fluster the soldier dragged King for some distance over a bed of rough gravel, scratching his face. Since no further sound came from the cave, King's principal aide crept cautiously inside and threw a noose around the grizzly's neck. All strained to pull the carcass out into the light, and then they could see that King's bullet had ripped through the roof of the bear's mouth, lodging in its brain.

"I have known . . . a lot of intrepid bear hunters," wrote a ranching partner years later, "but I have never known any but King with the hardihood to pay a grizzly a visit in the solitude and darkness of its own den."

The hunt of 1871 was to make a favorite campfire story. It under-scored a certain reckless side of Clarence King—the side which placed less value on his reputation as a scientist than on his credit as "a fellow not easily scared." And it was such deeds, so rash and unexpected, that aroused the imagination of his circle, the pleasure and despair of all his friends, the wonder of strangers. "Why, there never was such a man before!" exclaimed Rodman Gilder, on reading afterwards of King's adventures: "If he were alive I should not rest till I had met him."

Many men of the Brownstone Age, in the ease of clubhouse or salon, relived vicariously the experiences which Clarence King was pleased to share with them. "He had a gift for getting unending delight out of life," wrote Royal Cortissoz the art critic,

and for sharing it with all with whom he came in contact. His charm was not by any means for his intimates alone—indeed how could it have been, since it was, after all, but the artless expression of his nature? Brilliant scientist as he was, he had also something of the character of a poet, of the debonair adventurer who goes up and down the world seeking excitement or beauty, some new and vivid sensation, and, through the good fortune that attends such temperaments, finding what he sought by every roadside.

His nimble tongue and twinkling eyes—William Dean Howells de-scribed them as "blithe blue," though King himself called them hazel—

were universally welcome, in company of every sort from humble hardrock miner to lofty millionaire.

His explorations in the West impressed everyone who knew about them. It seemed to C. C. Goodwin, a graduate with Mark Twain of the Washoe press, that King had "explored almost every defile, climbed to the summit of every mountain and lifted the veil from every desert of the West." That, of course, was rank exaggeration; yet the services of the government bureau that King founded—the U.S. Geological Survey—gave satisfaction to the nation. The brilliance of his intellect, the sparkle of his wit, the significance of his scientific accomplishments, the charm of his rare excursions into belles-lettres and—not least of all—what John Hay called "the dazzling attractiveness of his personality" won him fame and a web of friendships which spanned the Atlantic. The degree of esteem that his associates felt for him was suggested by a further statement of Cortissoz: "A man who could hope for even one encounter in a year or two with a friend such as Clarence King . . . might reconcile himself to a desert island." It must have seemed to Cortissoz, as it would to Lloyd Morris, that King was "incandescent."

At his death in 1901, in spite of several years of balked achievement, his place in history seemed so firm that his bust appeared in company with many heroes on the bronze door cast for the Capitol in Washington—a display now mounted in front of the National Museum. For to many, as Van Wyck Brooks has said, he was the symbol—brilliant and mercurial—"of his American generation." Yet a few decades later, as Bernard De Voto added, King's name would survive in appraisals of American civilization almost solely through "his friendship with a person of considerably inferior intelligence, Henry Adams, and through a rumor of scandal that has been attached to him, but what he added to our civilization is not mentioned."

Over Adams, whom he captivated in the season of the bear hunt, he wove a spell that extended back beyond archaic horizons, according to the enchanted one himself—to *Pteraspis* in Siluria. The friendship was immediate, like the attraction of magnetic poles. Remarkable as Adams's circle of acquaintance was, he never claimed a marked capacity for friendship; his intimacies were few, especially in the bitter years which followed his wife's death. "One friend in a life time is much," he said; "two are many; three are hardly possible." He was not given to indiscriminate eulogy; he subjected some of his friends to appraisals as cynical as those which he gave the affairs of Washington or the world;

he weeded his attachments ruthlessly; and among them only John Hay, the protégé of Lincoln, remained as dear as Clarence King.* Their friendship—that of Adams and King—endured for thirty years, renewed whenever they met—in Washington, Quincy, New York, or among the Caribbean islands.

Its spell remained long after Clarence King's lonely death. And *The Education of Henry Adams* reaffirmed it in a manner that would never let it die. In those pages Adams recalled King as a "miracle . . . a bird of paradise rising in the sagebrush . . . an avatar." In retrospect,

King had everything to interest and delight Adam. He knew more than Adams did of art and poetry; he knew America, especially west of the hundredth meridian, better than anyone. . . . He knew even women; even the American woman; even the New York woman, which is saying much. Incidentally he knew more practical geology than was good for him. . . . His wit and humor; his bubbling energy which swept everyone into the current of his interest; his personal charm of youth and manners; his faculty of giving and taking, profusely, lavishly, whether in thought or in money as though he were Nature herself marked him almost alone among Americans. He had in him something of the Greek—a touch of Alcibiades or Alexander. One Clarence King only existed in the world.

In that opinion Adams did not shun agreement; he took pleasure in the wide regard which King inspired. He explained it on the basis of his own conviction that, in King, "men worshipped not so much their friend, as the ideal American they all wanted to be." King was unique, "the most many-sided genius of his day," the perfect representative of young America.

Considered alone, the tribute Adams paid to King's memory might suggest extravagance—the effervescence of one dazzled by a "bird of paradise." Yet it sounded across a reassuring obbligato offered by many articulate friends. James D. Hague, an intimate of King's for more than half a lifetime, collected several eulogies in the *Clarence King Memoirs*, published by the Century Club in 1904. From their pages emerged

*N. B. the claim Adams made on July 9, 1882: "We three, King, Hay and I, are as close to each other as middle-aged sinners can be" (*Letters of Henry Adams*, ed. Levenson et al., II, p. 464). A biographer of Hay would suggest that the relationship of the trio was that of two inhibited men in the company of a third, uninhibited one—a man whose "glorious impulses were [the others'] vicarious adventures" (Dennett, *John Hay*, p. 156).

portraits as brilliant as the profile in *The Education*; as, for instance, when John Hay, the Secretary of State, declared:

Clarence King resembled no one else whom we have ever known. The rest of our friends we divide into classes; King belonged to a class of his own. He was inimitable in many ways: in his inexhaustible fund of wise and witty speech; in his learning about which his marvellous humor played like summer lightning over far horizons; in his quick and intelligent sympathy which saw the good and the amusing in the most unpromising subjects; in the ease and airy lightness with which he scattered his jeweled phrases; but above all in his astonishing power of diffusing happiness wherever he went. Years ago, in a well-known drawing room in Washington, when we were mourning his departure from the capital, one of his friends expressed the opinion of all when he said, "It is strange that the Creator, when it would have been so easy to make more Kings, should have made only one."

The rare diversity of traits and talents that had delighted Adams and Hay had sprung from a blend of old New England stock. The surname King had come to Massachusetts as early as 1640. Daniel Kinge, the immigrant, may have been descended from Robert, Bishop of Oxford, as a family tradition held. If so, the line could then boast of a distant connection with the Plantagenets and claim a coat of arms that was described as "*Sable*, a lion rampant between three crosses crosslet, *or*."

Like many another English settler, Daniel Kinge had been famished for land, and he had set about relentlessly to acquire an estate around the village of Lynn. His aggressiveness and his dislike for paying debts had caused his name to be sprinkled freely through the court rolls of the day. To underwrite his ventures he had even taken sharp advantage of his father, Ralphe Kinge, a draper of Watford, England, whose will set the debt "at very neare one thousand poundes." Father Ralphe had begged help from the pastor of Boston, a family friend, to persuade Daniel to settle the obligation as soon as he was able—"which if he does not," the old man wrote, "my advice is that he may be strictly put to it by all such waies and meanes as my executors shall thinke fitt." The money was never pried from Daniel, however; and when he died at Lynn in 1672 he left much land to each of his five children.

Extreme parsimony had passed, along with Daniel's acres, to his son and namesake Daniel, Jr., known as the "Captain." Captain King traded for several years as a resident merchant in the West Indies; then he kept a tavern in the town of Salem, where he became the constable. He managed his affairs shrewdly, enlarging his estate until it measured nearly a thousand acres. Whatever Clarence King inherited from such grasping fists, it was not that touch of avarice which John Hay longed to induce in him as a counterbalance to ruinous generosity.

Benjamin, of the third generation of Daniel Kinge's descendants, more aptly foreshadowed Clarence King's temperament. He was of scientific tastes, was absorbed in philosophical studies, and he soon settled in Newport, Rhode Island, as a maker of "mathematical instruments." His specialty was quadrants and compasses for the ships which put in at Newport Harbor, but in 1756 he also made the "instrument to determine the latitude in order to run the dividing line" between Rhode Island and Massachusetts. And it would become a family tradition that he had helped Benjamin Franklin in certain electrical experiments involving the Leyden jar.

His dormered house on the corner of Church and High streets was to remain in the King family for generations. There Samuel, Benjamin's son, continued the family business, as he announced in the Franklins' paper. He also retained his father's shop on Thames and Pelham streets, where he painted honest though somewhat primitive portraits in his spare time. Cosmo Alexander, a Scottish artist of fashion, praised his work. But there was little demand for art in Newport; Samuel's commissions came at rare intervals. But one of his sitters was the most learned scholar in America, Dr. Ezra Stiles, who interrupted the posing to marry Samuel, in 1770, to his sweetheart, Amey Vernon.

The wedding connected Samuel King with some of the most distinguished families in Rhode Island. Amey's father, a wealthy merchant, was descended from the Vernons of Haddon Hall, and his name and arms ran back to Richard de Vernon, a crony of William the Conqueror. Amey's mother was a Ward—the daughter of Richard Ward, twice governor of Rhode Island; and a great-granddaughter of Roger Williams, founder of Rhode Island.

Marriage had not come between Samuel King and his painting, and he wielded an influence over several students who aspired to careers in art. Anne Hall and Edward Malbone practiced at his workshop studio, and both had vogues as miniaturists before their teacher's death. Gilbert Stuart received instruction from him, but his favorite pupil was Washington Allston. In the opinion of William Dunlap, the one-eyed critic and impresario of New York, Samuel King deserved immortality for stimulating Allston's genius; yet he died almost forgotten in his native Newport, years after his son had become an affluent merchant in the China trade.

By the time that Samuel King the younger was seventeen years old, no fewer than fifteen American vessels had entered the China run from ports like Boston, Salem, and New York. The spirit which had sent American privateers against the British Navy, during the Revolution, later drove American merchantmen to break the monopoly of the great East India Company. The Yankee *Fan Kuei* carried their trade to Canton, the only port then open in China. And there they bartered their cargoes for silks, nankeens, and chinaware, or cinnamon and tea—commerce which soon created merchant princes.

By 1802 the younger Samuel King had become the principal partner in the East India firm of King & Talbot, with a countinghouse on Front Street, in New York City. He would take turns with his associates in making runs to China to manage their dealings in the Canton hongs, the factories and warehouses where the China traders lived and worked. Legend pictured him as riding out typhoons and fighting pirate dhows, winning the trust of hong merchants and mandarins alike, and living in princely opulence at Macao. He married his cousin Harriet Vernon; and their children, with a double infusion of Vernon blood, were bred to trade and commerce. The sons sought, one by one, to follow their father's example—the first, Charles William, who had left Brown University in 1825 and sailed the following year to the American factory at Canton; and then Frederick, whose packet would disappear one day in a China Sea typhoon.

The third son—his name was James Rivers—had inherited the scientific tastes of his great-grandfather Benjamin, and if he had followed his inclinations he might have become a man of science or a medical doctor. But family interests drew him into commerce, and while still in his teens he entered the countinghouse of Olyphant, Talbot & Company, in New York City. There he learned the business of a China merchant in a house which had earned the highest reputation for its ethics. Soon the Opium War broke out, a disaster for trade. Still, James Rivers King could return to Newport by his twenty-first birthday and propose to Caroline Florence Little, going on fifteen, whom he had known since she was a small child.

Marriage with Florence would bring him no wealth, but her family was as proud as his own, and as well connected. It was said to be descended from Alfred the Great and three signers of the Magna Charta. Her father, William Little, whose premature death had cut short a legal career of much distinction, had been a scion of *Mayflower* ancestry, a gifted orator, and a student of languages. But his gentility had found its match in the bluestocking he had married, Sophia Louise Robbins, daughter of Asher Robbins, long a senator from Rhode Island.

Devout always, Sophia Little clung to the Moravian faith, and her daughter Florence had been baptized at the worn and warped meetinghouse which stood across the street from the old King home. A peculiar stillness marked the meetinghouse, as one of the flock later remembered—the stillness of meditation. But the brotherhood was dying out in Newport; the congregation had so dwindled that, by 1837, it could no longer support a parson, and Florence's mother would write in 1840 how her family lived in "a kind of hermit-like seclusion from all spiritual communities, not willingly, I assure you. Formed for hearty and warm and perfect fellowship, our souls long for pure Christian sympathy, for the spiritual mingling of hearts and souls."

Presumably, James King could offer Florence the "Christian sympathy" she desired; they shared, besides, an attitude of high seriousness, a yearning for culture, an appreciation of things of the mind. "I was very young when I became engaged to James King," she later admitted. "One of his first tributes was to bring me 'Buckland's Geology' to read and waken my mind to the subject." Science and courtship mixed well. They were married on September 5, 1840, by the Reverend Francis Vinton, rector of Trinity Church. But within a year, the family business called James off to China aboard an Olyphant ship, the *Clarendon*.

The mandarin had closed the Canton factories during the opium trouble, and James's eldest brother had returned to America, broken in health. Charles William King had made a name for himself at the hong of Olyphant & Company, known for its piety as "Zion's Corner." Four years earlier, in 1837, he had organized the expedition of the *Morrison*, ostensibly to return a few shipwrecked sailors to Japan, but in reality to open that hermit nation, and for his pains had received a cannonade from cohorts of the Shogun; but his account of the voyage foretold the doom of that quaint empire's isolation. Later historians would agree that Charles William King had understood the Orient as clearly as any American of his period. Like his cousin and partner, David Olyphant, he refused to deal in opium, and for that reason gained the reputation of being "a little queer." He also refused to kowtow to the imperial commissioner whose orders had closed the hongs. But his prestige remained so great that the exalted Mandarin had granted him an audience. Charles William had then seized the opportunity to mediate the troubles, a task so onerous that it helped to wreck his health.

When in 1841 the Chinese allowed the Canton commerce to resume, Charles William was not yet well enough to return to the Far East. It was James's time to make the run to Canton, regardless of his wife's condition, and at sixteen she faced loneliness with the self-command expected of her background. Florence King never claimed to be an intellectual woman. "If she were," she suggested in later years, "she would have escaped many needless travails." But her sympathies lay with the teaching profession; at heart she was a teacher; and hardly had she felt herself with child than she began to perfect her grasp of languages—of Greek and Latin and French—in anticipation of teaching them to her son or daughter when the proper time should come.

Her baby was born on January 6, 1842, a mild day for Newport winter. She named him Clarence Rivers King—Clarence no doubt because it suggested the lilt of her own name, and Rivers for her husband, who must have arrived in China by that time, after a six-month voyage. "The word *maternity* is underscored on my heart," Florence King would afterward claim, and in the absence of her husband her affections were concentrated on her son, the beginnings of an unshakable possessiveness.

They lived in the midst of a kindly, considerate family. Among immediate relatives was Aunt Caroline King, who remained a spinster and showered her regard on her nieces and nephews. There was Mrs. Little, Clarence's remarkable grandmother, the friend of prisoners, women in distress, and runaway slaves. There was also his great-grandfather, Asher Robbins, who had retired from the Senate and was now discharging the chores of postmaster, in Newport, while he worked at studies of Demosthenes and Homer. And of great importance too—a force, no doubt, in the child's development—was his Negro nurse, "an old family servant, for whom he ever after cherished a lifelong regard and affectionate sympathy." Perhaps in this relationship was rooted his later regard for the black race, among which he was to have many friends, whose companionship he would frequently seek.

It was a quaint town in which Clarence spent his early childhood; and it would remain so for years to come, with "an antique shabbiness" that impressed his friend of a later time—the novelist Henry James—as truly remarkable. It was a place of odd sights and sounds and smells, where carts hauling straw or yellow onions rumbled over the cobblestones of the main street, and cattle bawled on their way to market at the foot of Long Wharf, where one could catch the smell of rotting timber, the salty reek of harbor water, or the taint of fish. But it was a place that would always draw Clarence King back to its narrow streets. It was not hard for him to put down roots in a place so closely woven into his family's history.

"I have been at times all but morbidly aware of the power of local attachment," he later wrote, "finding it absurdly hard to turn the key on doors I have entered often and with pleasure. My own early home, though in other hands, holds its own against greater comfort, larger cheer."

Clarence King, in fact, fell in perpetual love with the old King house on Church Street, with its gambrel roof, its dormer windows, its rooms so redolent of cargoes from Canton. It was there years later, when he had become a famous geologist, that he wrote much of his important treatise *Systematic Geology*.

Letters that took four or five months from the Orient were exciting things to receive, and James King, it seemed, succeeded in making those exotic places—Macao on the river Pearl and the factories at Canton—sound nearly possible for Florence, encumbered though she was with a baby. The American hong, whatever its drawbacks, was a spacious building, three stories high; and on the second floor were drawing rooms and chambers, airy enough for even the climate of southern China. The Chinese no longer enforced bans against foreign women in the factories, and several ladies, both English and American, had gone there with their husbands.

And there was always the example of Charlotte King, the wife of Charles William, to give Florence courage. Charlotte had sailed on the *Morrison* expedition, and her calm nerves throughout the opium troubles had gained her notice as "something of a heroine." China held no terrors for her; she wanted to help promote "the moral welfare of the native females"; and she was ready to sail back to the Far East as soon as her husband's health permitted.

In 1843 Florence King considered taking passage on the *Huntress*, Talbot & Olyphant's new ship of six hundred tons. She knew that James was in need of her. But at the last moment she held back, anxious perhaps over the welfare of her baby, and instead of her sailing, Asher Robbins entrusted letters in the care of his good friend Caleb Cushing, the newly appointed envoy to the Chinese—"a packet of letters," he wrote, "to my grandson, Mr. James King, at Canton."

James, no doubt, found letters a disappointing substitute for the wife he expected to see, and the restricted life in the hong grew more oppressive. Not that it was a hard existence, even with all the long hours. "American merchants at Canton," as a visiting chaplain soon discovered, "preserve a style in living that does them credit as good livers. . . . Their tables were well furnished—their meals served in very creditable style, and the system of domestic arrangements . . . is among the most convenient . . . in the world." The Chinese servants were excellent in their way, but the monotonous life must have palled on James King. He grew to hate clerking, to hate keeping books, or preparing manifests for tea and silks, rhubarb, canes, and camphor.

Even the chance to help Dr. Peter Parker, the medical missionary, in the hospital which the great hong merchant Houqua had furnished rent-free, failed to redeem the life for him; and he found it impossible to exert the energy his brother Charles had brought to the China trade. He made no deep impression on his associates at the American factory. John Heard, of Boston, referred to him and his younger brother David, who had come out on the *Huntress*, as "nice fellows." But most hard-headed China traders had little use for dreamers such as James King.

" 'Tis fortunate Jim King's wife did not come out," concluded the supercargo of the *Huntress*; "for her husband, I think, is a poor coot, and probably will never be worth sixpence—he talks of going to Singapore on a visit and then return to the States." James King waited only till Charles returned from Manila, where he had gone for his health, which had failed again in the semitropical heat of Canton.

On reaching home James learned that death had struck at Newport in his absence. Asher Robbins had slipped on the ice during the winter, had taken to bed in his "quiet old house between a court and a garden," and then died, leaving the family deep in mourning. Aside from the pleasure of being with Florence again, and of seeing his son for the first time, James must have found these trying days; he soon had news of another loss, irretrievable for him.

Charles had never felt strong again, and so he, too, had embarked for home that summer, only to die on ship in the Indian Ocean. His body was cast into the Red Sea, and with it sank James's hope for a permanent residence in America. His remaining two brothers were now in China—Frederick, somewhat older than himself; and David, a lad of sixteen. But neither seemed equal to the place which Charles had left. It was only a matter of time, James knew, before he too must sail back to manage the King patrimony.

Clarence had the benefit of a father's presence for eighteen months (or thereabouts), long enough perhaps to make for his enduring infatu-ation with things Oriental, including what he later called "artistic Chinese cookery." King would write how "they who come home from living in China smack their lips over the relishing cuisine," and memo-ries of his father may have lurked behind the allusion. Had not plea-sures of the table been among the few indulgences free to clerks in Zion's Corner?

President Polk in Washington was always biting off too much to chew, some thought; and if "Fifty-Four Forty or Fight" missed bringing on a war with England, there was still the trouble with Mexico to make people wonder. Mrs. Little blamed the war on a combination of Satan and scoundrels who intended to spread the abomination of slavery. But the North was as much to blame as the South, she thought, because of its hypocritical compliance. She declared as much in the play she wrote called *The Branded Hand.*

"The North," as one of her characters argued, "cares not, so [long as] we help fill her purse, how many of her sons we imprison and brand. All the North wants is riches and luxury. There's a great deal of talk there, but it means nothing." Even the preachers in the churches smelled of guilt, and she had a bit to say about that, too, on the final page:

> Do not God's ministers for slavery plead,
> And prove it holy from the sacred text?
> Sleep then, Oh, foolish conscience, sleep again!
> The anthem of a thousand churches lull thee.

But what a puny brawl the Mexican War would seem compared to the Taiping Rebellion that roared over China! Ten provinces would be laid waste before the celestial inciter could swallow enough gold foil to assure his ascent into Heaven. Yet such strife could only hinder, not destroy, the China trade; the Treaty of Nanking had opened up new ports; the struggle for profits had grown intense. Never had competi-tion seemed so keen as when James King, in the spring of 1847, took ship again for China.

Months earlier, Florence had borne him a daughter, whom they had also named Florence—a delicate baby fated to die soon. James had left his wife with child again, and early that autumn Clarence had a second sister, named Grace Vernon. Winter passed, then spring; no word arrived from James King. And then one day in June, Florence awoke with a pounding heart. She knew that he was dead, and she felt so certain of the premonition that she wore a touch of black thereafter.

Summer passed with humid heat. At last a ship brought news that was no news at all, but with it fresh heartache. "It was on my twenty-second birthday," Florence wrote in later years, "that my youngest child lay dead while I heard of her father's death."

James had sailed on to Amoy, the newly opened port that faced the camphor island of Formosa. Fever raged there, a most unhealthful spot, and fierce typhoons had lashed the China Sea. James had died on June 2, 1848, the day of Florence's premonition. His death had come, according to report, from his going out "with camphor pack" to hurry some Chinese hands. He wanted to lose no time in returning to Canton for news of Florence's latest confinement. His body had stayed at Amoy, buried there perhaps on that "isle of the dead" by Dutch Reformed missionaries. "The pall of bereavement, and the manifold burdens of a sweeping family disaster," as a friend would write, had fallen on the young mother with "a force that would have completely crushed any but the mentally and morally strongest." In her double grief Florence King turned closer to her son, and as so often happens when a father counts for little, the son became his mother's satellite, in a close mother-son relationship which, in this case, would last throughout the life of Clarence King.

2

The Wind's Will

The year of world troubles—1848—was racing toward its close. An obscure sawyer had noticed the sparkle of gold in his California mill-race; the president's message to Congress, in early December, authenticated the news with pouches of gold sand. By Christmastime crowds had gathered at every Eastern port to start the run for California. Newport yielded its share of restless men; seventy-odd gold hunters prepared to leave on the whaler *Audley Clarke*, and many who stayed behind talked only of gold—gold—gold. "You can pick it up," they said, "like the Hebrew children finding manna in the morning."

Meanwhile, Clarence was six years old; the time had come to start to school. His mother was ready to teach him what she could. But she also wanted him to attend some good academy, and for the purpose chose a boarding school in Pomfret, Connecticut—Christ Church Hall, conducted by the Reverend Dr. Roswell Park. And so the early Newport days of Clarence King came to an end. His mother moved ten miles across the Connecticut line; and in Pomfret, which (as the James family later discovered) had "something quite Arcadian" about it, the Kings took rooms in a boardinghouse where a Mrs. Allen kept eighteen paying guests, half of them students.

Christ Church stood in a grove of evergreens, and there on Sunday mornings Clarence and his mother must have heard sermons which Dr. Park would soon collect in one of his frequent volumes. He was tall and spare, a West Pointer who had exchanged his military career for education and the church. He had come to Pomfret about five years earlier, after a stint as Professor of Natural Philosophy at the University of Pennsylvania, and in the classroom he looked as grim as he did on Sundays in the pulpit. It was his habit to wear a suit of austere black, with a collar as stiff as his pedagogical manner.

He kept a maple rod at hand, for he was "a strict disciplinarian." He tolerated no breach of conduct; nor did he hesitate to cane delinquent students, as one of the older boys (whose name was Jimmy Whistler) soon would learn. Another of Dr. Park's pupils—Louise Chandler, who came to be known as Mrs. Moulton, poet and dispenser of literary gossip—would long remember how Jimmy Whistler appeared one day "with a high, stiff collar and a tie precisely copied from Dr. Park's. Of course," Mrs. Moulton added, "the schoolroom was full of suppressed laughter. The reverend gentleman was very angry"; and the first time Jimmy Whistler "gave him some trifling cause of offense, the Reverend Dr. went after him with a ferule. The school was in two divisions—the girls sitting on one side of the large hall, and the boys on the other. Jimmy, pursued by the Dr. and the ferule, went around back of the girls' row, and threw himself down on the floor." There the master overtook the painter-to-be, the future authority on the Gentle Art of Making Enemies, and gave him a sound thrashing.

But the stern teacher offered solid instruction, as far as it went. He spurred his scholars on with appeals to their ambitions, a customary method; for in America, as everybody knew, a man of industry might reach the pinnacle of success. He might even leave his plow in a Pomfret furrow and, like General Putnam (whom Dr. Park mentioned in his book *Pantology*), take command of an army.

Clarence must have known the story of Israel Putnam and the wolf—the savage old she-wolf that had preyed on the whole countryside. He must have known how she had eluded capture year after year until Israel Putnam, though hardly more than a boy, had vowed to track her down; how he had cornered her in her lair and, winding a rope around his body, had crawled into the cave until he could see the animal's eyes. And then one shot had ended the nuisance. *

The boy's interest in science and nature began to show itself at Pomfret. His early religious training (Florence King had now joined the United Congregationalists) had covered the themes of Genesis, sometimes by demonstration. "Most people in youth," he later wrote,

have witnessed the "Moving Diorama of Creation." They have not forgotten the fiat, "Let there be light," uttered in sepulchral tones, by the hidden

---

* Concerning mention of the grizzly hunt of 1871 in the notes for James D. Hague's article on King for Appleton's *Cyclopaedia of American Biography*, King suggested: "You can putnamize over this if you see fit." In May, 1904, the *New York Post* review of *Clarence King Memoirs* would note the parallel between King's bear exploit and General Putnam's encounter with the wolf.

showman, and the sudden blaze of obedient gas light; nor has the procession of life, where, one after another, the cardboard beasts marched across the field of view, to slow melodeon music, escaped their memory; nor the religious comments of the man with the rod.

But how—precisely—did the biblical account explain the odd discovery he made one morning soon after his seventh birthday?

Winter had whitened the fields and hills of Pomfret. "In the severe January weather," as his mother later remembered,

he came to me . . . and asked if I could go a little way over the frozen snow to see something. . . . The "little way" proved to be about a mile, and the something was a remarkably distinct fossil fern in a stone wall. He asked me to explain how it came there. I promptly confessed my ignorance.

But Florence helped him to consult Hitchcock's *Geology*; and the fern opened a subject that would hold his interest for a lifetime. Florence encouraged him to collect all manner of rocks, plants, mosses, seeds— any natural thing that caught his fancy; "and," as she added, "from that time on my rooms became a veritable museum."

The pleasure Clarence took in nature won, no doubt, his teacher's approval, for Dr. Park appreciated the outdoors. His book of poems was not limited to religious or patriotic themes; it included several nature lyrics after the manner of William Cullen Bryant. Dr. Park was also versed in geology, a subject he had treated in *Pantology*, his "systematic survey of human knowledge." Among the illustrations of the book were engravings of animals long extinct—dinosaurs and pterodactyls, megatheres and mastodons. Moreover, Dr. Park took a liberal view of the seeming discrepancies between religion and science. He believed that "the book of nature and the book of revelations [would], when fully understood, be found to agree entirely, both being the work of the same infinitely wise and omnipotent Author." No doubt it was well for Clarence King, the future scientist, to fall so early into the hands of such a teacher.

But then, in 1852 Dr. Park resigned his Pomfret rectorship to become the president of Racine College. It may have been on this occasion that Florence King took Clarence to live "in the vicinity of Boston" for Latin School under a master named Calef. For a while the goal of his preparations seemed to be Harvard College. But Florence found the climate uncongenial; and soon she took him to live in New Haven. One reason for the move may have been a wish to be near her brother, Robbins Little, who planned to take a master's degree at Yale. Or was it a desire to give Clarence's bent for natural history a suitable environment?

The science of the world had been seeping for thirty years into the American mind through the pages of Silliman's *Journal*, edited in New Haven, and in 1853, in spite of theological obfuscation bred at Yale College, the place was considered the scientific capital of America. Its atmosphere would be exactly suited to encourage Clarence's devotion to nature and his attentive examination of it in the environs of the town. "His early acquaintance . . . with the birds, fishes and plant life of New Haven was something remarkable," he later reminisced in third person; "and these youthful [pastimes] undoubtedly had much to do with the development of [those] powers of observation that have played an important role . . . in his career."

Florence King rented rooms on Church Street. Near by lived the choleric pastor of First Church, the Reverend Leonard Bacon; and across the street stood the house of President Woolsey, who left by lamplight every morning to harangue the men of Yale at early chapel.

Clarence continued his studies under his mother's guidance; for Florence King, "a woman of most remarkable intellectual gifts" (whatever her claims to the contrary), was dedicated to his education, leading him with special sureness into books and literature. Her influence grew so apparent that a close friend came to regard Clarence's taste and perceptions as a "natural outgrowth of his mother's mind. . . . I never knew," the friend would add, "a mother with a keener sense of a boy's quality and characteristics or with a greater wisdom or power to develop the best possible."

She was gentle with him always; yet she governed him with a firm will, and he returned her affection. He obeyed all her wishes; if their relationship kindled any resentment or rebellion in him, it had sunk below the threshold of awareness; and soon after his death Florence could declare: "I have never known a more perfect human tie than that which bound my son and myself. We were one in heart and mind and soul."* Whatever burdens her attachment stored against the future

---

* "I have lost not only a devoted child," King's mother lamented in another context,

but the closest and tenderest *friend* whose sympathy in every thought and feeling was so entire that I cannot imagine a more perfect communion, even in the heaven where I expect to join him ere

(and the burdens would be great), these were carefree days for Clarence King.

He was growing rapidly, and with his robust constitution (though he was never large for his age) came a buoyant spirit, a need for unrestrained activity. Often as he bounded along Church Street or across the green where Yale men played at football or cricket, "his winning smile and agile movement" charmed the future president of two great universities—Daniel Coit Gilman, then the librarian at Yale. No suggestion of ill health, or shadow of nervousness, such as troubled his Uncle Robbins, affected Clarence.

It may have been overwork, hard study, which had frayed his uncle's nerves, for Robbins Little, ten years older than Clarence, had been a conscientious youth. He felt much better now that he had just completed a world tour aboard the Olyphant clipper *Wild Pigeon*. The ship had sailed out of New York in the fall of 1852, a contender in what the oceanographer Matthew Maury would call "the most famous race that has ever been run." It had been a sweepstakes around the Horn, with the *Wild Pigeon* pitted against three of the swiftest ships afloat. It had made no difference that her run to California—118 days—had lost the race. She had dashed on—thirty-eight days to Hong Kong and then up to Whampoa, where her cargo had been discharged and another taken aboard for the voyage home.

Still centered at Canton was the trading house that supported Clarence and his mother. James King's share of Olyphant & Company had been kept in the China establishment; his brothers, Frederick and David, had stayed as active partners; and the firm was known as Olyphant, King & Company till 1851, the year the senior partner (old and pious D. W. C. Olyphant) died. It was then reorganized as King & Company, the Olyphant heirs preferring to concentrate on the New York house.

King & Company prospered at first. As Shanghai grew in importance, a branch of the firm was established there. Then misfortune struck; Frederick failed to return from a coasting voyage; and, anxious

---

long. He came to me so early in life that I can say like Goethe's mother, "We were young together." No clouded look or hasty word ever marred the sweetness of our relation.

(Florence K. Howland to C. W. Howard, January 17, 1902, J. D. Hague Collection). Subsequently, she claimed that "her precious son" had been "the very center of [her] life" (*idem*, April 4 [1902], *ibid.*).

for his safety, David went in search of him, in a chartered steamer, along the ill-mapped shores of the South China Sea. He searched until "acute ophthalmia" struck him temporarily blind. But not a trace of Frederick King was ever found, and he was presumed to have perished in a typhoon.

David assumed charge of King & Company and, young though he was, earned a reputation for enterprise. While serving as consul for Prussia in Shanghai, he managed to free several Siamese vessels which the mandarins had detained; in gratitude the monarch of Siam appointed him commercial agent for the Kingdom of the Yellow Robe. Here was a chance to corner the foreign trade of Siam; therefore he sailed to Bangkok in 1855 and formed a third branch of his company there. Storms were gathering, it was true; but the crisis was to spare the heirs of James King for several months to come.

When, at thirteen, Clarence was ready for high school, he moved with his mother to Hartford, which supported one of the finest public high schools in New England. At first they lived at the house of Judge John M. Niles, who, as Van Buren's postmaster general, had placed Great-grandfather Robbins in the Newport post office. The judge had retired from Washington during the gold rush year and had taken up a quiet horticultural life, in a house on Main Street, not far from Charter Oak, the patriotic landmark which was hollow now and full of bees. The plain three-story building of Hartford High School stood but a short distance away, at the corner of Anne and Asylum streets.

All who sought admission to the Classical Division had to take "an examination in the primary rules of Arithmetic and other elementary studies." Clarence must have passed the test, for he was enrolled in "the Classical II Division" on October 15, 1855, and at once began to attend classes. There he joined a group of nearly thirty-five scholars, under the charge of Samuel Capron, a Yale graduate who tugged at his beard, or ran his fingers through a mop of curly hair while hearing recitations. He was known as "the Hartford Grammar School Master," and he gave his whole time to teaching the classics.

The Classical Division had descended from the Hopkins Grammar School, which had enjoyed a long tradition as the "Rugby of Connecticut" before merging with the public high school. It had lost none of its distinction in the merger, and had gained expanded facilities. It still provided pupils with a thorough grounding in Latin and Greek, for which it levied no tuition. Latin grammar, supplemented by readings, inaugurated the program; and after the first term came exercises in Latin composition. Greek began in the second year and followed a similar pattern, varied by translations from Latin into Greek, and vice versa; and with the third year came courses in ancient history, geography, myth, and antiquities.

It was a rigorous program, one that filled Clarence with conflicting feelings—with love for the classics, as literature, but contempt for the method of teaching them. After such instruction, he later explained, "countless young Americans . . . can attack Greek and Latin poetry with military precision, can form in a hollow syntactical square, and successfully receive the determined and bitter charge of attacking tutors; but where is there one whose lips have a single note of response to the melodies of the past; one young writer who has learned to drape the graceful garment of language around the firm body of an idea?"

It was possible, though, for a classics major to take courses in the English Division of the high school; and during his four years at Hartford, Clarence balanced his program with work in mathematics, modern history, and English. He was fortunate in having for English a stimulating woman who had been a child prodigy and was now, in the words of Harriet Prescott Spofford, "a very wonderful teacher, awakening in her pupils powers they did not dream of." Her name was Mary A. Dodge. She was only nine years older than Clarence himself, and as he would recall years later, "she still had the sweetness of natural womanhood." It was an open secret that she had begun to write under a nom de plume, and she would soon attain notoriety as "Gail Hamilton." She had charge of all work in English composition, and she taught, besides, the course known as "Elegant reading of English Literature."

Miss Dodge, a sort of watered-down and peppered-up Margaret Fuller, was a convinced abolitionist, and some of her essays had begun to appear in the *National Era.* Clarence, indeed, had been surrounded by discussions of the slavery issue. His mother had grown more abolitionist with the years, and his grandmother, Mrs. Little, whom he saw on visits to Newport, had crusaded for years against slavery. It had taken courage to join the abolitionists when she had done so, for they had numbered only a handful then, mostly women, and they had faced hostility even in the North. Mrs. Little had been one of the women for whom—eight years before Clarence's birth—the police had opened a narrow lane through the mob which had later dragged William Lloyd Garrison toward Boston Common, with a rope around his neck. She had aided the underground railroad; and she had poured her feelings against the Fugitive Slave Law into a short novel, *Thrice Through the Furnace*, much of it based on the lives of persons she had known.

The story would have anticipated Mrs. Stowe's theme had its publication not been delayed until the appearance of *Uncle Tom's Cabin*, by far the greater work. Clarence's grandmother herself called her book "a little bark" compared to Mrs. Stowe's "noble vessel." Yet, with its strange power, it doubtless helped to shape Clarence's deep regard for the Negro race. It must have been easy for him to sympathize with Gibby the slave youth who told much of the story, and he must have felt the pathos in the death of Gibby's mother, who had nursed her master's children. There were memories of his own Negro nurse to condition his response.

Mrs. Little was emphatic in her opinion of slavery, which, in her words, "uproots the domestic affections and destroys all purity of attachment between the sexes . . . the boast and safeguard of our Christian civilization." She had drawn an appealing figure in Gibby's quadroon sister, whose skin was as clear as amber. She had caused two whites to fall in love with her, without intending marriage. "No," one had declared, "there is a conventional toleration of another sort of connection. . . . I have no desire to run counter to it, and thus Marian shall be mine"; a resolve which condemned her to degradation. "Oh, Slavery," cried Gibby the fugitive, "where is there a fiercer fury than thou art?" Mrs. Little had proceeded to put an impassioned denunciation into the mouth of this fugitive slave, but the opinion was hers. * It was also that of Clarence's mother. It became his own as well, and among his schoolmates he secured the reputation of being an "enthusiastic abolitionist."

Through the winter and spring of 1856, while Mr. Capron drilled the class in Latin and Greek, the question of slavery raged across the land, as the chief issue of the coming election. By June the race had begun between John Charles Frémont "the mustang colt" and James Buchanan, "an old grey horse whose name was Buck," with former President Fillmore hardly counting. In Hartford, like most of New England, resentments left smoldering by the Kansas-Nebraska troubles found release in support of the new Republican Party and a vigorous rally

* "I remember during the fifties," King later wrote, "she ate no sugar but free-soil maple and refused Southern oranges, as they were to her mind 'full of the blood of slaves' " (King to Hay, undated [1888], A37865[26], Hay Papers [Brown University Library]).

against slavery. Even Judge Niles returned to politics, and before cancer could strike him down he had planned a new paper, the *Hartford Press*, to support Frémont.

In November, like most of New England, the people of Hartford cast their votes, predominantly, for the Mustang Colt. The new Republican Party won in most of the North, but Frémont ran second in the race at large. The struggle for freedom had only begun, however; and on that issue Clarence, though scarcely fifteen, predicted to his school friends an ultimate clash between the North and the South.

His best friend was a slender, dark-haired boy named James Terry Gardiner, * whom he had met on first coming to Hartford. It was a close friendship, and it would be a lasting one. "Mr. Clarence King and myself," James Gardiner later informed a committee of Congress, "have lived together since we were fourteen years old on terms of intimacy closer than those of most brothers." With a third boy, named Daniel Dewey, they formed a devoted trio—"Dan, Jim, and Clare."

Florence King compared their friendship with that of Jonathan and David. The boys themselves, having read *In Memoriam*, called it attachment in the laureate's sense and promised one another "never to get the world's bashfulness of saying 'love.'"† They addressed one

---

* Or James Terry *Gardner*, as he spelled his name at this time. Later he adopted the spelling *Gardiner*, at which King's mother congratulated him on regaining the use of his "i." In the interest of consistency the final spelling will be used throughout this book.

†King used the phrase "loved in the 'In Memoriam' way" in a letter to Gardiner on September 19, 1861, in connection with their feeling for one another; and on March 18, 1862, he confessed: "My love for you grows always and is a most absorbing passion. The deeper I feel the more it becomes an effort to express myself and at times I almost reason myself into resolving to be silent henceforth." Such expressions call up the question of homosexuality, in view of the intensity of King's attachments to certain male friends and his occasional outbursts of misogyny. In 1950 Lionel Trilling told me of his belief that King may have been enmeshed in "the vast complex of homosexuality that flourished sub rosa during the Victorian Era." He told me, further, of his hopes for writing a play dealing with "the suggestive friendship of King, Hay, and Adams"—a project that his busy life seems never to have found the time for. I can imagine with what alacrity Professor Trilling would have endorsed Gore Vidal's claim in the expansive historical novel *Empire* (New York, 1987) that "Henry Adams had always been in love—there was no other word—with [King] the geologist, naturalist, philosopher, world-traveler, creator of mining enterprises, [and] Renaissance man"; that indeed King was "the man [Adams] loved and envied above all others" (p. 273). My conclusion is that Trilling magnified out of proportion certain hints of a bisexual tendency in King and underestimated the decisive evidence for King's vigorous heterosexuality.

another as "Brother," especially in the letters which they exchanged, to exercise the letter-writing art that they were learning both at home and at school. At fifteen, as Jim would later recall, Clarence had learned to "write beautifully," under his mother's guidance; and he composed long screeds to his friends.

At the same time the three seemed inseparable in their leisure. Dewey wrote, "Truly we have had a strangely happy boyhood together." Saturday became the high point in their week during the school year; they would spend it sleighing up and down Washington Street, or in skating on the river if the ice allowed, or in tramping through the countryside in "costumes gotten up for the occasion . . . more pictur-esque than conventional." In such outings Dan and Jim became enthu-siastic partners in Clare's nature study. Gardiner would later recall: "He studied enthusiastically the botany, the bird and animal life, and the rocks, of the region over which we rambled."

A favorite jaunt took them across the Connecticut, to fields teeming with redwings, meadow larks, and bobolinks. There, too, they could catch the lisp of swamp wrens, the cry of bitterns, the furtive splash of muskrats in the meadow pools; and sometimes, under some maples near a tributary of the dark and still Hockanum, they would build a fire and lunch on chocolate and the trout they had hooked. And all the while Clarence's memory soaked up impressions—a process of unconscious photography. He was seldom at a loss to recall what they had seen or heard, his recollections coming with a sharpness that often amazed his friends. It was this faculty that would enable him to produce for his mountaineering papers, in 1871, minute descriptions of landscapes he had not seen sometimes for years, but whose slightest detail lay etched in his memory, ready for instant use. "He never, in fact, forgot any-thing," wrote William Crary Brownell, the literary critic. "Everything in the environment, whatever the environment might be, lay cosily in his mind in a state of the most complete realization."

For some time a quest for spirituality had been of deep concern to the three Brothers. They would often return to the subject in their letters, which they prefaced with hints of inner struggles or with observations on their souls' health. They begged criticism from one another, as befitted a "Brotherhood in Christ," and they prayed, "May God keep us true to Him and 'unspotted from the World.'"

Clarence and his friends were not alone in such earnest pietism. The tone of their letters sounded often like that of letters which Mrs.

Little—"the prisoners' friend"—wrote to men and women behind bars, unfortunates to whom she signed herself "your mother in Christ." Moreover, economic insecurities that now beset the country fostered an evangelical spirit that led to a great revival in the following year.

President Buchanan had been in the White House only three months when rapid declines in stocks and bonds presaged the business disasters of 1857. Soon railroads, trusts, insurance houses—a number of Hartford's own—were obliged to close their doors; and Clarence and his mother were, evidently, not long in receiving grim news of King & Company in the Orient.

The "bust"—for that was the common word now—had not been David King's fault; he had pushed the interests of the firm with vigor, and the bold risks that he had run would ordinarily have reaped handsome profits. Yet reverses had begun early in 1855, when commerce declined at Canton as a result of antiforeign bitterness. Then in December 1856 mobs of Cantonese had burned all of the foreign-owned factories, dwellings, and consulates in the city. King & Company staggered under the losses, and it was forced to remove, at a ruinous cost, what little remained of its goods to Hong Kong. The Chinese governor-general excused himself from all liability; he charged that British soldiers had set the fires, a lie that delayed the settlement of claims until the disaster of King & Company was complete.

The catastrophe came when money which David had sent to cover obligations at Shanghai had vanished, along with the steamer in which it had been consigned. All hands aboard had disappeared without a trace; and soon the panic had swept King & Company into limbo, and with it all the assets that Clarence's father had left invested. And now from the wreckage came the revelation that, under David's direction, the firm had reversed its stand on opium. Not only had it joined the opium traffic, but also, on going down in ruins, it left duties on the drug unpaid to the amount of ten thousand taels. The "bust" proved beyond salvage; and the heirs of James King soon found themselves with little more security than the hordes of unemployed who roamed the streets of America.

Since the death of Judge Niles, Clarence and his mother had lived with the family of an insurance official named James Bowles, also spelled Bolles. But Florence King must have wondered what to do before her resources came entirely to an end, and she reached a conclusion not surprising in a widow not yet thirty-two years old. Perhaps her decision was helped by the fatherly manner of George S. Howland, the owner of a white lead factory in Brooklyn. He could boast of a pedigree which, like her own, stretched back to the *Mayflower*. He had made good use of a legacy from his father, a Brooklyn landowner, and he seemed to have the right intentions. He was a graying widower who had buried three of his four children, and wanted to find another woman young enough to bear him a second brood. He visited Florence King at Hartford, and she must have given him cause for hope, notwithstanding his age.

It was a time of tension for Clarence, who must have resented Mr. Howland's intrusion. He seemed at seventeen to have reached a crossroads in his life, and he wondered what course to take. A crisis came in April 1859, when he withdrew from school without a diploma "because of illness"; an early attack, perhaps, of the melancholy which at intervals plagued his later life. The future loomed so dark that Clarence again took refuge in religion.* "My only comfort," he confessed, "is

* The record is clear that as a youth King was deeply devotional in an orthodox way and prone to claim, "Religion is my life." It is not so clear how religious he remained as he grew older and became more steeped in science. True, a certain traditionalism seems implicit in a later witticism. His religion, ran the Kingian quip, was like his teeth: both were inherited and, he fancied, both were sound. But such levity might well imply a conspicuous retreat from a once intensely pious bent, such as would not hold religion up as a butt for persiflage. The fact is, King rarely mentioned religion in his maturer years. Perhaps he pondered over it just as seldom, à la George Strong, the bachelor paleontologist whom Henry Adams modeled on King in his brief novel *Esther*. Possibly, then, something of King's later religious views may be inferred from Esther Dudley's interrogation of Strong.

"Do you believe in God?" she asked.
"Not in a personal one," Strong answered.
"Or in future rewards and punishments?"
"Old women's nursery tales!"
"Do you believe in nothing?"
"There is evidence amounting to strong probability, of the existence of two things . . . mind and matter."

Certainly King himself in his maturity continued to believe in God—maybe not in a personal God any more than George Strong did, though on occasion and possibly from force of habit he continued to use personal pronouns and anthropomorphic phrases like "the Divine hand" in referring to the deity. Thus, in his Sheffield anniversary address in June, 1877, he spoke of the primal cause of evolution as if it were a personal Being— "He who brought to bear that mysterious energy we call life upon primeval matter [and] bestowed at the same time a power of development by change." Yet the likelihood that King's mature concept of God transcended personal limits seems implicit in his pan-

that God who overrules all will be the father of the fatherless"; and he prayed "for patience and real humility." Yet how futile his prayers seemed beside the erotic fantasies that came in spite of all his efforts to suppress them.

"Oh, Jim," he wrote, "my hot nature must need a great deal of checking. I am sure my trying troubles must be sent for the purpose of teaching me to govern myself." He worked off much of his energy in walking or in riding horseback, especially on a Morgan mare that belonged to Mr. Bowles. And by the end of the year he had nerved himself for an invasion of Manhattan.

The ease with which he found a job as a clerk with William Brown & Company, flour merchants, was a surprise even to Clarence himself, for he chose to believe that no help had come from Mr. Howland. "My old enemy Pride," he wrote to Jim, "is laughing in its sleeve at my scorning assistance, both in carrying on my education and in procuring me a place. I feel I am my own man, dependent on no one, and if I fail no one but myself is to blame." And it pleased him to remind his friend of a summer prophecy "that I should do it all myself. *I have.*"

He settled down in Brooklyn, where his mother joined him near the end of January. Morning and evening he crossed to and from Manhattan on the Brooklyn Ferry, noting a two-cent fare in his pocket diary. His work in the flour business did not come easily; or at least he took it

---

theistic identification of the diety with Nature, as on the last page of *Mountaineering in the Sierra Nevada*. Not that such a tenet would preclude his ending letters to his loved ones with "God bless you," as if such benedictions invoked a personal deity; nor is it likely that King pressed the severe idea of an impersonal God on his Sunday school class of Crosse & Blackwell girls in the 1880s. Understandably, the final crisis of his life brought a renewed preoccupation with religious concerns, leading him to give as an urgent reason for wanting to live his discovery that he had "a message for the churches." Who knows, however, what that message was, for it cost King such an effort to speak that his companion of the hour chose not to ask him for an explanation. There is little probability that it involved such a bizarre epiphany as that which Gore Vidal offers in *Empire* (p. 274) as the central trauma of King's breakdown during the Panic of 1893. "When I went mad that day in the lions' house in Central Park," the novelist has King say between paroxysms of coughing during his fatal illness, "I was positive that I had seen God, and He was, simply, a huge mouth, maw, with teeth, sharp, sharp—and hungry, oh, so hungry to dine on us. That's why we exist, I thought, to feed Him." Such effects make for entertaining story-telling, but the tenor of King's final theology, whatever it was, was patently more reassuring. It enabled him to face death calmly and without fear.

with enough seriousness to feel "overwhelmed . . . on week days," while Sunday was "little more than a resting time." He did not understand that his perpetual weariness, that "perfectly fagged out" feeling, came not so much from the work itself at the South Street office as from his constant struggle to suppress forbidden feelings. He appealed to Jim for "all sorts of moral suggestions, counsellings," to help him fight his sinful thoughts. "It was very nice to talk about moral purity in a little city, but Great Jones!, Jim—how many more seductive, wicked, beautiful, fascinating, jolly, voluptuous, apparently modest, artful women there are to one poor chicken here; they show you their necks and bosoms without intending to, and all the abominable wiles they practice on a fellow . . . are mighty inflaming."

He found it hard, evidently, to concentrate on ledgers; for help he read the Psalms and went to vesper services at Grace Church. Then he hit upon the sedative of art, bought a season ticket to the Academy's exhibitions, and hypnotized himself on William Hart's autumn pieces or Albert Bierstadt's vistas of the Rocky Mountains. Another experience worth an entry in his diary was hearing Adelina Patti's crystalline voice in *I Puritani*, How much more satisfying than the grandest feast on oysters at Dorlon's, either raw, stewed, broiled, or roasted in the shell.

Meanwhile, Mrs. King made her wedding plans. Friday, April 13, as Clarence noted in his diary, became the "Great Day of Mother's Announcement," after which his reaction to the silence of his friends suggested the extent to which he had identified himself with her. He scolded Jim for having sent "no word of congratulations." He claimed, with an odd exaggeration, that all his friends "except you and Dan" had sent their best wishes, "and I am not a little hurt that my dearest chums should slight me at such a time." All excuses were meaningless, he added, and he requested Jim to make none. "Only do say *something*."

Jim Gardiner was probably not surprised to hear at this time of Clarence's growing distaste for business life, or that he had implored "Heavenly aid in eradicating the melancholy" from his heart. "What is to become of me is uncertain. Probably I shall remain where I am, but the scientific school or a farming life is not impossible." He could scarcely wait for each weekend, to escape into the byways of Long Island; and once, overtaken by a thunderstorm, with a rainbow arching the sky, he knelt on a bank of grass and "prayed God" that he "might always be as thankful" for such signs of hope and grace.

His mother married Mr. Howland in July 1860, and Clarence gained still another rival for her favor in a crippled stepbrother, nicknamed Snoddy.* But he seemed no longer driven to rebel. He curbed his "enemy Pride," and leaving the flour business without regret, accepted Mr. Howland's help to finish his education.

---

*King came to value John Snowden Howland highly, and his mother later wrote: "My step son is a helpless cripple, beautiful in mind and character but in body like an exquisite vessel of cracked glass which a rough touch might shiver in atoms" (Florence K. Howland to John Hay, June 11 [1882], A40157[1681], Hay Papers [Brown University Library]).

3

The Yale Years

By 1860 immense changes had begun to work in the mental climate of America. To the credit of the nineteenth century, as Clarence King would suggest, were "two intellectual achievements so radically new in kind, so far reaching in consequence, so closely bound up with the future of the human race, that we stand on the greatest dividing-line since the birth of the Christian era." He referred to the growing understanding of two principles—the conservation of energy and biological evolution.

Ingenious men had applied the first law with spectacular success, mastering the industrial uses of energy at an incredible rate. And now that Charles Darwin had published *On the Origin of Species* the second principle of the century was rapidly crystallizing. Not that young Clarence King could know so soon what iconoclastic power lay in Darwin's work. "But"—as he was to comment later on—"we live in the future tense." And he could sense while yet a boy the limitations of the unscientific point of view which, though entrenched at Yale College, would soon fall obsolete in the wake of Darwin's theory.

The college, with theologians and classical scholars glorifying the past, had few correctives for a curriculum that was so out of joint with the future. Over half a century later King's acquaintance, the publisher Henry Holt, would cite the Yale College of their day as "probably at its worst in mind, body, and estate. In mind it dated back for centuries." It was the most conservative of all the important colleges in America; it placed its emphasis on the study of the classics and gave but scant attention to social or scientific researches. The faculty included good scholars and men of the highest character, but they were thinkers to only a limited degree. It was at their type of mentality that King would one day aim his barb: "The classic is only a half man."

He would argue that "the man of exclusively classical education" had become "a half-quaint half-pathetic figure, as out of time as Don Quixote. Nothing is more curious than his bewilderment in face of the great mechanism of modern life. . . . His radical difference from the scientific-mechanical man consists in the fact that half of his brain has never been stimulated into consciousness and cultivated into activity. Not to know how nature and man manage the conversions of energy, not to see the early light of science beginning to penetrate and illuminate the very depths of space, to get no nearer than Job got to the binding together of the sun and worlds, to linger in archaic darkness as to the building of the earth, to stop where Aristotle stopped in conception of the process of evolution, is to be a man with half his brain unborn."

Or, as he would declare on another occasion: "There can hardly be conceived a greater calamity befalling a young man born with a talent for literature than to have him elaborately and expensively spoiled in an American classical college. Better far that he should be a cowboy, with a Bible and Shakespeare in his saddlebags, and the constellations his tent, the horse his brother, than to have life, originality, and the bounding spirit of youthful imagination stamped out of him by a competent and conscientious corps of badgering grammarians."

King must have begun to formulate such notions by 1860; for in contrast with Henry Holt he decided against enrolling for the academic course. He turned his back on Yale College, where uncle and grandfather and even great-grandfather had studied before him. He rejected it in spite of his preparation in language and literature and turned instead to a new department on the campus where science was quietly working its marvels.

The Yale Scientific School, but six years old although its antecedents dated back to 1846, had in force a liberal entrance policy. Not even a high-school diploma was required if one could pass the examinations in mathematics and the rudiments of physics and chemistry. King evidently passed the tests well enough, and in September he joined the unorthodox company of Yale "scientifics"[*] Under his full name, Clarence Rivers King, he registered for a three-year course in applied chemistry, at a fee of about two hundred dollars a year. Clarence was to complete this course in just two years.

---

[*] In *Clarence King Memoirs*, both S. F. Emmons and D. C. Gilman give the year of King's enrollment as 1859, but the *Yale Catalogue* and the *Yale Banner* reveal that it was actually 1860. King's letters of 1859 and 1860 and his diary for 1860 support this date; his signature as of the fall of 1860 in the volume labelled "1854–60 Entrance Book" in the records of the Sheffield Scientific School clinches the matter.

The science students were not bound by the same rules as the "academics." None of them was obliged to live in the dormitories of Brick Row. Clarence found a room at 71 College Street, only half a block beyond the Yale fence and not much farther from the common where his great-grandfather had watched General Washington review the local levies for the Continental Army.

New scientifics did not have to wait, like ordinary freshmen, to wear beaver hats or carry "bangers" for defense against uncivil townies. When one lived off campus, even if only a block beyond the fence, he had a right to carry protection. And Clarence presumably carried a banger like most other Yale canes—a thick staff of hardwood with the bark still on it; and he must have walked with it often, under his "much-loved elms," his face eager, looking very boyish for his eighteen years.

Almost every day he had to pass the Yale fence on the corner of Chapel and College streets, the most frequented spot on the campus. Little paint remained on the rounded rails after long and constant wear from Yale posteriors. But Clarence could never join the congregations at that roost; for there the scientifics were not admitted—they did not belong. As King would later write, "An American professor of a classical subject felt entitled . . . to look down upon a teacher of natural science, and by the same quaint sort of logic the Yale academic students excluded 'scientifics' from the boat and fence."

A superior attitude infected the college men; and as one of them latter remembered, "I regarded the studies of my contemporaries in the Sheffield Scientific School with a sort of contempt,—with wonder that human beings possessed of immortal souls should waste their time in work with blow pipes and test tubes." Not that such opinions disturbed young King; for him the hub of Yale could only be the science school with its laboratories, at the corner of Grove and Prospect, a short walk across the Yale grounds.

The stone hall, presented by the railroad magnate Joseph Sheffield, had been occupied since summer only. For the first time the two divisions of the school could operate beneath a single roof, with adequate space and facilities. According to Silliman's *Journal*, Mr. Sheffield had spared no means to turn the building into "a scientific establishment second to none in America."

It contained two complete laboratories—one for analytic chemistry "fitted for thirty special students"; the other for metallurgy, with several thousand specimens of ores and furnace products. Professor George Brush had lent his private cabinets, full of "preachers," as he termed the specimens, for all who cared for "sermons in stones." In addition, the science students had access to the college cabinets in the commons building behind Brick Row, and the combination could not be surpassed, many people thought, "by any mineralogical collection in the country." King so prized the benefits of Sheffield, as the school would be renamed before the year was out, that he begged Jim Gardiner to transfer there from Troy.

The keystone of King's program was chemistry—experimental, analytic, organic, and agricultural chemistry; but he also worked at physics and geology, including mineralogy and a special study of crystals. The number of his classmates was never large, hardly more than a score; and their method of work was entirely different from the discipline imposed at Yale College. It consisted mainly of laboratory experiments under the guidance of Professors Brush and Johnson. Small teams conducted independent experiments; they analyzed unknown substances; studied various chemical reactions, the behavior of acids, bases, and salts. In various ways they tested for themselves the facts and principles of science. The laboratories opened at eight in the morning; and except for lectures, or scheduled recitations, a man was free to work there according to his own conscience. It marked a revolution in New Haven, especially since the school rejected those agents of virtue which harried the life of Yale in general—formal marks, proctors, and compulsory chapel. Such a program struck many respectable people as a snare devised by godless radicals. But the freedom of inductive methods suited King's growing independence, and he was soon to write to Jim Gardiner, "I am happy in my studies." He did not neglect to supplement them with continued intensive attention to nature in the Yale environs.

As King settled into his scientific routine, the country swung into the most impassioned presidential contest since the days of Jefferson. "I have been studying the politics of the time," King had written months before. "I am more than ever a Wendell Phillips man, heart and soul with the philanthropic radicals." He evidently believed, like Phillips, that Abraham Lincoln could lead the Republicans and stand a chance of winning only because John Brown and Garrison and other militant abolitionists had blazed the way.

Not that in holding back from the Lincoln boom had King grown less hostile to slavery. He must have rejoiced in the Wigwam plank that branded the institution as morally wrong. But he doubted if Lincoln's avowed intent to restrict the practice within its current boundaries could solve the problem. For years Congress had wasted its energies in sterile debates on slavery issues; the delegates seldom had time for anything more. Nor would there ever be time, said the senator from Illinois, Stephen Douglas, who had defended his seat against Lincoln; never, that is, till slavery questions were banished from the halls of Congress and remanded to the people of each state and territory.

Not even Lincoln could split a rail more neatly than Douglas had split the Democratic Party by his wedge of popular sovereignty. Fire-eaters of the South, in choosing Breckinridge of Kentucky as their candidate, defended slavery as morally right; they vowed to push it into the territories under the sanction of the Supreme Court in the Dred Scott case and thus prepare the soil for new slave states. The Douglas faction clung with equal tenacity to hopes of settling the issue by popular will in each territory. And King could see no better solution for the crisis.

If the federal government owned the territories in general, had Congress the right to rule in favor of one or another sectional party? "I say, *No*," he wrote to Jim; "for if she does, she violates the right of one or another. Then the policy of 'Old Steph' comes in and says that Congress had nothing to do with it, that sovereignty belongs to the settlers. . . . Theirs is the right to say whether freedom or slavery shall be the institution." King thus hoped that popular sovereignty would prevail throughout the Western Territories. It would establish freedom there, he felt, assuming that the emigrants were mostly northern men.

But Douglas, with his compromises, had little chance at the polls; the Democratic split ensured Abraham Lincoln's victory in November 1860, and that meant trouble from the South. Though many Yale students seemed unaware of the ominous drift, King feared that the conflict which he and his mother had foreseen was drawing near. It was during the Christmas holidays that news came that South Carolina had bolted the Union, and by the New Year it looked as if the entire cotton bloc aimed to follow. Some southern students hoisted a white Palmetto Flag above Alumni Hall one Sunday morning, but the Rebel banner did not wave there long. It roused the northern boys more thoroughly than the dreariest message from the South.

Soon the Confederacy had been formed. Few people wanted war, but war appeared to be inevitable. Spring vacation in 1861 brought the news that Rebel guns had fired on Fort Sumter. And students from the South, cocksure of victory, faded from New Haven overnight.

Even then the full significance of the tragedy reached few of the men at Yale, and less than half a dozen responded to Lincoln's appeal for volunteers. To be prepared for local trouble, the classes organized some military companies and drilled on the green with a burst of zeal that soon cooled. But even such activity troubled King, whose opinions were colored still by the counsels of Wendell Phillips. Let the South march off, with flags and trumpets, and we will speed the parting guest.

As spring slipped by, he welcomed the wry irony in Dan's letters about the military furor at Hartford's Trinity College, where drills like those at Yale were held. "I suppose," Dan jested, "we are to go south and fight for *States rights*. I've become a regular fire-eater, and practice swallowing a few coals before breakfast every morning, just to keep in trim." But with the weeks it grew apparent that Dan's levity covered anxieties, a sense of guilt that neither he nor his friends had volunteered. King himself could not escape a mood of doubt, especially when the war reached Yale in the hearse of Major Theodore Winthrop.* Muskets cracked, a bugle sounded taps, and the hero was lowered into a grave across the street from Sheffield Hall. More students volunteered that summer, and fears began to mount that the war might last for years.

King's conscience was aroused, and he came to appreciate Dan's anxiety to enlist as soon as Mrs. Dewey would give her consent. He thought of joining the volunteers himself, and once he told Gardiner of that desire. But, with the letter posted, his stomach turned at the thought of having to kill others. He wrote that he was wrong in wanting "to push the bayonet. I was hot with passion . . . excited by the outrage at one of my pet ideas—'freedom.' God knows . . . I would not quail before death for my land, but the act [of killing] would crucify in me many of my noblest impulses. It is like tearing my soul in two."

At the same time he worried that Gardiner might think he lacked the courage to lead men. But he *would* be a leader, King protested; he

*Theodore Winthrop (1828–1861) was descended from the two Governor John Winthrops and from Jonathan Edwards, and was a relative of at least six college presidents. He had traveled widely after graduating from Yale in 1848 and, having devoted himself to literary work, had completed half a dozen volumes before he was killed at Great Bethel, Virginia, in one of the first thrusts against Richmond. His books appeared posthumously, favorite reading matter for King.

would make it the object of his life to lead others. "Don't think that because I show you my tender side, Jim, my weak side if you will, that I have no fire, no firmness, no mental power. Don't think that I never lead men, for in my way I do." As a devotee of campus athletics, he recognized the influence he wielded among his classmates.

The war did not discourage Yale men from taking sports in earnest. They came from every corner of the campus, gathering on the green or at the boathouse or in the new gymnasium; even the scientifics came, for, although barred from the organized sports of Yale College, they formed their own teams and crews. King took pride in his endurance. He delighted in competition; he skated in season, boxed, and played cricket. He became field captain of his baseball club, stroke oar of his crew, and a fleet captain of the Yale navy. "It's funny," he said, "how the fellows take me as a boating oracle. I've been consulted all about college on training theories." He pressed Gardiner harder than ever to come to New Haven, and, yielding at last, Jim enrolled in the spring of 1862.

That was the season from which James D. Hague, Clare's senior by six years and another friend for life, was to remember him as "an active, sprightly youth, quick to observe and apprehend, full of joyous animation and lively energy, which always made him a leader, whether in the daily exercises of the classroom and laboratory or in an impromptu raid by night on Hillhouse Avenue front fences, with the mischievous purpose of lifting off and swapping around in neighborly exchange the door-yard gates of lawns and gardens. 'Off fences must come,' he sometimes said of the gates, 'but woe unto him by whom they come—if found out.'"

During his last months at the scientific school King's program grew less exacting; still, it was a climactic term. Having proved himself a superior student, he had been elected to the Berzelius Society, a club regarded by some as a sort of local auxiliary of the American Association for the Advancement of Science. He had demonstrated many times how he could strike to the heart of problems under investigation and then, with intense powers of concentration, master all details. His teachers saw a touch of genius in him, and young Professor Brush, a protégé of Baron von Liebig, became his close friend and mentor, and pictured him years afterward as Sheffield's "greatest graduate."

Only one other teacher impressed King as deeply—James Dwight Dana, who had just returned from a convalescence in Europe. His quick energetic manner seemed a perfect complement to Brush's more subdued ways. He gave his "long course of lectures in geology" during King's final term, and some of his most memorable remarks came as digressions while he reminisced about the United States Exploring Expedition, which Captain Charles Wilkes had commanded. "Dana has the most vivid powers of description," Gardiner wrote, "setting before us . . . scenes from his travels." He seemed to enjoy the nimbus of romance that recollections of the expedition, which had set sail in August 1838, cast about his frail figure.

It was hard to believe that achievements of such dimensions had been crammed into only four years. Wilkes and his corps had proved the existence of a continent in the Antarctic; they had traced out two thousand miles of frozen shoreline there. They had surveyed numerous islands in the South Seas, hundreds of miles of coastline in both Americas. They had seen the mountains of California long before the Gold Rush; they had collected plants and fauna unknown before their own time. Dana had himself studied hundreds of unfamiliar crustacea, as well as the zoophytes which formed the coral reefs. *

That expedition had shown what government aid could do for science. A good start had been made in scientific exploration, and great accomplishments under the aegis of government loomed in the future, once the war had been won. The spirit of the work survived, meanwhile, through the bounty of certain state legislatures, the most significant work in progress being the Geological Survey of California, which Professor J. D. Whitney had launched in 1860.

King had heard much about the work in California. William Ashburner, one of Whitney's assistants, had visited New Haven, and his arrival had aroused much interest at Sheffield Hall. Second in charge of the survey was Professor William H. Brewer, a graduate of the scientific school, and he had kept in touch with Brush and Dana. Moreover, the State Geologist of California was himself the elder brother of the man who taught King German.

William D. Whitney, a Sanskrit scholar, had taken an interest in King, for King had shown the linguistic facility of his grandfather Little. They often chatted together and, besides dropping the latest word from California, "my German teacher [sets] me wild," King wrote, "with his stories of student life on the Rhine and walking excursions in Switzerland." Such contacts stimulated King's desire for further train-

---

*Mark Twain would write in his *Autobiography* that when he was a boy on the Mississippi, the name of Wilkes was as famous as Theodore Roosevelt's would later be. Wilkes was regarded as another Columbus who had discovered a new world.

ing. He began to dream of a trip abroad for graduate study. But already at work were the influences that were to send him west instead, for practical training in the field.

Meanwhile, his second year at Sheffield reached its end, closing a program of scientific studies that was then the best available in America, and in July 1862, he took his degree, a Ph.B. "with honor."* An anniversary ceremony marked the event at Sheffield Hall, but the scientifics had to wait another week for their diplomas, receiving them at the same time that seniors from Yale College received theirs, at Dr. Bacon's church on the green.

King's formula for a sound man included "prayer, hard work, and plenty of fun." He planned now to concentrate all summer on the final ingredient—with a cruise to Canada while training for the Yale regatta in the fall. After commencement he borrowed the gig *Undine* from his boatclub and had it shipped to Whitehall; and there with Jim, Dan, and a Quaker schoolmate named Sam Parsons, he launched it at the marshy head of Lake Champlain. Five hours of rowing brought them to Ticonderoga, and there they fished for bass and sturgeon to supplement their stores. As they continued down the lake next day, they had no inkling of how soon they would have to face a point of martial authority.

Since spring the Union Army in Virginia had, at best, won only indecisive victories. General McClellan had cried for more men, and Lincoln had promised reinforcements, even if a draft were necessary. Talk of a draft had sent throngs of apprehensive Yankees slipping into Canada; and so on August 8, 1862, the secretary of war forbade all men of draft age to leave the Union as long as military quotas remained unfilled.

Rewards of five dollars a prisoner had spurred the zeal of U.S. marshals, and wholesale arrests were being made along the Canadian border; but, unaware of Stanton's order, Clare and his friends rowed on, perhaps as far as Rouses Point. Eyes were scanning the lake for all craft headed north, and they were "apprehended and detained," on suspicion that the cruise was only a move to evade military service.

"We were obliged," Gardiner wrote, ". . . to go up to the U.S. office

* Both D. C. Gilman and S. F. Emmons, in *Clarence King Memoirs*, call King's degree a B.S., but Yale's *Quinquennial Catalogue* lists it as a Ph.B., and on occasion King referred to himself as a Ph.B.

and make affidavit that we were students and therefore exempt from the draft."

They were allowed to resume the cruise; but they read, no doubt, the editorial invective hurled at "recreant Americans who would desert their country." They skimmed down the Richelieu—through canals to avoid the rapids—and spent Sunday on the shore of Lake St. Peter. Then on to Quebec; but even Canadian journals, it seemed, indulged in contempt for battle dodgers. "Three times three groans," read one, "for the sneaking cowards!" And notwithstanding their jaunty uniforms (duck pants, straw hats, and shirts of ultramarine) the *Undine* crew must have found it hard to cut "the glorious swell in Canada" which King had planned. If they carried out their scheme completely, they rowed on down the St. Lawrence and up the Saguenay to fish for land-locked salmon. In the end they sent the *Undine* home by freight, took a steamer to Montreal, and then walked back to New York State.

Their detention had crystallized Dan's resolution to join the army. He had vowed to enlist at the first post they came to in the States, but delayed the step until they reached Connecticut. King bade him goodbye at Yale, and Dan hurried on to Hartford, where he joined the Twenty-fifth Regiment. The bloodiest battle yet of the war had just been fought in the woods along Antietam Creek; the Union cause was far from won; and no editorial thunder against Abe Lincoln's throttle hold on civil rights could have wholly eased King's conscience for having failed to go with his friend into the volunteers.*

---

*A search of Civil War enrollment lists (Director of War Records Office, National Archives, to writer, January 10 and February 1, 1950) fails to show that King ever registered for the draft. In seeking to account for his failure to fight, one should not overlook the influence of his grandmother Sophia Little and her Moravian faith. King's mother believed that he had inherited many of Mrs. Little's traits of mind. Mrs. Little remained staunchly antiwar, and King seems to have accepted her literal and unconditional interpretation of the Mosaic command, Thou shalt not kill. The sentiments of other relatives may also have swayed him. His Aunt Charlotte King so deplored the war that she virtually disowned her son Vernon King for volunteering in a Union regiment, and when Vernon fell near Richmond and his body was brought to Newport for burial she refused, according to Henry James, to permit his gallantry to be commemorated on the gravestone. In the final tally, though, it must be recognized that Clarence was not particularly unusual in avoiding military service. A large number of his generation, John Muir for example, declined to fight. In Muir's case it involved flight to Canada, but it was possible to purchase a substitute for one's place in the draft, an opportunity that many took advantage of.

4

Shasta, Here We Come

King had remained in New Haven till after the fall regatta. One day in October 1862 he stopped at Professor Brush's house and found his teacher reading a letter from his old friend, William H. Brewer of the California Geological Survey. Brewer had written how a small party under the leadership of Professor Whitney had climbed Mount Shasta to make the first controlled measurements of the peak, an operation which had aroused much interest, for Shasta was commonly thought to be the highest summit in the United States.

King listened eagerly as Brush read the letter aloud, and he could fairly see the Indian summer scene at the mountain base, where the strange insectivorous plant *Darlingtonia* grew. Brewer's account gave a vivid picture of the immense cone, tinged with alpenglow, towering above the twilight below. "And then the moon rose," Brewer had added, "and we sat around our cheerful campfire (for it was cold) and gazed still. And I got up from my blankets late in the night, when the moon's illumination was finer, to look at it by that light."

Brewer and his party had begun the climb when the moon was high. They had reached the topmost point by noon, a sheer needle of lava; and Brewer had not restrained himself in describing the wilderness which they had seen through the rifts in the mists that curled around the summit: Chain on chain of mountains rolling westward to the Pacific, some grizzled with snow, others dark with chaparral; the valley of the Klamath stretching northwest toward the Siskiyous; a roil of clouds in the east; then mountains again to the south, hemming the vast trough of the Sacramento. Haze had engulfed the valley, and above it towered Lassen's Butte, some seventy-five miles away. To Brewer that summit had looked "like an isolated island peak of black rock and white snow rising from this sea of smoke."

King drew a deep breath.

"That settles it," he said.

In the following January he wrote to Professor Brush at Sheffield that he had been reading geology since he left New Haven, "and have," he added, "pretty much made up my mind to be a geologist if I can get any work in that direction." To come to such a decision had not been easy; family tradition had pulled him toward a commercial life, and the issue whether or not he would enter business had remained unsettled for weeks. "His question is fully as hard to unravel as was mine," wrote Jim; "perhaps harder." Gardiner had turned to the study of law, at the school in Washington Square, which Major Winthrop had pictured as Chrysalis College in *Cecil Dreme*. He had hoped that King would room with him, in quarters which they could fill with books and pictures and make into "a cosy little den."

But Mr. Howland had moved the family—now increased by a baby daughter—to Irvington, an hour by train from Manhattan, and King could write, later, "My home was on the Hudson, near New York." Irvington was a small new village named in honor of the author of *The Sketch Book*, who had lived in Sunnyside nearby. King owned the works of Washington Irving, the 1860 edition; and it may have been now that he fed his interest in the West on Irving's account of Captain Bonneville and the fur trade; or now, that he read Humboldt, or Frémont's reports, or even the posthumous volumes of Winthrop, especially the Western novel *John Brent* and that poetic travel extravaganza *The Canoe and the Saddle*. King was evidently much impressed by Winthrop's "Siwash Odyssey," which skimmed across Puget Sound and traced a *via mala* over the Cascades to The Dalles.

His taste for mountains had also led to volumes on the Alps, including John Tyndall's glacier essays. Tyndall was a scientist writing, though a scientist with imagination, and the audacious hues of his scenes appealed to King's love of color. Only Ruskin's "mountain chapters" in *Modern Painters* seemed to give him as much sheer joy; for Ruskin, who had ranged across the same wild scenes, had brought to the mountains a painter's eye, a poet's heart—indeed a vastly more subjective and primitivistic feeling. As King would later write: "Ruskin alone, among prose writers on the Alps, re-echoes the dim past, in ever-recurring myth-making, over cloud and peak and glacier; his is the Rigveda's idea of nature. . . . To follow a chapter of Ruskin by one of Tyndall's is to bridge forty centuries and realize the full contrast of archaic and modern thought."

King read and reread Dana's new *Manual of Geology*. He geologized along the Hudson, and sometime late in 1863 he went to Harvard to hear Professor Louis Agassiz lecture on the subject of glaciology. The Swiss-born scientist, propounder of the ice-age theory, was now the most popular teacher of natural history in America, his reputation having attracted many young men from other schools and other communities. He was given to startling statements. "Gentlemen," he began, "the world is older than we have been taught to think. Its age is as if one were gently to rub a silk handkerchief across Plymouth Rock once a year until it were reduced to a pebble." Nothing in the professor's philosophy of science, however, jarred on King's religious convictions, which in fewer respects still cleaved to "a literal Bible." Agassiz was himself a deeply religious man who believed that each species of plant or animal was, per se, a "thought" of God.

King returned from Cambridge more sure than ever that his vocation lay in geology; in that field, his religious, esthetic, and intellectual interests all converged, and he approached the study of the earth as a quest for ethical and esthetic values fully as much as for scientific fact. "I have read in Revelations," he would write a little later, "of the passing away of the earth and all the beauty and grandeur of it. I read too of a new heaven and a new earth, beautiful in type. Well then, if this is transitory, why study so hard into all the intricate mazes of fact, which will be swept away and known no more? I look for lessons." King believed that God had "scented all with design . . . that lessons were taught in Nature which were not elsewhere, not as important perhaps as the 'law,' but still vital." He was thus still influenced by the gospel of his old schoolmaster, Dr. Park. No doubt he was also affected by ideas from Paley's *Natural Theology* and *View of the Evidences*, standard readings for the academics at Yale College.

He now took rooms in New York with Gardiner as they had planned, and Gardiner found his "jolly nature . . . as good as sunshine." Of an evening both would relax from study before a cheerful fire, with guests like Sam Parsons or King's bachelor uncle, Robbins Little, who was now a lawyer with an office in the city. They fell in with "the practical Ruskinites of the city"; along with Eugene Schuyler, who was Yale's first Ph.D., they joined an esthetic study group which met in a red brick house on Waverly Place, near Washington Square. There several young insurgents full of notions about the state of American art, and full of zeal to agitate those notions, bowed to their idols, Ruskin and the Pre-Raphaelite Brotherhood. This small circle of American Pre-Raphaelites, as they would soon be nicknamed, was led by Clar-

ence Cook, art critic of the daily *Tribune,* with help from Russell
Sturgis, later the art expert for the *Nation.* Also prominent in the group
was Peter B. Wight, the architect. Likewise two youthful painters of
the Hudson River School, Charles H. Moore and Thomas Farrer.

The young reformers styled themselves the Society for the Advancement of Truth in Art, and after several meetings they settled on articles
of faith. "We exist," they declared, "for the purpose of stirring up strife;
of breeding discontent; of pulling down unsound reputations; of making the public dissatisfied with the work of most artists, and better still,
of making the artists dissatisfied with themselves." These young icono-
clasts opposed the pettiness and prettiness fostered by the academies.
But for a more positive goal they pledged themselves to nothing short of
"a unified effort to revive true art in America." In architecture they
leaned toward the Gothic, found the Greek revival anathema, and
championed the functional, setting great store by plainness and simplicity. In appreciation of their stance, Ruskin would soon send his
blessings. Their watchword, proclaimed in their little magazine *The
New Path,* was TRUTH TO NATURE.

At this time, not having yet moved to his view of nature as syn-
onymous with the deity, King conceived of it as a veil drawn before
man's eyes, gross enough to render bearable the intense light shining
from the godhead. "Look at it then with gentleness and humble admiration," he wrote in a pocket notebook. "You, Clarence King, never
dare to look or speak of nature save with respect and all the admiration
you are capable of." He believed that it was the key to art and science;
and so he could turn from esthetics to his fondest study—geology—
without a sense of falling from a higher purpose.

He thought of going to Freiberg for more training in science; he also
thought of securing some practical work in the field, a position, say,
with Professor Whitney's survey on the Pacific Slope—"in any capacity," he declared, "from blow piper to mule driver." In return for Brush's
recommendation he promised to "do lots of collecting for Yale."

Later that year Jim Gardiner's health broke down from overexertion
in his law studies, and King found in the welfare of his friend further
incentive to heed Horace Greeley's admonition. He discussed his hopes
with his mother and made plans for a trek à la John Brent across
America. "It must have been a sense of the coming development of this
continent," Gardiner wrote," and a desire to be a part of it that led him
to plan, when we were twenty-one, our trip to the West across the
plains." Jim agreed to go, and postponed his examination in favor of the

customary cure for nervous exhaustion—a change of work and scene. They were joined by another friend, William Hyde, whose father owned a foundry in the bonanza town of Gold Hill, Nevada Territory, a few miles from the California line. King secured letters of introduction, and they were ready to start in April 1863.

On his last evening at home King sat up late with his mother, who could not hide her concern over reports of Sioux uprisings along the frontier. Nor did they forget, in their prayers together, to mention Dan Dewey—now with General Butler's troops somewhere in Louisiana. "If he lives," King said, "he will make a great man." They had no way of knowing that Dan's body had just been carried from a canebrake with a bullet in the head.

Having met at Niagara Falls, the three companions rode the railroad train west. They transferred to a branch line at Hannibal, Missouri, and King noticed a bearded man and woman, with two children, board their car. The engine shrieked (it was clad in sheet iron against guerrilla bullets), and the train lurched forward. The tracks had been laid for the Pikes Peak rush, and all smoothing had been left for a more convenient season, which had never come. The cars clattered and banged; according to one of the passengers, the ride was as rough as "a trip in a two-horse wagon over a rocky road." The children bounced on their seat, and out of sympathy King helped to feed them and to keep them amused during the later stages of the journey. He won the gratitude of their mother—and of her husband, too, who said his name was Speers. He was a horse-and-mule trader from St. Louis, taking stock across the plains. The same train carried his animals and his drovers. They would get together at St. Joseph—three covered wagons, a string of mules and horses, and an ambulance for the young ones and the wife. Speers invited King and his friends to join the company, and since they had planned to cast their lot with a suitable train they accepted the offer and agreed to help the drovers guard the stock in return for board.

In St. Joseph, busy, crude, and incredibly dusty, the boys bought ponies tough enough, they were assured, for the worst sort of desert. They put on leather clothes and leggings, rejoined the Speerses, packed their belongings in one of the wagons, and helped to get the cavalcade upon its way by May 1. "In that journey," Gardiner remarked of King (who had grown side whiskers like his literary hero Major Winthrop), "he showed his wonderful power of entering the lives and sympathies of every human being in the train, from the half-breed Indian hunter to the gaunt and bigoted Southwestern Missouri emigrant."

The Speers company crossed the Big Muddy on a new-built bridge. Beyond the bottomland thickets on the opposite shore, the road rolled across a green expanse of grass, the home of prairie hens and doves. The sky grew dark the second afternoon, then flashed with zigzags of lightning which drenched the plains in amethyst fire. Thunder crashed and roared and rolled, a tumult that made mock of heat storms in the East. Then the rain beat down in sheets. Successive nights of deluge all but stalled the caravan and made an anticlimax of the rawboned posse that barred the way near a dozen shanties known as Troy.

Before King could understand the trouble, he and Gardiner and Hyde were dragged into a frame hutch that served for court. A long-faced judge glowered down at them, and they heard themselves described as "nigger thieves." They were accused of having kidnaped free Negroes and run them back into Missouri, their lank captors looking more than earnest about the charge. But Mr. Speers rushed to the rescue. He vouched for their innocence. The judge dismissed the case, and King and his trailmates hurried from the quagmire court before the posse suffered another change of mind.

The stock and wagons slogged through the merciless mud, over parallel trails to the "Coast of Nebraska." Now and then they passed small bands of Potowatomis, first of the Indian tribes they would see. The lush grass of Kansas gave way to sweeps of sagebrush, mixed with cactus, aloe, and purple vetch. Bad weather lingered, and each new thunderhead filled the teamsters with dismay.

On the thirteenth day of the journey a marvel appeared in the western sky—a column of lightning that slid up the heavens like a luminous snake. Its head dissolved in a noon-like glare; then came a crash that made the earth tremble.* It was like a portent of ancient times and made King wonder what magic it held for Indians that slunk

---

* Fitz Hugh Ludlow, known as the "Hasheesh Eater," later described the wonder as he saw it from a Concord coach while crossing the plains with the landscape artist Albert Bierstadt. "If it were only possible to paint such things! But on canvas they would seem even more theatrical than they do in these inadequate words. In all the wrath of nature . . . there never visited me anything to compare in awful splendor . . . with this upward lightning stroke on the Nebraska plains" (*The Heart of the Continent*, p. 21).

at night about the camp. Could it promise more abundant buffalo? Old signs of the herds could be seen as the caravan neared the Platte. Buffalo paths which led from the river crossed the road at intervals.

Not far beyond Fort Kearney, King learned of a herd drifting north to its summer range. The news filled him with a yearning for the chase. He assumed the task of adding buffalo hump and tongue to their humdrum fare of cornbread, beans, and fatty pork. The pace of the cavalcade allowed him plenty of time. He engaged a local plainsman as his guide and traded his pony for one that was especially trained for hunting on the plains.

They got an early start the following day and had no trouble in finding the herd, a dark and somber line along the south horizon. As Theodore Roosevelt later wrote, "Mr. King reckoned that it must have covered an area nearly seventy miles by thirty in extent; the figure representing his rough guess, made after travelling through the herd crosswise, and upon knowing how long it took to pass a given point going northward. This great herd of course was not a solid mass of buffaloes; it consisted of innumerable bands of every size, dotting the prairie within the limits given." When among the nearest sentinels, the guide advised King to pick a single quarry and concentrate on it alone. King chose a young bull, and when it galloped off he spurred his pony in pursuit, Colt in hand. He chased it for about two miles, and then in a shallow basin he squeezed the trigger, firing behind the buffalo's shoulder. Spots of red sprang out upon its hide.

Suddenly the bull made a stand, its eyes glaring like fiery pitch. It dipped its head, then charged with a bellow, just as King's pony wheeled about, unsettled by the stampede. A solid front of buffalo stormed across the trough, hemming King's mount between their rush and the charging bull. The head of the wounded animal rammed into the afterpart of King's saddle. The impact hurled the pony to the ground, with its back broken, a crushing weight on King's leg; while, as if in a dream, he watched the bull wheel over them in a ponderous somersault. It gasped its last breath in the wallow where it had fallen.

A mile and a half of buffalo thundered by, with King estimating their number at about ten thousand head. Their horns glinted like a flight of spearheads, and their plunging masses split in streams around King's injured horse and the carcass of the bull. The ground trembled under their hoofs, and the pony screamed till King put a bullet through its brain. Then he waited, choking with dust, afraid that each moment might be his last.

Later the plainsman found him and hurried him off to an army doctor's care at Fort Kearney. The next day King boarded the Overland stage to overtake the Speers train. He was lame, but he had a story that would become a campfire favorite.

In the days that followed the Speers train rolled along the south bank of the Platte, whose lazy course was fringed by vivid green cottonwoods. Soon they passed through Ash Hollow, where General Harney had thrashed the Sioux, and near the forlorn town of Julesburg they crossed the river at a ford treacherous with quicksands. Near the end of May they rested on a once-grassy bottom between two popular landmarks of the trail—Courthouse and Chimney Rocks. No matter how these might pique King's curiosity as geological freaks, his lameness prevented him from riding with a friendly drover named Dick Cotter to carve his name like other emigrants at the Chimney's base. Nor for the present could he take side trips with Gardiner, who seemed engrossed in a family whom the Indian dangers had brought into the train. There were two daughters, both of whom wore bloomers, and Miss Amanda, the older girl, was not ill-favored in spite of numerous insect welts. It troubled King to watch Gardiner ride off beside her every morning. Not even the landmarks past Fort Laramie, where the monotony of the plains began to disappear—Independence Rock, Devil's Gate, and Ice Slough—kept him quite enough absorbed to forget his apprehensions over Jim. He could not feel certain of Gardiner's safety till Miss Amanda and her family had finally parted from the train.

He had regained the use of his leg meanwhile.* He could ride a borrowed horse, and he stood guard again every third night. And once while out with a comrade in search of "cold pure water," he rode to a mountain range eighteen miles or so from their route. On starting back he found that a party of "savages" had crossed their trail, and soon they came upon an Indian camp. With great uneasiness—for how could they know whether or not the warriors were hostile?—they hid in the brush all night, not rejoining the train till after dawn. At this date King's convictions about Indians were still "tinged with [what he would call] the most sanguinary Caucasian prejudices."

The caravan soon finished its pull across the "elephant's back"—at

---

*According to Theodore Roosevelt (*The Wilderness Hunter*, p. 195), King's leg had been broken in his mishap with the buffalo bull. The short period of King's convalescence, however, suggests otherwise.

South Pass—the June sky a deep blue, the Wind River Mountains gleaming like silver to the north. Several old trappers volunteered "an instructive history" of the pass—how buffalo had trailed through it from time out of mind, followed first by Indians, then by mountain men, who had shown the way to emigrants bound for Oregon. Last of all had come Frémont, over a well worn trail, but all America had resounded with praise of his "discovery."

King's party proceeded along the Overland stage route, down the Big Sandy, past the cut-off trail to Fort Hall. Rumors of hostile tribes increased, and every evening hungry Indians loitered near the camp. Doubtless King and his friends would have felt less easy still had they known the fears of the nearest Indian agent—that hordes of aroused Shoshones were ready to cut the road between South Pass and Bridger. Often, too, the wayside grass was "shaved behind the skin"; and men from the caravan had to search for forage. On June 21 they reached the Green River, a stream of pale beryl, much too swift for an easy crossing; and three days later they came to Fort Bridger, a prison now for nine hundred Shoshones, whose chiefs were ready to smoke the pipe with commissioners of the Great White Father.

The route through the Wasatch Range continued surprisingly easy, thanks to a series of interconnecting clefts that started with Echo Canyon, frequently precipitous, with walls of red sandstone. The geology fascinated King and, like a host of emigrants since the Gold Rush days, he and Gardiner kept diaries of their observations. Their youthful reflections, even in the galleries of the Wasatch, were to have seminal effects upon the career of each. Both were to regard much of their later achievements as "the natural outgrowth" of their trek across the continent.

On reaching the Weber Valley they feasted on the produce of Mormon gardens, including lettuce and green onions. Then on June 29 the valley of the Great Salt Lake unfolded before them, the lake shimmering like a plain of turquoise. The train rested in the public square of the city of Salt Lake, a spacious plaza watered by a cold snow brook. "The city was well laid out," wrote one of the party," but most of the houses at that time were adobe or sundried brick." Roses grew in the dooryards, and there were orchards of pears and apples, apricots and peaches. It was surprising to find such a place in the heart of the wilderness; there were brick stores stocked with luxuries, and the Mormons were hard at work on "the great tabernacle built of huge slabs of granite."

Before Mr. Speers could order the train on, a carriage drawn by two enormous mules rolled up, with Brigham Young inside, a square-jawed man with sandy hair shot through with gray. He was well informed about the Speers party, and he wanted to give them some advice before they moved into the great salt desert. He pleaded for understanding, not only for his own people but also for the marauding Utes. They would never regret it, the Mormon president declared, if they gave the "Indian a biscuit instead of a bullet." Brigham Young—notwithstanding a rumor of "forty-four wives and seventy-five children"—won the admiration of King and his friends.

"He was certainly chief among the Mormons," was their verdict.

Brigham's biscuit philosophy may have given them somewhat calmer hearts as they started toward the inferno of salt and alkali which stretched west beyond the lower edge of the Great Salt Lake. They followed the Overland stage road, the route that Captain James Simpson had surveyed four years before, and the Pony Express had used till superseded by the new-strung wires of Western Union. Before reaching the salt beds, Mr. Speers had casks and barrels filled with water from the last brackish spring; then the train pushed on at night. They came to an Overland stage station some forty miles out on the desert and found that the soldiers there expected nightly raids from the Goshutes of the region. Indian signal fires blinked balefully from the porphrytic crags that loomed from the plains beyond. "For three hundred miles," claimed another party who passed that way a few days later, "we rode expecting death in every canyon."

But no threat of danger could spoil the pleasure King and Gardiner took in the journey, and when a month of steady travel had brought them to the western edge of the Great Basin, Gardiner wrote: "Before we left the Plains we had become so fascinated with the life and so interested in the vast loneliness in these deserts . . . that I would gladly have turned around and traveled back over the same road." They reached the Carson River* on August 6, 1863, and there before them loomed the great Sierra, a barrier which, as King would later describe it, towered "high against the west, its summits snow-capped, and its flanks shaded by a forest of dark green pines."

King and his two companions parted from the train at Carson City, a few blocks of brash frame buildings, for Mr. Speers planned to lead the

---

*King's party probably took the Simpson route all the way to the Carson Valley, notwithstanding S. F. Emmon's statement that "their line of march followed the Humboldt River in Nevada."

outfit over the mountains without a delay, while King had opted for a brief pause in Nevada Territory. It was not a final farewell, however, for King was to see the train again at Sacramento—in a "large corral," as he would describe the scene, "and there in the middle were our old wagons drawn up in a line, Big John's, Dick's, and the ambulance. Under the shed in one long row were the stock, the dear old mules I had watched so many nights."

King went at once to see the latest wonder of the world—the Comstock Lode. Bill Hyde's father welcomed the three at his Pioneer Foundry in Gold Hill, a roaring boom town a mile below Virginia City. The Comstock settlements were perched like martins' nests upon the flanks of Mount Davidson, where "Washoe zephers" howled like demons above the clatter of a thousand stamps.

The wind was screeching wildly on the night of King's arrival. The pinewood building of Mr. Hyde's foundry creaked and shivered in the blast, but King fell asleep, along with thirteen other persons quartered there. The wind still raged when he awoke at one in the morning, and the roar of fire intensified its din. Half blind from smoke, he dashed from the building, from which sheets of flame were pouring into the wind. He had come near to losing his life in the conflagration, heavy sleeper that he was.

Everything that he and Gardiner owned—their money, letters, diaries, all their clothes but those in which they had gone to bed—were burned. But they were fortunate compared with Mr. Hyde, who had no insurance and who had been lamed by burns while saving his books. He estimated his loss at one hundred thousand dollars; but he started to rebuild as soon as the ashes were cold, and King and Gardiner may have helped on the job, though a friend later wrote that King found work at a quartz mill to fund their trip across the Sierra. Two weeks later they left for California, and having found it necessary to sell their horses, they planned to walk the entire length of the Placerville Road.

That highway had become one of the busiest freight routes in America, crowded with mule teams drawing wagons, schooners, even occasional Concord coaches. It would have been strange indeed had King and Gardiner not been able to catch a ride while trudging along the roadside. Soon a teamster stopped his wagon. He was on his way to Stockton; and when he invited the boys up on the seat beside him, they did not hesitate.

They rode across the divide and coasted down the western slope, passing continuously "the great Sierra mule-train,—that industrial gulf stream," as King would describe it, "flowing from California plains over into arid Nevada, carrying thither materials for life and luxury." Saturday night brought them to Placerville, which had kept a smack of Hangtown roughness. It hummed with passion over the state election four days off.

It may have been at the small hotel where the teamster had staked King and Gardiner to supper that a "Secesh loud-mouth," sporting a Colt revolver, began to impress his views upon the bar. As King listened, with his hands in his pockets, he scarcely realized that his interest might be taken for a challenge. The bully began to curse him for a Yankee and dropped his hand toward the holstered gun. He never drew it. King was unarmed, his pistol having burned at Gold Hill, but he thrust his thumb forward in his pocket like a hidden derringer. At the same time he snapped the quill toothpick he chanced to have, left over from supper. It made a sound like the click of a pistol lock, and the bully retreated through the doorway.

King turned to Jim, with a breath of relief. This country has a lot of sheep, he said, "—in wolves' clothing."

The teamster had to take the road the following morning, though it was Sunday. There was plenty of work in Stockton, he said, and he'd be pleased to haul them there. King and Gardiner sat down on a bale of hay and deliberated whether to travel on or to honor the fourth commandment. Conscience won, and they bade their friend goodbye; but feeling their clothes too rough for church, they climbed a hill behind the town, to read the Sermon on the Mount from Gardiner's freshly acquired New Testament.

On Monday morning, "footsore and travel-stained," they caught the stage and then the cars on the Central Pacific for Sacramento down on the yellow plain. The paddlewheel which they boarded at the river dock blew its whistle at four in the afternoon and swung into the muddy current. There were scores of men on deck, mostly sun-browned miners, with flannel shirts and high-topped boots, many of them drinking at the rosewood bar. One passenger in particular impressed King and Gardiner.

Gardiner had seen the man first. "Again and again," he wrote, "I walked past him, and at last, seating myself in a chair opposite and pretending to read a paper, I deliberately studied this fascinating individual." Gardiner was sure that the man was an intellectual and he called King's attention to the traveler.

King watched him for a moment. The stranger was perhaps the

roughest-dressed man on the boat, for he wore a battered hat, a coarse gray shirt, and a coat with threadbare elbows. He looked about thirty-five years old. Though he had a full brown beard, the lines in his weather-beaten face gave it a look of kindliness. King had never seen Professor Brewer, but he knew him at once.

Later, when they found him alone, smoking his pipe, King approached and asked if his name were Brewer. It was, the man replied; and then in Gardiner's words: "Clare introduced himself as a student from Yale Scientific School and was warmly received. He then introduced me and we all spent the evening together." William H. Brewer had not been home for three years, and he was eager for news of his friends in the East. King and Gardiner were just as eager to hear of his latest adventures in California.

The professor had, as a matter of fact, just finished a rapid reconnaissance of the Sierra Nevada from Tejon in the south to Forest Hill, just north of Placerville. Of the entire field party, only he and his packer, whom he had left behind with the mules, had been able to stand the hardships. But since he wished to run the reconnaissance through the northern ranges before the summer season ended, he was now on his way to San Francisco to talk with Whitney about replacements. It was a disagreeable task because of a shortage of funds. But they were skimming the cream of geology off the state that season; and with it, as Brewer liked to say, the finest scenery God Almighty ever made.

Only the cry of "Man overboard!" interrupted his good-fellowship. The paddlewheel did not tarry, for the captain learned that a passenger who lived upon the bank had decided to swim directly home. They steamed through the Strait of Carquinez, and the bay then lay before them. Across the water San Francisco sparkled on its sand hills, the monument of California's march (as King would write) "from barbarism to vulgarity." It had been a rapid pace; three years ago only sand had blown across the spot where Brewer's rooms now were. "Of course," he said, "you'll stay at my hotel."

In the morning King and Gardiner spent their last dollars on new clothes—light pants, pale vests, and frock coats that buttoned high about their necks. Then Brewer led them to the survey office, in a large three-story stone building called Montgomery Block. There the survey had filled three rooms with plant and geological specimens, stacked on shelves and stuffed in drawers and cupboards. And there Brewer was greeted by half a dozen men, for most of the corps had returned from the field. Professor Whitney struck the visitors as being of even "heavier caliber than Agassiz." The piercing look of his eyes, between a dome-like forehead and a steel-gray shovel beard, agreed with his reputation for perseverance, or what opponents were apt to call "mule-headedness."

King was well aware of the importance of the Whitney Survey—a work that President Eliot, of Harvard, later cited as "the finest State survey ever made." * King did not disguise his eagerness to join the corps, even as a volunteer without pay. It was clear that Brewer wanted his help, although he warned of Indian troubles to the north. The next day Whitney engaged King on a voluntary basis, and thus he joined the geologists—whom he would blithely term "those hammer-bearing sons of Thor."

Two days later he took leave of Gardiner, soon to be employed by the Army Engineers. He followed Brewer aboard a paddlewheel for Sacramento—a Bible, a book of sermons, and a table of logarithms in his duffel. At the state capital, where they laid over Sunday, King went to church for the first time since April. And what pleasure, he jotted among his notes, to be with worshippers again, to pray when they prayed, and sing when they sang. Brewer then parted from him to go for the pack outfit at Forest Hill. King himself went on to Grass Valley, the agreed place of meeting, where "a fair gelding" waited for him in pasture. Brewer soon arrived on an old roan mustang, following by grunting mules and Jan Hoesch, the Danish packer. Jan was introduced as a genius "in the intricate art of packing." He knew just how a load could best be carried; he was an expert judge of packsaddles; he understood all mulish whims and vagaries. And King at once became his understudy in how to pack their old mules, branded from head to rump like animated Rosetta stones.

As they pushed north, Brewer made notes on the geology and flora of the region. King followed his example, scribbling his own notations down in one of "Henry Penny's small improved metallic books." Their route included mining towns once prosperous, but now reduced by the failure of the placers. Nevada City, San Juan North, Camptonville, Galena Hill, Brandy City, Eureka—most had huge hydraulic diggings now, where whole mountainsides were being washed into coffee-colored

*Eliot would characterize Whitney himself as "a man of absolute integrity, independent to a fault, quick tempered and sensitive,—a somewhat troublesome subordinate, but a very considerate, just, and generous superior."

streams. Yet the pathos of decay hung over all. "You see it in a hundred towns and camps," King later wrote, "where empty buildings in disrepair stand in rows. . . . The cheap squalor of Chinese streets adds misery to the scene, besides scenting a pure mountain air with odors of complete wretchedness."

The more decrepit the town, the higher its prices. It cost the survey fifteen dollars for the three of them to share with seven whites and a pair of queued Chinese a garret in Poker Flat—"a miserable hole," in Brewer's opinion; and the following day King jotted in a notebook: "Poker Flat where we stayed last night is one of the most rudimentary of mining towns; and yet there, Professor B tells me, are houses of ill fame, hurdy gurdy and gambling [dives] of all kinds."

The trail grew rougher as they proceeded, through Whiskey Diggings and Potosi. They had now reached the heart of the northern gold region. Laboriously, they worked up the gorge of the Middle Feather River, then rambled through the uplands north and west of Honey Lake. One of the loveliest spots in the state, Brewer decided, as he attacked a steak which King had broiled to a leathery finish. "Thank God," he added, "I'm omniverous."

They found invertebrate fossils in Genesee Valley, and Brewer beamed with pleasure. Such pieces ought to shed much light on the age of the gold-bearing slates, and that was one of the questions which the survey aimed to answer. King recognized what a superb teacher he had found, and Brewer's interest reassured him that he had chosen the right career. They talked of many things around the campfire or on the trail, including the metamorphic versus the eruptive theory of granite. Brewer soon informed Brush how "well posted" he had found this Sheffield product and how valiantly King had argued for Brush's metamorphic hypothesis. It would take more experience in the field to bring King around to Brewer's view, later universally accepted, that granite was an igneous rock.

Meanwhile the nights grew colder, and it was necessary to head at once for Lassen's Peak, where Brewer proposed to study the lavas of recent eruptions. They packed the mules and made for Big Meadows, fording the Feather River, whose sedgy banks reminded King "of home." They tramped up the valley toward the cone which rose bare and desolate against the sky.

A raw wind howled across the mountain during their initial ascent, on September 26, probably the first time the peak had ever been climbed. King reached the topmost shaft, only to be blown back by the gale. Clouds obscured the landscape below, defeating the purpose of the climb. But Mount Shasta, seventy-five miles away, loomed from the mists, sharp and majestic—the peak which had drawn King like a magnet. He shouted to Brewer above the wailing of the wing: "What would Ruskin have said if he had seen *this!*"

A fierce snow squall delayed a second ascent until September 29. They began the climb by the light of the moon, an hour after midnight. King forged ahead, and again he was the first to reach the highest needle. "Here," he wrote, "I wrapped my blanket round me and looked out over the moonlit distance." It was a world of utter silence till Brewer clattered on to the nearest ledge.

Dawn began to flush the east. The form of Shasta grew more clear, its shawls of snow gleaming like coals. At last the sun appeared, a blaze of gold that tipped the lower sweeps of forest with green fire and flashed from a score of burnished lakes. Projected then against the western sky rose a mighty cone of cobalt blue, a spectral mountain, the arial shadow of King's titanic perch. Sight of it filled him with an awed rapture.

And yet of the whole panorama it was Shasta which held the deepest fascination. It drew his gaze again and again; its sweeps above the snow line stirred him so deeply that he burst, according to Brewer, into "rhapsodies of admiration." A rapport bound the two. "Although I have often reached great altitudes," * Brewer later confessed, "that day stands out in my memory as one of the most impressive of my life."

They remained on the peak for nearly ten hours, tracing out old flows of lava, taking compass bearings, and making sketches of topography. Tyndall's praises of swift glissades were on King's lips as they began the descent, and the invitation of steep snow slopes was irresistible. King had his way in spite of Brewer's cautions; and down he glided over the smooth white surfaces, four and five hundred feet at a stretch. According to Brewer's timing, he slid in less than a minute down a slope which had required an hour to climb, and "Ah, it was splendid!" King exclaimed.

They broke camp on October 1 and worked northward over lava tables toward Pit River. The cone of Mount Shasta, always in sight, dominated the scene; and a week later they crossed the pass at its

* The elevation indicated by their barometers for the peak, "scarcely 11,000 feet," disappointed Brewer. Almost all the heights computed by the California Geological Survey exceeded subsequent measurements. The U.S. Geological Survey cites the height of Mount Lassen as 10,457 feet.

eastern base, where a brook tinkled down from the snows, its water clouded with an ashy sediment. As they studied the turbid color, Brewer remarked that in Switzerland he would have called it a glacier stream.

And why not here? King wondered.

Brewer did not answer at once, but gazed at Shasta's dazzling mantle. He had crossed its upper reaches a year ago, and there had been nothing but snow underfoot. He had seen no ice, not a single crevasse. The milky color of the water must be due, he reasoned, to volcanic dust; so the Whitney reports would credit Mount Shasta with only scars from past glaciers. Yet King could not forget that turbid stream, and Shasta remained a magnet for years to come, a mystery, and an inspiration.

They moved northward then through blistered basalt formations until they came to Pluto's Cave, an extraordinary tubular cavern that extended just below the surface of the lava plain. They entered it beneath a high arch and made their way by candlelight for nearly a mile, with innumerable bats flicking past them in the still, heavy air. "It looks," wrote Brewer, "as if the surface of the great lava flow had cooled, but that the crust had broken somewhere lower down and a long stream of the fluid had run out, leaving a long, empty channel or gallery." At its head they blew their candle out in order to experience the complete, unearthly darkness there. Then they fired a pistol to note the quality of "its dull, muffled explosion." It was an experiment King would repeat at the identical spot seven years later and describe in his chapter "Shasta Flanks."

Soon the little party moved into Oregon, across the Klamath River, along the Cottonwood Road. The forests of the Siskiyous had donned the tones of autumn; frosts aggravated Brewer's rheumatism, and King suffered too. The field work had to be halted. So they struck back across the top of California, through settlements as dreary as any in the state, ending the reconnaissance among the redwoods around Crescent City. King was gnawing at questions that would keep him occupied for years. And he would always feel that the experiences of 1863 had shaped his career.

5

Rooftop of the West

On returning to San Francisco, King learned that Frederick Law Olmsted, an old Hartford friend and the architect of New York City's Central Park,* had become the superintendent of the Mariposa Estate. That famous grant, some seventy square miles in extent, had slipped from General Frémont's absentee control; the general's creditors had formed the Mariposa Mining Company and thrown its stock upon the market. But production at the mines had slumped, and Olmsted welcomed expert counsel, especially from William Ashburner, Whitney's associate.

Whitney decided to lend King's services too. The survey could thus accumulate more data, and King would have the chance to study one of the most important gold-vein regions in the state. He left with Ashburner for the grant on November 24, 1863, and after an overnight journey, arrived in the town of Bear Valley, a few red-roofed buildings along a shrunken stream. The valley paralleled a minor range which bore the sobriquet of Mrs. Frémont's father—"Old Bullion"—and sustained the Mariposa mines on its outcrops of the Mother Lode.

Problems of mining and engineering monopolized Ashburner's time, and King found himself left solely responsible for a general survey of the tract. He enjoyed the job; it required him to tramp for hours every day about the countryside. He grew quite fond of the oak-covered top of Mount Bullion, which he climbed whenever time allowed, especially on Sundays to escape the saturnalia at Bear Valley, where the "boys," like Artemus Ward's citizens of the Bay, remembered "the Sabbath day to keep it jolly." He called Mount Bullion "my Sunday mountain."

From a rocky seat there, King enjoyed gazing at the eastern Sierra, which ranged southward to a vast climax of silvery peaks. These the topographer Charles Hoffmann was to place near the sources of the

---

*During the early part of the Civil War Olmsted had also served as general secretary of the United States Sanitary Commission, predecessor of the American Red Cross, a taxing job that had undermined his health.

Kings* and Kaweah rivers. There could be no doubt of their towering height—perhaps they were even higher than Mount Shasta. On a Christmas trip to San Francisco, King talked of them as if they had stolen Shasta's place in his affections. The effect of his enthusiasm was less than flattering; Whitney wondered if he had begun to slight his investigations for Ruskinistic dawdling, and Brewer mentioned King's dislike for "unpleasant work" in a letter to Brush. Even Ashburner may have begun to form the unfavorable opinion that he later relayed to Brewer. King was "such a confounded little 'blow-hard,' " his verdict would hold, and his statements, when sifted, revealed such "little foundation that I have begun to class him with Fitz Hugh Ludlow, and don't put much reliance in any of his stories." But the sharpest cut at the time came from William Gabb the paleontologist, who made no secret of his contempt for a fellow who preferred to sit on a peak and dream all day over snow mountains in the distance instead of hunting fossils in the gold belt.

Plunged in gloomy revery as he rode back to the mines in the company of Hoffmann, King repledged himself to science. He would uncover that elusive link that Whitney yearned for (which, to be sure, Brewer and he had found at Genesee Creek, except that no one thought it "conclusive"), the fossil that would solve forever the riddle of the gold belt's age. He pressed his search for days, "smashing tons of rock" in the words of Hoffmann and wearing out his field hammer. Then, *eureka*! He found it in a gulch known as Hell's Hollow—"the object for which science had searched and yearned and despaired. . . . I was at pains," he wrote later, "to chip my victim out whole, and when he chose to break in two was easily consoled, reflecting that he would do as well gummed together."

Heartened, King persevered until he found more "plump pampered belemnites" at other places on the estate. Some turned up within twenty feet of the auriferous quartz of the Pine Tree vein. The riddle of the gold belt was solved—the upheaval had occurred in Jurassic times—and Whitney would give King credit for the field work. He wrote, "The geology of the Mariposa estate has been examined with some detail by Mr. King," then cited King's examinations of the dip and

---

*Spelled *King's* by Clarence King and the California Geological Survey. A formerly frequent use of the singular possessive helps account perhaps for a misconception sometimes encountered that Kings River, like Mount King at the head of South Fork, was named for Clarence King. It was called, rather, by the early Spaniards the River of the Holy Kings (*el Rio de los Santos Reyes*).

strike of the Mariposa slates, as well as his study of about 150 outcroppings of the gold-bearing quartz. King began to feel less like a tyro, especially when an established geologist, William Phipps Blake, tried to usurp priority for similar finds of his own.

In March 1864 King interrupted work at the Mariposa Estate for his first visit to Yosemite. Doubtless the excursion furnished exciting impressions to reinforce those in the pages he would write about his later sojourns in the valley and its environs. Then in April Whitney invited him on a trip to western Nevada to help on a study of rock formations there, a comparative survey which Whitney hoped might shed more light on the rocks of California. King joined the professor at Sacramento, where they took the Oakland stage—a mountain mudwagon—across the Sierra. Deep mud clogged the road beyond Placerville, and heavy snow toward the crest made it necessary to change to a sleigh. King stayed behind at Lake Tahoe to make barometer readings along the south shore, and on rejoining Whitney on the Comstock he found that his chief had decided to send him on a reconnaissance of the West Humboldt range, whose summits loomed snow-clad against the northeast horizon.

It appeared that Whitney had long pondered over the need for a geological section across the Great Basin. Such an undertaking was out of the question now because of the cost. But as soon as the California Survey could be completed across the Sierra, it might be possible to secure financial aid from the Central Pacific Railroad, now under construction; or Congress itself might be made to see the light. Whitney's visions revived the inspiration that had struck King on his transcontinental trip, rekindling his imagination. The difficulties of such a section seem insuperable; yet the first step could now be taken, and King hoped to turn the work in the Humbolt Mountains to good advantage.

He crossed the Carson desert with a small escort and marched along the west wall of the highly colored range. He climbed to the top of Star Peak, still crowned with snow, the highest prominence in the range. It furnished a fine view out over the wastes of Nevada, swept with yellow whirlwinds. Due west stood Lassen's Peak, soaring above the haze. King had time for only a cursory examination of the range and its companion chain to the eastward, and his report was not as full as Whitney might have wished for, yet the state geologist was to concede that Mr. Clarence King had made "some important explorations . . . in Nevada territory."

Meanwhile, King's wonder at the great white mountain masses at the southern extension of the Sierra had induced Whitney to authorize an exploration there. The survey's report in *Geology* would, in time, record how the glimpses which King had caught of them from Mount Bullion had led "to the belief that here were the most elevated summits of the range; and this fact, coupled with the circumstance that, unless explored during this season by the Geological Survey, this region might long remain a blank on the map of California, led to organization of a small party." King joined it on his return from the Humboldt country, a party charged with making the first systematic exploration of the High Sierra, "the new Alps."

Brewer headed the expedition; Hoffmann had consented to go as chief topographer, and Gardiner as a voluntary surveyor. King's crony of the plains, Dick Cotter, was hired as general aide and packer instead of Hoesch the Dane, on King's promise to take responsibility for the mules while Cotter learned the tricks of packing. They assembled in Oakland, where the animals were stabled; and there they called on the witty Irish forty-niner J. Ross Browne, a compiler of mining statistics who kept in touch with Whitney's work and whose humorous writing would anticipate Mark Twain. "We had a jolly time," Brewer noted; "he drew an amusing caricature of us, with our big boots, woolen shirts, and closely cropped hair." They found Browne's house almost as interesting as Browne himself; for in a quaint, not unattractive way Pagoda Hill, as it was called, mixed Chinese, Indian, Moorish, Gothic, Italian, and Russian styles of architecture.

Under way on May 25, 1864, the party trudged down the eastern side of the bay, reaching San José by the second evening. The buckskin which King rode gave him endless trouble, especially in Pacheco Pass, where to complicate matters the packs began to slip down under the bellies of the mules.

Drought had settled over California with an intensity never before recorded, the worst dry season within the white man's memory. Heat ranged from ninety-two to ninety-eight degrees as the party toiled toward the Central Valley. "No green thing meets the eye," Brewer wrote. A shimmering haze veiled the distance and blotted out the Sierra; a hot wind slashed across the pass. Dust covered the food and gritted between King's teeth at evening bivouac, and it was hard to breathe because of the stench from the putrid bodies of cattle that had died around the hole which furnished the only water in the vicinity. Buzzards and coyotes hovered about, glutted with carrion.

The tempers of all grew trigger-sharp as they pushed down the Butterfield stage road. King lost count of the dead stock they passed, dry as mummies. Carcasses dotted the plain, which stretched away completely bare except for occasional sprigs of sere wire-grass. Only mirages and dust devils broke the monotony. Once twenty-seven whirlwinds swept across the valley in a dismal train, whipping dust into the air in columns several hundred feet high. Now and then these pillars of dust would take the shape of slim shafts, which swayed back and forth like giant ropes. "At other times they rose in hollow, inverted cones, or a column would expand into a cone at some distance from the ground. At the junction of the column and the cone a fringe or horizontal cloud of dust would occasionally be seen, with many fantastic forms, in which column and cone were variously combined." These grotesque effects, which usually occurred between ten in the morning and two in the afternoon, were the emblems of that difficult crossing which cost the life of one of the mules. *

Its death throes awoke King and his comrades in the night. Nothing they could do, however, could save the animal, for the combination of poor feed, dust and alkali, heat, and poisonous water had left it a gasping ruin. It gave its last choke in the coppery dawn, and they left its body on the plain, another feast for the gorged vultures. But the mule's fate soon worked in King's favor; his stubborn buckskin was sentenced to the pack saddle as soon as another mount could be procured at Visalia, a languid village in a grove of live oaks. There a bankrupt Mexican agreed to part with his horse for a small sum of gold. It was a young bay gelding, with slim black legs and a blaze in his eyes and a light-hooved lope that recalled John Brent's superb black stallion. Having named him Kaweah for the river at hand, King saddled him at once, to get acquainted, while Brewer called on the local commandant of cavalry, from whom he was authorized to request an escort against Indians, should the need arise.

While still in Visalia, Brewer bought more rations than Buckskin and the mule Nell could carry. It was necessary to hire an ox team to haul the load up to the camp which they planned to establish at a saw-

---

* This crossing of the Central Valley cannot be considered typical, but the difficulties are not exaggerated. The drought of 1863 and 1864 ruined the early cattle industry of the state. King later described the scene: "Desolation such as drought has never before or since been able to make reigned in dreary monotony over the plains" (*Mountaineering,* p. 177). For years thereafter bleached skeletons littered the valley floor.

mill, sixty miles beyond. On the June 8 they started for the mountains, whose summits glistened above the nearer foothills. The temperature rose to a hundred degrees, and all felt sick in their saddles until they reached the trees in the foothills. There on Sunday King read aloud from the book of sermons he carried in his pack, and as the others approved, it became his Sunday custom to read some kind of religious fare.

The third day brought them to an amphitheater filled with conifers. There was a meadow, and a stream that rippled over granite sand on its way to the Kings. Brewer chose a campsite on a knoll, within view of the Thomas sawmill (later called Millwood), and they settled down for a week, to study the environs. Climbing various crags, King sketched the profile of the eastern crest, traced its drainage system, memorized its complicated form, and remained convinced of the superior height of the mountains there.

The trees which he passed on rides were magnificent, especially the giant sequoias. Months before, Brewer had heard reports of these southern groves, containing the largest Big Trees in the state; and the California State Survey would soon publicize them—"discover" them (as the Pathfinder had "discovered" South Pass). "The newspapers out there," Gardiner remarked in after years, "have hardly yet ceased congratulating us." They were camped not far from the throngs of Big Trees that would later be known as the General Grant Grove. They marveled at the size of one sequoia that stood on a ridge to the north of their bivouac. It was called the "King of the Mountains" and may well have been the giant that would, in another three years, be christened the General Grant Tree. The cinnamon-colored trunk towered 274 feet, according to their triangulation, and measured 106 feet around the base, nearly twice the girth of the largest tree at Calaveras. Before the "King" had been burned by a forest fire the circumference may have equalled 120 feet.

What impressed King most about the sequoias, beyond their size, was the foliage which flared from the boughs like a "mist of pale apple-green." "The Sequoia being in flower," he wrote, "we shot down a branch"; and that reminded him that "the great Humboldt would have been better off with a six-shooter, for he complained of being for years in the tropics without being able to examine the flowers of the palm which hung sixty feet overhead because he could hire no native to climb for him." Through the burned-out heart of one fallen tree they found they could ride a horse for seventy-six feet with ample room for turning. Brewer wrote to Asa Gray, the botanist, that "the whole party rode in by turns, 'to have the thing to tell of.'" Cotter managed even to gallop his mount inside the hollow, for it averaged nine feet high and was equally wide; and at the point of greatest expansion, Brewer stood erect in his saddle and could barely touch the top with his hand. In their droll way the local Indians spoke of the largest tree of all growing north of the South Kings, but the party lacked the time to make a search for it.

King spared time, however, to visit the Digger rancheria and watch the funeral of the chief's dead squaw. The body lay on a pyre of logs, the breast covered by a grass bowl and a papoose basket. The mountain basin echoed with the wails of the mourners, old hags with hair smeared with pitch and ashes. One aged tar-head hailed the sun as it set, snatched a brand from the nearby fire, and lit the funeral couch.

"Himalaya! Himalaya!" chanted the mourners.

Buck the chief wept as the flames licked through the papoose pouch of willow bark. The pitch fire burned intensely hot, and he suddenly staggered toward it, only to be dragged back by watchful tribesmen to his children. "Not a stoical savage, but a despairing husband, stood before us," King later wrote. This, clearly, was not the time for con-dolences, and so King left. Next morning he asked a good-natured Digger known as Revenue Stamp how the chief had fared in his grief.

"He whiskey drunk" the Stamp replied.

And who, King asked, was the fat girl with him?

"New squaw."

Rhetorical question: "Who shall say that our outcast persecuted red brother is not capable of all the sensations . . . the grief of our higher selves? *I* can," King scribbled in a notebook, "for I saw the widower married on the following day, bloated with feasting and drinking, swaggering about with a pair of States pants." Buck interrupted the celebration of his nuptials long enough to steal a prized silk hand-kerchief from King.

As soon as the hired ox team came with the supplies, King's party prepared to push on toward the never-melting snows. They cached part of the stores at the mill, broke camp, and leaving all known trails behind them, zigzagged through a wilderness of fir and pine and scat-tered sequoia, along the spur between gorges of the Kaweah and the South Kings. The route was so steep that the mules could hardly cling to the rock, and the best they could make was eight miles a day until they struck a cattle trail, freshly cut to the alpine pastures ahead.

They spent four days at Big Meadows, making side trips out from

camp. King and Cotter celebrated the summer solstice with an unsuccessful bear hunt, and before they could regain camp a violent snowstorm swept down from the peaks. All of the company had to burrow
under piles of brush on the lee side of high boulders, and when that
shelter failed them they built a bonfire of pitch-soaked pine knots. The
smoke guided to camp two U.S. dragoons who had come from Visalia
to ask Brewer to request an escort, for then their detachment, or part of
it, could escape from the terrible heat of the valley. The soldiers
promised that the escort would join the expedition in two weeks and go
with them "into the region possibly hostile."

Near the end of their stay at Big Meadows a huge mixed-blood
Cherokee and a butternut-clad Pike, who had camped nearby to hunt
for deerhides, offered them some haunches of venison and expressed
interest in their plans to explore the High Sierra. "From them," King
wrote, "we learned that they had themselves penetrated farther than
any others, and had only given up the exploration after wandering
fruitlessly among the cañons for a month. They told us that if we did
succeed in reaching this summit we would certainly be the first."

When the march was resumed, King took the lead, heading southeast across the meadows, past herds of gaunt cattle that Mexican
vanqueros had driven up from the plains to escape starvation. The
plateau swept in terraces toward the crest, and granite domes rose
bleakly out of the forest, The way was so difficult that they accomplished only a few miles a day, never more than eight. They had
reached an altitude between nine thousand and ten thousand feet,
where the sky was slate blue and only the soughing of wind, the murmur
of water, and the occasional cries of Clarke crows broke the silence.

On the last day of June, after King had killed an enormous rattlesnake, they veered to the north, toward the gorge of a stream known
later as Roaring River. This course, they hoped, would lead them to
their goal more quickly than the high divide; and soon they struck
moraines—smooth grades, miles in length, that promised an easy
highway to the ramparts of the crest. For the rest of the day they
plodded up the even incline till, reaching snow, they pitched camp in
an alpine basin beyond which their animals could go no further. "A
thousand upspringing spires and pinnacles pierce[d] the sky in every
direction," King wrote; "the cliffs and mountain-ridges [were] everywhere ornamented with countless needle-like turrets. Crowning the
wall to the south of our camp were series of these jagged forms standing
out against the sky like a procession of colossal statues. Whichever way

we turned, we were met by some extraordinary fulness of detail. Every mass seemed to have the highest ornamental finish."

At dawn next morning Brewer and Hoffmann left the bivouac, with barometer and theodolite across their shoulders. They planned to climb the massive pyramidal peak that filled the head of the basin, for they believed it was a dominant point in the final crestline of the Sierra. Their faces were drawn with weariness as they limped back into camp that evening and sank near the fire. They were silent for some moments before describing their climb, with its two false starts. They had not gained the top till two that afternoon. Then what a panorama! A hundred peaks, Brewer judged, all over thirteen thousand feet.

Barometic calculations indicated that the elevation of the rocks on which they had stood exceeded 13,800 feet. * An empty gulf had yawned before them, with sheer precipices and numerous small blue lakes. Five miles beyond rose a range with points higher than any summit near them. Hoffmann opened his notebook; and King, on seeing the sketches there, exclaimed in triumph. "I instantly recognized the peaks," he wrote, "which I had seen from Mariposa, whose great white pile had led me to believe them the highest points in California."

The ultimate crestline was unapproachable, Brewer feared. But King could not renounce his wish to explore it; for had he not read Tyndall, as Brewer recalled, "and thought no place was inaccessible"? The next morning he asked Cotter, whose "iron endurance" made of him a model climbing partner, if he cared to try for "the top of California."

"Why not?" was Cotter's debonair reply.

Besieged by both, Brewer yielded his permission, in spite of their dwindling supplies; and they began to prepare for the climb, rolling a week's supply of bread, beans, and venison in their blankets. "King is enthusiastic," Brewer wrote, "is wonderfully tough, has the greatest endurance I have ever seen, and is withal very muscular. He is a perfect specimen of health."

King and Cotter's arduous celebration of the 4th of July began with the first faint streaks of gray in the eastern sky. "Brewer and Gardiner," King wrote, "went with us to the summit of the western ridge just where Mt. Brewer rises. The view from there was wild and rugged beyond

* The U.S. Geological Survey cites the elevation of Mount Brewer (which Brewer's companions insisted on so naming) as 13,570 feet.

anything I have seen. . . . Brewer then tried to dissuade us from venturing further . . . but we had made up our minds to try." Both shouldered forty-pound packs, loads which their companions had borne thus far. King shook Brewer's hand, and when pressed for plans he had to admit he had only one—to stand on the highest peak, God willing. The climb which he now began with Cotter inaugurated, in the opinion of Francis Farquhar, Sierra historian, "a new era in American mountaineering. Never before had anyone attempted to traverse such a complex mass of ridges and canyons as those that confronted them."

In the south a procession of crags joined the two main crests of the Sierra, like the crossbar of a titanic H. It formed a divide between the headwaters of the Kings and Kern rivers, and King sensed that somewhere along it lay a possible route. Exactly where was another question; indeed the first problem was to reach it at all. Because precipitous pinnacles barred direct passage along the western crest to its junction with the transverse ridge, they tried an oblique approach. They worked down across several cirques which drained into the Kings, night overtaking them as they prepared to scale the divide itself and cross into the head of Kern Canyon. They bivouacked frigidly on a shelf of granite under an overhanging ledge, which sheltered them from the immense blocks of rock that came hurtling down the mountainside on being dislodged by the leverage of frost. After a few hours in their blankets they munched a starlit breakfast, then began to climb a steep snow slope. Cutting steps with their bowie knives, they worked their way upward for about five hours.

"It was now that our reata came into play," King wrote, "and we took turns in climbing the length of it, and pulling packs and blankets after us, reaching the top about noon. . . . What was our consternation to find ourselves, as we scaled the summit, on the brink of an almost Yosemite cliff!" They crept along the edge to a series of shelves and then, King added,

I tied the reata firmly about my body, and Cotter lowered me down to the first shelf; he then sent down the precious barometer and our packs. Next, he made a fast loop in the lasso, hooked it over a point of rock and came down handover-hand, whipping the rope off the rock to which it had been fastened, thus severing our communications with the top of the cliff.

Three hours of such work brought them to the bottom of the cliff, a feat whose description is said to be "the earliest record in the Sierra of the practice of roping-down." Then they made their way through fields of alpine grass towards the base of the peak that was their goal. They camped in a grove of lodgepole pines, rising before dawn to continue the climb.

High noon brought them to the summit and a view out over Owens Lake and seven ranges of desert mountains. It was a place of awful sublimity; the noon sky was "grave with noctural darkness." King wrote:

The earth blinds you with its light. . . . With an aspect of endless remoteness burns the small white sun, yet its light seems to pass invisibly through the sky, blazing out with painfully bright reflections, and lighting up the burnt sand and stone of the desert with a strange blinding glare. There is no sentiment of beauty in the whole scene. . . . Silence and desolation are the themes which nature has wrought out under this eternally serious sky.

The stillness there, in King's phrase, was like "the soundlessness of a vacuum . . . the waveless calmness of space" He broke it at once: "I rang my hammer on the topmost rock; we grasped hands, and I reverently named the grand peak MOUNT TYNDALL." *

That must have been after he had swept the horizon with a level and found that the granite under foot was not, as he had supposed, the highest point in the range, not the climaxing elevation for which they had reserved the name Mount Whitney. Within a radius of seven miles loomed other peaks with elevations equal to Mount Tyndall's, and at least two towered even higher. The nearest was a formidable pile of needles two miles away, and King named it Mount Williamson in honor of the Army Engineer officer who had surveyed one of the western railroad routes.

The loftiest summit of all, six miles or so to the north, resembled an aggressive flat helmet facing the desert, for King could see a field of snow there. "Mount Whitney," he wrote, "as we afterward called it in honor of our chief, is probably the highest land within the United States. Its summit looked glorious but inaccessible." It sat as a capstone for a region sculptured by ice into shapes that seemed purely Gothic in

---

* When King visited England in 1882, he is said to have "compare[d] mountaineering notes with his great compeer, Tyndall" (Bronson, *Cowboy Life on the Western Plains*, p. 354).

spirit—shapes that made King feel as sure as Ruskin that "the Alps [had] furnished the models for early cathedrals."

He longed to climb that helmetlike peak, and he resolved to find some possible route to its unrivaled crest. Limited supplies prevented him and Cotter from trying to reach it now; their food was barely sufficient, as it was, to take them back to their companions, and their worn condition increased the risks of climbing. Cotter's boots had gone to pieces, and in spite of strips of flour sack bound about his feet for whatever protection they might afford, he left a trail of blood as he walked.

"We were obliged," King said in his report to Whitney, "to take a new route home, but made the whole successfully, reaching the camp near Mount Brewer with our bones and our barometer whole, although twice on the way Cotter came within a hair's breadth of losing his life, and once I almost gave myself up." * They mustered strength enough to dash into camp at full speed, their shouts answered by the voices of their waiting friends. That night as they all reclined around their campfire, Brewer said: "King, you have relieved me of a dreadful task. For the last three days I have been composing a letter to your family, but somehow I did not get beyond 'It becomes my painful duty to inform you.' "

It was Brewer's opinion that the Mount Tyndall climb was "by far the greatest feat of strength and endurance that [had] yet been performed on the Survey." Even Whitney later added: "[King] deserves a gold medal for his pluck."

Brewer defined the diet to which the party had been reduced as "partial starvation." It was urgent for them to hurry back to the cache at the sawmill; and in doing so they passed Big Meadows, where the military escort waited, seven soldiers fitted out with carbines, mules, and a month's supply of rations. Brewer was ill, with an ulcerated tooth that resisted all of King's attempts to pull it with a bullet mold, and King insisted on going with him in search of a dentist. They rode all night to Visalia. When the ulceration broke, Brewer's relief was so

---

* Cf. Francis Farquhar's remark: "The difficulties of the descent, as described by King, are hard to account for. Perhaps one should accept the offer King once made to [J. D. Hague] who challenged some of his statements, that he would 'throw off five degrees for a flat acceptance, or, otherwise he would conduct him personally to the scene.' Those who have been on the scene would, I believe, demand more than five degrees" (*History of the Sierra Nevada*, p. 147).

frank that King dared beg him for permission to climb the Kern Sierra for an attempt on the helmetlike peak which they had named Mount Whitney.

Brewer consented, gave him a hundred dollars for expenses, and told him to rejoin the party on August 1 at Galen Clark's Ranch—or Clark's Station, as it was also called. King secured an escort of two cavalrymen, a pack horse, and rations for a two-week trip. He left Visalia on July 14, with the temperature ranging between 108 and 111 degrees in the shade, and entered the mountains the following day by way of a new trail that a cattleman named Hockett had opened along the south fork of the Kaweah River.

"I rode until nine in the evening," he wrote in a note for Whitney, "when we came to the 'Hog ranch.'" That rude establishment—"two acres of tranquil pork"—was set near a meadow high in "the most magnificent forest in the Sierras." Here he prepared to stay over Sunday to rest the horses, a break that would give him scene and circumstance for a portrait, a blend of fancy and fact concerning a family of chronic wanderers. One frequently saw such families in the West, and months before he had talked with one of them, rolling down from Oregon, the pathos of their lot prompting him to note in his field book: "poor restless people who come from a better land."

Later King developed the theme: "That brave spirit of Westward Ho! which has been the pillar of fire and cloud leading on the weary march of progress over stretches of desert . . . that restless spirit which has dared to uproot the old and plant the new, kindling the grand energy of California, laying foundations for a State to be, that [will] fill an immortal page in the story of America, but when, instead of urging on to wresting from new lands something better than old can give, it degenerates into mere weak-minded restlessness, killing the power of growth, the ideal of home, the faculty of repose, it results in that race of perpetual emigrants who roam as dreary waifs over the West, losing possessions, love of life, love of God, slowly dragging from valley to valley till they fall by the wayside."

Such were the Newtys—as King would christen his pig-herding friends—a mother and father, one full-grown daughter, two ague-ridden children, whom he found sharing the chaos of a common bed, before a pyramid of glowing coals. Rarely had he found it so hard to open conversation, but he managed with something about "a pleasant camp-spot here."

The wife, pipe in mouth: "They's wuss, and then again they's better."

The old man added: "Does well for our hogs. We've a band of pork that make out to find feed. In fact, the pootiest hogs in Tulare County—nigh three thousand"; and so the conversation got under way, though what King chose to tell about himself impressed the woman, obviously, that he was "not up to her standard." For one thing he admitted that he had never shot a coon, a confession which was "something of a staggerer" to the big girl Susan, six feet long if an inch, who had been holding one of her size-eleven feet in the air to trace the patterns of the firelight with her toes. Later King learned the reason for her start, for Newty said: "Don't mind the old woman and her coons . . . She used to say no man could have Susan who couldn't show coonskin enough of his own to make a bed quilt. But she's mostly over that now."

Susan showed King the hogs before he turned in that night, and he awoke the next morning with "the distant roar of swine" in his ears. On going with Newty to the corral, he drew from the old man the story of his wanderings; first from Pike to Oregon and then successive recessions south, with pigs and plunder. What next? Why, on to Montana provided the hogs could be put into bacon; and then—who knows?—perhaps Texas.

When King and his men broke camp, old Newty remarked that he and Susan would go a piece with them, to hunt for hog feed. The old man saddled a shaggy pony; the girl threw a sheepskin over a mustang and mounted with an Amazonian leap. Then side by side the three rode off through the forest, the soldiers having gone ahead. At last the old man beckoned King aside and managed to get the proposal out: "Thet—thet—thet man what gits Susan *has half the hogs!*"

King's Mosaic view of pork was much too deeply ingrained; he rode away with the Pike County version of *au revoir* resounding after him. "Say, you'll take good care of yourself." And his traveler's tale of the Newtys of Pike, if not a literal record of what occurred at the hog ranch, had yet the tang of truth. It fixed the lineaments of the perpetual migrant and caught the pathos of human retrogression. "I took pains not to overtake my camp-men," he concluded, "wishing to be alone; and as I rode for hour after hour the picture of this family stood before me in all its deformity of outline, all its poverty of detail, all its darkness of future."

The trail crossed a plateau covered with meadows and stands of pines. The improved lap ended at a bridge across the main branch of the Kern River, and there King called a halt for the night. They followed an Indian path the next day, presumably northward to the plateau east of Kern Canyon. Then they turned east and followed another branch to its source, north of the peak which King called Sheep Rock for the bighorn on its flanks. They toiled then through a pass south of King's goal, a weary climb according to the official report.

"In the midst of every difficulty," Whitney wrote, "Mr. King worked for three days before he could reach the base of the mountain whose summit he was endeavoring to attain." His choice of route was poor, too far to the east, and he was stopped by a soaring wall, three or four hundred feet from the top. He called it impossible, and ceased to climb.

Doubtless King would have reached his goal had he chosen his way with more care and less headlong impetuosity. "But he seems to have had a genius for finding the wrong routes," Farquhar would observe concerning this attempt. Later climbers were to wonder at his difficulties; but, "It's easy enough," as Brewer pointed out, "to climb a mountain when you know where to go." King was a pioneer with nothing of record to help him.

Of the descent, King noted,

When I hung up the barometer, a bitter wind was blowing. It hailed and snowed and the clouds closed in around me, shutting off all view. I had been all day abroad and the fatigue and excitement exhausted me greatly, so much that although chilled through I could scarcely prevent myself from lying down and sleeping. A strange carelessness came over me, making me reckless in the descent. I was obliged to make an effort to keep myself from running over the most dangerous debris slopes.

Defeat of the moment did not check King's optimism that a feasible way would still be found to the top of Mount Whitney, and he regretted that time did not permit a further search on this occasion. Attainment of the summit would remain a goal with him for years. It was fitting, in the meantime, that his present failure should yet win praise from Whitney, for he had determined the main features of the topography of the Kern Sierra—an area which might otherwise have remained a blank on the survey's map.

King dismissed his escort on returning to the plain. He rested at Visalia, thawing out the last trace of alpine cold and becoming reaccustomed to "such articles as chairs and newspapers, and to watching with unexpected pleasure the few village girls who flitted about." It may have been on this visit, also, that he vied "with the best vaqueros of Visalia, in bronco-riding contests, for the bravos of the elders and the smiles of the señoritas." Then he set out for the agreed upon place of meeting. One hundred and twenty miles of road and trail lay before him. "I dared not attack its monotony," he wrote, "by any unusual riding; and having settled [Kaweah] at our regular travelling trot,—a gait of about six miles an hour,—I forgot all about the dreary expanse of plain, and gave myself up to quiet revery."

He did not record the drift of his thoughts, but he knew the character which the region bore. One traveled the Millerton Road at his peril, and seldom at night; for, as King had heard, "a certain class of Mexican highwayman" still robbed and murdered over the whole Tulare plain.

It was King's custom to carry a pistol for protection against such lawless riffraff; indeed, he might have really noticed at Visalia such characters as he would picture in "Kaweah's Run"—two Mexican mountaineers who watched him draw a small amount of gold at the Wells Fargo office. "I observed them enough," he noted in story context, "to see that the elder was a man of middle height, a wiry, light figure and thin hawk visage. . . . His companion struck me as a half-breed Indian, somewhere about eighteen years of age, his beardless face showing deep brutal lines." A fancy such as King's required no more, it seemed, to inspire a tale of high excitement; for, according to a friend, he could make a better story out of a streetcar ride than most men with the best of material.

"Kaweah's Run," certainly, was the sort of yarn a born raconteur might spin to relieve the monotony of a hot and wearisome ride—"an adventure with Mexican bandits," as King would cite it to his editor, "in which I am pursued for days and escape in the night saved by the sagacity of my horse Ka-we-ah."

Background details so circumstantial that they might have been culled from field notes were to make it a plausible narrative. King paused in story Ruskinize as he doubtless did in fact: "I was delighted," he wrote,

to ride thus alone, and expose myself, as one uncovers a sensitized photographic plate, to be influenced; for this is a respite from scientific work, when through months you hold yourself accountable for seeing everything, for analyzing, for instituting perpetual comparisons, and as it were sharing in the administering of the physical world. No tongue can tell the relief to simply withdraw scientific observation, and let Nature impress you in the dear old way with all her mystery and glory, with those vague indescribable emotions which tremble between wonder and sympathy.

And he revealed much of himself, his abiding delight in dark flesh tones on the female form, in his description of an Indian woman whom, presumably, he saw at a trailside rancheria; a "woman of splendid mould," he wrote, "soundly sleeping upon her back, a blanket covering her from the waist down in ample folds, her bare body and large full breasts kindled into bronze under streaming light."

Many readers were to take his tale for sober truth, even in California. But factual record pointed otherwise. "Of the ride to Clark's ranch [at Wawona] via Millerton and Mariposa," King reported to Whitney, "I have nothing of interest. I arrived at Clark's at 10 AM Aug 1st, according to orders, and waited until the party came in."

During the wait he came to know Galen Clark, a bearded, middle-aged man who "looked like the Wandering Jew and talked like a professor of belles-lettres." King also found that Frederick Law Olmsted was camped at Wawona with his wife and children, as well as Mr. and Mrs. Ashburner. Olmsted was still in delicate health, but he could relax among the majestic trees of Wawona, for he was on vacation from his managerial duties at Bear Valley. King spent several days with the Olmsted party, eating trout and venison prepared by an artful black cook and "squiring the ladies on rides and entertaining them with stories of his adventures."

Brewer and the others were more than three weeks late. All looked gaunt and worn, and Hoffmann had become too lame to walk or ride. But the story of their movement north gave the expedition's history an impressive finish—how they had followed an Indian trail down into the South Fork of the Kings, a gorge surpassing Yosemite for the height of its cliffs; how, unable to find a way up through the head of the canyon, they had climbed to the northern rim and made a camp between two principal forks of the Kings; from where, five miles away, they could see three peaks surging nearly 13,000 feet against the sky. They had named the tallest one, which sheered away in enormous cliffs on the northwest side, Mount Clarence King; the lesser ones Mount Gard[i]ner and Mount Cotter. They had also seen and named the Palisades.

They tried, then, to find a route directly north, but the region proved impassable for the animals, and the only remaining course, except retreat, lay over the crest to Owens Valley. Crossing a pass later named the Kearsarge, in the wake of several hardy gold prospectors, they reached the Owens River by July 28, then marched up the valley while Indian fires signalled their progress from heights on either side. On August 2 they recrossed the divide through a saddle which Brewer judged to be the highest American pass yet trod by horses.

They camped in favored Digger retreats along the Middle San Joaquin, passing the days in rides through almost impenetrable terrain. The nights turned freezing, and food grew scarce. Their ragged clothes had to be patched with old flour sacks. Buckskin went lame, and one of the soldiers was lost for days. Hoffmann's rheumatism became acute, while an abscess developed in his left thigh. Even Brewer, who had lost thirty pounds, felt thoroughly worn out; and so on August 23 he brought the expedition in to Wawona, with Hoffmann lashed to his saddle.

Thus ended one of the greatest feats of exploration in the history of the Sierra—a reconnaissance which added to the map of California an area "as large as Massachusetts and as high as Switzerland." The whole company had performed admirably, but King's exploits seemed to stand out as a special feature of the 1864 campaign. As he himself would suggest, "The same elasticity and endurance which had won him the stroke oar of Yale made him the most active mountaineer among his associates of the survey."

6

End of Apprenticeship

King helped to nurse Hoffmann while Brewer made a trip with Olmsted to the Yosemite Valley and then on to the high country of the Tuolumne. Yosemite had become a famous place; nearly a thousand visitors had admired its wonders during the past ten years. The state survey had backed a movement launched by such public spirits as Dr. John Marsh, Starr King, and Jessie Frémont to make it "a public pleasure-ground"; and Senator John Conness had carried the gospel back to Washington. He had engineered a bill through Congress granting the valley and the Mariposa Grove of Big Trees to the state as a permanent park; a measure which President Lincoln had signed while King and his friends were exploring the High Sierra.

Now in September 1864 Governor Frederick Low accepted the grant pending action by the state legislature. Under the governor's terms the valley and the grove were to be managed jointly by an eight man commission, including Whitney, Ashburner, and Galen Clark, with Olmsted serving as chairman. In addition Clark was appointed a special warden with the title "Guardian of the Yosemite Valley and the Big Tree Grove." But, first of all, it was necessary to fix "the locus, extent, and limits" of the park; and the board chose King and Gardiner to conduct the survey for that purpose. They were charged with running a boundary line, with gathering data for a map, and studying the geology of the region.

King and Gardiner had taken Hoffmann to San Francisco, but they prepared in a week to return to the mountains. The Yosemite survey would be a race against approaching winter, and the work must be completed before the legislature met in December; so they took the Mariposa trail at once, with Cotter and two mules, and reached Yosemite by October 5, 1864. There they were joined by three assistants—two of them old habitués of the valley and one a hand of the Mariposa Company. Soon Bill Hyde, their comrade on the plains, also volunteered his help.

They commandeered two empty cabins under the pines near Black's Hotel. To the north rose the half-mile chute of Yosemite Falls, now almost dry, its rill vanishing in fine spray above the floor of the valley. Wind and frost had chilled away the summer haze, and King and his friends reveled in the dawnlight which streamed next morning through their doorway. While still in their blankets they decided upon a climb to find a starting point for the work.

King scaled the northern wall, along with Gardiner and Cotter, and camped that night near the brook which "emotional Mr. Hutchings" had named the Virgin's Tears. They moved to the brow of El Capitan the following day for an unobstructed view of the valley, the floor stretching three thousand feet below them, a brown and yellow carpet, seared by drought and blazing with orange streaks where frost-bitten cottonwoods lined the Merced. A turning sweep of their eyes commanded a full exposure of the range, from base to summit, a wilderness of domes and ridges rolling back to the gleaming crest.

"It was during these first general views," King wrote, "that I conceived the idea of the whole Merced country having a common origin, and the consequent necessity of studying it as a unity, if I wished to learn its history." The conundrum of the place challenged his resourcefulness, and King gave most of his attention to it during the next two months, while Gardiner ran the boundary. They gave each other help, but each remained accountable for his own mission.

They began the survey on October 8, at a huge pine not far from El Capitan. For a week Gardiner laid the boundary in a northeasterly direction, a mile or so from the brink, as Congress had decreed. The line crossed woods and ridges of bare rock; and when chaining became impossible, the work was continued by means of triangulation.

In pursuing his geological work King managed to climb most of the heights around the north wall, including the highest pinnacle of the Three Brothers. Once he crept to the lip of Yosemite Falls, silent now that the stream had frozen. He measured the drop, and his figure of 2,537 feet sheared a hundred feet or so from Brewer's measurement.* He also climbed North Dome, which overlooked the Illilouette, then ranged between North Dome and Lake Tenaya, where polished bedrock shone like glass. He ascended Mount Hoffmann (named for his

---

*Neither figure was correct; the measurement now accepted for the total drop is 2,425 feet.

colleague), then followed the tracks of ancient ice flows down Yosemite Creek. Striae convinced him that a glacier from Mount Hoffmann had merged with ice that had overflowed from the upper Tuolumne and ice which had ground down through Tenaya Canyon, to become the main glacier in Yosemite Valley. The Illilouette and Little Yosemite had contributed to the stem; and as King studied the scars above Hutchings House, he figured that the glacier had been a thousand feet thick.

His inner eye invested the "old ice engines" with terrible grandeur. Yet drawn to the theories of his chief, he failed to recognize the glaciers as the chief builders of Yosemite Valley. Not that he could subscribe to Whitney's theory of subsidence, which held that the bottom of the gorge had "dropped out." He did suspect that, in some cataclysmic dawn, the forces of shrinkage had rent the tableland asunder, leaving a fissure in the semiplastic rock; the subsequent ice rivers had, in his opinion, merely smoothed out the pristine fault.

As soon as King had finished the work around the northern walls, he decided to climb the Obelisk, which he would rename Mount Clark for the Guardian of Yosemite. It was the center peak in a mountain group southeast of the valley. He chose Cotter for companion; they packed two mules for a week's excursion, then headed up the Mariposa Trail on October 21. On reaching the south plateau, they left the trail and struck across the tableland.

The first signs of storm appeared next day, but with their goal in view King found it hard to turn back. "I yielded to my constitutional sanguineness," he wrote, "when my judgment said return, and pressed on hoping for a favorable change of wind. I took the precaution to make a sketch of the country as we advanced, and to this alone I think we owe our lives." The blizzard which King would depict in "A Sierra Storm" caught them on a great moraine, but after a grim eight-hour struggle they regained the Mariposa Trail, and the valley opened before them just as the storm swept by.

Winter was at hand; there was little time to spare. The whole party came back to the plateau on October 25, to launch the final stages of the survey. "Gard[i]ner and I," King noted, "decided upon the line for our [south] boundary and arranged the closing triangles." The area thus delimited amounted to only twenty thousand acres, a far cry from the vast extent of Yosemite on its becoming a national park a quarter-century later. Meanwhile they sent the chainmen for grain at Mariposa, and while they were away King tramped about the south cliffs to measure various points. Climbing out on Cathedral Rocks, he planned the topographical survey of the valley floor below; a job he began the next morning and finished two weeks later, assisted by Hyde, who chained courses and worked up the findings in a sketch.

Another storm then broke, also to be limned in "A Sierra Storm," and it cut the field work short. A thousand cataracts streamed down the cliffs, and the Merced overflowed its banks. The rain became snow. Soon the trails would all be blocked. "On the following morning," King wrote, "we determined at all costs to pack our remaining instruments and escape."

It took Gardiner and himself nine hours to reach the sheep hut between Yosemite and Wawona. There they met Cotter, returning from Clark's to help with the gear. He was worn out, but he insisted on going on with King instead of resting at the hut. "The storm increased to a tempest," King wrote, and exhaustion forced them to travel slower and slower. Cotter sank, and might have perished in the snow had King not lashed a long neckscarf around him and hauled him like a husky dog in harness. They reached Galen Clark's cabin at two in the morning, and there they rested till Gardiner overtook them in the teeth of a new snowstorm.

Funds of the state survey had been exhausted, and fresh appropriations appeared remote. Brewer had shipped for home already; Whitney had been in the East for months; and on reaching San Francisco, King and Gardiner also thought of home. They presented plats of the boundary and copies of their notes to Olmsted, who was also planning to return to New York to resume his city parks work. Then they caught the SS *Moses Tayler*, bound for Nicaragua.

The steamer arrived at San Juan del Sur in time for Christmas. A blue and white carriage whisked them over Commodore Vanderbilt's macadam highway to the shore of Lake Nicaragua, where they had to wait for a boat. King found it no hardship to rest for a week or two in the "slumbrous haze of the tropics"; for he found the women attractive there—especially the "bewitching black-and-tan sister" who strummed a guitar while brewing chocolate for his breakfast.

As a type, the Nicaraguan "virgin" aroused his affection. He would never have patience with the ubiquitous Yankee who doubted her morals; and when a few years later he reviewed the travels of a professor from Vasser he found that gentleman's ineptitude in science scarcely less ridiculous than his opinion on tropical women, or their "laxity of manner and *morale*." Was it that the professor looked for no higher characteristics? "Kingsley in literature," King declared,

and Jerome [sic] among painters make the same gross mistake, that fullness of animal means absence of moral nature. It is only Story [the sculptor] who seems to catch the sensuous innocence of the tropical woman. His "Lybian Sibyl" embodies it. Her soft full outlines, and air of nerveless repose, suggests the twilight, the palm and the wind-swayed hammock.

In similar fashion, the Nicaraguan "virgin" epitomized the lushness of the country that King and Gardiner had to cross.

It was a world of heightened color. Shark fins circled the steamboat which bore the travelers over the lake; whistling ducks and egrets sailed across the water or perched on mats of floating weed. The steamboat churned into the San Juan River, the only outlet, and the water turned a pale yellow during its drift to the Caribbean. "Splendid flowers," as King would remember, "wreathe and drape the trees with veils of viny growths; enormous leafage lines the river banks; blazing orchids, stately palms, bend toward the sea."

King reported to Whitney in Boston; then he went home to Irvington, and nearly at once to bed. He was ill for weeks with malaria which he called "old Greytown fever," blaming it on the Nicaraguan swamps. He made a slow recovery, yet he managed to finish his notes and send them on to Whitney. He was not yet sure of the future; he still thought of a year's study at Freiberg. But Whitney promised to "favor, promote and uphold" his plans; and King suspected that, with reasonable luck, the California Survey would continue to furnish the best field training available. He resigned himself to staying on with Whitney until he was ready to launch a survey of his own. Jottings in his notebooks suggested his bold ambition—jottings like:

THE U.S. INTERIOR SURVEY
C. R. KING, SUPT.

In taking stock of his qualifications, King labeled his knowledge of astronomy as only "a little." That science was fundamental in running surveys across large areas; so as soon as he felt recovered he hurried up to New Haven and took Professor Lyman's famous course. He renewed old ties at Sheffield, friendships with men like Dana, Johnson, and Brush. He saw much of Brewer, too, now filling the chair of agriculture; and his former language teacher, the brother of his chief, wrote: "We enjoy having him here . . . and my real respect for his ability, as well as my liking for his disposition and engagedness in his work, grows every time that I see him." A few days later King and Gardiner went to Boston and told Whitney of their decision to remain with him while they prepared themselves "for further good work."

A mournful sequence of events was soon to unfold in the national drama—Appomattox, the pistol shot at Ford's theater, the slow train to Illinois. "The war was over," King wrote later of the period. "Lincoln's wise and generous character had disappeared from the stage. The nation and its people went out as from some black tragedy into the sunlight of every day, and resumed a suspended life." King himself worked with restless energy, much alone, and sometimes ill with relapses of "old Greytown fever."

Through it all he kept in touch with Gardiner, who concentrated on the map of Yosemite, which was published two years later in *The Yosemite Book.* That was before Hoffmann discovered errors in the valley floor which King had drawn from Bill Hyde's sketch. The twists he gave the Merced, whether from his own carlessness or from mistakes by Hyde, would prove so wide of the actual course that a new plat would have to be made. Whitney was disgusted and with characteristic bluntness pronounced King's share of the map "a complete sham." Moreover, he had judged King's notes unusable for *The Yosemite Book.* Much of this animus stemmed from his dogmatic rejection of King's observations on glacial striae in the area, a matter on which Whitney's views would in time be proved completely wrong. But King had much to learn yet, and on his return to Irvington his apprenticeship continued with the plat he made of the Kern Sierra.

The summer of 1865 passed. King's mother was occupied with two young children now, for another had come that winter, a boy whom she had named George Snowden for Mr. Howland. "The country lived and laughed again," King wrote. "Everyone went his way." And soon he booked passage on the *Henry Chauncey,* a huge Pacific Mail side-wheeler, to return with Gardiner and the Whitneys to the West that fall.

The first volume of *Geology*, which Whitney had seen through the press, helped to thaw the chill at Sacramento. Yet the financial condition of the state survey had not improved when King arrived in California. There were no funds for a survey of desert regions, such as Whitney had promised in the *Geology*. But the state geologist hoped to induce the Army to sponsor such a reconnaissance.

It required time to convince the military of its need for the work; but by December 1865 arrangements were concluded, and King and Gardiner were "hung on General McDowell's office for the winter." They were ordered to Prescott, Arizona, where McDowell planned to make a tour of inspection. Their mission was "to explore the unknown parts of Arizona" for the purpose of finding routes for military roads.

General Irvin McDowell furnished them with instruments, including photographic gear. King had asked for a chance to test the uses of a camera in the field; and an amateur photographer, Charles A. Brinley, joined the company before they took ship for San Pedro. They started ten days before the general's entourage. "I quite envy them the privilege of a winter in Arizona," Whitney wrote, "and only hope they will be prudent and not let the Apaches get their scalps."

The work promised adventure. The territory nourished a pack of gaudy scoundrels—horse thieves, rustlers, highwaymen, and gamblers, all with trigger fingers; and if outlaws were not scourge enough, the Indians made the hair on every head uneasy. Not a week passed without some depredation, and the Army had retaliated with a huge manhunt, a campaign of extermination. A survey there might prove hair-raising— literally.

The ship dropped anchor near Dead Man's Island, and at Drum Barracks King drew provisions, an ambulance for the instruments, horses, and an escort of volunteers who looked like desperadoes. The survey ought to be safe from Indians now; but who, he wondered, would protect them from their protectors?

King's party headed inland just after Christmas. An odometer clicked off the miles to the plaza in Los Angeles, where King lodged with his friends at the Bella Union, billed as the best hotel in southern California. On Sunday morning they watched Los Angelenos saunter to mass with game cocks under arm, then afterwards form a ring behind the Church of Our Lady, where they waited for the priest to start the cock fight. But King and his comrades did not linger in the pueblo in view of its reputation as the toughest town in the entire state. Their road veered eastward, abreast a chaparral-covered range then known as the Sierra Madre,* and soon they passed the San Gabriel Mission, hedged in by prickly-pear cactus nine feet tall. Cajon Pass took them across the mountains, and their road swept down to the cottonwood-sheltered bed of the Mojave River. Soon the river vanished in desert sand, and there was no grass for the horses until they reached the Colorado. After crossing it, they started over the Prescott road, and there their worries began in earnest.

The Indians of the region—Yavapais and Hualapais of fierce Yuman stock—were on the verge of war, and King was warned against them at Fort Mohave. Sometimes reconnaissance work would take him and Gardiner ahead of the escort, as on January 24, 1866. Suddenly two Indians sprang from a juniper thicket, barring the way with arrows aimed and drawn to the arrowhead. King noticed Gardiner's hand reaching for his Colt.

"Don't," he cried.

One of the Indians hissed like a snake, and at the signal fifty more "savages" poured from behind scrub junipers—tall bronze warriors, all but naked, each holding his bow and arrow ready. They wore no paint, a good sign, but they looked anything but friendly. The Indian in command made signs for King and Gardiner to dismount and then undress. Escape was impossible. They got down from their horses and laid their revolvers on the ground.

Surely the escort must be close behind. King saw hope in delay; and when the Indian pointed to the barometer case on his shoulder, he slowly unslung the instrument and thrust the long tube forward, as if he were aiming at the horizon. He tried to muster enough Spanish to make the Indians understand. *Big new gun. Whoom! Shoot big distance.* He held their attention for nearly a quarter of an hour. Then Gardiner tried to interest them in the compass. The Indians grunted at it in disdain. Some of them began to gather sticks of cedar, others to prepare buckskin thongs for the torture. Within a few moments, unless something happened, both captives would be stretched on the ground, with heaps of coals searing their chests.

The fire crackled; King could smell the smoke. But the delay had served its purpose. King and Gardiner had not yet taken off their

*The present-day San Gabriel Mountains, which were so named by the California Survey.

leather breeches when the escort rode into view, as in a present-day Western, and seeing the trouble, deployed and charged. "There was no doubt," as a friend who knew the West would write, "that King's presence of mind, coolness, and ingenuity saved the lives of his friend and himself." The Indians scattered, and only two were captured— prisoners whom General McDowell, on overtaking King's party, hand- ed over to a friendly Hualapai chief for judgment.

"The young men are mad for war," the chief said, but he promised to hold them in check for the next two days, time for the expedition to reach the plain near Prescott. Beyond that time he could give no assurance. Indeed, the next mail driver was murdered near the spot where King and Gardiner had faced torture, and nothing could raise King's estimate of such "savages." They had, he later declared,

but one passion in life—assassination; one bequest from father to son—the tiger love of human blood; one mental activity—treachery. As observed by early Spanish students, the Apache* differs in no wise from the astonishing devil whose lodge is to-day decked with the bloody scalps of last year's pioneers. He is the same whom we have lately seen in the person of Cochise, demurely drawing down the grin of hell into the oily counterfeit of a brotherly smile, and "swapping" platitudes with a certain childlike general, while his picked warriors only a few miles away danced a veritable *can-can d'enfer* around a writhing soldier whom they grilled for a pastime."

A garbled report of King and Gardiner's ambush reached Fort Mohave, and J. Ross Browne, who was then at the fort, was to carry back to the East the "painful rumor . . . that Gard[i]ner had been killed."

Meanwhile, General Mason had sallied out to meet McDowell and to conduct the party to Fort Whipple, where a major general's salute hailed their arrival, on January 26. The garrison bore no resemblance that King could see to campaigners on a campaign; yet he was at first

---

*King believed that the Hualapais who had captured him and Gardiner were Apaches and always called them so when recounting this incident. In retelling King's version of the episode Rossiter Raymond at first designated the Indians as Apaches, then called them Hualapais, apparently thinking the latter were of Apache stock. So, too, did Gardiner in the manuscript "The Trail Between the Cedar Bushes," which compounded the confusion by identifying the friendly Hualapai chief as Iritaba, who was actually the head chief of the Mohaves. Emmons's account simply spoke of Apaches.

encouraged by the promises of General Mason, to whose staff he and Gardiner and Brinley were now attached. They were assigned a new escort of seasoned cavalry. They worked up the topography along the Prescott road, then settled down to await provisions—above all, mules. The wait stretched out for three weeks.

At last transportation arrived for the instruments—four mules, wild-eyed, pot-bellied, and emaciated. Indeed, they were on the verge of collapse, for they had been fed on worthless marsh grass until they could scarcely totter. They moaned with hunger and tried to eat anything loose in the snow—pine cones, pieces of buckskin, or cotton rags. By afternoon King had them packed and moving up the Mint Canyon road, but after a few steps each one lay down to rest.

"We first unpacked the one who was reclining on the sextant," King reported, "and rescued that valuable instrument from imminent de-struction, and then devoted ourselves to the one long frame that weighed heavily on the transit theodolite. These attended to, they were all allowed to rest and all hands hoisted the animals to their feet and readjusted their packs." The process had to be repeated every few minutes, but after a mile the weakest mule was left to die in the middle of the road—hardly a propitious start for the exploration of "unknown parts" of the territory.

Excellent forage grew at the second bivouac nine miles from Pres-cott. King let the animals graze for a day or so and gain strength, while he and Gardiner studied the environs. They climbed a mountain known as Granite Peak, which made them an excellent topographical station. It was, as King observed, the "bold terminus" of the Sierra Prieta; from its summit the general structure of a wide area became clear, and Gardiner claimed that their map brought out "for the first time the true general direction of the system of mountain ranges in northern Arizona."

It took them a week to nurse the mules around the flank of Granite Peak to the edge of Skull Valley. They were now due west of Prescott, with the Sierra Prieta sprawled between; and of the possible routes across the crest Indian Pass struck them as having the best conditions for a road. King next proposed to hunt for a route to the basin of Bill Williams Fork. He secured a view of the intervening Santa Maria from a cone above camp, and led the party into its watershed, which they explored in all directions. It would be hard to imagine a region more vexing to travel, King decided, or one which could offer fewer induce-ments to settlement, in spite of the grass on its mesas. The idea of a direct road from Prescott to Bill Williams Fork struck him as futile. "Even if built," he wrote, "[it] would never be travelled."

The survey had scarcely been begun, but the enlistments of the escort had expired. The soldiers insisted on being mustered out, and King could do nothing except head for the nearest Army post. A march of two days brought them to Camp Date Creek. There King's request for new men and rations went ignored. General Mason's whole campaign impressed him as a sham. It seemed that the general was "drunk most of the time and care[d] for nothing when sober except to add to his list of mining feet." King lost hope of reorganizing his endeavor on the spot, so near the end of March he agreed with Gardiner to look for help in California. They headed for Los Angeles, in a hard journey across the Colorado Desert, an ordeal that would afford King a robust nine pages for his sketch "The Range." "Spread out below us," he would remember, "lay the desert, stark and glaring, its rigid hill-chains lying in disordered grouping, in attitudes of the dead." Then arriving in friendlier country, they rode past rolling hills covered with vernal grass and groves of live oak trees, at last reaching the city; after which King hurried up to San Francisco to lay the Arizona impasse before General McDowell at the Presidio.

The general could spare no further resources, his brusque tones dashing all hope for the work in Arizona and earning Whitney's praise of him as "the greatest ass that ever wore epaulets." "K and G have got some valuable results however," observed the state geologist, who assumed that the two would rejoin the California Survey. But King hesitated, and his reluctance caused Whitney to suspect, as he wrote to Brewer, "that King wants to get more glory by doing something on his own hook. I shall advise him then to go to Nevada, where he can have a glorious field, plenty of room and no competitors." Whitney had sensed exactly what King wished to do, but after several days King decided to bide a little longer under Whitney's wing.

He accepted the post of assistant geologist, then spent the rest of May in working up the Arizona data, which as "A General View of the Prescott Region" J. Ross Browne would publish in his 1868 report on mineral resources west of the Rocky Mountains. Then after preparing for a summer campaign in the central Sierra, King left the Bay early in June with a cook and a botanist. They rode across Pacheco Pass, gold with ripe wild oats and overlooking "miles of orange-colored flowers" that swathed the floor of the Central Valley. Far beyond, "rose three hundred miles of Sierra half lost in light and cloud and mist, the summit in places sharply seen against a pale, beryl sky." In five days they reached Bear Valley, where Whitney soon joined them with Brinley and Gardiner. All went on to Clark's Ranch. "Another day's end," wrote King, "found us within the Yosemite, and then for a week we walked and rode, studied and looked, revisiting all our old points, lingering hours here and half-days there, to complete within our minds the conception of the place."

Meanwhile a human skull had arrived at the survey rooms in San Francisco. It had turned up—or so the story ran—under 132 feet of volcanic ash in a mine near Angel's Camp in Calaveras County. Less than overawed by the find, a miner named James Matson had given it to a grocer, who had passed it on to a certain Dr. Jones at Murphy's. It was the doctor who had surmised what interest the fossil might have for science. "This knocks the hell out of Moses," he was heard to say before he rushed it down to San Francisco.

As soon as the work in Yosemite Valley was finished, Whitney left King in charge of the field party and started off for Calaveras to study the scene of the find. Was it a hoax? Whitney thought not, although the shaft, he learned, was flooded with water. He cross-examined everyone concerned with the discovery, and convinced himself that the skull had come from the depth reported—truly a "bony fide find." He had no doubt that it was a relic of the Pliocene. The Calaveras Skull, as an editor named Bret Harte observed, "exactly fitted a theory promulgated by the survey of the extreme antiquity of man on this coast." The fat began to fry in scientific fires; and in the hustle no one bothered about the Angel's Camp dentist who deplored the theft of a cranial showpiece from his office.

Bret Harte's muse, indebted to Holmes and Longfellow, responded to the turn of events: "Speak, O man less recent! Fragmentary fossil! / Primal pioneer of pliocene formations" ran his plea in the *Californian*. He suspected that the state geologist might have "slightly antedated" the *calavera's* age. He wanted the story straight from the fossil's mouth; so the ancient teeth thrilled with nicotinic juices, and the Skull replied between expectorations:

> "Which my name is Bowers, and my crust was busted
> Falling down a shaft in Calaveras County,

But I'd take it kindly if you'd send the pieces
Home to old Missouri!"

It was rather to Cambridge that Whitney shipped the pieces; Cambridge where a decade later he would still be fighting for his theory of the Tertiary age of man—a hypothesis King was inclined to accept, for he himself would find a pestle under Tuolumne Table Mountain that suggested immense antiquity for man.

In the meantime King had restocked for a circuit of the Merced Group, Mount Clark having retained its lure. "There was in our hope of scaling this point," he wrote, "something more than mere desire to master a difficult peak. It was a station of great topographical value, the apex of many triangles, and, more than all, would command a grander view of the Merced region than any other summit." From a camp at the mountain's base he climbed with Gardiner to the sharp south edge of the Obelisk just before the sun went down on July 11, 1866. It was sometimes hard to keep from slipping, burdened as they were by instruments; and the rest of the climb provided King with the drama for one of the most exciting passages in all his writing.* Not that subsequent climbers could duplicate the extent of his perils.

They reached the top with shouts of relief. King stepped down to a lower niche and scribbled impressions in his notebook. The isolation of the peak, which gave him a sense of hanging in air, permitted views in all directions. One scene aroused his admiration especially—the several dark spires which fretted the southern end of the Ritter Group. These tips, almost needlelike, seemed sharper than any pinnacles he had ever seen, and he gave them a name that would persevere for its aptness—the Minarets.

While Whitney was introducing the Calaveras Skull to scientific circles, King's party continued to explore the Merced Group. They climbed most of the major summits, and one of them King ascended twice. It was Black Mountain, among whose spacious amphitheaters John Muir was to find his first live glacier five years later. King over-

---

*Gardiner, also, left a rousing account of the Mount Clark ascent. See Farquhar, History of the Sierra Nevada (pp. 150–151) for the quotation of a climactic excerpt from it. It rivals the dramatic force of King's statement, but the style falls short of King's distinction.

looked the glacier, but he referred to one of the amphitheaters as "the ancient den of a glacier dragon." From Black Mountain, on July 31, he studied the San Joaquin basin, where the sun struck fire in the haze, making it glow like burgundy. Across the abyss, Mount Ritter slowly dimmed to a dark purple.

During August he led his party up the San Joaquin. They camped beside a lake choked with lily pads; the next day brought a skyline piled with cumuli, and the wind bore threats of storm. King and Gardiner trusted that the thunderhead would blow away, and began to climb Mount Ritter, which bristled with spires. Within a shaded cul-de-sac they came upon a field of ice two hundred yards wide and a half mile long. It had moved some fifty feet since winter, as they could see, for a deep crevice yawned between it and the mountainside. It was a small glacier, but under the influence of the preconceptions of their chief, they failed to see it as such, and the honor of finding the living glaciers of Mount Ritter had to wait for John Muir. All the other ice fields there must have struck King and Gardiner as slopes of packed snow.

Up they struggled toward the summit on the western side—the only side that looked at all approachable. The storm broke, driving them back when about four hundred feet from the top. With stores exhausted, it was necessary to retreat to Clark's Ranch, and Mount Ritter had to wait for John Muir to scale its loftiest turret ten years later.

Whitney's instructions left much country yet to be covered, and King got his party into the field again as soon as they had filled their packs at Clark's. There was scant time to make a decent report, much to Whitney's annoyance. King merely hinted at "capital adventures"; and now, he added, they were off to regions beyond Mount Hoffmann. They crossed the Little Yosemite and made their way to the upper Tuolumne, beyond a pinnacle known as the Unicorn. They forded the river and camped at Soda Springs in Tuolumne Meadows, from where they made excursions around the plateau.

King followed the river to where it dashed into a series of wild cascades and where the open basin closed in a gorge. He penetrated the canyon only as far as a mighty falls, the lip of which cut off his view of the lower chasm. A brief search revealed no passage forward, and it seemed to him that to go further would be impossible for "any creature without wings." He turned back, excited by his discovery, the more awesome because it must, for the time, remain unexplored. Could it be, as he suspected, a rival to Yosemite? He let anticipation whet his fancy; and the reports that circulated allowed the Grand Canyon of the Tuolumne to surpass Yosemite in grandeur.

But it was necessary now to turn to the wild peaks northeast of Soda Springs. King again paired off with Gardiner; they climbed Mount Dana twice, then rode a moraine "like a graded highway" to the slopes of the tallest mountain. They tied their horses in a high meadow, then finished the climb with blanket packs, reaching the summit over a windswept ridge which gave them "some uneasiness." The gale drove them into a crack in the granite and gave them a night of intense cold. Yet they regarded the mountain—another first ascent—with a certain fondness. King wrote that because of its "firm peak with titan strength and brow so square and solid, it seems altogether natural we should have named it for California's statesman, John Conness." In thus honoring such an influential patron King proved himself to be an astute politician.

The idea of an interior survey, independent of Whitney's explorations, was still working in his mind, and he discussed its problems with Gardiner while they sat on peaks like Mount Conness, and looked out over the blue and purple reaches of Nevada. King was becoming an accomplished geologist, and Gardiner was perfecting his grasp of the mapping techniques he had learned from Hoffmann. The rapid triangulation method had served them well all summer, and Gardiner felt sure they could carry the system over the Great Basin and the Rocky Mountains. Quickly, then, the outlines of King's project came into focus. He thought of hitching it to the railroads, then abuilding, for he knew that such a step would help him secure aid from Congress.

The more he thought of a survey of his own, the less importance he attached to the work in hand. A ride through Mono Pass and down Bloody Canyon to Mono Lake, a northward swing through grim volcanic country, and a circuit back across Sonora Pass and down the Stanislaus—all were prescribed movements which he made without great concentration on results. A telegram from his mother brought him news of Mr. Howland's death from brain fever; and as King would later tell his friend Henry Adams, "I found myself at 24 years of age with eleven people dependent on me alone." Such sudden responsibilities pressed him for a decision. He sent his resignation to Whitney and brought the expedition to a close.

Reluctant to accept King's withdrawal, Whitney offered him sole charge of the economic geology of the state survey. But King declined and, instead, asked for Whitney's endorsement of his plans for work in the interior. Whitney's first reaction was to refuse, since he had some doubts as to the feasibility of King's idea. But soon he relented and notified Senator Conness that King was "well qualified to make geological and geographical explorations." King's hopes soared as he engaged passage home. He was taking the most decisive step of his career, and in his pocket was an emphatic recommendation from Colonel R. S. Williamson, of the Army Engineers, for whom he had named the pinnacles near Mount Tyndall.

Right, Clarence King, in 1863 or 1864, at the outset of his career. He was then serving as Volunteer Geologist on the California Geological Survey under Professor Josiah D. Whitney. In the fall of 1863 he made his first field trip, in the company of William H. Brewer. *Courtesy of the late Francis P. Farquhar.*

Left, James T. Gardiner, King's life-long friend, who made the transcontinental trek with him in 1863 and also served on the California Geological Survey. Between 1867 and 1873 he acted as second in charge of the Fortieth Parallel Survey and its chief topographer. He managed King's affairs after the latter's death in 1901. *Courtesy, The Bancroft Library.*

VIEW OF THE SUMMIT OF LASSEN'S PEAK.

Above, Lassen's Peak, wood engraving from a field sketch by Clarence King in 1863. It was published in J. D. Whitney's *Geology*, Vol. I, 1865. The mountain is viewed from the southeast, at a distance of about three miles from the summit, and the sketch represents some 2,000 feet of vertical height. *Photograph by Caroline Lawson Hinkley.*

Facing page, Mount Clarence King in the Sierra Nevada. This peak, rising 12,909 feet, sheers away in enormous cliffs on the northwest side. It was named in the summer of 1864 by the exploring party of the California Geological Survey, at the same time that neighboring mountains, not quite so tall, were named for James T. Gardiner and Richard Cotter. *Photograph by Ansel Adams. Courtesy of the Ansel Adams Publishing Rights Trust. All rights reserved.*

Above, Field Party of 1864, Geological Survey of California: James T. Gardiner, Richard Cotter, William H. Brewer, and Clarence King. Cotter later claimed that his hand rested on Brewer's shoulder to signify his confidence in their leader in the field. In its exploration of the High Sierra, this party named Mount Whitney, Mount Brewer, Mount Tyndall, and the Palisades, among other landmarks. *Courtesy, The Bancroft Library.*

Right, William H. Brewer, second in charge of the California Geological Survey from 1860 through 1864. In August 1863 King and Gardiner met him on a paddlewheeler that steamed from Sacramento to San Francisco, and thus began a life-long friendship among the three. Brewer's observant letters home were gathered in 1930 by Francis P. Farquhar in the classic *Up and Down California in 1860–1864*. *Courtesy, The Bancroft Library.*

Left, Clarence King at the age of 27, at Washington, D.C., reproduced from *Clarence King Memoirs*. In late 1869 King had just completed the first three seasons of the Fortieth Parallel Survey, the extent originally authorized by Congress, and thought that his field work was over. *Courtesy of the Library of Congress.* Right, Josiah D. Whitney, Professor of Geology at Harvard College and Head of the California Geological Survey, under whom King served his apprenticeship, from 1863 through 1866. Brewer claimed that King picked up the idea for the Fortieth Parallel Survey from Whitney. *Courtesy of the Museum of Comparative Zoology, Harvard University.*

Above, The Fortieth Parallel Corps en route across country, photographed by Timothy H. O'Sullivan circa 1868. The scene, more pleasant country than much of the Great Basin, may be in eastern Nevada, where they found areas of considerable fertility. *Courtesy, The Bancroft Library.*

Left, Clarence King, posing as if pausing in a rope descent of a rock face, circa 1869. King describes his and Cotter's feats with the rope in his chapters on Mount Tyndall in *Mountaineering*, and Francis P. Farquhar cites his account as "the earliest record in the Sierra of the practice of roping-down." *Courtesy of the Rare Books and Manuscripts Division, The New York Public Library-Astor, Lenox and Tilden Foundation.*

Facing page Above, Clarence King in the camp site near Salt Lake City, October 1868. The black man on the right is Jim Marryatt, who would become King's valet. This photograph by Timothy O'Sullivan served as an illustration for King's gift book *The Three Lakes*, dated Christmas 1870 and limited to three copies that were presented to his half-sister Marian and two of her playmates. *Courtesy of the Rare Books and Manuscripts Division, The New York Public Library-Astor, Lenox and Tilden Foundations.* Below, Timothy O'Sullivan's group photograph of the Fortieth Parallel Corps in camp near Salt Lake City, October 1868. King stands in the center, and Richard Cotter of the Mount Tyndall climb of 1864 rides the tent pole. *Courtesy of the U.S. Geological Survey, Denver.*

Above, Clarence King in field dress at Uinta Lake, Utah. This O'Sullivan photo-graph served as an illustration for *Clarence King Memoirs*. Here King carries a cistern barometer slung over his shoulder, as in the photograph of the California Survey field party of 1864. *Courtesy, The Bancroft Library.*

7

Along the Fortieth Parallel

Postwar America was a land of opportunity. The Civil War had transformed the entire life of the nation, and had launched the American economy on a course of unrivaled expansion. The country cried for new blood, new brains, new courage; and to the lure of wealth and power and reputation rose thousands of young men, some of them surprising candidates for achievement and fame.

Henry Adams later wrote,

No one could yet guess which of his contemporaries was most likely to play a part in the great world. A shrewd prophet in Wall Street might perhaps have set a mark on Pierpont Morgan, but hardly on the Rockefellers or William C. Whitney or Whitelaw Reid. No one would have picked out William McKinley or John Hay or Mark Hanna for great statesmen. Boston was ignorant of the careers in store for Alexander Agassiz and Henry Higginson. Phillips Brooks was unknown; Henry James was unheard; Howells was new; Richardson and La Farge were struggling for a start. Out of any score of names and reputations that should reach beyond the century, the thirty-years-old who were starting in the year 1867 could show none that was so far in advance as to warrant odds in its favor.

Clarence King, in January 1867, had not yet reached his twenty-fifth birthday and looked even younger, but he was eager to make his bid for the laurels America offered the young and the bold and the clever.

On arriving home he had found that Mr. Howland's losses were beyond recovery, a financial debacle whose full extent and suspicious circumstances King now learned of for the first time. Anxiety over his family's welfare caused him to waver in pushing his plans for a geological exploration. He hesitated to count on congressional favor and, for more security, thought of hunting work in the mines of Colorado. There he would not be quite so far from home.

It was Brewer's reception in New Haven that tipped the scales in favor of exploration, for Brewer was optimistic about King's plan and gave him a glowing endorsement. It was addressed to Edwin Stanton, still the secretary of war and the most powerful bureaucrat in Washington. In approving King's proposal Brewer stressed the dearth of reliable information about the region the transcontinental railroad was to span. Professors Dana and Agassiz gave King further recommendations, also pointing up the mysteries of that unamiable country.

The public had once called it the Great American Desert. None of the previous expeditions sent there by the government—those of Frémont, Howard Stansbury, John Gunnison, E. G. Beckwith, and James H. Simpson—had accomplished more than simple reconnaissance. They had lifted the mountain and desert regions from the shrouds of myth, but at best they had provided only a rude, tentative, disconnected outline of the geography between the Great Plains and California. No really authentic map had yet been made. The best was the atlas of General G. K. Warren, adequate perhaps for military use, but not for scientific purposes, owing among other things to its small scale (1 : 3,000,000). King's plan for a continuous geological section, underpinned by detailed topography based on careful and accurate triangulation, would go far to bridge the gaps in the scientific knowledge of the West.

To the recommendations of his scientific backers King added an array of social introductions and political endorsements. "My credentials make me a good fellow," he doodled in a notebook. Then, leaving Gardiner at work on a map of the central Sierra, he hurried down to Washington. His beard was smartly groomed, his face was aglow with hope, and his mind was firm with what Gardiner called his "consciousness of power to persuade men. . . . With everybody he made friends," Gardiner explained.

As I look back . . . I can see that this gift of friendship made possible the carrying out of our plans which never could have been accomplished on their mere merits. It was this gift of winning men's feeling that brought to him at Washington the support of the strong men who aided him to create the Fortieth Parallel Survey.

The city, he found, had not yet lost the air of an armed camp, especially near the old brick building where Stanton held his office. The secretary, with a few curt words, could send a battle-seasoned general flushed and shaken from the room. Yet with an audacity that a friend would call "sublime," King handed him Brewer's letter and set about explaining his proposal.

The War Department had never doubted the expedience of a continental railroad. Rails would give the Army increased mobility in the Indian wars—an excellent reason for pushing the tracks across the interior. But even more important, King argued, would be the economic effects of the rails. The region which they would unlock for settlement bore little resemblance to the worthless wastes depicted by obsolte geography books. The mountains, he said, were not barren,

but full of wealth; the deserts are not all desert; the vast plains will produce something better than buffalo, namely beef; there is water for irrigation, and land fit to receive it. All that is needed is to explore and declare the nature of the national domain.

And that was what he proposed to do along the route chosen for the tracks through the Rocky Mountains and across the Great Basin, in a belt one hundred miles wide and—as it would develop—eight hundred miles long.

The plan impressed Stanton, who conferred at once with the chief of engineers, Brigadier General A. A. Humphreys. The general, himself a skilled surveyor who had conducted a topographic and hydrographic exploration of the Mississippi delta and who, moreover, had administered the Pacific Railroad Surveys, was well qualified to judge King's plan. Colonel Williamson's letter had aroused his interest, and after studying King's proposal he reported:

There is reason to believe that extensive coal beds exist in the eastern portion of the region designated, which, of itself, is a sufficient reason for a geological examination of the belt in question, in view of the scarcity of timber along the route. The geology of the other portion of the belt is unknown, and its determination cannot fail to prove of material value to the interests of the government and country.

King also secured an endorsement from Professor Spencer Baird of the Smithsonian Institution. Then he turned his attention to Congress. "If you want to get a man red-hot," he would be quoted as saying, "you must go at him white-hot." That was how he went after senators and congressmen—white-hot, and among those who grew red-hot in response was the junior senator from California. How fortunate, King discovered, that he had named a Sierra peak Mount Conness. Senator

Conness not only became an advocate of King's plan, but he also succeeded in swinging a number of his colleagues behind it, and wound up by attaching it to the appropriations bill then pending.

The measure authorized the secretary of war "to direct a geological and topographical exploration of the territory between the Rocky Mountains and the Sierra Nevada," always including the route of the Pacific railroad. A proviso prescribed the use of funds already voted for wagon-road surveys through the public domain. The bill passed on March 2, 1867; and thus King, as Henry Adams would later write, "had managed to induce Congress to adopt almost its first modern act of legislation."

Five days after President Johnson's signature on the bill King received a letter naming him U.S. Geologist in charge of the Geological Exploration of the Fortieth Parallel. "It was a truly American phenomenon," wrote Charles Loring Brace,* amateur of science; "here was a young man of twenty-four [sic] who had already . . . proved himself one of the most daring of living explorers and now was appointed by the Government to head the most important American scientific survey of this generation." At Stanton's office King noticed a glint in the secretary's eyes, a smile on the full lips.

"Now, Mr. King," Stanton cautioned, "the sooner you get out of Washington the better—you are entirely too young to be seen about town with this appointment in your pocket—there are four major generals who want your place."

King prepared a plan of operations and sent it to the chief of engineers, under whose bureau the exploration would be made, and to whom King would report directly, with no intervening chain of command. Then he took Stanton's advice. He went to Newport for a rest at the old King house on Church Street, where General Humphreys sent him instructions that incorporated all essentials of the plan: "and as I sketched them myself," King wrote, "they naturally satisfy me."

Thus it became his official aim "to examine and describe the geological structure, geographical condition, and natural resources" of a wide strip between the border of California and the Rocky Mountains. He

* In search of health Brace became King's fellow traveler on the voyage to California in 1867 and left a brief account of the journey in a book called *The New West.* Considered somewhat of an authority on race, he shared with King a deep regard for the Negro people.

was ordered to study rock formations, mountain ranges, and intervening valleys; to examine mines and mineral deposits, especially of coal; and to gather data for a topographical map. He was ordered also to make a study of weather conditions and to gather specimens of the plant and animal life. He could expect to receive one hundred thousand dollars to finance the work for three years, and General Humphreys authorized him to engage two assistant geologists, three topographical aides, two collectors, and half a dozen camp men. He also received permission to hire a photographer, and there would be a military escort, bringing the strength of the party up to thirty-five men. King's personal salary was set at $250 a month, plus a per diem allowance in the field. That would enable him to keep his mother and her family; so he accepted the job "with pleasure."

He began to organize the corps at once, for he hoped to sail by May 1. J. P. Iddings, who knew King later, would write that he could imagine the enthusiasm with which he developed the enterprise "and the romance with which he must have enveloped it." Gardiner joined the force as principal topographer, and second in charge, turning down the chair of geodesy in the Lawrence Scientific School at Harvard. Eyestrain had forced him to leave the map of the central Sierra unfinished, but he came at once to New York City, where the Olyphants had lent King an office. There Gardiner, his sight improving, helped in the task of choosing instruments, and King selected other assistants only after consulting with him.

They agreed to take as second topographer a Swiss named Henry Custer, who had worked with the Northwest Boundary Commission; and somewhat later F. A. Clark, who had "chained" in Yosemite, joined as third topographical assistant.

As chief aide in geology, Dana recommended James D. Hague of M.I.T., a most felicitous choice. King had admired him since the day they had met in 1862. Hague had studied at Harvard, Göttingen, and Freiberg; and he had done considerable work as a mining engineer, including a stint in the South Seas. Neither his carefree manner nor the "gentlemanly love of ease" which Gardiner ascribed to him would prevent him from teaching King and the corps a number of things about their business. His younger brother Arnold, a slender, quiet, intense young man, had studied with King at Sheffield, and King accepted him as second assistant in geology.

The junior Hague then introduced a friend from Boston, Samuel

Franklin Emmons, who had graduated from Harvard before going abroad for special training.* "It's just the type of work to suit me," Emmons exclaimed. But King had no authority to place a third geological assistant on the pay roll. He was delighted, therefore, to hear that Emmons was willing to work without salary for the experience. This completed a geological team that bristled with promise. For the photographic work, King hired "a wet-plate artist" named T. H. O'Sullivan, who had helped Mathew Brady photograph the war. †

Professor Baird recommended Robert Ridgway for the assignment in zoology. Ridgway was a boy of seventeen, but he had made such professional pictures of birds that King did not hesitate to take him. Another careful draftsman applied for the botanical position—W. W. Bailey, to whom Asa Gray had written: "Mr. King desires a young man who shall at the same time be an accomplished botanist. As the two things are incompatible, I think you will do as well as anybody."

"I was summoned by telegram to meet Mr. King in New Haven," Bailey wrote. "I found him in bed and indisposed, but full of fun and anecdote, and he kept us all . . . in roars of laughter. He asked me a few pertinent questions." And as the answers satisfied him, King hired Bailey on the spot.

All things considered, King's selections for the corps were brilliant choices, as witnessed by the professional eminence that most of them would afterward achieve. It made no difference that several were personal friends, in view of the remarkable company that King kept. By the end of April everything was ready, and the expedition could be called "the best equipped by training of any that had thus far entered the field of American geology."

Yale College gave the men a farewell dinner, and some of them sailed from New York on May 1, 1867. King followed ten days later with the rest of the party. He was weak from fever, yet ready with soaring

---

*Mary Hallock Foote later described Emmons as "tall, spare, rather harsh featured but distinguished looking, a somewhat hawklike profile deficient in chin, black hair, marked eyebrows, an open-air color on his thin cheekbones. When he rode he was one with his horse and went cogitating along, rolling cigarettes and lighting them with the flint and steel in a little silver box that he always carried" (A Victorian Gentlewoman in the Far West, p. 181).

†Timothy O'Sullivan was full of his war experiences and often bored his campmates with long tales of adventure with the Union Army. "One would think he had slept with Grant and Mead," complained W. W. Bailey, the collector of botanical specimens, "and was the direct confident of Stanton." But O'Sullivan was a first-rate photographer and made photographic history with the King Survey.

optimism to launch what Henry Adams was to call "one of the classic scientific works of the century." Even Whitney granted that he stood upon the threshold "of as fine a career as ever was offered to a scientific man." The morale of all was high, and King later declared:

> If I succeeded in anything, it was in personally impressing the whole corps and making it uniformly harmonious and patient; and I think I did that as much as anything else by a sort of natural spirit of command and personal sympathy with all hands and conditions, from geologists to mules. As I think back I wonder, at my age, taking command as early as I did, that I should have carried through all the necessary steps to thorough control and organization.

King shared a cabin with Custer on the hurricane deck of the *Henry Chauncey*, and eleven days out of New York the steamer slipped into the harbor of Aspinwall. "This is a most forsaken hole, dirty and nigger-infested," Bailey wrote. "The coconut trees are its only charm." Heat oppressed the passengers as they walked from the wharf to a waiting train. They slumped in cane seats inside the cars, but as the engineer delayed departure the sultriness became unbearable. The travelers drifted out, one by one, to catch whatever breeze that stirred. King himself sauntered to the rear platform, from where he could watch a pretty woman from Peru. She had two children, one a baby in arms, the other a boy who insisted on playing some distance away.

Suddenly the train jerked forward. There was no whistle, and passengers dashed to regain their seats. In the confusion the mother looked at the moving cars, then back at her boy. She darted to the edge of the platform and thrust the baby into King's hands. Then off she ran to her other child and began to drag him toward the train. But the engine had gained in speed, and she gave up the race. King could only hope, as he waved the baby, that she realized how gravely he took his new responsibility.

It was not a duty to assume lightly. In the humid heat of the Isthmus one could almost believe the legend that for every cross-tie on the road a human life had paid. The train rolled through a jungle of mangroves, palms, and banana trees trailing long lianas. Unimpressed by such luxuriance, the baby began to make demands which King was helpless to supply. Cars in Panama did not even carry water, much less milk.

But as they clattered past sudden clearings, the views of the natives, children as bare as the day they were born, and women whose light chemises revealed breasts of every shade from fawn to ebony, suggested to King that abundant supplies of what his charge needed might be found at the railroad's end. And on arriving in Panama City, after a ride of forty-seven steaming miles, he set about the business, with the baby in one hand and a parasol in the other to shield it from the sun.

He trudged among the adobe ruins, in search of a woman willing to mother his charge for the afternoon. Soon he heard some words in English, and at a small but tidy house he discovered a family of Jamaican mulattoes. The housewife looked healthy, in her late thirties, and she had a nursing child. King's story set her laughing merrily; she took the baby and told him to go for a walk while she refreshed it, both inside and out.

King was further relieved to learn at the station that another train was due to follow from Aspinwall, so he returned to the house of his Good Jamaican, where he remained in high spirits till the second train arrived. It brought the mother, who relieved him of his charge; and then he made his way to the wharf, through swarms of natives hawking shells, parrots, or tropical fruit. A small tug carried him out to the SS *Constitution*, riding in the bay.

The ship was soon gliding along the coast of Central America, and then of Mexico, and "it seemed as if we were taking a pleasure trip," wrote Bailey, "as indeed we were. Often the ship sailed near enough to the shore for us to see the great conical volcanoes, towering against the sky. One of our greatest sources of amusement," the botanist added,

was to gather around Clarence King and listen to his innumerable stories. We little suspected then, matchless as we deemed his power, that we were really listening to one of the great raconteurs of the world. [In another context Bailey likened King to Scheherazade.] For him to start a story was but a signal for a crowd to gather. Our own little group became secondary to a large audience embracing all sorts and conditions of men. In reading his books you, of course, get something of his charm, but to know King at his best one had to hear his voice, and above all his musical, infectious laugh. As he hypnotized us—so, in later life did he thrill the Prince of Wales and the best circles of all lands, either social or literary.

The steamer docked at San Francisco before dawn on June 3, and King awoke Gardiner at their appointed meeting place, the Occidental Hotel. They made their headquarters at Colonel Williamson's office while King saw old friends, dined at the Union Club, secured equipment from the local quartermaster, and hired a crew of camp men.

These included Dick Cotter, who had just returned from two years in northern Alaska. There he had served with an expedition to connect America with Siberia by means of a cable across the Bering Strait. On being abandoned by Eskimo companions in the dead of winter, he had suffered such a harrowing ordeal that his faculties were affected. "His mind is much dimmed," wrote Gardiner, "but his glorious heart is as warm as ever. I have hope that affection and sympathetic treatment may restore him." Cotter would spend at least two seasons with the King Survey, and then would settle in Montana.

In the meantime King could not leave San Francisco without calling at the rooms of the state survey in the Montgomery Block. There Whitney, who had called him "more of a promiser than a performer," proved to be in a sensorious mood. He was annoyed that Gardiner's map of the central Sierra remained unfinished, and he chafed over King's delay in reporting on the field work of the previous season. King's success with Congress and the War Department may have caused the state geologist a touch of chagrin, in view of his own indifferent luck with the California legislature.* And his attitude did little to salve King's pride. "King is evidently not inclined to take advice," Whitney wrote after their meeting. But the fragmentary report which King eventually submitted deserved less scorn than Whitney heaped upon it. †

On June 6, in the company of Baron Ferdinand von Richthofen, the German geologist and geographer, King took passage on the steamboat to Sacramento. His corps had pitched camp in a stand of cottonwoods a

---

*The situation was in reality more complex. King would always claim that the idea for the Fortieth Parallel Survey had germinated during his trek across the West with Gardiner in 1863. On the other hand, Brewer believed that he had taken the idea from Whitney, elaborating it and improving it, "especially in the matter of the maps." Both explanations appear to be correct, for as noticed in chapter 5, King's original inspiration had been bolstered and reinforced by the thinking of his chief. But Whitney seems to have expected him to launch a survey in the latitude of Arizona, where King had worked in the winter of 1866. King's announcement of an exploration along the fortieth parallel came as a distinct surprise, and Whitney had to cancel plans to operate in central Nevada himself during the 1867 season, so as "not to be in King's way." Thus, when viewed in the light of these facts, the ambivalence of his attitude toward King becomes more understandable.

†Confused as the report is in places, and neglectful of the later phases of the 1866 reconnaissance, it yet contains some fine passages. Though Whitney rejected it for use in *The Yosemite Book,* King found it helpful in writing *Mountaineering.* Specifically, the climax of "Merced Ramblings," recounting the dramatic conquest of Mount Clark, duplicates several paragraphs of the report almost verbatim.

mile or so from town—a bivouac of the sort that served King's corps for season after season in the field. The several wall tents contained wooden bunks supported by stakes, and under them were stored the field trunks. A rack for saddles and a washstand stood before each door flap. Various colors waved from improvised poles—the American flag, the geological flag with two white hammers crossed against a red background, and the astronomical flag with a single white star on a field of blue. A trench served the cook as a stove, two bars of iron holding pots and kettles over the fire, and a round iron cook-oven was settled in a pit where it baked bread "to a charm"—as one of the party claimed. "It is wonderful what good victuals we have in camp. I challenge Delmonico to surpass our boiled mutton and caper sauce." Here the corps settled while perfecting arrangements for the field. Tenderfeet like Bailey learned to ride the mules, while Emmons and the Hagues examined mines in the foothills, and Ridgway scouted the countryside for birds and their nests to ship to the National Museum. For his large wet-plate camera O'Sullivan readied a mobile darkroom.

Governor Low's secretary had advised Gardiner as to the proper man to see for mules and wagons—a certain Ben Crocker who had fitted out the exploring parties for the Central Pacific and who knew what the deserts and mountains demanded of stock and gear. The light which the survey promised to shed on reported coal measures was of such importance to the railroad that its president, Leland Stanford, called at camp in person. From that interview developed a long and sustained cooperation between the railroad and King's corps. King depended on Crocker's judgment in making up the train, and the wagons and animals thus assembled were to serve the corps superbly in the relentless terrain ahead. The men were much in the saddle at Sacramento, testing the qualities of mules and horses, which they branded with two crossed hammers.

King had hoped to be on the road by June 20, but a remittance of gold pieces had not come from Washington (coin rather than paper being the necessity in the West); besides, snow still choked the mountain passes. King postponed the departure, and the heat of July struck before the corps began its sally across the plain—eleven men on horses, a pair of freight wagons and a thoroughbrace loaded with instruments, each drawn by four mules and followed by extra animals. The caravan took the Donner Summit road into the forests of the foothills, while King remained behind to make some last arrangements.

He followed ten days later, past Auburn, Colfax, Dutch Flat; then past the mining town of Alta where, as he would learn, the corps had paused for Sunday, camping in a glen where Ridgway had identified the calls of russet-backed thrushes, shifting Ariel-like among the thickets; then on to Cisco, terminus of the Central Pacific, where the corps had rested while a blacksmith had repaired the wagons.

The railroad had tackled its most forbidding barrier in the fourteen miles ahead. There the granite had ruined tools and resisted black powder till the Swedish inventor Alfred Nobel had patented a new explosive—nitroglycerin. Slashes in the rock marked how well that stuff had done its work. Shoals of coolies could be seen, in loose blue shirts and basket hats—"China boys" who shoveled and carted and blasted granite from the cuts, and who, at Summit Tunnel, were chiselling away at a quarter-mile passage through the rock. The higher King climbed, the deeper grew the drifts of snow, until in the topmost stretches of Donner Pass he faced accumulations eight feet deep. Then came the swift descent.

King overtook his men on July 15. They had pitched the first work camp at a place in Truckee Meadows known as Glendale Crossing, near where the city of Reno would mushroom a few months later with the advance of the Central Pacific. *Ciénegas* along the Truckee furnished grass for the animals, and there were truck gardens at the settlement, which added vegetables to the doves and waterfowl hunted for the table by a young mulatto named Jim Marryatt. He was a tall youth, whose face lit up at talk of exploration. King learned that he had attached himself to the corps at Colfax. He claimed Liverpool for his birthplace, though it later developed that he had run away from home in Jamaica, going to sea as a cabin boy, and had wound up in California. He was a good cook, and Gardiner had hired him as "cook's mate" at Alta, the next stop. Marryatt had lost no time in making himself "a necessary institution." Indeed, he would outlast all the other camp men and in the end become King's personal valet.

The corps, customarily in the saddle by six A.M., made preliminary excursions during the next few days. King accompanied Gardiner and J. D. Hague to the top of Peavine Mountain, which served as the first geodetic station. It gave them splendid views of the profiles, so harsh and barren, of the Truckee and Virginia mountains, and of the robin's egg blue of Pyramid and Winnemucca lakes. Directly east, the vista reached far beyond the Big Bend of the river toward the principal field of their task.

King had worked out his plans for the season, the corps to cover by fall a block of country a hundred miles wide by a hundred and fifty miles in length. The block stretched from the border of California to the Shoshone Mountains—fifteen thousand square miles across the midriff of Nevada. Geological and geographical work had to go hand in hand, not an ideal arrangement. But no geological investigation would be worth the effort, King was sure, unless it could be based on correct topography. As John Wesley Powell would put the matter, "[King] gave practical recognition to the fact that a good topographical map is the essential basis for accurate geological work." And so, in the absence of adequate maps, it was necessary for the corps to make an atlas of its own.

In its trigonometrical basis the work approached the character of a geodetic survey; indeed, King and Gardiner received help and advice from Professor Hilgard of the United States Coast Survey. They adopted theodolites, as in their California apprenticeship, to carry a continuous system of triangulations across the country, from mountaintop to mountaintop. Rock cairns, when necessary, served as signals. Distances had to be computed at first from an astronomical base, the sextant and zenith telescope providing geodetic checks at astronomical stations. Later a measured base line was employed. Systems of secondary triangulations would be run inside the major triangles, and tertiary systems within the secondary, and by means of these all topographical features could be placed. Relative altitudes were determined by observations of cistern barometers; and the topographers, working with compasses and gradienters, would sketch the surface configuration around each occupied station. They would sketch it in both profile and relief, a method exactly suited to the bleak, bare landscape of Nevada. The scale of the atlas would be four miles to the inch, and the geological maps would employ contour lines in place of hachures, the vertical interval between the lines amounting to four hundred feet. Hill shading on the geographical maps, on the other hand, would be accomplished by meticulous brush-work and then copied on stone by means of crayon.

The geologists, meanwhile, would correlate their work with that of the topographers; they would gather data for geologic sections of all the country surveyed. They would collect thousands of specimens in the course of a season—fossils, rocks, and minerals, even samplings of water from springs and lakes. They would observe and describe the features of the land in pocket notebooks as methodically as the topographers depicted them in sketches.

On returning to camp from Peavine Mountain, King found that the escort, twenty cavalrymen from Fort Churchill, had reported for duty. What a hard-looking set they were, all wearing knives in their boots, some so drunk they could hardly stay aboard their horses. Their actual usefulness would always be a matter for debate—four would desert the first season. "They give us more worry than the Indians," Bailey complained. And as time went on, they would be employed more and more in merely looking after the animals. But King, ever mindful of his narrow escape from the Hualapais in Arizona, always wanted them along. They were suited to a rough country, and their presence now suggested that the campaign was under way in earnest. Soon King moved the base to Big Bend, thirty miles downstream. The settlement of Wadsworth would soon spring up near the campsite, but now only an abandoned shanty stood there amidst the grass and sunflowers.

King divided the corps into two main work details. The first group, under Gardiner, went to explore the Truckee Mountains; the other, Custer's party, proceeded to the next range eastward, the Hot Springs Mountains, which bordered Carson Sink. Bailey and Ridgway had begun, meanwhile, to comb the region for specimens of plants, birds, and animals. They worked along the riverbanks and through the canyons of the Virginia Mountains. Then King sent them both to Pyramid Lake with O'Sullivan the photographer, and they accepted an invitation from H. G. Parker,* the local Indian agent, to ship down the river in his sailboat, the *Nettie*.

The Truckee had never been navigated before, and when the men returned, they brought King a tale of rapids that had snagged the *Nettie* on a half-submerged rock. Pyramid Lake had stirred Ridgway, not because of the island of rattlesnakes he had found there, though it provided items for his collection, but because of the multitudes of white pelicans. He told of their trip to Anaho Island and how the birds had taken flight at their approach with such a thunder of wings that they could scarcely hear one another speak.

But pelicans in the desert were not, in King's opinion, the queerest inhabitants of Nevada. Scattered along the rivers or at the desert springs was a squatter type which seemed unique. Most of them had

*A spirited raconteur, Parker had quickly become a favorite with the Fortieth Parallel Corps. He was an amateur taxidermist who skinned and stuffed many specimens for Ridgway's zoological collection.

once been California bound, but they had stopped along the road, sometimes to earn a precarious living by making wild hay.

It amused King to distill the type into a campfire story—one that never happened as he chose to tell it (or as it survived in a friend's version), for King could see no harm in slight invention to entertain old comrades. It bothered him little to switch a field trip with Brewer from the mountains of California to the wastelands of Nevada, or to add two imaginary characters, a cayuse wrangler famous from the Fresno River to the Sacramento, and a gunman from Virginia City, on vacation as a packer since the graveyards on Mount Davidson were full. While riding back from the Humboldt country, this hypothetical party had pitched its camp at a spring where a desert rat named Tison had squatted down with a Paiute squaw and a flock of "half-breed incidents." The intrusion gave the old outlaw, contrariness incarnate, endless bother. He felt compelled to shoot his watchdog because it had let King touch it without biting back. It riled him even more when, on a bet, the bronco buster rode his meanest mustang to a collapse. "With a six gun," the old cutthroat yelled, "I'm a wolf off'n the headwaters of Bitter Creek, and it's shore my time to howl." But then the gunman from Virginia City did a few clever things with his revolver, and the wolf concluded it was time to "*re*-tire from the shootin' business." Tison had only one more claim to superiority—his fancied luck at cards. He looked at Brewer, whose professional dignity belied a passion for seven-up. The challenge was too much to resist, and Brewer went to the old man's 'breed-infested cabin. He returned at midnight with the news that he had won the entire establishment—cash, spring, cabin, stock, squaw and second generation down to the nursing papoose.

Shortly after sunrise old Tison charged up to the spring. "It was all on the squar'," he howled, "when you handled my dog and rid my pinto and shot the livin' lights outa my hanker for a gun. And the game last night was on the squar' too till I git the winnin's chucked in my teeth. But you cain't go makin' a fool outa me. I came yere to tell you that thar's gonna be trouble unless thet prissy-lookin' feller *takes at least the squaw*."

So much for fiction. As a result of making camp at Big Bend, King was soon confronted in fact by one of this captious type. On hearing of the corps, the owner of the collapsing shanty came back and complained of trespass. He had never secured title to the land. Yet he demanded $260 for the grass King's stock had eaten and the driftwood that Marryatt had gathered along the river. The grass was valuable enough, scarce as it was in the arid reaches of Nevada, but King scoffed at the claim. * He smiled at the stranger's uneasiness when the camp men drifted near, their curiosities aroused by the argument. The fellow edged toward his horse, hinting of mayhem if he ever caught a certain scientific gent *alone*. The threat amused King; he knew the fellow was a sham; when they next met on the desert—both alone—the stranger made a swift "retreat into the sandhills."

The appearance of another odd figure took a more congenial turn. Tall and spare and covered with dust, the wayfarer sank to the ground from weariness. He was barefoot, for as he explained, heavy boots had punished his feet more than rocks and stones during his trudge across the Sierra. King took a letter of introduction from his trembling fingers and found it signed by a friend from Hartford. It presented Sereno Watson, former physician, teacher, and farmer, who, moreover, had taken the chemical course at Sheffield. A shy, inhibited misfit, he could offer no eloquent testimony for himself. But he was like his name, "always serene and cheerful," and something in his determination to join the corps tugged at King's sympathy.

King had no vacancies to fill, and delay of funds had forced him to support the expedition for weeks out of his own purse. He could take Watson only as a volunteer in topography, but the exhausted man snapped at the offer, too abjectly eager for a just suggestion of his worth. King could hardly have foreseen that Sereno Watson would in time become one of the most distinguished botanists in America.

The spectacle of Dr. Watson learning to ride a mule kept King and his men amused. But after marching across the Carson Desert to the Humboldt Sink—the Battle Lakes of the old fur trappers—the corps had reason to value a doctor, even if only one who had left his profession. Here was "the worst place between Missouri and Hell," according to local inhabitants. Floods of the past year had filled the shallow lake near which the corps pitched camp. Green-scummed marshes spread extensively along its western shore, and miles of oozy muck waved with banks of tules. The stench of decayed vegetation fouled the air, nauseating in its rankness. Even the sulphur-laden water stank like rotten eggs. But the worst torment arrived at night—clouds of mosquitoes dense enough to smother a candle's flame.

* Mark Twain (in *Roughing It*, I, p. 174) suggests the value of hay in Washoe at the time of his arrival in 1861: $250 a ton.

"None of us pretended to sleep after the first night," Bailey wrote, "but walked about attempting to beat off these fearful pests. Bars were of no use, and the 'pesky devils' would get under our blankets and scorch us until we would 'git up and get.' " The touches of fever the men had developed at Sacramento flared again—the "mountain ail," which in its virulence resembled typhoid fever more than the ordinary ague. King attributed it, at least in part, to their brief exposure on the Isthmus. One by one the corps was forced to bed.

Between chills King felt weak, and his head light, but he continued to work, in desperation as the effectiveness of the corps dwindled. Through the next few days he examined the natural dam that held the waters of the Humboldt back and studied the mountains that walled both sides of the sink. He had to drive himself on a trip with Emmons to check geology in the Hot Springs Range, which reared from the Forty Mile Desert. The mountains were aptly named for the scalding pools at their base where many an ox train, crazed from thirst, had been parboiled. The sun baked the bare rock and the heat rebounded as if from a furnace. Pulsations danced before King's eyes—of light and darkness alternating—and he crawled into the shadow of a ledge of sandstone. His consciousness contracted round the pain that seared his head; all grew dark, and then King knew that he was blind. He managed somehow to reach his horse, his hazel eyes fixed in a blank stare, and Emmons led the way to camp.

A week in the Humboldt Marshes had prostrated the corps. In hope that flight from the stagnant water might bring them relief, King ordered his men to march by easy stages upstream to the mining town of Oreana. They made camp in a field of sunflowers, and there King began to recover, regaining his sight. But the fever raged among his men. It was necessary, he decided, to leave the river to escape the miasmas on which he blamed the trouble.

For an asylum he chose a wild ravine ten miles away in Wright's Canyon, deeply sculptured in the strangely colored rhyolites of the West Humboldt Mountains. The main bivouac was pitched beside a stream that chattered all night long through willow and aspen and bushes of buffalo berry but sank with the noonday heat into a string of silent pools. The invalids, almost three-quarters of the company, were packed on mules into an airy retreat a mile or so higher in the canyon. There they suffered periodic attacks for more than a week. Then a shift in the wind and a falling barometer warned of a storm, and King found it necessary to get the sick men under shelter. He led the train across the range to the silver town of Unionville, in Buena Vista Canyon, a larger settlement now than the "eleven cabins and a liberty pole" that Mark Twain had scorned six years before. It had reached its zenith, and then its decline, the upper town "showing only a line of roofless buildings where"—as Bailey recorded—"the magpie and coyote love to linger." As the cabin which served as jail contained but a single prisoner—a murderer chained in the cellar—King hired it for his ailing men.

Only Clark and O'Sullivan, besides two camp men and a soldier, remained strong enough for strenuous duty. A sense of impending failure oppressed King, driving him to undertake much of the field work he had planned for others. "Mr. King was untiring," Bailey noted, "and did the work of two or three." He left the sick in Gardiner's charge. Then with Clark, one soldier, and an Indian guide, he marched south to the Stillwater Mountains between Salt Valley and the Carson Sink.

On September 22 he climbed with Clark to the summit of Job's Peak. A thunderhead drifted toward them, and from the tickle at their hair roots they knew that heavy electrical charges had begun to generate. Soon the air sizzled like bacon in a pan, and as the cloud rolled near, the rocks sang like a plague of mosquitoes. A distant bolt of lightning brought relief, but the tickling and the frying resumed almost as soon as the thunder reached their ears. Though the theodolite clattered on its tripod, King, anticipating no danger, set the cross hair on the initial signal. He leaned to observe the angle. Suddenly the air exploded; the sky and the mountain reeled together; then he saw Clark bending over him, staring at his arm and side where the bolt had struck. The damaged theodolite lay twenty feet away where it had been knocked against the wind.

"I was staggered and my brain and nerves severely shocked," King wrote. His right side turned the color of coffee. The skin peeled off, and it took a week for his distress to wear away, though after the first retreat to camp in Salt Valley he refused to let it interfere with work. In two weeks more he and Clark had finished their reconnaissance, not only of the Job's Peak chain but also of the Paiute Range, directly east of Unionville. *

On returning to that melancholy town King found the corps improved in health. Bailey and Ridgway had discovered the West Hum-

* Now better known as East Range.

boldts to be a rewarding field for their collection; and Custer soon returned from a trip to the Humbolt Valley, where he had resumed his topographical work. Although the corps had not completed the area King had planned to cover that season, he thought it wise to turn back now and fill the gaps in their summer's work, especially in the lowlands where they had been routed by disease. Redividing the men, he sent a party under Emmons to survey the Black Rock country, along the northern edge of their belt of operations, and to carry the work westward to the border of California. At the same time Custer's group went on with the topographical work through the Humboldt region. All were instructed to meet at Glendale Crossing in November.

Then King boarded the Boise stage with J. D. Hague, who had finished a study of the Humboldt mines. They headed for the Owyhee district in southern Idaho, which rumor boomed as the greatest strike of gold and silver since the Comstock. Some of its ores assayed three thousand dollars a ton. Because the mines would soon depend on the railroad for supplies, King considered them relevant to the proposed report on economic geology. He spent three weeks with Hague in the shafts at Silver City.

Free passes on the stage lines then carried them into Oregon. At The Dalles a most exciting paleontological display awaited their attention—the first Oligocene fossils which Dr. Thomas Condon had taken from the John Day Basin, forerunners of the fossil bones which O. C. Marsh would harvest from the Oregon beds to help in the confirmation of Darwin's theory. Weary from his travels, King retired early, but was soon roused by a knock on the door of his hotel room. He opened it to a lean, dark-haired Irishman who explained that he had read of the U.S. Geologist's presence in the evening newspaper. King "was soon [dressed] and ready to talk geology with his enthusiastic guest, and the next forenoon was spent in the Condon home, looking over the unique treasure gathered there." The intense and eager fossil hunter was greatly encouraged by King's praise, and it would be King's privilege to carry the news of Condon's remarkable discoveries to colleagues in the East—to his friends at the Smithsonian, to J. S. Newberry at Columbia and Marsh at Yale. Meanwhile King and Hague steamed down the Columbia River, through country Theodore Winthrop had described so vividly. They turned south at Portland, staged to Sacramento, and then across the Sierra.

The chill of November had crept into the air by the time King arrived at Glendale Crossing. A few of the corps had preceded him there, and King found them quartered in an old house in the meadows. Custer, he learned, had suffered a bad relapse while working near Oreana; but Gardiner had gained sufficient strength to carry on the work. He had completed the main triangulations for the season, and he reached the Meadows shortly after King's return. During the next few days the work was completed in the Truckee section; it was carried back to the California border and closed with the Black Rock survey to the north.

Emmons brought his party to Glendale Crossing on November 26, having covered a region infested with hostile Bannocks. They were villainous demons, and Emmons had feared an attack, especially after finding the body of a teamster riddled with bullets and arrows. But as most of the escort had gone on the trip, his party was much too strong to tempt the Bannocks. Relations with the Paiutes remained much better; they were friendly, and King had gained the confidence of chiefs like Captain Sou and Old Winnemucca. The young men would bring trout to sell, a welcome addition to the camp fare; and early in December several warriors from Old Winnemucca's reservation came to ask King to be their emissary to Parker, the superintendent.

They brought the scalp of a Pit River Indian, one of those troublesome raiders from across the California line. The Paiutes had killed him as he tried to steal from their herds, and now they wanted King "to send the scalp to Parker, with a note stating the circumstances which had put it in their hands."

King felt relieved on ending the field work of 1867, short though it fell of first objectives. It was no small accomplishment to have carried the survey over more than twelve thousand square miles of what he believed was "the most difficult and dangerous country . . . on the continent." The geological collection contained over three thousand specimens of rocks, minerals, fossils, salts, and ores; it represented every rock formation that the corps had examined, and marked a good start toward illustrating the mineral wealth along the fortieth parallel. King sent General Humphreys an enthusiastic report. "In spite of the most adverse circumstances," he wrote, "and almost overwhelming pressure of work, the few of us who kept our health have, by great effort, turned a threatened failure into a very complete success."

No longer was science the mere camp follower of military reconnaissance. "Eighteen hundred and sixty-seven . . ." he later declared, "marks, in the history of national geological work, a turning point, when the science ceased to be dragged in the dust of rapid exploration and took a commanding position in the professional work of the country."

King settled part of his corps at Carson City to work on specimens and plat the topographical notes. But as the hub of his winter program he planned an examination of the Comstock Lode. Therefore he chose Virginia City as his principal base. "Virginia City! Chaste name for a riproaring bonanza town that knew no day or night, fed red-gaitered, tobacco-chewing, whiskey-drinking hard-rock miners and lightened them of the burden of gold and silver coin that jingled in their pockets." It was a loose-built town of brown, wooden houses and red brick stores that hugged the treeless slope of Mount Davidson, where not a sprig of green could be seen. The buildings along the parallel streets stood on ground above the mines, and were already settling down into cavities produced by the cave-ins in the tunnels, a fact that seemed to concern no one overmuch. Through the streets streamed coaches, wagons, and "mountain schooners," the last being prodigious freight vans drawn by a dozen mules apiece and bearing merchandise of every sort—furniture, machinery, stoves, glass, all manner of foodstuffs, wines, tools, even pianos—all that luxury required or money could buy. Virginia City might be remote from the outside world, but it compensated for its isolation with excitements of its own, especially those of the stock market. All day long, day in and day out, the streets boiled over with stock speculation.

Indeed, the Comstock was now booming after the slump of 1865. The restless spirit of America seemed concentrated on Mount Davidson, busy as a great ant hill. King and his colleagues slipped into the furious tempo of the place, for the work before them was immense, the time short. King rented rooms at the Ophir House for himself, Emmons, and the Hagues, "within sight of hundreds of dumps and within sound of the gentle note of the quartz mill." It was an ideal center for their sojourn, close to the mines they had to study and near enough to Carson City for King to keep his eye on the party there. Before December ended, he could write: "I am the busiest man in town, hard at work from morning till night. No time to write my friends, and yet no time to forget them either." All the while Jim Marryatt kept the geologists happy as their cook.

8

From Washoe to the Rockies

And then came the worst winter that Washoe settlers could remember; it was even worse than the year before. Rains turned the Carson River into a flood, and it threatened to swamp the White House, where King had quartered his Carson City detachment. Yet on slogging down into the valley, he found the men in good spirits. "We dine in a smaller house near by," wrote Bailey. "But this unrecorded river intervened. . . . At last we settled down to the prospect of swimming for our meals." Between drenchings, however, they found the White House snug; and King went back to the Comstock, satisfied that all was well below.

Worse storms followed; the "Washoe zephyr" beat at Ophir House, forcing entrance at every crack. But no degree of bad weather could prevent King and his geologists from running their study of the lode. Mine superintendents allowed them to trace company charts and gather data underground. Then in February King called his photographer up from Carson City to take pictures of the Savage and the Gould & Curry tunnels nine hundred feet below the surface. It was a pioneer experiment with light from burning magnesium wire, and it proved a great success. O'Sullivan's shots of conditions in the shafts and stopes included the havoc of a cave-in. *

In the meantime King discovered that a Washoe winter could be a time of gaiety. Virginia City, indeed, seemed pleasure mad; lamps blazed all night in a hundred saloons, where faro tables existed for a single purpose, to lighten the patron's purse, and only women of tarnished reputation seemed in evidence; women who, a correspondent from the Bay remarked, had "a pet way of jerking up one side of their fabrics when passing gentlemen in the street." Gambling and vice

* See William H. Goetzmann, *Exploration and Empire*, pp. 623–27, for possibly the first publication of five of these extraordinary plates, documenting "the frightening everyday life of [the] Western silver miner." As far as Robert Taft could find (*Photography and the American Scene*, p. 285), O'Sullivan's plates included "the first 'interior' mine views made in this country." They were not the first underground photographs, however; pictures had been taken of Mammoth Cave the year before.

119

were, inevitably, the recreations of a place dedicated, like the Comstock, to a struggle for silver and gold.

And yet gentility and refinement were not entirely lacking. A number of respectable ladies raised the moral tone of Washoe, and frontier observance held them as safe from approach as each might choose to be. Some could afford to accept bouquets from bright young men in government service. King jotted in a notebook, "Flowers for Mrs. Baldwin," and enjoyed a pleasant evening at the home of that resplendent matron, wife of Judge "Sandy" Baldwin, partner of "Big Bill" Stewart. She was the *grande dame* whom Mark Twain (the senator's recent secretary) had lampooned in the *Golden Era*, the lady whom Twain had admired to see "arrayed in a sorrel organdy, trimmed with fustian and figaros, and canzou fichus."

Social entry was assured for the young men of the fortieth parallel when she took them under her wing. King dressed the part of a dandy; the clothes in which he appeared on the streets of Gold Hill or Virginia City were as spruce as those he had worn in Newport or New York, a low-crowned wide-awake topping his ensemble. He wore tight-fitting trousers of light-colored doeskin with a stripe down the side. The tone of his vest was more subdued, but a gold watch chain flashed across it; his coat was darker still, but against it pale violet or lemon-colored gloves made a jaunty contrast. His mustache flourished, and a neatly clipped beard covered his jaws and chin. He liked to carry a cane in town, and frequently he dressed as formally as any swell from Fifth Avenue, in a clawhammer coat and white tie. This was the dandy whom men of the corps called "Kingy," the debonair spark whom Mrs. Baldwin exhibited in her parlor.

One young lady in Mrs. Baldwin's circle struck King as especially charming, a schoolteacher whose last name was Dean. She was "worthy of all praise," Emmons agreed, and she was soon known as "Deany" to the fortieth parallel men. "Deany" and "Kingy"—they made a pair. King received her bid to the Leap Year Ball which "the unmarried and marriageable ladies of Virginia, Gold Hill, and Silver City" had arranged for gentlemen who were "also unmarried and marriageable." It was Deany's evening to take the lead; she called for King in a sleigh; she paid the bills, and then she saw him home again, as all the ladies did their beaux.

It marked the beginning of a romantic attachment that stirred King deeply. He called on Deany; they dined together, skated together, sleighed along the mountain roads or down into the valley—in a rig "most aboriginal," observed Bailey—two government mules spangled with sleighbells and harnessed to a boxsled with a huge cow chime in front. They would jangle off with friends to a special institution of the valley—the Hot Springs Bath House—for swims in the tepid water that spewed from the rocks there.

Gardiner was showing interest in another Comstock "specimen," also a schoolteacher, but as King would grant, "as charming a little recent vertebrate as was ever collected." Her name: Josephine Rogers. The four of them went to dancing classes together, to sociables at a choral society, and to prayer meetings at the Reverend Mr. Taylor's church. Then came the Bachelors' Party which several young men promoted in return for the Leap Year Celebration. As the *Territorial Enterprise* foretold, it was the gayest occasion of the season, an all-night dance, laced with champagne and whiskey. "A few got tyght," wrote Emmons. At about this time, something led King to jot a few of his thoughts in a notebook labeled "private."

To man he assigned "the larger nature," to woman "the more perceptive"; woman's nature was more intuitive, man's more analytical. But both, he believed, "should be equally logical, equally critical and creative." Equally tender in feeling, too. It was a fallacy, he thought, "to suppose woman all tender and man all strong." He rejected the conventional oak and vine as suitable symbols for modern love, as they failed to suggest complete union. The substratum of love should be "physical mergence," and its unifying function "the essential part of marriage." King felt that physical union was "as necessary to proper love as the planet for history." It encouraged "progressive companionship" in the intellectual sphere, he believed, and in the spiritual realm it marked the fulfillment of divine law for human beings.

The pretty schoolteacher had scored; King was in love. But as the spring of 1868 approached, he had to prepare for another campaign, which called for trips to San Francisco to buy supplies, to locate mules, and to gather all available information on the regions he planned to explore. There was a private mission to perform too; which done, King headed back for Washoe, delayed only by the snowstorm that raged across the Sierra. He reached Virginia City on Easter Day, with a diamond ring, and Deany announced their engagement.

All was ready by early May for the second campaign. Two camp men came with the mules that King had bought beyond the mountains, and the animals of the previous year were rounded up from winter pastures.

It reassured King to note the high morale of his men, who numbered twenty-seven that season, not counting the twenty soldiers of the escort. As Emmons wrote,

After we had rested up at Virginia City during the winter, where King had provided us with comfortable quarters and good food, he inspired us all with his own enthusiasm . . . and we went at field work again . . . sometimes with snow up to our middle. With him nothing was impossible that was worth doing, and whatever was worth doing at all, was worth doing in the very best possible way. And his enthusiasm was so contagious that however we might doubt the possibility of accomplishing a given project, we were always willing to try it after a talk with him. And the very most difficult things he generally undertook to do himself. So that in all his corps every one felt the impulse to make his best effort if only to please King.

The men were proud to be members of the Fortieth Parallel Survey, and the esprit de corps soared.

Two detachments took the field on May 8, 1868. Emmons led the first group to Austin in the foothills of the Toiyabe Mountains, with orders to survey the entire chain. The second group, under Custer, accompanied by the state minerologist of Nevada, left for the Big Bend of the Humboldt to secure the topography east of Unionville. Dr. Watson served as botanist with the party, having replaced Bailey, whom malaria had forced to return home.

King himself had to stay near Carson City to answer the trespass charges filed by the cantankerous squatter who had threatened him months before. The suit, however, did not keep him from joining Ridgway on a trip to Pyramid Lake, where the pelicans had returned to nest. Spring had softened the harsh landscape along the way; lush meadow grass rippled in the wind. There were blazes of peach blossoms along the trail, and cottonwoods shimmered in early leaf beside the Truckee. Here was beauty for a painter, just the thing to fire the enthusiasm of the new camp man who accompanied them—John Henry Hill. Hill was an accomplished watercolorist, for King had begun the practice of taking artists on the exploration. King had met him in New York, where Hill had followed the American Pre-Raphaelites, his work having won high praise from the editors of the *New Path*. He was a devotee of mountain scenes, and preferred painting in the open air to working in a studio. Bailey had predicted that he would "find the weird scenes of the desert valleys and rugged mountains of the Great Basin an inexhaustible field of study." Be that as it may, Hill was to leave the survey after only a single season, and when asked what the scenery of Nevada was really like, he would quip with laconic finality—"Hell."

Meanwhile, the pelicans grew more numerous the nearer the three visitors approached the lake. The birds, they found, had begun to breed on Anaho Island, a dozen miles from where the Truckee emptied into the lake. The males were standing guard beside their mates. Then all thundered into the air, and the sand lay covered with exposed nests, each holding a single egg. While Hill sketched, Ridgway gathered more than a hundred specimens for shipment to the National Museum, a supply for exchange with other institutions.

It seemed doubtful for a time whether the specimens would ever reach civilization, for Ridgway and Hill had an Indian scare. A band of outlaw redskins, more of the Pit River malcontents, had attacked the Paiute settlement at the lake. "They [took] with them," Ridgway wrote, "practically all stock on the reservation except the ponies ridden by the defenders. The raiding party was a large one, and we doubtless would have been wiped out had not their plan for surprise been divulged by the escape of a reservation Indian whom they had captured with intent to kill."

King had left the reservation before the trouble began and so had only pleasant memories of the excursion, especially of his visit to the friendly Paiutes. He assured a friend years afterward that some of the happiest moments of his life were spent around Old Winnemucca's lodge fire while he listened to Paiute chants and legends and groped back through accretions of time for an inkling of their origin. He admired these people for their virtues; he found that the old chief was as trustworthy as Frémont had found his father Captain Truckee years before. The Indians were intelligent too. "Princess Sarah," Old Winne-mucca's daughter, had been schooled by Catholic priests in California; and soon her quaint volume, *Life Among the Piutes,* would be hailed as one of the first significant expressions of the Western Indian in print. Already King was on his way to becoming a staunch defender of the native American.

He returned to the Comstock by the end of May 1868, and he spent the early days of June in geological studies of Mount Davidson. He had the good fortune to find that the former mineralogist of the state was willing to sell the private notes he had made in the early days of the Comstock. Cave-ins had long since closed the upper reaches of the vein to study; and King informed the chief of engineers that, lacking these older data, "the record and description of the mines would be imperfect; with them I can unhesitatingly say that we have the most thorough account of any great silver mining district in the world."

A statement on the character and the structure of the lode was taking shape in his mind—a long chapter that would contradict the opinions of Whitney and a dozen other experts who regarded the Comstock like a great cheese, all consumed but the rind. King had found that geological conditions there did not preclude the possibility of further bonanzas. "The examples of other great veins," he soon wrote, "all that we know of the mode of deposition and chemical transmutation of silver ore, rather favor the idea of continued silver occurrence in depth."

And indeed eight years later the Big Bonanza, the greatest strike of all, was to justify his optimism beyond all expectation.

King left Washoe on June 18 and took the Overland Road for Austin. Emmons had pitched a camp on the outskirts of town, in a gulley choked with buffalo berry and aspen trees. There the various groups converged, the military escort reported for duty, and all "cele- brated . . . with becoming festivities."

Austin now ranked second to the Comstock as a mining center of Nevada. It could boast of eleven mills; there were three churches, one of them built by Methodists from the proceeds of fifty thousand dollars worth of wildcat stock foisted at par on widows and orphans in the East. Now the mortgage had been foreclosed and the building transferred to the Presbyterians. "Parson Stewart told me this," King wrote; and it was just the kind of yarn one expected of a boom city where even a train of camels could be met upon the street. Austin might well have been the scene of King's "celery story."

He had stopped in such a town, according to Arnold Hague, after a rough time in the mountains, and gone to the best hotel for a square meal. A weather-beaten miner in a red shirt joined him at table. Between them sat a dish of young celery, King's favorite appetizer. "Glancing at the dimensions of the miner, and his hungry look, King became anxious about his own share of the celery, and to make sure of it secured a fine stick before the meal began. The miner looked at him sharply, but said nothing. After the first course King ventured to secure a second piece, an act still more keenly observed by his neighbor, who, King thought, was only waiting to make up his celery average later in the meal. As he did not do this, King kept on, until only one fine bunch was left for manners, or for the miner if he chose to take it. When the latter was evidently through with his feast, and leaning back began to pick his teeth with a fork, King laid aside his scruples and took the remaining piece, the best of all. The miner again eyed him sharply, evidently much surprised, but merely said—'Stranger, you're shore hell on grass.' "

At Austin, King reshuffled his men into three new groups, to explore east as far as the Great Salt Desert. King's party surveyed the ranges west of the Reese River, the haunts of numerous wild mustangs, then headed across the Shoshone Mountains. On reaching Carico Lake, one of the escort took French leave, a desperate character whose later career ran to murder. Although he had supplied himself with survey instruments, his absence was not detected for about twelve hours, time for a good head start. King knew that this desertion, if not prevented, would ruin the morale of the other troopers—especially now that they were about to enter the territory of Indians thought to be hostile. So, regardless of the long delay, he took the sergeant in charge and started after the culprit.

"I chased him one hundred miles," King wrote, "across the desert and through the mountain ranges of northern Nevada . . . trailing him like a bloodhound."

On the second day he saw that the soldier had headed for a pass in the Havillah Mountains.* King left the trail, rode in a wide circle, skirted the end of the range that night, and reached the opposite side before the sun had risen. There, picketed near a spring, stood the soldier's horse; the man himself, as King surmised, had camped in a nearby thicket. There was undergrowth enough for an ambush, and it gave King a worrisome moment; yet he left his horse in the sergeant's care and, with his revolver drawn, stole upon his quarry, who was busy over a campfire.

"I captured him in a hand to hand struggle in which I nearly lost my life," King wrote, "and only saved myself by dodging his shot and cramming my pistol in his ear in the nick of time. I lodged him in Austin jail, and the fact of his capture forever reduced the soldiers and the working men of the survey to obedience."

The mountains streaked in a northerly trend across King's belt of survey, "rank beyond rank of parallel ranges," he observed, "strange in

*Now better known as the Sonoma Range.

form and unusually . . . bright in color." Snow in the high divides made it necessary to move at night when the crust had grown hard enough to bear the animals. Even then the party suffered bitter hardship. In one instance thirteen hours were required to cross a single saddle, a distance of only two and a half miles. The snow had drifted more than thirty feet deep there, and "men and animals were frequently lost from sight."

Such difficulties, however, did not keep them from reaching Ruby Valley in time for their rendezvous. On August 9 King led his party along the piedmont of the Ruby Range, in the wake of locust hordes that drove like snow through the air. He stayed at the camp which Emmons had made before pressing on to the Utah border, a base where Ridgway and Watson had spent a month in making prolific collections.

Ridgway's favorite "specimen" was a western kingbird he had christened "Chippy." He had bought it from a Paiute who had robbed a nest and had nursed it along on grasshopper minces until it could feed itself. It had learned its name, and it followed the men like a puppy, teasing for locusts, of which it never grew tired. Its favorite perch was a guy rope of a tent, but during the midday heat it would retire beneath the umbrella which shaded the wet- and dry-bulb thermometers—provided that someone else had stayed in camp. The bird hated solitude; it refused to stay behind whenever the men went out on trips, and it often rode on Ridgway's shoulder or on the barrel of his gun. It remained the mascot of the corps until it disappeared one day, presumably the breakfast of a hawk.

When the personnel had reunited for briefing, King gave further assignments, reserving for himself the task of winding up the reconnaissance of the Ruby Range.* His party struck camp near the end of August and followed a northward course along the foot of the mountains. The range had grown more rugged, and King moved in short side tours around the peaks and through the canyons. A certain stream that plunged down in a constant flow to Franklin Lake aroused his curiosity, and the story of his climb to its source was to make a Christmas letter two years later to his sister Marian, whom he addressed therein as "My dear Marie."

Jim Marryatt had saddled their mules, King wrote:

And we rode up the mountain gorge, following as closely as we could the willow covered bank of our brook. As we ascended, the cañon grew dark and narrow, its huge rocky walls towering up against the sky and covering us with

---

*Commonly known as the East Humboldt Mountains in King's day.

deep gloomy shadows. At last we reached the lap of the mountain and came there upon the edge of the stone-bowl and were charmed to find the brook flowing from a lovely mountain lake.

King at once pronounced it Lake Marian in his sister's honor, and he told her how "the whole face of the mountain smiled as if it liked the name." But though he would mention it boldly in his report and include therein a picture of it captioned Lake Marian, the name could hardly compete with the fame of the Overland Mail, and subsequent maps would carry the designation only as Overland Lake.

King's party crossed the range through Secret Valley, and worked along the edge of Clover Mountains, reaching Humboldt Wells by mid-September. The other divisions converged there, and after resting briefly King sent two parties out again to cover parallel belts at the northern edge of the exploration. He himself started for southern Idaho with a small group, including the artist Hill, to study the measures of coal reported there.* The old Emigrant Trail led back through Thousand Spring Valley and across the Goose Creek Mountains, where forty-niners had lowered their wagons down the cliffs by means of rope. King examined the so-called coal along Goose Creek, finding it a humbug, merely black lava. Then he pressed on into the basin of the Snake, through a monotone of sage along the Boise road.

A dull throb pulsated underfoot long before he could see the black zigzag which marked the course of the Snake River. It lay six miles beyond the highway. But King and his men urged their mules into a gallop and dashed to the edge of the gorge. It was an awesome scene: "a monotony of pale blue sky, olive and gray stretches of desert, frowning walls of jetty lava, deep beryl green of river-stretches, reflecting, here and there, the intense solemnity of the cliffs, and in the centre a dazzling sheet of foam." Tents were pitched on the precipice lip which overhung the Great Falls, and from his camp chair King could gaze through veils of mist into a Dantean gulf.

The rock through which the river had cut its way proved to be "lower paleozoic and tertiary volcanic," and that precluded the presence of coal, the object of his visit. But the account he wrote of his sojourn at the Great Falls was to find a place in Bret Harte's *Overland Monthly* two years later. While the six and a half pages of print would entitle King to only twenty-five dollars, a sum that Harte "forgot" to pay him, the

*King slipped, evidently, in dating this trip as 1869 in *Systematic Geology* (p. 591).

critical notices were more encouraging. One reviewer called King's sketch "the gem of the October issue," finding in it "the fidelity of a photograph and the picturesqueness of a landscape painting." Such a response stimulated his hope of culling other papers from his notebooks, and of filling a volume which he considered calling *Sierra Tramps.*

On leaving the gorge of the Snake, King staged to Salt Lake City, where his corps reassembled by the middle of October. They found Gardiner there with his bride, whom he had married at Virginia City on September 7. The men stored their field equipment at Camp Douglas and put the animals out to pasture under the sinister eye of Porter Rockwell, leader of the Danite Avengers. Then King discharged the camp men, all except Jim Marryatt the mulatto cook, whom he had decided to take back East as a general helper. The corps started for home a week later, boarding the Union Pacific at Green River City, and all received a month's furlough on their arrival in the East.

It pleased King to report that the season of 1868 had ended in complete success. The corps had fallen but a trifle short of the goal he had set for the year—to survey the authorized belt as far east as the Great Salt Lake. Only a fringe south of the lake had not been covered; and that, he decided, could occupy the men next summer while they waited for the snow to melt in the Wasatch Mountains. Certain points stood out from the welter of facts which the corps had amassed. Traced and charted were the shore lines of a Pleistocene lake that had sprawled across Nevada, its arms flung out for enormous distances, its bed as large almost as Erie's and many times as deep—the same extinct sheet of water whose tufa traces King had erroneously reported, in 1864, as "coral reefs in the desert." It would be his privilege, nearly a decade later, to give it a name; and he chose to honor the French explorer who had written nearly two hundred years earlier of a dead American sea more briny than the ocean—the first mention, it was once thought, of the Great Salt Lake. No matter that the Baron de la Honton had been a fraud, his tale sheer fabrication; the aptness of his shot in the dark ensured remembrance. King fixed his name to the Pleistocene water— Lake Lahonton—whose shore lines he had traced across the face of Nevada.

Then, too, a distinct transverse section of the Great Basin had emerged from the fortieth parallel work. Frémont had used the term *Great Basin* to designate a depressed region where no stream could reach the sea, but popular use had extended the name to the entire expanse between the western ramparts of the Rockies and the Sierra Nevada. As such, it comprised no single geographical unit, an observation that Captain James H. Simpson had made as early as 1859, although unknown to King, for Simpson's report was not yet published. Quite independently, King's work revealed that a central plateau rose to a mean elevation of about two thousand feet above depressions on either side. The whole area, therefore, included three separate regions—first, Nevada Basin with its mute remains of Lake Lahonton; then the plateau of eastern Nevada, blessed with fertile soil in spots like Ruby Valley; and last, the basin of northwest Utah. There another sheet of water—even more vast than Lake Lahonton—had shimmered during the Pleistocene, and of it the present Great Salt Lake was only a shrunken vestige. During this particular season and the next, King and Emmons and Arnold Hague traced the terraces of its shores for hundreds of miles, only to lose the honor of naming it and of first describing it in print.

Professor Dana had thrown the pages of the *American Journal of Science* open to anything King might want to say for priority's sake about his work in progress. But in general King preferred to hold his facts for full reports, at the risk that others might anticipate his contributions, as would actually happen in the case of the ice-age lake of Utah Basin.

For there were rivals in the field, not counting the grid surveys which the General Land Office was pushing into the better-watered areas where settlement was springing up to the west of the Missouri River. But the same Congress that had authorized King's exploration had voted a small appropriation for the General Land Office to conduct a geological survey of the new state of Nebraska; and Dr. Ferdinand V. Hayden, a seasoned explorer, had been named as geologist in charge. Hayden's appropriation was renewed in 1868, and he devoted the present season to exploration in Wyoming, with plans to shift down into Colorado during the coming year when his operation would achieve separate status in the Department of the Interior as the U.S. Geological and Geographical Survey of the Territories.

Major John Wesley Powell had also begun scientific work in Colorado, at first supported by various colleges in his home state of Illinois. He would soon be granted aid by Congress, though not before he would, in 1869, launch his first epic descent of the Green and Colorado rivers. It would be a fearless plunge into the unknown, from the Union Pacific crossing to the mouth of the Virgin River nearly a thousand miles below. On receiving federal support in 1870 Powell's organization would come under the jurisdiction of the Smithsonian Institution, where it would remain until 1874. During that year it would be transferred to the Interior Department as the second division of the Geological and Geographical Survey of the Territories. Three years later its designation would change to the U.S. Geographical and Geological Survey of the Rocky Mountain Region.

Meanwhile, the year 1869 witnessed the military reconnaissance in Nevada and Utah that led to birth of still another Western exploration—a geographical survey conducted by Lieutenant George M. Wheeler of the Army Engineers. At first Wheeler's work would be limited to topographical reconnaissance, but he would soon add geology to his mission. The full name of his operation: the U.S. Geographical Surveys West of the One Hundredth Meridian, and like King he would report to the chief of engineers. *

It was the geologist of Wheeler's expedition, Grove K. Gilbert, who soon anticipated King on the Pleistocene lake of Utah. He was to name, describe, and chart it in a tentative way before the geological volumes of the King Survey could appear in print. "Thus by accident of publication," as Gilbert himself admitted, "King and his colleagues lost that literary priority in regard to Lake Bonneville to which they were fairly entitled by priority of investigation."

Field work for 1868 had produced fifty large storage boxes of geological and natural history specimens, which King had shipped to Washington. Watson's collection had proved that flora of the Great Basin was richer, more extensive than anyone had dreamed. But what impressed King's scientific friends in the East most of all were his charts of the Comstock Lode. He showed them at Yale, where he had bid for laboratory space for Arnold Hague's chemical work on the problem of silver reduction. Had the men at Yale hesitated to grant him laboratory facilities, the Comstock data would have won them over; of that King had no doubt. Brush and Brewer and Benjamin Silliman, Jr., were all

---

* In retrospect King would compare his survey favorably with the others. He believed that, on the whole, it "was the most complete and comprehensive in its aims, the best in equipment and organization and the most successful in the accomplishment of its mission" ("C. K.'s notes for [Hague's] biographical notice of him," King Papers). He judged that in many significant respects the Fortieth Parallel Survey had taken the lead, while the others followed. King's opinion had much to recommend it, notwithstanding the fact that the relative lack of settlement in the area examined would seriously undercut the practicality of many of his results.

impressed, and so was Alexander Agassiz, the austere guest whom King now met at Silliman's house. Brewer wrote to Whitney that the Comstock maps were superb.

"Indeed superb," came Whitney's reply a few days later, when King had shown a set at Cambridge; high praise in view of Whitney's coolness over King's success, or his disparagement of King's Sierra notes ("incomprehensible," was his verdict), or his contempt for King's "assiduous cultivation of Silliman's friendship." Anything to do with the younger Silliman, whose controversy with Whitney over oil in California would lead to disaster for the California Survey in the state legislature, was anathema to Whitney.

King went to Washington in November 1868 and set up office in a brick house on H Street, where Italian urchins sang "Santa Lucia" for pennies under the windows. Gardiner was there to watch routines, so King could concentrate on pulling the right political strings. Funds had been exhausted, and he faced a hard campaign for more.

King conferred with General Humphreys, and even with General Grant, the president-elect. Grant appeared at the fortieth parallel office and wrote a commendation of the survey, only to delay sending it to the proper committee on Capitol Hill. King was despondent (or so Emmons claimed in his diary): the Army appropriations bill was passed without further provisions for the survey's operations. But King still had the backing of Baird and Joseph Henry, with the prestige of the Smithsonian Institution behind them; and Senator Conness advised him to have no fears, that friends in Congress would see that he had a third season in the field. King could count on help from Blaine and Fessenden of Maine and from Edmunds of Vermont. Still he played a cautious hand and sought the support of other politicians. He had met a truculent squint on approaching Benjamin Butler, now a congressman from Massachusetts. Butler had been a political general, and his hatred for regulars such as Grant had grown to include the entire roster of West Point graduates. He regarded King's connection with the Army Engineers as something less than a recommendation, but his squint relented at King's description of the corps.

"You mean to tell me," Butler rumbled, "there're no West Pointers in the outfit?"

All were civilians, King assured him.

Then, by God, the general thundered, he'd see the measure through. He did; his committee provided for King's work in an ammendment to a civil appropriations bill that was both large and exceedingly miscellaneous. The incident was of the sort that would enable a friend to say: "[King] won men with ease, and used that power to good purpose." The bill reached the Senate on March 2, and on the following day King listened in the gallery to the voting. The *ayes* had it, and he could breathe freely again—especially when the chief of engineers informed him that his salary had been increased to $360 a month, "the highest pay given to Civil Engineers employed in the Engineer Department." It matched the pay of a full colonel on active duty.

King planned now to push the volume on mining, and leaving Gardiner in charge of the office, he entrained for Boston with Emmons and J. D. Hague. En route they paused in Manhattan to attend Offenbach's *Orfée aux enfers* and to view an exhibition of John Henry Hill's watercolors, including scenes of Mount Shasta and Virginia City. Then on to Boston, where both Hague and Emmons preferred to work at their own firesides. King himself could muster little enthusiasm for the city or, as he claimed, "the east winds and the Adams family and the general snobbery of solid knowledge and the organ and a great many other institutions which one must either worship or be snubbed as a barbarian."

He may have begun his Comstock chapter now, a work dictated to a clerk sometime in 1869; but he soon left Hague and Emmons to finish their shares of *Mining Industry* alone. His mother's health drew him to Newport, where he felt compelled to spend the month of April, not very happy, his patience taxed by Mrs. Howland's reaction to his engagement. "Only a sense of duty keeps me here," he wrote, with a compulsive feeling that made him add: "I have nothing to do but yield gracefully. . . . I shall stay here until I go West."

King arrived in Salt Lake City on May 15, 1869, not early enough to attend the golden-spike ceremony which joined the railroads at Promontory Point, notwithstanding rumors that he did. With him came his Uncle Robbins Little, as well as John Olmsted, the nephew-stepson of Frederick Law Olmsted—both primed for a lively campaign in the Utah wilds. King found that Emmons had gained permission from Brigham Young to make camp on the old lake terrace above the city, and tents were pitched there, with flags flying. The survey's livestock was fat from winter pastures, but the equipment stored at Camp Douglas had been rifled by deserters. Much of it had to be replaced, and most of May slipped by before King could put his outfits into the field.

First, he sent a small detachment under Emmons to resume examination of the desert south of the Great Salt Lake. Then he rented a boat—the *Eureka*—and launched a crew for a survey of the lake itself, a job he entrusted to the charge of N. R. Davis, a new man recommended by years of naval service during the war. King himself led a third division to the barren mountains north of the lake.

Nothing could relieve the dreariness of the scene, not even the interest King and his party took in searching for the long dry outlet of Lake Bonneville. Land contours to the south precluded any flow in that direction. "But," as King wrote, "the divide between the Utah Basin and the depression of Snake River falls below the level of the upper terrace, and it is therefore clear that the lake poured its waters into the valley of the Snake, and thence through the Columbia into the Pacific Ocean." He found in 1869 what he believed had been the ancient passage into the Snake valley. But Gilbert's subsequent work placed the spillage not where King presumed, but in Red Rock Pass, at the head of Cache Valley. There a channel could be seen in the rimrock, a great floodgate through which a torrent had thundered like Niagara on its plunge to the Snake. And King conceded "all praise" to Gilbert's elucidation of the problem.

It was still June when King and his men completed the survey north of the lake. During the course of that endeavor they had met a Mormon with four wives and a home arrangement that gave King much amusement. The plural family lived together in a house with one large room. A bed stood in each corner, and eight children slept in the middle of the floor.

Next King sent his party under Gardiner into the northern Wasatch, whose peaks soared above the snowline; a range which, for scientific interest, King considered "second to no single mountain block in the world." Emmons had also left the desert, to run a reconnaissance of the southern part of the range. So it was time, King judged, to transfer the main base to higher ground where meadows furnished better feed for the stock. He returned to the Mormon capital to arrange the move, but found a disconcerting message awaiting his arrival.

The Army Engineers had authorized him to march east as far as the Great Divide, to join the expedition Whitney had brought from Harvard College to map the principal ridge of the Rockies. No government funds could be directly spared for Whitney's operation. But someone close to the engineers had recommended that King's appropriation might be turned to double account. It was a preposterous notion, in King's opinion, and he felt enormous relief on finding the order spiked with nullifying provisos. The shift, he was informed, must not conflict materially with his own work, nor prove too costly.

"I am convinced," he replied, "that any such coöperation would seriously if not fatally interfere with this work." And assuming that Humphreys would endorse his decision, he packed at once into the middle section of the Wasatch, to locate a pivotal base far west of the Continental Divide. "After much roaming," he wrote, "I decided on a spot . . . in Parleys Park"—twenty-five miles from Salt Lake City. The base was reestablished there before concurrence arrived from Washington or before he learned that a copy of his letter had been forwarded to Whitney.

The sharpness of that note may have been caused by the smarts King felt from the criticism of several colleagues who thought he had grown too big for his breeches. Professor D. C. Eaton, whom he had invited to botanize with the corps that summer, had taken offense at the timing of the invitation, as if the schedule of the corps could be adjusted to the whims of guests. Eaton's displeasure mattered only because of its effect at Yale. But it angered King to learn that even Brush, his "best Yale friend," should be astonished at "his fallen condition."

"That I ordered Eaton into the field is simply false," he protested. He deplored "Army arrogance" as much as anybody, but it annoyed him even more to see how few appreciated what mental stress the survey cost him. "It is my last scientific labor," he declared, "and in the midst of all its deep complications . . . it seems as if my friends should be considerate and rather seek to excuse a hasty act than to flare up at it."

But whatever his irritations, King retained his sense of humor; and that same day he answered J. D. Hague's appeal for "foonds" with a touch of whimsy. "You address me as one who possesses that which may be remitted. Now I can tell you how pleased I am; continue to think so." He could send no money "for great state reasons." But how much sweeter his life would be made by the thought that now he would hear from Hague more often. "That is a deep joy to unremittingly yours . . ."

Much as his humor endeared King to his men, they placed even greater value on his respect for social amenities, even in the wilderness. He made their bivouacs, like the base at Parleys Park, as comfortable as his means allowed. "One of the rules of the Fortieth Parallel Survey," as a friend later recalled,

was that its members should be as civilized as practicable, especially at meals. The men believed in a good and varied diet, well cooked and served; and when the accounting officers of the War Department demurred at passing a bill for currant jelly, they were met with a threat to charge up at the rate of beef the venison furnished by members of the mess. By such means the geologists preserved both their digestions and their adaptability to social life.

It startled Rossiter Raymond the federal commissioner of mining statistics, who visited King in camp that summer, to meet a "polished gentleman . . . in immaculate linen, silk stockings, low shoes, and clothing without a wrinkle." The dinner surpassed in style any which Raymond had tasted west of the Missouri. Such attention to comfort may have earned King the reputation of a sybarite. But in his opinion it was safe to play the rude pioneer only if one came but seldom to the wilds.

Survey matters took King at intervals to Salt Lake City, but he would return to Parleys Park as if to a summer idyl. "King, always a delightful companion, was especially so in camp," wrote the older Hague. "Everybody missed him when he went away and was glad when he came back. If any discontenting grievances, dissensions or difficulties had arisen during [his] absence, they all vanished before his genial presence and cheerful spirit as soon as he returned"; and that was how matters now stood at Parleys Park. In leisure moments King's men caught trout in the stream and furnished the cook with waterfowl and venison. Curious Utes added a genre touch to the scene; a new guest painter, Gilbert Munger, who had engraved plates for the Wilkes reports, seemed "enchanted in a gentlemanly sort of way, sketching on four-foot canvases." Professor Eaton was "up to his highest speed in plants," cured of his pique and spurred by Watson's zeal; while Ridgway nursed a brood of hawks, and proved that the kingbird Chippy had not been quite unique. Another nestling, Chippy II, developed all the traits of its predecessor, keeping the whole camp entertained until it too made a breakfast for the hawks.

The field groups reconvened in mid July—even the crew from the lake appeared. Violent squalls had capsized the *Eureka* twice, and on one occasion heavy waves had nearly battered it to pieces. Davis and his companions had clung to the hull all night, in danger of drowning. Their eyes had burned, and they were nearly maddened by thirst. But now they were finished, and their work constituted the most extensive review of the lake since the Stansbury expedition. It revealed that the lake's surface had risen nine feet since Stansbury's time and that its size had grown by more than 600 square miles, changing its whole configuration.

King now reshuffled the *Eureka* crew among his other squads. In a week the men were ready for the field again, and he felt sure of reaching the Green River Divide, which he had set as the eastern limit of his work. He again took personal charge of a field group, with plans to explore the middle strip ahead, flanked by Gardiner on the north and Emmons on the south. King's party marched through Echo Canyon along the Union Pacific, making studies of the coal measures opened for exploitation there. On meeting the Bear River, they veered south and climbed its valley to some of the wildest scenes in America. "The rocky Uinta towered above my camp," King wrote, "and the sparkling Bear River flowed past my bed." His party combed the alpine rocks and forests, each man absorbed in his own particular task, with O'Sullivan taking spectacular pictures. The high peaks overlooking cirques and lakes and glacial canyons drew King like lodestones. Among those he named and climbed was Mount Agassiz, another first ascent.

The crest of the ancient Uinta, he concluded, had once exceeded Himalayan heights, before the torrents of the Tertiary had worn away thousands of feet of solid rock. Its height had been reduced to less than 20,000 feet when the ice ages came, to lock it in a hood of glaciers grander than the system of the Alps. Glaciers had chiseled out the cirques and vast U-canyons and left in their wake the hundreds of lakes that shone in polished basins. Floods of meltwater had thundered down the canyons, and the Bear had been the main source of Bonneville Lake. Thus King read the story in the scored Uinta rocks, a record that moved him deeply.

And yet the more practical tale that season was of coal. King's work on the measures along the Union Pacific confirmed that the carboniferous strata on either side of the Uintas held "a practically inexhaustible supply of coal"—news which congressmen, senators, and railroad magnates could all appreciate.

August 1869 had nearly passed when the corps returned to Parleys Park and prepared to withdraw from the field. King sent several men to stations in the East. Three detachments of the rest began to retrace the belt of survey in parallel courses from the Great Salt Lake, their purpose to fill the gaps in the accumulations of data and to check all doubtful observations. King remained in the Mormon city only long enough to auction off the greater part of his worn equipment, Brigham Young attending the sale, as well as George Francis Train, that curious character who had helped promote the Union Pacific, and whose whirlwind tour around the globe would inspire Jules Verne with the character Philéas Fogg.

King overtook one of his parties inside the border of Nevada; and taking the Humboldt route, they reached Argenta by the end of September. J. D. Hague had come from the Colorado mines, and King now joined him in a dash for San Francisco. There he bought Oriental bric-a-brac, and held a breakfast at the Union Club in Bret Harte's honor. Hague later recalled how King amused those present with a story of what had just occurred on the street below.

Four well-known geologists, Whitney, Hayden, Blake, and myself, coming from the four points of the compass, had run into a general collision . . . and being all unspeakably hostile at the moment, owing perhaps to their different views concerning the "chunk of old red sandstone" on the Stanislaus or the true inwardness of the "Calaveras Skull," had finally dodged each other in silence, but with eyes glaring scientific hatred.

The incident suggested more concerning King than Hague perceived or cared to admit; for, having come from a wearing campaign, King felt utterly weary of the scientific life. Somewhere in Utah he had written of his "intense yearning" to finish up with his "analytic study of Nature and drink in the sympathetic side" of himself. It may have been the sheer weight of science from which he recoiled in the street, to seek relaxation in the company of art.

Perhaps, too, his feeling of weariness stemmed from his languishing courtship. That King had hoped to marry Deany in the autumn of 1869 seemed implicit in his remarks to Hague concerning supervision of *Mining Industry.* "There are private reasons," he had written, "which you can guess (but you must not more than guess them) why I do not want to fall to work printing next October." But King returned to no wedding in Nevada.

Who knows what happened there except that he and Deany never married? King suppressed all reference to her in his notebooks, and she would remain a spinster for the rest of her life. It was very likely he, not she, who broke the engagement, yielding to the urgencies of an over-possessive mother.* "Duty," he would later declare, "has stood between

*In "So Deep a Trail," p. 146, Harry H. Crosby claims that King took Deany east with him in the fall of 1869 for a star-crossed meeting with Mrs. Howland, and that seems a likely statement. "Just what had happened to [his fiancée] at Newport King did not reveal, except to say" when he next saw Gardiner "that she had returned to [the West]."

me and almost every good thing." And *duty* in King's vocabulary meant his endless obligations to Mrs. Howland.

He confessed to Henry Adams in later years, that it was family responsibilities which had made him "refrain from marrying the woman" he wanted for his wife. He rationalized the break as for the best, no doubt, and once remarked to J. D. Hague: "I would never marry a woman anyhow, *just because I said I would.* That is the poorest possible reason men or women can ever have for marrying each other. People who marry without any better reason than that must surely come to grief." But there may have been more to the matter than that. King may have already come under the compulsive spell of dark skin color and primitive make-up—may have already begun to feel a deep-seated aversion to the refined white woman as sexual partner. It was a compulsion that would mold his life in a strange way.

King worked till late November on completing his study of the Comstock Lode, and was the last member of the survey to return East. As far as he knew at the time, he was ringing down the curtain on the field work of the Fortieth Parallel Exploration, and he perhaps felt a certain fitness—a certain symmetry—in closing his labors so near the point where they had begun in 1867.

9

Mountaineering . . .

King found, in December 1869, that the first year of the Grant administration marked no visible improvement in affairs at Washington. This was the season when Henry Adams noted in all departments of government "confusion, cross purposes, and ill temper that would have been scandalous in a boarding school of girls." King felt no deep desire to settle "among the Philistines." He thought of staying only long enough to write and publish the fortieth parallel reports, and he hoped with his constitutional optimism to finish the work within two years. Then he might settle down as a teacher of science, perhaps at Cornell, where Andrew White appeared to favor the fortieth parallel work.

The immediate future, King realized, was the most significant interval in the life of the survey. The final impact of the work would depend on the quality of the corps' reports, and for that crucial effort he rented rooms on G Street, in a building where creakings in the dead of night convinced Jim Marryatt, his "man of all work," that poltergeists had joined their ranks.

The noises, apart from effects they had on Jim, interfered in no way with his corps' progress. The topographers continued platting field notes on a scale of four miles to the inch. Ridgway described a total of 262 species of birds, to finish the ornithology by spring. *Mining Industry* was brought to a satisfactory close. In spite of a siege of fever and excruciating rheumatism, King had contributed a chapter on the Green River Coal Basin, in addition to his paper on the geology of the Comstock Lode. Arnold Hague had summarized his findings on the chemistry of the Washoe process and recommended improvements that would save the Comstock smelters millions in formerly lost silver and gold. But the bulk of the volume comprised the papers which J. D. Hague had compiled with the help of his brother and Emmons on the principal mining districts from the Comstock to the Colorado gold fields.

"The reports of the expedition are so voluminous," King wrote to Humphreys, "and the preparation of MSS requires so much of my time that my own investigations are falling behind." Nevertheless, he worked long and hard over notes and specimens in his effort to solve the riddles of the Cordillera. He referred fossils to Fielding Meek, Hayden's collaborator, who had examined specimens for Whitney. He also ordered chemical analyses and microscopic sections to be made of items in the rock collection, for he was determined to ground the work on a firm lithological and petrographic basis. He met with scientists at the Smithsonian, and exchanged data with John Wesley Powell, the one-armed veteran of Shiloh, who had just made his first voyage down the gorges of the Green and Colorado. Major Powell briefed King on the geology of that region and invited the Fortieth Parallel Corps to hear his lecture on the river expedition. There were social calls as well, and occasional visits to the White House for presidential receptions, while for exercise King took horseback rides or walks with Emmons and Gardiner.

But Washington grew oppressive. King regretted that he had placed his headquarters there. His corps seemed handicapped by the distance from the laboratories at Yale, and there was no adequate geological library in the capital. Relocation at Sheffield had grown imperative, and King secured permission from General Humphreys to make the move.

Yet he had scarcely settled down in New Haven when he learned that certain congressional "friends" were engineering new appropriations for field work in the West. He telegraphed to his chief for clarification and received in reply an order to take the field. King did not mind foregoing a rest at Woods Hole with the Spencer Bairds. But it was another matter to plunge into abrupt improvisations which could promise only doubtful results in view of the lateness of the season. He counseled the general to hold the campaign over for the following spring, advice provoked in part by an attack of the "gouty rheumatism" that was to become chronic and afflict King off and on for the rest of his life.

But "Humphreys' walkin' papers" stood, consigning King to "wusser pickle / Than any brine of ocean"; or so he wrote his friends at Woods Hole, in a dialect apology for his sudden nonappearance " 'mong the shell-heaps and the sea." As he explained,

Mappin' up wat's called out West
Bustin' rocks for Uncle Sam
Tearin' holes in pants and vest
Eatin' semi-fossil ham—
That's wat fell ter this child's lot.

In the end King secured permission to restrict the work to a study of the quiescent volcanoes along the Pacific Coast, "the sources of the lava flows which have poured eastward from the Sierra Nevada and the Cascade ranges into the Great Basin." It would be a feasible project for so brief a season. He would need only a few men to pursue the new plan, and several could be left in Gardiner's charge, to keep the work going in New Haven. For the western assignment he chose two clerks, the topographers F. A. Clark and A. D. Wilson, the geologists Arnold Hague and Emmons, with "good Jim Marryatt" to serve as camp man.

The trip was of great importance to Jim, whose sensitivity to spectral things had reached a climax. One night soon after Humphreys' order he had galloped down from his attic room and gasped out that he had seen his mother. King thought he must be dreaming, and said, "Go back to bed."

But Jim stood firm. His mother had stood on the stairs, he said. "And I came down—right through her."

The next morning King received a telegram from a black parson in San Francisco. A woman, it said, had come to the Bay in search of a son named Marryatt. King wired back that he would send Jim west by the next train. He followed with the rest of the party, and they reached the Coast on August 12, 1870. Among the first visitors to his hotel were Jim and a light-skinned Negro woman.

"Well, I declare," the woman exclaimed, "And how's the baby?"

King had a merry "confab with Jim's mother," wrote Emmons in his diary, for she was the Good Jamaican who had come to his rescue in Panama City in 1867.

Days of hard work followed. "At first glance," wrote Emmons, "it seemed a physical impossibility to organize and outfit a field party at that late season, but our chief, Mr. King, was a man of infinite resourcefulness." He appealed to General J. M. Schofield, at the Presidio, and received a complete outfit for the summer. As O'Sullivan was not available that season, having gone with an expedition to Panama in search of a feasible canal route, King engaged Carleton E. Watkins, the

San Francisco photographer, whom he considered "the most skillful operator in America." * And once again Gilbert Munger volunteered as guest painter.

The *Overland* circle had taken the artist up with enthusiasm, and King found time to spend an afternoon at Bret Harte's office, to chuckle over jokes and limericks in the company of Harte himself and Charles Warren Stoddard and Ina Coolbrith while "looking at Munger's sketches, putting snow into Lake Marian, and desecrating Starr King's knob." Perhaps King told about the ghost which Jim had seen, to plant the seed in Bret Harte's fancy ("one half fact and t'other half whim") for another ghost and another Jim with a very different ending; and Harte prevailed on him to polish off his impressions of the Great Shoshone Falls.

And then the little field party was off for the mountains, crossing the Sacramento plain through a shimmer of August haze that veiled, in King's words, "the Californian exuberance of grain-field and orchard." He was mounted on a white horse; the others on mules. The first tier of foothills beyond Chico brought relief from the oppressive heat, and soon the sky-piercing cone of Shasta, with "its pale, rosy lavas enamelled with snow," became the center of their lives. They pitched their tents in Strawberry Valley, at the ranch of a local guide named Sisson, while Arnold Hague and assistants journeyed on to Mount Hood in northern Oregon.

"Shasta from Sisson's is a broad triple mountain," King wrote,

the central summit being flanked on the west by a large and quite perfect crater whose rim reaches about twelve thousand feet altitude. On the west a broad shoulder-like spur juts from the general slope. The cone rises from its base eleven thousand feet in one sweep.

Three days slipped by in preparation for the climb, and the morning of September 11 dawned clear and cold. King's party rode on mules as far as the animals could carry them. Then with shoulder packs they toiled to the top of the secondary crater, later named Shastina. It was neither a perilous nor a taxing climb, but it gave King a sense of expansion such as he gained from all high elevations, "the instant and lasting reward" of his labors. The height had a strange effect on his perception of time

---

*Even more skillful, in King's opinion, than that curious Englishman Eadweard Muybridge, who would be the first to film animal locomotion (by horses, as it happened) and whom King had advised to go and photograph Yosemite. It was advice that Muybridge had taken in 1867, and would again in 1872, to become the chief rival of Watkins as picture-taker of the park.

and space. "The hours hurry by with singular swiftness. Minutes or miles are nothing; days and degrees seem best fitted for one's thoughts."

He gazed down into the gorge that yawned between Shastina and the main peak, and what he saw there wiped out for the time his abiding interest in vulcanism. Before him lay a field of ice, sweeping down and around the cone on which he stood, its face torn with blue crevasses. The view recalled the autumn of 1863 when he and Brewer had seen the turbid rill on the eastern flank of the mountain, something that had haunted King for seven years.* They had spoken of glaciers then, and Brewer had ruled them out on the sides of Shasta. But now King had no doubt that here indeed was one. No doubt whatever, though Dana, Frémont, Brewer, and Whitney had all failed to see it on their visits to the peak. Whitney, Dana, and Agassiz had even declared that no true glaciers remained inside the United States, exclusive of Alaska. But there the monster lay, at least three miles of it, a "shattered chaos of blue blocks." King named it Whitney Glacier in tribute to his former chief.

Shortly after dawn next morning he started with his men across the saddle which joined the lesser cone with the main summit. It took them four hours to reach the topmost ledge. To the east King saw a second glacier, "crowded out from the foot of an immensely steep *névé*." But the northern sides of Shasta were cut from his view; eager to see what they might hold, he walked to the edge of a prominent spur and gazed down on a system of three huge flows of ice. They seemed to cover the whole north side of the peak, distance making them look like a single sheet of ice. He summed the matter up for Humphreys as a "somewhat startling discovery."

Yet King's elation could not obscure one baffling question. How could every scientific visitor overlook such quantities of ice? The riddle solved itself when after another arctic night King led his men down the south side of the mountain, along the trail of earlier climbers. "From the moment we left the summit," he wrote, "we encountered less and

---

* "That was an illustration," Brewer later wrote, "of the way in which [King's] retentive as well as perceptive mind stored up, and ultimately used, the facts and suggestions it had once received." Brewer mentioned another instance of this faculty— how King had responded to his (Brewer's) idea in 1863 of using photography in geological surveys and had applied it for the first time in the Arizona reconnaissance of 1866 and then on a large scale in the Fortieth Parallel Exploration. It was a practice quickly emulated by the other surveys in the field, until "the camera [became] an indispensable part of [survey] apparatus. Many similar instances," Brewer added, "might be given in which King did the things of which others had [only] dreamed" (*Clarence King Memoirs*, pp. 323–24).

less snow, and at no part of the journey were we able to see a glacier."
Whitney's party, like those of Dana and Frémont, had climbed Mount
Shasta from the wrong side—at least for seeing glaciers.

King sent Emmons on to Mount Rainier in Washington Territory.
For a week thereafter he and Clark explored the southern flanks of
Shasta, finding only dapples of ice and snow, mere relics of vanished
glaciers. Then they packed their mules for a circuit of the mountain
and rode off through the forest. A long climb brought them to the
second stream of ice which they had seen from the summit, its frozen
cascades disappearing under accumulations of detritus.

King later summarized an event of that day in a letter to George
Frederick Wright, of Oberlin College:

I was attracted by a sudden grating and rushing sound in the middle of the
region of debris and witnessed a very interesting phenomenon. The ice which
underlaid the moraine blocks had evidently melted from the percolation of
warm streams and the access of air through either moulins or crevasses. The
rotten ice gave way under the load of debris and thousands of tons of rock sank
down, leaving a conical pit a hundred yards in diameter and not less than a
hundred feet deep.

On two occasions King and Clark barely escaped going down themselves with avalanches of groaning boulders.

King wondered over these subsidences, and with a flash of scientific
imagination grasped the solution of a problem long debated among
geologists—the problem of how glacial kames and drumlins were created. Were not the ice streams of Shasta building small examples of
such phenomena, there before his eyes?*

* Cf. the remarks of Professor Wright in *Proceedings of the Boston Society of Natural
History*, XIX, 59: "I cannot doubt he had hit upon·the solution of the vexed and long
mooted problem concerning the formation of 'kames.'" Also, in *The Ice Age in North
America*, p. 288:

Mr. Clarence King would explain them [drumlins] as marking places of the great continental
glacier where streams of water which had run for some distance in superficial channels along the
surface of the glacier and collected a great amount of *debris* from the medial moraines, had finally
plunged through a *moulin* into a deeply hidden subglacial river.

Wright continues in a footnote: "I do not know as Mr. King has anywhere published
these views, nor, indeed, as he would now be willing to own them, as here stated. They
were given me in personal conversation, and contain so much that is worthy of
consideration, that I venture to repeat the theory."

On returning to their base camp where Munger and Watkins had striking studies to exhibit, King could add a thought or two to his dialect message to Woods Hole.

> I've clum' 'mong alpine mountains
> And forest that's all pine too.
> I've drinkt at bitter fountains
> Whar some took whisky in lieu.
> Not even all them postage stamps
> Left by the late J. Astor
> Would tempt this sorry child again
> To shin the cone of Shaster.
> I'll bet that old Excelsior,
> For all he's reckoned limber,
> Couldn't dodge them rollin' rocks
> Nor shy that rottin' timber.

Such gulch and mountain doggerel ran with a current vogue in 1870. King had packed a volume of James Russell Lowell's dialect verse along the fortieth parallel, and now, as he would observe, "All the world was reading Mr. Bret Harte's 'Heathen Chinee,'" for "Plain Language from Truthful James" had exploded on the public in the September issue of the *Overland.* No doubt King's letter produced smiles at Woods Hole. But literature could bear the loss when King declined to follow such pastimes further. Even the more serious verse that Shasta drew from his pen, perhaps to fill an hour on the mountain slope, faltered instead of taking flight. His best efforts were "The Stone Giant's Bowl" and "The Ice Dragon's Nest," both lyrics of thirty rhymeless hexameters associated with the mountain lakes he had named for his sister and two play-mates.* King had these poems printed in a handsome gift book, illus-

---

*Henry Adams claimed that King knew more about poetry than he. The statement is curious when verses by King are compared to "The Prayer to the Virgin of Chartres." It must be admitted, none-the-less, that a pleasing fancy plays through King's lines, as when he personifies an ancient Uinta glacier as a "white-ice terrible dragon," who

> grew while the sky, ever clouded, buried the peaks in a snow-drift;
> Then, dragging his long icy body with slow irresistible movement,
> Crawled through the crags and the gorges, till, from his den in the mountain,
> Reaching the verdurous valley, froze with his breathing the pine tree.

But the choice of the *Evangeline* meter was not happy. It may be that King composed more poetry than has survived, but on the basis of the fiew poems I have seen, either in print or in manuscript, he cannot be treated seriously as a poet.

trated with O'Sullivan photographs, to please the children when Christmas came in 1870. The gesture mirrored the tender side of his nature; the book had a great deal of charm.* And yet how far superior was the prose that his leisure produced—prose which sometimes rose to no mean order of poetry.

To dispell the ennui of remote camps he had turned to recasting the notes in his field books. He had already tasted mildly of the pleasures of publication. The account he had sent to Whitney on climbing Mount Tyndall had gone into the *Geology* of 1865 almost verbatim, and there was the paper on the Prescott region which J. Ross Browne had published in his report of the mineral resources west of the Rocky Mountains. But King had a secret wish to reach a broader audience than special readers of technical matter.

He had spun some of his mountain narratives, he claimed, against the monotony of his stage coach ride with J. D. Hague into Idaho and Oregon. Soon, as he told Hague's wife, he "planned to write them [down]"—yarns like "Kaweah's Run," to intersperse transformations of his notes on climbs about the Sierra. According to Emmons, King's method of composition consisted in his working everything out in his mind down to the slightest jot and title before setting pen to paper. Once this preliminary headwork was done, he would write "with such ease and rapidity that the words actually flowed from his pen." Any necessary revisions were liable to strike him as irksome. In this peculiar manner he continued transmuting his notebooks, hoping to fashion something that might "go" in literary journals. It was an experiment, he told Emmons, to see if the mere description of scenery could be made into popular reading.

It was a pleasant game for King, to be taken up and put aside according to his mood, and so it had progressed but slowly over the months and years. Real stimulus came when editors began to show an interest. James T. Fields of the *Atlantic Monthly* had heard King speak in March 1869, before the Thursday Club of Boston. King's picturesque impressions of Yosemite and the Great Falls of the Shoshone had put

---

*Its title is *The Three Lakes; Marian, Lall, Jan, And How They Were Named*, and besides the poems it features lithographic reproductions of two autograph letters by King concerning the naming of the lakes. I examined the copy in the rare book room of the New York Public Library, one of the three copies that constitute the original edition. The item is readily available, however, in Francis Farquhar's reprint, with introduction, in the *Sierra Club Bulletin*, Vol. XXIV (1939), No. 3. Farquhar also issued it as a pamphlet in a limited edition.

him under a spell. The editor had then invited King to send him some "sporting articles" for the *Atlantic,* enough to make a book. King agreed, though he was not to be hurried. In fact, it was not to Fields, but to Harte that he gave his first article, his picture of the falls of the Snake, which (as noticed before) appeared in the *Overland* for October, 1870. Soon he also obliged Harte with reviews of certain authors of scientific presumption, which he dashed off on his return to the Bay.

In the meantime he had pushed to a happy conclusion the campaign he had begun with such grave misgivings. After six weeks around Mount Shasta, he had moved down to Lassen's Peak and found it as rich as ever in geological interest. Then he had turned his exploration eastward over the Madelin Plain, to close with earlier work in Nevada. At the same time glaciers appeared galore. Hague and Emmons brought news of discoveries on Mount Hood and Mount Rainier. King was elated. "The discovery of active glaciers and the knowledge we have gotten of the volcanic period," he felt secure in reporting, "are among the most important late additions of American geology." He requested Humphreys to keep the matter private until his return, and then in December he hurried first to Yale and then to Harvard to break the news to his scientific preceptors. He was asked to speak before the Connecticut Academy of Science; Dana must have a report for the *American Journal of Science,* and to reach a wider audience King decided to give a more popular version to Fields, a "sporting article" at last.

He found himself cast in Boston as a sort of John the Baptist, harbinger of the literary nova that blazed in the West. His friendship with Bret Harte was an open sesame to the "somewhat famous Saturday Club." The Brahmins had asked Harte to Bemares, and they wondered whether the lion was tame enough to feed with the sacred cows. King would indeed be among the first to welcome Harte on his arrival in New York a few weeks later. But now on the last Saturday of December he became almost a lion himself for having run with the true big game out West. He went to the Parker House with Fields, the flowing-whiskered liaison officer of the Boston literati.

Agassiz, King's old master, had not been well enough to come. But there were others of the rarest caste—Dr. Holmes as cheerful as a bobolink; the gentle Emerson, soon to visit the West and link King's name with glaciers in his journal; there was even Longfellow, with his patriarchal mane. The gracious translator of Dante spoke with measured dignity, and when he inquired of the *Overland's* brain and Harte, he spaced not only his words but syllables as well:

"Is he a *gen-i-us?*"

A moment of silence followed. King meant no rudeness when he gave the first answer that entered his head:

"Why, as to that, Mr. Longfellow, everybody knows that the country possesses no *three-syllabled genius* outside of Massachusetts."

Whereupon (according to John Jay Chapman, * who preserved the story) "the gloom of offended Saturn" closed over the company. Not even Dr. Holmes dared to chuckle, though afterward he sought King out and pressed his hand.

In Chapman's opinion, King had struck on what laid Boston by the heels. "Why didn't those gentlemen laugh? They were the wittiest set in America, fond of laughing, collected at lunch for the very purpose of joking. Yes, but not at *themselves,* and not in response to the jest of a new, raw outsider. Had Dr. Holmes himself made the quip, it would have been repeated all over Boston." But Clarence King was only a Hartford and New Haven wit or, at best, a joker from Newport. He would value, nevertheless, his memory of the Saturday Club; the freeze was mutual, therefore unimportant. He had never really warmed to the Hub because he had always found it so chilly. "Boston was 1,387,453 years under the ice," he once remarked, "and then the Adamses came."

Enthusiasm in the *Atlantic* office over active glaciers dissolved any inhibitions King had felt about submitting his papers to "the organ." In February 1871 he reached a business agreement with the publisher James R. Osgood for a popular-styled book, to incorporate the pieces after their magazine appearance. Such arrangements took on interest in the light of a legend which King himself may have encouraged.

He claimed, in the context of the story,

that having written the sketches in order to beguile the tedium of life among the scenes described, and having sent them to the *Atlantic Monthly,* he was surprised on his return East, to see in the window of a book shop a volume lettered on the back, "Mountaineering in the Sierra Nevada—King," and wondered how another man of his name should have been in his neighborhood without his knowledge. It turned out that Mr. James T. Fields had not

---

*The families of King and Chapman had long been on terms of friendship; King's grandmother, Mrs. Little, and Chapman's grandmother, Maria Weston, had been sisters-in-arms in the abolitionist crusade. Chapman himself achieved a certain notoriety through an act of self-castigation in which he held a hand in the fire until it was burned useless, to be sheathed thereafter in a perpetual black glove.

only accepted the sketches for the *Atlantic*, but had collected them into a volume *without* consulting the author, who was indeed beyond the reach of consultation.

However well such a story, if King were indeed responsible for it, pointed up a taste for garnished facts, the truth was far more commonplace.* Fields had first suggested the book in the spring of 1869, and Osgood had bargained for it only days before King mailed the introduction, a general paper called "The Range." † There was some discussion between author and editor as to a suitable title for the projected volume. Inclusion of the word *geology*, which King favored, was vetoed as "too heavy ballast," but evidently *mountaineering* passed muster.

King followed "The Range" two weeks later with "Through the Forest," descriptions of the early phase of his High Sierra explorations in 1864. This second paper, in his opinion, lacked the interest of the first, though he thought it might "do," in connection with his third and fourth offerings—a two-part narrative of his conquest of Mount Tyndall, which he posted by the end of March. These Mount Tyndall sketches, whose publication Henry James would notice in an article of his own on a book by John Tyndall, departed in particulars from the rigid truth of King's field notes, but they gained in general interest over the barer, more sternly factual account Whitney had published. It was a

---

*In *Garrulities of an Octogenarian Editor* (p. 136) Henry Holt noted King's cavalier habit of dressing stories up for effect. Something happened at a dinner party that caused Holt to say to himself: "By telling such and such a lie, I could make a splendid joke of that." King promptly told the lie, Holt remembered, and his resulting story produced immense laughter.

† The succinct geological history that King sketched in "The Range" afforded a miniature preview of the cataclysmic drama he was to stage in *Systematic Geology*. Consider, for example, these half a dozen sentences on the volcanic scenes of the late Tertiary:

From the bottom of the sea sprung up those fountains of lava whose cooled material forms many of the islands of the Pacific, and, all along the coast of America, like a system of answering beacons, blazed up volcanic chimneys. The rent mountains glowed with outpourings of molten stone. Sheets of lava poured down the slopes of the Sierra, covering an immense proportion of its surface, only the high granite and metamorphic peaks reaching above the deluge. Rivers and lakes floated up in a cloud of steam and were gone forever. The misty sky of those volcanic days glowed with innumerable lurid reflections, and, at intervals along the crest of the range, great cones arose, blackening the sky with their plumes of mineral smoke. At length, having exhausted themselves, the volcanoes burned lower, and, at last, by far the greater number went out altogether (*Mountaineering*, pp. 3–4).

gain, however, that would irk a sober critic like John Muir, who remarked on reading of King's heroics: "He must have given himself a lot of trouble. When I climbed Tyndall, I ran up and down before breakfast"—even greater hyperbole in the opposite direction.

"I am at a loss," King confessed, "in deciding about the fifth of the Atlantic series. My choice lies between an adventure with Mexican bandits . . . and an account of a day in camp of a family of perpetual emigrants, an undescribed type of Western people, a social deformity which impresses you pathetically and drolly at once. Which?" King solved the problem by sending both.

And each provided a highlight for the series, the first tense with suspense and excitement, the other brimming with the humor and sadness of the human lot. The seed of the Newty family was a terse reminder King had jotted in a notebook in 1864. "Pathos of chronic emigrants," it read; "describe their camp and history." The type, however, had been depicted more often than King suspected. George Derby (alias John Phoenix), Alonzo Delano (better known as Old Block), Theodore Winthrop, Bayard Taylor, J. Ross Browne, and Bret Harte had all added touches to the literary image of the Pike, that protean figure who hailed from Pike County, Missouri (and by extension all Missouri, Arkansas, and southern Illinois) and whom Bayard Taylor had defined as "the Anglo-Saxon relapsed into semi-barbarism." No one, however, had excelled King's handling of the type. What if in matters of detail the Newtys did not duplicate the actual "folks" of "the hog ranch" that King had passed in 1864 on his way to the Kern? They yet conformed to a class which he had studied with mingled sympathy and repulsion from his earliest days in California—"that race of perpetual emigrants who roam as dreary waifs over the West." King not only made the Newtys, with their acres of potential bacon, a pathetic symbol of retrogression; he had also painted, as Wallace Stegner would declare, "one of the best and subtlest portraits of the Pike in our literature."

"Wayside Pikes," the composite sketch as published in the *Atlantic*, also featured an expansive bore whom King had met somewhere near Lake Tahoe, one Yank Clement (also spelled Clements), really no Pike at all, since he hailed from Vermont. Under King's pen he flourished rich and strange, though renamed Hank G. Smith, artist, and made a native son of California. King had no scruple about projecting something of himself into the ebullient bumpkin and making him the mouthpiece for a few Pre-Raphaelite mots that came straight from

King's heart. Hank aspired to make "himself famous as the delineator of mule trains and ox-wagons; to be, as he expressed it, 'the Pacific Slope Bonheur.'" King had caught the Clement likeness all too well, and Yank (alias Hank) would be all set to "take it out of him," except that King's frank bonhomie when they met again would appease Yank's resentment. * King's character sketches intensified the demand of Howells for more and even better works from King's pen—for "the fullest study of varieties of human nature which we as yet know only by glimpses."

As for "Kaweah's Run," King's derring-do brought his friends of the California Survey more amusement than conviction. They knew that nothing of consequence had happened on the Millerton highway; they knew, also, that King the raconteur was not a man to hold back anything worth telling till the spirit moved his "literary pen." Brewer conceded that the sketches were the best descriptions of the Sierras he had seen, but added that "in all personal adventures" King had drawn upon his imagination. Nor could Bret Harte resist injecting similar innuendo into a gift inscription—"To Clarence King, author of Geology of the fortieth parallel and other works of fiction." Not even J. D. Hague, loyal and ever certain that his idol could "perceive things which others might see without perceiving or hear without understanding," would insist that the breathless chase along the Millerton Road had happened as King told it.

And yet how well "Kaweah's Run" reflected the temper of the scene, of not only what might have happened, but what too often *did*! The head in the glass jar that passed for Joaquin Murrieta's † had been pickled in alcohol at Millerton eleven years before, but the West was

* A long-deferred deference to the feelings of Clement may have been one of King's reasons for buying the plates of Mountaineering in 1889 in order "to suppress the book." It was Simon Newcomb's understanding that King had quashed it "because some of the characters described in it were much hurt by finding themselves painted in the book" (The Reminiscences of an Astronomer, p. 259).

† It is possible that "Kaweah's Run" was suggested by the infamy of the bandit Murrieta. Indeed King may have seen Brewer's paper-bound copy of Joaquin Murieta: The Brigand Chief of California, which an anonymous rewrite man had pirated for The California Police Gazette in 1859 from The Life and Adventures of Joaquin Murieta by "Yellow Bird" or John Rollin Ridge, the half-Cherokee poet and journalist. It was from Brewer's copy, perhaps a unique survival of the Police Gazette pamphlet, that the Grabhorn Press republished the book in 1932, with an introduction by Francis P. Farquhar. King may also have taken a cue from "A Dangerous Journey," the melodramatic sketch that J. Ross Browne had included in Crusoe's Island the year King rode the Millerton highway.

still harassed by highwaymen, as even Whitney could testify when he lost a purse to one on the Placerville Road. King's tale rang true, and many who did not know the inside facts would take it unquestioned. In surviving perils, the *San Franciso Bulletin* would observe, "[King] attains a success that might well make any one of Jules Verne's heroes forever hold his peace, quieting himself in reflecting how much stronger, after all, than fiction is the truth—well told."

"When you have read the papers," King entreated Fields,

... kindly tell me what you honestly think of them and how . . . I may better the rest of the series. . . . Much may be said in a line,—as hereafter I advise you to stick to geology—or—less local flavor, too much rubbing the plate with garlic spoils your salad—or some similarly mild form of admonition; it must be mild you know, else I promptly retire back into science.

The editor's admiration encouraged King to polish the sequence off with two more papers—a description of the great ice storm which had stalled his Yosemite survey in 1864, and a piece called "Shasta," which recast the story of his 1870 ascent in a manner more consistent with the style of the entire series. He asked that the manuscript be sent at once to the printer, so that he might see the galleys before his departure for the West.

The significance King attached to his glacier studies had shaped his original plans for the season. His interest in ice had not diminished since the days when he had listened to Agassiz lecture. And from his point of view the glacier problem now provided the most arresting challenge in "the finishing up period of Western geology."

On comparing the ranges of temperature over the Cordilleras, he concluded that the climate was still cold enough to form glaciers. It was therefore far from easy to explain how and why the systems of the past had perished. Excessive aridity loomed as the cause, though why the climate had turned so dry remained a mystery. King felt the need of more conclusive field work like that of his last campaign; and in proposing to turn his studies so wide of his prior course he enjoyed the support of Dana, Whitney, and Agassiz, all of whom offered to send their recommendations to the chief of engineers. King preferred to manage the shift in his own way. He suggested to Humphreys that further work to the east on the fortieth parallel would merely cover terrain from which Professors Marsh and Hayden had already "skimmed the cream." This was intended to permit the general to discover advantages in the plan which King had broached already in his announcement of active glaciers—to examine Mount Baker, Mount St. Helens, Mount Adams and possibly even San Francisco Mountain, for the purpose of preparing "a complete series of maps and studies of all the great isolated volcanic cones of the Western United States."

But then a development followed which King had not foreseen—the reaction to his assumption of priority in the discovery of living glaciers inside the United States. A "hornets' nest" of counterclaims began to buzz. No one disputed the credit he deserved for recognizing the true character of the Mount Shasta ice.* But soon King and his friends at New Haven learned how others, elsewhere in the country, had noted live glaciers, one as early as 1833.

The furor did not destroy the value of King's work, for prior finds had contributed little to solving the scientific problems raised by the ice. Publicity, nevertheless, exerted restraining effects on General Humphreys, who found that King's proposal could "hardly be considered authorized under any existing act or appropriation." King therefore changed his plans for the 1871 season and prepared to carry his survey across the Continental Divide. This incident marked a rare instance of interference on the part of Humphreys. Through the life of the exploration King enjoyed maximum freedom in his relations with his chief and the Army Engineers. In general he was allowed to conduct his field operations as he saw fit, and the military maintained a strictly handsoff policy as regards his science.

The elms of New Haven had leafed forth some time before he put his corps aboard the overland cars. Five days brought them beyond Green River City, and King established his base on Black's Fork not far from Fort Bridger. He had two wagon trains in the field by early June, and then proceeded to San Francisco, to buy supplies and hire packers for the high mountain work ahead. In his roundabout return to Wyoming he took time for a ride down the east front of the High Sierra, as far south as Mount Whitney. He offered General Humphreys several scientific reasons for the trip. But none of them could wholly disguise his

---

*But that he was the first to do so was another matter. King seems not to have been aware that Israel S. Diehl, on climbing Mount Shasta in October, 1855, had reported seeing "fearful glaciers," a statement quoted by J. M. Hutchings in *Scenes of Wonder and Curiosity in California* (1870), p. 206.

personal wishes, Mount Whitney's challenge and the value he set on reaching the top, to be the first white man to tread "the summit of the United States."

The Carson City stage had brought him to Lone Pine by June 18, 1871, and three days later he started for the summit with a French mountaineer who chanced to be on hand. They climbed all day in spite of the storm that had broken across the range, shrouding the peaks "in a cloud of almost indigo hue." Tea and boiled beef before a log fire restored their spirits that evening, and the following day, though having (in the words of a subsequent expert) "stumbled on the only difficult route," they reached the top. "I dared not think it the summit till we stood there, and Mount Whitney"—or so King thought—"was under our feet." He engraved their names on a silver half-dollar and left it in a hollow on the highest ledge.

Swirling clouds prevented them from seeing that the peak was really that which King himself had named Sheep Rock.* Sunlight played on the western crest across the Kern. But clouds had blotted out the whole procession of eastern summits. The true Mount Whitney burst but once from its shrouds of deep gray, gleamed for a moment, then faded back into the storm's heart, and King mistook it for Mount Tyndall.

Of this error, no suspicion crossed his mind until he learned how his barometric readings, carefully checked at San Francisco, had pared four hundred feet from the accepted altitude of Mount Whitney. "For a moment," he confessed, "a sense of doubt came over me lest I had been mistaken." But a check of Hoffmann's map convinced him, as plotted there, Mount Whitney tallied with the summit of his climb. He blamed the discrepancy on some freakish swing in pressure during the storm, and so dismissed his doubt that somewhere in the seething gray he had missed his goal. It was the most spectacular error of his climbing career, and it would be the source of much chagrin to King when two years later he read the letter in which W. A. Goodyear had disclosed the fiasco to the California Academy of Sciences.

Goodyear, like King, was a graduate of Sheffield. He was blessed with abundant whiskers and even more abundant self-esteem. He believed

*Officially designated Mount Langley by the U.S. Board on Geographic Names. The Board's original name for the peak was Mount Corcoran, and it was thus marked on earlier maps. "Langley" is a highly relevant designation in view of Samuel Pierpont Langley's association with the general area. On King's advice in 1881 he chose the crest of Mount Whitney as the site for his observations on the amount and quality of the heat sent by the sun to the earth.

that King saw "many things through a strange magnifying glass," and he took pleasure in gibing at King's blunder. The wonder, of course, was that the slip had not been caught before; for, following King's ascent, a number of people had coaxed their mules to the cairn on Sheep Rock, thinking it marked the apex of the country. King read and reread Goodyear's embarrassing report while "traveling in the overland car to California in September, 1873." And as soon as his movements permitted, he hurried down to Visalia, "to settle the status of Mount Whitney"—as a local editor sneered.

He took the Hockett Trail, as in 1864. Two companions rode with him and, letting their mustangs set the pace, they wound through the forest to the Kern Plateau. There they found the uplands denuded of their former lush grass by flocks of voracious sheep—John Muir's "hooved locusts"—which had been herded up from the plain below. At their camp in a wild glacier-shaped canyon that swept down from the bogus Mount Whitney, King fell ill of dysentery, and was immobilized for three days. But on feeling better he climbed on west of his route of 1864, till his goal loomed through a spacious cirque. Through his field glass he could see that "it was a simple brief walk of a few hours to the summit." He reached the fissured crest on September 19, a little before noon.

This tardy success, coming after the passage of nine brimming years, had a strange importance for King. * Others had won the honors of first ascent, three "fishermen" from Lone Pine who claimed explorers' rights to supplant the name of Whitney with Fisherman's Peak, a claim that was doomed to failure. King supplemented the record they had left with a scrawl of his own, the note which John Muir would find a month later, the entry ending with "All honor to those who came before me." King's barometric readings reduced the anticipated height to 14,887 feet. † Even so, it remained the highest mountain in the United States,

* As Farquhar writes in the Preface to his edition of *Mountaineering*, "Clarence King was almost alone among Americans of his day in having the desire to climb remote and difficult peaks. His actual accomplishments in that field entitle him to respect as an eminent pioneer in American mountaineering." In a thin booklet entitled *First Ascents in the United States, 1642–1900*, Farquhar underscores King's achievements by crediting him with first climbing Mount Lassen, Mount Tyndall, Mount Clark, Mount Conness, Mount Agassiz, Mount Langley, and a height in the Ruby Range he calls "White Cloud Peak." It is admittedly an incomplete list because of the "vague character" of the King Survey reports in respect to mountaineering details.

† The elevation now cited for Mount Whitney by the U.S. Geological Survey is 14,494 feet.

Alaska excepted—"the true Mount Whitney," as he would write, "the one we named in 1864, and upon which the name of our chief is forever to rest. It stands, not like white Shasta, in a grandeur of solitude, but about it gather companies of crag and spire."

Meanwhile, in 1871 King had returned to the East to check the printing of the contour sheets for the geologic atlas. There was much to crowd into the next few days—the proof sheets at Julius Bien's in New York City; and pleasant hours in New Haven, where, at the herbarium of D. C. Eaton, Sereno Watson furnished him with a report on fortieth parallel botany, soon to be hailed as a monument in its province, and to remain for decades as the only reference book on the flora of the Great Basin. King even made a hurried journey to Newport, where the necessity faced him of taking Bret Harte to task.

Harte had a relaxed attitude about debt; in San Francisco he had earned a reputation as a sponger and welsher, and King considered him "a literary highwayman of the first rank"—not that it undermined his fondness for the man.* On seeing him that winter in the wake of his astounding contract with the *Atlantic*, King had reminded Harte that his stipend for the Shoshone Falls paper had never arrived. Harte had searched his memory, to no avail.

"Now, Harte, you know very well that you fobbed my money."

"Bless me, did I really do that? Well, we'll soon settle that!"

Harte had then invited King to Delmonico's, where they ate a good dinner. When the bill came, Harte searched his pockets.

" 'Pon my soul, King, I changed my trousers before coming out and left my purse at home! Just pay the check for me, will you?" And he had the assurance to ask for cab fare home, to boot.

And then Harte had decided to summer at Newport. King had given him letters of introduction, and King's friends were lavish in hospitality while the lion had searched for "a modest little cottage." The cottage turned out to be a mansion which rented for four thousand dollars.

---

*King once declared, according to Thomas Donaldson (*Idaho of Yesterday*, p. 357), that Harte "never paid a debt that he could dodge; he was the most successful borrower on record. . . . King said that whenever Harte succeeded in 'landing' a man for a large loan, or whenever he outwitted a creditor, he would hurl himself on the floor and yell in paroxysms of delight." These allegations about Harte, if not distortions of Donaldson's memory, may be illustrations of King's technique of exaggeration and overstatement to make a story. Even so, his aspersions on Harte pale beside those of Mark Twain, who knew Harte even better.

Harte entertained like a nabob; he used the name of King's family "with outfitters and tradesmen, and staved off all creditors"—till word of the operation overtook King in the West. King returned as soon as possible, took the nabob firmly in hand, paid his bills for a month, and then withdrew all further patronage.

King hurried up to Cambridge next; and there Fields' assistant editor, William Dean Howells, handed him the proofs of a mountaineering paper. To Howells, who looked on King with hearty approval, the latter's

blondness was affirmed rather by his blithe blue eyes [*sic*] and fresh tint than by his light hair which was cropped close on the head where it early grew sparser and sparser. He was of a slightness which his figure did not afterwards keep, and he was altogether of a very charmingly boyish presence, heightened in effect by his interest in explaining the pith hat which he had by him on the desk where he was reading the proofs.

The wilting heat of the Cambridge summer prompted him to advise such a hat for Howells himself. "But," the assistant editor added, "he met me even more sympathetically on the ground of literature, where he professed to envy me my associations."

King's senior by just five years and a fellow Cervantista, Howells was not yet Pontifex Maximus of American letters, but his enthusiasm seemed irrepressible. What he liked he liked fortissimo, and he liked King's writing, to judge from his praise. Three of the sketches had run since May, and the rest were scheduled to appear by the year's end, seven* in all, or more than half of King's projected book. Howells later confessed how he had shared all of his "chief's admiration of those vivid and graphic papers"—adding:

In my perfectly contented ignorance of every intellectual or moral interest outside of literature, I regarded the brilliant and beaming creature before me simply as a promise of more and more literature of the vivid and graphic kind, and of a peculiar quality unequaled in the performance of the new California School with which I classed him.

King furnished six more chapters for the volume, including eighteen pages on his latest ascent, the high point, he believed, of his mountain

---

*The equivalent of eight chapters as they appeared in book form. In *Mountaineering,* "Wayside Pikes" became two sketches, as King had first composed them; namely, "The Newtys of Pike" and "Cut-off Copples's."

adventures. There was a rather unembellished account of the Yosemite survey in "Around Yosemite Walls," affording a peg on which to hang "A Sierra Storm," which Fields had excluded from magazine publication. A sketch called "Merced Ramblings" managed to include King's vignette on the Shoshone Falls, though it tended to violate geographical unity. It also contained bits on his finding the fossils which dated the Mother Lode's gold-bearing slates and on his victorious assault on Mount Clark. He rounded out the Shasta adventures with a chapter on his one hundred-mile excursion around the flanks of the mountain.

King closed the book with a wry essay on the people of the Mother Lode. He had observed enough of Sierran society to know it better than most whose inclinations ran to barrages "in pica"; not that he overlooked the foibles of "the boys." He tried to understand their heritage from a day when even gold was less pervasive than blood and bullets. He made wry sport of early attempts at civil law and vigilante justice; yet when brushing up a story he had heard from Parker, the Indian agent at Pyramid Lake, his laughter covered a certain grimness, since the tale was true in essence. The boys of a nameless mining camp had voted "a fair jury trial" for a "doggone Lubricator" charged with stealing two donkeys and a horse. The boys wanted to "rope 'im up with all the majesty of law"; and so when the jury said, "Not guilty," they yelled, with fingers on their guns, "You've got to do better than that." Deliberations were then resumed.

"Your *opinion*, gentlemen?" the boys inquired a half hour later.

"Guilty."

"Correct! You can come out now. We hung him an hour ago."

Just before sundown the local barkeep decided to sweep the dust from the poker-room in which the court had sat, and when he opened the back door he wondered for a moment at seeing the missing horse drowsing under an oak tree and the two burros chewing on a dusty pile of playing cards. It then occurred to him that they had been there all day long.

After its publication in February 1872, King would dismiss *Mountaineering* as "a slight book of travel." Yet it was more than the trifle his disparagement suggested, more than a mere testimonial to his own receding youth. It was a significant souvenir of an era that was passing even then. It was also "one of the very few books," in the estimation of W. C. Brownell, the literary critic, "that have a clear title to be called unique. . . . It stands so completely by itself that it is hard to find the comparison that fits it." There was perhaps a parallel in Washington

Irving's *Sketch Book,* which it resembled in approach and structure and in its engaging melange of fact and fiction. King had also taken a cue from Ruskin's *Modern Painters,* writing with an artist's eye, like a true American Pre-Raphaelite, and saturating his prose with the "color-glory" of the Sierra. There were paragraphs among King's pages in which one out of every dozen words denoted a color, *beryl* being a special favorite.

Such color effects served to accentuate the sharpness of the book's visual imagery, that graphic quality which so delighted Howells—word pictures, say, of sapphire lakes shadowed by spiry ridges, of luminous cloud banks and foam-fretted rivers, jagged precipices rosy with alpenglow, glacier-scored gorges, or waterfalls like torrents of snow. Often King's descriptions read like the prose of an articulate art historian writing of richly executed landscape paintings. His photographic memory and precise recall made for scenes that teemed with details, all ringing true. Sometimes, however, his exuberant fluency sinned against his style with more adjectives than suited a taste for leaner prose. Sometimes, too, a cumbrous geological term or a precious classical allusion or an overlooked cliché might jar on the reader's ear. But King's irrepressible gusto usually prevailed. Vitality was the essential virtue of the book; King had managed to imbue it with the same vigor that marked his life style.

As a consequence, *Mountaineering* was charged with emotion, an ingredient much in vogue in the adventure writing of the day. But a special feeling infused King's dedication to the sublimer moods of nature, as in the mountain-climbing chapters. These pages made up the heart of the book, in line with the title, and in them King banished all restraints. The spine-tingling embellishments and the exaggerations of the Mount Tyndall sketches would, in particular, lead a twentieth-century writer-mountaineer to equate them with a work upon the Dolomites that had been sarcastically "announced in a weekly review under the heading of 'Fiction.'" Yet no fictional elements in the Mount Tyndall story would keep Francis Farquhar from citing it as "likely to stand as one of the classics of mountaineering literature."

Scarcely less important than the mountain-climbing scenes were the genre paintings of Western types, at which King proved himself so deft. How neatly these vignettes, so slight in plot, so rich in psychological thrust, pointed up the acuity of his eye! He sketched the Diggers, Pikes, and highwaymen (even the ebullient backwoods artist and his Sarah Jane, as Californian in her way as a vast potato or a massive pear) with such telling verisimilitude that the effect was out of all proportion to the number of words needed for their depiction. The humor which played like sunlight over King's characters was often hilarious, but it never turned mordant or sardonic. One also found pathos, sympathy, and excitement there, and King's genre painting fused diverse and often contrasting elements in diverting blends that created a demand for more and encouraged extravagant expectations of major works of fiction from his pen.

The whole of *Mountaineering* was so steeped in the flavor of California that its identity as "local color" was quickly perceived, and the sketches were linked with landmarks of regionalism like Harte's stories of the Mother Lode. But neither King's local color nor his evident romantic tendencies could obscure his book's position as an original of American realism. This, notwithstanding his subsequent denigration of the excesses of realistic fiction. At the same time his volume was clearly a travel book, a narrative of exploration; and like *Two Years Before the Mast* or *The Oregon Trail* or *Roughing It*, it would be hailed as a leading example of the American travel genre. As William Goetzmann would declare,

King's *Mountaineering* had one of the great stories of Western exploration to tell, and it told it superbly well—so much so that it belongs with [such] classics [as Irving's *Captain Bonneville* and Powell's *Colorado River*] which helped forge an image of the West as an exotic place fit to match the imagination of a Moran or a Bierstadt.

In this context, Goetzmann would find *Mountaineering* to be "the prime Ruskinian document of the age."

The book might have been a better one, however, had King restrained his penchant for exaggeration; better, too, had he pruned redundancies along with those unbridled touches of the colorful and picturesque which some readers would find excessive; and better, above all, had he achieved a greater and more seamless unity.* Still, with all such faults the book was a minor masterpiece. Gertrude Atherton, who knew the scene, was to find it the one "impeccable classic" she judged

---

*Of some of these blemishes King was aware, and they were in part responsible for his buying the plates from his publisher. The posthumous edition issued by Scribner in 1902 carried a note that the book had "long been out of print . . . owing to the desire of the author to make certain emendations in the text, a work that the arduous acitivities of a professional scientific life left him no leisure to perform."

worthy of reading over again year after year. And on its merits King would win a permanent, if unobtrusive, niche in the history of American letters. *

Meanwhile King had returned to the West by August 5, 1871, and veering from the Denver road, he made for the uplands west of Greeley

* In general critics have registered approval, and a few of their assessments follow: Howells (*Atlantic*, C: 604) found King "worthy to be ranked with [John Burroughs] for the charm of his science," and the "freshness and force" of King's expression gave one "a new sense of the value of descriptive writing" (*ibid.*, XXIX: 501). Henry van Dyke (*The Lamp*, 1903, pp. 299–300) called *Mountaineering* "more attractive" than either Irving's *Astoria* or his *Captain Bonneville*: "If there has been a better book of familiar travels in unfamiliar places in America I have never seen it." In *Clarence King Memoirs* (p. 251) Edward Cary found that "the real literary merit" of the book "justifies its claim as an American classic." Theodore Solomons, a literary mountaineer (*Overland*, 2nd ser., XXVII: 478), pronounced it "the first real literature of the Sierra"; and "nothing of published travel in the Alps," he claimed (*ibid.*: 637), "possesses greater fascination." Henry Seidel Canby (*Saturday Review of Literature*, XIII: 7) assigned it to "that small but distinguished nature library which is one of the features of American literature" and judged it "one of the obligatory books for readers who would know their country." To Franklin Walker (*San Francisco's Literary Frontier*, p. 287) it was "probably the most exciting book ever written about mountain climbing." Wallace Stegner (*Literary History of the United States*, II, p. 865) called it "in many ways the most delightful book of its decade"; its publication (*ibid.*, III, p. 272) could be considered along with that of Mark Twain's *Roughing It* as "the high-water mark of frontier literature that belongs properly to belles-lettres." Van Wyck Brooks (*New England: Indian Summer*, p. 187) rated it "as fine as the *Oregon Trail* or [*Two Years*] *Before the Mast*. Neither Parkman's book nor Dana's had anything better than King's sketches of mountain characters, the Newty family, the Digger Indians, the 'Pacific Slope Bonheur,' or the spirited chapter *Kaweah's Run*, in which he described his escape from the Mexican bandits. What made the book unique, however, as Parkman's and Dana's in their fields—one for the plains, one for the ocean—was its special feeling for the mountains. John Muir alone in later years approached in veracity and splendour King's pictures of the ice fields and the gorges, the granite corridors filled with the tumult of water, the arrowy rushing of brooks, silent and black as night, like the void into which Dante looked through the bottomless gulf of Dis." In *Literary Lodestone* Dixon Wecter called *Mountaineering* "a classic of scientific description, gaiety, charm, and often hilarious humor"; and in the *San Francisco Chronicle* (Aug. 17, 1958) W. H. Hutchinson judged it "better than Harte and the equal of Twain." Surprisingly, the rare detractors include Henry Adams in his notice for the *North American Review*. He found the book, though "agreeable reading," rather a trifle that showed "only the superficial qualities of a lively raconteur." It was his opinion that it "errs perhaps in carrying sensationalism too far. . . . The danger . . . loses its artistic effect by repetition. Even the actor becomes careless and breaks his neck at length from mere inattention, while the reader becomes distinctly sleepy."

"in a light four-wheeled buggy, over a trail hardly fit for a commissariat mule." He knew, on reaching Estes Park, that Arnold Hague's bivouac, could not be far beyond, somewhere on the flank of Longs Peak. But night was at hand. Lodgings could be had from a Welshman named Griff Evans, in an unchinked cabin roofed with saplings, hay, and mud. A fire crackled on the hearth inside, and "luxury provided a room and one bed for guests."

It was there, a short while later, that a fortieth parallel mule brought a frail rider even shorter than King by some three inches, with an auburn goatee and a beautifully drooping mustache—a rare and intensely polished young man in whom some truculent senator could fancy the semblance of a begonia. It was Henry Adams, who had lost his way, and was famished after a day of fishing in the park. The encounter was a dramatic one. He fell into King's arms; and their friendship, in the words of *The Education of Henry Adams*, "was never a matter of growth or doubt." Actually, they had met before. Adams had come with Emmons to the survey rooms at Washington in the spring of 1870* and had gone with the fortieth parallel men to hear Major Powell lecture on the Colorado River; and now in 1871 scarcely a month had passed since their paths had crossed again in Cheyenne, where Adams had appeared just as King was starting for the East.

Adams claimed that "professing" at Harvard had kept his blood thin, and he had jumped at Emmons's invitation to spend the summer in "a country wilder than Siberia." The two new friends now "shared the room and the bed and talked till far toward dawn," and the comradeship of a lifetime flowered.

Their tastes in art and literature were in accord, and King must have envied Adams for knowing "almost everybody in the country who could write." Adams, moreover, could appreciate paradox, fossils, and geological strata; he shared King's admiration for the genius of Agassiz, whose lectures had stimulated his curiosity more than all the rest of Harvard put together. Each one's appeal for the other lay in the sheer polarity of their natures; but Adams credited King's attractiveness to his education. He saw in King a paragon of knowledge and training, and nothing could seem more moving to one who was to make *education* the shibboleth of his life.

"In 1871," wrote Adams,

---

* Indeed it is not unlikely, according to evidence in Emmons's diary, that King and Adams had met as early as 1869.

[I] thought King's education ideal, and his personal fitness unrivalled. No other young American approached him for the combination of chances—physical energy, social standing, mental scope and training, wit, geniality, and science, that seemed superlatively American and irresistibly strong. His nearest rival was Alexander Agassiz, and, as far as their friends knew, no one else could be classed with them in the running.

Indeed, it seemed to Adams that "with ordinary luck he would die at eighty the richest and most many-sided genius of his day."

"Everyone who met him thirty years ago," Adams would say in another context,

remembers how he bubbled with life and energy, and how his talk rippled with humor and thought quite new to our rather academic life in the East. . . . No other place except the Sierras has produced in our time the same sense of freshness, and no one else had its whole charm except King. At least so thought those who knew him. We would, at any time and always, have left the most agreeable man in Europe and America to go with him. We were his slaves, and he was good to us. He was the ideal companion of our lives.

In the opinion of Adams, King showed such little egoism "that none of his friends felt envy of his extraordinary superiority, but rather grovelled before it, so that women were jealous of the power he had over men, but women were many and Kings were one." At the crest of unbroken achievement, King could convince his devotee of such a lack of egoism simply because he betrayed no doubts about himself; he took his diverse capacities for granted. And the drive permitted by his self-assurance did not fail to galvanize a soul as torn with self-mistrust as Henry Adams. Adams might call it "abnormal energy." But he could not resist its fascination; he saw in King so much of what he missed in himself.

How well such deference must have answered obscure needs in King himself! Adams attributed something of the Greek to him, "a touch of Alcibiades or Alexander." But secretly, too, there was somewhat of Narcissus, a hunger for recognition of his own self-estimate, intensified perhaps by some dim notion of an Achilles' heel. This was the reason he could never return the devotion of his friend in equal measure. Inner necessity forced him, rather, into the role of enchanter. Adams closed the circuit when, inhibited and shy, he seized on King as his ideal, as "a kind of young hero of the American type."

On the following morning, August 6, Hague's surveyors mounted a station on top of Longs Peak, then closed the work in that area. Adams approved of their departure. Colorado, within five years of statehood, was much too civilized for one who had come for regions wilder than Siberia. King took him on to Bridger Basin, where the landscape was harsh enough for even an atavism from New England. There they continued their conversations, which persisted in memory like a benediction: ". . . after all," wrote Adams after many years, "the odor of youth and the pine forest is a little sacred, like the incense of the mass. We had ideals then, ambitions, and a few passions. . . . They were as fresh and exciting as the air of the Rocky Mountains, and the smell of the camp-fires in which we talked till the night grew tired of us." Or until Emmons, in the High Uintas, exerted his claim as host and carried Adams off for a two-week "stunner" in the canyons of the Green; after which, on September 1, the visitor started back for his drudgery in the East.

In the meantime, King had returned to Cheyenne, where he formed a partnership with N. R. Davis to run cattle on the open range. He then marched with Hague's party into the grassy sweep of North Park, now veiled in the smoke of distant forest fires. The murk prevented triangulation, and while they waited for the air to clear, the topographers amused themselves as best they might. One of them blazed gigantic letters on a mountain slope, a call for imitative magic—USE BROWN'S WIND PILLS.

No cleansing winds arrived, however, and for weeks King restricted the corps to geology. But the delay in topographical work threw both field groups behind schedule. In explaining the consequent lag in topography, he called the summer's work the "most arduous" in his experience. "Drought, forest fires, canyons, remote supplies of forage . . . lofty snow-clad ranges, and wide plains regions through which artificial signals have to be used, and most of all, an almost uninterrupted smoky atmosphere, combined to give constant trouble."

Triangulations could not be resumed until an early snow cleared the atmosphere sometime in late September. By then King had rejoined Emmons somewhere near the apex of the Uinta Range, not yet known as Kings Peak.* They proceeded down the valley of Henry's Fork, the

---

*The highest peak in the Uintas and in Utah bears Clarence King's name," writes Wallage Stegner in *Beyond the Hundredth Meridian*, p. 192; and Rufus Wood Leigh in *Five Hundred Utah Place Names* (Salt Lake City, 1961), p. 47, agrees that the designation *Kings Peak* honors Clarence King, although this origin cannot be conclusively

haunt of lawless mountain men who were as polygamous as Mormons, with tastes that ran to Indian squaws. Old trappers' trails gave access to the surrounding heights, and the corps worked up "a large portion of the Uinta range not previously examined."

"We then forded Green River," King wrote, "and made a depot camp about twenty miles east . . . in a range not noted upon any map." After surveying these nameless mountains, they worked into the chasms of the Green—into Horseshoe Gorge and Red Canyon—and then beyond Browns Park where, at Ladore, the current sluiced through the heart of the range. It was thwarting work, for frequently the water foamed from wall to wall, and the cliffs soared thousands of feet into the air. King now began to ponder a new idea, a plan for a boat trip of his own down the gorges of the Green, and of the Yampa as well, so as "not to be outdone by Powell." But when at the campaign's end he broached the expedition to the chief of engineers, General Humphreys again held him to his original course, in order that 1872 might be the survey's final season in the field.

Meanwhile, a blizzard caught King's party in the Escalante Range and pinned them down for five days, the cold killing one of their pack mules. They dug themselves from deep snowdrifts and pressed on to the Yampa River, where a two thousand-foot precipice ended their progress southward. They edged along the brink for two days before they found a crossing near the Yampa's junction with the Little Snake.

---

authenticated by the U.S. Board on Geographic Names. In any case, Kings Peak (13,498 feet) was evidently not so named by anyone in King's corps, for the expression appears on neither the topographic nor the geologic atlas of the King Survey, nor is it listed in the indexes of the Fortieth Parallel Report. Apparently the name first appeared on a U.S. Geological Survey map in 1905 (the Gilbert Peak quadrangle), and the Executive Secretary of the U.S. Board on Geographical Names (letter dated Sept. 8, 1987) conjectures that this may have been a deliberate move to commemorate King posthumously by the bureau he had founded. The biographical compilation on King by Clifford M. Nelson of the Geological Survey states that other geographical features named in his honor include Clarence King Lake near Mount Shasta, King Crest on the Grand Canyon Rim in Arizona, and King Peak in the Directors' Range of the Thiel Mountains, Anarctica. Interestingly enough, Enos Mills's *Rocky Mountain Wonderland* mentions a Mount Clarence King located five miles southwest of Longs Peak, and the name is said to have appeared on certain early twentieth-century maps. But it has not endured, in spite of having received the endorsement of the Colorado Geographic Board and the Colorado Mountain Club in 1931. That same year the U.S. Board on Geographic Names doomed the name when it reaffirmed an earlier decision to designate the peak Mount Copeland for a pioneer settler in the area (see the Board's Sixth Report, issued in 1933).

Another blizzard struck while they were tracing the sources of the Little Snake, and they were caught with nothing to eat but a few "hot rocks" and whatever game they could find in the wind and snow. "After the storm," King reported, "we got some more provisions," but he refrained from telling the chief of engineers that he had been foolhardy enough to follow a grizzly into its lair and kill it with his single-shot Ballard. On they persisted, reaching Fort Bridger by November 2.

Ill from exposure, King took to his bed on reaching San Francisco, but success had outrun disaster—he had brought the campaign of 1871 to a satisfactory close; and the praise of Ashburner, chief of mining experts on the Coast, suggested the height of his prestige—"C.K. . . . the most remarkable product of the age!"

10

King of Diamonds

The reputation of King's survey increased with the success of *Mining Industry*, which J. D. Hague had seen through the press in 1870. Though numbered Volume III, it was the first fortieth parallel report to be published, and it set a high standard for those to follow. Demand for it was immediate, and the War Department received requests for nearly three times the number printed. Scientific critics such as Whitney in the *North American Review* praised the profusely illustrated text; the *American Journal of Science* called it the most important contribution yet made to mining literature in America. In general, its reception served to quiet congressional anxieties about the practicality of the King Survey. It failed, however, to impress a certain tool of railroad, bank, and mining interests, the Honorable A. A. Sargent of California. In the Senate Sargent had called the Comstock charts a costly fraud. "Not one foot of the explorations mapped out here in gaudy colors," he ranted, "was made by Clarence King or any man in his employ."

Such a stricture called for instant rebuttal. King sent a sharp reply from San Francisco, and J. D. Hague, now a private mining consultant, caught the overland cars for Washington, where he met Emmons, who had come from Boston. There in the Capitol they faced the senator and won a public apology for the "error." That did much to still criticism; and before the end of 1872 another development would have such impact on the public mind that it undercut all further censure of King's work.

Meanwhile, King was to lose himself in a brief Pacific idyl.

Weeks of rest at Rancho Sanchez, where he had taken winter quarters, failed to restore his health. "He is quite weak and looks very badly," wrote his clerk; and a more complete vacation seemed imperative. King asked for a leave of absence for himself and Arnold Hague, and early in February 1872 "the Hague-King Company," as the travelers styled themselves, took passage on the *D. C. Murray* for the Sandwich

Islands. They were still under way on the seventeenth, the publication date of *Mountaineering*; and nearly three weeks slipped by before the headlands of Oahu loomed from the sea.

Here was Charles Warren Stoddard's Island of Tranquil Delights—a wharf heaped high with bananas, papayas, guavas, and cane, with stacks of exotic fish, and hordes of islanders, white and brown and yellow, with girls in ilima leis. For years the port had been a whaling center second only to New Bedford, sending its whalers to the Arctic seas for oil; and, never hostile to a pun, King noted in his pocket memo book the girls who "blubber while they're gone."

But the Hague-King Company lingered at Honolulu only long enough to catch a paddlewheeler—the *Kilauea*—for the island of Hawaii. For two days more they cruised along foam-girdled reefs where the ground swell roared and weird fish streaked through submarine tangles. Then the steamer nosed into the curve of Hilo Bay, and there a sky-piercing welcome pealed across the water. Brown Kanakas swarmed around the pier and laughed and chattered, ready to mangle King's name into something sounding like "Kinika."

Hilo had no lodgings like the Hawaiian Hotel in Honolulu, but the townsfolk opened their homes, and Hague and King found themselves in the brown frame house of the local sheriff. It was perhaps the same hospitality that welcomed Henry Adams in after years; and it was down the falls behind the house, as Adams would verify, that the plunge of "old-gold girls" held King bewitched.

Stoddard, his poet friend,* would later describe the scene:

Resigning themselves to the resistless current, their folded feet tapering like arrowheads, their hands clasped high above them, they stretched their lithe length in ecstasy as they sank into the curved crest of the cataract and shot down with the descending flood, a flight of shadows over the shimmering surface of a screen.

They wore garlands of flowers around their necks, and the spell they cast was intensified by the state wherein King found himself, marooned on "a very Pisgah of celibacy." His "story of the Hilo cataract" would grow so lyrical that "it was received with incredulity by skeptics at home." But the old-gold magic was to linger—a memory to tease the fancies of sympathetic friends; and when long afterward John La Farge

---

*An inscribed copy of Stoddard's *Poems* would be found among King's books after his death.

found tawny beauties of his own in the coconut paradise of Robert Louis Stevenson, there was enchantment still—at least for a while:

Pretty girls, with arms thrown out and bodies straight for balance, their wet clothes driven tight to the hips in the rush of water, had a look of gold against the gray that brought up Clarence King's phrase about Hawaii and the "old-gold girls that tumble down waterfalls." In the plunge and the white foam, the yellow limbs did indeed look like goldfish in a blue green pool.

And when the painter caught such creatures on his pad, Henry Adams felt obliged to tag the picture "for Clarence King's satisfaction."* Indulgent friends would thus uphold King's fetish of the dark complexion or—in the euphemism of Henry Adams—his fondness for the archaic woman.

Polynesian gaiety roused a responsive chord in King; and according to a confidant, he would always number among his "dearest hours" those which now danced by "in a merry Kalakauan fête." He never tired of wandering through the cane or palms from hut to hut with his small Hawaiian wordbook bound in sheep, or of breasting combers on the beach, "himself [as] daring and swift in the water as the lithest brown maid or sturdiest islander of them all." His satisfaction exceeded, if that were possible, his keen delight in the Paiute Indians on the shores of Pyramid Lake. He must have taken a special pleasure in the company of the island's "governess," the Princess Keelikolani, whose house was shaded by a massive umbrella tree and brakes of bamboo, seventy feet tall. Years later when disclaiming any aspiration to rule an island (even one in the Caribbean), he told a friend: "I had my chance in Hawaii where I came perilously near falling in love with the Princess." Still, he remained the man of science—a specialist in eruptive rocks. And where could he find a more instructive book on vulcanism than the slopes of Mauna Loa, where lavas had burst from a thousand fissures not three years before? From his host's veranda one could see a smudge along the skyline—smoke from Kilauea, a prime attraction for geologists, even geologists on vacation. The Hague-King Company could not resist the world's most famous firepit. They secured horses with Mexican saddles and rode them through candlenut and ohia trees into a maze of lava flows, their pathway looping and twisting for thirty miles

*See for example the reproduction facing p. 210 in La Farge's *Reminiscences of the South Seas*. To King's hypercritical eye, however, not even La Farge's most exquisite watercolors could do full justice to the "primeval glow" of Polynesian "old-gold girls."

to where Volcano House sat hunched on Mauna Loa. The crater of Kilauea yawned below them, moaning like an anguished surf.

It was on March 1, 1872, that King and Hague climbed down into the pit. There a molten lake lay ringed in fire, its surface glazing over from time to time with a grayish crust. Suddenly a jet spewed up and licked across the surface of the crater. "Numerous little branchlets," King observed, "spurted out from the sides of the flow and ran along the depressions of the basaltic floor for a few feet and then congealed." Again and again he shattered those eerie skeins to study their sections—glass at the top, but muddied with crystals toward the bottom like sugared fudge. It pleased King to find a parallel to Darwin's notes on basaltic flows in the Galapagos Islands. It was only a minor experience; yet in a characteristic way it added to that store of fact and understanding which was making King a world authority on volcanic phenomena.

King and Hague reached the Golden Gate on March 26. They had overstayed their leave by more than a week. But the voyage had been so calm that they would call the Pacific "different from other oceans." Peaceful days of old-gold girls and lomi-lomi had done for their health and tempers all that Rancho Sanchez had failed to do, and they now felt ready for another campaign.

Gardiner had kept the office work at Montgomery Block well under control, consolidating geology and platting maps, and soon the corps began preparing for the field. They made a camp on the edge of Oakland, serenaded by meadow larks; and by late April King had sent most of his men on their several assignments. Parties under Emmons and Arnold Hague entrained for Winnemucca—Emmons's group to survey neglected stretches north of the Humboldt, Hague's group to make a swift review of stratigraphical data on mineral deposits along the fortieth parallel. Gardiner set out for Cheyenne with a third group to finish topographical work in Wyoming and Colorado, and now O'Sullivan rejoined the survey after his stint in Panama and a season in the field with Lieutenant Wheeler.

King himself undertook a study of the ancient glacier system of the High Sierra, a work necessary to underpin the climatic generalizations he planned for his summary volume, Systematic Geology. Winter had burdened the range with the heaviest snow of years; drifts blocked the way as King and two assistants worked up the ridge between the Fresno and the Merced. The tusk-like horn of Mount Humphreys loomed across the mazes of the San Joaquin; but the deep snow obliged them to stop far below the crest and make a semipermanent camp, where King fell ill with "mountain fever." He left his men with instructions to move forward as soon as the melting snow permitted, and then retreated to civilization for a week in bed.

As soon as he could stir again, King made a tour of his field groups in Nevada and Wyoming. On returning to San Francisco, he learned that the westside approach to Mount Humphreys remained blocked; so he sent orders to his party to cross the range through the nearest open pass, and strike for the peak from the desert side. He planned to rejoin them later in the season. Meanwhile drafting problems claimed his attention, and he worked for days with an artist at Montgomery Block to develop a method for shading topography on the atlas.

Montgomery Block had appealed to King, with its interior jungles of palms, its lobby and billiard room as hazy as Indian summer with the smoke of cigars. It was the haunt of engineers and mining men, and there one heard sub rosa news from all the mining districts of the West. There were bona fide revelations, much conjecture, many wily tips from market riggers; for now in 1872 the city had slipped into a craze of speculation worthy of the Arabian Nights. The most extravagant stories gained attention—whispers of silver mountains richer than the Comstock or of new Golcondas in the desert.

No one with normal senses could have missed signs of the gem-stone fever during that hectic summer. The question of precious stones had become about the most urgent thing since Coronado's quest for Cibola. Newspapers printed rumors of diamonds and rubies, often captioned "News from the Diamond Fields," though no one seemed to know where the fields could be. Speculation had settled on Arizona when, in late July, the banker William Ralston filed incorporation articles for a firm with the jaw-breaking title San Francisco and New York Mining and Commercial Company. It was capitalized at ten million dollars; it could boast of a board of directors that included a former governor of the state and the American representative of the Rothschilds. William M. Lent was elected president; Ralston of the Bank of California served as treasurer, and the resident directors for New York were a pair of generals—Samuel L. M. Barlow, an able corporation lawyer, and George B. McClellan, who had opposed Lincoln for the presidency. Another general—Benjamin Butler—acted as legal representative. Such eminent frontage stimulated excitement, especially when fortified by the tray of uncut gemstones that appeared in the window of William Willis, the foremost jeweler of San Francisco and the secretary of the company.

"I had been so absorbed with the legitimate work of the Exploration during the summer," King later wrote, "that it was quite impossible for me to devote any attention whatever to the consideration of the reported diamond discovery."

Nevertheless, one facet of the business could not fail to pique his interest—the association of Henry Janin with the firm as expert consultant. King knew Janin as a man of skill and integrity, an expert who seldom failed, although as Emmons would quip, he had made his reputation "by condemning most every new scheme he was called to report on." What a reason for pause that Janin, always so cautious, now served an enterprise which promised to yield "gems worth at least a million dollars a month."

Disclaimers notwithstanding, King noted the "wonderful story" that papers like the *Alta California* had to tell. "We have thus commenced with Mr. Janin," the *Alta* read, "because he is well known here, and it is mainly on his statements that the confidence rests." Janin, whose report the columnist claimed to have read, had inspected the mystery fields and from a ton and a half of gravel had washed a thousand diamonds, four pounds of rubies and a dozen sapphires. He had then claimed the best grounds for mining—three thousand acres under the provisions of Sargent's recent mining law.

The entire report appeared on August 10—a guarded document, and yet how much in character to all acquainted with Henry Janin. "I would say," his conclusion ran, "that I consider this a wonderful discovery; and one that will prove extremely profitable; that while I did not have time enough to make the investigations which would have answered very important questions, I do not doubt that further prospecting will result in finding diamonds over a greater area than is yet proved to be diamondiferous, and finally, that I consider any investment at the rate of forty dollars per share or at the rate of four million dollars for the whole property, a safe and attractive one." Coming direct from a man like Janin, it made the mystery seem more plausible.

That was how the diamond question stood as King left San Francisco for another round of field work in Nevada. He rode the cars to Elko, a mushroom town in the Humboldt region. Hague and Emmons had left Nevada; they were busy now in Colorado and Wyoming. But King found his chief clerk waiting at the station with an outfit ready for a three-week tour of country south of the Central Pacific, where it was King's aim to establish systematic connections between the geology of Hague and Emmons.

The task led him once again into the Ruby Range and then into the Pinyon Mountains across the sage-dotted valley of the South Humboldt. It meant inspecting mines at boom towns like Bullion City, hunting fossils on weathered slopes, camping at wild-hay ranches or at Paiute wickiups, climbing into the saddle at dawn, riding forty miles a day, over Indian trails or wagon roads hock-deep in alkali, passing only occasional days at rest in camp. His party skirted Diamond Desert in the final week of the trip and, coming on the Eureka district, studied the mines at Mineral Hill, famous for swindles. Then they doubled north again, reaching the Central Pacific at Humboldt Palisades.

Much of the trip had taken him far from the telegraph or beyond reach of frontier presses, so that the days slipped by in a large part free of the gemstone mania. It was different in San Francisco, where wildcat companies were springing up with forces poised to cover the fields as soon as their whereabouts could be learned. A later tabulation would establish that at least twenty-five such companies were incorporated in 1872, with a total capitalization of nearly a quarter-billion dollars. Some of the more aggressive firms sent agents into the washes around old Fort Defiance, Arizona, where Kit Carson had found "rubies" years before. The rest seemed to watch and wait.

Even certain solid inmates of the Block appeared "on the tiptoe of expectation." It was clear that a rush was brewing. San Francisco had gathered pressure like a donkey engine with its safety valve shut. But the complex claims of King's survey left him little time to puzzle over extraneous mysteries; and while he prepared for a final assault on the ice conundrums of the Sierra, he could only promise himself that he would "give the subject [his] careful study" as soon as the regular work was done.

Having left the Bay on September 8, King packed across the mountains by way of the upper Merced and Tuolumne canyons. By prearrangement he met in Owens Valley a friend from Irvington, the landscape painter Albert Bierstadt. Bierstadt, master of the gigantesque, was one of the most applauded artists in the land; or, as King had put into the mouth of Hank G. Smith: "It's all Bierstadt and Bierstadt and Bierstadt nowadays!" What Hank went on to say mirrored King's own opinion as a long-convinced Pre-Raphaelite: "What has [Bierstadt] done but twist and skew and distort and discolor and belittle and bepretty this whole doggone country? Why, his mountains are too high and too slim; they'd blow over in one of our fall winds. . . . He has n't what old Ruskin calls for."

Whether or not King liked his friend's style, he welcomed Bierstadt's company for a few weeks in the Sierra.* Having found the advance party near the head of Bishop Creek, they spent some twenty days around the spire of Mount Humphreys and among the scoured heights of the Evolution Group. Bierstadt filled portfolios with his sketches, while King studied the traces left by the ice rivers that had once crawled down from the crests. His men took constant barometer readings to measure the elevations of recessional moraines left by the glaciers on retreat.

King felt satisfied with the findings of the trip—"a rich harvest" concerning the vexed problem of the ice epochs. It was now October, and he led his party down again into Owens Valley, where he observed the effects of a great earthquake earlier in the year. They marched south to Independence, then crossed the divide again at Kearsarge Pass, the same treeless gap which Brewer had tramped in 1864 while King was trying to scale Mount Whitney. The trail led down into the gorge of the Kings, almost through the shadow of the peak which Brewer had named Mount Clarence King.

Meanwhile, the diamond fever had mounted higher than ever. Newspapers exulted over what appeared as certain confirmation of Janin's report. George D. Roberts, a shrewd mining sharp, had recently returned to the Bay with several moneymen from a trip to the secret fields. His purpose had been to explore the holdings, he told the press, not to work them; for the place was much too high for operations so late in the year. The ground was covered with snow, but his party, with jackknives only, had found 186 diamonds. There could be no question now, everybody thought, about Janin's examination of the property. Roberts's report, according to the *Bulletin*, "renewed the excitement, and little else is talked about on California Street but diamonds and rubies. . . . A fact that is so easily demonstrated as the existence of

---

*When King came to buy Bierstadt paintings for his art collection, only one of three would be of a mountain scene in the American West. The other two were Italian views—one of Roman ruins which overlooked the Campagna, the other of an untended garden with somber cypress trees.

diamonds in that country should not be longer one of doubt and suspicion."

The firm, it appeared, planned to keep the exact location a secret only until it received a patent for its claim. As that could happen at any time, King must have felt uneasy over his delay in looking into the matter. At Visalia he and Bierstadt caught the train for San Francisco, leaving the rest of the party to march at leisure back to the Bay.

King reviewed what facts about the diamond discovery had come his way. All the clues were meager, with little meaning in isolation; but when King pieced them together, they spelled out neither Arizona nor New Mexico. He later wrote:

I knew from the condition of the [Little] Snake, Bear* and Green Rivers, . . . at that time unfordable, that [the diamond party] had not gone to Arizona, as alleged, and from the report of Janin I had learned that the discoveries had been made upon a mesa near pine timber.† From a knowledge of the country, I was certain that there was only one place in that country which answered to the description, and . . . that place lay within the limits of the Fortieth Parallel Survey.

It must have struck him with a mixture of satisfaction and misgiving, but one thing was certain. Nothing so important as diamonds within the boundaries of the exploration must go unstudied a moment longer.

He reached the Montgomery Block on October 18, finding Emmons, Gardiner, and Wilson waiting for his arrival. And where, came their first question, did he think the diamond fields could be?

"Not in Arizona," King replied. He told them of his well-considered surmise: the Tertiary beds of Vermillion Basin. Diamonds *might* be found there—around the mountains of Browns Park.

The very location! the others exclaimed. "Curiously enough," King could later inform General Humphreys, "Mr. Gardiner and I had reached . . . an identical conclusion as to where the spot was."

King now learned how Emmons and Gardiner had chanced to ride

*The Yampa.

† In "So Deep a Trail," pp. 18–22, Harry H. Crosby reports that Gardiner later told a daughter that this innocent-sounding though telltale clue, along with others, was gained not from Janin's published report but from a few unguarded remarks made by the expert during dinner with King and Gardiner after King's return to San Francisco. They had deliberately "happened" on Janin at a restaurant where they knew he regularly dined.

from Wyoming on the same train that had brought the Roberts party home. Suspecting the business of that ragged crew, they had put their heads together and schemed to find out all they could. For a start, Gardiner managed to chat with the outfit's civil engineer, whose name was Malcolm King. And then on reaching San Francisco they had launched a systematic (though very casual-looking) roundup of every fact they could worm from anyone connected with the venture. Wilson joined the cabal, along with J. D. Hague, and they met each day to compare notes. What they succeeded in sleuthing out in a week's time "as to the water supply for washing, timber, lay of the land, and various other things that would mean nothing to the ordinary individual" was trifling enough in itself, but combined with their knowledge of the country it proved enough to place the fields within a radius of fifteen miles.

This conclusion jibed with certain facts that Wilson supplied. Late in August he had heard of a pack train fitting out from Green River Station, the Roberts expedition, as it would develop, and later still he had seen their tracks at Browns Park on the brink of the Green. They had not been out long enough to have gone much further, certainly not to Arizona.

Emmons and Wilson waited for King's permission to hurry back to Wyoming. Winter was near, but King had made his decision: "I determined to go there." They would ferret out the fields at once, in the utmost secrecy, cloaking their movements "under the guise of survey work," to be reported as such to the War Department. They would not even mention diamonds, except as "carboniferous fossils."

"It was in the interest of pure science," Emmons would claim, "and in the hope of discovering the true matrix of the diamond, that [King] undertook [the] investigation." The volunteers for the search spent one day in preliminary preparations. Gardiner elected to stay behind to work on the atlas, but on the twenty-first Emmons and Wilson caught the overland train for Fort Bridger, where a number of the survey mules were stabled. To forestall suspicion King delayed his own departure until the following day. He reached Wyoming on October 24, rejoining his men there.

They had secured provisions and had hastily assembled a camp outfit, including sieves which Emmons had hid among their boxes of supplies. To the curious they explained two long-handled shovels as an emergency precaution in case they were snowed in again, as during the season before, and had to dig themselves out. Four days were lost in the wait for saddles that Arnold Hague now sent from Laramie, and snow had actually fallen before they could take the trail on the twenty-ninth, a party of six, counting two camp men and a cook. Their necks were wrapped in long, thick woolen mufflers that King had provided, and the wind blew so bitterly that several flannel shirts, all worn at once, were scarcely proof against the cold. Balls of ice from wading thinly frozen streams sheathed the legs of the worn-out mules and "rattled as they went like rude castenets." The six advanced, King wrote, "with terrible marches to Green River Canyon," where they made a success-ful ford at Browns Park, then headed up the forlorn cleft which Frémont had called Vermillion Canyon, and then up the mountain beyond which lay their destination.

On November 3, the sixth day of the march, they pitched camp at a small spring in a gulch near the western end of a mesa that had once served as a geodetic station. They were now in Colorado, having fought the gale on a twisting course for 150 miles. The elevation was high, some seven thousand feet. The wind still blew, but brought no snow, and the earlier snow had melted. "Likely ground" could not be far away if their calculations were correct, and they started to search for it at once.

They rode down the gulch, "and in fifteen minutes," King wrote, "I found upon a tree a water notice, claiming the water rights of the stream." It was signed by Henry Janin, and dated Golconda City. They soon located other mining notices, and in another hour they came upon a shelf of coarse sandstone which jutted out from the imposing mesa. It was bare and swept by wind and stained with iron, but here all tracks converged.

"Throwing down our bridle reins," Emmons wrote, "we began exam-ining the rock on our hands and knees, and in another instant I had found a ruby. This was indeed the spot."

Gemstone fever hit them hard, and kept them searching the sand-stone floor as long as daylight lasted. Each discovered several rubies, but diamonds were harder to find, set off as they were from myriad grains of quartz by only a steely luster. They found three diamonds between them, no more. But as Emmons remarked, "That night we were full believers in the verity of Janin's reports, and dreamed of the untold wealth that might be gathered." No wonder Ralston the banker could think about shifting the lapidary center of the world.

Dawn broke none too soon for resuming the search. The two camp men had not been told of its object, and to get them out of the way,

King sent them hunting, a plausible assignment since there was no meat in the larder. No sooner had the camp men disappeared than King and his associates fell to work, and while tracing the boundaries of the claim, they found the picks and shovels used by the Roberts party in addition to their celebrated jackknives. They concentrated on the table rock again, and King wrote: "We . . . lay down upon our faces, and got out our magnifying glasses and went to work, systematically examining the positions of the stones and their relation to the natural gravels." They paid special attention to the ant hills which dotted the grounds, all a-glitter with the "limpid grains of quartz" which the ants had left on their conical dumps.

On some of these hills they found rubies in plain sight; and when they dug into the hills, especially where others had hunted before them, they turned up still more gemstones. One could understand how Janin could talk about a million dollars a month; for at the edge of the shelf where it sloped away into "Ruby Gulch," King harvested forty-two rubies from a single screening of sand. Diamonds also cropped up in greater numbers, but the manner of their occurrence bothered King. There was a disturbing regularity in their ratio to rubies; for every dozen rubies uncovered one was sure to find a diamond. "We both concluded that this had a rather suspicious look," wrote Emmons. And then when King found a precious stone perched insecurely on a knob of rock, his doubts increased.

"The diamond," he wrote, "lay directly on top, in a position from which one heavy wind or the storm of single winter must inevitably have dislodged it." He called Emmons and Wilson together, pointed out the stone, and said he thought it was a fraud. * They at once agreed

---

* Thomas A. Rickard (A History of American Mining, p. 395) gives credence to Asbury Harpending's version of the detection "that King obtained his clue from the finding of a cut stone by a German member of his staff, and there is evidence," Rickard continues, "to corroberate this statement, the man that detected the evidence of the lapidary's art being a certain Schmidt, who had had some experience with gems" and who later told Harpending of how he had helped King in the search for stones at Diamond Mesa; how indeed he had called King's attention to a half-cut brilliant with the remark: "Look here, Mr. King. This is the bulliest diamond field as never vas. It not only produces diamonds, but cuts them moreover also." An amusing anecdote, apparently indestructable; but a careful review of primary evidence shows it to be no more reliable than Harpending's statement (The Great Diamond Hoax and Other Stirring Incidents in the Life of Asbury Harpending, p. 234) that King telegraphed to the directors of the diamond firm instead of racing back to San Francisco with his bleak news; or the

to a plan to test the entire matter, and next morning they began a far more systematic examination.

Emmons described the work. "We brought up our sieves," he wrote, "and tried the earth around the rock in various directions. When the earth had been disturbed, we would almost always find rubies." The siftings also produced amethysts, emeralds, sapphires, garnets and spinels—an unheard-of combination in nature. But where it was clear that the ground had not been trampled, intensive search brought nothing more precious than grains of quartz. "Next we took the ant hills," Emmons wrote; and at the base of many, they found small holes that must have been made by a stick pushed through the crust. On tracing the course of each stab, they seldom failed to meet with a cluster of rubies. Untampered ant hills proved barren, however. The implication was unmistakable; the hills were salted, and near each salted mound they found the "storm-worn footprints of a man." To prove their conclusions beyond a doubt they told the camp men of the nature of the investigation and had them spend the fourth day digging pits to bedrock where the specific gravity of diamonds should have concentrated them had the occurrence been genuine. They screened samples of earth, and when they washed the siftings at the brook the results silenced all further question. The "new Golconda" was a swindle.

King now discovered that their trail had been followed from Fort Bridger. A lone horseman rode into camp, "a stout party, city-dressed, and looking very much out of keeping with his surroundings." His greeting was, "Have you found any carats?" He said his name was J. P. Berry, and he claimed to be a diamond merchant and mine promoter, formerly of New York. He had spent "a peck of money" trying to find the diamond grounds, and had kept the railroad watched at several points all summer. He had, at the present moment, eight henchmen

---

statement (p. 235) that Goodyear's gibes about the Mount Whitney fiasco broke King's heart and that "he died a few months later." Harpending's account is dead wrong at several points where it touches on King. In particular, there was no German—named Schmidt or otherwise—with King's party. Of course one might expect the apochryphal cut stone to crop up in a romantic diversion like *The Dangerous Angel* (New York, 1953), which Clarence Buddington Kelland contrived about the Diamond Swindle for the *Saturday Evening Post*; and predictably, Kelland's passage on King's exposé rounds off the cumulative evidence of fraud with the clincher: "But, most damning of all, was the finding of a cut diamond!"

hid on a nearby peak with spyglasses trained on King's outfit, and his business ethics quickly glimmered through his words:

"You say it's a swindle? What a chance to sell short!"

"No," King said. "It's bad enough as it is."

Here was a mischief maker entirely capable of touching off a stampede in the dead of winter—a rush that could end in wholesale death from blizzards. Something must be done to circumvent his scheming; and around the campfire that night, with Berry's bivouac in plain view, King and his men hatched a plan of action. The railroad was 150 miles away by trail, but only thirty-eight as the crow flew, not so far but what they could sometimes hear—or fancy they could hear—the faint and long-drawn wailing of a whistle. King proposed to make a cross-country ride at once to the nearest station, at Black Buttes forty-five miles away. He would catch the train for the Coast and do what he could to expose the fraud before a rush for speculation purposes could be engineered. Emmons would meanwhile lead the pack train to Bridger by the route they had come in order to foil suspicion.

Dawn had not yet broken when King slipped out of camp with Wilson for company. The two rode all day across the exasperating terrain of Cherokee Bad Lands, and far into the night "with only the stars as guides," reaching Black Buttes in time to see the approaching light of a locomotive and for them to jump on board the westbound passenger train, the mules following in a box car. They reached San Francisco on the evening of November 10, and King lost no time in seeking Henry Janin out.

Gaslight burned throughout the night in the expert's rooms at the Occidental while King detailed his findings. Dawn found Janin shaken, if not as yet convinced, and later that morning he took King to the diamond directors. They were gathered at Ralston's office in the Bank of California.

"I have hastened to San Francisco," read the letter which King had prepared, "to lay before you the startling fact that the new diamond fields on which are based such large investments and such brilliant hope are utterly valueless, and yourselves and your engineer, Mr. Henry Janin, the victims of an unparalleled fraud."

King made clear that it was his sense of duty as a public officer that had compelled him to come before them and state the facts. He spread on the table samples of the stones his party had gathered; and by precise descriptions of the landscape and cogent references to the company's florid map—marked with Discovery Point, Ruby Gulch, Diamond Flat and Sapphire Hollow, all in appropriate colors—he convinced his hearers that he had in fact examined the claim.

King's final opinion, as he had summarized it in the letter, was devastating. Gemstones existed in places where nature alone could never have sown them, but did not exist in places where the laws of nature would have carried them, without stint, had the occurrence been honest. He could only conclude that some designing hand had salted them with a fraudulent motive. It was the work of no common swindler. The culprit knew enough to select a spot where every geological parallelism added a fresh appearance of honesty. The locality was in fact so astonishingly considered and the salting so cunning and artful that it came as no surprise that even Mr. Janin, hampered by lack of time for exhaustive study, should have been deceived.

King may have magnified the adeptness of the deception out of consideration for Janin, who would remain his friend for life. He insisted that the facts be published at once. To a hint that a delay might work to his own advantage he replied:

"There's not enough money in the bank of California to make me delay publication a single hour. If you don't [publish], *I* will. But," he added, "it will come with much better grace from you."

He recognized, however, that the board's wish to verify his disclosure was justified, and when Ralston proposed to send another expedition to the grounds King volunteered to repeat the trip. General David Colton, red-haired trouble-shooter for the railroad and now general manager of the diamond firm, assumed leadership of the party, which included Janin and two leading share-holders, E. M. Fry and John W. Bost, formerly the surveyor general of California. It was a bitter journey. The air swirled with snow and the wind howled, and it turned so cold that, if Emmons's hearsay statement can be believed, "even the whiskey froze in [its] bottle." Janin worked with the general, and King stood ready to help them at any moment.

As Henry Adams claimed in later years, the young men of the fortieth parallel had California instincts and were quite like brothers to Bret Harte, caring little for simplicity and much for things complex. What King saw at Diamond Mesa must have filled him with a wry amusement, all the more so as the lines of the inner story grew more clear. It must have piqued his sense of humor to consider how two "honest miners," Philip Arnold and John Slack, had come one night two years earlier to George D. Roberts's office with a sack they wished to leave in his safe, it being too late for the banks.

What was in it? Roberts had wanted to know. *

"Rough diamonds," Arnold had blurted out, then bit his tongue. But that—so the story went—was as far as Roberts had got with his pumping, although he had known the miners for years. They remained vague about their diggings, except that they lay in hostile Indian country.

Most interesting was the rumor that the jeweler Willis had seen the sack that very night and appraised its contents at a hundred thousand dollars. One could also appreciate the promptness with which the news of diamonds had reached the ear of Roberts's friend, the banker Ralston, and even more, the speed with which the banker had called the miners to his office. They remained as evasive as ever. They had the richest mine in the world, and they intended to keep it. Arnold did, that is; Slack agreed to sell his share for a hundred thousand dollars. Then the banker insisted on sending an agent out to the new Golconda.

On one condition only, Arnold had said. Let the representative wear a blindfold. It was here that General Colton entered the story, for he was a steady man, of unimpeachable judgment in spite of his having served as Senator Broderick's second in the duel with Justice Terry. Ralston had much faith in the general. So off he had gone at blindman's buff as soon as the party had left the railroad, running around in circles, taking four days to cover the distance a crow could fly in a couple of hours. But General Colton had found the diamonds, rubies, sapphires, emeralds, garnets, and spinels; and Ralston could feel sure of replacing Amsterdam as the lapidary capital of the world.

It must have amused King, also, to hear how Arnold had never batted his eyes when Charles Tiffany, back in New York City in the presence of Horace Greeley, who thought he might be president soon, had valued a sack of the gemstones "at a rajah's ransom." Nor had Arnold's aplomb deserted him when the men who might bring capital to the venture insisted that the ground be shown to Henry Janin, the expert who had never been wrong. "Why not?" said Arnold, and Janin

* Coincidentally, Roberts would die on the same day as King at nearly the same hour, and their obituaries would appear in parallel columns on the same page of the *New York Times* on Christmas morning, 1901, along with a brief account of the Diamond Swindle.

was shown so well that he figured twenty men could work the fields to the tune of a million dollars a month.

King watched him bending over ant hills on the rim of Ruby Gulch—watched him making careful check of the soil, in various parts of the mounds, and also in the space about them—tests which proved without exception that the hills had all been doctored, for the sand at deeper levels panned out barren. Janin reworked the refuse of his older workings and found rubies as before, and he pointed out a spot which the "honest miners" had suggested as a prospect. He had passed it up then, he said. He had not wanted to act on hints. But when he examined the spot with Colton, they picked up rubies in such positions that the stones could only have been planted there.

"It would have been as impossible for nature to have deposited them," the general wrote, "as for a person standing in San Francisco to toss a marble in the air and have it fall on Bunker Hill Monument."

In Ruby Gulch they retested the pits which King's men had sunk to bedrock and found the gravel gemless. Even the places where Janin had turned up diamonds before were unproductive now—indicating that the miners who had helped him sift and pan had contrived to slip gemstones into the sand before it was washed. The truth was bitter, but it was clear. The expedition returned to San Francisco by November 25 and laid the facts before the directors.

"During the forenoon," reported the *Alta*, "great throngs of people gathered on California Street, anxious to glean some information as to what General Colton's message would be." The directors met at noon in Ralston's office, where after hearing the dismal confirmation they voted to publish King's letter. The story had to compete with that of Greeley's death. But it was the stuff that makes front pages.

The *Chronicle* expressed a general consensus when its editor declared: "We have escaped, thanks to GOD and CLARENCE KING, a great financial calamity." The *Bulletin* was equally certain that the diamond fraud had come near "being one of the most disastrous [swindles ever perpetrated]. In thirty more days, but for the timely exposé by Clarence King, no less than twelve million dollars of stock would have been put upon the market." The debacle might have reached the proportions of a Mississippi Bubble. Several bankers thought as much, and King found himself the toast of the season.

"Who's the King of Diamonds now?" Whitney asked. "And isn't he trumps?"

The course he had followed could not be praised enough by a half-incredulous press. "Fortunately for the good name of San Francisco and the State," ran one editorial, "there was one cool-headed man of scientific education who esteemed it his duty to investigate the matter in the only right way, and who proceeded about his task with a degree of spirit and strong common sense as striking as his success."

The editor of the *Overland* asked King for his personal version of the episode. But King had advised General Humphreys of the true intent of his trip to the Green only after his disclosures had been released by the diamond directors. Now, on asking leave to oblige the *Overland,* he heard the first sour note in the midst of his triumph: first a telegram of refusal, then a letter of rebuke. As the diamond fields were located within the boundaries of the survey, "it was eminently proper," the general admitted, "that they should have been included in your operations." But the way the results had reached the public had provoked official displeasure, and Humphreys made it clear that "established order" decreed that "the Engineer and War Departments are the first to be informed of the results of their own operations."

The *Overland* had to be satisfied with striking off a few puns in the column "Etc." "A Benedict Arnold once sought to sell his country. Whether our Arnold be a Benedict is not announced, but in any case, the country seems to have been sold. According to Shakespeare, *Duke* Clarence had a fearful dream, in which he saw 'Invaluable stones, inestimable jewels [sic] / All scattered in the bottom of the sea.' But Clarence *King* had fearful waking—for *he* saw them all scattered on the *surface of the land.*"

The allusion probably amused King. But much more interesting was the news that broke when a grand jury was summoned. In its investigation curious facts turned up—such as the testimony that General Butler had received a gift to make sure that a clause covering diamond placers should appear in Sargent's mining bill; or the news obtained by a private detective that Arnold and Slack had made two trips to Amsterdam and London to purchase fifty thousand dollars' worth of stones. It was they, it appeared, who had started the run on "niggerheads," as diamond dealers called flawed beauties in the rough. American jewelers, including Tiffany, who had overvalued the stones, excused themselves on the grounds that their experience had, after all, lain only with polished gems. The jury returned indictments, but the culprits had decamped. Slack was never seen again. But it was common knowledge that Arnold had gone home to Kentucky, where he bought a safe to hold his half a million dollars, before starting up a new bank.

News would arrive later that a rival banker had shot him in a gunfight and that he had died from the complications of subsequent pneumonia.

It was Ralston who bore the main brunt of the hoax King had punctured. He repaid losses by associates from his own purse, and then, placing his receipts under glass, he hung them on his office wall. It was a cheap escape at that, costing him only about $250,000. The outlay seems to have had no connection with the run on his bank that would force its suspension in August 1875 and lead to his death from apparent apoplexy while he was swimming in the Bay.

In the meantime King's rewards, though largely intangible, were gratifying in the extreme. Not least among them was the fact that he now had unassailable answers for the Sargents in Congress. For once and all the diamond exposé had established the practicality of the Fortieth Parallel Exploration and amply justified congressional appropriations for its operations. As the *Nation* observed, "This single exposure, the work of a few days in appearance, the result of several years in reality, has more than paid for the cost of the [entire] survey"—a figure which, when the work of King's corps was finally completed, would stand just short of $600,000.

Exploding the diamond swindle was the capstone of the fortieth parallel field work. Except for subsequent rechecks of specific problems the expeditions of the survey had come to a close with the 1872 season, an endeavor of six years duration and heroic proportions. "As a great and epic feat of exploration and adventure," runs the judgment of a present-day historian, "the King Survey surpassed everything else that had been done [to explore] the latter-day West except perhaps Major Powell's dramatic descent of the Grand Canyon."

11

The Pass Beyond Youth

"There are turning points in all men's lives," King wrote in March 1874. "It is thus with me about mountaineering, the pass which divides youth from manhood is traversed, and the serious service of science must hereafter claim me." He believed in his pledge, especially in his farewell to the mountain peaks.

The rigors of field geology had left him tired and worn; he had ached in bone and muscle on closing the 1872 campaign, and he was prey to spells of melancholy. Because he needed a mild climate for recuperation in 1873, he again took winter quarters in San Francisco. Only a few miles of city, sand, and water separated the survey rooms from the home his mother now set up in the village of Brooklyn across the Bay. Oakland had just absorbed the village, but all was yet, in Charley Stoddard's phrase, "a kind of wildwood or wilderness." There King kept the carriage he had shipped from the East, and he spent much leisure with Mrs. Howland and the children, making the trip by ferry back and forth across the Bay.

Emmons soon relieved him of the chore of making disbursements, and King found it no hardship to part from the members of his corps who had caught the train for home. They were to push their assignments forward in the East, while King himself supervised the atlas sheets that were taking final shape at Montgomery Block. He could also report, "My own geological work progresses well."

San Francisco was eager, meanwhile, to honor the King of Diamonds. After the gemstone furor his social vogue matched his professional status, whose sudden enhancement the historian H. H. Bancroft was to later affirm by the exaggerated claim that "young as he was, King had acquired a reputation and a position second to no scientist in America." Such praise was nothing less than puffery, Bancroft's judgment warped possibly by the magnetism of King's personality. Still, it was a fact that King's standing had soared in the wake of the diamond exposé, and the publicity generated by that bizarre incident had made him the lion of the hour. To many onlookers the new éclat gave him a certain glamour, and as an admirer would later describe him, he appeared "full of color, and surrounded by an atmosphere of romance." He was caught up in a social extravaganza that was "tropical in rankness," and found himself invited to more drawing rooms than he cared to visit. He was persona grata at strongholds like the mansion of James Ben Ali Haggin (of the oddly Moslem-sounding name), whom he addressed merely as Haggin, admitting a certain familiarity; strongholds like the palazzo of General Colton on the crest of Knob Hill; or the Taylor Street house of George Hearst, whom King never liked. ("You remember," ran his quip, years later, "that . . . Hearst was bitten on the privates by a scorpion; the latter fell dead.") He found Millbrae, the peninsula estate of D. O. Mills, much more appealing.

But tired as he was, he preferred solitude as a remedy for his illness. Sometimes he retreated entirely and walked through the countryside, or drove in his carriage, wrapped in introspective moods. These times of withdrawal were excellent medicine; there settled over him, he wrote, "a soft gentle dawning of my boyhood's simpleness of mind." And he felt in such moments "like one freed from a terrible dream. The whole world," he added, "seems different, new, hopeful." He had need of this resurgence of optimism in the face of news that now came from Gardiner, in Washington, D.C. The latter was leaving the Fortieth Parallel Corps for higher pay from Dr. Hayden, and he justified his move on the grounds that field work under King had been completed, and he wished to go on as an active field geographer.

Gardiner's desertion ("base desertion," according to an unsigned letter to the Nation) came as a blow to King; only one other experience, he declared cryptically, exceeded the shock. He begged his "Brother" to reconsider; and in doing so he betrayed his dismay at finding his closest friend allied with a "Christless man" in conflict with the Army Engineers. To go on working year after year as a field geographer could only end in unfulfillment—a sterile life. "I am convinced," he wrote with intense emotion, "that science goes on and progresses at the expense of those absorbed in her pursuit. That men's souls are burned as fuel for the enginery of scientific progress. And that in this busy materialistic age the greatest danger is that of total absorption in our profession. . . . We give ourselves to the *Juggernaut of the intellect*."

Notwithstanding the vow he would make in 1874, King shrank from "that Dantean purgatory" that engulfed the scientist lost in his work. He longed for a life that would let him "ripen," yet feared he would never attain it in the wastes of geological field work. Such a life seemed only for those with a settled home, for those who could keep a family without want and cultivate the finer graces of civilized existence. Such a life, he feared, was not compatible with the impoverishment or the enforced asceticism of the absorbed scientist.

No power on earth, he promised himself, could draw him into another geological survey.* It was a young man's job, and he felt no longer young, although he was only thirty-one. He had done more than his share of a young man's work, but he had crossed the divide now and left the slopes of youth behind. Rheumatic aches and a glance in the mirror convinced him of that. His hair was receding above the temples, and growing sparse on top, and semi-baldness, clearly, was in store for him. His figure, too, was gaining in girth, at the expense of that "boyish presence" which had always suggested his being younger than his years. There was a hint of actual stoutness to come. But his will was firm; he remained determined to put his findings into form and underscore their significance; though not at the price of a full life, if he could help it. "King"—as a later associate, Bailey Willis, put the matter—"was a student of geology, but not a devotee of the science."

His story now became a knot of tangled impulse—devotion to duty and distraction from it; a yearning for self-fulfillment—for a life of the spirit, and yet a life of the senses too; a search for health, for relief from his heavy moods and from pains of the body; and through it all a grinding scrabble for wealth, a struggle that was to grow no less exhausting over the years. In spite of his scorn of money, financial inducements (no less than reasons of health and duty) had kept him in California after the diamond fraud.

No measure of Congress, in 1873, barred scientists from serving private interests while drawing federal pay. And now that King had determined to make money, he found it natural to follow the lead of J. D. Hague, who prospered as a mining consultant. King accepted commissions that came his way in the wake of the diamond exposure; and while nursing back his health he studied prospects for men who could pay for every report a fee equal to a year's salary from the government. Whitney observed, "The King of Diamonds has all the

---

*Gardiner told a committee of Congress: "Mr. King announced to me by word and by letter, now in my possession, that he intended to retire from the business of conducting western surveys" (Forty-third Congress, 1st Session, House Report 612 [serial 1626], p. 70).

work he can do now examining mines and . . . never charges less than $5000 for looking. . . . Some people are born with silver spoons in their mouth; others with gold ones set with diamonds."

It was honest work and within the law; but there were people who spoke in innuendo. It was hard, no doubt, for Whitney to reconcile his pupil's great success, much less his breakfasts with Silliman, Jr., with whom Whitney was still feuding over the oil question in California. Better had King sipped orange juice with the Devil himself, in Whitney's opinion. "I hear all sorts of stories about King," he gossiped grimly. "I fear he has got on a slippery pathway"—an allusion, perhaps, to rumors that King had approached a certain politician in the interest of a newly formed corporation, the Sierra Iron Company.

King had accepted stock for a study he had made with Hague of certain iron beds along the upper Yuba. The affair had been in order; King had asked for a leave of absence; he had done the work on his own time; and his reputation for integrity continued unimpeached, notwithstanding Whitney's doubts.

King's reputation did not even suffer when he became involved in silver litigation in Nevada. There an honest man had been defined as the "son of a bitch who would stay bought"; Nevada courts appeared to exist for the sole purpose of settling brawls over ledges of incredible wealth. The orgy of theft and bribery and subordination which had rocked the Comstock for a decade had moved to Ruby Hill; and there two mines—the Richmond and the Consolidated Eureka—battled over a cavern of ruby silver which both had tapped in a limestone hill.

That winter King received a summons to testify before the court as an expert witness. He found it convenient to visit Eureka, since numerous Paiute place names on the atlas could be verified nowhere better than among the nearby Indians themselves. Old Winnemucca, with a stick in his nose and feathers in his cap, was as friendly as ever; around their fires the Paiutes gave King the information he desired; and that was warrant enough for the trip, not to mention the figure he cut before the Eureka court. The Nevada press in reporting his testimony tagged him as "the eminent mining expert."

Underground, he had estimated that more than three million dollars worth of ore lay in sight. His cable to the owners of the Richmond led to a truce in the suit. Their agents bought the contested zone at the opposition's price.

Miners began to raise more ore than King had predicted, and that consolidated his reputation with "the Richmond people." They hired him to keep an eye on "their bullion business in New York," and he began a connection which, in some degree or other, endured for years. King could have become the manager of the mine, but fortunately he declined the position. The rival mines were fated to work in chronic friction, which finally reached the U.S. Supreme Court. C. C. Goodwin, an early colleague of Mark Twain, described the atmosphere of that prolonged suit as "filled with whispers of combines to defraud, bribery, double dealing, perjury." To testify in the midst of such corruption could jeopardize the name of a witness; and yet, in 1877, when greater knowledge induced King to reverse himself on Ruby Hill geology, Goodwin could detect not "so much as a shadow on the stainless shield of Clarence King's integrity." As a witness, he was "an honest partisan"—a partisan all too honest for any great enrichment of himself.

All such stints of experting King took with the utmost seriousness, as fellow authority Rossiter Raymond would attest. "I have known, in my time, many mining experts, and their personal methods of studying cases," Raymond would reminisce:

But I never met King's equal in insatiable desire to find out beforehand anything that anybody else knew or could know, whether it were relevant and important to the case in hand or not. I can remember him as going into a mine at early morning, taking his lunch with him; coming out late in the afternoon; bathing and dressing for dinner; then, aroused by some casual table-talk, putting on his underground clothes again, and spending the greater part of the night in the mine, just to 'settle the point'. . . . In general, his exhaustive preparation and wonderful general knowledge, reinforced by his alert self-possession, ready wit, and unfailing good-nature, made him a most effective expert witness and a terror to cross-examiners.

And then came the matter of the Emma Mine, the infamous Emma in the Wasatch Mountains. It, too, came under King's eye in 1873. Soon after its discovery, it had produced enough superior ore to make it famous in mining circles. In due course one hundred thousand tons had been "rawhided" down the trails of Cottonwood Canyon; ore that yielded up to seven hundred ounces of silver per ton. Suddenly, then, the owners had thrown the mine on the market for only $350,000; Ralston the banker had taken an option, but let it lapse; Whitney condemned the bonanza as a kidney of ore that did not continue in depth. But then for a fee and a promise, Silliman, Jr., had called "it a true mineral vein"; which was all that certain promoters needed to float it on the British market for nearly five million dollars. That was how the matter stood when, in June 1873, a new manager retained King to make an investigation.

This commission followed his second round of work at Eureka. He traveled on to Salt Lake City, meeting Emmons, whom he had called from the East; and they reached the mine by June 8. There a scene of desolation met their eyes. Deep snow had slipped down the mountain-side and left a wrack of smashed and twisted buildings. King found the mine itself in a dreadful state; ore reserves had been gutted. No precautions had been taken against caving, and all search for new deposits had come to a standstill. The wherefores of such ruin, he decided, were problems "which it were the highest charity to solve on the theory of stupidity." And having little hope for the mine's future, he minced no words in his report: "The great Emma 'bonanza,' the object of such wide celebrity, the basis of such extravagant promises, is with insignificant exceptions worked out, and the future of your company is hung on a mere geological chance."

Rumblings of scandal began to roll across the Atlantic. It dawned on owners of Emma stock that they had been fleeced of about two million pounds. British-American goodwill languished. Watchdogs of Congress learned that a senator from Nevada had collected fees of more than a quarter million dollars on Emma transactions; while no less a figure than the American minister to England had assumed, for favors rendered, the "attitude of a 'puffer' at an auction sale."

The scandal threatened to soil King's name. Certain men were eager to discredit him, in order to guard themselves from exposure. An attempt was made to stigmatize his report as a fraudulent humbug, written *before* he had seen the mine. But with the truth upon his side, he found it easy to defend himself, and by forthright speaking he turned the incident into a source of further acclaim.

Meanwhile, in June 1873 he had merged his study of the Emma with a review of Utah geology. Emmons helped him to settle certain problems of orography, along the Wasatch Range. Then back they went to the summer swelter of the East, for there were bullion affairs which King must arrange in New York City, and talks he must have with General Humphreys. But at last came a rest, a brief retreat with Emmons to the White Mountains of New Hampshire; then a few days at Newport, where Henry Adams brought his wife for a weekend visit.

They had just returned from a European honeymoon, "bobbing up on this side of the ocean like a couple of enthusiastic soap bubbles." She was a "charming blue" whom Adams had married a year before—wealthy and witty and twenty-eight. Her name was Marian Hooper, but friends knew her as Clover, and her admiring circle soon included Clarence King.

By September he was ready to return to the West; he had gained permission to conduct a roving one-man check of problems in the field, and now he began the trip which brought his comedy of errors around Mount Whitney to a close. It was on September 18—the day Jay Cooke turned Wall Street into a shambles—that King trained his field glass on that looming helmet of granite and saw that it was an easy walk to the top. On achieving it next morning, * he descended into Owens Valley. There he expatiated on the unsporting inclinations of the three trout lovers who had beaten him to his goal; he deplored their intention of barring Whitney's name from the apex of the United States and, by right of first ascent, of calling it Fisherman's Peak. Lieutenant Wheeler would mark the mountain so on his atlas, and moves would be made in the state legislature to vote the name into law. But in the end "Fisherman's Peak" would endure no better than "Bigler Lake," laid down by an act of legislature. Time deferred to King's choice; "Mount Whitney," like "Tahoe," would finally prevail, on maps and in the public mind.

King took pains to set the record straight about his role in the Mount Whitney story. On reaching Independence, he telegraphed the news of his success to J. D. Hague. "The many friends of Clarence King," read the *Bulletin*, "will be glad to learn that he has recently made an ascent of the true Mount Whitney." The paper carried a short account of the peak's history, mistakes included, from the time Brewer's party had sighted it and named it in the summer of 1864. Hague then expanded the notice into a full-length article, and Benjamin Avery published it in the *Overland*.

King could justify his detour through the High Sierra by geological studies it allowed him to make in the White and Inyo mountains, east of Owens Valley, investigations tempered by dashes of ethnological musings. "A week after my climb," he wrote in the postscript to his chapter about Mount Whitney,

* As narrated in chapter nine.

I lay on the desert sand at the foot of the Inyo Range and looked up at Mount Whitney, realizing all its grand individuality, and saw the drifting clouds interrupt a sun-brightened serenity by frown after frown of moving shadow; and I entered for a moment deeply and intimately into that strange realm where admiration blends with superstition, that condition in which the savage feels within him the greatness of the natural object, and forever after endows it with consciousness and power. For a moment I was back in the Aryan myth days, when they saw afar the snowy peak, and called it Dhavalagiri (white elephant), and invested it with mystic power . . .

This was the drift of my revery as I lay basking on the hot sands of Inyo, realizing fully the geological history and hard materialistic reality of Mount Whitney, its mineral nature, its chemistry; yet archaic impulses even then held me, and the gaunt, gray old Indian who came slowly toward me must have subtly felt my condition, for he crouched beside me and silently fixed his hawk eye upon the peak.

At last he drew an arrow, sighted along its straight shaft, bringing the obsidian head to bear on Mount Whitney, and in strange fragments of language told me that the peak was an old, old man who watched the valley and cared for the Indians, but who shook the country with earthquakes to punish the whites for injustice toward his tribe.

I looked at his whitened hair and keen, black eye. I watched the spare, bronze face, upon which was written the burden of a hundred dark and gloomy superstitions; and as he trudged away across the sands, I could but feel the liberating power of modern culture which unfetters us from the more than iron bands of self-made myths. My mood vanished with the savage, and I saw the great peak only as it really is, a splendid mass of granite . . . ice-chiselled and storm-tinted, a great monolith left standing amid the ruins of a by-gone geological empire.

Clues to the character of that empire were the object of his quest; he searched for Paleozoic fossils, cracking rocks diligently, a pith hat shielding his head from the sun. He crossed the desert mountains by way of Soldiers Pass and worked north along the White Mountains as far as Aurora. Luck favored him, and he achieved his aim, "finding," as he explained to Humphreys, "the first recognizable fossils ever taken in this region, and materially enlarging our knowledge of the Paleozoic ocean." He collected rocks, too, which belonged to Dana's Archean system; rocks which suggested that he had located the western edge of the ancient sea which had broken against a great Azoic mass of land and rolled to the east as far as Colorado. In dwelling on these difficult problems King helped to provide his summary volume with a set of special maps; small charts that would indicate, as he wrote his chief, "the evolution of the continental forms in our section of the country, beginning with the earliest insular occurrences of land and progressing through each successive elevation, showing, as no words could, the mode of continental growth."

King devoted the rest of his tour to a study of the relations between the silver-lead deposits of Nevada and rocks from the Silurian period. He staged to Pioche, with its booming silver mines, its seventeen whisky hells, and a populous graveyard. There in October 1873 he collapsed and lay for several days in bed, a fugitive from "geology in the face of exhaustion." The whole tour had been a struggle against ill health, and it would continue so to the end, as if to confirm the remarks which Henry Adams had made in the *North American*:

In works like that of Mr. King the wonder always is that a day passes without accident. If he is not dragging or riding a mule up or down a perpendicular precipice, he is shooting at bears, getting struck by lightning, or catching rattlesnakes by the tail. There is no end to the forms in which life or health is risked in these adventures; yet however great the momentary dangers may be . . . they are not so wearing nor so fatal as the risks of alkali plains or the river sinks, where health is surely undermined.

But soon King was up again, mixing government duties with private commissions, that fruitful combination that would win both praise and censure. He could parry the thrusts of his critics nicely enough; all private examinations such as he had made at Pioche enriched the background of his report; and by means of his findings he could refer the silver districts of the whole Great Basin to their parent formation. His itinerary included Hamilton, high in the White Pine Mountains; Eureka, where the Richmond thrived; and then the bleak Toiyabe Range, where he remained for the rest of November to study that derelict gamble of Hague's and his—the Murphy Mine.

Once the Murphy had boasted of a rich chimney. It had then seen days of poor ore and poorer management. By 1872 the stopes were barren, the mill silent. Hague and King had gained title and by the spring of 1873 they had the Twin River Mining Company in operation, Hague serving as president, and King as one of the four trustees. High-grade ore had been uncovered, but it did not last, a fault shearing the vein away. It took a gambler's nerve to cut blind drifts, in hopes of finding the ledge again. But as King studied the Murphy, his optimism rose, and he told the superintendent to blast away.

So the work on the Murphy continued, with new drifts and tunnels. The outlays devoured the treasury, till King and Hague were compelled to gut the mine and mill the ore in sight, and then "abandon the thing forever." They broke even, indeed a little better than even, but no resounding success inaugurated King's career as a hard-rock mining man. It would be his great misfortune not to see how aptly the Murphy, so rich in promise, so fraught with grief, typified his later search for El Dorado.

King hung his hammer up in November 1873 and rode to San Francisco at the expense of the London *Times*. A commissioner representing the English paper was waiting to take his testimony on the Diamond Swindle, for one of the parties linked to the fraud had sued for libel. The publishers had taken a philosophical view of the action and prepared to establish the truth of their reports. King lodged himself in rosewood comfort at the Grand Hotel and talked freely of the exposé. His deposition was later read at the trial in London, published verbatim in the newspapers, and made his name well known across the Atlantic, where the sales of *Mountaineering* exceeded those at home.

King's stay on the Coast was short on this occasion, scarcely a week; he left with regret, and soon told a friend: "My years in the Sierras and the plains of California, Oregon and Nevada were the happiest I have ever known or ever expect to know." He might have mentioned San Francisco; for much though he disparaged the sham of society there, he had yet gained a train of friends in the city. Many were birds of passage like himself; others were San Franciscans for life.

Among the latter was a comrade King had found at the Union Club, a Swedenborgian crony old enough to be his father; the "Bachelor of San Francisco," as clubmates called him, but one whom King referred to as "my dear philosopher, my valued anachronism, my friend of the book and owl." The Bachelor was adept at drawing out both friends and corks from special bottles at the Union Club. His name was Horace F. Cutter, but he impressed King's circle as a blend of Wilkins Micawber, Socrates, and Don Quixote. Perhaps an index of his eccentricity was his unshakable belief in sea serpents.

He loved Spanish literature, and he found delight in the ways of Spain which lingered on in California. In that he shared a zeal with King, who took pleasure in wandering through the Spanish missions and hearing stories about Junipero Serra and the Hispanic settlement of California. King and the Bachelor had found a lasting bond in the pages of Cervantes. *

King later reminded him,

You cannot have forgotten the morning we turned our backs upon San Francisco, and slowly rambled seaward through winding hollows of park, nor how mist drooped low as if to hear the tones of fondness in our talk of Cervantes and the Don, nor how the approving sun seemed to send a benediction through the riven cloud-rack overhead.

It was after we had passed the westward edge of that thin veneer of polite vegetation which a coquetish art had affixed to the great wind-made waves of sand, and entered the waste of naked drift beyond, that we heard afar a whispered seaplaint, and beheld the great Pacific coming in under cover of a low-lying fog, and grinding its white teeth on the beach.

Still discoursing of La Mancha, we left behind us the last gateway of the hills, came to the walk's end and the world's end and the end of the Aryan migrations. We were not disturbed by the restless Aryan who dashed past us at the rate of 2:20 with insolent flinging of sand, a whirling cobweb of hickory wheel, and all the mad hurry of the nineteenth century at his heels. . . . By the fire in our private breakfast room we soon forgot him, and you led me again into the company of the good knight. Even Alphonso must have felt the chivalric presence, for all unbidden he discreetly hispanized our omelet.

There was reason, it seemed, for Louis Janin's pronouncing this crony the Dictator of the Union Club; the Bachelor could be eloquent when something engaged his fancy, which was most of the time. He had arrived in California wearing a high silk hat and a frock coat, in time to join the Vigilance Committee, and he had remained to deal in several speculations such as " 'corners' in whiskey, tobacco, turpentine, oatmeal, or macaroni." Indifferent success since Vigilante Days had failed to curb his zest for chasing rainbows. "I have enough for my necessities," he liked to say. "What I wish now is enough for my eccentricities." The fact was, "He delighted in schemes, projects, and enterprises of every sort," wrote J. D. Hague, "and was never without something in hand for promotion." One of his dreams appealed to King in his eagerness for a "business plan of life," and he lent his name to the Bachelor's scheme for

---

*The bond was so close between King and Cutter that J. D. Hague wrote a lively sketch on the Bachelor and included it in *Clarence King Memoirs*, along with King's letter to Cutter on "Mambrino's golden helmet."

exploiting an immense estate in Lower California—"the largest private landed estate in the world," so Cutter claimed.

The project had just the correct blend of precarious elements to fire the Bachelor's spirits, an enterprise centered near Magdalena Bay. There Benjamin Butler's syndicate had secured a grant some ten years before and hired J. Ross Browne to run a survey. The general's colony had failed, though not before the worth of archil had grown apparent— that lichen which covered the shrubs and cacti of the lower peninsula. Supplies of it from the Malabar coast had long been used as a dyestuff in Europe, the "crottle" of Scottish weavers, running the gamut of blues, and making fast all other dyes employed with it. It sold for around three hundred dollars a ton on the British market, and such a price guaran-teed that the largest supply of it on the planet would not go long unpicked.

Sure enough, a lank, laconic Irishman by the name of Hale—Joseph P. Hale, or Don José, as he preferred to be called—had consulted with engineers at the Montgomery Block and in 1871 had sent hundreds of thousands of dollars' worth of equipment down to Magdalena Bay. Rivals had appeared—Mexican, German, and French promoters with money enough to corner land—but Don José had put his wits to work, and five ships bulging with archil had sailed for Europe, to glut the market, break the price, and drive the competitors into bankruptcy.

Their ruin was Cutter's chance, apparently. He plotted to secure control of forfeited land—to make himself a baronial "haciendado"— Don Horacio, as he was dubbed by Don Clarencio King. Affairs of the fortieth parallel and bullion business carried Don Clarencio east before the project could mature or fail. But J. D. Hague obliged him with occasional bits like "Cutter is going it blind on his land scheme— advertising for widows and orphans and referring to you in *great* capi-tals"—and doubtless sending Whitney's eyebrow to the limit of its arch.

The scheme was doomed to failure, like so many of Cutter's dreams. Not so, however, with Joseph P. Hale; at his death in 1893 the world would learn that he had become one of the greatest landlords of the century. King had placed his wager on the wrong Don.

King felt on returning east in December 1873 that he had forever crossed the pass beyond youth. He found that financial disaster had all but paralyzed New York; banks were closing; business houses were toppling, and there seemed no end to the crisis. The New Year dawned sullen and cheerless, and King lay just as cheerless, suffering from another siege of illness. Emmons would later explain that although "King was a man of remarkably robust physique, and showed throughout his physically arduous life powers of endurance that [were] rarely equalled, . . . he was subject to sudden and almost unaccountable breakdowns in which he suffered intensely." His recurrent troubles included asthma, malaria, and above all a devastating "rheumatism"—some form of severe arthritis. Moreover, his gourmet love of fine wines and rich foods was of little help to a distressing case of gout. King's doctor drew a distinction between the gout and the rheumatism, but they may have been connected. Certainly they were connected in King's mind, for in several letters over the years he would deplore his "gouty rheumatism."

For months King's health refused to mend. Rheumatic agony threw him "into a condition which," as he described it, "forbids [every]thing but rest." It prevented him from trying to place the Hite Mine of Merced Canyon with Eastern capitalists. It would keep him from testifying in hearings on the western surveys before the House Committee on Public Lands. It would even oblige him to postpone yet again, then finally abandon, his "darling project" on the great volcanoes of the West.

It was during this trying season that King decided to relocate his corps in Manhattan, even though he had never really liked New York as a place in which to live. It was too expensive, and seemed too comfortless; and as he had once informed Professor Brush, it lacked "the quiet fossilizing tendency" he longed for after his "many years wandering in the wilderness and [his] exciting sojourn among the Philistines at Washington." He loathed "the din and dust of it" and "the wail of suffering" and "the crashing juggernaut car of modern life," which seemed so implacable there. And yet all things considered, King found New York to be the best place for his headquarters during the final period of desk work. Moreover, it seemed to be the most convenient base for his private ventures, his "business plan of life."

At his direction Emmons, who seems to have succeeded Gardiner as second in charge, rented offices at 47 Lafayette Place, not far from the Astor mansion. Around the corner stood Cooper Union, which sponsored the American Geographical Society. The presence of Rossiter Raymond had made the Union a center of mining and metals inquiry; for besides his duties with the Cooper-Hewitt interests, Raymond was still serving as U.S. commissioner of mining statistics. He was also running the American Institute of Mining Engineers, and King saw in him a valuable ally. But in that shaded cul-de-sac stood an even greater stimulus to research—the Astor Library, with one of the most magnificent hoards of books in the city. Here King's uncle, Robbins Little, soon took charge as director, and King himself served as trustee. Meanwhile, the geological collections had come from Yale, and the survey's quarters were fitted out for work and study and gracious living. Emmons had even hired a butler.

King remained on duty through his "long and painful illness," and there were only occasional breaks in routine. Brewer came down from Yale, and King told him all he knew about the forests of the fortieth parallel; for Brewer was serving on a special committee "to memorialize Congress" in the interest of forest conservation; an effort that was to smooth the way for a national forestry service. Then during May 1874 King spent a leave in California, where he confided to Hoffmann that he was studying law on his own, "so as to perfect himself as a Mining Lawyer, that is, to examine Experts in Mining Cases." He would in time secure an extraordinary command of mining law; but for the present, while on the Pacific Slope, he wore his geological hat and examined coal seams on the rancho of the late Dr. John Marsh, who had worked tirelessly for the establishment of Yosemite Park. A month later King was back at his desk in New York, reporting to General Humphreys that every branch of the fortieth parallel study was "in a flourishing and advanced condition." The atlas was now finished, and Julius Bien had received the last sheets for printing.

King had resisted pressure to speed the remaining work at the expense of thoroughness. "The day had passed in Geological Science," he told the general,

when it is either decent or tolerable to rush into print with undigested field observations, ignoring the methods and appliances in use among advanced investigators. It is my intention to give this work a finish which will place it on an equal footing with the best European productions and those few which have redeemed the wavering reputations of our American investigators.

The task called for assimilating a vast amount of detail, and King and his staff continued to lavish pains on every phase of the work. They launched a study of Western rocks, from the angle of chemistry and microstructure, and King had more than a thousand thin sections prepared from representative specimens, to be used as slides for microscopic analysis. He had sent Emmons to Europe to observe the methods developed by British and Continental surveys and to collect books of reference not available in America. King also instructed him to buy the finest microscopes that he could find in Germany.

Emmons secured the microscopes; and at Leipzig he induced Professor Ferdinand Zirkel, pioneer of microscopic petrography, to come to New York and oversee the work on the fortieth parallel rocks. Eccentric though he was, Zirkel was an original thinker, the man for whom King had named Mount Zirkel in Colorado; and the prospect of his arrival kindled King's enthusiasm. King exulted in the microscope's "comparative certainty," as he wrote to Brush, at detecting mere traces of elements in the rocks, and he counted on Zirkel to make the most of their specimens, to correlate them systematically with known European types. This was new work, as there had been no one in America with a command of Zirkel's specialty.

Not that the German's conclusions were to be entirely free from error. "We have been told," wrote J. P. Iddings long afterward, "that he was much influenced by the eloquent and forceful exposition of King and his associates regarding the nature and occurrence of the rocks." Iddings believed that King's ideas may have warped Zirkel's judgment to some extent. At any rate the reexamination which Arnold Hague was to make of the whole collection revealed that the specimens which Zirkel had labeled trachytic belonged to another category. Zirkel's memoir (Volume VI of the Fortieth Parallel Report) would, nevertheless, become a kind of spectacular pair of seven-league boots in speeding forward the petrographic phase of American geology; it was to create a veritable revolution in its province.

Questions of the glacial age continued to claim King's thoughts. His observations on Mount Shasta had suggested the origin of kames and kettle holes in New England, and he had followed his glacier studies in the West with a trip with Emmons to the island of Naushon in the summer of 1873. They had spent five days on the island, one of the Elizabeth Group off Buzzards Bay, Massachusetts. King noted glacial features similar to some he had seen in the West, and concluded that the island contained part of a vast terminal moraine left by the continental ice sheet that had covered New England; a moraine that could be seen at the head of Cape Cod, the Elizabeth Group marking a seaward extension that reached as far south as Staten Island. He returned to Naushon from time to time, perhaps in the summer of

1874, certainly during the summer of 1875, and he also cruised about Martha's Vineyard. He did not have time to follow up his studies of the glacial relics there. But his observations stimulated other students, G. F. Wright in particular, and their systematic work on the till of the ice sheet led, in the words of Emmons, to "the most important advance in the science of glaciology since the days of the elder Agassiz."

King's studies had satisfied him that the ice sheet had covered only a large part of the East and North. Conditions had been different in the Great Basin and the Cordilleras. No continuous sheet had developed there, only systems of local glaciers which had ground down from cirques, along the crests of the Rockies, the Cascades, and the Sierra Nevada. Their "actual ploughing erosion" had determined the characteristic contours of the gorges he had studied season after season. He could find no evidence that any other agent had given the U-canyons their present distinctive form. That was true even of Yosemite, although he thought its antecedent must have been a fissure in the range.

In *Mountaineering* King had mentioned Whitney's theory that a great subsidence (not merely a fissure) had shaped the valley during a plastic condition of the rock. He had never accepted it, as some believed he did; but he found himself drawn into the controversy that his former chief now waged against a Scottish nature lover who had come to the valley in 1868. John Muir, "that shepherd," as Whitney called him in derision, was no ill-educated dunce; he had studied five semesters at the University of Wisconsin, longer than King had spent as an undergraduate at Yale; and one of his teachers, Dr. Ezra Carr, had been a student of Agassiz. The shepherd knew, in fact, a thing or two about glaciology; and what he saw in Yosemite did not square at all with Whitney's verdict on the genesis of the valley, especially now that Whitney had rejected King's reports of glacial relics there. No matter how clearly King's moraines or ice striae had stared Whitney in the face, he had declined to recognize them on his visits to the valley, and had decided that the evidence King had amassed of a former glacier there (even as published in the *Geology* of 1865) was all an error. Whitney flatly asserted in the *Yosemite Guide-Book* that no glaciers had "ever occupied the Valley or any portion of it": and he dismissed all claims for glacial erosion as based on "ignorance of the whole subject."

"Nonsense!" Muir had said in effect; an opinion that he had published in the New York *Tribune* as early as 1871, and then in the *Overland.* Now in 1874 that magazine carried further essays from his pen, a series captioned "Studies in the Sierra," which showed emphatically—for that shepherd could write—that Yosemite owed its birth entirely to glacial action. King differed only in degree upon that score; his views on the glacial history of the valley came nearer to Muir's than they did to Whitney's theory of the "dropped block." A sense of loyalty to his former chief may have underlain his antipathy for Muir throughout the glacier controversy. Or it may have been a sense of personal pique that motivated him, for Muir had succeeded in places where King had failed. The east face of Mount Whitney, which defeated him in 1864, had not daunted the wiry Scot, the first climber to win the top by that approach. Muir climbed Mount Ritter, too, where King had turned back; and he had made his way down through the Great Tuolumne Canyon, which King had found impassable on a single attempt.

"I am sure," Muir had scoffed in the *Overland*, "that it may be entered at more than fifty different points along the walls by mountaineers of ordinary nerve and skill." *

The jibe had come in the wake of Goodyear's derision, and it must have stung King to the quick. Muir's successive disclosures of living glaciers in the Sierra struck only scorn from him, as bitter as Whitney's. He had seen these glaciers, a number of them at least. He regarded them only as fields of snow, and he was to hope, in a sharp footnote, "that Mr. Muir's vagaries will not deceive geologists who are personally unacquainted with California, and that the ambitious amateur himself may direct his evident enthusiastic love of nature into a channel, if there is one, in which his attainments would save him from hopeless floundering." Time and unbiased experts were not to find it hopeless floundering, however; in the end they pronounced Muir right, far more right than wrong.

King was never to meet Muir, ill luck for both. Had they come together, they doubtless would have agreed on many things, and their grudges might have melted in the warmth of mutual love for the Range of Light. At any rate Judge Goodwin, who knew them both, could imagine them "walking side by side all day over Yosemite trails and

---

* Robert E. C. Stearns, the naturalist, had come to King's defense (*Proceedings of the California Academy of Sciences*, V: 156); he did not wish to question the motive or the taste of Muir's remark, he had said, "or to explain why Mr. King did not explore the valley *at the time referred to.* Yet he found it "[un]reasonable to suppose that, if an experienced mountain-climber like Mr. King had really desired to enter the valley, he would have been deterred from doing so by obstacles of an ordinary character, as no person can with truth deny to him the possession 'of ordinary nerve and skill.'" See also *Mining and Scientific Press*, XXVII (October 5, 1873): 214.

hardly speaking and then at night see them enthusiastic over the great day they had enjoyed."

King's health had now improved, restoring that "dash about him" which had delighted H. H. Bancroft, the bookseller turned historian. King had met Bancroft through Gardiner, who had some family connection with the historian, and he had dined at Bancroft's house in San Francisco. He had also patronized Bancroft's Library on Market Street; and the diligent historian, whom he met again at Yale in the autumn of 1874, claimed to see in him his "ideal of a scholar"; for King, he wrote, "could do so easily what I could not do at all; he was so young, with such an elastic brain, trained to do his most ambitious bidding." This, no doubt, was sincere praise, coming as it did from one who had spent a fortune on books and manuscripts. Bancroft was now the grand khan of a literary factory; he dreamed of a many-volumed chronicle of Western America; and he had come east with a wallet of testimonials, his baggage bulging with proof sheets of his first production, *Native Races of the Pacific States*. King could not forget the courtesies he had received at Bancroft's Library on Market Street. He asked what he might do to help.

A review, of course. Bancroft was well acquainted with *Mountaineering*; he had cited it in his text; and he considered King ideally qualified to do a review by virtue of what Henry Adams was to call his "picturesque intimacy with the manners of the Apaches and the Digger Indians."

"I'll do my best," King promised.

And so in October, with a dozen pages committed to the *Atlantic*, King packed *Native Races* off to the mines of Colorado. He had hired himself at one hundred dollars a day to testify for the Dives Company at Silver Plume, in a suit against the encroaching Pelican Mine. To prepare for his testimony it was necessary for him to spend many of the following days underground—or as the miners sang to the tune of "Bell-Bottomed Trousers"—

> Down in the Dives
> Underneath the ground
> Where no ray of sunlight
> Ever could be found,
> Where the brightest silver
> Is scattered all around . . .

And then came days with a phalanx of lawyers, including two future United States senators—Henry M. Teller and Edward Oliver Wolcott—who prepared to argue the suit before Judge Belford, sometimes known as "the red-headed rooster of Georgetown."

Yet King found time enough to range through Bancroft's compilation, and it roused a warm response in him. Here was a monument which for vast romanticism and disregard for the scientific method was to strike Henry Adams as "a disgrace" to American scholarship and which spurred him to urge Lewis Henry Morgan to scalp the chronicler down to the neck; but King was inclined to find no serious fault. He was aware that Bancroft was not the sole author, for the historian made no attempt to conceal his methods. They did not matter; King was himself engaged in a joint endeavor, and he gave *Native Races*, as Howells recorded, "twelve pages of unalloyed praise."

The review concentrated on *Wild Tribes*, the first volume of the work; and King assured Bancroft in November of the pleasure it gave him to reread the book: "Of its excellence as a piece of critical literary combination I was fully persuaded from the first, but only on actual study do I reach its true value. . . . It is simply fascinating to the student who realizes the vital value of savage data." Yet it was no slight task, he found, to deal with a book of such breadth. It was not possible even to "intimate the varied class of material," and he fell back on the plan of following the author "from the Arctic coast down to Panama, tracing the prominent changes and elements of development." The review appeared in the *Atlantic* for February 1875, and it helped to launch *Native Races* on a spectacular course.

At the same time the Pelican-Dives struggle grew in fury. No morbid will to compromise infected the leaders of either faction; each maintained its own saloon, its own brigade of thugs to stand picket, charge, or battle for ore. Each company strove to outdo the chicanery of the other, and a ghoulish climax came when a small fortune in stolen ore—of the highest grade—was spirited out in coffins lowered for the bodies of men killed in the fighting underground. Tempers flared so viciously in court that the judge kept two pistols on his desk. But then in May, after a Dives mercenary had murdered one of the Pelican's owners in a public livery stable, both factions felt the time had come for a settlement.

As King's report had roused the interest of several financiers, a San Francisco company made an offer for the vein. The negotiation failed, however. And then with irony almost weird the owner of the Dives died from natural causes while returning from the Bay. That melancholy stroke opened the way at Silver Plume for a peace of exhaustion; the Dives fell beneath a sheriff's hammer for only fifty thousand dollars, to the main surviving owner of the Pelican; though the final twist was not to come for another five years, when the consolidated mines sold for five million dollars.

Meanwhile King fell ill again. It may be that the present Rocky Mountain sojourn was the occasion of the hernia he sustained from the attack of a recalcitrant "Colorado mule"—a rupture that would cause him nearly to die when it reopened in 1882. In any case, on returning east he confessed, "I have been . . . confined to my bed more than half the time," and the pain and prostration forced him to advise the chief of engineers that at any moment he might have "to relinquish work." Yet he managed to keep the desk work going, and by summer he could report that basic researches had been completed on notes and collections. The paleontologists ("those scientific autocrats") to whom he had consigned all tell-tale fossils had finally returned the stratigraphical determinations on which much of the final work depended. King was now ready to write the crowning volume of the Fortieth Parallel Report, *Systematic Geology*. Its creation dominated the next span of his career.

12

Systematic Geology

In the spring of 1875 King leased a flat on lower Fifth Avenue, in a somber building which Mabel Dodge described long afterward as a house with "a blank look like a face that hides its thoughts." It was not an unusual place for the Brownstone Age, lugubrious for all its frosted glass and knobs of silver, but it stood in a genteel part of town, in what might be called "a citadel of aristocracy." King was to live there for several years while he brought his treatise to a finish.

He had welcomed to his hearth the year before a cub from Whitelaw Reid's Great Moral Organ, the daily *Tribune*. This young man, whose name was Edgar Beecher Bronson, had covered the trial of his Brooklyn kinsman, Henry Ward Beecher; he had taken down the proceedings word for word, and a long trial it had proved to be. The avalanche of words had driven him from the job, exhausted. But the shorthand practice had made him an excellent secretary, as King discovered.

An editorial symbiosis soon flourished at 23 Fifth Avenue, King dictating, Bronson taking the words down as fast as King could speak them. The manuscript of *Systematic Geology* grew by page and chapter under the roof where Mabel Dodge and John Reed in a later time were to curl the hair of Bohemian Gotham. King cheerfully said that "just three people" would care to read the tome, but specified not one of them.

In their occasional intervals of leisure, King would say of an evening, as Bronson later remembered, "Get a stick, Ted, and come on." Then came rambles in search of adventure in meaner parts of town. Sometimes they found it, too—as on the night they saw a patrolman clubbing a tipsy sailor for no good reason except that he was a limey. It was just before dawn, in a dark alley of the Thompson-Sullivan Street area (then known as "Africa"), and Bronson would remember: "Without a word or an instant's hesitation, King handed me his stick, pitched into the policeman with his good bare hands, and pounded him to insensibility. Then before the policeman could recover sufficiently to summon aid, we went hotfoot home." The mauled sailor was with them, and King gave him temporary shelter.

As Howells later wrote, King's sympathies were universal. And if he prowled tenement purlieus out of feeling for the poor, it did not lessen his delight in brighter parlors of the rich or cultured. He found himself welcome at Mrs. F. A. P. Barnard's where polished throngs drifted between coffee urn and chocolate pot at her "Sunday night collations." There would be her husband, president of Columbia College. There, too, King might see his staunch friend, E. L. Godkin, red-haired editor of the *Nation*; or Colonel George Waring down from Newport; or the John Bigelows or the Parke Godwins, the Richard Henry Stoddards, or the Bayard Taylors. Or General Francis Walker might be there, just in from Sheffield, where he served as the new professor of economics. Or one might meet the painters R. Swain Gifford and Eastman Johnson, or the sculptor Quincy Ward, who could turn an anecdote as neatly as a bust in marble. Or there would be less crowded evenings at the Philip Schuylers', where King amazed the Reverend James Freeman Clarke with word-pictures of Yosemite; evenings, too, at the Frederick Law Olmsteds', where other guests were apt to be the likes of Calvert Vaux, Charles Loring Brace, H. H. Richardson, or William Cullen Bryant.

King was equally welcome at Peter Cooper's house on Lexington Avenue, or at Ringwood Manor, the country mansion of Abram S. Hewitt, who was Cooper's son-in-law and a member of Congress. Guestbooks at Ringwood became, in time, "almost a register of high society"; but few of the visitors excelled King in winning Hewitt's regard. Their intimate association was to fill Hewitt, as he confessed to Seth Low, with "an admiration for [King's] attainments and his character that may possibly warp my judgment." The esteem was mutual.

There were also hilarious invasions of "Holtdom," as Henry Holt the publisher called his house; and there, one evening, King found himself placed at the end of a long table, facing his friend John Hay, who sat at the other end. Holt had reasoned that each would keep the conversation going in his vicinity. Instead to the great amusement of their host, they fired away at one another "the whole length of the table, and hardly anyone else said a word."

It was Hay's motto that "friends are the sunshine of life"; and he, as much as King, had a genius for friendship—this special "worder of foreign topics" for the *Tribune* who had won the heart of President Lincoln when he was scarcely out of Brown and had gone to the capital as a presidential secretary, to be flung into the vortex of the Civil War. King would himself remark upon those experiences of Hay:

The friend, the intimate of the President, living with him in the White House, sustaining, day after day, relations of the close confidence, he saw the whole complex progress of events, and from the very force of position gained an accurate knowledge of the truth of that swiftly made history. . . . He knew from the lips of his chief the motives, estimates, and intentions of the man, and bore a share of that Atlas-load of desperate perplexity and incalculable care which rested with crushing weight on the shoulders of Lincoln.

Then had come appointments to Paris, Vienna, and finally Madrid, where Hay had served under General Sickles, then minister to Spain. There he had begun *Castilian Days*: "A group of masterly pictures," as King wrote later, "of a land and people with glory and greatness behind them; a land in the afternoon of life." Fields and Howells had run selections in the *Atlantic* the same time as King's Sierra sketches, while Hay's Pike County ballads—"Little Breeches" and others—had taken the country by storm. * King found in John Hay's writing a "diamond-like brilliancy" and in the man himself a comrade for life.

Meanwhile, on the first Friday of every month, spring or winter, came banquets of the Round Table Club, which King now joined, a score of the wittiest *bon vivants* in New York City. Godkin had started the club with a half-dozen other advocates of free trade: "a cause for which at that time"—so one of them suggested—"many people were ready to dine." And dine they did, seven times a year at the Knicker-

---

* In an unsigned sketch carried by *Scribner's Monthly*, VII (April, 1874), King told how Hay (pp. 737 f) had read the verses of Bret Harte on coming home in 1870 when "all the world" was talking about "The Heathen Chinee." Poems like "Chiquita" set Hay thinking.

He saw how infinitely finer and better than nature they were, but, having been born and brought up as a Pike himself, he saw that they were not nature. He wrote "Little Breeches" for his own amusement—at least we have heard this is his account of the matter—to see how a genuine Western feeling, expressed in genuine Western language, would impress Western people. . . . The ballads were written within a few days of each other; two of them in a single evening.

It followed that sometime in the 1870s Hay should have become a good friend of Harte, to whom he later wrote: "I do not know what heaven meant by creating so few men like King and you. The scarcity of you is an injury, not only to us, but to yourselves. There are not enough of you to go around, and the world pulls and hauls at you until you are completely spoiled" (Geoffrey Bret Harte, ed., *The Letters of Bret Harte*, p. 194).

bocker Club, while free trade was all but forgotten in talk that was its own reward. It was New York's answer to Boston and the Saturday Club; and here King could bandy persilflage with raconteurs like Hay or that "animated-prism" John La Farge—or Dr. S. Weir Mitchell, who was about to launch a second career, that of novelist—or William C. Whitney, the traction magnate—or William Graham Sumner, down from Yale.

Then too, on Saturday nights, came wonderful "pow-wows of roast oysters and ale," as John Fiske called meetings of the Century Club. This was the organization that Mark Twain had called "the most unspeakably respectable club in the United States, perhaps." It had sprung from the Sketch Club years before; the poet Bryant was its president, and it figured in New York fiction under thin disguises—as the Pyramid in the novels of Robert W. Chambers; or as the Philomathean in a tale by Paul Leicester Ford, the little hunchback marked for violent death. Here gathered an "aristocracy of art and literature"— or, as King himself remarked, "the rag-tag and bobtail of all there is best in our country." He himself had become a member in December 1874, on the recommendation of Hay and Quincy Ward.

He would remain a loyal Centurian for the rest of his life. He was a visitor at the clubhouse whenever he was in town, and a leader of effervescent talk in the billiard room or over oyster platters or Bass's ale. Few Centurians left so deep a trace upon the memories of their fellows as King. The artist Maitland Armstrong claimed that "no better talker ever lived, nor any with a readier wit." Nor had William Rainsford, rector of St. George's Church, ever "heard a conversationalist so versatile, so brilliantly clever"; he considered King more eloquent than Abram Hewitt, and that was saying much. The sweep of King's talk at the Century, according to Edward Cary, the club's necrologist, ranged "from the true rhythm of Creole gumbo to the verse of Theocritus, from the origin of the latest *mot* to the age of the globe, from the soar or slump of the day's market to the method of Lippo Lippi, from the lightest play on words to the subtlest philosophy"—a sweep of interests that seemed unending to many of his hypnotized clubmates, and always expressed with utmost felicity. "The trouble with King," exclaimed another Centurian, "is that his description of a sunset spoils the original." Still another compared his stories to tales from the Arabian Nights, and William Crary Brownell claimed that "inattention was impossible in his presence." James L. Ford, the journalist, recalled visits to the clubhouse where "I heard Clarence King talk as I never heard any one talk before or since. He could take the most commonplace topic and blow it into a succession of many-colored bubbles as a child blows soapsuds or a glass-blower fashions his material."

The effects were aided by King's voice, baritone, resonant, and perfectly modulated; and by his smile—"the sweetest smile" that Robert Underwood Johnson had "ever seen on the face of man." He had a way of heralding his sallies of wit—a tossing of the head, a twinkle in his eye, a clearing of his throat, followed by a spontaneous half-chuckle, half-snort through his nose. Then would come the witticism—often some sparkling gem which, like the bon mots of Tom Appleton, passed current among his friends.

King's wit seemed never to fail him. According to one who knew him best, he "diffused over every conversation in which he was engaged an iridescent mist of epigram and persiflage." The puns and quips, the jeweled phrases, the jokes and stories which fell from his lips were, evidently, legion, but as the Century had no Boswell, they were allowed to perish, leaving only a bright tradition.

When talking art with Quincy Ward or Eastman Johnson, John La Farge or Homer Martin; letters with Brownell, Edward Cary, or F. Hopkinson Smith; or national affairs with Joseph Choate, Whitelaw Reid, or William Maxwell Evarts—King always had something his friends wanted to hear, and they listened, as Cary remembered, "till the smoke-dimmed lights were turned down about us." William Rainsford, also, recalled such scenes long afterward: "When Clarence King crossed swords with Mr. Hitchcock of the *Sun*, . . . a circle would gradually gather round, till the room was full of silent men listening to Clarence King. It was a unique tribute paid to extraordinary brilliancy of wit, wisdom, and learning." On recalling those Century Saturday nights across the busy years, Nicholas Murray Butler, president of Columbia University, would reminisce: "If there was a group from which came shouts of laughter and merriment, it was pretty certain to be gathered about Clarence King . . ." There were other names on Butler's list, but King's led all the rest.

In commemorating King as raconteur after his death, John La Farge would recall the "poetic completeness" of his recitals:

Whenever he came back from a trip, things had happened to him which only the mind and eye of a constant enjoyer of human nature could have met with. If only he had written them out! They will probably have perished; and yet even the very names of the tales, as we have christened them, contained the proposition of picturesque and strange amusement. Who that has heard the story of the Hen and the Gondolier but has wished to see it written out to give an example of the serious chances of Western life?

King talked away whole books in his performances—friends who wrote were sure that he "threw away upon the transitory entertainment of a few what might have been the enduring delight of a multitude." No less a judge than John Hay would finally testify "to the literary treasures he squandered in his daily and nightly conversation"—how King

poured out in inexhaustible profusion his stores of fancy and invention. There were scores of short stories full of color and life, sketches of thrilling adventure, not less than half a dozen complete novels, boldly planned and brilliantly wrought out,—all ready for the type or the pen, which now—an infinite pity!—are only the stuff that dreams are made of.

Hay was convinced that if only King had buckled down and put on paper the literary wealth in his matchless talk, "he would have been a great writer."

Of course, King meant—or said he meant—to write his stories down. Once in Bronson's presence he said to Mrs. Howland, "Mother, I *must* write a novel." And when she wondered whether his years as a field geologist were proper training for creative writing, he countered: Why not? Geology depended on imagination—who could actually *see* any deeper into the earth than anyone else? King felt, as a matter of fact, that his life in the wilderness had been the "best training conceivable in constructive imagination."

His desire to write a novel had also been mentioned to James Osgood, who had succeeded Fields as publisher of *Mountaineering*. But "Alas!" King answered when Osgood asked about his progress: "The novel remains in a foetal state lacking only a little time to be born." He promised, though, to "gird himself for the story" as soon as *Systematic Geology* was off his hands. "Are you going to publish it?"

Osgood would have done so, likely enough, if King had ever sent a manuscript. Howells waited eagerly for the book, and afterward wrote, "I believe that [King] vaguely meant to write a great work of fiction. . . . He was supposed to have by him the beginning of a novel, and perhaps he had." But King kept the secret of what had, or what had *not*, been committed to paper, and Howells decided: "It was rather something to

bluff inquiring literary friends with, to dream over and fancy finishing."
Perhaps King felt that friends like Howells, so lyric in praise of *Mountaineering,* expected too much from his pen, and so he remained at strained relations with it. He once remarked "that after the *Scarlet Letter* New England was a sucked orange and the craftsmen were always slipping up upon the peel." Did he have a fear of slipping too?

Friends later spoke of a volume "nearly if not completed in MS," containing three stories of American women—"one of the Rocky Mountains, one of the Californian* and one of the semitropical type." It must have been among King's manuscripts that were lost or destroyed. All the fiction that would remain among his posthumous papers comprised some hastily scrawled paragraphs on life in a paddle-wheel steamer making for Greytown through "the liquid lap of the Caribbean." In addition, a few random notes suggested a tale of pioneers in the vein of *John Brent.* These were notes of a plains crossing, of "a man taking blooded horses to California," not unlike the trek King made with the Speers train in 1863. Though only scattered jottings, they hinted of lust on the desert, and of spiritual growth on the mountain heights, the hero wondering at the secret effects induced by the scene. A young mother camped not far from his bivouac arouses his feeling so strongly that he must cut his arm until the ideal of Motherhood and God prevails over his passion. An arrow drives by while he chases hostile Indians; its sound recalls a rattlesnake hiss or the tragic *sh-h-h* of Rachel, the celebrated French actress.

King's notebook mentioned a broken engagement, after which the hero sees the woman drown—sees "only her white hand above the water"; then her cry awakens him on the gray hills. Had King intended to deal with the story of Deany, whom he had renounced at Virginia City? Who knows? † But he must have planned unhappy moments for the novel; cruel symbols came to his mind—like the hawk with the bluebird in its talons, the hawk which lit on a bleaching skull or on the

---

* Whether this story of the Californian type was the work King fleetingly referred to as "Santa Rita" in later letters is not clear. It probably is not, for he projected "Santa Rita" as a major novel, hardly slight enough to be squeezed between two comrade stories in a single volume.

† And also, who knows what Henry Adams meant by his note to Henry Holt on January 7, 1899? "As for Clarence King," it reads, "why doesn't the tramp publish his own novels? He has a dozen in his desk." Concerning King's novels, however, it appears that Hay's remark on the stuff of dreams is more correct.

cross at the head of a miner's grave and tore its prey to pieces. Such were the hints of what King might have written but for the dearth of time which he was always to lament. Yet these were hardly the fragments which, if granted to the world, as Howells suggested, would have confirmed his early promise.

Why King never bothered to give his stories permanent form baffled his friends. Howells believed it stemmed from an unconcern with literary status that left King prone to renounce what sketches he had done rather than publish new ones. Bronson attributed the failure to sheer profusion of endowment—to "a mind so tireless and fertile that by the time it had sketched one brilliant literary picture another was clamoring for the recorded expression none ever got." Perhaps the problem was no more complicated than Lawrence Clark Powell's judgment that King was much too sociable and gregarious for the lonely work of writing or Rossiter Raymond's speculation that King's peerless talk in hours of conviviality "exercized and fatigued the same faculties [that it would have done] if it had been penwork." At any rate, King the talker seemed to "do in" King the writer. Raymond believed that a further hindrance to his literary activity was a lack of time and energy owing to his need for making money at geology and mining engineering. No doubt temperament was a factor, too. King was by nature an impulsive, romantically spontaneous writer and never seemed to develop the discipline for composition of a more plodding sort, especially editing and revising; and when spontaneity failed to work, the result was liable to be no writing at all. It was an irony that, at the same time, King had to contend with a discriminating critical faculty that would not let an imperfect work become public. He himself would later explain his unfulfilled promise by the naive or perhaps not wholly candid view that the door to pure literature seemed always shut in his face. That being the case, if indeed it were the case, he seemed to lack sufficient urge to kick the door down.* Yet King was not the only member of the Western School to thwart the hopes of early readers. Even the biggest medicine man of the Overland tribe had come on fallow days now.

* If destiny and literary sweat had made King a more dedicated author, it is likely that his permanent resistence to the writing act, what he lightly labeled "driving the quill," plus his penchant for talking, would have confirmed him in dictation, like Henry James in his later phase. Even at this point in the middle seventies his work with Bronson on the manuscript of *Systematic Geology* proved the congeniality of that method.

King saw much of Bret Harte in these middle seventies—a chastened Harte. After years of constant moving while burning talent to boil the pot, the former editor of the *Overland* had come to a temporary halt a few doors north of King's Fifth Avenue flat. It was not surprising that Harte, having lost his bearings, had disappointed his *Atlantic* friends, nor that they had refused to renew his sumptuous contract. He had turned to lecturing; his name had drawing power still, but most who heard him were forced to admit that he lacked dynamics on the plat-form, and that he had killed some of his better stories by laughing "before the audience had time to."

It would appear that for his talk on the "Argonauts of '49" he had bor-rowed details from *Mountaineering*; he had furbished up King's lynching story (". . . take your time, gentlemen," Harte's boys tell the jury; "only remember that we're waitin' for this yer room to lay out the corpse in!"). And he had rung a change on King's allusion to the Sierra muleskinner who had snorted, "Me swear? . . . No, I can't blaspheme worth a cuss. You'd just orter hear Pete Green. *He can exhort the impenitent mule.*"*

But in the end Harte had failed on the platform. And now he was failing with novels and plays—a broken man, whose life had turned nightmarish. King saw him become

the victim of absurd fancies which drove him to excesses as ridiculous as they were costly. He became firm in the belief that gaslights in rooms were poi-sonous; accordingly, he purchased fourteen French lamps at twenty-four dol-lars each—and presented them to the landlord in lieu of rent. . . . Whenever he moved . . . about all that the respective landlords had to show was a collection of furniture installed by Harte, installed but infrequently paid for.

Often Harte, unable to sleep, rose with dawn and, like King himself on occasion, roamed about the city in search of coffee or a cocktail. When King heard him speak of the odd characters then abroad, he urged Harte to put them on paper. But Harte had reached a stalemate; only the flimsiest journalese resulted, and in 1877, for "Mornings on the Avenues," the *Sun* paid only a hundred dollars—a sad fraction of what a Bret Harte story had once commanded. "I could not," he later

* Harte shifts the scene to a mountain camp meeting where a saintly sunbonnet sits in judgment on the teamster. "Why, Miss," the astonished skinner replies, "you don't call that swearing, do you? Why, you ought to hear Bill Jones exhort the impenitent mule!" *Tales of the Argonauts*, pp. xxviii–xxix.

wrote, ". . . again go through what I did in New York the last two years . . . I passed there."

Something drastic had to be done to salvage his fortunes, even his sanity—lest, as one friend remarked, "his creative faculty . . . be crushed and perish utterly." King joined a rescue movement, along with Hay and others. "Bret's friends," as one of the circle wrote the secretary of state from 23 Fifth Avenue, "have agreed that if he can be made consul to Nice he can be saved to literature." And they appealed to Secretary Evarts to grant him the appointment "as an aid to [the] country's literature." Nice proved unobtainable, and Harte's supporters had to settle for Crefeld, Germany. But Harte was grateful for even that, especially since his friends kept working in his behalf. "I at once pitched into Evarts and others," King advised him, concerning a drive to get him moved to Glasgow. "Evarts has been particularly busy, but is well inclined. I think the matter can be soon arranged"; as indeed it would be.

King's own struggles against ill-health continued. At times he felt recovered, only to suffer relapses. And then how sharply aware he was of the slower tempo of his life! Yet he valued what seemed to him a more philosophical outlook, and he wrote: "From the calmness of my present eddy in life I can take views of life which are more broadly true than I could in more active days." At such moments he yearned to settle down in respectable ease—to leave forever the frontier hurly-burly, as Bret Harte had renounced in 1871 what Mrs. Howland called "the pseudo-civilization of California."

King's mother enclosed her indictment of the West in a note to D. C. Gilman, a note congratulating him on his return to the East. Gilman had resigned as president of the University of California to found at Baltimore the first graduate faculty in America on German lines. He became president of the Johns Hopkins University on Washington's birthday 1876 and at once invited King to lecture there as a nonresident professor. King discussed the matter at Baltimore in March and found the prospect pleasing. Johns Hopkins was taking the best available men in America and Europe. But though the bid was renewed at later intervals, King was never free enough from other commitments to accept.

During the seventies he learned how much the arbiters of science valued his status. He had been elected in 1872 to the American

Philosophical Society; in 1874 to the American Institute of Mining Engineers; also in 1874 to the Geological Society of London; and three years later to the American Geographical Society. In 1877, also, he joined the American Association for the Advancement of Science; and as time went on he became an associate fellow of the American Academy of Arts and Sciences, a corresponding member of the Boston Society of Natural History, and a founding member of the Geological Society of America. But his most coveted honor had come in April 1876 when he was elected to the National Academy of Sciences. Membership indicated achievement of the highest distinction in American science, and King enjoyed the prestige of becoming the youngest man so honored during his own lifetime. Not that it made of him a zealous academician: he seldom attended meetings of the societies he belonged to, and never contributed to their proceedings. The politics of science had as little appeal to him as the politics of government, which he mistrusted—with reason, no doubt, in that devious year 1876.

As Henry Adams later observed, King was a loyal Republican "chiefly [from] love of archaic races, sympathy with the negro and Indian and corresponding dislike of their enemies." It was an attitude of King's whose intensity only grew with the succeeding years. * Eighteen seventy-six now brought much to provoke it, with the Freedmen's Bureau having become a mare's nest of unparalleled dimensions, and with the Sioux and the Cheyenne poised to cut Custer down with all of his men, a Pyrrhic victory for the Indians that would lead to endless grief. But the Centennial year held still other grave concerns, and not least among them was the gangrene in the civil service, which had never seemed more virulent, as the frauds of the Whiskey Ring came to light. King hoped for something better, and so on May 10 he joined the new Republican Reform Club of New York City "from a profound sympathy," he wrote, "with its efforts to purify the public service."

The club was only a part of a movement now gaining strength. Henry Adams, Carl Schurz, and Henry Cabot Lodge were nursing plans for a "party of the centre." Their efforts led on May 16 to an Independent Conference at the Fifth Avenue Hotel, and though the delegates

---

* King's profound feeling for the darker races was reflected in the interest he later took in an orphaned black boy from Alabama, who in his words "has had to work from the cradle up and [doesn't] even know his letters." King had him placed in the care of a black family in New Haven and remitted money to Brewer to pay for his board and lodging, clothes, and instruction from a tutor. See letter to Brewer, dated 15 May [1892] (HM 27833, Huntington Library).

endorsed no candidate for the White House, Charles Francis Adams, the principal speaker, advocated Benjamin Bristow, exposer of the whiskey frauds. If the Republican nomination could be seized for Bristow, the need for an Independent Party would disappear, and reformers could support the Republican ticket with greater assurance. Leaders like Schurz sought therefore to build up pressure for Bristow, and they made their influence felt at all the new Reform clubs.

King's enthusiasm flagged as this pattern grew clear, and he balked when the New York club named him as a delegate to work for Bristow's nomination. The panel listed men like Joseph Choate, John Jay, Alexander Hamilton, and Theodore Roosevelt. But King had no faith in Bristow's chance at Cincinnati; and he issued a public statement that the club, if pledged to Bristow before the convention, would, in his opinion, suffer defeat with him and thus "impair its effectiveness in the campaign." Unlike Schurz or Adams, he did not despise the leading contender, Blaine, who had once got up from his sick bed to vote for a bill in King's interest. "He stands by his friends," King told Howells. But when the nomination went to General Hayes instead, King was satisfied. He remained the steady Republican who—in the words of Adams again—"never for a moment conceived that there could be merit in other ideals."

Newport tugged at King in the meantime. He had gone there often, to be with Mrs. Howland and "the juniors"; and now he installed a part of his staff for the summer of 1876 in the old King house on the corner of Church and High streets; a house still "bright with the rich fabrics, grim with the weird carvings and the porcelains and fragrant with the strange scents of the Far East." The leisure of a former age had never quite abandoned the town. It had clung to its rotting wharves, its rows of gray old gambreled houses, even while it turned resort and became a watering place for wealth and fashion. It was a town of concentric circles, and King could move in most of them at will.

He needed only to walk down Church Street into the heart of Old Town to meet the haycarts of his youth. But a stroll along the walk on the other side of the island carried him past a chain of chateaux—the strongholds of an encroaching high society. Much of that part of Newport's population was Fifth Avenue, transplanted for the summer; many of the faces he had seen that winter in New York City. Here New York and Boston met; their smart sets mingled according to formulas crystallized in the pose of Ward McAllister.

Here, also, many an artist or intellectual came for the season—
George Bancroft, for example, to work at "Roseclyffe" on his history; or
Alexander Agassiz as busy as a coral polyp on marine biology at Castle
Hill; or John La Farge, who had installed himself at a cottage off Old
Beach Road, where he mixed meditation with his painting (for he was a
thinker and a writer as well as an artist) and guarded his solitude. King,
in whom La Farge fancied a resemblance to Dante Gabriel Rossetti,
valued the acquaintance more than Bancroft's, or even more than that
of Agassiz, and their friendship flourished here as cordially as in New
York.

Other mutual friends stood ready to jog the cultural conscience of
the island, and King could come and go in their interlacing circles. He
enjoyed the literary nights at Colonel Waring's, where one was likely to
meet the playwright Boker or the wit Tom Appleton, or General
Butler, as stentorian as ever, or Kate Field or Fanny Fern. Colonel
Waring was vice president of the Town and Country Club, a group for
literary teas, which Julia Ward Howe had named for its Boston proto-
type. Mrs. Howe, as magnetic as she was dowdy, had remained its
arbiter for half a decade; and many of its teas were held at her summer
retreat in Lawton's Valley. Science was not neglected on the programs;
one might hear, among the poets, an astronomer like Maria Mitchell, a
biologist like Agassiz, or an alienist like S. Weir Mitchell. On at least
one occasion King himself spoke on some aspect of the West.

Or there were dinners with another founder of the Town and Country—Thomas Wentworth Higginson, a strange alloy of milksop and
bravado, the result, as King suggested, of having been "sired by a
second-class Greek and damned by a Puritan mother." Colonel Higginson regretted in print that he had not been born a woman. But he
carried a saber scar on his chin for having tried to rescue Anthony
Burns from Boston Court House. He had snorted off to Kansas in the
days of John Brown, and then he had led a regiment of free black men
through the Civil War, and King honored him for his love of the Negro
race. The colonel had groomed Helen Hunt—who had just become
Mrs. Jackson—for a career that would reach its climax in *Ramona*; he
was also the unheeded mentor of a shy and unknown poet named Emily
Dickinson. King had brought him and H. H. Bancroft together, and
Higginson had fired an enthusiastic review of *Native Races* off to *Scribner's Monthly*. But he was even more enthusiastic over King's work; he
claimed that he turned to *Mountaineering* "when other books fail, and
there is no mood which it cannot meet"; nor could he recall any other

"book of personal travel" that seemed "so fascinating in every page." And soon he offered King the benefit of his long experience as a writer—suggestions for revising and perfecting the style of *Systematic Geology.*

Then in August 1876 something occurred of singular interest to the scientific coteries of America, the arrival of Thomas Henry Huxley to lecture on the theory of evolution. In London Gilman had told him of the fossils O. C. Marsh had brought to New Haven—the prehistoric horses, in particular, which Marsh had gathered from the John Day Basin, on a lead from King. Huxley had gone to Yale and there engrossed himself "in birds with teeth, and reptiles without 'em, to say nothing of other paleontological wonders which to a confirmed Evolutionist are worth all the journey across the Atlantic." Or so he reported to John Fiske on August 9, 1876. On the same day King received a wire from Marsh to come and join the conclave; and when he did, he encountered friends like Gilman and Joseph Leidy there, at Marsh's cluttered showplace of a house.

The Descent of Man had provoked a storm over Darwin's ideas. Opponents of evolutionary doctrine called it mere speculative theory, hardly science. But Huxley smiled on seeing Marsh's series of horse fossils. He could now declare that biological evolution was "a matter of fact and history as much as the monuments of Egypt." What did it matter that he had to change his lectures where they concerned the horse? That line of descent was proved beyond all doubt, and Huxley considered the specimens at Yale one of the most important collections in the world—indeed, he claimed, "the most wonderful thing I ever saw."

King had long valued Marsh's collection, joke as he might about it. He had warned Marsh about shipping such quantities of fossils down to sea level lest he shift the earth's center of gravity and throw the whole world out of kilter. He had no doubt that the angel Gabriel, in view of all the skulls in Marsh's possession, would give his first blast at Yale: "Think of the time he could save by starting here." And how strange it was that, among so many bones, Marsh had "never got a rib." But then, King liked to add, what use would Marsh have for a wife? For a dyed-in-the-wool collector like him only a harem would do.

Nevertheless, King had a stake in Marsh's fossils. So many had come from along the fortieth parallel that the holdings at Yale "constitute important proof of our geological conclusions." For that reason he desired to add to his report a monograph by Marsh on vertebrate paleontology, illustrated by numerous plates of fossils. Huxley had helped to choose from "the cream of the whole collection enough to fill one volume"; and the mail soon brought King a letter confirming his judgment of the specimens.

"It is of the highest importance to the progress of biological science," Huxley wrote, "that the publication of this evidence . . . should take place without delay."

That was the urging King needed. General Humphreys agreed. Marsh's proposed memoir on extinct birds with teeth—*Odontornithes*—received official sanction as Volume VII of the Fortieth Parallel Report; and when it finally appeared, Marsh's first book-length treatise, the aged and failing Darwin himself joined in the general praise. "Your work on these old birds," the great scientist wrote from across the Atlantic, "and on the many fossil animals of North America has afforded the best support to the theory of evolution which has appeared within the last twenty years."

It was a triumph for King as well as for Marsh.

Huxley's tour had made cultural history, and a few months later King remarked: "Huxley alone, among prominent evolutionists, opens the door . . . in his proposed evolutional geology" for a union of the truth in the two schools, uniformitarianism and catastrophism: "Looking back over a trail of thirty thousand miles of geological travel, and after as close a research as I am capable of, I am impelled to say that his far-sighted view precisely satisfies my interpretation of the broad facts of the American continent."

King had speculated hard as to the course and manner of evolution as he worked on *Systematic Geology*. When invited to speak at the Sheffield commencement on June 26, 1877, he took the occasion to give his views in a paper that he called "Catastrophism and the Evolution of Environment." The ceremony marked the thirty-first anniversary of the school, and a number of graduates had returned. Some assumed that King's address would anticipate the trend of *Systematic Geology* and serve as "the first expression . . . as to the bearings of his survey on the theory of science." He did not fail his audience on this score, although some were bothered by his bold conclusions. Even Marsh, as a mutual friend reported, "got very warm before King finished and used his fan vigorously."

The outdoor facts of Western geology had carried King to a view midway between uniformitarianism and outright catastrophism, or more accurately put, a view that regarded "geological history [as] a dovetailing together of the two ideas." His stand, if it had to be labeled, might be called "modified catastrophism." But then, he observed, "the admission of even modified catastrophism, namely, suddenly destructive, but not all-destructive change, is, of course, a downright rejection of strict uniformitarianism."* King recognized the consequence of that rejection, and he called it "nothing less than an ignited bomb-shell thrown into the camp of the biologists," who seemed to build complacently on a uniformitarian basis, presuming there was nothing in the geological record to disprove it.

Marsh fanned, but King went on. He conceded that most of the earth's history was uniformitarian in character. But he denied that uniformity was the sole law or that the present rate of terrestrial change was adequate to explain the grander features of Cordilleran history. These could be correctly accounted for only by granting that dynamic rates had sharply accelerated at intervals in the past, with catastrophic effects on all living things. His six-year exploration along the fortieth parallel bore witness to instance after instance of change in the earth's crust that had occurred with catastrophic rapidity—instances of tilting, upheaval, subsidence, faulting, and folding; and to this catalogue of crustal mega-contortion he added the massive volcanic extrusions of the Miocene and Pliocene that had innundated vast areas with molten lava. Last, he cited the climatic enormities of the Ice Age, culminating

*This aspect of King's thought bears a striking resemblance to the present-day concept of "punctuated equilibria" espoused by scientists who hold, much as he, that long intervals of slow and gradual geologic and biologic change have been "punctuated" by brief times of extremely rapid, even catastrophic change. In support of this position, Stephen Jay Gould, coauthor of the Eldredge-Gould model of "punctuated equilibria," describes "modern geology as a blend of Lyell and the catastrophists" and declares that much of the "current advocacy for punctuational change represents nature reasserting herself against the blinders of our previous gradualistic prejudice. Geology, more than any other discipline, has been mired in this prejudice. Lyell put us there for a host of complex reasons that had little to do with the empirical world as he observed it. We should acknowledge his influence by recognizing that some processes do tick along in the gradualistic tempo. But we should reject gradualism as a restrictive dogma. Punctuational change, with rapid flips between stable states, may characterize more of our world. As geologists, we should pay special attention to the punctuations in our record, for we have systematically ignored them and may well have missed the dominant tempo of natural change" ("Toward the Vindication of Punctuational Change," in *Catastrophism and Earth History: The New Uniformitarianism*, ed. William A. Berggren and John A. Van Couvering [Princeton, N.J., 1984], pp. 13 and 31).

in floods of such incredible magnitude that the epoch could aptly be termed the "age of water catastrophe." After every cataclysm, as he read the geologic record, had come some change in existing species. "I confidently assert," ran his argument, "that no American geologist will be able to disprove the law that in the past every one of the great breaks in the column of life coincides with datum points of catastrophe." During such crucial times only the most plastic forms of life could survive. "When catastrophic change burst in upon the ages of uniformity," he declared, "and sounded in the ear of every living thing the words 'Change or die,' plasticity became the sole principle of salvation."

He cited, as a prime example, the horse whose fossil bones had been assembled by Marsh and checked by Huxley:

These two authorities, whose knowledge we may not dispute, assert that the American genealogy of the horse is the most perfect demonstrative proof of derivative genesis ever presented. Descent they consider proved, but the fossil jaws are utterly silent as to what the cause of the evolution may have been.

I have studied the country from which these bones came, and am able to make this suggestive geological commentary. Between each two successive forms of the horse there was a catastrophe which seriously altered the climate and configuration of the whole region in which these animals lived. Huxley and Marsh assert that the bones prove descent. My own work proves that each new modification succeeded a catastrophe. And the almost universality of such coincidences is to my mind warrant for the anticipation that not very far in the future it may be seen that the evolution of environment has been the major cause of the evolution of life; that a mere Malthusian struggle was not the author and finisher of evolution; but that He who brought to bear that mysterious energy we call life upon primeval matter bestowed at the same time a power of development by change, arranging that the interaction of energy and matter which make up environment should, from time to time, burst in upon the current of life and sweep it onward and upward to ever higher and better manifestations. Moments of great catastrophe, thus translated into the language of life, become moments of creation, when out of plastic organisms something newer and nobler is called into being.

Whitelaw Reid published the address in the *Tribune,* and it later appeared in the *American Naturalist* under the shortened title, "Catastrophism and Evolution." At Godkin's request Henry Adams reviewed it for the *Nation,* and King's ideas prefigured a major theme in *The Education,* a strand in Adams's stark philosophy of history. Moreover,

King's statement added fuel to the debate on evolution that raged on both sides of the Atlantic. It also served as a topic for argument in itself, and started G. K. Gilbert planning "half a dozen controversial papers." Uniformitarianism might be overdone in geological circles, Gilbert agreed, "but King is certainly 'out' in the opposite direction at several points." King found himself also castigated by a spinner of Darwinian theology at Princeton, Dr. James McCosh, who countered with "archaic argument full of truth and rich in fallacy." The paper impressed the botanist Coulter, and at Harvard C. S. Peirce, the founder of Pragmatism, compared King's theory, in significance, with Darwin's reading of Natural Selection and Lamarck's "inheritance of acquired characteristics." It seemed to Peirce that probably all three modes of evolution had been at work in shaping species, but King's, he was inclined to think, had been "the most efficient." * Brewer would claim, however, that with the passing of time King modified these views, though in what particular respect was not specified.

King could now advise General Humphreys that the work of the Fortieth Parallel Survey was all but finished. During the past twelve months he had seen three publications through the press. First had come Zirkel's memoir on the composition and structure of the various kinds of rock in the survey's collection. It was numbered Volume VI of

* "A third theory of evolution," Peirce wrote, "is that of Mr. Clarence King. The testimony of monuments and of rocks is that species are unmodified or scarcely modified under ordinary circumstances, but are rapidly altered after cataclysms or rapid geological changes. Under novel circumstances, we often see animals and plants sporting excessively in reproduction, and sometimes even undergoing transformations during individual life, phenomena no doubt due partly to the enfeeblement of vitality from the breaking up of habitual modes of life, partly to changed food, partly to direct specific influence of the element in which the organism is immersed. If evolution had been brought about in this way, not only have its single steps not been insensible, as both Darwinians and Lamarckians suppose, but they are furthermore neither haphazard on the one hand, nor yet determined by an inward striving on the other, but on the contrary are effects of the changed environment, and have a positive general tendency to adapt the organism to that environment, since variation will particularly affect organs at once enfeebled and stimulated. This mode of evolution, by external forces and the breaking up of habits, seems to be called for by some of the broadest and most important facts of biology and paleontology, while it certainly has been the chief factor in the historical evolution of institutions as in that of ideas, and cannot possibly be refused a very prominent place in the process of evolution of the universe in general." *Collected Papers* of C. S. Peirce, Vol. VI (*Scientific Metaphysics*), p. 17, par. 17 (6.17).

the Fortieth Parallel Report. Volume IV had quickly followed it, composed of Ridgway's *Ornithology* and two papers on invertebrate fossils, the keys to dating and correlating strata. The first of these papers on paleontology was by Fielding Bradford Meek, the other by James Hall and Robert Parr Whitfield. In addition, Emmons and Arnold Hague had finished *Descriptive Geology*, a full account of the geographical and geological features encountered along the explored belt, arranged like the atlas sheets in a sequence from east to west. Its publication as Volume II in the spring of 1877 had left Hague free to work on the rock and mineral cabinets and make the thousands of specimens ready for transfer to the National Museum; "which done," King joked, "American petrography is safe." After June, he alone remained on the rolls of the corps, and *Systematic Geology* hovered on the verge of completion.

To supplement his own observations, King had drawn extensively from the work of his entire corps for the raw facts that he fused into his statement; but "all deductions are my own," he claimed. In the main, his method followed the sequence of geological time; he started at the base of the geological column and marshaled the important facts he and his colleagues had gathered on all successive formations. At the same time he made a consistent effort to correlate data from different areas and to "construct a continuous piece of geological history." He had compressed the whole into fewer than eight hundred pages.

The first of King's eight chapters served as a foreground; the four which followed traced the transformations of the region, as recorded in more than 120,000 feet of rock laid down through four major eras—from the Archean to the Cenozoic. Chapter Six contained his stratigraphical summary. The entire scope was so vast—involving as it did the longest section any geologist had yet worked out with comparable care—that King could claim without fear of contradiction: "It has rarely fallen to the lot of one set of observers to become intimate with so wide a range of horizons and products. . . . This Exploration has actually covered an epitome of geological history."

The pressure of immense overloads eroded away before the coming of the Paleozoic sea, King reasoned, had metamorphosed sedimentary beds of the Azoic Age into crystalline schists. These along with granites, gneisses, and quartzites made up the Archean bedrock, sixty thousand feet thick, as King's corps had discovered along the fortieth parallel.

King needed many pages to record the Archean outcrops there and to fix their stratigraphical relations. But unconformities always distinguished them from the Paleozoic strata, so that he could reconstruct a plausible topography for the close of the Archean Era. It consisted, he wrote, of "a great Archean mountain system built up of at least two sets of non-conformable strata," and these he referred to Laurentian and Huronian horizons. The lofty ranges of crumpled strata were sculptured into broad, smooth forms and were not sharply furrowed by erosion, like the mountain chains of later eras, although mechanical dislocations had produced astounding rifts and precipices. Still, according to King's spectacular reconstruction, the configuration of the Archean ranges within the area surveyed agreed in a general way with that of the present Cordilleras. Orographical movements along lines of weakness coinciding with the Archean chains and the faults therein had largely determined both the area and structure of the modern system.

Yet all traces of change between Archean and Paleozoic times had been wiped out along the fortieth parallel. When the geologic record next divulged its secrets, a profound ocean washed against a continent that had lain west of the present land of Nevada. Its waters extended eastward over pre-Cambrian ranges and broke only around the island summits of the Wasatch and the Medicine Bow. For undetermined ages great east-flowing rivers bore detritus down from the western land and covered the ocean floor. Nearly forty thousand feet of sediments accumulated at the western edge of the sea, but tapered to thirty-two thousand in the Wasatch zone and to only a thousand in Colorado and Wyoming. These deposits of the Paleozoic were divided by King into four groups—first, "a purely detrital Cambrian"; second, "the great limestone series," whose thickness of eleven thousand feet suggested "enormous intervals of the continual sway of profound ocean"; third, the Weber Quartzites, ranging up to ten thousand feet thick; and last, two thousand feet of limestones from the Upper Coal Measures. He summed the era up as "two periods of mechanical detritus, interrupted by one and followed by another period of deep-sea lime-formation."

Then a severe orographical change had occurred; strangely, the continent west of the Paleozoic shore line in Nevada sank, instead of rising higher, after having discharged detritus for unknown ages into the eastern sea. That ocean floor now rose and became dry land as far as the Wasatch, and in its turn the new Mesozoic continent discharged detritus into the ocean, westward, thus reversing a process that had lasted for an era. By the close of the Jurassic Period, twenty thousand feet of sediments had accumulated. Then occurred a sudden upthrust, a lifting and folding of the ocean floor; and the shore line receded as far as the western base of the present Sierra Nevada. The lateral force of the earth's shrinking crumpled and crushed Triassic and Jurassic deposits in a wrack of almost indistinguishable folds, and a long chain of mountain islands rose from the ocean, the mountains known now as the Coast Range.

No disturbance of comparable fury had racked the area east of the Wasatch. There a shallow sea continued to billow east as far as Kansas, overlaying Carboniferous beds with thick Cretaceous sediments.

But with the close of the chalk period came "one of the most important orographical movements of the whole Cordilleran history." The entire interior of the continent rose. The Great Plains replaced the inland sea; the Uinta and the Wasatch Mountains—for an extreme example of how King read the geologic record—towered no less than thirty and forty-four thousand feet respectively—over five and eight miles above sea level. These heights represented no gradual uplift in King's scheme of things, but an upheaval both sudden and necessarily catastrophic. Such a heaven-assaulting upthrust was in diametric contrast to the views of Powell, who argued that erosion had kept pace with a slow elevation of the mountains, thus accounting for the passage of the Green through the heart of the Uintas at Ladore. With the ranges reared so loftily in King's picture, he saw the Eocene as consequently a time of intense erosion. Enormous rivers swept their scourage down into four fresh-water lakes, which successively filled the Vermillion Basin during the period. Two similar lakes later coexisted through the Miocene, one filling a counterpart of the present Great Basin—the other, vast portions of the Great Plains, especially after the sinking there which ushered in the Pliocene.

Then had come the baleful fires which King had painted in his sketch "The Range"; volcanic chimneys blazing along the coast of America, like a system of titanic beacons; molten avalanches seething from innumerable ruptures along the ranges and across the plateaus. King had reserved his seventh chapter for a close analysis of the products from those massive eruptions; his studies confirmed the law which his friend Ferdinand von Richthofen had laid down in 1866 on "the periodic succession of volcanic rock" and enabled him to give a slight refinement of its statement. He also framed a hypothesis to account for subterranean fusion and for the creation of all the various kinds of lava. But he declined to go further in that direction till more was known of the internal physics of the earth; and as it was, he wrote, "I have trodden far enough, perhaps too far, on the thin crust of physical conjecture." But he had raised a problem that was to pique his curiosity for the rest of his life.

Meanwhile, prior to Chapter Seven, King touched on crustal movements which, as the Pliocene ended, had tilted the Great Plains south and east, giving drainage to the sea. The Great Basin, farther west, buckled in the middle, and two depressions were formed, one near the Wasatch Range, the other near the Sierra Nevada. Both collected meltwater as it rushed down from the systems of glaciers which grew on the mountain heights, contemporary with the continental ice sheets. It was for the westward lake that King had chosen the name Lahonton, while confirming Gilbert's choice of Bonneville for the other, the immense forerunner of the Great Salt Lake, and from his study of these Pleistocene bodies of water, or their remnants, King was able to reconstruct the region's climactic history during the Quarternary: two wet cycles of raging torrents dividing three of desiccation. The last dry cycle, of course, had continued through the present.

King closed his text, in Chapter Eight, with Orography, or the nature of mountain building, as he had found it in the regions of his exploration. It was a difficult chapter that worked out a correlation of "mechanical history" with the stratigraphic record; and having remained "on the ragged edge" of it for months, he finally interrupted it for the sake of his health and for a trip to his cattle ranges in the West.

But the manuscript of *Systematic Geology*, described by a later historian as "only a trifle less dramatic than Genesis," was ready for type by early 1878. And when the volume was published the following autumn, in a sumptuous format with chromolithographs from Munger paintings and monochromes of O'Sullivan photographs, it won swift acclaim. "Mr. King's graceful pen never showed itself to better advantage," the *American Journal of Science* declared; and G. K. Gilbert would soon inform President Hayes, "Few American geologists have undertaken as wide a range of theoretic and economic studies [as Clarence King] and none have acquitted themselves with greater credit."

There was wide agreement that *Systematic Geology*, in its splendid "get-up," represented the high-water mark of government publishing in America, and the book quickly became a model for official monographs to follow. In the *Nation* Henry Adams suggested its reissue in a less expensive format as a textbook for schools of technology, thus foreshadowing the coming generation of geology students who would be required to read excerpts from King, along with Dana's *Manual*. "Our government has produced much excellent scientific work," Adams wrote, "and has gained a high reputation for its publications; but if it has produced anything more creditable than this survey, we have not yet seen it." President Rogers of M.I.T. had no doubt that King would take rank among the most distinguished of scientific explorers, and in James Hall's opinion he had "earned for himself a position among geologists second to no man in the country." Actually, by 1879 King was fast approaching the zenith of his scientific career, though his prestige as a scientist would persist through fallow days, with the reputation of *Systematic Geology* holding firm. After his death Edward Cary the literary critic would rate his cross section of the western Cordilleras as "probably the most important single contribution [yet] made to the scientific knowledge of the continent." At the same time Emmons would argue with partisan enthusiasm that King's treatise was very likely the best "summary of the great truths of geology . . . since the publication of Lyell's *Principles*."

Years later Herman LeRoy Fairchild would suggest that the systematic study of the West since 1867 had produced probably "the most brilliant chapter in the entire history of geology," and King's name was prominent among those he mentioned as responsible for the achievement. In 1933 George P. Merrill, head curator of geology at the National Museum, would cite "*Systematic Geology* [as] masterly," adding that "no more thrilling picture of the growth of the cordilleran country has ever been written." Advances in science, however, were to date some of King's contributions; successors in the study of the fortieth parallel regions would reorder various of his stratigraphical determinations; and as time went on, subsequent geologists would cite his statements less and less in their papers, especially after those on whom he had exerted personal influence had passed from the scene. But advances made by later researchers could not displace King's book as a classic in its field, nor could growing silence about it erase its significance in the development of American geology. It meant, rather, that what remained of value in King's book had passed into the common content of the subject. *

* Mustered here are the opinions of a few representative scholars who, subsequent to Merrill, have commended King's contributions. In 1943 Merle Curti wrote in *The Growth of American Thought*, p. 505, that "King's work in revealing to the scientist the nature and significance of many hitherto unknown regions in the mountain West was of first importance." Carroll and Mildred Fenton retained King on their popular roster of those who tower over the field of earth sicence—see *Giants of Geology* (1952). In the opinion of the Fentons he was one of those pioneers who had "exerted a general

influence upon geologic progress" (p. ix). In *Science in the Federal Government* (1957) A. Hunter Dupree recognized that King had "adopted unprecedentedly high standards" and that "from his work a comprehensive view of the geologic hstory of the mountain region of the West emerged. Although he paid attention to the mining industry, King's real aim and real triumph was in pure geology" (p. 196). In 1962 Richard A. Bartlett (*Great Surveys of the American West*, pp. 207–08) pointed out, "King felt that his scientific conclusions were safe, and for the most part they have withstood the test of time. . . . King's *Systematic Geology* remains to this day a classic in the field of historical geology." Four years later William H. Goetzmann, in *Exploration and Empire*, pp. 463–64, called it the "great synthesis of Western geology," which had at last discovered "the Great Basin in all its complex history . . . and incorporated [it] into the sophisticated world of science." Then in 1982 J. W. H. Monger and G. A. Davis underscored the basic soundness of King's treatise in the paper "Evolving Concepts of the Tectonics of the North American Cordillera" which they contributed to *Frontiers of Geological Exploration of Western North America.* It was their contention that "Cordilleran tectonic studies were firmly established by Clarence King, who in 1878 recognized the long evolution of the Cordillera" and deduced "the major events of Cordilleran history." They observed that in subsequent years "King's discoveries were investigated, elaborated and, in some cases, refuted, but the picture of Cordilleran tectonics he presented is readily recognizable today" (pp. 215–17). No doubt the latest edition of the *Encyclopaedia Britannica* intended some kind of consensus in its current opinion that *Systematic Geology* "is considered a masterpiece." It is an appraisal not universally shared, however. The two principal biographers of Powell, for example, have downgraded King's scientific achievement in comparison with that of their subject. William Culp Darrah, in *Powell of the Colorado*, p. 251n, held that King is "generally overrated as a geologist"—a judgment that Mr. Darrah reaffirmed in our long conversation at Gettysburg about King and Powell and the Western surveys. In *Beyond the Hundredth Meridian*, p. 388, Wallace Stegner has taken the similar position that King's geology, like that of Hayden, "has suffered much more . . . with time" than the work of either Powell, Gilbert, or Dutton.

13

Cattle Baron

The years of King's devotion to the Fortieth Parallel Survey had seen the Cattle Empire spread across the Great Plains. Grass was the natural basis for the industry; the High Plains north of Texas held the lushest grasslands on the continent; and herds of Texas cattle—tall and rangy longhorns—had begun a steady movement north. Abilene, Kansas, became a cow town in 1867, the year that King had launched his exploration; the year, too, that he had prophesied that "the vast plains will produce something better than buffalo, namely beef." By 1868 the Loving-Goodnight trail had pushed through Colorado, as far as Cheyenne.

Cheyenne was sprawled on a plain that swept in swells to the westward mountains; a plain wrapped in a gray-green monotone of grass, bunchgrass, buffalo grass on which the longhorn "Southerners" fed and grew fat. By 1869 the territory had found a bonanza business. Two years later, from sixty to eighty thousand head of stock grazed the rangeland near Cheyenne, and Henry Adams found the countryside too civilized, too full of "farms" and cattle, for a wilder-than-Siberia summer.

So Adams had roughed it up to Emmons's camp in the High Uintas, while King remained on the Laramie Plain, to meet his former field assistant N. R. Davis. Both had watched the cattle business spreading across the plains; both had perceived a golden chance for profits; and from their meeting was born a partership to raise cattle on that sea of grass, a firm that Davis undertook to manage. They styled it N. R. Davis & Co., not that Davis was at first a full partner. King had furnished the initial capital of $8,380, a shoestring start; but the firm weathered blizzards and the panic of 1873, and the opportunity for profits in the years ahead seemed extraordinary. A steer worth five dollars at birth would gain in value up to forty-five dollars, or even sixty dollars, after cropping grass on the open range for four or five years at practically no expense to its owner. "That is why our cattlemen grow rich," exulted the *Breeder's Gazette*.

King was not a frequent guest at Stonehenge, the ranch which Davis had claimed on Owl Creek, some twelve miles out of Cheyenne. King had confidence in his associate; he had soon accepted him as an equal partner, and let him run the business with a free hand. To the casual observer Davis *was* the business. The editor of the *Cheyenne Sun* was, therefore, not quite sure how much his readers knew of "the celebrated Geologist," whether indeed they knew at all that he was a stockman of the region. "Mr. King," he wrote for their enlightenment, "is a much younger looking man than is commonly supposed, and quite stoutly built. As we saw him starting out yesterday for his ranch we could not see why he should not grow up with the country and become one of Wyoming's cattle kings."

That was in 1877, the date of King's vacation from *Systematic Geology,* the visit he liked to call his "Rocky Mountain summer." He had come for the benefit, first, of the mineral waters at Manitou Springs and then of "strenuous rest" on the ranges where his livestock roamed. He could be proud of the strides the **ND** ranch had made in the years since Davis had knocked together a log cabin near the source of Owl Creek, just south of the Colorado line. Stonehenge was known now as one of the finest ranches near Cheyenne, with a string of blooded horses and herds of longhorns that mingled with Iliff stock along the forks of Crow Creek; holdings that Davis had enlarged the year before by buying more "Southerners" up from Texas.

A spacious frame house with wide piazzas had superseded the first rude cabin, now a bunkhouse for the **ND** hands. Stables stood south of the house, and near them were corrals with walls of mortar. There were no enclosed pastures. Fenceless prairie rolled away in every direction, with grazing for the herds and for Hayden's *mulada,* which Davis wintered every year. Centered there on Owl Creek, a brook narrow enough to spring across, the partnership of King and Davis prospered; and small wonder, with all the grass.

The first year had brought increases of nearly 25 percent on King's investment. Prospects had looked so bright in the summer of 1872 that he and Davis had not hesitated to expand the firm. There had been no trouble in finding the means; both Emmons and Gardiner were ready to put their savings into cattle, and together with F. H. Sheldon, who had read barometer for the survey, they had made a purse of fifteen thousand dollars and King had signed contracts with them in August 1872.

Under the terms agreed upon, N. R. Davis & Company had bought more Texas cattle, ranching them along with **ND** stock, though under separate brands. * The three investors retained ownership to the cash extent of their investment, but the company had control for a five year period. At the end of that time Davis and King were entitled to 50 percent of the accumulated increase.

The arrangement had been a happy one—so lavish in gains that two hard winters (1872 and 1876) had made little difference. But now the contracts had expired, and the time had come for a settlement, as soon as the roundup could be finished. King and Davis had decided to make an outright purchase of the **ESG** herd (as they termed the Emmons-Sheldon-Gardiner cattle), and all agreed on a leading stockman to referee the transaction—a Harvard man named Thomas Sturgis. The head of Sturgis, Lane & Goodall, one of the largest cattle companies in Wyoming, Sturgis currently served as secretary of the Wyoming Stock Growers Association.

The roundup had begun when King arrived for his Rocky Mountain summer. The *Greeley Tribune* reported in August 1877 that Davis was "busily engaged with quite a force of herders in tallying the whole [ESG] herd." **ND** hands were sweeping the range from end to end, and Sturgis supervised the tally of stock which they corralled. They had soon rebranded more than six thousand head, a figure that did not include the beef steers. These were tallied in the fall, when gathered for shipment—fifteen hundred of them, as the count proved. **ND** punchers drove them to Cheyenne, and on to the trains for Chicago, sixteen head to a car.

When Sturgis had finished his "judgment of the beef," Gardiner wrote: "We were thoroughly satisfied with the way in which the trust was executed." It brought the investors profits of over 180 percent; and the firm of King and Davis became sole owner of all remaining stock; which made it, according to the Greeley paper, "the largest cattle owner in Weld County." Already the income King received from cattle far exceeded his salary from the government, but he was content to plow much of it back into the business. †

There could be no doubt that grazing had long since recovered from the crash of 1873. Publicists were now writing of "bovine el dorados . . . beef bonanzas." It became a fad for young men from Ivy League col-

---

*Each a combination of the King-Davis brand (**ND**) and the last initial of an investor—$^{ND}_E$, for instance, in the case of Emmons's share of the herd.

† According to the Journal of N. R. Davis for 1871–79 (Rollins Collection, Princeton University Library), King's share of profits for 1878 amounted to $30,249.

leges, backed by money out of Boston or New York, to take up ranches on the High Plains and run herds for market in Chicago. "There is," King said, "a fascination about [the] wild, roving, adventurous life of a ranchman which . . . captivates young men of birth and education, especially when there is money in the business."

It was easy enough for King to arrange for capital in the East to underwrite as a grazing partner some young man like Edgar Beecher Bronson, his secretary since 1874, when John Hay had brought the two together. King had galvanized Bronson with stories of the West— "tales," as the latter described them, "to fire the love of adventure latent in most youngsters; tales that fired mine and turned the tables of my life, turned me from newspaper work then my trade and made me mount a train the very day after my work with him was finished, ticketed straight away to Cheyenne." Bronson had reached Owl Creek in June 1877. At King's request Davis taught the young man the rudiments of the cattle business, and King soon felt the moment had come to launch another ranching firm, with money largely from Peter Cooper. At once the question of where to locate posed itself.

The range was overstocked below the North Platte River. But off to the northeast stretched the ancestral lands of the Sioux and Cheyenne. Only a handful of white men had gone there, besides the miners in the Black Hills. But there were a half a hundred kinds of grass just waiting for cattle now that the buffalo were disappearing. The government had signed a treaty with the Sioux that pushed them back into the Bad Lands and opened their hunting grounds for exploitation.

King knew that bands of warriors still roamed the territory, men embittered by the treaty. So there would be plenty of risk in taking cattle there, but nowhere could better grass be found; wondrous grass, wrote a cattleman of Cheyenne: "Nothing but grass and more grass, the blue joint with ripening heads, good as corn for fattening, and mossy stretches of buffalo grass curling closely to the ground and making unexcelled winter feed." King therefore made plans with Bronson for him to pioneer new ranges in that last frontier.

He instructed the young man to buy a herd, and Bronson picked Alex Swann, of the Duke of Wellington nose, to learn from, for Swann was considered the canniest buyer in Cheyenne. An education followed, of which Bronson wrote:

Everywhere that Alex went the tenderfoot went too. Every herd Swann examined, I was seldom out of earshot. . . . Finally a day came when he refused a bunch about my size (716 cows, each with a calf by its side) on a difference of a dollar a head with the seller, and when he was gone . . . I got the seller to split the dollar and bought the bunch.

It was a herd that had been lately driven from Utah.

Bronson took possession in September 1877 at Cooper Lake on the Laramie Plain northeast of Cheyenne, and with a few experienced hands he began to drive the herd through the Laramie Hills. The drive was a heavy responsibility for a youth of twenty, and so it was hardly strange that King's own movements corresponded so closely with Bronson's trail. King later advised General Humphreys that on September 18 he had undertaken a prolonged trip north of his former work, "from the region of Fort Fred Steele eastward to the Niobrara River," a trip that took him over some of the most impressive fossil beds of the West, those through which Buffalo Bill Cody had lately guided O. C. Marsh on the expedition from Yale.

On the trail Bronson branded the herd with Three Crows and earmarked the cattle at the same time. Then he drove them across the southeast corner of Wyoming to a winter camp on Cottonwood Creek. There he had an exasperating brush with rustlers and was obliged to trail seventy-six cows as far as Deadwood, where he demanded—and collected—payment for the entire lot. Then King told him to leave the stock on Cottonwood Creek under the weather eye of a "thoroughbred old Texan brush-splitter," and the two returned to New York City to put the last touches on *Systematic Geology*. By January 1878 they had the manuscript in final shape, ready for submission to General Humphreys, and King sent Bronson back to Wyoming with instructions to find a permanent range.

With a single companion the young man scouted for sixty days without meeting another human being, and King reported to the chief of engineers that he was "out of mail communications in Wyoming somewhere on the Niobrara." Bronson trailed down that stream, the Running Water of the Sioux, then veered north to the White River. There in the northwest corner of Nebraska he found the range that King had sent him to find—six hundred square miles of "rolling hill country, open timbered with pines like a park; with springs of clear, cold water breaking out in almost every gulch; with tall, white limestone cliffs to north and south that gave the valley perfect shelter against winter storms, and all the land matted with juicy buffalo grass." Bronson claimed twenty miles along the head of the White River and twenty miles along the Niobrara; he located the home ranch on a small creek a few miles south of Fort Robinson. That was a wiser choice than he knew at the time. Some scourge—smallpox no doubt—had destroyed an Ogallala camp there long ago, and left the place tabooed as *Wi-nogi-waka-pala*—that is, as Ghost or Dead Man Creek. It was thus safe from marauders. He would later claim to be the first man, bar one, to have run cattle in "what had been the favorite home camping ground of the main band of Ogallala Sioux."

Bronson recorded the Three Crows brand at Sidney, Nebraska, which he described as "a hell-hole." Then he regathered the herd and drove it to the new location, the range surrounding Deadman Ranch. He built living quarters there, with a stable under the same roof, and there he kept horses constantly saddled in case of attack. From time to time he would send King word of his operations, including his touch and go with cattle thieves, and King concluded that his protégé had "a special talent" for the cattle game.

Bronson justified his confidence and, like Davis, assumed a respected place among the cattle bosses who looked to Cheyenne as the capital of their domain. King had him join the Wyoming Stock Growers Association, of which Davis was soon to become the president, and both helped to organize the Cheyenne Club, whose name would carry around the world. It became the center of sociability for the area, especially after a luxurious brick clubhouse was built, with a billiards room, dining hall, and comfortable sleeping quarters. It pleased King that his partners maintained a paid-up membership for him, and he sometimes stayed at the clubhouse during his later visits to Cheyenne.

The cattle boom continued. King believed that he had passed from the financial insecurity of science to the possibility of a fortune. And so enthusiastic grew his accounts of Davis and Bronson's operations that capital became available in larger amounts. Abram S. Hewitt of the Cooper-Hewitt iron works was interested in the Deadman Ranch. And neither Dull Knife's bloody escape from Fort Robinson nor the last stand of his followers on the Three Crows range could upset the arrangements King had made for forming a New York corporation for further underwriting the Three Crows herd.

King received a long letter from Bronson about the uprising—how Dull Knife's band had been starved in an effort to break resistance; how the Cheyenne had leaped through the prison windows, overpowered the guard, and dashed in a body through the night, warriors and squaws and children; how they had run toward Dead Man Creek to seize the Three Crows horses and were turned away from that goal only by pursuing soldiers; how they were then hunted down and wounded or killed almost to a man because they would not surrender. "What a story of butchery and disgrace," Bronson concluded.* And he asked King, after detailing Dull Knife's provocations: "Can you who know so much of the Indian imagine anything which would sooner arouse his simple, suspicious mind to distrust of the good faith and fair promises of his captors, and impel him to the first act of desperation which opportunity should offer?"

The account made King so indignant that he copied the story out and sent it off to Carl Schurz, now secretary of the interior; "only leaving out," he said, "such mention of the ranch as might fix the letter on [my man]." News of the trouble did not bother Hewitt, however, and in 1879 the Lakota Company, Ltd., was formed, capitalized at one hundred thousand dollars. Hewitt and Edward Cooper, the mayor of New York City, subscribed two-thirds of the stock between them, while King and friends like Gardiner and Raphael Pumpelly took the rest, King's share amounting to ten percent. The arrangement permitted Bronson to enlarge the Three Crows herd until it numbered about eight thousand head, both Texas stock and "Westerners."

In the meantime ND herds grew even faster. Quincy Shaw—the Shaw who had summered with Francis Parkman on the Oregon Trail in 1846—had listened to King's plea for backing and had approved it to the extent of $125,000, a sum he placed to the credit of N. R. Davis & Company late in 1878. Shaw's brother-in-law Alexander Agassiz provided one hundred thousand at the same time, while Gardiner added twenty thousand more. The money, King felt sure, would be doubled in three or four years, with handsome profits for himself and Davis, though somehow it seemed a bit too easy. Would such swiftly accumulated wealth be good for the moral sense of a Christian gentleman? It disturbed King to watch the growing materialism of the times.

"Ours is a vulgar, but remarkably active civilization," he would write, with the further observation that it was given over "to the energetic pursuit of personal prosperity and the struggle for material good." His conclusion was that "of all ages and all lands this is the one where for the mind's and the soul's sake a brilliant struggle must be made to stem

---

*Bronson would retell the story of the Cheyenne Outbreak in considerable detail in Chapter VII of *Reminiscences of a Ranchman*, a book he would dedicate in 1908 "to the memory of Clarence King."

the almost irresistible current." But how could one square convictions like that with a personal battle for wealth?

"Clare and I," wrote Gardiner,

have had to face this matter in a practical form, passing as we have done from the humble pecuniary inheritance of science to cattle kingdoms in the West: and at our last meeting in New York we pledged to one another the promise that however rich we may become we will by simple living, and use of our money for others, do our part to stem the tide of selfish extravagance.

So much for conscience.

King knew that herds had been accumulating on the ranges of the Far Northwest, descendants of cattle driven across the plains; and having secured capital, he turned Davis in that direction for new sources of stock. January 1879 found Davis scouting the finest range in eastern Oregon, on the western slopes of the Steens Mountains—or Stein's, as the name was commonly spelled. The range was overstocked there, and cattlemen were anxious to sell their herds. Davis signed contracts with several grazers, including Peter French, the rising baron destined for a bullet in the back. French had established a ranch in Blitzen Valley, and stock which carried his large **P** brand had struck Henry Miller, the cattle king of California, as the finest cows he had ever seen. They were steady Durhams for the most part, more docile than Spanish longhorns, but efficient rustlers on the range.

Davis arranged for twelve thousand head to be conveyed to King and himself in the early spring. He bought 150 horses in California to mount the drive, and had them herded across country to the Steens Mountains. King met him there in April, after a wearing time in Washington, and they prepared to launch the drive. They hired a force of fifty drovers; they had more horses and wagons shipped from Owl Creek, and on the appointed date the transfer of the stock began. They were "cut out" and tallied by class, the steers from the cows and the calves, all receiving trail brands, a lazy **D** combined with French's **P**.

Nearly a month passed in getting the cattle ready for the drive. But in early May 1879 four or five trail herds started in a leisurely amble that would take them across the Owyhee River and up the basin of the Snake, eventually into Wyoming by the Lander Cut-off, and then along the Sweetwater River, a trail longer than the long trail up from Texas.

Official cares drew King back to the East by May 14, the day he wrote

Adams that he had "had a very interesting journey into Oregon, [seen] some most striking geology and got over 12,000 cattle started on their march for Colorado." But the drive was scarcely under way, and he could follow the progress of the herds only from reports—reports, too, of the Bannocks on the warpath, killing cattle. The herds moved at different rates, the steers about ten miles a day, the cows and calves scarcely five, no more than what the stock might walk if merely rustling on the range. One band of cows and calves had barely reached Fort Hall when cold weather struck, and they were turned loose to winter near the river. Another herd stopped farther along the trail, near the Big Bend of the Bear. But five thousand steers had reached their journey's end near Medicine Bow, Wyoming—worse luck for them. There was insufficient time for them to "season," and the terrible cold killed nearly 20 percent of the herd.

"I have been a great deal alarmed" King wrote as the spring of 1880 approached, "from a series of newspaper yarns, reporting the whole country between Oregon Station and Cheyenne snowed under, and the last blade of grass eaten off. . . . The fact is, I have got my annual scare." And for sufficient reason. "The wealthy firm of N. R. Davis & Co.," read one paper from Wyoming, "have men out skinning the dead steers which dot the surrounding country. Out of a herd of 5,000 turned loose last fall, 800 or 900 gave life up as a bad job on hogbacks and in gulches." Still, the loss fell short of pure disaster, and King received word that the herds in Idaho had fared much better.

When spring came, Davis put some of his cowboys on the westbound train; they picked up the **ND** remuda, which had been wintered near Fort Hall. Then they gathered the cattle along the Snake River and the Bear; the only mishaps during the drive occurred at the ford of the Green, some of the cattle drowning in the current. Where to graze the new arrivals had been a problem. Davis filed a claim, under the Desert Land Act, for a site near Elk Mountain, a landmark on the Cherokee Trail. He had claimed rights to the range between Elk Mountain and Medicine Bow Peak. But the steers from Oregon had crowded the region and left no room for the cows and calves.

"I suppose," King wrote, "there is nothing nearer to you than Hat Creek big enough for our band." He hated to think of Davis's "vibrating on a buckboard over that dreary Laramie road"; but there was no alternative. Davis appraised the Circle Bar Ranch, of Warren and Guiterman, now for sale on Hat Creek, a tributary of the Cheyenne. With the ranch went rights to six hundred square miles of range between the Cheyenne and the Niobrara, most of it lying in the southwest corner of Dakota Territory. King secured the purchase money from Shaw and Agassiz, $120,000; and the last contingents of the Oregon drive were herded across Wyoming to the Circle Bar range.

Grass had grown short along Owl Creek, and Davis was also forced to drive many of the ND cattle up to Hat Creek. He prepared to weather another "glacial winter," the worst for nineteen years, as it developed. Yet the herds came through in fair condition. The holdings of King and Davis now totaled twenty-five thousand head of mixed stock, * and the firm ranked as the third largest cattle grazer in Wyoming. With an interest in such vast expanses of range, King had come to think—so Marsh would joke—"that he owned the Rocky Mountains."

While the boom was at its crest, King arranged for still another protégé to start a ranch—Owen Olmsted, the frail but plucky stepson of his old friend Frederick Law Olmsted. In this matter King had again turned to Davis, placing young Olmsted in his hands in 1878 for a two-year apprenticeship. But this, King promised Davis,

is positively the last appearance of CK in the role of cattle benefactor. I have set up the last man. I have shipped you the last Kid. I have trespassed for the last time on your good nature, as to these infernal boys. I have graduated with honors and I am done. I have had all the credit of it, and you have had all the work. Heaven must eventually reward you for my fun.

Owen thrived under Davis's tutelage, and by the spring of 1880 he was judged ready to launch out on his own. In April King raised the money for Owens' firm, the Rocky Mountain Cattle Company, and helped to organize it under the laws of New York. It was capitalized at thirty-five thousand dollars, with Hewitt the principal stockholder, along with Henry Cabot Lodge. King himself made only a small investment, but he assumed responsibility for getting Owen started on the range. At first he thought of locating Rocky Mountain cattle (to bear the brand 82 85) on the Laramie Plain near Medicine Bow. But since the ordeal there of the ND steers did not recommend that choice, he turned to the region of Pumpkin Buttes, between the Powder River and the Belle Fourche, west of the Black Hills. That was 150 crow-flown miles to the north of Elk Mountain, but the climate was milder, and

* By January 1, 1882, the figure had increased to thirty thousand, according to the *Black Hills Pioneer.*

there was plenty of room. With a draft from Hewitt, Owen bought some fifteen hundred head of Oregon cattle and drove the herd to Pumpkin Buttes. Then he bought fifty halfbreed English bulls to improve the beef quality of the stock. At his new ranch he built a cabin and corrals with the help of three hired men. "Thriftily, he acted as his own foreman, and he worked alongside his hands in all weather, sometimes spending sixteen or eighteen hours a day in the saddle. He must have supposed the rugged outdoor life was invigorating; in any case, he did not know he was ill until he collapsed."

The Fates had allowed young Olmsted only eighteen months after the purchase of his herd, barely time to get his operation well under way. Then he was dead at twenty-four, and a temporary foreman notified King that he was holding the Rocky Mountain Ranch and cattle for further instructions. Owen's brother, John Olmsted, went out to the ranch and looked the business over for the stockholders, and on the basis of his report King set the value of the herd at twelve or thirteen thousand dollars more than the original cost. "Altogether," he added, "Owen had made a very good start." But what to do with the start was another question. King studied the matter, and at his suggestion the **82 85** cattle were merged with the holdings of Olmsted's nearest neighbor, a young Vermonter named Bartlett Richards, who ran the Ship Wheel Ranch near the Belle Fourche. Richards assumed the trust and would manage it faithfully, though he was to appear as something of a "heavy" in *Old Jules*, the Western classic by Mari Sandoz.

In the meantime returns on Davis and Bronson cattle increased with every shipment to Chicago. There were drives, moreover, to the Rosebud Agency for government issue to the Sioux, and profits mounted in spite of serious problems.

Like problems of the grass. It had become so scarce at Owl Creek and Elk Mountain that Davis had considered selling off the cattle at Elk Mountain prematurely. King had counseled him to hold them if at all possible, for they would be hard to match. They were retained, but the combination of poor feed and subzero weather did them much harm before the winter of 1881–1882 could turn mild. "Elk Mountain was a kind of Waterloo," King admitted; "still the showing is so good that I am almost inclined to bet on a million at the time of division."

There were signs, however, that the boom might break at any time. Davis and Bronson were apprehensive, and they brought their qualms to King. The persistence of trail drives—from Texas on the one hand and from Oregon and Utah on the other—and the plethora of capital that boom conditions attracted from both the East and overseas had overstocked the range too much for further profitable breeding or fattening of cattle. Certainly, too, the open range was passing, with the steady influx of "grangers" and their fences, and just as certainly the law of weather averages would hold its court. King knew how cruel that law could be, having seen the Great Drought in California strew the rancho lands with carcasses. Hence his sage agreement with his partners that they should not trust their luck too long and go on "betting," as the saying went, "against God Almighty and a sub-Arctic winter." Sooner or later the inexorable weather cycle must turn against them.

King felt such uneasiness about impending disaster that he advised selling the Lakota holdings after the fall roundup of 1882. It made no difference that the roundup produced such lucrative shipments of beeves that 1882 would be called the Golden Year—it was time to abandon the cattle business. Yet Hewitt felt that good conditions would persist, an opinion he had such confidence in that he not only declined to sell his share of the company, but also insisted on buying his partners out—brand, crop, and wattle. Nothing King might say from England, where he had gone in the spring, could discourage him, and Hewitt closed the deal in person for $285,000. He merged the Rocky Mountain assets with the Lakota Company, making Bartlett Richards the manager of the combined enterprise and setting him on a course that would lead within a few years to his controlling the most extensive cattle operation in Nebraska. Bronson, on the other hand, moved to Texas on leaving the Deadman Ranch and with Cooper-Hewitt backing took up a spread in the Pecos Valley, a venture King declined to join, though Gardiner, Arnold Hague, and Henry Janin did.

King could not have parted with his Lakota interest at a wiser time. The price of cattle had reached a peak in May 1882, and the fall of that year marked the divide between the fat years and the lean on the northern plains. Understandably, King could not relax until he had also sold the principal assets of N. R. Davis & Company. He scouted about in England, where the investment pot was boiling and where bankers favored the cattle industry in America, and prospects opened in London scarcely four months after the Lakota sale. He reached agreement with Richard Frewen, brother of Moreton Frewen and manager of the Powder River Cattle Company, and Frewen carried a proposition to British friends, including the Earl of Dunraven. They formed the Dakota Stock and Grazing Company in the spring of 1883 and paid a half million dollars for the Hat Creek Ranch, 16,830 head of cattle and rights to the vast range on which they grazed. The sale brought King more than $120,000 as his personal share, not counting the modest block of shares he retained in the company, jointly with Davis.

That was the last large harvest provided by his partnership with Davis. A horse ranch remained at Owl Creek, at which the principal stud was a noted stallion named Huerfano, but the dividends dwindled, and the Elk Mountain homestead was abandoned entirely. King was prepared, he wrote, "to pocket the profit or loss with a smile"; but there was less profit and more loss, especially after the calamitous winter of 1886–1887, which left the range a frozen shambles. When spring came and the beleaguered stockmen rode out to take account they found dead animals "piled in the coulees. Poor emaciated remnants of great herds wandered about with frozen ears, tails, feet, and legs, so weak that they were scarcely able to move." The Great Freeze, which changed the cattle industry forever,* would have spelled disaster for King had it come a few years earlier, or had he not read the warnings in time to voluntarily close his books as Cattle Baron.

King's experience as a cattleman had woven one more skein of color into the varied pattern of his career. But during these years he enjoyed yet another notable achievement, one that will be dealt with in the next two chapters. It was an accomplishment of major significance for his reputation as a government scientist, and of major benefit to the nation—a success in which he took justifiable pride and satisfaction. "What I did in and from Washington," he later remarked, "had the effect of ending a period of chaos in national geology, of founding a new and higher order of science in America."

---

*Cf. Moreton Frewen's remark on July 3, 1887, to his wife, one of the fascinating Jerome sisters and aunt of Winston Churchill: "From what Dick [Frewen] writes it is all over with cattle in Wyoming and Montana, more than half of them are dead this past winter, the business can never recover [from] such a blow as that" (Frewen Papers, microfilm reel 2).

Left, Samuel Franklin Emmons, close friend and colleague who shared King's interest in mining geology and who became a leading economic geologist of the day. He contributed to *Clarence King Memoirs* and wrote the memoir of King published in 1909 by the National Academy of Sciences. *Courtesy of the Library of Congress.*

Above left, Henry Adams as Assistant Professor of History at Harvard in 1872, a year after his celebrated meeting with King at Estes Park in the Colorado Rockies. Incandescent praise in *The Education of Henry Adams* has been the chief means of keeping King's name alive. For Adams King was not less than an avatar, the "most many-sided genius of his day." *Courtesy of the Harvard University Archives.* Right, Bret Harte, local color pioneer for whom King and John Hay pulled wires for his appointment to the U.S. Consular Service, first at Crefeld, Germany, then at Glasgow, Scotland. Harte had edited the *Overland Monthly* in San Francisco when King contributed to that journal. *Courtesy of the Huntington Library, San Marino, California.*

Major John Wesley Powell, conversing with a Southern Paiute. This photograph was taken by Jack Hillers in 1874 while Powell served as chief of the Second Division of the U.S. Geological and Geographical Survey of the Territories. In 1881 the Major succeeded King as Director of the U.S. Geological Survey and acted in that capacity until 1894. *Courtesy of the Yale Collection of Western Americana, Beinecke Rare Book and Manuscript Library.*

Left, William Dean Howells, circa 1881, celebrated American novelist and critic, who was the warm friend and sometime editor of Clarence King. A fellow Centurian, he contributed his reminiscences of various meetings with King to *Clarence King Memoirs.* He also attended King's funeral. *Courtesy of the Massachusetts Historical Society.*

Right, John Hay, poet, novelist, historian, and statesman. A sketch by J. W. Alexander published in the *Century Magazine* as an illustration to King's essay "The Biographers of Lincoln." Hay's praise of King fairly glows in *Clarence King Memoirs.* He served as Secretary of State under McKinley and Theodore Roosevelt. *Photograph by Caroline Lawson Hinkley.*

Above, Arnold Hague, geologist and esteemed assistant to King on both the Fortieth Parallel Exploration and the U.S. Geological Survey. He was coauthor with S. F. Emmons of *Descriptive Geology*, Vol. II of the King Report. He later devoted many years to an intensive study of the Yellowstone country. *Courtesy of the Huntington Library, San Marino, California.* Above right, Clarence King in the green velvet suit of his European tour, 1882–1884. In 1883 he was painted in these clothes, said to be cut like Oscar Wilde's, by the Swedish artist Anders Zorn. One version of Zorn's portrait went to John Hay, the other to Baron Ferdinand de Rothschild, later reproduced in Gerda Boethius' biography of Zorn. *Courtesy of the Huntington Library, San Marino, California.* Right, James D. Hague, mining engineer, with a copy of *Clarence King Memoirs*, of which he was the principal editor. He had served as the first geological assistant of the Fortieth Parallel Survey and was the chief author of *Mining Industry*, Vol. III of the King Report. *Courtesy of the Huntington Library, San Marino, California.*

246

Left, John Muir, the naturalist and early conservationist who bested King and J. D. Whitney in a running controversy over glaciers and the origin of Yosemite Valley. Muir later became the principal founder of the Sierra Club. Unfortunately he and King never met, a pity, for their antagonisms might then have dissolved in the glow of their mutual enthusiasms. From Francis P. Farquhar, *History of the Sierra Nevada.*

Left, Abram S. Hewitt, iron magnate. He was King's patron in Congress and his partner in the cattle business in Wyoming and Nebraska. After his service in Congress he became the Mayor of New York City on defeating Theodore Roosevelt and Henry George in a spirited three-way race. *Courtesy of the Library of Congress.* Right, John La Farge, artist friend of Clarence King and Henry Adams, in an oil portrait painted in 1902 by his former student Wilton Lockwood. La Farge, who claimed that King fitted into the ways of artists, wrote his memories of their friendship for *Clarence King Memoirs,* of which he was an editor. *Courtesy of the Library of Congress.*

247

The Corps of the California Geological Survey, photographed in San Francisco during the Christmas season of 1863: Chester Averill, William Gabb, William Ashburner, Josiah D. Whitney, Charles F. Hoffman, Clarence King, and William H. Brewer. *Courtesy, The Bancroft Library.*

King's Camp overlooking the Shoshone Falls of the Snake River, October 1868. The photograph was taken by Timothy O'Sullivan, photographer not only for the King Survey but also for that of Lt. Wheeler in 1871. King's color-drenched description of the falls first appeared in the October 1870 issue of Bret Harte's *Overland Monthly* and was then incorporated into *Mountaineering. Courtesy of the National Archives.*

"Summits, Wahsatch Range, Utah," chromolithograph from a study by Gilbert Munger, published as Plate I in Clarence King's *Systematic Geology*. The King Survey, with a base located at Parley's Park, explored and mapped the Wasatch Mountains during the season of 1869. *Courtesy, The Bancroft Library.*

Left, Brigadier General Andrew A. Humphreys, Chief of Engineers, to whom King reported as U.S. Geologist in charge of the Fortieth Parallel Survey. Humphreys thoroughly understood the complexities of survey work, for in the 1850's he had administered the Pacific Railroad Surveys. *Courtesy of the Library of Congress.*

Left, Clarence King, Director of the U.S. Geological Survey from 1879 to 1881. This portrait was published in the annual report of the Geological Survey following King's death in Phoenix, Arizona. The report also contained a fitting memorial sketch on King. *Courtesy of the National Archives.* Right, Marian Howland Townsley, King's beloved half-sister, whose fresh and delicate loveliness charmed Henry Adams in the middle 1880s. Against her mother's wishes she married Lieutenant Clarence Page Townsley, who would rise to the rank of brigadier general and command the Military Academy at West Point. *Courtesy of the Huntington Library, San Marino, California.*

251

James T. Gardiner, Clarence King, and Richard Cotter, in camp outside of Sacramento in the summer of 1867. Note how the harrowing hardship that Cotter had recently suffered in northern Alaska had caused him to look much older than in the photograph of the California Survey field party of 1864, taken only three years before. *Courtesy, The Bancroft Library.*

14

Establishment of the U.S. Geological Survey

Tension had grown between the various surveys of the government during the later years of King's work on the Fortieth Parallel Exploration. As a result of the rapid settlement of the West, he wrote,

the expeditions [had] assumed a sudden prominence. Their results were eagerly looked for and the corps were brought into ambitious rivalry, both as to the territories which were to be assigned to each and the appropriations which were sought in Congress. What may be termed the feudal period of Federal scientific works was at its height.

There was a need for improved policies and organization.

Joseph Henry had raised his voice in favor of reform as early as 1874. "We are inviting thousands of foreigners to come here," he had reminded the National Academy of Sciences, "and we ought to be able to tell them what we have to offer. For this purpose a survey of the whole United States should be made. We have three organizations for this purpose—the Coast Survey, the Engineers' survey, and this civilian survey"—the last a reference to the corps of Hayden and Powell. Henry argued that no wrangling should occur among these organizations, that their efforts should be coordinated, their accomplishments unified. Let the academy study this matter, he urged, and pilot the necessary reform.

But Henry was an old man; he failed to press his plan, and by May 1878 he was dead. The Smithsonian Institution, during his tenure as secretary, had become a strong influence, however, in shaping scientific policy for the government. So the question of Henry's successor aroused keen interest. Spencer Baird, having served long as second in charge, seemed likely to follow as chief—not that he could count on undivided support in scientific circles. For some time before Henry's death, other names had sounded in the councils of the influential—names of men like Julius Hilgard of the Coast Survey, or Simon Newcomb of the

Nautical Almanac, or even King, in spite of his business affairs which, scientific friends now feared, beguiled his mind from pure research.

Alexander Agassiz let it be known that he did not actually oppose King, whom he considered as "one of the few mining experts . . . who are entirely honest." Yet it would be "a hazardous experiment," he believed, to entrust the Institution to a man committed to giving professional evidence in a field so rife with temptation as mining. He preferred the astronomer Newcomb, and even Hilgard preceded King as his second choice. But it was Baird who emerged triumphant; the regents gave him their unanimous vote even before Henry had been laid in the grave; King could thus congratulate an old and valued friend, for from the start of the Fortieth Parallel Survey he had been able to count on Spencer Baird's good will.

But Henry's death had also emptied another significant post—the presidency of the National Academy of Sciences. And as time was to prove, this fact would have a crucial bearing on the question of the surveys, and on King's future as well; for into the breach now stepped his close friend O. C. Marsh to serve as acting head of the academy pending the next election of officers, for Marsh had become vice president a month before. Stress over the territorial surveys had grown sharp in Congress, but in the gathering crisis King could scarcely have gained a stauncher ally, in a more strategic place, than Marsh was to prove in the next few months.

King himself had predicted a national survey. He had claimed in 1868, according to Emmons,

that if we carried out our work successfully and creditably, it would result sooner or later in the organization of a permanent Geological Survey of the entire country, and that, with a country as rich . . . as ours, it would prove, if conducted on thoroughly scientific principles, the greatest geological survey the world had ever known.

Yet for years he had adroitly avoided becoming embroiled in feuds with rival organizations—even in the spring of 1874 when the House Committee on Public Lands had opened hearings on a proposal to merge the Western explorations. The trouble had flared acutely after parties under Hayden and Wheeler had clashed in Colorado the previous summer; and in the subsequent dispute, civilian versus military control of Western exploration had emerged as the central issue: the Interior Department versus the Army Engineers. Hayden had willy-nilly become the hard-used champion of "unification under civilian control."

King's basic sympathies had been shifting to the principle Hayden defended. He recognized that the claims of the military were becoming anachronistic, and yet he wondered how one in his position could move into Hayden's camp, as Powell and Gardiner had done, even on principle. The moral demands of his situation did not permit him to testify against the engineers. He had pleaded with Gardiner to temper his defection from military control:

In your too excited language about the Engineer Corps I see that you do not realize the advantage we owe them, that you forget how it looks to be under their flag and working against them, and do not attach enough weight to the fact that you are in honor bound to complete for them the work which is in your head and hands.

King found himself in a quandary which merely increased with time.

It had not been sheer coincidence, then, that ill health had sent him west in time to miss the week-long hearings of 1874. The quarrel had reached a stalemate during his absence. The Interior and War departments were represented by their respective secretaries, and President Grant wrote in support of the military. Powell rallied eloquently behind Hayden. But after all the rhetoric the Public Lands Committee reached a judgment that resolved precisely nothing.

Meanwhile, the tensions had grown against a background of greater issues—notably, the rape of the public domain by interests long entrenched, rapacious, unyielding in their efforts to thwart reform. But the slow recovery from the panic of 1873 had encouraged moves in Congress for economy, and legislators questioned the wisdom of handing money out to several uncoordinated corps, whose duplication of effort was estimated at 25 percent of their total work. King, his own work all but finished, now felt he could take a more overt stand.

"The four chiefs," he wrote in third person,

maintained their rivalry in camp and in Congress. Amongst them King and Powell felt most strongly the evils of the want of correlation and discipline of the whole service; and it was mainly through their combined influence that the conduct of the surveys [again] became a matter of Congressional investigation and the National Academy of Sciences was drawn in as advisor to the government.

"Powell," he admitted, "led this movement in Washington." But that was not to denigrate the substantiality of his own role. Historical opinion over the years would differ about it, and about who was primarily responsible for achieving the final consolidation of the western surveys. Yet in 1966 the nice assessment of William H. Goetzmann would reaffirm the fundamental part that King had played. "King and Powell were both prime movers in the consolidation struggle," Goetzmann would find in *Exploration and Empire*, his careful muster of evidence making it clear "that King had a role in [this] struggle fully as important as that of Powell." The basic reason why Powell ordinarily received more credit was, as Richard B. Wilson would suggest, that the major "worked in the public's eye while King worked behind the scenes, leaving no trail."

The question of the surveys had come to a head in 1878 when the House Appropriations Committee voted to block all further survey funds until some plan for reorganization could be found. "It was mainly through King's influence among the leading scientific men of the country," Emmons wrote, "and his tactful management of affairs in Congress that [a] crisis was averted." The executive departments answered congressional queries with recommendations full of claims and counterclaims. Then Abram Hewitt, King's closest friend in the House and (in the judgment of Henry Adams) "the most useful public man in Washington," inserted in the Sundry Civil Appropriations Bill a resolution directing the National Academy to study the survey problem and form some plan for reorganization.

Probably Hewitt's move was prompted by advice from King, an eventuality in line with Thomas Donaldson's subsequent claim that the U.S. Geological Survey "came as a result of King's suggestion." Donaldson, who would serve with King and Powell on the Public Lands Commission, was in a good position to learn the inside facts. His claim, moreover, would be supported by Goetzmann's later extrapolation from the scanty evidence available on the matter. "[Wallace] Stegner," according to Goetzmann's review, "points out that Hewitt took credit for suggesting that the Academy's help be sought in the consolidation question, whereas S. F. Emmons credited King with the idea. It seems most likely to me that the idea originated with King, who was on very good terms with the members of the Academy, particularly Marsh. King, in turn, must certainly have made this proposal to his friend and business partner Hewitt, who based his claim for credit on his role in Congress. There is no evidence that Powell originated the proposal. . . . [But] Emmons, who was also a business partner [of King's], was in the best possible position to know King's relationship with Hewitt." Later Mary C. Rabbitt would reach a like conclusion in her searching history of the U.S. Geological Survey.

As acting president of the academy, Marsh took the matter into his personal care. In August he consulted King, in addition to the council of the academy. King advised two civilian surveys, one for economic geology, the other for topographical mapping, and in due course Marsh adopted his view. But of more immediate importance, consultations like those with King and the council led to Marsh's prompt formation of a special committee to deal with the whole involved question of the surveys and the public lands. His choice of committeemen, running heavily to geologists, included some of the most distinguished scientists of the day: Professors James Dwight Dana of Yale, William B. Rogers of M.I.T., William P. Trowbridge and John Strong Newberry (both of Columbia), Simon Newcomb, and Alexander Agassiz; whereas Marsh himself was to serve as chairman ex officio.

Marsh had avoided naming any member of an existing government exploration. That decision brought a loud protest from General Humphreys, for the Army Engineers could see no chance in such a panel for military control, even though Trowbridge was a West Point graduate; and in answer to Marsh's call for recommendations Humphreys' chief assistant spelled out further sharp dissent. At the same time more favorable replies came from the Interior Department—statements from Powell and Hayden and Commissioner James A. Williamson of the General Land Office—and these gave the committee a basis for deliberation.

The sixteen-page recommendation submitted by Major Powell briefly restated the plan for land reform that he had recently published in his *Report on the Lands of the Arid Region.* Here was a succinct and studious blueprint for Marsh's committee to sponsor and, with it, to foster the cause of civilian authority over a consolidated geological survey. No one had contributed more to the drive for land reform than Major

Powell, and aside from his call for combining the Western surveys the main thrust of his program aimed at an audacious reformation of the policies and practices of the General Land Office, whose masses of records he censured as "a gigantic illustration of badly directed scientific work." No one knew better than he how controversial his program threatened to become, which seems to have been one of the reasons he barred himself, at least among his confidants, as a candidate to head a consolidated geological survey.

Marsh's committee was sure to recommend against control by the military—a course that would eliminate Lieutenant Wheeler as a choice for geological director; at the same time Hayden was unaccept-able to at least four members of the committee. Even his former teacher, Newberry, had turned against him and advised both Hewitt and Garfield in 1877: "Briefly . . . Hayden has come to be so much a fraud that he has lost the sympathy and respect of the scientific men of the country." Newberry now regarded him as "simply the political manager of his expeditions." He had hired relatives of his political patrons and spent much money on photographs, which had been passed about with "an eye to political effect." Hayden's methods had, without question, antagonized a majority of the committee, and they assumed that he must be scuttled. Some of them quietly turned to King as a possible candidate; and he found the challenge hard to ignore, eager though he had been to retire from government service.

To serve as geological director would mean shelving the novel he had promised to write for Osgood. It would also mean that certain business propositions would have to be struck from his calendar. His interest, for example, had been aroused in the Speaking Telephone, which many considered a toy, but in which advances had been made not only by Alexander Graham Bell, but also by Elisha Gray, Amos Dolbear, and Thomas Edison. The latter inventors had pressed Bell's patents with applications of their own, and a savage fight for control of the field had developed, with much litigation.

King considered the invention as one of the great developments of the age. "We shall whisper around the globe," he was to prophesy, and he predicted refinements "which will give at once a legible and audible record of the pulsations of human speech, and thus end that tedious and retarding conventionality, the alphabet." Meanwhile, if properly managed, the telephone would make millions for its owners, and King arranged with several of the parties concerned to combine patents. "The control could be secured for four hundred thousand dollars," a son of Abram Hewitt later wrote. "Mr. King brought to my father the proposition that control be secured." *

Hewitt had called in Edward Cooper for a conference. Old Peter Cooper had come, too, his single good eye flashing like a coal at the mention of litigation. "I am too old a man now to go into any new venture," he said, "but this is a good business, because everyone wants to talk." He doubted that the current litigation could compare with the trouble that had pestered him when the first Atlantic cable had snapped; and remember, he reminded, "I made a fortune out of that."

He urged buying up the telephone claims, but the cautious views of Hewitt and Edward Cooper prevailed. They convinced King that litigation costs would mount too high, and so he allowed the options to lapse; which left him a freer man for the post of geological director should the appointment come his way.

He waited for Marsh's committee to act; and then, in September 1878 he went to Cambridge and called on Whitney, whose availability for the post was an open question. "The [real] object of my visit," King later wrote to his former chief, "was to ask you in all frankness first if you would be a candidate for the directorship if Congress created the office, to which you decidedly said *no*; secondly to enquire how you felt about throwing your influence for me." And to that, too (as King informed Brewer), Whitney had "answered with equal promptness and every outward sign of cordiality that I was '*the only person to be thought of*.'" And so feeling assured of Whitney's support, King sent a "confidential letter to a friend" on the committee; and his hat was henceforth in the ring, however secretly.

King followed developments closely. He conferred with Marsh and Hewitt, Newcomb and Powell. All accepted him as their candidate, and King gave his sanction to the major's plan. He drafted editorials to run in the *New York Times* and the *World* and the *Sun* when the time was ripe. "Then," he promised, "I will open the ball in a very lively manner." In the meantime, Major Powell had asked to appear before

---

*This may well have been the "valuable business engagement" of which King advised the Engineer Bureau on December 26, 1878 (telegram to Chief Clerk, King Survey Letter Book). The exact lines of King's plan are not clear; but according to Ralph Mooney, Historical Librarian, American Telephone and Telegraph Company, "This, apparently, was an attempt to break the Bell patents by lumping together all possible claims against them. Such action was taken many times" (Mooney to writer, December 9, 1955).

the committee when it was ready for action. His arguments were persuasive, and in the end the committee's "Report on the Surveys of the Territories" incorporated all the main features of Powell's program, while at the same time conforming in a general way with the "lines laid down by [King]."

Briefly, it focused on the collective surveying operations of the General Land Office, the newly renamed Coast and Geodetic Survey, and the Hayden, Powell, and Wheeler surveys (the King Survey having been excepted because its work was done). The committee recommended that the aforesaid operations be divided into two categories— "surveys of mensuration" and "surveys of geology and economic resources of the soil"—and that two bureaus be authorized within the Interior Department to implement these sharply distinguished missions. A modified Coast and Geodetic Survey, further renamed the Coast and Interior Survey, should deal with "all questions of position and mensuration." To enhance the accuracy and economy of this mission the committee judged it to be "absolutely essential that there should be only one geodetic system, one topographic system, and one land parceling system," all to be administered by the superintendent of the Coast and Interior Survey. The second bureau, named the U.S. Geological Survey, should consolidate the three existing Western surveys and should deal with all "questions relating to the geological structure and natural resources of the public domain." Finally, the committee urged the appointment of a public lands commission to consider the codification of the public land laws and to report to Congress a standard for land classification and valuation.

At a special session of the Academy on November 6, King joined a company of some thirty-seven members who arrived at Columbia College to sit in judgment on the plan. After three hours of debate, Marsh put the report to a vote, and the *Ayes* carried, all but one member voting so. The lonely *Nay* was cast by Marsh's bitter adversary in the Battle of the Bones, the paleontologist Edward D. Cope. Cope, who had attached himself to Hayden and Wheeler in the field, quarreled violently with the provision to merge the purely geological work sponsored by the government. The basic reason for his opposition was, of course, his implacable hatred for Marsh. He could see that a geological program inaugurated under Marsh's aegis would have no place for Copean paleontology. It would freeze him out, as surely as it threatened to eliminate his patron Wheeler.

Hayden, for his part, seemed comfortable with the plan, caught though he was between two millstones—an unsympathetic committee on the one hand, a hostile military on the other. It was left to the engineers to exceed Cope's objections; they denounced the academy's report as soon as it appeared in print—especially General Humphreys, who, as Newcomb remarked, "opens the fight by a sort of hara-kiri." He sent his resignation to the academy, as a gesture of protest. Understandably, the academy declined to accept it, but not before Captain Carlisle Patterson, superintendent of the Coast and Geodetic Survey, had rushed to offer the general active sympathy as a fellow officer.

Both Powell and Hilgard kept King posted on Patterson's views; and Hilgard assured Marsh, concerning the directorship of geology, "I am rooting for King, for whom I entertain a foolish affection. But Patterson . . . does not know King personally." An obvious move suggested itself, and Hilgard asked for the pleasure of bringing the two together. This he did on King's next visit to the capital, and King vindicated Hilgard's belief that he and Patterson were "just the people to strike up a great friendship." The Coast and Geodetic Survey from that day forth harbored no further opposition to the academy's proposal or to King's unheralded candidacy.

Meanwhile Marsh carried the plan to strategic executive offices; he secured the approval of Carl Schurz, secretary of the interior; of John Sherman in the Treasury Department, of Baird at the Smithsonian, and even of President Hayes, "so far as he had the report before him." Thus the plan had formidable backing when it went to Congress in December, 1878. "It was directly referred to the Appropriations Committee of the House," King wrote, "[and] in committee it was discussed with great fulness." Hewitt became its champion, guiding it across a bog of committee politics, with help from John D. C. Atkins, a one-armed colonel from Tennessee. Soon the matter seemed so firmly under control that Newcomb could advise Marsh at Yale: "There is little doubt of the whole thing being put through the House very soon. Then the fight will commence in the Senate. There is where we want King. . . . Senators should be interviewed without delay"; for the opposition was hard at work already in the upper chamber.

King received his cue—the time had come for him to present his credentials. He hurried down to Washington in early January with letters to the president from Howells and his wife. The *Atlantic's* editor claimed that his sole grief against King was "that a man who can give us such literature should be content to be merely a great scientist." Mrs. Howells recommended King to her "Dear Cousin Lucy," the president's wife, as "the most accomplished man of his age in the country."

King took rooms at Wormley's Hotel, an old-style Southern caravanserai, run by a suave mulatto, which seemed to have a special appeal for senators and congressmen who had no Washington homes of their own. From there King could soon report that he was "in the thick of the fight." He at once began to press his double objective—passage by Congress of the academy plan and his own campaign, still muted and unobtrusive, for geological director. He found the legislative prospects excellent, thanks to Powell's unfailing energy as a lobbyist and to Hewitt's astuteness in the House. Hewitt had incorporated the academy's plan in a bill for which he had requested King's advice, going (in the words of Allan Nevins) "into the subject thoroughly with [him]." The upshot was that King himself would write a crucial portion of the measure—the clause that would "create the office of Geological Director and define its duties and field of action." The secretary of the interior had been requested to furnish a prospective draft of this clause, and after consulting with the committee, as King explained afterwards, "[Schurz] committed the drafting to me. I then enquired of Mr. Hewitt . . . whether the field was to be considered as the public lands or as the whole United States. He plainly told me that the Survey was to be made to cover the whole union and I used in this sense 'National Domain'"—a phrase whose ambiguity King did not then foresee or the oceans of embarrassment this ambiguity would later cause him. On approval by Schurz and then the committee, his draft of the "enabling clause" went verbatim into Hewitt's bill.

Hayden seemed "outwardly for the bill, but his soul," as King could see, was "in a distracted state." The Army Engineers, of course, were pitted against it; but the most powerful opposition of all came from the Western bloc in Congress, led by "old Perplexity," Representative Thomas N. Patterson of Colorado. He would soon be damning the proposed legislation as fraught "with disaster to the West and its landed interests." Such stalwarts were ready to fight reform with all their resources, seeing that any change in customary methods of land disposal threatened the heart of their power. It was King's opinion that "the land rings [were] rampant."

"The contest here is a tremendous one," he wrote, "having waked up no end of bitterness and consolidated a powerful lobby." But King expected victory. "The main thing is to get the bill through," he declared, "and to that end I bend all work." He kept at his "struggle with Congress," going at senators and representatives "white-hot," as his phrase would have it. Day after day he met with friends of the press like E. L. Godkin at Wormley's or the house of Henry Adams. He wrote letters and gave advice, and was interrupted in the work only by his old recurrent fever and a brief trip south.

In one respect King's position was at first embarrassing—he was still attached, in a formal sense, to the Army Engineers, who opposed the course he worked so hard for. But on January 18, 1879, he closed his financial accounts with that bureau and requested General Humphreys to relieve him officially from his charge as U.S. geologist. The general complied; the contradiction was thus removed from King's position, and he could act with more effective freedom in the accelerating politics in which he found himself.

Not that his days in Washington were wholly devoted to politics. For relief from Congressional deserts he could turn to the oasis which Clover Adams had made at 1501 H Street. Henry Adams had left the *North American Review* in the year of President Hayes's peculiar triumph. He had resigned from Harvard as well; and after a brief sojourn in New York, to work on the Gallatin papers there, he had again turned south to Washington to be, as he put it, the "stable-companion to statesmen whether they liked it or not." He had spent the last two winters with Clover on H Street, where the *Life of Albert Gallatin* was drawing to a close. Here Clover sparkled, so gay a hostess—"the lady of infinite mirth," as Henry James would soon portray her, in elegant Mrs. Bonnycastle in his brief nouvelle *Pandora.*

Clover's dinners of six or eight, like Bonnycastle parties, were "the pleasantest in Washington," even if a bit exclusive. ("Hang it," Mr. Bonnycastle would be made to say, ". . . let us be vulgar and have some fun—let us invite the President.") These cordial gatherings in the Adams drawing room constituted what a subsequent historian would call "the most noted salon this country has ever evolved." Yet how welcome King was made there; his hosts called him their "prop and stay," their swan, their bird of paradise; and after dinner they would sit together before the fire, for winter or summer a fire burned on the Adams hearth, and on their talk would ripple. It was conversation that enchanted Raphael Pumpelly, the golden-bearded giant—conversation which Henry Cabot Lodge would praise as the best of talk, shot through with wit and humor. It glittered with anecdote, but it was serious too. It brimmed with the knowledge of men and books.

If only confidants were present, Adams might read a chapter from the manuscript he called "Democracy." It was the unsparing story of the investigation by Madeleine Lee of the nature of political power in Washington, and only a few like King, the Hays, Holt, and Godkin knew that he was writing it. The readings were hugely diverting, and King left the Adams hearth refreshed for new encounters with the senators, who had impressed his host like so many "angry monkeys."

Hewitt's bill had weathered condemnation by the engineers, and now it withstood the first onslaughts of the land rings too. But in February 1879 when it escaped from the Public Lands Committee, it faced a Congress of deeply split opinion. Party lines crumbled in the open debate—the Republican Garfield stood with the Democrat Hewitt, bulwarks both in the House. Hewitt, like King, had rooms at Wormley's Hotel. There on occasion, as King explained to Carl Schurz, "Mr. Hewitt kept me incessantly occupied over the surveys." Out of their huddles came Hewitt's eloquent address of February 11, 1879, hailing his bill as a safeguard for America's "heritage of the future." Hewitt urged Congress to take appropriate steps lest that birthright be "mortgaged to grasping corporations or to overpowering capitalists." It was a magnificent effort, perhaps Hewitt's finest speech; but close upon its delivery came the shock of defeat. The bill fell in the House, and the fight seemed all but lost in the Senate as well. Only a compromise could save the cause, and lights burned late at Wormley's Hotel.

To quiet the apprehensions of the land rings, the substitute measure introduced in the House by Horace Page of California dropped all phrases aimed at changing the public land system with its parceling surveys that abounded in corruption. The revision mentioned neither "mensuration" nor the Coast and Interior Survey; and thus watered down, it became acceptable to the Western bloc in Congress, although it authorized a consolidated geological program under the authority of the secretary of the interior and the creation of a Public Lands Commission to examine and codify the public land laws. The clause King had drafted remained intact.

The bill named a salary of six thousand dollars for a director whom the president should choose: "Provided, That this officer shall have the direction of the Geological Survey, and the classification of the public lands, and examination of the geological structure, mineral resources, and products of the national domain." No personnel of the bureau could hold a private interest in any lands or mineral wealth within the province of the survey, or make examinations for any private party or corporation therein. The measure discontinued the organizations of Hayden, Powell, and Wheeler, except that in actual practice the latter's operation would be allowed to persist in the Army Engineers insofar as it was needed for military purposes. At the same time the measure directed that all collections made by government surveys be sent to the National Museum when no longer required for work in progress.

Although the proposed legislation was now relatively inoffensive to the land rings, Hewitt took no chances on its passage. He attached it to the Sundry Civil Expenses Bill, and it was enacted on March 3, 1879, during the pell-mell rush of voting that closed this session of Congress. An unobtrusive clause in the act appropriated twenty thousand dollars to complete and prepare for publication the contribution of the Powell Survey to American ethnology, with the proviso that all the materials that Powell had collected concerning American Indians be transferred to the Smithsonian Institution. This insured a suitable berth for Powell and an operation that would develop into the Bureau of Ethnology. But for Hewitt, whose career in the House of Representatives would close with the present adjournment of Congress, the legislation authorizing the Geological Survey provided a fitting climax for his twelve years in Washington; and in retrospect he would cite his role in seeing it through the vicissitudes of hostile politics to final passage as his most substantial achievement in Congress.

When the contest for the directorship of geology moved into the open, Hayden was apparently in the lead. He had assumed that Powell, not King, would be his chief rival, and with almost paranoid zeal he had planted spies to report on every movement Powell made about the capital. He had not reckoned on King's strength until a partisan warned that King would be his "strongest opponent." King himself, once his mind was set, was not the reluctant candidate that would sometimes be pictured.* He actively courted the support of influential men, and on

* The seeds for this reputation of reluctance were sown by King himself, who masked his eagerness for the appointment by an air of nonchalant indifference, well illustrated by his letter of February 19 [1879] to William H. Dall of the Smithsonian:

I feel now as I always have that I dont care a pin about any position in the gift of the government for my own sake. It would be a very great sacrifice socially and pecuniarily for me to leave New York. If however the administration should ask me to take the Geological Directorship I should do so in a cheerful missionary spirit and do the best I could. A letter from Boston received a little

approaching Senator Blaine he frankly said, "Mr. Blaine, I want that position! It is a case of a man seeking the office; not the office seeking the man."

He later wrote of the contest that followed: "The leading scientific men of the country took sides, and . . . all sorts of pressures, legitimate and otherwise, were brought to bear upon President Hayes." It had been no secret to King that Hayden was "moving heaven and earth to get the President's support." Hayden's devotion to publicity over the years, his profligate distribution of reports, his tireless attention to congressmen, and his connections with scientific societies the world over brought him vast advantages now. Recommendations on his behalf poured into the White House from organizations, politicians, and private citizens—sometimes even geologists. "It has been said, I do not know how truly," Simon Newcomb wrote, "that the number of these testimonials exceeded that received by any other scientific man" in the United States. The president was overwhelmed, and except for Carl Schurz's intervention, he might have appointed Hayden as soon as the bill was signed.

King had Major Powell to thank for spurring Schurz to action. King had been Powell's choice for director from the first. They had met as early as 1870, and had cooperated cordially on the correlation of the geological work of their respective surveys; concerning which Powell had written in 1874, "In this course I conferred with Clarence King himself and from time to time we compared the results of our studies and rendered each other mutual aid." The soaring regard that Powell had developed for King's ability came shining through the letter he now sent to Garfield in the House:

King was the pioneer and founder of a whole system of survey work which was novel and original, exactly suited to the region and which . . . will on the whole be the only practicable system for the far West. To have grasped the difficulties of the problem at the very outset of the work and to have planned beforehand a system of operations for overcoming them rapidly and easily . . . indicated in King an orderly, sagacious, logical mind which places him among the truly great men of science in the estimation of those who know how to appreciate his work.

---

while since quoted you as saying that I had "withdrawn from the contest." Now I have never been *in* a contest. I am simply waiting about in the neighborhood where lightning can conveniently strike me if inclined

(Box 13, Dall Papers).

It was therefore understandable that Powell should throw his full support behind King's candidacy, especially in view of his avowed distaste for Hayden; and on March 4, 1879, he appealed to Secretary Schurz, through Atkins in Congress, to block Hayden's nomination by any means possible. The factions were thus locked in a last test of strength; it had become clear, as King afterward recalled, "that one of the two rivals must be crushed."

But he could soon remark with confidence: "I have the inside track." Even the cold shoulder from friends he had counted on—Whitney at Harvard and Dana at Yale—could do him no real damage. Whitney had sided with Hayden and blocked a faculty recommendation of King from Harvard, a move that Brewer excused as the whim of an old man; and though stung by the desertion of his former chief, King wrote him a letter that was surprisingly deferential under the circumstances. "I do not doubt," he said, "that your reasons are sound and good [and] I have no blame for you in this matter. I believe you always act fearlessly and as you think strictly right."

But then, more than equalizing the Harvard fiasco, "a stentorian letter" in King's favor reached the president from Yale, signed by men like President Porter, Brewer, and Marsh. The latter two had sent personal recommendations as well. Further endorsements came from Columbia, Johns Hopkins, the University of Pennsylvania, New York University, the American Museum of Natural History, and the State Museum at Albany. King was backed by the chiefs of several state surveys, including Gardiner at the helm in New York; and he received the written support of every member of the late committee of the academy, except Dana, who straddled the fence. Alexander Agassiz assured him in a letter that found its way to the president's desk that he would rather see no other geologist as head of the new survey.

Schurz advocated King in spite of accusations like those of Cope, aimed at King's connection with private mines during his service as U.S. geologist. The secretary, in General Walker's words, "was from the start a tower of strength, and Hayden was beaten before he began, though it was still desirable to make the President feel that King's appointment was the best thing."

Among those who lent their support to this end was the mining expert, Rossiter Raymond. Long a close associate of Hewitt in the latter's private iron concern, he had followed the consolidation battle in Congress with rapt attention, frequently addressing it as editor of the *Engineering and Mining Journal.* In his editorial for March 8 he gave

King's candidacy an oblique but forceful endorsement, pointing out how

> much depends upon the action of the President in choosing the right man for this great enterprise. If the geological survey were an established institution, with its rules, methods, and traditions, there would be less danger in placing at its head a man of mediocre ability. But the Director now to be appointed must create his institution as well as administer it. The impulse now given it will determine its future. The manner in which it is conducted for the next two years will either fix it as a recognized and esteemed branch of the public service, or expose it to utter overthrow, and doom the country to recurring chaos in this department. . . . If the new Director is wise, he will understand that his primary object must be to ascertain and make known the resources of the public lands. Let him boldly put the economical problems first, and win public respect for scientific work by showing, even to the unscientific, what benefits it can confer upon the community. Let him imitate the sagacity of Clarence King, who published first of all his volume on the Mining Industry, and last of all his theoretical deductions in continental geology.

On March 11 newspapers carried a premature announcement that King had won the nomination—a ruse perhaps of the Hayden forces to lull King's advocates into false assurance. If so, the ruse failed. King's staunchest backers—men like Powell and Newcomb, Hewitt and Atkins—were determined to press every advantage. They had divided the campaign work among themselves, doing what they could in the daytime, meeting with King at Wormley's in the evening, or at the newly christened Cosmos Club, where King had enrolled as a founding member. In their evening conclaves they would compare notes and, in the words of Newcomb, "ascertain the effect of every shot, and decide where the next one should be fired." Powell was especially trenchant in his opposition to Hayden, whom he condemned as "a charlatan who has bought his way to fame with government money and unlimited access to the Government Printing Office."

It was the personal force of King's supporters which in the end clinched his victory at the White House. Both Newcomb and Powell secured personal interviews with the president to counteract the influence exerted by Hayden enthusiasts. At one of these meetings Newcomb mentioned the name of Professor Newberry, who had led the Ohio State Survey while Hayes was governor.

Would the president give much weight to *his* opinion?

"Very great weight indeed," the president replied.

So Newberry was summoned to Washington. Marsh came too, at a word from Powell, and with him Brewer, determined to compensate for Whitney's defection. In the conference that followed, Brewer explained King's pioneer work to the president; he gave King credit for bringing modern topographical methods into federal surveying, the method King and Gardiner had learned in California. Brewer later explained that he did not know that Hayden had tried to usurp the credit for introducing those improved techniques. The president listened closely. "And had I been a witness on the stand in a trial at court," Brewer would add long afterward, "I could not have been cross-examined much closer." But with the main dates and facts firm in memory he gave the chief executive "the history in detail."

Hayes seemed convinced of the hollowness of Hayden's pretensions. Fresh in his mind, no doubt, was the response of President Eliot of Harvard to his request for a confidential opinion: "Dr. Hayden . . . does not command the confidence of men of science. I have often heard [him] discussed among scientific men, but I have never heard either his attainments or his character spoken of with respect." Eliot favored Whitney for the new post, but he did not oppose King, and he had concluded: "The appointment of either Professor Whitney or Mr. King would be regarded by American scientific men as well-earned, as creditable to the government, and as full of promise for the future of the Survey. The appointment of Dr. Hayden would seem to them discreditable, discouraging and unpromising."

So after a final talk with Schurz the president announced, on March 20, that King's nomination had gone to the Senate to be confirmed. King remarked, once more in third person: "There was a certain fitness that of the two candidates King should be chosen first Director of the Survey; he had thrown himself heart and soul into the movement for consolidation, while his antagonist Hayden had never clearly declared himself for the obliteration of his own corps."

No report issued from the Committee on Public Lands till April 2. Then the doors of the Senate closed in executive session, and land-ring stalwarts bared their claws. Old charges were hurled that King had "received enormous fees from private persons for his services while . . . drawing a salary from the Government." But friends in the Senate defended him ably, and Adams wrote that "King's victory was crushing." The nomination was confirmed on the afternoon of April 3, 1879.

Great was the jubilation in King's camp. Hope inspired the day, for men like Emmons, Pumpelly, Gilbert, and Arnold Hague had promised to join his staff. And even as King hastened to southeast Oregon to launch a cattle drive back along the Oregon Trail before the burden of office could claim him, plans were taking shape in his mind—plans to make a reality of his promise to Brewer that "the world never saw such a survey as we will have."

Henry Adams wrote to Marsh: "Our fight ended so satisfactorily that we shall never be happy till we've had another and got licked. King is now in Oregon, I suppose, but we want him back already—that is, *I* want him."

15

Director of Geology

After returning from the West in May 1879, King took his oath on the twenty-fourth as director of the U.S. Geological Survey. He could not hire a corps till the end of the fiscal year, but planning for the survey became his chief preoccupation at a temporary base in New York City. "It was left very much to me to decide early policy," he later declared. Still, he kept in touch with Secretary Schurz and now and then hurried down to Washington for consultations.

Feeling the need of seasoned models, he proposed a six-month tour of Europe to study established surveys there before committing himself to a program. But the secretary, understandably, vetoed King's proposal; and King plunged at once into the throes of shaping up his plans. The size of the task was disconcerting—indeed, it seemed so much a threat that he remarked to Major Powell, "I feel like a condemned culprit ascending the gallows but"—he added—"I suppose you are right in predicting that when my blood gets up I shall enjoy being hung."

Congress had charged the survey with two principal functions—to study the geological structure and resources of the national domain, and to classify the public lands. The act had not bound King expressly to a third responsibility. But at a nod from Carl Schurz he had come to a "verbal understanding" with General Francis A. Walker, census superintendent, to provide the impending census—the tenth—with statistics on the mineral industries of the nation. These were intricate assignments, and their precise achievement required King to know exactly where he was headed.

He knew well enough the course he ought to take, although he doubted his authority to do so. "A Geological Survey," he wrote before the year's end,

. . . may be either wholly in the nature of pure and speculative science involving theories of the origin of the globe and the histories of continents, or

271

it may be directed to the vigorous study of the position, nature, extent, uses and values of the mineral products, such as soils, metals, coals, mineral fertilizers, building stones, clay, etc., which are the foundations of human industry and the basis of national wealth.

A case could be made for either aim. King was by no means hostile to the claims of pure science; he was to keep an active interest in speculative geology for the rest of his life, and it was natural for him to add: "Geology studied and practiced from the side of abstract knowledge has heretofore yielded, and always will be made to yield, results which are indirectly of value to civilization, as so much addition to the sum of knowledge, so much enlightenment and education." But the law behind the survey implied a more practical program; practical motives had inspired both the framers of the legislation and its staunchest supporters, and in the struggle for the directorship King's practical experience had been his strongest asset. He could now see no logical alternative to charting a pragmatic course.

If for no other reason, such a course recommended itself to address two overriding problems of the day—the national monetary crisis, on the one hand; the crisis in the production of industrial steel, on the other. The first problem turned on the requirement by the Bland-Allison Act that the secretary of the treasury purchase from $2 million to $4 million worth of silver every month for coinage purposes and on the need that a large reserve of gold be held in the Treasury to underwrite the resumption of specie payment for "greenbacks" at a time when gold production had been in decline for over twenty years. The second problem turned on the fact that the nearly unlimited reserves of iron ore in the United States did not at that time guarantee an adequate supply of the particular kind of low-phosphorous, low-sulphur pig iron required by the processes then in common use by American steelmakers. Consequently, it was necessary to import ores of suitable composition to insure the continued industrialization of the country. The government's need for gold and silver in the currency crisis and industry's need for steel urged the immediate systematic investigation of the mineral resources of the nation; and bowing to the common sense of such a course, King made his decision.

"Without in any way seeking to undervalue or discourage the pursuit of pure geology," he declared, "I submit that practical or economic geology is the branch for this government to pursue first. . . . We do not know within a hundred million dollars what our annual mineral yield is. . . . I submit that such knowledge is a national necessity."

So far King needed to fear no opposition; the wisdom of his stand was evident. It justified his promise to the census, and Congress had clearly provided for the geological program it suggested, even to the point of turning the survey into a potent ally, mentor, and catalyst for the mining industry. But when King reached the question of extent, the geographical range of his field work, he ran into trouble. His proposed program logically called for national scope, and King believed that the work should extend "over every acre of the United States." And yet hardly had he begun to lay plans than an ambiguity in the law confounded him. What did Congress as a whole mean by "national domain"? King relayed his apprehensions to Carl Schurz with the query as to "whether we are to confine the operations of the Survey to the public domain"—by which he meant the public lands of the Western states and territories—"or whether we can go into the old states." King preferred the latter course. But whatever Hewitt or Atkins and other sponsors on the Hill had meant by "national domain," he felt growing doubts that Congress at large had intended it to cover the whole United States, and Schurz was inclined to agree. Thereupon an opinion as to the legal sense of the term was asked of the attorney general, who ruled that " 'national domain' meant the public lands to which the United States had not parted title." If this decision appeared to set King's course, it was the leanness of his first appropriation—only one hundred thousand dollars—that fairly forced the issue.

King willy-nilly restricted the work of the survey proper to public lands in the West, at least—he consoled himself—until Congress should grant him more money. It did not mean that he had renounced with any finality the aim of nationwide operations, and he opened the question with his friends in Congress. He asked for a definition of the doubtful term, and the House Appropriations Committee framed a resolution which applied *national domain* to the "whole territorial area of the United States" and authorized King to "extend his examination into the States." But in the Senate a cry of "States' rights" went up like the Rebel yell, and there the resolution foundered in a pigeonhole.

On July 7 King submitted his plan of operations for the fiscal year. It was approved, and he started forming his organization. First he structured the Geological Survey in two overall and independent divisions, under the headings of Mining Geology and General Geology. In the field he hoped to decentralize his organization enough to avoid some of the practical difficulties that had beset the several surveys in the past. The long treks between winter quarters in the East and field work in the West had cost dearly in time and money. King planned to save much of this expense by dividing the public domain into four large districts— each with headquarters where the men might work the year around, after the fashion of the Coast and Geodetic Survey.

To each of these districts King assigned a geologist-in-charge at four thousand dollars a year. Emmons headed the Rocky Mountain Division, which stretched from the Mexican border up to Canada. It included New Mexico, Colorado, Wyoming, Montana, and the western fringe of Dakota; and Emmons decided to place his office at Denver. A second area, called the Division of the Colorado, coincided with the southern part of Major Powell's explorations—the canyon and plateau region between the Rocky Mountains and the Great Basin. The major had long planned to describe the Grand Canyon environs; but now he delegated that task to Captain C. E. Dutton, his assistant in the field, and orders were extended which had detached Dutton from military service and assigned him to the Interior Department. King did not consider this arrangement permanent. As soon as Dutton's monograph could be completed, he planned to merge the Colorado district with the Division of the Great Basin, with headquarters in Salt Lake City. He had appointed G. K. Gilbert head of the Great Basin operations, a logical choice in view of Gilbert's work on old Lake Bonneville, which King requested him to finish. At the same time Arnold Hague was named geologist for the Pacific Division, which included all of Washington Territory, and most of Oregon and California. And so the four main districts began to crystallize.

By July 24 King had hired a force of twenty-one men—geologists, topographers, and clerks. Their work was to be coordinated from a central Washington office, in what had been a private home on the corner of 8th and G streets: "a large brick house prettily carpeted and papered, and full of handsome mahogany desks." But King had begun to feel the pinch of funds already. He could allot no money for work in paleontology, and only the most essential map work could be inaugurated. "I should consider it a calamity to the Survey," he explained to Lieutenant Wheeler, "to be obliged to execute any considerable topographical work." Already much of King's funding was allocated to projects that could scarcely be considered in the mainstream of his program. The best example was Hayden's work. Since President Hayes had failed to place that disappointed antagonist elsewhere, a niche had been decreed for him in the new survey, as a principal geologist at four thousand dollars a year, to continue work on Hayden Survey publications all but independent of King's control. *

At the same time twenty thousand dollars was earmarked more relevantly for the census of the mineral industries, in line with King's agreement with General Walker. Congress had directed the general to reinforce the usual staff of enumerators with a select corps of special agents—experts on various phases of the national economy—and it was appropriate that mines and mining had been chosen as a field for special assessment. As Walker had pushed King's nomination for the geological directorship, relations were cordial between the two, and they had easily reached an understanding on the conduct of the joint inquiry. Its purpose would be to determine "the character, extent, and total influence of the mining industry"; and to accomplish that, King and Walker had agreed to pool manpower and resources from their respective bureaus, the Geological Survey assuming scientific direction of the work, while the Census Office retained administrative control. This was the scheme of things that made it possible for the survey to conduct, during King's tenure, a complete appraisal of the mineral resources of the nation.

The mineral review, unlike the survey's regular business, had to be extended into the "older States," where King had no assurance of authority to act. Still, this negative factor was more than balanced by the comfort that such work "would tend at once to popularize the Survey." Pumpelly agreed to direct the operation, "exclusive of the precious metals and mineral oils," though he spurned a permanent place with the government, and committed himself to a couple of years

* See "Ferdinand Vandeveer Hayden: The U.S. Geological Survey Years, 1879–1886," by Clifford M. Nelson, Mary C. Rabbitt, and Fritiof M. Fryxell, for a corrective to the common view that Hayden's last years were withdrawn and unproductive. The paper establishes that, in spite of recurrent illness, Hayden managed to make a not inconsiderable contribution to knowledge. The authors add, however, that "not all Hayden's efforts were constructive. Although he was grateful to King for his appointment in 1879, Hayden believed that he had been unjustly denied the directorship of the Geological Survey and secretly opposed King and his policies. By covertly providing James Dwight Dana of Yale and [Archibald] Geikie with such negative information on the survey's program as he could obtain for their editorials in the *American Journal of Science* and in *Nature,* he tried to aid efforts by Dana and others to prevent King from securing congressional approval to extend the survey's operations east of the Mississippi River" (*Proceedings of the American Philosophical Society,* CXXV [June 1981], 239).

or so only because of the rich rewards in publication that the census promised. King gave him ample latitude in the conduct of the work and let him establish his office and laboratory in "the historic old Vernon House" in Newport. Pumpelly had his program under way within two months, with a force of fifty-seven men, detailed mostly from the Census Office and paid from General Walker's funds.

"Having a free hand," Pumpelly wrote,

I decided to lay special emphasis on the iron ores as underlying the fundamental industry of civilization. The census of the other minerals could be confined largely to the usual statistical methods. My plan was to have every mine and every known outcrop of iron ore, from Canada to the Gulf of Mexico and from the Atlantic to the Pacific, examined geologically, and systematically sampled for chemical analysis.

His operations represented only a part—though the greater part—of the census work that King had committed the survey to, but months must pass before the precious metals census could be put into effect. Meanwhile, a more pressing problem demanded King's attention—the question of the public lands.

He had discussed that urgent issue with many people on his last trip west. "And in general," he reported to Schurz, "[I] confirmed my original idea that the two great difficulties are the mineral and the irrigable lands." King was especially interested in the mineral lands; he had begun to assemble court decisions under the local mining laws of the West, as well as the statutes themselves, in order that the problems of mining and the mineral lands might be studied in their legal context. But there was little more to do until the ambiguities were resolved in the clause charging him with responsibility for classifying the public lands.

King, happily, did not have to wait long for a classification policy; the Public Lands Commission authorized by the Act of March 3 soon supplied it. King was an ex officio member of the Commission, along with James A. Williamson, head of the General Land Office, and he promptly asked for Major Powell to be included, "because he is the originator of the reform and has more facts than any one else." The request was granted, and at Powell's acquiescence King expressed his satisfaction. "*Hamlet* with Hamlet left [out] is not to my taste," he

assured the major. Then the president added two more members—
A. T. Britton, a land attorney in Washington; and Thomas Donaldson,
who had saved the George Catlin collection of Indian paintings for the
nation.

The commissioners met on July 8, 1879. They chose General Williamson president and Britton temporary secretary till Captain Dutton
became available for the post; they agreed on a general approach to the
land problem, and consulted with various members of Congress before
they undertook a four-month tour of the West. And though the whole
vexatious problem of classification lay before them, they reached a
decision that the Geological Survey could not classify lands either as a
condition for sale or in advance of sale without obstructing the rapid
settlement of the frontier. With that as a guide, King could put his
corps to work without clashing with General Williamson's organization.

He would declare in his annual report:

I have . . . concluded that the intention of Congress was to begin a rigid
scientific classification of the lands of the national domain, not for purposes of
aiding the machinery of the General Land Office, by furnishing a basis of sale,
but for the general information of the people of the country, and to produce a
series of land maps which should show all those features upon which intelligent agriculturalists, miners, engineers, and timbermen might hereafter base
their operations, and which would obviously be of the highest value for all
students of the political economy and resources of the United States.

It was a significant step in shaping the course which the survey was to
follow.

Meanwhile, King took the train for Cheyenne for the first stage of
the Western tour. He had promised much of his time for Land Commission duties, but cattle affairs detained him in Wyoming, and he arrived
in Denver only after his colleagues had convened. There the commission began its investigations; it heard the opinions of prominent citizens of the state and launched a canvass that would cover every state
and territory west of Kansas and Nebraska—only the extreme Northwest excepted.

As the work went on, King and his fellow commissioners sometimes
sat in a body; at other times they separated for side trips. Captain
Dutton mailed circular letters, along with copies of Major Powell's arid-

lands report, and questionnaires were published in journals and newspapers, with an invitation to interested readers to respond. In the end the board could say that it had reached "the most intelligent people in the West," and had secured "opinion from those whose long experience and thorough practical knowledge of the working of our present land system gave to their advice a special value."

King, as usual, had several irons in the fire; but he had requested Eliot Lord, his clerk, to travel with him on the tour, and with Lord's help he succeeded in combining numerous survey duties with Land Commission chores. He had, in fact, planned his itinerary to include visits to the survey units in the field, beginning with the Rocky Mountain Division. Emmons, his tall frame decked out in "riding clothes of Indian-tanned buckskin made by his London tailor," was still in Cheyenne, but he had sent a party under A. D. Wilson to begin work on the Leadville district, in the Mosquito Mountains. Leadville had boomed for over a year now—a tatterdemalion junktown of false fronts, board shanties, log huts, caves, and canvas tents. It had more than a hundred saloons and an equal array of gambling houses and thirty-five places of even worse repute. It was one of the busiest mining centers in the West, and King could see, as he advised Carl Schurz, "where practical geology can gain laurels in making a volume on the two wonderful silver-lead districts—Leadville, Colorado, and Eureka, Nevada." Projected books on both lodes had taken a preferred place on the survey's publication schedule, and King now rode to Leadville with his enthusiasm high.

He found Wilson hard at work, assisted by a brother-in-law of J. D. Hague—young Arthur Foote, who had dared to bring a wife to the West. Her name was Mary Hallock Foote, and King knew her from New York as an artist of talent whose sketches were bringing her recognition. Already for the publishers of *Mountaineering*, she had illustrated Longfellow's *Hanging of the Crane* and *The Skeleton in Armor*, as well as the Holiday Edition of Hawthorne's *Scarlet Letter*. She could also talk, and to Colonel Donaldson, who went with King to call on her in a small log hut on the edge of town, she seemed "well read in everything." Years later she would give her own version of the visit: "Clarence King came out with the Land Commission and never was there better talk (I at least have never heard better) than we used to have by our stone fireplace."

She had not yet published her fiction about the West, but she was jotting down her ideas, and much of *The Led-Horse Claim* would doubtless be on paper before her husband packed her away from Leadville. Later her prosaic description of a U.S. survey party in *John Bodewin's Testimony* would ring entirely true:*

The party are in camp now in the woods back of our cabin. There is no better company this side of the range than you'll get around their campfire of an evening. No ceremony—pot of beans or oatmeal or what not, boiling on the coals for tomorrow's breakfast—boys in their buckskins—not one of them but your daughter might dance with, or dine with, or gallop across country with, as she happened to find them. They're liable to turn up almost anywhere, those fellows—at the swell clubs in New York or London, or the President's reception, or digging their way up some mountain-peak above snow-line.

While King explored the Leadville boom, others in the commission party canvassed southern Colorado and New Mexico. Next the commission moved to Cheyenne; then on past Medicine Bow where Elk Mountain loomed in the distance above the range where King's trail herd from Oregon would pass the winter. The next stop was at Salt Lake City, and King took rooms at Walker House with Donaldson and Britton for the period of their stay.

* D. W. Brunton, a Colorado mining engineer, wrote in "Technical Reminiscences" (p. 10): "Conditions in Leadville during its early days are so truthfully and graphically portrayed in Mary Hallock Foote's most interesting novels . . . that it would be a waste of time to describe them here." Leadville provided the données and the scene for three of her novels. But in her long career Mrs. Foote published thirteen other books of Western fiction, and from her pages emerged the sharpest picture of the mining frontier since Mark Twain's *Roughing It* and the better tales of Harte. Public interest in the West ensured a modest vogue for her work during the ascendency of Howells, whose manner she adopted. Yet a far better novel than any she ever wrote is Wallace Stegner's *Angle of Repose* (Garden City, 1971), which drew from her then unpublished "Reminiscences," to re-create imaginatively the lives of Mrs. Foote and her husband Arthur under the fictional names of Susan Burling Ward and Oliver Ward. Part IV treats their Leadville experiences, including the visit in 1879 of King and Donaldson under their actual names. This episode also presents S. F. Emmons, Henry Janin, Rossiter Raymond, and Helen Hunt Jackson under their real names, while J. D. Hague appears in fictive guise as Conrad Prager. King, "glitteringly" characterized (the tag is Stegner's), is mentioned at later points in the narrative, but makes no further entry on stage. The vast success of *Angle of Repose*, which won the Pulitzer Prize, rekindled interest in the works of Mary Hallock Foote, and several of her books came back into print, and in 1972 the Huntington Library brought out her "Reminiscences" as *A Victorian Gentlewoman in the Far West*. On p. 181 therein she remarks, "We reached the height of our preposterous social brilliance that summer in Leadville when Clarence King arrived from Washington with members of the Land Commission in tow—huge Tom Donaldson being one of them. 'He's such a unanimous cuss,' King said of him."

Eager to impress, a party of Latter Day Saints took them to see an irrigation project which had made the desert green. King and his friends rode down to Lehi in a private car with several bishops and a troop of laymen, "an assembly of forty Mormon saints and many foreign sinners." During the excursion Brother George Q. Cannon enlightened King on the economic basis of Mormonism; in the course of which he claimed that a healthy Saint could manage four wives without trouble or strain, and would be serving God in doing so, at least in Utah, where there was an excess of women. Had Mr. King observed "the exquisite beauty of Mormon women"?—a disconcerting question, to which King murmured a noncommital reply. He was more impressed with Mormon canals. *

Back in Salt Lake City he fell ill, his malaria-ridden liver no match for the poor champagne the commission received one night at dinner. Donaldson wrote that "King and Britton glanced stealthily at each other when they drained the first glass. When the second was served, King fairly turned blue." "My God, I'm poisoned," he exclaimed as they returned to Walker House. The rest of his stay in Utah was a bout with illness, though he forced himself to keep on the job.

The survey units working out of Salt Lake City were in various stages of activation. The Division of the Colorado had launched a prompt continuation of Major Powell's former work. The major, who had not yet joined the Western tour, retained an understandable connection with the Colorado Division. Back in July he had seen two topographical parties off for the canyon country—one to the Uinkaret Plateau, the other to the Kanab region, along the northern rim of the Grand Canyon. They were hard at work there now, and with them were geological parties under the leadership of Charles Walcott, the youthful paleontologist whom James Hall had referred to King.

Operations in the Great Basin Division, King discovered, had not

---

*King had long nourished a desire to write something on Mormonism. When Howells had entreated for more mountain sketches in the early seventies, King had written his demurers from California: "I have no ambition to reel out of my notebooks more mountain climbs to get the public tired in their knees. Then too the mere artistic need of avoiding an anticlimax in the *Atlantic* would compel my shocking death in just three numbers." Instead therefore of more mountaineering, King had proposed something about the Mormons, provided Howells promised to run it unsigned. "I have further work in Utah," King had explained, "and should not like to be done [in] by Danites." The idea simmered on in his mind, his interest in the Mormon experiment continuing strong, but in the end the aim would come to nothing, like most of his later impulses to write, the pattern of his life remaining too restless and unsettled to foster work with the pen.

begun so promptly. Gilbert had been detained in Washington, and preparations for the Bonneville exploration were not complete. King helped with arrangements, borrowed instruments from the Coast and Geodetic Survey, and left two thousand dollars from his own pocket for Gilbert to buy whatever else the work required. Gilbert put the expedition into the field in early October, in time for a three-month trip through northwest Utah and the adjacent sections of Idaho and Nevada.

Meanwhile, the Land Commission moved on. One detachment staged to Butte, Montana, while King struck west for the mines at Eureka, where F. A. Clark had started topographical work. Eureka belonged in a geographical sense to Gilbert's province. But the Great Basin was so vast that King had made Gilbert responsible for only its general geology; he assigned the economic studies to George F. Becker, professor of mining at the University of California. King planned for Becker's work to include the geology of Eureka, to be laid down on Clark's new map; and when the commission reached San Francisco King conferred there with Becker, a young, light-hearted savant, full of drive and industry. They agreed on a quick look at mining districts scattered across the Great Basin, pilot work for planning monographs in the series King wished to publish. The examination was to coincide materially with the impending census of gold and silver mining, and Becker started without delay for southern Utah, with orders to double back to Eureka and Bodie before the end of the year.

General field work in the Pacific Division had to wait, King decided, though he planned for Hague, eventually, to launch intensive studies of the quiescent volcanoes of the Pacific Coast. King himself gave most of his time to the Land Commission during his stay in California. His party took rooms at the Palace Hotel, now boomed as "the grandest hostelry in the world," and there the commission reconvened for public testimony. They also questioned men at Marysville, in a region once rich, now sicklied over with the slickens from hydraulic placers. And then, as in Utah, they inspected a pioneer irrigation project down in Kern County, where canals of cold snow water were turning the plain into a garden.

King considered the tour a brilliant success. "The Geological Survey booms," he wrote to Schurz, "and the Land Commission is homeward bound, having faithfully investigated nearly all questions and sounded the chief people everywhere."

The commission met in Washington that December to digest the testimony, and from its discussions came a preliminary report. The majority's stand was not so radical as Powell's, although they accepted his thesis that most of the West—about 40 percent of the United States—was too dry for agriculture without the boon of irrigation, too dry indeed to profit from many features at all of a land system determined by the more humid conditions of the East. Yet the majority, King included, had no wish to scrap the current system wholesale; it was too deeply rooted, with too many rights already vested in it. They wanted, rather, to readjust it to the special conditions of the West. They declined to sponsor any changes which, in their opinion, might impede the rapid settlement of the frontier; and they embodied their recommendations in a bill which covered the land system in its entirety—a bill which provided for a rational system of classification, a gradual reduction in the price of unsold land, and the adoption of Powell's pastoral homestead. The commissioners attached it to their report and sent it to Carl Schurz.

Not that it would make much practical difference. When the bill reached Congress, it fared no better than other bills which Powell had offered in his arid-lands report. Congress would have no part of these reforms—at least for the present.

The work of codifying the land laws engaged the commission throughout 1880. But King was now so absorbed in survey problems, and in the census, that he could spare the Land Commission little time. Powell, too, was busy with other matters, principally his concern with the affairs of the Bureau of Ethnology. So they left the codification to a committee formed of their three remaining colleagues. Britton compiled several volumes of public-land laws, and Donaldson wrote a history of the public domain, soon published by Congress. Little else would henceforth bear witness to the commission's labors, and another attempt to rationalize the public-land system of America came virtually to naught.

For month after month Pumpelly had received a steady stream of iron-ore samples, and now in 1880 King was ready to tackle gold and silver. He summoned Emmons and Becker to Washington and bade them draw up plans for gathering statistics on the entire precious-metals industry of America. He aimed for their investigations to provide the most accurate index of the production of gold and silver that had ever been made; and he also intended to demonstrate the actual state of the business through facts on methods used in ore reduction.

King believed that both objectives should prove of the greatest practical value to mining men.

At the same time, he reserved the inquiry into mining laws and mining civilization as his own special responsibility. Having already begun to gather legal data on Western mining, he proposed to do for that branch of law what Britton had undertaken for the laws on public lands in general. "I don't know that you realize how important the local laws, regulations, and customs are," he remarked to Emmons. "I am most anxious to have a full collection bearing on that point."

King wanted to give a truthful picture of the life which had developed at the mines, an essay on the habits and the customs of the types who flourished there. Among those he planned to describe were the prospectors—"men whose experiences," wrote a *Tribune* correspondent after a talk with King,

have had more of romance than [those] of any other in this country, but of whom the people know little. The poor man, with his "grub stake," carrying his blankets, climbing the mountains with all his earthly possessions . . . on his back, and the learned professor employed by bonanza kings and Eastern millionaires indulging in the luxury of a pony ride and a pack animal, will be introduced.

At King's request, Becker and Emmons devised a series of schedules for the inquiry. They analyzed the best reports available on American mines and reduction works, and then worked out a list of questions to secure what information they needed. They were pioneers. "We worked hard and long," Becker would later remember. "We were in almost daily consultation with King, who was well informed on the whole subject, but I do not remember that he ever made any material change in our plans. We also had prolonged sessions with Gen. Francis A. Walker, . . . who was thoroughly agreeable and agreeably thorough."

King saw much of the general in Washington. Both had joined John Hay, the new assistant secretary of state, in keeping house "in a scrambling sort of way" in a "bachelor Castle," as Hay described it, at 1400 Massachusetts Avenue. There, Hay added when inviting Howells for dinner, "Clarence King [was] a sufficient attraction, if the feast consisted of a cold potato." The trio also had a private dining room at Wormley's, where they could lunch with guests, and "I doubt whether there ever was table-talk more brilliant," Becker would later reminisce, "than that to which we listened in that room." King always spoke in a gentle voice, Becker observed, but sometimes he said startling things. "Yesterday at dinner a guest asked him if the red pepper were hot. It's granulated hell, replied King." Informal, merry, irradiated with wit and good fellowship—such was the atmosphere in which the minerals census reached its focus.

The sensitive character of the gold and silver industry, King knew, ruled out the usual methods of gaining statistics. One could count on few returns from posted questionnaires. So King, like Pumpelly, had decided to send trained men to make personal inspections of every mine that yielded appreciable amounts of gold or silver or mercury, and of every mill and smelter. The plan and schedules were approved, and King sent out his agents on June 1, 1880, more than half a hundred of them. Emmons took charge of those working in the Rocky Mountain area, while Becker supervised the men assigned to the Great Basin and the Pacific Slope. King allowed them to push the work without interference, and when their funds ran low he lent money from his own pocket, to ensure that not a single working day was lost.

The census had its moments of excitement: claim jumpers thought one of Emmons's assistants was a spy, and nearly killed him in a Leadville shaft. But there were comic moments too: country postmasters mistook Pumpelly's small pouches of iron samplings for silver or gold; some posted guards over the sacks for twenty-four hours a day, and nothing appeared to cause the mails more trouble—unless it was the redwood stump, two flat cars long, which an agent on the West Coast had mailed to the Forestry Census, "postage free."

During the year King's agents visited 1,967 deep mines, 325 placer developments, and 438 reduction works of every kind. The result was an avalanche of more than two thousand reports. Time and available funds were both inadequate for the perfection he desired, but never before had such a series of technical data been amassed on Western mining—of that he could be sure.

King looked forward to working with Emmons and Becker on reducing the data on gold and silver to printable volume; Pumpelly would do the same for the results on iron and other minerals. General Walker had reserved several volumes in the census series for their findings. But King had also planned for the census work to provide material for the memoirs he expected to issue under the survey's imprint. For a beginning, his publication program called for at least a dozen volumes.

There would be a general treatise on the production of gold and silver: King planned to write it himself. Emmons's field work pointed toward the promised volume on Leadville, a treatment of both the mining and the geology of that district; while Arnold Hague agreed to do the companion memoir on Eureka. The Big Bonanza had made a fresh investigation of the Comstock necessary, and King now parceled the subject out as special projects: Becker assumed responsibility for the geology of the Comstock; Eliot Lord for a history of the mines; and W. R. Eckart, an engineer from San Francisco, for the mining and milling equipment found in use there. Thus, half the publications which King projected were, in some way, related to the gold and silver mining of the West. Three additional volumes would also deal with the West—Gilbert's study of Lake Bonneville, Dutton's description of the Grand Canyon region, and Marsh's monograph on *Dinocerata*, an extinct order of gigantic Eocene ungulates.

There could be no doubt that the geographical province of these works conformed with the law, even in Marsh's case, since Marsh had worked at his own expense. The propriety of the remaining volumes was not so clear, although they accounted for about a quarter of King's publication schedule. They included Pumpelly's studies on iron and coal and a memoir by R. D. Irving on the copper rocks of Lake Superior—none of them centering in the established areas of the survey. What attitude Congress would take toward this move of the survey into the states was problematic. Even Secretary Schurz found it prudent to write in his Annual Report for 1879–1880 that "care has been exercised that only census employees should be detailed to work in the region east of the one hundredth meridian." That was not strictly true, but one could hardly be careful enough in view of the opposition which the survey had aroused in the Senate.

Schurz luckily knew why Senator Dawes of Massachusetts had blasted King as "an extravagant humbug." It was King's mistake in failing to ornament a reception given by the senator's wife.* But no matter how absurd Dawes's petulance was, it did not help King's bid for a program of national scope. The favor of Senator Blaine was also strained at present, for on the appearance of *Democracy* in print he found no faint resemblance between himself and Silas Ratcliffe, the glaringly corrupt politico of the story. Henry Holt, the publisher, had given the novel

---

* The Dawes reception was not the only social event which King was obliged to miss that season. In describing a dinner given by Mrs. Elizabeth Cameron, the sparkling young wife of "Senator Don" of Pennsylvania, Julia Parsons remarked: "Clarence King was ill and could not come" (*Scattered Memories*, p. 66).

anonymous launching, true to his promise; but capital gossip seemed to fix on King, among others, as its likely author; and it would be attributed to him by the Library of Congress, and catalogued under his name. It seemed futile for him to disown it. Senator Blaine, along with his house guest Gail Hamilton, who had been King's high school teacher, cut him coldly. King's stock now reached its lowest ebb in the senatorial club, and urge as he might the passage of his resolution, it simply languished in the Appropriations Committee.

Undaunted by this somber rebuff, he requested Congress to authorize the survey to issue annual statistics on the mineral resources of the nation—a mission it could effectively achieve only if allowed to operate freely over the whole United States. King assumed that reason must prevail in the end, even in the Senate, and he formulated long-range plans accordingly. To the original districts of the survey he proposed to add four additional areas east of the hundredth meridian: two districts in the Mississippi Valley and two in Appalachia, one north of the Mason-Dixon line, the other south of it.

Leading geologists endorsed the proposal, but the antagonism of the Coast and Geodetic Survey stiffened resistance in the Senate. Booth of California called King's plan "preposterous." A nationwide program might be accomplished "in a perfunctory manner," he admitted. "But compared to a thorough geological survey of the whole United States, anything that can be done under this plan would be like a bird scratching on Mount Davidson to develop the mineral wealth of the Comstock lode three thousand feet below." So King's resolution remained blocked indefinitely, and even funds to carry on the status quo appeared to be in considerable jeopardy.

"I shall be bound hand and foot here until the first of July," King wrote. "Politics and dinner parties have so engrossed Congress that they have not done any business this year. In consequence, we shall . . . be gasping and drinking cold lemonade and delving for appropriations until midsummer."

The need to dance attendance on the wives and daughters of congressmen and senators exhausted King's patience, though fortunately by now he had the social assistance of a young hound from the Owl Creek kennels. The pup had become King's namesake, someone having dubbed him "Rex"; and as King informed his ranching partner, Rex had "his head fondled and petted by all the girls in Washington, until before long he will have a bald spot there, like mine."

The social rounds included evenings at the Schurzes', where the secretary played Chopin, which delighted King, whose taste in music was catholic, ranging from Beethoven to the latest popular fare. There were also levees at the Evartses', where King rubbed elbows with lions like George Bancroft or Secretary Sherman. Or there were Mrs. Hayes's Saturday receptions. The Marine band would blare as bigwigs marched into the East Room, the president leading, with some matriarch like Mrs. Astor upon his arm—in a constellation of jewels—followed perhaps by Mrs. Bigelow Lawrence (whom Adams had used as a model for Madeleine Lee) prancing along with Aristarche Bey, the Turkish minister. Senators and congressmen supplied a multiple representation—wives, daughters, cousins, sisters. But King might see real friends there too—the Schurzes again, or the Evartses, and once even the Howellses, who had introduced him to the president, "with an enthusiasm which he deprecated as 'din.'" Once, too, he had gone with Becker, who had come to Washington with wifely admonitions to restrain his cigarette ashes from "Mr. King's tea cup, or the President's best china vases." Guests dined well at the White House, but they did not "wine" there; Mrs. Hayes decreed abstention. She even served coffee with fish, though one could take tea if he chose, or unspiked punch or lemonade. There was always plenty of lemonade.

Yet lemonade and the dances paid in adequate funds for the Geological Survey, and an accelerated program was assured for the coming fiscal year. King had organized effectively; the survey flourished at the end of its first year, and its success had prompted Dutton to write Sir Archibald Geikie in praise of the director's achievement:

Mr. King is more than justifying all the high expectations which attended his appointment & his skill & ability to organize & administer have proved to be of the highest order. He succeeds in everything—& he is enthusiastically loved by everybody. He has drawn into the survey the best geological talent of the country.

But success had its price; the work had left the founder of the survey utterly weary.

King fretted and chafed under the demands of administrative details; for was he not, as Bailey Willis would describe him, "a restless spirit to whom responsibility was irksome"? Recurrent malaria and rheumatic pain gave his patience no chance to revive, and it seemed that each new onslaught of disease ate deeper into his endurance and left him more vulnerable than before. In this state of health he feared his chances for a mining fortune might be running out, an apprehension scarcely allayed by the restrictions which Congress had placed on the business interests of survey personnel.

King had not completely severed his private mining connections, and his desire now grew to turn his time and energy more to that account. He had recently joined a pool to finance a search for mining properties in Mexico, and reports from south of the border suggested that his fortune lay in that direction. Hence his decision in June 1880 to step down from the directorship of geology.

King claimed that he had accepted the post on a "distinct understanding with the president that he should remain at the head of the bureau only long enough to appoint its staff, organize its work, and guide the forces into full activity." That now had been accomplished, and he planned to resign on July 1, 1880. On June 11 King advised Schurz of his determination, but at an urgent plea from President Hayes he agreed to remain in harness a few months longer.

He started west at the end of June, assured of leave whenever he found it necessary to look into his private affairs, and though his life for the rest of the year became a web of mining transactions, complicated by ill-health, he remained intensely concerned with the precious-metals review and the program of the survey as he found it working in the field.

Emmons, whom he saw in July, was still preoccupied with Leadville mines. In Salt Lake City, Gilbert and Captain Dutton were preparing to take the field, Gilbert for another Bonneville expedition and Dutton for further surveys of the Canyon Country. King continued west before their wagon parties began to roll, but by the end of summer both campaigns had justified his confidence. Gilbert fixed the south profile of the ancient lake; Dutton worked up the geology of the Uinkaret Plateau, while two of his detachments surveyed the Kaibab and the San Francisco Mountain.

King himself had reached the city of San Francisco by mid-July, and he summoned Becker for further talks. Becker had started his work on the Comstock late in April. He had interrupted it only long enough to mind his part in the precious-metals census, and both assignments were under control. King was so pleased that he raised Becker's salary to that of full geologist, and at Becker's solicitation he engaged Carl Barus, a Würzburg Ph.D., to make galvanic measurements of ore bodies. This work was to be the survey's first experiment in geophysics, and though it might fail of conclusive results it testified to King's foresight in recognizing the value of physical methods in geological research.

King could feel pride in his bureau, and on his return from Arizona and Sonora (where mining matters had taken him in August and September)* he composed the first annual report of the Geological Survey. It was not a long document; King sketched the history of the organization; he described the work in progress; he included letters from his division leaders, repeated his case for extending the survey across the nation, emphasized the need for informing the public on natural resources, and announced the publications program which he had inaugurated.

As he did not wish to entrust the manuscript to clerks in Washington, he had the document printed in San Francisco and sent printed copies to Schurz in early November 1880. † "The summer campaign has been wholly successful," he could add, and he talked less of resigning, till friends like Becker began to hope that he might, after all, remain as chief.

But private ventures cried for his attention. He left the survey to run on its own momentum for the next two months while he returned to Mexico, to the scene of another extravagant hope. Sinaloa proved kinder to his health than had Sonora; it was storms and flood, not fever and dysentery, which delayed his return to San Francisco, weeks behind schedule. He remained in the West till early February 1881; then urgent telegrams called him back to Washington for a last struggle over appropriations for the coming year. He found the capital crowded for the impending inauguration, when an old friend of Western exploration was to claim the White House—General Garfield, political meteor of the day. Wormley's had no accommodations, unless King shared a room with a senator from Maine.

But Henry and Clover Adams, just back from Europe, had leased the

* As narrated in chapter sixteen *infra*

† See U.S. Geological Survey *Bulletin 100* (pp. 17–18) for bibliographical details. King's private edition comprised 500 copies. The official edition was published as a congressional document. Then the secretary of the interior ordered a further edition of 750 copies, which was issued separately.

Corcoran house on H Street, and they snatched King away from the crowded hotel. Was he not the dearest member of their circle—an unpredictable spirit who seemed so romantic that they would introduce him as "Our Byron."

Clara Hay had come to Washington for the remainder of John Hay's tour as assistant secretary of state. A close friendship had flowered between the couples, and King discovered himself in the center. They would often meet for tea or for dinner, these intimate five, and for talk from the heart—Clover, full of charm and high spirits, delighted by social gossip which she could relate with wonderful powers of mimicry; Clara, more subdued, not so brilliant as Clover perhaps, but more solid, more stable, her figure a shade too stout; Adams, witty, ironic, but not yet clouded with pessimism; Hay, the rival of King as raconteur, a poet besides, as full of jokes as King was full of puns;* and King himself, beloved of them all. Henry James deemed their society "the most entertaining in America."

They called themselves the "Five of Hearts." As a token of their close freemasonry they had stationery printed with five small hearts in Chinese red, as on a playing card. The pips were placed in the upper left-hand corner, and the letter paper was a simple luxury whose prompt consumption King advised, "as the shuffle of years might make clubs trumps before we realize it." There were also napkins and a silver tea-set embellished with five hearts, all of which may have been a jest at first; but if so, it was a jest that came to be taken at least half seriously. The Five of Hearts were not to become a capital fixture, however. Hay was ready to leave the State Department and with it Washington, and the impending change in administration would bring an equally decisive shift in King's circumstances.

"I know nothing of [King's] intentions for the future," Arnold Hague remarked; "and so far as I know no one else does." Carl Schurz did, however; and so did Powell, who later confessed that he had tried "to persuade [King] to remain at the head of the work even up to the very last week of his term of service."

But the die was cast. With survey funds assured, King submitted his

---

*Clover Adams preserved a sample of King's puns. After one of her skye terriers had come home with an affected eye, he diagnosed it as a "tom-cataract" (*Letters of Mrs. Henry Adams,* p. 277). Another sample was preserved by Henry Holt. When told of an oil magnate's having given "a very conspicuous house" to a favorite relative, King quipped: "Oil's well that ends swell" (*Garrulities of an Octogenarian Editor,* p. 136).

resignation on March 6, 1881. When President Garfield asked him to withdraw it, King went to the White House and explained his reasons in person. "Sir," read his statement for release:

Finding that the administration of my office leaves me no time for personal geological labors, and believing that I can render more important service to science as an investigator than as the head of an executive bureau, I have the honor herewith to offer my resignation as Director of the Geological Survey.

It was not entirely a frank statement, but it served the purpose. When Garfield saw that King would not change his mind, the resignation was accepted "in a letter of graceful regret."

King had not considered it necessary to secure Powell's consent before proposing him for the post. Garfield consulted with Spencer Baird, the major's superior, and half an hour later he sent Powell's nomination to the Senate to be confirmed.

All was done, as Powell claimed, "without my solicitation and without my knowledge"; and all very quietly, too, in an effort to keep the matter from Hayden, as it was thought he might try to block the appointment. The truth was, however, that Hayden had known for some time of King's desire to step down and had swallowed the bitter pill that Powell would be his successor. The Senate accepted the major's nomination on the 18th of March, while allowing him to retain the reins of his cherished Bureau of Ethnology. It was a popular choice in most quarters: "a choice," as one editor declared, "that will be welcome to all who know anything about the Survey." Powell could be counted on to build wisely upon the foundations which King had so soundly laid.

King's tenure as director of the Geological Survey had been so brief that its significance would sometimes be underestimated, and the traditional view of the early history of the survey would come to hold that Major Powell, "with his broad view of science and advanced ideas of land and water in the West, is the heroic figure," looming over both King his predecessor and Charles D. Walcott his successor. Mary C. Rabbitt's intensive study of the history of the survey would lead her to believe that another view could legitimately be taken, and she would suggest

that the importance the Geological Survey achieved in its first 25 years, in fact its longevity, should be attributed not to the broad view of science taken by

John Wesley Powell, but to the foresight of Clarence King in organizing the survey's research to aid in the industrial progress of the country while seeking ultimately the advancement of science and to the perspicacity, administrative skill, and seemingly limitless energy of Charles D. Walcott, who held that the Survey's field was geology and not all science, who directed its research toward the aid of not just the mineral industry, as envisioned by King, but of all industries and practical undertakings that would benefit from a knowledge of the Earth and its resources, and who insisted that basic and applied science cannot be separated.

16

Treasures of the Sierra Madre

King had left the capital, confident he had turned the Geological Survey over to able hands. He was confident also in his belief—oversanguine, to be sure—that he was a "power behind the throne." He assured such favorite assistants as Becker that their interests would be protected.

A minimum of dislocation followed. Major Powell launched no overnight reorganization, beyond merging the clerical forces of the survey and the Bureau of Ethnology. He favored centralization in Washington. But till adequate quarters could be obtained there, he kept the regional offices King had established in the West. He indicated that he would push King's publications program toward completion, changing it only in a small degree. King had genuine reasons for the pride and pleasure he took in his successor, this one-armed fighter with the shaggy, rust-red beard. Indeed, within a year Powell sailed jauntily over the hurdle that had caused King so much embarrassment. He beguiled authority from Congress to extend the work of the survey over the entire country by the shrewd but simple strategy of requesting—and gaining—an appropriation "to make a geological map of the United States."

But by then it was apparent that King's highly practical implementation of the will of Congress by establishing the survey as the ally, first and foremost, of the mining industry did not square with Powell's inclinations. The major had only a minimal interest in mining. The breadth of his preoccupations went far beyond the scope which Congress had prescribed for the survey, and with the energy of a wheelhorse he set about redirecting his bureau's mandated mission to suit his own views of what the nation needed to know about the public lands and to serve an older, less directed tradition of science that held that everything about a subject must be learned before that knowledge could be applied. He launched innovation after innovation without advice or guidance from self-styled powers behind the throne, and it took him no more than three years to radically transform King's original plans and organization. The new program relegated mining geology and mineral statistics to a minor consideration in an establishment that emphasized topography, geological mapping, and paleontology, and that studied matters as diverse as forest distribution and the problems of irrigation, and that increasingly implemented measures more closely connected with agriculture than with geology. In fact, under Powell's direction the Geological Survey not only abandoned its initial alliance with the mining industry, but even formed a firm alliance with agribusiness, including animal husbandry; and with all his ebullient drive the major continued to foster irrigation as the indispensable means of sustaining agriculture in the arid West. No wonder that successive moves were to generate in Congress to move the Geological Survey from the Interior Department into the Department of Agriculture.

Meanwhile a new phase had opened in Clarence King's life. On returning to New York City in the spring of 1881 he had taken rooms at Brevoort House, a block south of 23 Fifth Avenue. Expensive, richly furnished, this hotel could boast of one of the most discriminating cuisines in town. It catered to wealthy foreigners, and the European atmosphere appealed to King, as it did to several of his friends, whom he met there for wine and Continental cookery. They included cronies like Philip Schuyler, fat and genial General Samuel Barlow of the erstwhile diamond firm, and even John Hay, who had come to New York to run the *Tribune* while Whitelaw Reid was on his honeymoon in Europe.

At this time King began to yield more and more to the hedonistic ideas which had always appealed to him. Yet this was a difficult season for him. His stubborn ailment racked him mercilessly, and he complained to Emmons: "My physicians shake their heads and tell me that it will take several months yet to tell whether this outbreak of the malady is going to be curable or fatal." He felt that in rest lay his best chance for recovery; and, "One after another," he confessed, "I am trying to relieve myself of labours." The wonder is that he managed to cope with as many responsibilities as he did.

The connections he still retained with the Geological Survey were without further salary, and he remained only unofficially responsible to the Census Office for the statistics on precious metals. The few government chores still under his direction were centralized in quarters lent by the American Museum of Natural History, a citadel of salmon-dark granite overlooking Central Park. There on moving from 23 Fifth Avenue King had left his scientific library—more than four thousand books and pamphlets—and there the final work had been done on the fortieth parallel rocks. There King had also quartered Carl Barus after the electrical experiments at Washoe and Eureka, and together they planned extensive geophysical researches that were to keep Barus busy for years. King had been eager for the survey to follow up Barus's work with more geophysics: a program to discover such physical data as those which, missing still, had balked his speculations on subterranean fusion. The matter was crucial to King's catastrophic geology. As Adams had pointed out in the *Nation,* so long as he framed no laws to govern the cataclysms he charged to geological history, "he will have simply succeeded in depriving us of Lyell's system without offering us a system of his own."

King hoped to supply that lack in a book he thought of naming *The Upheaval and Subsidence of Continents.* It was part of the private investigations, the "valuable work as geologist out of harness," that he had promised himself to do on resigning from the directorship; and essential to it would be the work that Barus had now undertaken—the work of exploring interactions of the primal materials of the globe under conditions of extreme heat and pressure.

Geophysics, nevertheless, seemed so remote from the main objectives of the survey, as it was shaping up under Powell's direction, that it won but lukewarm sanction from the major. Only the salaries of Barus and his associate were covered by the latest budget, and King was obliged to equip the physics laboratory himself. It was a strain on his purse. But he accepted the burden and sent to Europe for the best instruments available for the purpose.

At this time King also consolidated the last phases of the precious-metals work at his museum rooms. His field agents had amassed twenty-five thousand pages of manuscript, besides stacks of executed schedules. King hoped to digest most of this information himself; but, as he had written to General Walker: "It is plainly apparent that delegating all I possibly can, there must still remain for me eight solid months of labor. With all the intimacy acquired by years of study of the mining regions, I was still unprepared for the amount of work which piles up for me personally."

He summoned first Becker, then Emmons, to help with the compilation. But even so, the work ran on so long that it was necessary to warn the census chief: "Volume I will follow 'the Lord knows when,' and He has not as yet vouchsafed any information." Shortly afterward, in May 1882, ailing health forced King to surrender charge of the work completely, though not before, as Becker later acknowledged, "all the most important questions were settled [so] that credit for the general conduct of the work belongs entirely to him." There had been a preliminary bulletin—*Statistics of the Production of the Precious Metals in the United States*—published by the Census Office in 1881. The final report of the tenth census would incorporate two further volumes, including King's compilation of mining laws. But his sanguine plan to skim the cream of the entire study into a single memoir covering "all the striking features of the industry"—*The Precious Metals*, which he had promised for the memoir series of the Geological Survey—would never be realized. It would be another casualty to his persistent rounds of ill health and the furious pace of his ongoing struggle for the fortune that glittered in his dreams.

King's retirement from public service had brought surprise to many of his supporters—to others, disappointment. The press had received his statement to the president, and some reporters had read between the lines: "It is understood," one of them wrote, ". . . that the private business of 'experting' is much more lucrative to him than the Directorship of the Survey, and that he will again follow his profession of mining engineer." There was the lure of Mexican gold and silver, and he was now free, barring illness, to follow the old Conquistadores. That was King's main reason for leaving Washington, whatever his public admissions. He had wanted to push his mining ventures in Mexico, unhampered by the responsibilities of public office. He dreamed of wresting from the Sierra Madre one of those glittering fortunes which passed for supreme achievement in America of the 1880s.

If the national mind had reached any focus at all after the Civil War, it was concentrated on wealth and all that wealth could buy. And the business way of life, because it opened the door to power and luxury, seemed the inevitable one for energetic young Americans. Just as the hardiest Frenchman in Froissart's era had turned to war, and the hardiest Englishmen in Hakluyt's time had turned to the sea, or to exploration, so now in America business claimed young men of strength and vision. King could not escape its compelling attraction. Not that he wholly approved of it: his mind and his heart seemed deeply divided concerning all that came with the acquisition of wealth.

The common values of the day had impressed King as shallow,

shoddy, even evil. He had a sharp indictment ever at hand for what he termed "our hopeful level of Philistine vulgarity." American plutocracy struck him as a "simian circus," eager to ape the gaudiest shams of the Old World. Once he remarked after a banquet with a millionaire, "These people have bought the scenery of society, but the play isn't going on." And once he asked, "What are you going to do with such a people?" Yet his amused contempt for the new rich had never slackened his urge to join their company. His lust for wealth grew so insatiable that he turned his back unbothered on a career that had marked him, in John Hay's phrase, as "the best and brightest man of his generation."

This defection was fostered by King's growing weariness with science—and the scientific mentality which on occasion he roundly excoriated. "I am forced to admit," he wrote in the *Forum*,

that the purely scientific brain is miserably mechanical; it seems to have become a splendid sort of self-directed machine, an incredible automaton, grinding on with its analysis or constructions. But for pure sentiment, for all that spontaneous, joyous Greek waywardness of fancy, for the temperature of passion and the subtler thrill of ideality, you might as well look to a wrought-iron derrick.

The fact was that King was choking on a thinness of emotional atmosphere. It was a common affliction, almost a national suffocation, that went with the commercialization of American life after the Civil War. King felt it as a blight nourished by the science of the age, the science from which he recoiled in fatigue and disgust.

He did not seem to care that, as a mining promoter, he was jumping from the skillet into the fire. "He was so constituted," according to his friend Brownell, "as fastidiously to desire to make the most of the Epicurean principle, to get the best out of its practice"; and to him the business life seemed the sensible means to that end—the way to the wealth that would enable him, among other things, to cultivate his "private life," refine it till it had the grace and distinction of a work of art. Such were the reasons he wanted wealth—not to possess it for its own sake. Hence his quip that the streets of Heaven were paved with gold "just to show how little they think of it there." But the intrinsic value King set on gold, so trifling in itself, would hardly lessen his scrabble for it, the incessant struggle that would dominate his later life.

It was true that he still made money on his cattle in the West, and would do so until 1883; but he needed much more for the princely life he dreamed of, especially for the patronage of artists that he planned. "Behind this," wrote John La Farge, "there was a great mirage of a possible future of some mine, the very record of which was in itself romantic. When the resulting fortune should come, the artists were to have a chance, were to help make use of it for beautiful things." Such hopes of affording bountiful patronage to the arts had fanned King's fascination with the histories of treasures—not least the fortunes of gold and silver mined from the ranges of Mexico since the days of Cortez. From 1879 his *ignis fatuus* had been the gleam of Mexican bonanzas; and nothwithstanding his commitment as director of the Geological Survey that year had marked the beginning of his feverish investigation of Mexican mines—his quest for lodes that had fostered Mexico's reputation as one of the richest mining countries in the world.

By 1879 Porfirio Diaz had given the land three years of peace, and a new era seemed to be dawning. The strong man had offered concessions to foreign capital, and American empire builders had responded with deals for Mexican railroads, Mexican telegraph lines; and posses of Yankee mining men—wildcat promoters as well as scouts for American nabobs—had swarmed into the mountains and deserts of the northern states—into Chihuahua, Sonora, Sinaloa. Not even dread of Apaches could stem that tide of gold-hungry men, which included King's old friend of the diamond swindle, Henry Janin.

It was Janin's practice to ferret out historic gold or silver mines which had slumped or failed because of drownings or obsolete methods of work. Mexican owners were often loath to change their customary ways; they worked the mines in much the same manner as in the sixteenth century. Thus profits came hard; and unprogressive proprietors could make more money by leasing their holdings, or selling them outright, to invading gringos. Sometimes they would sell well-opened mines of proved merit for less than mere prospects up in the States. Janin took options on such properties for later resale to American syndicates, and he was out to place just such an operation when the Land Commission had come to San Francisco in 1879. King had settled down in the Palace Hotel, where Janin had bubbled on about the Minas Prietas (the "Black Mines"), a flooded lode of gold and silver in the mountains of Sonora. The shafts were located in the general vicinity of the legendary lost Tayopa—the Mine with the Iron Door—which many believed to have been the richest single treasure-hold in all the world.

Spanish priests had worked the quartz vein of Prietas in the eighteenth century till Indians drenched the countryside in blood, and then for many years the shafts had lain neglected. The Marquis of Coloma, a grandee of Spain, had claimed Prietas then, and worked the vein for silver down to the heavy water level, where his crude method of draining (by means of rawhide buckets carried up notched tree trunks from level to level) was bound to fail, and the stopes lay swamped for decades more. In 1860 an English company had taken over the principal mine and drained it of water, tapping ore of immense richness, and several million dollars worth of gold and silver was produced in the course of operations. The story was not ended, King believed. There were still bonanzas waiting for capital and ingenuity to lick the problems of production.

King rushed his proposals to his Eastern friends—Alexander Agassiz, Henry Lee Higginson, and Quincy Shaw, ever on the alert for a new Hecla or Calumet, as their fabulous copper mines in upper Michigan were called. They rose to King's bait with an offer of more than half a million dollars for control of the workings at Prietas, which was secured from the current owner, a Mexicanized Yankee named Don Ricardo Johnson. King agreed to become the manager, for an interest, and asked for a tenth part more to be held for him at bedrock price until he could raise the purchase money.

His friends lost no time in forming the Minas Prietas Mining Company, with the New York banker James J. Higginson as president. They capitalized it at a million dollars and opened an office at 62 Cedar Street, which King hastened to make his New York business address. His mining involvements quickly increased: he now advised his Boston millionaires to buy a second bonanza that Janin had brought to his attention.

It was not an old mine—the Harshaw, located in the Patagonian Range of southern Arizona. But the early production sounded phenomenal. There was a forty-foot vein, fully opened, the widest vein King had ever run across; and it was rich with horn silver. Control could be had for six hundred thousand dollars, and King's friends in Boston responded promptly. They bought up the original company, and in March 1880 they formed their own corporation—capital stock: two million dollars.

King took Harshaw shares for his services, and then bought more stock at bedrock price, though he had to keep the business quiet in view of the mine's location. It was not compatible with his position as director of the survey and the restrictions laid down by Congress. But the matter was easily managed: Gardiner, one of Harshaw's new trustees, carried King's stock in his name, along with his own.

There was no need, however, to act so stealthily in Mexican ventures, and King agreed to direct a fund for exploring the flooded old Rosario Mine in the mountains of Chihuahua. The move would come to nothing, however. Other Americans beat King's men in a jockey for location, and he stopped the work before expending much of the exploration fund. His reason: "I can't afford to be connected with a fiasco."

Other skirmishes of his scouts proved more encouraging. They turned up an excellent prospect in a drowned old silver mine in Sinaloa eighty miles north of Culiacán, where the *zona templada* enjoyed an eternal spring, with temperate days and cool, crisp nights. The mine, like the Rosario, could be reached by mule trail only, and it went by the ominous name of Yedras—"Poison Ivy" in Spanish. But the six-foot vein had put its owners on Easy Street before subterranean streams had made the mine a sump. Yedras was on the block now for two hundred thousand dollars. At a nod from "the Boston people" King hired Pumpelly (whom he considered the best geologist on the survey's staff) to make an examination. Pumpelly reached the mine around ten o'clock one night, and pressed for time because of having to "catch the first steamer from Mazatlán," he worked around the clock. "It was one of the hardest jobs of my life," he later confessed. "Like a convict stonebreaker, sitting on the ground with a rock between my legs for anvil, I broke and quartered samples [of ore] for twenty-seven hours." But then he fired back an emphatic recommendation, claiming $1,800,000 worth of ore in sight; and King's agent, George Tew, closed the purchase in May 1880.

The Yedras Mining Company was chartered by early July, with a million dollars' worth of stock, and with James Higginson again installed as president. King took a fourth of the shares at about two-fifths of the par value, most of the rest having been subscribed by his Boston friends. They insisted that the mine be run as a close corporation, to avoid all smack of speculation, which meant that, while Hay and Gardiner had paid for a large percentage of King's subscription, they received none of his stock, merely rights to share in his profits. That was a legal fiction, perfectly legal and purely a fiction, but everyone was happy. King not only became a trustee of the new company, he also agreed to manage Yedras in addition to Prietas.

He kept in touch with the mines through weekly reports. He authorized the shipment of hoists and pumps for the works at Prietas. He also studied plans for a new mill there of forty stamps, and pondered the question of suitable treatment for the stubborn Prietas ore. "The West is covered with the wrecks and debris of new processes," he bantered, "and I am always a little shy of anything unless it has ruined a few good people." At first the Prietas ore was treated by means of pan amalgamation, then with the Russell process of lixiviation.

At Yedras King ordered a survey of the ground and approved the action of his man in "denouncing" nearby claims. An owner, to hold his mine under Mexican law, must work it for a certain period every year; a claim not worked the specified amount of time could be "denounced" and made to revert to the state. It could then be bought at a government sale, sometimes for a song. The Yedras Company increased its tract by such maneuvers until it reached a mile in length, a cause for much rejoicing, for as King remarked: "Outcrops of the vein trace themselves along the surface of the hill nearly the whole length of the denounced properties, and we are likely to open bonanzas at any point on the outcrop." The future looked bright during the summer of 1880, the time of King's next trip to the West.

Urgent problems, nevertheless, had arisen at the mines. Someone must go to Prietas at once to make some fundamental decisions about the mill and furnace construction there. "This cannot be deferred a moment longer," King maintained; and as soon as government duties allowed, he himself set out for Sonora. It meant passing through a region scourged by Victorio's warriors, a land where victims of Apache viciousness were sometimes found spread-eagled over ant hills, their bones picked clean by the great black ants that could strip a skeleton between sundown and dawn.

King knew little of the country's language: "Only that little Spanish," he once suggested, "so much more embarrassing than none." But he had taken a Spanish dictionary on the stagecoach out of Tucson, and fell to memorizing words in spite of the torrid heat. All the verbs were in the infinitive, and he got no help from Spanish grammar; but by the time he reached Guaymas, as John Hay later wrote, "he was master of a highly effective and picturesque jargon which delighted the Mexicans and carried him triumphantly to the mines."

He began at once to bargain with pack- and wagon-train operators; hauling contracts had to be completed as soon as possible, for it would take two months and monopolize most of the wagons in Sonora to bring

the mill machinery, lumber, and building iron to the mine from Guaymas. He could not risk letting someone else tie the trains up; for as he
wrote: "That would leave us out in the cold till next spring. As it is, we
have got in ahead of everybody for up-freight from the coast to Hermosillo, and are likely to breed a furore in that charming city."

The mine lay in the bluish sierra to the southeast of the city, the road
to it running through country crawling with Indians, revolutionaries,
and bandits of every description. Back in the tumbled mountains the
wily chief Cajeme had drilled a force of Yaqui followers, who were to
terrorize the countryside for years to come. All developments at the
mine would have to be conducted on the edge of Yaqui insurrection.

King reached the village of Las Prietas after "the most bruising and
battering sort of all-night travel." It was the season of summer rain; the
temperature was 90 degrees by night, 110 by day. He had fallen ill with
amoebic dysentery, complicated by an extravirulent strain of malaria;
pain gnawed at his belly, his face turned the color of an orange, and he
lost thirty pounds. "The whole of Mexico would not tempt me to go
through that experience again," he wrote. Yet he managed to make a
thorough examination of the property.

His studies confirmed prior evaluations of the mine; and he predicted
that, barring some unforeseen change in the ore below water level, the
opened portion of the lode should earn the company a net profit of a
thousand dollars a day. "So far as the vein and ore go," he reasoned,
". . . the enterprise stands on as safe a foundation as is possible in any
mine that has not met the critical change of passing below the water
level." The water problem, however, would have to remain an open
question for another two hundred feet down. So during the rest of his
five-week stay King concentrated on engineering matters, and he felt as
optimistic as fever chills and the gripes of dysentery would allow.

On his return to Arizona in September he stopped at the Harshaw to
check the new mill, only to learn that the fabulous ores of the upper
levels had yielded to an enormous "horse." That was mining lingo for
an invasion of barren country rock that impoverished a formerly rich
vein. Hint of the development had reached the East, and one of King's
friends in Boston had wired back the importunate question: Was it true
that there was a horse in the mine? In reply King telegraphed: "The
mine is a perfect livery stable." Chaffing aside, the horse was a prime
disaster, as unexpected as it was overwhelming. There had been no
forewarning, no premonitory signs of it. Indeed, not two months
before, Gardiner had left the mine "at a bright cheery heat . . . over the

ore in sight"; and so confident had been the superintendent's report, which King had read on his way to Sonora, that King now exclaimed: "I was wholly unprepared for the sudden climax at the mine, and experienced a shock to the feelings which perhaps may have been heightened by the depression of mind and body I had suffered."

One thing bothered him especially; he had asked Gardiner to sell his Harshaw holdings at a profit, to meet other pressing commitments and to relieve himself of any conflicts over legal restrictions. And he feared that the move might look as though, without advising his benefactors, he had acted "in some intimation of the [vein's] condition."

Soon, however, the "geological Micawber" revived in King; he recovered his constitutional optimism, and assured his friends in Massachusetts that "skillful work" should develop more rich ore near the surface. "I do not doubt," he wrote, "that somewhere in the length of the lode we shall find a bonanza extending downward. . . . It will be hardly short of a miracle if the ore does not make into a chimney somewhere. Such a long rich bonanza on the surface means more below—somewhere—and I believe we shall get it." He virtually promised to make the Harshaw repay investment in the early future.

The mill did in fact continue to handle a hundred thousand dollars' worth of ore a month. But the Boston trio decided to sell, their first furtive moves plunging the Harshaw stock to a fourth of its nominal value. Then came mutters of "Fraud!"—although aggrieved parties could bolster their charges with nothing more sinister than the plain fact that someone, at the bitter news, had sold quickly and sold first.

Harshaw might have pointed a moral to King; but if it did, its force did not prove strong enough to shake him out of what Theodore Winthrop had called "the bitter bad business of quartz mining." On arriving in San Francisco he found Henry Janin overflowing with enthusiasm about another mine—a modest one this time—at Grizzly Flats near Placerville. It was worth inspecting, Janin insisted, and King rode out to the mine himself. The small bonanza, bright with sulfurets, looked good to him; he was also impressed with the possibilities in an abandoned ore chimney, so impressed that he wired Shaw and Agassiz for purchase money. J. D. Hague joined the pool a little later, and they formed the Mount Pleasant Mining Company to float the works at Grizzly Flats.

Mount Pleasant never quite equaled King's hope for it, but it paid for itself in the next few years, and produced some tidy dividends, in spite of several bullion thefts. The mine lay in the heart of Black Bart's country, where stages were being waylaid in the 1880s; and after several robberies on the road King's superintendent began to search for some means of foiling the thieves. Once he had a lead brick cast and covered with gilt till it looked like gold, then gave it to the stagecoach driver to surrender at the next holdup instead of the bullion that would be hidden inside the coach. Between shipments, however, the fake ingot was left about the office at Grizzly Flats—a sore temptation to the Chinese cook, who yearned to die in China. He stole the bogus gold one day and started out of the mountains, with men from the mine in pursuit. He started to fire as they overtook him, and received more lead in return—this time without gilt.

In Sinaloa, meanwhile, the Yedras bonanza was "going down gallantly," and reports led King to hope for a million dollars profit on the ore in sight. High ratios of antimony and arsenic, however, had made the ore rebellious, and a stubborn reduction problem developed. King was aware of the dire results such troubles could have if not corrected, and he approached the matter gingerly. In addition to furnace roasting for the ore, he thought of adopting some type of lixiviation, instead of pan amalgamation. Several Mexican mines were now leaching their ores with hyposulphate of lime and showing good results. But "I'm unwilling," he decided, "to take any steps toward the creation of reducing works until I've seen the mine." He caught the boat for Sinaloa early in November, "ill," as General Walker heard, "shaken with fever, and heavily out of pocket."

The muttering of local revolution had scarcely died away as King debarked at Mazatlán. He staged to Culiacán, where men and horses were available, and they struck into the sierra, over primitive trails, through thick subtropical forests. The remote site of Yedras brought King among a simple people of Aztec descent, the men large-bodied and well proportioned, the women sparkling specimens of olive-brown beauty. King greatly enjoyed their friendly greetings, their laughter, their naive embraces of welcome. "He has fallen in love with Mexico and its people," wrote a friend; "the Mexican Indian exceeds even the Kanaka in his admiration and respect." The natives of Yedras accepted him as a kind of feudal lord, a Yankee hidalgo armed with power over their small world, especially since his company had leased the Rancho Valgame Dios, which surrounded the mine and supported the village of Yedras.

Stands of pine grew on the rancho, and the lease gave rights to the timber. King had shipped a whole sawmill from San Francisco; mules had borne it piece by piece up the tortuous trails to the mine, and its double circular saws could handle the heaviest timber the mine required. Lumber lay stacked on a flat below the mine tunnel—posts and beams and planed boards awaiting King's decisions. Hundreds of thousands of bricks were being fired, and piles of stone quarried for masonry. The mine had spurred the whole countryside to new activity, and the work slackened only for Sundays, holidays, cockfights, and revolutions.

At King's request the bonanza winze had been carried down to a hundred feet below the tunnel level, and the ore body was explored by means of side drifts. It turned out well, perhaps not as well as the sanguine foreman had predicted, but King felt cheered. He raised his plans for the mill from thirty stamps to forty, and allowed for power to go still higher.

He turned also to the question of transportation, a pressing one for a place as hard to reach as Yedras. Pack mules now supplied the mine with freight, and bullion intended for San Francisco had to be loaded on muleback also, and carried under guard to Culiacán, a slow, inviting prize for bandits. King made plans to replace the trails by a wagon road, and mule *conductas* by wagon trains, regardless of cost, for Yedras had infected him with extravagant dreams of development.

He was ready now for the horseback travels he had planned to take with Janin and others through the western Sierra Madre. This was the jaunt that would prompt Clover Adams to write, "He bloweth where he listeth and official traces cannot keep him in the shafts"—a jaunt which put over a thousand miles beneath the hoofs of his mule before he was ready to come home.

No one rightly knew what treasures lay hidden in those austere ranges, but the legends were fantastic. Somewhere, for example, in the mountains back of Yedras, on the floor of one of those great gorges which the Mexicans called barrancas, lay the famous lost Naranjal Mine, a mine so rich that its owner had paved the path with silver between his house and the church nearby. King's scouts had not recovered the lost Naranjal, but they had lined up mines for him to see in at least three Mexican states; but before he regained the coast the second rainy season of the year had swooped down with cloudbursts and raging rivers. Back in Washington, Clover Adams wrote: "We hope daily to see him, but he is so reckless of life and strength that his friends feel uneasy."

At one place the flood swept away his gear, and he lost all his papers and money. He had to wire for more leave, and his return to San Francisco was delayed for weeks. Storm kept him in Mexico through Christmas, and he became " 'compadre' to several pretty girls," a brotherly relation, as his friends contended, "with a dash of the cavalier servant's [sic]." His feeling for the brown girls was an intensification of the earlier wonder with which the native women of Spanish America had inspired him, the admiration which he had suggested in the *Atlantic*:

Whoever has strolled at dusk where palm-groves lean to the shore, and watched the Indian women sauntering in the cool of evening with a gait in which a ripple of grace undulates—whoever has seen their soft, dark eyes, and read the expression of tenderness and pathos which is habitual on their faces, can but feel that here simple nature has done all she can for woman.

When he could again set out for San Francisco, he was "anxiously awaiting a dispensation . . . to stand as Godfather to a Mexican baby—with a pretty Godmother." Perhaps the woman whom he called "Madonna of the Corn Stack."

The prize of King's Mexican tour had been another historic group of mines, thirty-nine shafts at Sombrerete, Zacatecas. Though formerly among the most productive mines of Mexico, they had lain for years unworked, at the base of a mountain which looked like a Mexican hat. Title could be secured by simple relocation, and King's skirmisher, George Tew, took possession for the syndicate. As soon as King could return East, he placed the prospect before his wealthy friends, finding it hard not to exaggerate the promise of Sombrerete. Much of its history read like pure romance.

Humboldt had lauded Sombrerete in glittering phrases, had cited one of its veins as the wealthiest "yet discovered in the two hemispheres." Soldiers of fortune had found it shortly after the Spanish conquest, and Sombrerete was soon pouring vast treasures into the coffers of Spain. Two veins, six hundred feet apart, continued yielding docile ores all through the seventeenth century. The quantity was sometimes fabulous. Around 1675 one vein—the Veta Negra—started producing at the rate of twenty thousand dollars a day, a bonanza that endured for years. A decade later the 20 percent royalty claimed by the King of Spain had reached a total of $12 million. Then ground water had filled the shafts; and the mines had lain undisturbed for nearly a century, till the House of Fagoago came to grips with the problem.

During the first year, the Fagoagos found nearly $2 million worth of ore in one vein; and when they dug a crosscut to the second vein they struck a huge pocket of ruby silver. It was stubborn ore, as hard to work as it was dark and rich, and for its reduction they built a patio with eighty-four *arrastras*, large mule-driven mortars, the ruins of which could still be seen. The ore took years to work, but produced $11,500,000, a fortune that made the head of the house a great grandee—the Marquis of Apartado.

The revolution came in 1810, driving the Fagoagos from the mines, and Sombrerete fell into the hands of native *buscones*. They leased the ground to an English syndicate, and a few years later the English struck another bonanza, one that realized $13 million in less than a year. But the Mexican owners refused to renew the lease when it expired; they wanted to work the mines themselves. But they failed in their struggle against the water—a total defeat; and Sombrerete languished again, idle and deserted, until King's scout found the property and denounced it.

The grounds extended for nearly two miles along both veins—a tract which had yielded $150 million, if official figures were only approximately correct. The principal shafts were deep, nine hundred to a thousand feet deep, but King was sure the ore descended in depth. All signs indicated a lower junction of the veins, and that determined the course he planned to follow. He decided to pick two shafts for operations—say the San Francisco and San Pedro *tiros*. They were about three-quarters of a mile apart, and full of water. Let two pumps be brought, better ones than Sombrerete had ever seen, to drain the shafts. Then retimber them and dig them deeper, to perhaps two thousand feet, where, if King's speculations were correct, the Pabellón and Veta Negra veins came together. The width of the ore body at that point should equal that of the two veins combined.

Such a plan would require time and money, but the stakes were staggering. King dared hope that Sombrerete still held wealth comparable to the treasures wrested from her veins in the past; he also believed that given adequate means and the proper machinery he could find it and reduce it at great profit. That was what he proposed to his friends in Boston and New York; and when his enthusiasms were aroused, as now, he could muster what Bronson would call "wizard fluency and eloquence of expression."

King carried his point, and scarcely two months after resigning the geological directorship, he arranged to found the Sombrerete Mining Company. Most of the corporators were the same people who had backed Yedras and Prietas. On May 11, 1881, they signed a certificate of incorporation which specified $5 million in capital stock. "The plan seems a stupendous one to Mexican miners," wrote one correspondent of the project, "but to men who have worked 3,200 feet underground in the Comstock mines of Nevada, it is child's play." King was soon to learn, however, that the development of Sombrerete was hardly child's play.

He became one of the five directors of the company, along with Agassiz and Shaw; and at the first board meeting they chose King president as well. As superintendent he selected his former field mate of the California Survey, Charles Hoffmann, whom he had hired, in the first place, to map the grounds at Yedras and Prietas. On completing grade-curve charts for the first two mines, Hoffmann proceeded to Sombrerete, where he settled down for two years' service "until all the machinery was set up and part of the mines drained." During that time King would lean heavily on his advice.

Meanwhile, King received $750,000 for the development of Sombrerete; he authorized the purchase of "everything necessary for running the mine on the most approved methods." His agents ordered two large hoists from San Francisco, duplicates of a model built for the Anaconda Mine at Butte. They also bought four powerful sinking pumps, air compressors, and tools and machinery enough to equip a machine shop, a carpenter shop, a smithy, and a sawmill—six hundred tons of hardware that must be borne on mules for hundreds of miles across the sierra. Heavy machinery had to come in parts, no single section weighing more than three hundred pounds, the limit of each mule's burden. It would take four thousand mule trips to equip the works, and long trains must toil up and down the mountains from ten to fifteen miles a day. Freight charges would, in the end, exceed one hundred thousand dollars, or twice the original cost of the gear. No wonder the Mexicans had the saying "It takes another mine to work a mine."

King decided to concentrate his efforts on the San Francisco shaft, to explore the Pabellón vein. It was clear that Sombrerete, with so many problems to be solved, could not produce immediate dividends. Meanwhile King's associates wished—indeed, demanded—quick results from the mines at Yedras and Prietas.

In the second year of King's management, the mine at Prietas had begun to net a few returns, slimmer by far than what King had counted on. The time it had taken Prietas to wipe out capital overdrafts had run so long that King could feel no real encouragement over the gains. It was a stern fact that the profits had come from working the best, indeed the most accessible, ore in the mine; and they struck him as hardly a fair return on the capital. The outlay at Prietas would eventually reach almost a million dollars, without a satisfactory solution to the problems of reduction. Faro or rouge et noire was safer than hard-rock mining, King had once remarked to Clover Adams. Prietas must do much better, he declared; and in mid summer, as soon as his census work permitted, he hurried west for a brief conference with his assistant manager, and together they plotted a strategy of hopeful exploration.

King asked the superintendent to open a lower level and, in secret, to push four faces to the edge of the adjoining property—the old Creston Mine which King had examined the year before. If clandestine assays proved sufficiently rich, he planned for Prietas to absorb the Creston. Then by leasing further ground (like the nearby Verde) he could assure the mill of sufficient ore to warrant twenty additional stamps. Prietas would then be able to count on sheer volume for a worth-while profit, even from indifferent ore.

Meanwhile, machinery troubles curtailed production. The combined gold and silver for the second half of 1881 scarcely exceeded two hundred thousand dollars—which left so small a sum after operating costs were paid that King warned his assistant: "There is a general feeling here of disappointment over Prietas." Spare no effort at the mine, he urged, till dividends could be paid, from twenty-five to thirty thousand dollars a month. "Nothing less," he added, "will retrieve what looks at this distance like a probable failure."

So the year 1881 dragged out in preying suspense. His health had improved for only temporary snatches. On returning from California, he had paid the Adamses a visit at Beverly Farms, "only to be put to bed and nursed," according to Henry's report. King rested there while Adams worked through ancient files of newsprint sent from Harvard College, and as the Essex marshes grew damper still, the friends may have renewed their dream of sailing to the South Seas before the next census and of sucking oranges there till they died. It was something to jest about at any rate, though Adams knew that King would never be ready, in spite of his enduring love for old-gold girls.

But Beverly Farms put King on his feet in time for him to repay the

Adamses' kindness. In New York, Henry and Clover paused on their journey back to Washington; and the Five of Hearts—for John and Clara Hay were also there—gathered as guests of King's for feasts at Delmonico's, of duck with hominy or turkey stuffed with chestnuts. They would go to a play, or to *opera bouffe* or even to *Patience*, Gilbert and Sullivan's light-hearted "spoof" of Oscar Wilde's estheticism and the latest musical hit from London. But this was only a dash of cheerful counterpoint in King's more solemn pattern of mines in Mexico and castles in Spain.

He had entered another pool, this time for promoting a mine in Chihuahua. He had envisioned profits of a quarter-million dollars; yet nothing went according to plan. "I have wasted all my autumn placing Salido," King complained, "and never saw such uphill work before." The market, in his opinion, was as dead as Julius Caesar. His personal loss neared twenty-five thousand dollars, and the fiasco cost him much of his interest in Mount Pleasant, that splendid little mine at Grizzly Flats.

These reverses preceded another siege of illness, more critical than ever. An old hernia had reopened, an injury King had suffered years before when "a Colorado mule," as he reminded Adams, "tried to go through me, saddle and all." Aggravated by malaria and the strain of overwork, the trouble nearly killed him, according to Adams's report. It subjected him to "forty minutes under aether and knife," then prostrated him for weeks at Brevoort House, and forced him to delay a long-scheduled return to Mexico. Alexander Agassiz had gone to visit Mayan ruins in Yucatán, and the two had agreed to meet in Mexico City for a six-week horseback ride together across the Sierra Madre Occidental to the Gulf of California. "I [shall] have an excellent companion in Clarence King," Agassiz wrote with evident satisfaction. King himself considered the trip important for the future of his promotions; he planned a tour of inspection, first to Sombrerete, then to Yedras and Prietas. It was necessary to convince Agassiz of the promise of each mine, to show him by firsthand evidence that each mine justified full confidence in its future.

But while King nursed his strength, word came from Agassiz to cancel the trip entirely. The barbarous two-wheel carts of Yucatán, each drawn by three mules at a gallup, had shaken him up so hard, to the detriment of an old circulatory trouble, that Agassiz lay almost as ill as King himself. Additional horseback travel, he declared, was "out of the question." That was unfortunate, since the management of the mines could have used some of Agassiz' common sense.

Nothing more unpropitious than the cancellation of the tour could have struck King's chances for drawing more working capital from the Boston trio. In financial matters the three held together clannishly, and they were now solidly united in demands for greater profits before dropping more funds into what they labeled "Mexican sinks." Meanwhile little good news arrived from the mines to give King encouragement. The difficulties had grown more grievous than ever at Prietas, especially in the case of the new mill, whose machinery had to be "brought hundreds of miles on mules [and] was scattered all the way from the Pacific coast." King therefore pinned his hopes for quick returns on Yedras, where there was a comfortable quantity of ore in sight. Moreover the Yedras mill, unlike that at Prietas, was nearly ready for operation, and King believed that another year would see the mine earning extensive profits—provided that capital could be found to keep it working in the meantime. But the Boston triumvirate had lost all faith in Yedras; they wanted out, and though they feared King's temperamental optimism had impaired his judgment, they named him agent to arrange for the sale of the Yedras Mining Company.

So, like many another Yankee with a "good thing" in his pocket, King turned to London and Paris, where his sister Marian had gone before him. He confided his last census responsibilities to Becker and Emmons and on May 6, 1882, boarded the steamer Britannic in Henry Janin's company. The ship eased away from the Tenth Street dock, and in spite of ailing health and a qualm or two about the voyage—he confessed to feeling "green in advance"—he approached one of the most agreeable periods of his life, a transatlantic holiday.

17

European Interlude

The weather proved ideal for a voyage, and the White Star liner sheared through bright days and starry nights. King anticipated no very long stay across the Atlantic, a few weeks at most in Great Britain and on the Continent. But he intended to make the most of his holiday before sailing home in July or August. "He broke out with a thousand pranks and paradoxes"—or so it seemed to the poet-banker with an immaculate forked beard who shared not only King's table but his "Clarentian prenomen" as well. King introduced himself and found in his dapper messmate (who was a Centurian like himself) another lasting friend.

"Freedom was what we both needed," Edmund Clarence Stedman wrote of their meeting, "and my own reserve was at an end the moment I saw him changed from the dignitary to the veritable Prince Florizel." (Robert Louis Stevenson's *New Arabian Nights* had just appeared.) King's "frolic was incessant and contagious. . . . He jested, fabled, sparkled, scorned concealment of his delight." And flipping a gold double eagle, he made unending wagers with Henry Janin on nearly everything they met.

The *Britannic* coasted around the tip of Ireland, through peaty smells that blew across the waves from a multitude of chimneys. Then it glided up the yellow Mersey to its dock at Liverpool. King went straight to London and took rooms at the St. James Hotel, where he talked of Yedras and its virtues, hoping to interest the proper people. His American backers had authorized him to sell control of the mine for a million dollars, but King's incorrigible optimism had seized him again, and he was convinced that Yedras could bring much more on the British market. "Investors in mining property," he wrote soon after, "seem always to have preferred taking great chances to smaller but safer investments." He hiked the price to half again what his partners had asked. A glib but plausible Yankee schemer, who gave his name as George S. Sedgwick, appeared at King's hotel and proposed to locate

purchasers for a 5 percent commission. King accepted Sedgwick's proposition, but reserved the right to veto any buyer who did not please in
every way.

Now King was ready to storm France, though not before driving his
friends to Epsom Derby in a rented tallyho as payment of a wager. It was
a kind of national fête, with the crowds roaring like a wild surf when
the race was run; and Stedman would later "cherish a fading tin-type
exhibit of [their] group on the tallyho, lifting [their] cups, with King as
toastmaster."

He hurried to Paris the following day, leaving apologies for the
American minister—James Russell Lowell, to whom he had an introduction from Adams, but who had heard of his arrival in England and
wished to make him welcome. King lingered a week in the French
capital, "city of wit and rapiers," as he was to call it, "of art and
epigram, of polished intelligence and graceful extravagance." All Paris
seemed to fling "her sparkling life gaily into the light, as the waters of
the *grandes eaux* are tossed to the sapphire sky." The American diplomat there was Levi P. Morton. King had first made Morton's acquaintance at the Adamses' house, in the company of Sandy Bliss, Morton's
business partner and a stepson of old George Bancroft; and "If ignorance is Bliss," King had later quipped, "what the devil is Morton?" The
fact was that Morton might have become president of the United
States, had he deigned to run as Garfield's mate when the bosses of the
Republican convention had given him the nod before turning to Chester Arthur. Morton had wished to grace the Court of St. James's, but
when Lowell was sent instead, he solaced himself with the post at Paris.
There he presided over the American colony, where the brightest star
was Mrs. John W. Mackay, whom King recalled—not quite correctly—
as "a barmaid" on the Comstock. Though business matters concerned
him mainly, King's first Parisian week began what Stedman called his
"social life in France." He regained contact there with his Aunt Charlotte King (widow of his Uncle Charles William), who had renounced
America after her return from China and whom Henry James would
describe "as a character of characters and a marvel of placid consistency."

As in Mexico, King's linguistic talent now carried him over difficulties. As a boy, he had learned to read French well, but did not speak
it. He now took the spoken idiom by storm, at first making "havoc of
genders, moods and tenses"; but "in a few weeks," according to Hay,
"he was speaking the language with perfect ease." French was the

tongue in which he resumed negotiations over Yedras with the Paris financiers he had contacted before leaving America. They expressed interest, but were in no hurry to close a deal. While they considered, Sedgwick introduced King to others who moved in the banking circles of France; two of whom—promoters named Willett and Cavallier—set out with encouraging vim to gain the attention of potential buyers. With the problem of Yedras thus addressed, at least for the present, King felt ready for a dash to Spain, his "consecrated realm of Don Quixote."

He had mastered Castilian by now and had read a shelf of books on Spain, and as Adams would remark, "He loved everything Spanish, even the Spanish inn." The Iberian visit became a highlight of his travels, a very pilgrimage for one so enamored of Cervantes. He dressed for the trip in a green velvet suit, with pale stockings, oxford shoes, and a jaunty tam-o'-shanter completing his costume. His knee breeches were cut somewhat like Oscar Wilde's; and thus decked out, he raced across the Basque provinces, down to Madrid, insatiable for the "artistic and historic wealth under which"—as he surmised—"Spain fairly groans." He swept through the galleries of the Prado, and his sympathies seemed to comprehend the entire range of Spanish art, from primitives through Velasquez down to Fortuny y Carbo. He reveled in Spanish music too, in the wild offbeat of gypsy melodies, the syncopated airs of Málaga or Andalusia—music of a type he had learned to love in Latin America.* He frequently left the slow trains along the way, and laid over in cities or pueblos, in what Washington Irving had called the true way to tour Spain—with "an ample stock of good humor, and a genuine disposition to be pleased." He liked the Spanish people because they seemed so natural, so seldom academic; there was something to please him even in their densest ignorance.

"You have had a great war in your country," said a minor dignitary.

"Yes, very destructive, very exhausting; but thank God, North and South are beginning to be friends again."

"Are you of the North or of the South?"

"The North."

"Do you not find it very trying to have those Chilenos in your Lima, señor?"

---

*On July 31, 1950, Miss Eleanor Hague, the elder daughter of J. D. Hague and a collector of Latin American folk music, told me that such music became a special favorite of King's, rivalling in his esteem all but the most preferred classical selections. Its rhythms held him fascinated.

But why should he try to extend the Spaniard's picture of the American hemisphere to cover anything north of the land of Cortez? He liked the Spanish people just as he had found them; he claimed a nice respect for the savor of their scallions, and only admiration for their country where "the very kiss of passion burns with the mingled fire of love and garlic." To enjoy the true flavor of the provinces he scoured the byways on a mule, over sun-drenched plains, and no spot was too forlorn to deny him some pleasing or picturesque effect—the trunk of some gnarled olive tree, or the ruins of a windmill etched against the gray horizon, or a flock of lately shorn sheep filing across the landscape.

He went through the mines of Almadén, the greatest mercury mines in the world, and he studied the copper district of Rio Tinto, just as he had examined the iron fields at Bilbao while passing through Biscay. Then on he journeyed to the Rock of Gibralter, bristling with fortifications, to conquer which for Spain his good friend Don Horacio Cutter had dreamed of schemes involving explosive balloons. He crossed the straits to Morocco and, like Mark Twain, stood in awe before Tangier, so like a figment of Scheherazade's.

On his return to Spain, he recalled his talk with Don Horacio in the hollows of Golden Gate Park, and resolved to honor his friend with "Mambrino's golden helmet," the barber's basin which Don Quixote had won and worn. Many a fine new basin could be had at Seville or Córdoba, but only an ancient one would do. The search led him to a decayed posada somewhere in La Mancha, and a faded sign above the door read *Barbería.* There hanging from a wrought-iron bar, King found his prize—"a barber's basin of battered and time-stained brass, the morning light just touching its disk of green."

A bronzed widow some fifty years old answered the knock of King's Spanish guide, who, lank and thin and hollow-eyed, informed her in an equally hollow voice: "Señora, the gentleman is a lover of the good Don Quixote."

Her quissical glance seemed to answer: "So is everyone. What of that?"

"My friend is *Americano.*"

"¡*Válgame Dios*!" the woman cried, now thoroughly interested. "All the way from Buenos Aires! No? Then from Cuba, of course! Yes, yes! My father's cousin was a soldier there, and married a woman as black as a pot."

"No, señora, my friend is from another part of America; and he has come here to buy from you the old brass basin above the barbería door."

"¡*Pobrecito*!" she said. "You take care of him! He is"—and one of her brownish index fingers touched her head—"a little wrong here."

The guide declared gravely that King was "perfectly clear."

"Why then in the name of the Blessed Virgin does he want of that old basin with a hole in it?"

King chose that moment to interpose, "It seems very droll, my good woman, does it not? But I have in my own country a charming friend whom I love very much. He is called the Bachelor of San Francisco, and he has never seen a Spanish barber's basin, so I want to carry this as a gift to him. We have no barbers' basins in America."

"¡*Caramba*!" she exclaimed, "what a land! Full of women as black as coals, and no barbers! My father's cousin had a beard like an Englishman when he came back, and his wife looked like a black sheep just sheared. As to the basin, señor, it is yours."

Later, in Paris, King wrote of the quest in a long letter to Don Horacio, an Irvingesque idyl of color and charm, a lively *jeu d'esprit*. He covered the manuscript with blue embroidered silk cut from a robe of Cervantes' time. "But at the last moment," he confessed, "what I had written seemed so lacking in local color . . . that I put it [to] one side"— until, that is, his mother read it. Then at her encouragement he sent it to his friend, along with the basin in its patina of pale green. He gave a copy of the manuscript to another Cervantista, John Hay; and later still Richard Watson Gilder published it in the *Century Magazine*, along with a few changes and additions that King had made. [*]

"Hang the *Century* people," he exclaimed when the sketch had appeared in print. "Behind my back they corrected my Spanish and blundered."

In the letter King's style was perhaps too elaborate, too richly orchestrated for so slight a theme; and his friends, whom the piece delighted, were inclined to overrate it. Royal Cortissoz called it "a golden page of literature"—"the most exquisite tribute to [Don Quixote] in the English language"—and he placed it "among the finest things ever written in America." "The Helmet of Mambrino" is hardly as good as that; yet its charm suggests, along with that of *Mountaineering*, what King's mark

---

[*] The barber's basin remained as a cherished keepsake in Don Horacio's possession until his death shortly before King's, and then it was lost. The futile search for it is detailed by J. D. Hague in *Clarence King Memoirs*, pp. 99–115. In the end one like it was substituted for the original and hung on a wall of the Century Club as a memento there of Clarence King. Don Horacio's copy of King's letter also came into the possession of the club and is preserved in the library.

in American literature might have been had he given more of himself to writing instead of becoming a novelist *manqué.*

London drew him back later in the summer, laden with spoils—with silks and shawls, laces and Spanish fans, with paintings he had bought in Paris, including watercolors by Fortuny.* Like Henry James, he found "London in August" a rewarding place and explored it with great diligence. He would visit afoot so many various neighborhoods, with such eager curiosity, that before the close of his English interlude a sympathetic friend could claim with understandable hyperbole: "He has walked over London until he knows it better than any Englishman ever did, and is . . . fairly enchanted with London, or rather English, life." Meanwhile, he amused Howells, who had just arrived from America, with his talk of the city, of the eating places of the London poor "where you could buy for a penny a slice of wonderful pie which included the courses of a whole dinner in its stratification." Like Stevenson's Prince, he enjoyed the foreign cafés in Soho best, but he was also partial to one or two in Whitechapel.

London had, in fact, so fired King's interest that he delayed day after day, to Howell's huge diversion, a visit to the country house of Sir John Clark in Aberdeenshire. He would buy his ticket to Scotland from time to time, then wire Sir John to expect him later. But he did at last go, and gave his keenest attention to Scotland's geology; and while in Glasgow, he salaamed to Sir William Thomson, later Lord Kelvin, whose early paper on the age of the earth had stimulated King's own work in geophysics. "What a lofty flight . . . King must be making among the savants of Her Majesty's realm!" exclaimed the aforesaid friend over King's visits not only with Sir William Thomson but also with scientific peers like Tyndall and Huxley. "In my mind's eye I see their open-mouthed stare when they find the hero of the fortieth parallel, slayer of the diamond swindle, and bonanza wizard to be a peach-skinned blonde young man with a desperate relish for ballet and a blush like a virgin." But King had many things to discuss with Sir William, especially his projected work on subterranean fusion in col-

* Henry James would soon report to John Hay: "I have seen our genial Clarence, who is as genial as ever, though talking a little too much for one's nerves, perhaps, about Fortuny & other £5000 people & things" (James to Hay, December 5 [1882], A37835[11], Hay Papers [Brown University Library]). "Clarence is truly a festive nature," James would add to Clover Adams, "and has more watercolours even than you" (*Letters of Henry James*, ed. Edel, II, 408).

laboration with Barus and Hallock, and he received heartwarming encouragement from the eminent British physicist.

But Scotland, cold and gloomy with rain, could hardly hold King long, and he hurried back to London in September. He took lodgings at what he called "the best hotel I ever saw," the Bristol in Burlington Gardens, later moving to number 6 Bolton Street, across from the flat of Henry James in Piccadilly. The latter part of town appealed for its atmosphere of weather-stained quality. All was old and dingy there, the houses gazing askew into the treeless sweep of Green Park. But a better location could hardly be found, according to Edmund Gosse, for "the impassioned student of London life and haunter of London society."

Society there betrayed no qualms over Americans of means and leisure; it simply absorbed them and asked no questions. "One wandered about in it," Adams had claimed, "like a maggot in cheese." And King found it so congenial that he matched even James's enthusiasm for the "Londonizing process." He dined out almost as frequently as James himself, who was said to spend a part of each day on a couch, resting his lower back, and conserving his strength for his nightly bouts at the dinner table. Both had flung themselves into what a mutual friend was to call "an infectious orgy of idleness and frivolity."

A gathering that stood out was a dinner both attended at the Hotel Continental—a literary banquet that had brought together some of the sprucest Americans then in England. The guests included Edwin Booth, Laurence Hutton, William Laffan, Moncure Conway, Thomas Bailey Aldrich. Osgood the publisher was the host: he was trying the Old World now, after floating down the Father of Waters with Mark Twain; and there were two of Twain's chums from Nook Farm— General Joseph B. Hawley, who had served as president of the Centennial Exposition, and Charles Dudley Warner (Twain's collaborator on *The Gilded Age*), who had just toured Spain, incensed that he could not find a codfish ball in the whole Iberian Peninsula and as bored with all things Spanish as King had been enchanted. * Howells came too, and

---

* Warner rubbed King the wrong way several times during the years of their acquaintance, as on the occasion of their dining together just before Osgood's banquet: "It was a shock to me," King reported, "to find that we could not talk for a week together about Spain. I admitted his discovery that they had no fish balls. I waived the whole garlic question. I said that I too had heard that Puritanical practices were not universal in Andalusia, that the women had from time to time, etc., etc. I followed him for an hour along the quiet stream of guide-book impressions and color-blind memories, which to him mean Spain, and then I tried to launch out with him into the depths and up to the

John Hay, who was now in Europe to finish in secret the novel he called *The Bread-Winners*. It was an open secret, though, to some of the diners; Howells had read a part of the manuscript, and Aldrich wanted it for the *Atlantic*, provided the author's name came with it; but on that score John Hay would never yield.

As for *Democracy*, both Howells and Warner were sure they knew the author—to wit, John W. DeForest, a revelation which neither King nor Hay gainsaid. They were content merely to disclaim all credit of authorship and go on playing the quaint game of Henry Adams, even at Osgood's dinner, while Warner and Howells so sagely went astray. But in an expansive mood, King offered to Howells a cherished Fortuny; for as Howells would later explain, "He had much of the Arabian Nights in him and liked to shine in a surprising munificence." And over their wines the company talked of his sable majesty, Cetewayo, the current toast of London; or they debated the splendors of Bayreuth and the recent première of *Parsifal*. Wagner was greater than either Beethoven or Schiller, someone said. Oh, yes, replied another; a greater poet than Beethoven, a greater musician than Schiller.

Even Bret Harte had run down from Glasgow at Osgood's invitation—a Harte surprisingly different from the broken man who had left New York five years before. His fortunes had mended in Europe; the British had taken him to their bosom, and he gloated over the change. He chuckled over the portly waistlines of his friends, of King and Howells especially; not that time had spared Harte himself. His hair was silver now, in contrast with his dark mustache; but silver became him in some theatrical way—"like a French marquis of the *ancien régime*," said Howells. "Or like an American actor made up for the part," another added, maybe King.

Harte had returned to writing plays. He had resurrected the Luck of Roaring Camp for the stage, but had changed the baby boy into a girl, and brought her to Paris, for adventures with other roving Californians. He enjoyed the collaboration of a Belgian diplomat's wife, a Madame Van de Velde, who had taken him into her London home. Harte, in fact, spent more time in London than he did in Glasgow, where King and Hay had persuaded Secretary Evarts to have him transferred as consul. For form's sake he kept his Glasgow address and had his dinner

---

heights of Spanish genius and character, and I was enraged with him because he had not cared enough to try to think himself into it all" (King to Hay [September 3, 1882], A37865[5][2], Hay Papers [Brown University Library]).

invitations sent there for forwarding to London, and the replies sent back for the proper postmark.

At the time of Osgood's dinner Harte had only one more act to write for *The Luck of Roaring Camp,* and when it was finished he took both King and Hay to hear him read the play at Madame Van de Velde's house in St. John's Wood. The Luck had adventures indeed; for Harte, as Adams would later suggest, was one of the few American writers who dared, in his day, to deal with sex. But something was amiss; and King, like Hay and Howells, was never quite sure if Harte's plays were just "too bad for the stage, or else too good for it."

King set great store by Bret Harte's company, whether at dinner with Hay or Howells, or at home with George Smalley, the London correspondent of the *Tribune,* or during sallies together into the least respectable neighborhoods, to chaff barmaids together and see the other side of London life. Thus began the intermittent slumming that would punctuate King's English sojourn, during which he would make "studies of the lowest strata of London life." On some of these excursions he would have the company of Henry James, whose diffidence about invading such "gruesome and out-of-the-way parts of town" King would remember years later and imagine the author having "gather[ed] up a few unmistakably good invitations and button[ed] them in his inner pocket, so that there should be no mistaking the social position of his corpse if violence befell him." The adventures may well have furnished James with the sort of detail that would serve him well when he came to describe the London proletariat in *The Princess Casamassima.*

At intervals King frequented a specially unsavory quarter known as Seven Dials, consorting there with all sorts of sinners—barmaids, apple women, sailors, and thieves—all in the interest of local color for a projected volume of stories about ten women of the lower depths, stories that he aimed to tell in the local vernacular. For this purpose he duly recorded "reams of notes on dialects whole fathoms below the strata touched by Dickens in *Oliver Twist.*" A literary object had thus become the excuse for his slumming. But there was no denying the fascination he found in it, as in his earlier forays into the bleakest warrens of New York City, for the range of King's empathy was as broad and inclusive as Howells would claim it was. He sometimes went with gold coins clinking in his pocket, heedless of danger from the shoals of thieves; and it was said that to a comely barmaid whose name was Elizabeth he tossed an antique gold piece, with the quip, "An Elizabethan sovereign." It was an expensive pun.* But that was King's way: "He was not rich, as rich men go," wrote Howells, "and that was why he could afford pleasures that rich men, as they go, cannot or will not permit themselves."

Still, he won the esteem of one of England's wealthiest men, the widowed Baron Ferdinand James de Rothschild, and he might have borrowed Heine's pun on sitting down with another member of that family—"We became famillionaire." Howells soon wrote to Warner: "The young Baron Rothschild has taken a fancy to Clarence King (as if that man had not luck enough already!) and wants to live with him." To Henry James the baron "appear[ed] to be unable to live without [King]," and Stedman termed their comradeship "blood-brotherhood." King advised "Ferdy" on art and bric-a-brac, or on how to furnish his palatial country house at Waddesdon, a house for which wealth was doing its utmost. As the baron's main connection with the family business was to spend its money, he had plenty of time to cultivate his taste for art. His collections—Renaissance paintings, gold and silver carvings, bronzes and enamels, jewels and crystals—were destined for the British Museum, and his country house became a show place of the nation, the chief sight of Buckinghamshire.

It was perhaps there in the smoking room amongst rare objets d'art that King chatted tete-a-tete with the Prince of Wales, blue-eyed and pleasure-loving, an intimate of the baron's. Edward esteemed Americans and American ways, and when the host complained of a headache, the prince urged him to retire, adding, "King and I will get on

---

*A gambit, too, in King's play for literary raw material: "Think of it, Hay," a friend reported, "He goes down to the lowest dive at Seven Dials, chirps to the pretty barmaid of a thieves' gin mill, gives her a guinea for a glass of 'bittah,' [and] gets the frail, simple thing clean gone on him. Then [he] whips out his notebook and with a smile that would charm a duchess asks her to tell her story. Naturally she is pleased and fires away in dialect that never saw print, which the wily geologist nails on the spot. Of course she is a poor, pitiful, wronged thing who would have been an angel if she had been kindly treated and taken to Sunday School when she was a child—they are all so, you know. Think, Hay, of ten such girls, with their plump red cheeks, their picturesque slang, and their pert ways corralled in one book written for a General Moral Purpose and dedicated to her most Benignant Grace, Lady Stanley, who is quite as charmed with Frascuelo [King] as the barmaids. I suppose, rather let us say *hope*, that King is walking through all these narrow slippery places upright and unstained as an archangel" (Frank Holcomb Mason to John Hay, January 18, 1884, A39958[22](2), Hay Papers [Brown University Library]).

well enough together"—as indeed they did. * And later King would reminisce about the Prince of Wales's set—"the young arch-worldlings [who] went ingenuously about showing their vaccinations to one another, and exchanging boyish congratulations and condolences."

It was perhaps King's acquaintance with the Prince, certainly his standing in the Prince's circle, that insured éclat for the outing he soon conducted for "a Sunday school class" of factory girls from Crosse & Blackwell's, preservers of pickles and potted meats. He had volunteered to teach the girls on Sunday afternoons in a manner "not quite orthodox, perhaps"; and finding them so direly ignorant of the charm of trees and grass, he chartered a train to take them for a picnic in Windsor Park. † Out of the castle walked the Queen herself, to stroll among King's breathless charges and to take a cup of tea from one of their trembling hands. Philanthropic sorties among the underprivileged did not tarnish King's position in beau monde drawing rooms, social chores of that sort being quite in vogue. Had not James Russell Lowell just dedicated a home for working girls in Brixton Road? Even Baron Rothschild cherished a reputation for charity work around Waddesdon—work that would soon help him to gain a seat in Parliament.

It was at the baron's table that King now met the famous Lady Dalhousie, whose radiant hair had fascinated Gladstone. She enjoyed King's stories, including his tale of the diamond fraud; and he dined with her at Hereford Gardens, a social center of the day. There Ouida the novelist often came; and there, too, King met Lord Randolph Churchill's brother-in-law, the all but legendary Moreton Frewen, whose brother Richard had just bought the Circle Bar Ranch from King and Davis. The spectacular Frewen brothers had been the first men to run cattle on Powder River, and at their home ranch they had built a house that looked like a royal hunting lodge, and they had kept relays of horses posted at intervals across Wyoming to bring guests at a gallop from the railroad two hundred miles away. The relays also brought fresh

---

* Sometime after the publication of Clarence King Memoirs a copy was sent to Edward VII, and on Memorial Day, 1905, E. C. Stedman wrote to J. D. Hague, editor of the volume: "Now if Lord Knollys [the royal secretary] will only beguile the King into reading the 'memoirs' of our King, Edward VII may invite us all over to the next Derby Day!" (Courtesy of the late Miss Marian Hague.)

† In connection with King's active sympathy for many "in the submerged fraction" of society, Hay spoke of having "introduced him once to a woman of eminent distinction, one of the first writers of our day. After he had gone, she said: 'I understand now the secret of his charm. It is kindness'" (Clarence King Memoirs, p. 125).

potted flowers from Cheyenne, so that lady visitors might wear corsages at dinner. Moreton Frewen owned the **76** brand, which Owen Wister was to fix in the folklore of the West when he came to write *The Virginian*. But Frewen denied the tale which had amused the whole of Cheyenne—of how he had bought the **76** herd for double its value, the seller having run the cattle around a butte while Frewen counted them twice. Like King himself, he played for the highest stakes, and dreamed always of a fortune in the offing—as now, from a scheme to ship American beef to England on the hoof. Frewen was as eloquent as King when he described "the millions of lean cattle in Wyoming and Montana which could be fattened by the English farmer. . . . As they were full-grown cattle, the time necessary to mature them for market would be short, as compared with Irish store cattle."

Stentorian praise from "Uncle Sam" Ward, the brother of Julia Ward Howe, had prepared Moreton Frewen to admire King. They hit it off together, as one cattle baron with another. Forty years later Frewen would claim how bright his memory of their first encounter had remained, and he liked to compare King's personal charm with that of Lord William Beresford. It was perhaps typical of King's impression on the hunting and shooting set in England, where his gift for social relations led, in John Hay's words, to "a facile conquest of hearts." Hay notified Adams in the fall of 1882: "Socially [King] is the same as of old. He is run after by princes, dukes and millionaires, whom he treats with amiable disdain. He never answers a letter and never keeps an engagement, and nobody resents it." Hay insisted that nothing described more aptly King's success in British high society than "the well-worn phrase of Dickens, He was 'the delight of the nobility and gentry.'"

Preoccupation with the British upper classes, as much as King's interest in the pretty wantons of the dives, set ideas spinning in his head; and he was moved, he said, "to do a droll thing, namely to write a companion volume" to *Democracy*. Nothing promised a more complete contrast to the tales he planned on the ten wenches of Seven Dials, for the new project would bring Madeleine Lee to London "in search of the fine old English code of society, morals and statesmanship." The more King pondered the idea the more his enthusiasm grew. He made notes on British high society even more voluminous than his "reams" on the London underdogs, and the novel assumed a scintillating shape in his mind. At first he called it *Monarchy*, then *Aristocracy*. In his fancy, it mimicked the Adams style and featured a suave young peer modeled on Lord Randolph Churchill. It would also involve the Prince of Wales and Mrs. Langtry under the sheerest disguise, amidst a diverse cast of personalities in the public eye and a few characters borrowed from *Democracy.* King soon let John Hay know that he was so "full of ideas about *Aristoc*" that there would be no delay in his "getting at it." Like the ten stories of the slums, it was something to fill odd moments of his English visit; and it added point to his time among the "swells" at the Savile or the Turf Club, or to weekends at country houses like Waddesdon Manor. The project thrived on the aristocratic demand for his company—a demand so enthusiastic that, when he could not accept an invitation, his cronies would say, "It's a cold day for the dukes."

"They dine me too much," King confessed to Hay, "but they are diverting." He added that his dinner companions for the following evening—an evening in December, 1882—would consist of "H.R.H., the Duke of Cambridge, Huxley, [the Marquis of] Hartington, Dean of Westminster Escott, Matthew Arnold, and a lot more to the number of 24, all swells. So it goes day by day, till I am fatigued"—though no air of weariness could disguise the satisfaction he gained from his social vogue. His popularity flourished so great that a friend was moved to call him "the phenomenon of the period. The whole British aristocracy, scientists, literary men, and particularly women from duchesses to barmaids are climbing over each other to get at him." Later the same friend exclaimed: "How the English Mother and her callow brood do spread their nets for that man!" Not that nets could inhibit him from taking debutante or matron alike on fair-weather excursions in the boat he kept for rowing on the Thames. All the while, as he informed Hay, there crept over him a "sneaking desire to be a little, just a little, English."

No wonder, then, that the English stay ran on so long that friends at home began to ask about him in dismay. "Poor King!" exclaimed Adams, ". . . he must have got naturalized as a British subject, and married an Irish peeress"; or, somewhat later: "Be not mad at my calling King mad, for mad he certainly is"—though, as Adams concluded, he was sure to be forgiven. In his total abdication from care, he had sent his Boston friends no word in months about the Yedras promotions, leaving them in what Adams termed "Egyptian darkness." King reasoned that, having nothing of moment to write, there was little point in writing; but Agassiz actually speculated that he must have lost his balance. "He acts most strangely to the eye of a by-stander," Adams admitted. "In Boston they talk pretty freely about him and of course his friends are dumb because they know nothing about him."

King had gone to Paris again that fall, Cavallier having aroused the interest of a syndicate associated with the Banque Franco-Egyptienne. The head of the pool requested an option to buy the mine at the price King asked for it, ten million francs. And while he waited for the deal to mature, King settled down at the Grand Hotel, where Hay and Henry James had lodgings, the latter having crossed the channel to gather impressions that would appear in *A Little Tour in France*. Pleasant days followed. The three took breakfast together, roamed the boulevards, and prowled in shops and galleries, where it seemed to James that King bought "watercolours and old stuff by the millions." He reported to Howells that King was "a charmer. He charms all the bric-à-brac out of the shops." In the words of Leon Edel, James "watched [King] with the eyes of a story-teller and a lover of character." He called King "the most delightful man in the world," one who worked "magic spells"; and he would remember their days in Paris together as having had "a sort of fairy-tale quality, & the genial King, as I look back at him, strikes me as a kind of fairy-godmother." But in the long run he had mixed feelings, reservations. All the King magic could not prevent him from concluding that the charmer, when viewed objectively, was "a queer, incomplete, unsatisfactory creature"—one who seemed "slippery and elusive, and as unmanageable as he [was] delightful." What a contrast to the idolization of Hay, who would later confess to James his reaction on hearing at Cannes that King was in Paris: "I felt like taking the first train there! I said to myself—'Ah, where *he* is, there is my true country, my real home.'"

Abruptly, King's agreeable stay in Paris was cut short by news of Cavallier's sudden death and simultaneous word from Sinaloa that the newest tunnel at Yedras had turned out barren. The upshot was that negotiations with the prospective buyers in Paris collapsed, leaving the Yedras affair no further along in essential respects than when King had first arrived in Europe.

His social ties in London, though, had brought him into financial circles there; and he was soon preparing the ground for launching an English corporation to acquire Yedras and the surrounding rancho. In these moves he acted on advice from Henry L. Higginson, who had come to Europe chiefly to search for musical timber to build into the Boston Philharmonic Orchestra, the dream of his life. It was Higginson who suggested the services of a certain Captain Pavy, of the Debenture Trust Company, who proved more effective than Sedgwick in finding the right subscribers and underwriters. Pavy interested men of name and substance, but they were cautious, and King complained to Hay that "not even the geological processes are so slow as a London company." But better news arrived from Yedras, and the Anglo-Mexican Mining Company was finally registered on August 23, 1883, with an office in Cannon Street.

The capital stock was listed at £325,000, in five-pound shares; and under King's terms the company was committed to pay $1 million cash for the Yedras properties plus four hundred thousand in paid-up shares. King accepted a place on the board of directors, along with a baronet, a member of Parliament, and a major general in the British army. He also agreed to become the managing director, at a salary of £600 a year. The board sent a British engineer to examine Yedras. He sustained King's estimate of the ore in sight and reported the mill to be the finest he had ever seen, "and probably the finest in the world." The company's prospectus was published lavishly, along with King's report and that of the British engineer. Stock was floated on the London market, and the first installment of the purchase money was paid to the Yedras Company in America. King had glowing hopes for the Anglo-Mexican Mining Company, and he confidently projected Yedras as "a mine of long life and abundant yield." But his appointment as managing director he regarded as anything but a full-time job.

Meanwhile King plunged without restraint into the currents of estheticism that swirled through England, indeed through most of Europe. He played the esthetic game with zest and vigor, resuming his dashes around the Continent. Just as he had breezed through Spain and basked in France, he added other lands to his itinerary—Holland, Germany, Switzerland, and Italy, where he sought out the picturesque and paid homage to the finest works of art. His eye for color and form delighted friends like Hay, whom he impressed as one already steeped in the scenes of their visits, as if by deja vu. His instinct for esthetic values seemed as sure as his intuition in scientific matters.

The beauty of Nature, King liked to say, had always attracted him more than her structural order, and so at heart he felt more like an artist than an engineer. He gave free rein now to that side of his nature, his "art-loving mind," as his own phrase ran; and in so doing he won respect as a connoisseur of art. King's outlook was that of an artist without his actually being one, as was said of Oscar Wilde. It was an attitude that was likely to prove expensive. But King the everlasting optimist could see no reason to spare expense, dead sure that Mexican silver would make him a millionaire for life. So on rushing about Europe, he bought art objects with what Hay called "unerring judgment and unflinching extravagance." Dealers kept him informed of their acquisitions, and he was constantly adding to the collection he had begun in the States—to his store of carved furniture, Yaqui blankets, Aztec vases, fans of painted silk from Japan, and Samarai swords inlaid with gold and silver and set with pearls.

In his collecting compulsion, King was a proper son of his time, the age of highboys and whatnots cluttered with bric-a-brac, of houses as smothered in objets d'art as any curiosity shop. One of the earliest pieces in his possession had come from the Centennial Exposition in Philadelphia—a Japanese screen with a scene from a feudal romance. He continued for years to add Oriental items to his collection, prizes such as his forebears had brought home from China, along with their cargoes of tea. King's love for all such things had begun in his boyhood when he had fondled bric-a-brac at the old King house in Newport.

So he felt entirely at home in the furor over Oriental art that had swept across Europe, prompted in England by Whistler and Rossetti, whose collections had raised it to the status of a cult. The spectacle of King's unrestrained purchases of objects from the Far East moved Hay to gentle rebuke in a poem he called "A Dream of Bric-à-Brac (C. K. Loquitur)." It sounded rather like a fugue of De Quincey's, this dream by C. K. of a ride through "fair Niphon . . . reclined in [his] jinrickashaw." His rickshaw-man pulled him to a china-shop, fragrant with exotic smells; and there he saw "A sight to make the warm heart glow, / And leave the eager soul no lack,— / An endless wealth of bric-à-brac." "I saw,"—as Hay reported C. K.'s words—

> bronze statues, old and rare,
> Fashioned by no mere mortal skill,
> With robes that fluttered in the air,
> Blown out by Art's eternal will;
> And delicate ivory netsukes.
> Richer in tone than cheddar cheese,
> Of saints and hermits, cats and dogs,
> Grim warriors and ecstatic frogs.

There were masks of sandalwood in C. K.'s vision, and the walls of the shop were rich with pictures of storm-washed pagodas and trees with small brown monkeys clinging to the boughs, like dabs of fuzzy hair.

Priceless porcelains littered the shelves—Imari pots and Ming dishes, a gold and gleaming punch bowl, several five-clawed dragons fighting over a few bronze censers, and an insolent Dog of Foo who sniffed at the aromatic smoke that curled up from them.

While C. K. wondered over all these cunning devices, it seemed that all the intangible beauty of the place became concrete before his eyes in the form of a girl of Old Japan. She held a gilded fan, which scattered fragrance through the room; and when he kissed her, she responded with a silvery laugh, and every treasure in the room seemed to hear her and react. Even the monkeys on the wall awoke with impudent chatter. Then a throng of travelers from various lands, including a Coptic priest, choked the room, pointing brazen fingers at C. K. and shouting with mockery as they vanished.

"And who were your friends?" he asked the girl.

"They come," she answered, "whenever a man makes a fool of himself."

Fool or not, King remained infatuated with Oriental art. He kept on the alert for prize pieces from the Far East, for painted screens and fans and blue-white porcelains, and he sometimes presented sets of Japanese chinaware to special friends. He collected things from the Near East too—like gold brocades from Damascus or richly patterned prayer rugs out of Turkey. But even more attractive to him were beautiful things of European provenance, and everywhere he went, not just in the galleries of London or Paris dealers, he purchased items that pleased him by virtue of some rare or luxuriant quality. Had he not brought from Spain the most opulent matador's regalia he could find? And there were antique coverlets, one of which he had bought from the couch of an impecunious doña; also chests and coffers, sanctuary statuettes, bas-reliefs, altar veils and frontals, even chasubles from the Renaissance.

King would sometimes lend his treasures to friends; it pleased him to see them displayed and admired. But he also arranged to store a part of his spoils at the studio flat which Sedgwick, his go-between, had taken in London—a move which later caused King regrets.

Had he disposed of some of his rose Du Barry brocades? a friend inquired one day.

"No," King answered. "Why do you ask?"

Because, the friend explained, he'd seen them worn at a fancy-dress ball.

Upon investigating, King discovered that much of what he had stored at Sedgwick's flat could not be found. Sedgwick had an explanation ready—that someone posing as King's agent had come and carted them away. Not a very convincing story, and King felt sure that he had been gulled. Nor was it to prove his only mortification at Sedgwick's hands. Yet King declined to prosecute him, out of pity for Mrs. Sedgwick and the bright young daughter Nannie—Anne Douglas Sedgwick—whose popular fiction would someday make her name well known on both sides of the Atlantic.

King's infatuation with bric-a-brac had in no wise eclipsed his love of paintings, which he also collected. Besides Gérôme's "Red Flamingoes," acquired from Morton, he had oils by three American painters who were personal friends—R. Swain Gifford, Bierstadt, and Munger. He now renewed his comradeship with Munger, recalling old mountaineering days at the painter's studio, or in his houseboat on the Thames; for having impressed the British swells in California with Yosemite studies, Munger had shipped his canvases over to London, where he had forthwith fallen in with John Millais and become a prodigious success. About this time King also discovered Anders Zorn, a pyrotechnic young Swede who shared his enthusiasm for the sun and the warmth and "unacademic" women of Spain. A coming man in King's opinion, Zorn had opened a studio in Brooke Street, and there in his green velvet suit sometime in October 1883, King sat for his portrait—a bold aquarelle in the new impressionistic mode. In one version the picture went to Baron Rothschild. In another it would hang for years in John Hay's parlor. King found Zorn's work "ingenious . . . but life-like," and so he commissioned the artist to paint a portrait of Marian as well.

Oils of the Dutch school had a special appeal for King, and he bought both old and recent examples—landscapes, still lifes, genre pieces, and marines. As John Hay testified, "He became at sight the friend of Mesdag and Israels." In addition he collected Italian, German, and Flemish primitives; and he became an enthusiast over the watercolor renaissance then under way. Many, perhaps most, of his pictorial acquisitions were in that medium. He supplemented his Fortunys with many another drawing and watercolor from the Latin countries; cherubs attributed to Correggio, for example, and various genre pictures of Italian life, scenes from Venice and Marseilles by Felix Ziem, views of rural France by Henri Harpignies, studies of lions and tigers by Barye, and alpine scenes by Gustave Doré. The latter were among the last works by that burly Alsatian, the fruit of a recent tour of Switzerland.

King went with Hay to Doré's atelier in the rue Bayard, a rendezvous for Parisian writers and artists. Soon he was fraternizing like an old messmate with the bull-necked painter, the illustrator of his beloved Cervantes. According to Hay, they planned a trip together "to Arizona to sketch the war dances of the Apaches." It seems that the artist was not aware of King's frigid opinion of his Inferno scenes—"those hard, theatrical conceptions with which Doré had sought to shut in our imagination. That artist," as King had deprecated him in *Mountaineering*,

has reached a conspicuous failure from an overwhelming love of solid, impenetrable darkness. There is in all his Inferno landscapes a certain sharp boundary between the real and unreal, and never the infinite suggestiveness of great regions of half-light, in which everything may be seen, nothing recognized.

But what did King's opinion matter now? The artist would be dead in a few days, his great peasantlike strength no proof against the onslaught of a particularly virulent pneumonia.

Though Doré's Swiss scenes were things of beauty, the true token of artistic superiority for an esthete based in London was apt to be a Turner sunset, and only watercolors by Turner could fully satisfy King. He had begun to collect them back in America, and preferred them above all other pictures in his possession. Not even the Welsh scenes by David Cox that he prized so highly could rival them in his affection. Indeed, he had favored Turner ever since the days in Greenwich Village when he had pored over Ruskin's *Modern Painters*.

Ruskin had of course proclaimed that his greatest pleasure would have been in buying every Turner he could find and in passing his days at Brantwood between his garden and his gallery. But now that he had launched his drive for the workingman's museum, the old prophet urgently needed money; he had begun to sell even his venerated Turners when King met him by sheer accident at a London dealer's. King did not recognize the old man with Father Time's beard and the turquoise colored eyes. But something he said "when argu[ing] upon a number of subtle points which to him were evident" so captivated Ruskin that he asked King up to Brantwood as his guest. There in the midst of exquisite Botticellis King completed his conquest; and Ruskin, in Hay's report to Howells, took him "to his heart and poured lyric toffy all over him." Moreover, he offered King his choice of the two best Turners that still remained in the house by Coniston Water.

"One good Turner deserves another," King replied, and he bought them both. Perhaps they were his roc's egg, the supreme trophy he had promised himself to Stedman on the *Britannic*.

There were several American watercolors in King's collection, one being an Indian-summer prospect in the Rockies by Samuel Coleman; and now at bohemian dinner tables he sometimes met another American—Edwin Abbey—whose art he admired. Abbey's illustrations for the poems of Robert Herrick had made his reputation in England, where he seemed serenely at home; and King engaged him to paint a tenderly sentimental picture on the theme of "an old song."

Abbey used as his model for the young woman singing at her harp the American actress Mary Anderson, who had just played Rosalind at Stratford after having declined Oscar Wilde's *Duchess of Padua*. She was tall and statuesque and rather long of neck, in the art fashion of the day, just the type of slender beauty Abbey loved to paint; and in the picture, over which he fussed for months, her stature grew and grew until when "The Old Song" was finally shown, it provoked *Punch* to gentle raillery in one of its sallies against "culchah." King was thus denied possession for another year, for Abbey insisted on rubbing "our Mary" out and doing the figure over again.

Mary Anderson had meanwhile come to be the muse of William Black, the long mustached purveyor of gorgeous Scots romances and an eager collector of Yankee friends. King dined with him several times, along with Abbey, Harte, and Hay, at Black's old rambling house in the Strand, where Peter the Great had lived in his London days and Dickens had taken chambers for David Copperfield. Black's confreres included Matthew Arnold, and it may have been at Black's intimate table that King and the poet-essayist cemented their friendship. On hearing of Arnold's approaching lecture tour in the United States, King invited him to spend "a quiet week" at Mrs. Howland's house in Newport and there enjoy "the last of autumn while . . . finishing [his essay on] Emerson." King won the admiration of the poet, who was moved to praise his charm to close friends, and their association seems to have provided a high point in King's dining out. Before Arnold sailed for America King gave him a letter of introduction to John Hay.

The note reminded Hay of how he had always overweighted his pan of the social scale by piling up acts and words in King's favor. "Now I am going to turn the balance," King said, "and bring down my side with a run by making you acquainted with Mr. Matthew Arnold & his family.

No lecturer can escape a visit to Cleveland & Cleveland means light or darkness according as one enters your door or not." Thus, the Arnolds would stay with John and Clara Hay on going to Ohio; and how well for Arnold, as King would learn, for on the afternoon of the lecture Hay stopped by the theater to see how the tickets were moving. The sale was slow, and so in a characteristic gesture he bought all the remaining tickets and had them presented to the students of the local university. Arnold would never know the reason for his Cleveland triumph and must have formed an exaggerated notion of the extent of love in Ohio for Sweetness and Light.

Meanwhile, the rounds of dinners continued as long as King remained in London. He liked to overeat, as he would own to Howells, and as if to prove his point, he slipped into more dining groups than ever. Two of them were Anglo-American fellowships, the Kinsmen and the Rabelais Club.

King joined the Kinsmen at their June dinner, 1883, at the Blue Posts Tavern, a feast which rivaled Osgood's banquet months before; and he found the Kinsmen all convivial spirits—Edwin Abbey and Osgood, one-eyed "Polyphemus" Laffan, Laurence Hutton, Brander Matthews of Columbia College among others. It was Matthews, an admirable raconteur himself, who defined "a master of conversation" as the "talker who could [hold] his own against John Hay or Clarence King."

Edwin Abbey had drawn the Kinsmen's emblem at the head of a menu rife with barbarous French puns: a hoop-bellied John Bull pumping the hand of a spindle-shanked red Indian, each clutching a brimming glass; for the Kinsmen aimed to meet and dine and drink and talk on either side of the Herring Pond and to narrow the pond in the course of their festivities.

The eating and drinking they held important enough, the talk even more so; and along with King they acquired some of the most remarkable talkers in England: a trio, first, of incomparable bookmen—Austin Dobson, Edmund Gosse, and Andrew Lang; then Comyns Carr of the Grosvenor Gallery; George Boughton, the English-American landscape painter; Linley Sambourne, sly cartoonist for *Punch*; and Alfred Parsons, who had painted a watercolor for King's collection. There were other Kinsmen absent in America—Barrett the actor, Mark Twain, Elihu Vedder and Frank Millet the painters, Julian Hawthorne, and H. C. Bunner; and among the others soon to join were William Black, Aldrich, Howells and Harte, and even Henry Irving, who gave each Kinsman his autographed "bone," a standing pass to the Lyceum Theater.

Larger and somewhat longer established was the Rabelais Club, founded by the Romany Rye from Philadelphia, Charles Godfrey Leland, who devoutly wished it "to coruscate—whizz, blaze and sparkle, fulminate and bang." Exactly such a wish might be expected from one who had fallen in love with Lola Montez years before. Equally in order was the claim of the secretary, Walter Besant, that the Rabelais admitted only two classes of members: first, those who could swear on oath that they had read the works of the Master diligently; and second, those who could make an affidavit that they had *not* read them with particular care. Forty or fifty free spirits had passed the Pantagruelist test when, sponsored by Bret Harte, King and Hay were admitted to the club. The Rabelaisians gathered around the dinner table half a dozen times a year, sometimes at the Savile Club, with Lord Houghton presiding. Not that they quite lived up to the expectations of the founder or achieved their published aim—to lay "the priggism of the day." But how could their talk be less than rare when men like Leland, DuMaurier, Meredith, Hardy, Saintsbury, Lang, Lowell, Hay, Howells, Harte (who would be the next president), and Henry James forgathered?

Clarence must be having a gay time, thought Becker, back in New York. King, in fact, had enjoyed his English visit so much that he called it his "first long dream in life." He wrote few letters, never having been a sedulous correspondent, and so none of his American friends knew when to expect him home. Long overdue, he set December 20, 1883, as the day for his sailing; but the date slipped by, and King stayed on in London, against a backdrop of flaming orange and scarlet sunsets, Krakatoa's stagy legacy from halfway round the world. What his motives were for lingering there in London his friends could only surmise; perhaps the uncertain state of his health was reason enough. But there were business reasons too—annoying snags in the Anglo-Mexican promotions.

The economic frosts that had settled over England with the panic of 1873 had never completely melted away. Investment capital proved tighter now than King had anticipated. Anglo-Mexican stock moved slowly on the market, while the underwriters whom Sedgwick had brought into the scheme turned out to be men of straw. As a consequence, the Anglo-Mexican Mining Company failed to muster the next installment of purchase money when it fell due; and King's remissness in the crisis alarmed his friends in State Street. It was bitter news to them that he had allowed the payment to be postponed without a clearance from Boston or New York. They were afraid that King had jeopardized their interests, along with his own.

It grew apparent that King was not the Dedicated Businessman. He had moved into the business sphere almost solely for wealth, not for the sake of business itself or the business life; he had no real desire to become a magnate of industry. The whole drift of the leisured life that he now cultivated pulled him in the opposite direction. He still dreamed of gaining millions from his Mexican mines; he continued to dream, too, of turning millions to the use of contemporary artists, and of making himself a new Lorenzo. But ill-health, infatuation with excessive refinement, with art as something divorced from common pursuits, had sapped his will to close with the problems of business or finance, or to concentrate on the means of turning his dreams into reality. He must have placed inordinate value on his time, to have fancied that he earned his salary as managing director. He seems to have only seldom gone near the office in Cannon Street.

"I now have a slight hope," Emmons declared in June, 1884, "that in consequence of Blaine's nomination King may be back this summer." Emmons's hunch was right—King promised to sail, and he wrote of the trip to J. D. Hague:

I look forward with great interest to leaving my home in England, and visiting your new and extraordinary country. All the phenomena of a sudden, unfinished civilization such as yours, will afford me the greatest amusement and keenest study. I am anxious to see what your Broadway and 5th Avenue look like, and whether the vaunted beauty of the American girl approaches that of her calmer and heavier sister over here. Then, too, accustomed as I am to our well regulated and orderly methods of politics, I shall take a great interest in observing the passionate activity, and the corruption of your system.

Chaffing aside, I do feel very much like an early Briton, and approach the idea of America with intense curiosity. It is impossible for me to realize that I have been away only two years.

He sailed for home with his cargo of art in early September, shortly after dining with Lowell at the Bristol Hotel. The minister seemed more English than the English themselves. Yet who could say if his attachment to the British Isles was felt more deeply than Clarence King's? King's affection for Britain prompted a friend to remark to Hay: "In my mind's eye, dear boy, I see the Savant of the Fortieth Parallel lost to his native land. He may live in America from a sense of duty, but he is like Mr. Henry James a London man at heart henceforth forever & ever." "Ah, happy England!" King himself could say in retrospect, but his departure had left, in Hay's words, "the entire Chamber of Peers in mourning."

18

Silver Clouds and Darker Linings

Clarence King, like Henry James, had found a Great Good Place in the Europe of art and tradition. It gave him a vantage point for a calm appraisal of life in America, and he now came home with a sharpened sense of American civilization. How estranged it seemed to him from the life he had left in England! "We are far more Roman than English," he concluded, and it was not a cheering discovery.

King had read Mommsen; he could see, he thought, a broad resemblance between the United States and the second phase of the Roman Empire. The social scene in America had assumed the character of its ruling delirium—a blatant preoccupation with power and sheer size. Within a year King would write:

The chief experiences of the Roman people were what ours have been—war, trade, and sudden expansion into national greatness; an expansion so rapid and immense as to overshadow and mar the serenity and order of social life. Material prosperity and political administration were the leading pursuits. Rome and America have loved luxury and pomp. Each civilization might be called a political success: both must be judged social failures. Rome loved the big; it seemed in harmony with the prodigious growth of Roman population and the gigantic spread of the imperial system. Size, brute mass, the big figures of the Census are our pride.

King shuddered at the motiveless frenzy he found in New York, the city of noise and speed and size, where in the years of his hegira abroad the longest suspension bridge in the world—the Brooklyn Bridge— had been completed. How oppressed King felt under what he termed "the crushing weight of the zeitgeist," which had crystallized as the supremely antagonistic force in his life! How subtly and yet profoundly alienated he felt from the spirit of a society where moneylenders had become dominant, where materialism was rampant and the arts were sterile! Such a society he indicted as "a nervous disease."

336

The circus mechanics of the presidential race seemed to prove that America had lapsed into a moral coma. The candidates—Blaine and Cleveland—had begun to butt each other like two bighorn rams above the clouds, two rams who filled the lower canyons with the din of their clashing. Oddly enough, King did not recoil from the tactics of his old political idol, now labeled in campaign song as "the continental liar from the state of Maine."

Indeed, King's loyalty to Blaine had never wavered, even through transitory strains created by the appearance of *Democracy*; for in spite of *Democracy*'s moral he remained blinded to the extent that Blaine was a symptom of national disease. The railroad scandals, the Mulligan letters, even Blaine's aloofness from Civil Service reform had left King, like his fellow stalwarts Howells and Hay, unshaken in his faith that here was a man for the White House. " 'In our bones' we felt it the right thing," wrote Howells, whom King had met on Boston Common shortly after his homecoming and with whom, respecting Blaine, he was in instant agreement.

But who was concerned with the real issues? "No one," Henry Adams had decided. "We are afraid to discuss them. Instead of this, the press is engaged in a most amusing dispute whether Mr. Cleveland had an illegitimate child, and did or did not live with more than one mistress, whether Mr. Blaine got paid in railway bonds for services as Speaker; and whether Mrs. Blaine had a baby three months after marriage." Bitterness grew between the factions, and religious bigotry was fanned. Not even King escaped a private fear—or so he confided to Mrs. J. D. Hague—that the Catholic Church might prove to be a political menace.

Here was the popular prejudice on which the Republican drive soon ran afoul. In New York City Blaine neglected to right a spokesman's blunder which branded the Democrats as a party of "Rum, Romanism, and Rebellion"; and the fate of the campaign was sealed, apparently, when in addition he dined at Delmonico's surrounded by a train of millionaires. The election came and went. While the outcome hung in doubt, enraged Democrats trooped up and down Fifth Avenue, though seldom so far as Brevoort House, where King had taken his quarters. Some carried banners; others chanted: "We'll hang Jay Gould to a so-o-o-u-u-ur apple tree." When the election count came in, King learned that his idol had lost New York by scarcely more than a thousand votes, and with New York, the White House. "For Blaine I am truly sorry," he wrote. "There is not gratitude enough in this people to keep him in the sunshine. The shadows will gather about him henceforward; neglect will succeed abuse. His sun has set!"

So the flag drooped at half-mast before that stronghold of Republicanism, the Union League Club, where King had joined another dining group, the XX Club, composed of a score or so of his New York friends. But there was only limited anodyne in old social ties; King felt restless, uprooted, and he confessed to D. C. Gilman that he found it hard to cast anchor: "The rush and whirl of New York life, the detestable social pressure of the place are so thoroughly antagonistic. . . . But for the crime of forsaking one's own country, I should live in London without hesitation." Like so many of his cultivated contemporaries, he felt nostalgia for the English capital, wrapped in its "blessed fog, a mercy in gray." And more than once he considered fleeing back across the Atlantic, in the veritable exodus of harried Yankees who sought, in Europe, what Henry James was to call the Great American Sedative. Instead, he settled down to the comparative opiate of socializing, "devoting his energies to dinners and balls in New York" while deploring the attendant pressures of such a life.

For the present King was living literally out of a trunk—or so he claimed one day at Ringwood, Abram Hewitt's country mansion. Henry Adams would put the matter in a different light, claiming that King worked hard "to support royal tastes, but live[d] like a vagrant." Sometimes, however, King would forsake his New York rounds to retreat to Newport and become an intermittent boarder at his mother's house on High Street, where enthusiasm for art and social service flourished, where his mother spent her leisure writing money-raising letters for a Charleston art school, where George Howland wistfully talked of becoming a painter, and where King's benevolent old grandmother—Mrs. Little—still remained an active friend of prisoners and delinquent girls. But King's family could seldom hold him long at home; he felt smothered in the anxious atmosphere of Mrs. Howland's house, and he would hurry back to New York City, sometimes by train, sometimes by coasting boat, a trip he made at least once in the company of Brander Matthews.

In this unsettled state, King was obliged to store the greater part of his art collection in a windowless vault, down in the basement of the old Studio Building on West Tenth Street. That large three-storied hull of red brick, a short walk from Brevoort House or a little longer from the Brunswick (where King would live later), was an undisputed center of New York art, a hive of busy painters and sculptors. It was there that Henry Tuckerman had written his *Book of the Artists* and Emanuel Leutze had fortified the national hagiolatry with scenes like "Washington Crossing the Delaware." William Chase maintained a studio there, crammed with curios and bric-a-brac; and John La Farge had worked there, off and on, since the close of his apprenticeship in Europe, a bronze and urbane giant who painted with vibrant colors and made ingenious plans for opalescent glass—glass that was calculated to glow like curtains of jewels between the observer and the light.

And there in his studio that smelled of chemicals and paint, La Farge treated special comrades like King or Adams or Royal Cortissoz to candle-lit suppers tossed together by a Japanese retainer. His talk, according to Cortissoz, was better even than Whistler's. And King, who returned La Farge's hospitality, delighted in the real appreciation that gleamed in the artist's almond-shaped eyes at the items he pulled from trunks and boxes down in the gas-illumined storeroom he called his "10th Street den." "By the bye," King would say, "I have a Turner or a Millet somewhere here"; and what he produced was always fit, in La Farge's judgment, to hang in a museum.* He even ordered something by La Farge for his collection—a small study of water lilies, two open blossoms and a bud floating on leaves which curled and flaunted their purple lining.

King shared La Farge's love for stained glass, and concerned as both men were with questions of style, it drew them together in earnest discussions of how the memory of General Grant might best be hon-

---

*The quality of the nearly one hundred oil and watercolor paintings listed in the 1903 auction catalogue of King's collection seems to have been generally distinguished. But to put his role as art amateur in perspective, it should be mentioned that the scope of King's interest in painting had noticeable limitations. This was true even in the American field where, alert as he was, much of the finest art of his day seems to have escaped his attention. As David Dickason points out, "A modern observer can look back on [King's esthetic adventures] and marvel at the omissions as well as the commissions chargeable to his artistic sense. George Innis, James McNeill Whistler, Winslow Homer—all older than himself, and all significant painters—seemed not to come within his ken. Thomas Eakins, Albert Pinkham Ryder, Mary Cassatt, Frank Duveneck—almost his exact contemporaries—produced memorable work during King's lifetime, and apparently went unappreciated by him" (*Art in America*, XXXII [Jan. 1944]: 51). He seems, moreover, to have ignored the work of a number of artists coming into prominence during the last years of his life. So, however honed King's esthetic sensibilities, the range of his appreciations as a connoisseur of painting appears to have been patently less than comprehensive.

ored. A million people, one August day in 1885, had watched the procession that bore the hero's coffin to a temporary tomb on Riverside Drive. Grantism and its scandals had been forgotten; only veneration for the hero of Appomattox remained, and a clamor had gone up for a fitting mausoleum. King read the symposium run by the *North American Review* and gagged over demands for something in a strictly American style.

What did the people want, he wondered—an Indian earth mound? Or a Mayan ruin? Those were strictly American monuments, he pointed out in an unsigned paper, "Style and the Monument." Strictly American, but as suitable for the tomb of General Grant as a Siamese pagoda. Nineteenth century America had, in his opinion, found no characteristic style in art, no style that fitly expressed the ideals of the American race, simply because that race did not as yet exist, nor could it exist till all the different peoples of the land were melted down into a single racial alloy. Only when there were "no more Irish or Germans, Negroes and English, but only Americans belonging to one defined American race," could a true American style emerge. So let the monument designer, he argued, surrender all pretensions to a national mode and guide himself by the ideal of felicity alone. He would be building for a thousand years upon a historic spot. Let his work project the spirit of civilization in America; with that, King had no quarrel. But in his opinion that spirit harmonized with none of the manners of Egypt, Greece, or Gothic Europe, and enough incongruous mixtures of those styles disfigured the American scene already.

Only a Roman style would suit. "To no canons of taste or crystallizations of styles," King wrote, "can we turn and find ourselves less strangers than among Roman works." Grant himself had impressed King as of a type with Roman captains in the second century. His proposal therefore called for "a round Roman tomb of noble dimensions treated as to its details in Romanesque style." The circular Roman motive struck him as the highest expression of dignity, and Romanesque refinements would permit the advantages of modern architectural engineering, even the use of steel and glass. Cortissoz considered it an "astounding project that King talked over with [La Farge]."

"Our notion," the artist declared in retrospect,

was to have filled the drum, or perhaps even the curves of the dome, with the richest and deepest of figured glass, built, if I may so express it, into the walls of the structure, . . . a looking forward to a future which is certain to come. . . .

This imaginary tower would then have been like the glory of the interior of a great jewel in the day, but at night would have sent out a far radiance . . . making as it were a pharos, a lighthouse . . . dominating the river as well as the land.

But worthy as La Farge would always hold King's plan, it proved too visionary for civic approval in 1885. Eventually the Monument Committee chose plans for a Greek shrine—a squat cupola on top of a square sepulcher—the like of which (King had implored) let there be none on Riverside Drive. None at least until "we sit in white *kitons* in the cool of the day, within the classic shade of Jones' Wood, to discuss and speculate on the essence of tragic love, and, if baffled, adjourn to consult the oracle in Hoboken."

Another of King's architectural dreams—that remained, alas, but the stuff of dreams—was the house he hoped to build around his art collection, a very poem of a house, an example of how a man of taste might domicile himself in contrast to the torrential vulgarity flooding America. He surmised that what he longed to do was nearly unique this side of the ocean, where, as a rule, the houses were crimes against good taste. The American people, it seemed to King, had contrived to strew the land with heinous incongruities "from Bangor to San Diego"; even so universal a thing as a drawing room was likely to be, in his opinion, "a mere wreck of styles, a maelstrom into which all sorts of works of decorative and pure art are . . . sucked down together into mutual ruin." How many monstrosities one could find for every room of distinction! King wondered sometimes if there were more than a dozen superior drawing rooms in all the land, and his hopes survived only because he actually did, now and then, stumble upon a distinguished interior. He praised, for instance, "a white Louis XIV oak room," which he had found with happy amazement in a mansion on Fifth Avenue— "a true authentic example of the very acme of French decorative skill . . . and actually here in New York!" Miraculously, every detail of the room seemed in perfect keeping with the whole.

All details must harmonize in like manner in the house which he reared in his imagination. He allowed La Farge to catch fleeting glimpses of it in their conversations, and the artist would remember one of its rooms in particular, "where high up, above windows and doors, a manner of frieze should run around a large space filled with the most beautiful of stained glass." King had chosen scenes from *The Divine Comedy* as the decorative motif. But the dream was obliged to wait—to wait, alas, until it flickered out—upon the exigencies of business and King's nomadic life.

Not that under such circumstances the elegance of his collections remained entirely hidden in the shadows of the Tenth Street vault. He took pictures and bric-a-brac to his mother's house in Newport, and he continued to lend beautiful things to friends like J. D. Hague, who had settled his family in the fashionable upper end of town. There in Hague's living room Edwin Abbey's "The Old Song" would hang for years, along with its companion piece lying on the library table— King's valued copy of *She Stoops to Conquer*, which Abbey had illustrated and inscribed. There, too, King would bring, or on occasion send, acquaintances to admire a few choice pieces—"my little treasures," as he called them—primitive oils or stained glass, a Flemish cabinet, silver teapots, bowls or vases. Or he would lend pictures for display at the Union League Club, or to special art events like the Antoine Barye memorial exhibition or those of the Decorative Art Society—a hint of what he aimed to do as patron of the arts whenever his bonanzas came in.

For King still dreamed of winning a fortune in silver and gold. He reshouldered the management of Sombrerete, a burden he had laid aside during his holiday in Europe. The board of directors named him president again in the spring of 1885, and he left for Mexico on another trip in a long succession of journeys that would prompt Stedman to remark: "We seldom met when he had not just come from a distant region or was departing for some other point as far. In this wise I could not free myself from the illusion that he was a kind of Martian—a planetary visitor, of a texture different from that of ordinary Earth-dwellers." Late or soon, King's travels took him back to all of his mines—Yedras, Sombrerete, and Prietas.

Affairs at Prietas had reached their nadir in the summer of 1882 when the mine had been closed on the heels of a damning report by Pumpelly. Pumpelly had so seriously underestimated the Prietas vein that he had labeled the mine "a desperate failure." Then a yellow-fever terror had paralyzed the district. Conditions had mended there, however, since King's return from Europe, and the Prietas shafts had been sunk another six hundred feet, a large body of lean ore now keeping the mill in operation. Even a surplus began to accumulate in the treasury, in sharp contrast with Yedras, where labor problems had pushed a chronic crisis to the verge of disaster.

The Yedras natives had proved to be unsteady workers. They refused to stir on religious holidays, and it seemed as though every other day was a holiday. As the foreman declared, "Only one who has handled a gang of Mexicans who scarcely know the difference between a roasting furnace and a bread-oven . . . can appreciate the difficulties." It did not help to import Italians as replacements; they merely deserted. Chinese coolies were to prove a better choice, though in the end (after King's departure from the management) only Yaquis from Sonora would solve the problem conclusively.

At Sombrerete King found that George Tew, who had replaced Hoffmann as superintendent during King's European interlude, had fared better with labor, having brought down twenty-five hard-rock miners from Virginia City to replace the Mexican workers. As much the perennial optimist as King himself, Tew had retained his faith in the mine, and he swore, "It will make us all rich." The pumps had been set to work two years before—a spectacular ceremony, blessed by the local priest, while shouts had gone up from at least eight thousand natives who had congregated from leagues around. "The greatest day that Sombrerete ever saw," Tew had telegraphed.

Then months of pumping had passed, and Tew succeeded in draining the San Francisco shaft. He retimbered it down to the seven-hundred-foot level, where a large body of medium-grade ore had been uncovered. Profits, King knew, would depend on how the problems of reduction could be met. The ore was rebellious; it did not respond to the modified patio process used in the ancient hacienda which the company had acquired. Tew now worked a portion of it by concentration, the rest by leaching after it was roasted in a furnace. He shipped the products to the States for sale, a costly operation, even though the newly constructed Mexican Central Railroad had come within twenty miles of the mine.

Tew had begun to drain a second shaft, in hopes of cutting the Veta Negra at twelve hundred feet, but the cost was staggering. Soon the fiasco developed that Hoffmann had foreseen upon his being relieved by Tew. Hoffmann had taken a dim view of his successor, who, he was convinced, did "not know the first principles of deep mining"; and he had informed Whitney: "I am satisfied that his management from sheer ignorance . . . will cost the company a great deal of money in a short space of time. I feel sorry for King and Prof. Agassiz, who very likely have no idea of the true state of things." It was not reassuring testimony to the soundness of King's judgment that he continued Tew in charge as the quandaries at the mine multiplied. Under Tew's superintendence the working capital melted away, and then the ore receipts; and as the crisis mounted, King could foresee no further drafts from his friends in Boston. They were, in fact, as eager now to sell their Sombrerete interests as their shares in Yedras, and King had to scrabble for money in other quarters.

He captured the interest of three New York capitalists—John J. Astor II (son of the "Landlord of New York"), Pierre Lorillard the tobacco magnate, and Frederick Billings, once president of the Northern Pacific Railroad. Led by Billings, they formed a pool to operate Sombrerete under a long-term option to buy it for $750,000. The work was resumed upon that basis, and Tew remained as sanguine as ever. King still dared to hope and scheme; the possibilities were dramatic. As Bliss Perry would suggest long afterward, a Joseph Conrad might have spun another *Nostromo* around a mine like Sombrerete "and the fortunes that came and went like sheet-lightning in the sky."

Tew had, in the meantime, spied out other eclipsed lodes in the Sierra Madre, and King's nostalgia for Great Britain was steeped in anticipation of floating more mines on the London market. "I will fill you up," Tew had said, "as fast as you can unload, and most of these things hav [sic] not been looked at carelessly either. . . . You know how much mule back wriding [sic] it takes me to find a mine I can recommend." King knew indeed; yet he also perceived the futility of pushing new ventures before his first promotion had reached some satisfactory issue. It was a disconcerting fact that the condition of the Anglo-Mexican Mining Company had not improved since his return to America.

"There is no efficiency here," wrote one of the English corporators. The president of the company was absorbed in his own affairs; the secretary slighted the office; the accounts were allowed to fall behind, sometimes for months; and King's associates in the United States still waited for the balance of the purchase money, nearly a million dollars. They smoldered with wrath and blamed King for the muddle.

On a dash into Mexico, King reassured himself that the Yedras vein was as rich as he had always held; that once the labor and reduction problems were resolved the mine would produce with laudable success. More working funds were needed in the meantime. But how could one raise money on the mine as long as the owners on opposite sides of the ocean remained at loggerheads? Who would invest in such a confused snarl of ownership? King redoubled his efforts to break the impasse and managed at last to engineer a compromise whereby the long-suspended sale could be completed. Quincy Shaw, acting for the Three alone, agreed to accept unissued Anglo-Mexican shares, at par, in lieu of the long delinquent purchase money. The Yedras Mining Company was then dissolved; and Shaw received its assets, to be held in his hands until Anglo-Mexican dividends equaled the full amount that had been advanced by the Three. The agreement recognized King's equity, to be surrendered to him when all indebtedness to the others was discharged. Sometime in 1886 he used the guarantee as security for a loan from Hay and Gardiner—forty-five thousand dollars, with which he paid up the shares that stood in his name, the money keeping the works at Yedras going. Soon production began to exceed expenses.

But the Boston associates were far from impressed. Shaw countered all good news with a shrug, or he grumbled that King would "make a waste and frittering of any value there may be." Agassiz discounted the bullion that Yedras had produced; he gibed at King's effort as a specious straining for effect—"as a sort of see what I can do, at an outrageous sacrifice of ore and money." King must go, he said. Let someone else attempt to salvage that "infernal sink." The fact was, Agassiz fumed, had he paid more attention to Calumet instead of to King's "moonshine enterprises in Mexico," he would now be rich enough to underwrite his wildest dreams.

The three consulted; then Agassiz sailed for England, with proxies for the annual meeting of the Anglo-Mexican stockholders. He found affairs chaotic at the Cannon Street Office and was inclined to fault King for the trouble. "The more I see of this Yedras business," he wrote to Higginson, "the less . . . I understand the total absence of common sense [in] King." In January 1887 Agassiz packed the Anglo-Mexican board with men of his own choice, then forced King's resignation as managing director. William N. Olmsted, the secretary, was named instead; and on turning over his power of attorney in New York, King stepped down from the management of Yedras forever—at a time, ironically, when the mine had ceased to be a complete white elephant. *

* The labor problem at Yedras was alleviated during King's tenure by the importation of coolies from Hong Kong. As a result the mine began to produce so well that within two years the Anglo-Mexican Mining Company would declare a dividend of 30 percent. Thereafter, with the use of Yaqui workers, returns would average 10.6 percent a year until 1898, when the ore began to fail. When the affairs of the company were wound up about a year after King's death, the King interests received a settlement of twenty-six thousand dollars.

Brilliant success in King's youth and early maturity had not prepared him for failure in middle age; and as friends observed, he slipped more frequently now into enervating "spells of depression." "When the life and buoyancy of good health departs from a man's body," he wrote from one of his plunges into melancholy, "the poor mind grows weary and the thousand and one duties of daily life lie like heavy burdens which must be again and again lifted up by an effort of tired will. Thus with me the days and weeks seem like an insurmountable wall always in front of me." During such dark intervals he would retreat into what he called "the old wounded beast way that I have had since [childhood] of hiding myself when I am sore and unsuccessful."

The cause of one transient despondency was a stroke of ill luck at the Brunswick Hotel, to which King had moved from Brevoort House. At his new quarters "an unreflecting chamber maid" had pitched his ac- cumulated manuscripts into the trash—"a horrid loss," he informed Hay. "All my MSS—including what little I had done on the English novel, all my London notes, my unfinished Hadrian and the odds and ends—all gone." * What he needed at this point was some of the literary resolution of Carlyle, who had redone *The French Revolution* from memory after a careless servant had burned the first draft. King himself remained immobilized and would apparently never replace the lost manuscripts. Naively he projected the general cause of his malaise into what had become, for him, an increasingly hostile milieu; and he was inclined to agree with Adams—à la *Democracy*—that commer- cialized society had shaken his nerves to pieces.

The amoral excesses of individualism in practice, the ethics that regarded chaos as normal, which installed greed as a cardinal virtue and placed financial achievement before integrity, now left him in a chronic state of shock, yearning for escape, but ensnared in a web spun of his own vacillation. For what had stalled King was, as much as anything, a fatal cleavage in himself; in one recess of his divided self he lusted after William James's bright Bitch Goddess while in other depths he burned with a fierce contempt for the greed and hypocrisy, the callousness and cruelty that made for Business Success on the grand scale. King yearned for wealth, but he hated it too, hated the materialistic values that love

---

* The riddle of Hadrian seems to have intrigued King. In the *Century Magazine* for October 1886, he reminded readers of "the difficulties of knowing a man like Hadrian, and [of] how neither the dull biographies of his day nor the brilliant pages of Gre- gorovius can solve the enigmatical nature of the great artist emperor."

of money encouraged; above all, he hated the application of money standards to every function of society.

And this was a conflict fraught with disaster. Much of his failure at Yedras—his failure, for instance, to conclusively solve the labor problems there—had stemmed from his own deep conflict, and the hesitation it produced. Howells would later note King's "feeling for [the people] who do the hard work of the world, that others may enjoy their ease." Indeed, his desire for silver and the power that silver could buy had never burned intensely enough to destroy his sympathy for the native work-gangs underground, and he remained powerless to drive them with the ferocity common to captains of industry. The Boston trio had found such weakness in their managing director an intolerable extravagance. Measured by their business gauge, King's stature shrank to that of a sentimental incompetent, fit only for drawing up prospectuses. In such a prosaic way the *Zeitgeist* conspired to beat him down.

But how typical a story for a time when America put no premium on its men of finer grain, when it gave its laurels to those of coarser mold, mere money-grubbers distinguished for little else than compulsive avarice! The nation had found its ideal in the multimillionaire, and the hog with the highest heap—as Howells would soon lament—ran off with "the prize in our national cakewalk." For the rest it was a complete route.

Not a few of the best, most sensitive men of all—intellectuals, artists, poets—refusing to join the exodus, had gone down in the general wrack. There were magic lights among them, obscured in that garish day: old, outcast Whitman, for example, viewed askance by proper burghers, though trailed by adoring dogs or children down the streets of Camden; or a weary Melville, morosely silent, having cursed the goddess of market place and mine, "the arch-strumpet . . . harlot on horseback"; or the artist Ryder, eccentric refugee from a hostile world.

In such a world success could be as dangerous as failure. In defense of his integrity La Farge was now retreating, in spirit, into the art of the thirteenth century; and Howells, who had settled in New York City, faced the hazards of new fortune there with questioning bewilderment, his gentle spirit and good intentions no proof against his mounting fear that American civilization, without real equality, was coming out all wrong. He toyed with socialism, read books by Tolstoy, books by Henry George, who lived a street or so away—the theoretical Mr. George who had just defeated theatrical Mr. Roosevelt in the race for mayor but lost in turn to King's old benefactor, Abram Hewitt. The word of congratulation was, "We knew you'd do it, Mr. Hewitt!" although to what purpose was another question. Hewitt, as mayor, installed gas lamps designed by Stanford White outside his house and then rolled up his sleeves against the Tammany Hall that had put him in office. He had become an ailing old insomniac who slept, at best, a few hours in the dead of night, as if success on such terms were as disconcerting as downright failure. But of all King's intimates who seemingly had their heart's desire, none had found the incubus of the era more impossible to sustain than Clover Adams.

Tragedy had struck the Yellow House on H Street on December 6, 1885. King was in New York City that Sunday afternoon, talking with Emmons and Arnold Hague about the latest attacks in Congress on Powell's conduct of the Geological Survey. He did not hear the news till later—how Henry and Clover had taken their breakfast at noon, as was their Sunday custom; how Henry had gone for his usual stroll, leaving Clover in her room, the room where she had written each Sunday the weekly letters to her father Dr. Hooper; the room where she had brooded over his memory, perhaps over unendurable recollections of his final days when she had worn herself despondent nursing him, a wasted old man slowly sinking under the agonies of angina. She had never recovered from shock, never regained "that bright intrepid spirit" so dear to her companion Hearts, but had gone into seclusion on coming home to Washington. She had been dead of potassium cyanide for an hour when Adams found her crumpled before the fire.

King seems to have misinterpreted the first announcement of her death, and not understanding that Clover would be buried in Rock Creek Cemetery outside of Washington, he waited in New York, expecting to meet Adams on his way to Boston with Clover's body. King's brief, rather strained, but deeply felt letter of condolence was dated December 10, four days after the tragedy. Meanwhile, "I hoped . . . you might summon King and me to be with you at the last," John Hay wrote to Adams from the Brunswick.

But Adams hugged his grief in loneliness and silence, and his friends could only surmise what he had thought and felt through his macabre vigil. Had his longing for children burdened Clover's spirits with a cross she no longer had the strength to bear? Or worse, had anything he had said or written sown the suggestion of suicide in her distraught mind? Adams could not or he would not say; the chapter was closed—a secret, in his phrase, between himself and eternity.

Yet a short book he had published under the pseudonym Francis Snow Compton while King was still in Europe—the novel *Esther*—had gained a strange provocative significance with Clover dead. Besides King and Henry Holt the publisher, Adams trusted only one or two of his closest friends with the secret of its authorship.* But how precious he held the book, his "melancholy little *Esther*," as he referred to it. He claimed that it was written in his heart's blood, and that one chapter of it was dearer to him than all of his long History. There was no need to explain that there were personal echoes in the story.

Not that *Esther* was autobiographical in any strict sense. Still, no one acquainted with Clover could have read it without finding it redolent of her presence, or without a poignant feeling that Esther's doubts, all her religious uncertainties, reflected those which had torn at the very base of Clover's peace of mind. For how true, how perfectly authentic, seemed the portrait that Adams had drawn of a sensitive woman able neither to accept traditional dogma nor to achieve contentment in unbelief; Esther, like Clover herself, had been caught in one of the towering conflicts of the day, had found herself unable to reach a haven or to weather the storm. And at her father's death Esther's despair had grown unbearable. It was "worse than anything she had ever imagined; she wanted to escape, to run away, to get out of life itself, rather than suffer such pain, such terror, such misery of helplessness." She was fond of children—other people's children—but knew in her heart that she was good only for telling them stories; she had none of her own in which to forget despair, as Clover herself had none. That was Adams's sharpest cut of all, not even softened by the devoted sympathy for

---

*Adams gave King permission to admit Hay to the secret, and King sent the latter a copy in June 1886, and invited him to guess who had written it. Hay divined at once that Adams was the author. In King's next letter, on Independence Day, he explained:

[Adams] conceived the quaint archaic project of putting forth the novel without any notices or advertisements to see if a dull world would do their own criticizing and appreciate his work. Later [there] came to his mind a second reason why he should let the novel lie where it had fallen in the silent depths of American stupidity and that was a feeling of regret at having exposed his wife's religious experiences and, as it were, made of her a chemical subject *vis à vis* religion. . . . Later when Dr. Hooper died of heart failure, as the old man in *Esther* died, he felt that it was too personal and private a book to have brought into its due prominence.

King then ventured this opinion: "I think it far more compact and vivid than *Dem-[ocracy]* but one of the most painful things imaginable" (A37865[23][3], Hay Papers [Brown University Library]).

Esther that he assigned to George Strong, the bachelor paleontologist, whose irrepressible gaiety rivaled King's among the Five of Hearts.*

King had perceived the logical imperative of Esther's despair and self-loathing, and he complained that the ending his friend had given the novel was intrinsically false. He declared that Adams should "have made Esther jump into Niagara as that was what she would have done."

"Certainly she would," Adams agreed, "but I could not suggest it."

Perhaps he had made a mistake in telling King about the book, Adams remarked to John Hay, but that was done: "Now let it die," he begged. It was like the grave, a private place; he could not bear to admit the public. And as a defense against intrusion he claimed that, with Clover gone, he too had perished to the world.

Soon he fled to Japan with John La Farge, too late in the season for Nirvana, it was true, but also much too early for sex; for Adams affirmed that "in spite of King," sex was only a scientific classification in Japan. There was plenty of public nakedness, and phallic worship was as universal as the sun, but "the Japs are monkeys," he reported; ". . . the women very badly made monkeys." There was no escape for him in Old Japan, not even in buying bric-a-brac for King and Hay. So on he moved; he seemed contented only when in motion, as he claimed, and asked "no better than to wander on." And when he came home, it was to play the mordant mandarin, who trailed vitriol over the American

---

*That George Strong was modeled on King can be seen in such passages as the one which follows:

When . . . Professor Strong walked down Fifth Avenue to his club, he looked, to the thousand people he passed, like what he was, an intelligent man, with a figure made for action, an eye that hated rest, and a manner naturally sympathetic. His forehead was so bold as to give his face a look of strong character, which a dark beard rather helped to increase. He was a popular fellow, known as George by whole gangs of the roughest miners in Nevada, where he had worked for years as a practical geologist, and it would be hard to find in America, Europe, or Asia, a city in which someone would not have smiled at the mention of his name, and asked where George was going to turn up next

(*Esther, A Novel*, pp. 19–20). Adams used other friends also as models. One can see in the mural painter Wharton the talents and some of the traits of John La Farge, and the beauty and charm of Catherine Brooke, the girl from Colorado, were suggested by the loveliness of Elizabeth Cameron. The parallel between Esther's father and Clover's is unmistakable, and something of Phillips Brooks, Adams's cousin, may be found in the Reverend Stephen Hazard. To read *Esther* as a sort of roman à clef does much to relieve its pallidness as a Novel of Ideas, for though not strictly autobiographical, it is nevertheless rich in biographical significance. "The whole book, in fact," as Otto Friedrich observes in *Clover* (p. 298), "can be read as a terrible confession and a terrible prophecy."

scene. But King was ready to agree on everything in the mandarin mood. "If being diametrically opposed to the United States is to be a Chinese," he remarked in 1887, "I am one."

Of the Hearts who remained, the most stable were the John Hays; they were better adjusted to the facts of the Gilded Age. Spectacular luck had followed Hay since the hour Lincoln had called him to the White House; he had married a fortune such as King had dreamed of making; he had taken the place of his father-in-law as a trustee of Western Union and a champion of conservative values. He had made *The Bread-Winners* a vindication of private property, for private property seemed to Hay both fount and foundation of civilized order, notwithstanding the doctrines of Jesus or Gautama or the implications of much of the world's greatest literature. His credo was nicely suited to one now hailed as the "Laureate of the Republican Party," in view of the lines on which the party was evolving. His attitudes had also earned a name for Hay as a realist of letters.

"To be a realist in that sense," King wrote of him, defensively,

is simply not to be driven from a normal, sound conception of the material and external facts of life, by the powerful current which surges through the channels of thought and feeling of all poetic natures. The greatest realist is he who can keep his feet always on the solid bottom while wading deepest into the foaming river of life, and such is Hay.

A rich man now, Hay could afford to devote his years to a labor of love, like the most detached of scholars.

Since leaving the State Department, in 1881, he had given chiefly of his time to the epic life of Lincoln which he and John Nicolay had planned to write since their days at the president's side. In 1886 the exhaustive work—a million and a half words—was all but finished. And when the *Century Magazine* bought the manuscript for serial publication, King agreed to write a long advance notice for the journal's October issue. It was not a review so much as a graceful sketch of the two biographers—indeed it was called "The Biographers of Lincoln." Indirectly it was also a tribute to the friendship abiding between himself and Hay, a friendship such as King had called "a mitigating circumstance in life." He was careful, however, to give evenhanded treatment to the two writers and felt only surprise to learn of Nicolay's disappointment in the handling of his part.

King had conferred with Hay before writing the sketch. But in general his pressing business involvements seldom carried him down to Washington, where the Hays now lived next door to Adams in one of the Romanesque houses that H. H. Richardson had built for the Hearts on Lafayette Square. There King would sometimes send his sister Marian for a taste of society on the Potomac under Clara Hay's shelter-ing wing. Marian found it "bliss" and impressed Henry Adams as "look[ing] very fresh, delicate and pretty." And on rare occasions King himself would give his friends a day—"never more than that," as Hay complained, "and then there is a jubilee among the Four of Hearts— even the vacant chair seems less gloomy when he is there." *

King now waged a desperate struggle to recoup his luck in Mexico. He feared sometimes that Fate had forged the chains of labor forever to his legs, and he confided to Adams, "I shall never in time and space get beyond their tether or their clank." Yet he had managed to rouse himself from the illness and depression that had claimed him after his ouster from the helm at Yedras; and he darted through Mexico, in Hay's simile, "like a meteor" blazing over the problems of Sombrerete. "There seems to be great recuperative forces about him always," Hay added; "he gets out of bed for a ramble of five thousand miles and thinks nothing about it."

Large reserves remained in sight at Sombrerete; the mine gave promise of yielding adequate amounts of ore indefinitely. But the grade had fallen badly, as frequent assays showed, and no remarkable profits could be made, King feared, unless Tew's methods were improved. The nature of Sombrerete ore demanded a larger reduction plant, a better mill of an altogether different style. King had convinced Billings of the necessity of such improvements, and his plans had received approval. They provided for the use of mechanical roasters instead of the old reverberatory furnace, of Eckart rolls instead of cumbersome crushers, and of various other innovations to perfect extraction while minimiz-ing the need for labor. The Santa Rosa Mill, as King named it, promised to be the finest mill in Mexico, geared to handle a hundred tons of ore a day. Indeed, it would have over six times the capacity of the old mill that it was replacing.

* Adams wrote in The Education: "Since 1879, King, Hay and Adams had been inseparable." The statement is quite misleading if taken as literal truth. They remained in close sympathy, however, and their friendship was seemingly not affected by the death of Mrs. Adams. Hay and Adams saw more of each other than either did of King.

King reached the mine in March 1887 and found it looking admirable. "But," he wrote, "I devoted but little attention to it; my struggle was wholly on the surface of the ground, to find a place for our great Hacienda, which is now to be built. I was on a mule from morning to night." After breaking ground at Sombrerete, he traveled up to El Paso, a brawling new rail center, where the previous year he had organized the National Bank of El Paso, becoming a trustee and principal stockholder. "[The] bank has proved a great success," he could now write, and the triumph encouraged him to lay plans for a second bank somewhere in California. This project, plus his plans for Sombrerete, carried him next to San Francisco, where he ordered the construction of Sombrerete's new equipment, including the largest Stetefeldt furnace in the world.

How pleased he was to be in California, the land where he would rather settle than any other, England excepted. As he moved about the state, after his consultations on the mill with the engineers of the Union Iron Works, he combined the search for a new bank site with a study of various ranchos in the interest of the novel he was working out in his mind. He tentatively called it "Santa Rita," possibly for the principal character (who seems to have been anything but a saint), or for an imaginary rancho, the story's setting. The double mission took him soon to southern California, where a rage for associations with Helen Hunt Jackson and *Ramona* had gotten under way, to flourish for the next three decades.

King had read *Ramona* with immense pleasure, finding it "the gospel truth" about the Mission Indians. He approved the characterization of Alessandro, judging it "not much overdone." Where the book struck him as suffering "from a man's point of view [was] Ramona herself, whose only natural act was her perfectly bovine love for her buck. A little sense of humor and a few jets of melted lava in the love passages would have made it a remarkable book."

King found the main treatment of *Ramona* not a bit like what he planned for "Santa Rita." "[Still,]" he wrote, "much of my local color will have to be changed," and he now looked for new details to incorporate into his story. "I lived again in the dear old ranchos," he informed Hay—notably Camulos (the home of the del Valle family), now growing famous as the original of the Moreno rancho in *Ramona*. It was located in the Santa Clara Valley, halfway between Santa Barbara and Los Angeles, and since there was no hotel nearby, visitors were housed on the ranch itself. King found that Charles Dudley Warner had preceded him there by a couple of weeks. "He made himself vastly at home," King wrote, "[and] turned a sweet young girl out of the room in which Padre Salvierderra . . . is supposed to have slept." Señora del Valle, the model for the fictional Señora Moreno, had made Warner welcome; and according to her story, he had asked her "to unpack all the family Lares and Penates"—the heirlooms which Mrs. Jackson had so lovingly described. These included a golden rosary and an embroidered altar cloth, as well as the first communion gown of Señora del Valle's mother. There was also the Indian crepe shawl of her grandmother, for which Warner had had the effrontery to offer $16.75. That was more than the shawl was worth, he said, but he really needed it because of his friendship for Helen Hunt Jackson. "The barometric pressure was rather low over Warner about this time," King wrote, "and he left in disgust the next morning."

It was probably at Camulos that an Indian woman named Luciana captured King's attention, to give his quest for local color a breathtaking boost. She must have been a startling example of what he termed "natural woman," for he described her "as near Eve as can be" and at once planned to use her as a literary model. "I escaped from her by a miracle of self-control," he informed Hay. "I rode with [her] alone in the mountains among the straying cattle. The world was all flowers, and Luciana's face was the most tender and grave image of Indian womanhood within human conception. I had an almost overpowering attack of—, well, *Locksley Hall*." The two reined in their horses at a mountain spring, among live oaks dewy with fog from the nearby Pacific, while orange poppies blazed in the grass. They dismounted, and gazed out over the gray ocean; "and then," King wrote, "I came as near it as I ever shall."

Evidently this poignant experience—Luciana would haunt King's thoughts for a long time thereafter and her name would crop up in more than one subsequent letter—marked a high point in his researches for "Santa Rita." No doubt the encounter would have illuminated his compulsive weakness for the "archaic woman" had it ever received literary expression. But "Santa Rita" would never materialize. As King remarked later, he would "have the gentle tonic of perpetual gestation, the . . . pride of an important bellyful, with none of the throes of printing." In what Howells would call his "indifference to literary repute" he would never make the tedious effort it required to put the novel down on paper; he would keep "for his reward the aesthetic delight he had" in working out the details of the story in his head—and then in talking them away.

Had "Santa Rita" ever been written down, the novel (notwithstanding King's diligence in searching out authentic local color) would doubtless have eschewed the realism that had fast become a staple of the day—the literary development which, ironically enough, King's *Mountaineering* had so aptly pioneered. More and more in his dedication to the Ideal King chafed at the commonplace factualism pervading contemporary art and letters, comparing it with "prints from the detective camera—little snapshots at the casual attitude of society, which forever surprise us as the horse photographs of Muybridge do. [But] I have bought a photo of the Venus of Milo," he assured Hay,

and read the *Antigone* again to take the taste of realism out of my mouth. . . . I prefer the Milo to that plaster knee of the little French slut we saw in a studio with all the droll realism of the goose flesh & the adhering hairs. You can learn as much about women from the Milo as you can from all the distorted creatures who crowd the pages & canvases of modern art put together.

Meanwhile, the search for a new bank site took him further south, and the splendid harbor at San Diego and the prospect there of head-long urban growth were all he needed for a decision—San Diego was the place for his second bank. Like "Santa Rita," this project was destined to remain an unfulfilled dream, but now, as much as the charged image of Luciana, it filled King with a warm glow—a glow that persisted all through his homeward journey. It heightened his pleasure in the fleeting landscapes through which he traveled, even the harsh vistas of Arizona. "Those white alkali plains," he mused, "stretching on into the very sky, with their mirages, and the looming blue-and-black mountains, and the pale green shafts of gigantic cacti, and the occasional figure of an Indian [make] the most striking scene in America." The train clattered on, via El Paso, and at last into New Orleans, where King laid over at the St. Charles Hotel for the purpose of taking care of a delicate responsibility.

While yet in San Francisco, he had described the mission to General Barlow in a letter marked *Confidential!* and rounded off with the caution: "Lastly pray consider this as sacredly private & in the classic words of our friend Blaine 'burn this.'" His cryptic message suggested a situation squarely in the bailiwick of George Washington Cable. There had been "thrust" upon him, King explained, a woman

whose character and history form together one of those strange dark lines of Southern history which any friend of Southern men in ante bellum days understands all about. Fortunately for my piece of mind the old quadroon who has fallen into my hands is seventy years old and white haired. These two stubborn facts will easily protect me from an eye like incandescent lava. If I ever have her permission I will tell you her story and your eyes will open to new chapters in American political biography. . . . At the death of one of the greatest statesmen in our history her slender affairs fell into the trusteeship . . . of a gentleman of the old school who with his wife have been true & faithful to her. That man was my legal advisor in Mexican matters and in 1881 in going to his office I saw the heroine of this letter & had five minutes casual talk [with her]. I then learned nothing of her and had no dream of seeing her again. But from that hour it seems she set her heart on having me as the guardian of her little affairs. My friend, himself over 75, is now in failing health & has (to shorten the tale) laid on me the solemn charge of her welfare.

The purpose of King's letter had been to ask from Barlow an introduction to some New Orleans lawyer who could look after questions of land titles, and he added: "I want to be in the hands of a man not under 60, if possible one who knows about such histories & who has outgrown idle curiosity. I should think, if there were some fine old character among the French Creole lawyers, that would be best." King expected to inherit the old quadroon's "invaluable papers" upon her death and perhaps had thoughts of himself making literary use of them, but his subsequent letters to Barlow remained entirely silent on how her "slender affairs" were at last worked out.

For King, meanwhile, a prime attraction of the city was his favorite gumbo, the delight he promised to pour over the soul of Henry Adams. To Hay he explained: "I have been promoted far beyond French restaurants in New Orleans"—meaning that two or three middle-aged women of the city had taken him to their hearts and consecrated hours of gumbo for his pleasure. Like Lafcadio Hearn, he thought of New Orleans largely in terms of exotic cuisine; and yet, all gumbo notwithstanding, this visit seems to have been the occasion for his savoring common red beans there. It happened that, on overtaking Charles Dudley Warner at the St. Charles, he went with him to meet Grace King, the new young "Southern Woman of Letters." Warner, who had helped her place her first story, was an old family friend, and the measure of his familiarity was his presuming to invite King to lunch without first alerting their hosts. But there was only red beans and rice to serve, cried Miss King's "Mamma"; for it was Friday, a Creole fast day. But Clarence King, "*a l'aise* with cordial people, made himself *persona grata* . . . helping himself two or three times out of the great flat dish of red beans and the platter piled up with well-cooked rice." It may have been on this occasion that Grace King inscribed the volume of her work that would be found among King's books after his death.

Limited capital aggravated King's mining problems on his return to New York City. He learned that, pending observation of the Santa Rosa Mill in operation, the Billings group had declined to exercise their option to buy Sombrerete. Billings, it seemed, was loath to risk more money on the gamble. But the old plant remained at work, and every dollar it produced beyond the costs of operation was spent on completing the new mill.

Various difficulties slowed the work, delaying completion. When timber at Sombrerete was exhausted, King was forced to bring more of it from Durango, a slow and expensive move in the rainy season. And the new machinery, shipped by rail into Zacatecas, met with long delays on the final stage of the journey, for storms had ruined the roads. The mill, in spite of all King's urgings, would not be ready to make its maiden run till the spring of 1889, a crucial point in King's career, as his principal hopes for a fortune must then revolve on the Santa Rosa's failure or success.

He sometimes questioned whether the stakes were worth the struggle; there were moments when he wanted nothing more than to flee from his business entanglements. "Were it not for my family cares," he wrote to Adams in 1887, "I would gladly wander on anywhere a mule or canoe could bear us and search till death for the garden of Eden or the fountain of eternal wit, or any other thing we were sure not to find." But if such a retreat, or if flight to Europe or to some primitive coconut isle were not in his power, he still might find some hideaway, in an unspoiled corner of America, for occasional solace from civilization. Why not some peaceful part of the down-East backwoods such as Pumpelly had discovered for himself near Dublin, New Hampshire?

King had toured the mountainous parts of New England during the summer of 1885, hoping to find such a spot—"a really rural place with plenty of water for scenery and boating. . . . And at last," he wrote, "I came upon Sunapee Lake an hour out from Concord." Twelve miles of shining water, whose shores rolled back against dark wooded hills, where farms straggled through forest lands more rocky than Scotland. The land was cheap—a thousand acres for only six thousand dollars. John Hay had run up at a letter from King and had found the tract enchanting; he wanted half of it, if King should buy. And they would invite a few friends—Adams, of course, and perhaps Howells, whom Hay would promise an acre or two for the pleasure of his wit and wisdom, or Henry Holt, or D. C. Gilman, or Whitridge, who had "married the daughter of Matthew Arnold." All of them would build inexpensive lodges, share the costs of a garden, stable, and even a boathouse, and make what King believed they could—"a charming summer colony." It would be the ideal place in which to moon and write, or as he flippantly put it, "drive the quill."

For the next three years King spent a part of each summer there, sometimes with the Hays, sometimes with George, Marian, and their mother. They would ride horseback, boat, and "watch the dark shadows of Sunapee Mountain paint themselves on the still surface of the lake," and the peace recalled King's old expansive moods. It was "a delicious vein" in which Hay found him; "he ought to write his novel now." But the peace, King feared, was too fine to endure; some vile hotel would rise there, he surmised, "and noisome people like [those in] Howells' novels" would flock from "honest, disgusting middle-class Boston, and still later Dudley Warner"—or Deadly Warning, as someone quipped—would arrive "with a second-class artist and drag the lake into *Harper's*. Alas!"

But the negotiations dragged on; and by springtime, 1888, when King ran up to the lake with the John Hays, he could ill afford the best of bargains. "Ten minutes before we got there," Hay later wrote, "we looked each other in the three faces, . . . and all at once we said in chorus:—'We don't want the place!' and each begged pardon of the other for changing our minds." The Hays, however, had only to see the lake again, to fall in love with Sunapee all over. They bought the tract for themselves alone—twelve hundred acres of wild fir woods, where they built a summer home, the Fells, and Hay discovered a refuge in which "to cultivate his kinship with Omar."

No doubt King's principal motive for dropping out of the Sunapee arrangement was the clandestine love affair that now absorbed him in New York—a bizarre alliance that would, in time, add innumerable complications to his life. The union had to be kept secret from even his closest friends, making participation in the colony he had planned awkward if not impossible.

Sometime late in 1887 or early in 1888, several months after his emotional encounter with Luciana, he had noticed a young nursemaid at the house of an acquaintance in lower Manhattan, a Negro woman more than twenty years his junior. She had a pleasant face, a warm dark-brown complexion, with splendid white teeth and the black kinked hair of the Negro race. The shade of Ada Todd's skin, like the ample proportions of her figure, fit the specifications of what Henry Adams would call King's "dream of unfair women"—a vision that Adams would claim that he had heard about for over twenty years.

For color—a dark skin tone, as hallmark of the archaic, the quality that had moved King so deeply in his encounter with Luciana— remained his enduring fetish. * Race did not matter, it seemed, so much as complexion. "He has a peculiar weakness for color . . . especially when it is on a fair cheek," Emmons had once remarked concerning "the dusky fair ones of Mexico." And Adams: "If he had a choice among women it was in favor of Indians and negroes"; though King had also admired the women of Polynesia. All had swarthy appeal. Amber, bronze, old-gold, or even coffee browns and black—something in all these deeper skin tones roused his voluptuous nature, excited him as women of his own complexion could seldom do.

King in fact, as Adams noted, "had no faith in the American woman"—woman, that is, of the Nordic type. All the refining influences of his background—education, civilization, puritan Christianity, not to mention the anxious demands of a doting mother—had combined to make the customary white woman forbidden in his eyes, even physically repulsive. "To kiss a woman"—white, of course † —"and feel teeth through her thin lips paralizes me for a week," he wrote about this time. Thus, from his role of voluptuary of the primitive and exotic King could swing to that of bitter misogynist. How he mistrusted the young female of his own class, the "prim little Puritan maiden, sharp as a stock-broker, and with an unabridged dictionary of a mind"; while her more phlegmatic sister in the West, the girl he had chatted with on certain piazzas, had wearied his taste with "something of the same flatness and sugary insipidity" that marked the California grape. "Woman is too

---

* In a review of the first edition of *Clarence King* Walter Magnus Teller suggested the term *melanophilia* for the compulsive love of dark skin color such as King's and, it might be added, that described by Tennyson in *Locksley Hall*.

† That King's aversion was directed specifically to white women is conclusive in its context. "This snarl," he continued,

is because I am just in from passing Sunday at Tuxedo, and my grievance is that I didn't want to kiss the beings there. Their little minds squirm and contract under the [stimulus] of light conversation, as a dead frog curls up his wiry toes at the galvanic touch, but I am not deceived by their involuntary simulation of life: I know they are dead.

one-sided," he remarked to Bronson one day; "too one-sided—like a tossed-up penny—and I want both sides or none." King had spoken in jest, to explain why he had never married, and yet how truly the quip betrayed his opinion of modern woman. Portraits of the type which bored and repelled him could be found everywhere in the realistic fiction of the period; and all the fictional characters, he assumed in disgust, were "more or less true to the human model."

"Think," he wrote in 1888,

of the stunted and petty women and their incredible meanness, of the primeval monkey-scale of their average intelligence; remember how few wholesome, sweet, strong women are found in that army of distorted, diseased creatures who march between the covers of English fiction, laden down as they go with all the tragi-comic foibles flesh is heir to, and all the conceivable deviations from noble and normal womanhood, and then reflect how French realism has flung woman naked in the ditch and left her there scorned of men, and grinning in cynical and shameless levity over her own dishonor. Or, to come nearer to home, recall the pretty, brightish, smug little people who are made with inimitable skill to illustrate the sawdust stuffing of their middle-class democratic society.

Out of it all, is there one figure for weary eyes to linger upon: one type of large and satisfying womanhood, natural in the rare and ravishing charm of a perfect body; sweet with the endowment of a warm, quick, sympathetic temperament; sound and bright in intellect; pure and spiritual, with a soul [unshaken by] the jar of modern conflict? Is there any more womanhood in them all, English, French, and American put together and fused into one, than can be learned in a single hour before that Greek Venus in the Louvre, who is only perfect goddess because she is perfect woman?

The plain fact was that King had found his ideal—as Henry Adams would note again—in "types more robust" than the modern white woman, types that were best equated with the primitive force of the Magna Dea. "It was not the modern woman that interested him; it was the archaic female, with instincts and without intellect . . . rich in the inheritance of every animated energy back to the polyps and the crystals." King was frank about the matter with his closest friends. "Woman," he had confessed to Hay in 1887, "I like best in the primitive state. Paradise, for me, is still a garden with a primeval woman." Adams was sure that King, moreover, instinctively "regarded the male as a sort of defense thrown off by the female, much like the shell of a crab, endowed with no original energy of his own." Man without woman was only a crumbling husk, and to her he must always return for the energizing contact that stayed his threatening disintegration. Concerning the biological superiority of women King quipped: "We press the button, and they do the rest."

It was unabashed paganism, this sophisticated primitivism of King and Adams, this passion for the archaic female. Adams would soon sublimate it in veneration for the Virgin of Chartres, for him the unifying symbol of the thirteenth century, a medieval transformation of the Magna Dea, the chaste and chastened Venus of the Church. But King had turned to a more immediate type, like the sculptor Story, who had bodied forth his ideal of womanhood in the Lybian Sibyl, large-bosomed, luxuriant, frankly African. No doubt King had seen the statue in the home of Henry Cabot Lodge before it went to the National Museum; and it was not wholly coincidental that he had found his favorite modern sculpture in its Sphinx-like face, with its low brow, its long eyes, its full lips, poised above broad shoulders, full breasts, and legs that Story himself had called "the largely developed limbs of . . . the real African type."

King, indeed, had been fond of Negroes from childhood days when he had basked in the solicitude of his dark-skinned nurse.* It was his custom to defend the black race, which he considered better at heart than the white; in his opinion Negroes seemed more wise about human relationships. He kept a Negro valet—Alexander Lancaster—who spoke like a cultured Englishman; he praised the stories of George Washington Cable about the people of color in New Orleans, thought them finer than Bret Harte's work, and more likely to endure. It amused him, further, to startle friends like Robert Underwood Johnson, the

---

*James D. Hague has left an anecdote—no doubt one of King's originals—that illustrates King's regard for the colored race. "He had many friends among the negro people," Hague began, "and often sought their companionship when opportunity offered." Once on a visit to a Georgia gold mine he attended a Negro church in bitterly cold weather. The barnlike meeting-house had no means of heat except for the hot stones many old women had brought "rolled up in flannel petticoats or other comforting wrappers." Touched by their fervent spirit, King told the shivering congregation that he would buy them the largest stove in Dahlonega, a promise he promptly kept. Two or three years later, on a second visit to the mine, King chatted with the white driver whose buggy carried him from the railroad station, and during the conversation he inquired about the colored church and whether the stove he had sent was doing well. "Doing well!" the driver exclaimed reproachfully. "I should say so! There ain't a fence-rail left in this neighborhood within two mile of that meetin-house" (*Clarence King Memoirs*, pp. 406–9).

conservationist and champion of Yosemite National Park, with "a bit of bravado (no doubt) that miscegenation was the hope of the white race."

No wonder, then, that King had responded so deeply on meeting Ada Todd. She was probably no better educated than a primitive Greek Venus; indeed she seems to have been next to illiterate (when years afterwards, she was asked in a court of law to spell the last name of John Hay, which she pronounced "Hayes," her reply would be: "Y-A-S"). But King felt in her all the energy that signified for him the essential woman, and her "chocolate hue" aroused the compulsions of his color fetishism. She fascinated him. "There are certain women . . . ," he had written years before, "who place men under their spell without leaving them the melancholy satisfaction of understanding how the thing was done. They may have absolutely repulsive features, and pretty permanent absence of mind; without that charm of cheerful grace before which we are said to succumb. But they manage to assume command."

Ada seems to have done exactly that. King found her irresistible and besieged her with ardent, although furtive, courtship. They soon became intimate, and details of "comparative gynecology" slipped into his letters to the closest of his friends.

And, "Ah, my dearest," he would later write to her, "I have lain in my bed and thought of you and felt my whole heart full of love for you. It seems to me often that no one ever loved a woman as I do you. In my heart there is no place for any other woman and never will be. My whole heart is yours forever."

They must have talked of marriage, legally possible at that time for a white and black in New York, although not in certain other states. But King discovered compelling reasons why a wedding between himself and Ada could not be made of record. It would create inevitable scandal, in view of his public character. "I wish it could be intimated in my life and engraved on my tombstone," he had once told J. D. Hague, "that I am to the last fibre aristocratic in belief." There was no escaping the fact of such a public image: aristocrat and "blue blood," of a fine old Newport family. No matter how adroitly he had justified the liaison to himself, he knew that others without his tolerant views on race would hardly understand. The scandal would be a grievous embarrassment to his friends and family, for the society in which they moved feared scandal worse than it feared disease. And should his mother learn of it, he knew that, in her precarious state of health, the knowledge would only kill her.

Therefore he took elaborate pains to guard the secret. He revealed neither his true name nor his occupation to Ada, but borrowed the given name of his father and called himself James Todd in her presence, and she would not learn for many years that his rightful name was Clarence King.

Yet King respected the value she placed on a wedding ceremony, and he consented to the ritual, as long as no marriage certificate was involved. The ceremony occurred in September 1888—or so Ada would later claim. The place was 149 West Twenty-Fourth Street, the tenement flat of her aunt Mrs. Annie Purnell, on the edge of the Tenderloin district, haven of pickpockets, swindlers, and armed thugs. "An organ, a Bible, and other religious trappings" had been installed in the house; and clad in a full dress suit, King had slipped a gold ring on Ada's finger, and they were named husband and wife by a Reverend Mr. Cook, the colored minister of a Methodist church on 85th Street.* "It was the first wedding I ever saw," a small girl, then six years old, would later claim, "and I guess I remember it. They had a cake with white icing and candles—chocolate and all kinds." And later King himself would write to Ada: "Ever since I put that ring on your finger I have worked and prayed for you and will do so till God parts us by death. . . . God bless you, my own, my only one."

After the ceremony he took her in secret on some of his trips—to Washington, Newport, and Boston. But the risk was too great, he feared, in their moving about together in places where he was known. He found it much easier to arrange a double life in New York City where, as in London, one could drop from sight, it seemed, by simply crossing the street. For a time, while he kept his rooms at the Brunswick, across from Delmonico's at Fifth Avenue and 26th Street, he settled Ada across the bridge in Brooklyn. He rented a comfortable house for her on Skillman Street, where he could go to her at night when he was in the city; and he let it be known to curious neighbors that James Todd was a porter by occupation. And there in Brooklyn Ada gave birth to the first of their five children—a son whom King would call Leroy.

What had become of "simple, natural marriage?" he had once asked Howells. Where was "the chastely amorous old institution of wedlock in which two decent people took refuge to escape from the hard egoism

*N.B. the statement of Lawrence Clark Powell: "As lover, husband, and father [King's] story can never be fully known, for his white kinfolk are said to have destroyed the evidence that was in their hands" (*California Classics*, p. 137).

of their own individual lives?" King dared hope that he had rediscovered it in a union which had, before the law, no status beyond that of libertine and kept mistress.

"And meanwhile," Adams wrote, perhaps in double entendre, "he was passing the best years of his life underground. For companionship he was mostly lost."

19

Panic

The relief from tension which King had found in his marriage was lost in the complications which followed. The step had brought him into conflict with a dominant trend of the day—the concern of his set for social correctness. He found it a formidable challenge, and the strains of a double life grew difficult to bear. There could be no relaxation in his vigilance to keep his dual roles completely separated.

The mounting stress did nothing to sweeten his opinion of the society from which the secret must be guarded, and his conviction grew that the social fabric of America was falling into tatters. King's impulses, nevertheless, remained gregarious. He was still preeminently a social being; and the more he concealed one part of his life from his social peers, the more he looked to moor the other part in their company, or the more he looked for their approval of his public character. After his marriage he became more than ever a clubman, and his haunts included some of the most exclusive clubs in New York City.

He had retained his membership in the Century Association, where he basked in his vogue for wit and charm, and Stedman still considered him "Stevenson's Prince-with-the-tarts" incarnate. He made a habit, too, of the high yellow dining room of the Union League Club, and he joined still other organizations: the Players of Edwin Booth, in 1888, a group dedicated to brotherhood between theatrical men and leaders in the kindred fields of art, letters, and music; the Tuxedo Club, at Pierre Lorillard's Tuxedo Park, a piscatory Four Hundred bound together in the interests of exclusive fraternity and gamey fish; and the Boone and Crocket Club of Theodore Roosevelt, a hundred eminent big-game hunters who pledged themselves to foster "manly sport" with the rifle, outings in the wilds, and the conservation of big game. In the interchanges between these hunters, King may have told of his buffalo hunt in 1863 (for did not Roosevelt know all about it?), or of his bear hunt in 1871, or perhaps even of his escape from a charging elk which had, at the critical moment, impressed him "like a first-class hat-rack on a mule."

He joined the Downtown Club, the dignified Knickerbocker Club, even the Metropolitan, or (as someone dubbed it) "the millionaires' stable." This had just been organized by Pierpont Morgan, who housed it in a gleaming Italian palace on Fifth Avenue, a creation of King's hearty clubmate Stanford White, whose next designs were of a new clubhouse for the Century. This, too, became a mansion in the Renaissance style, and both were resorts of King when he was in Manhattan. Each issue of the Social Register during the *fin de siècle* named either the Century or the Metropolitan or the Union League Club as his address. He found them expedient places to hang his public hat. While lodging at a club, he could come or go at the call of his profession or the tug of his secret life without provoking difficult questions. Moreover, such a living arrangement made it easier to cultivate the protective myth of confirmed bachelorhood by dropping seemingly casual remarks like "It always takes years for me to realize that I have not got to marry a woman."

And yet whatever the satisfaction that King discovered in his clubs, it failed to ease his qualms over the deterioration of his intellectual life. He had deplored his "silence and general nonproductiveness" before his marriage. In compensation he engaged in bouts of hard, intensive reading and claimed to be "refreshed by the intellectual climate." Even those historical interests whetted by his work on the tenth census had stirred in him again, and John Hay could assure mutual friends that he was planning "vast historical works."

But always at his back pressed the weight of business involvements, aggravating his inner stresses, which drained away his energies and dulled his zest. "Now in middle age," as he posed his quandary to Henry Adams in 1889, "I am poor, and what is worse, so absorbed in the hand to mouth struggle for income that I see the effective literary and scientific years drifting by empty and blank, when I am painfully conscious of the power to do something had I the chance." On approaching fifty, King provided the melancholy spectacle of genius running to waste.

The sight of his sterile exertions troubled friends like Hay and Adams, who offered more than once to play the patron for the books they yearned for him to write—things they had heard him talk away before some friendly hearth till the night and all their eyelids grew weary together. King might borrow from friends on a business basis, but he was not prepared for outright patronage; and as he struggled on, there were only brief, occasional breaks in his literary silence, a bit now and then like "Artium Magister" in the *North American Review.*

This was his castigation of the dead-alive methods used in American schools and colleges to teach the classics—"the pestilent . . . system which neglects art and exalts grammar"—the system which had surfeited King at school in Hartford. He disparaged neither the classical spirit nor classical forms; he asserted his own love of classical art and letters. "Greek poetry and art," he suggested, "were, and are, and always will be as fresh as flowers gathered at dawn with the night-damp still upon their petals." And he saw in classical literature, next to an exalted religion, the most humane leaven available for the vulgarity of American life. It was his conviction that with proper teaching "the splendid ideality of antique thought and feeling [could] become a part of a young nation, [and] the lofty classics of the Greeks and Romans [could] be made of inestimable value in the creation of American character." But he could not find one good word to say for the current American methods of teaching. Pendantry and grammatical torture stifled the very faculties they were supposed to train, and left the pupils "systematically worried and finally ruined for polite letters or high art."

There were demurs to King's opinion. One arrived from President Gilman at Baltimore, and King admitted that the Johns Hopkins staff "must certainly do better classical work than the old treadmillers." Another came from Rossiter Raymond, whose manner with a pen reminded King of a mule he had once met on a Rocky Mountain trail. On noting the look in the animal's eyes he had asked the attending packer, "Is that mule vicious?" "No," the packer answered. "But he's kinda versatile with his hind hoofs." Raymond, who was "versatile" with his pen, tartly declared that he was not sure what King did actually propose. What did he offer in place of the system he had condemned? King answered the question, somewhat parenthetically, in a later essay called "The Education of the Future."

He found it easy enough to suggest avenues that education was to take; avenues it would open by further application of the prime discovery of the age—the conservation of energy; a line of thought that Henry Adams was to push to startling lengths in *A Letter to American Teachers of History.* It was impossible to ignore the question of energy, whether in education or in other spheres; it was so clearly the chief preoccupation of American science, one might even say of American civilization. "No sooner," King reflected, "is a phase of energy or of the great law of its universal conservation marked out in the laboratory of the physicist than the genius of some mechanic turns it to practical account." There was no end to the process that King could foresee; the march had just begun, the most stupendous movement in history, and it would proceed, he suspected, until the human race had hitched its wagon, if not to the metaphorical star, then "to the great universal power that moves the stars."

But of the other great discovery of the age—biological evolution—the world had made but meager use; that is, as compared with its vast potentialities for the moral and physical improvement of the race. Spacious advance into that province lay in the future, but it was there, King mused, that man would find the wisdom to conquer half the ills that flesh was heir to. "This is the age of energy," he wrote; "the next will be the age of biology."

Certainly biology—which meant heredity, and which implied psychology—would frame the pedagogical techniques of the future; and one example would be the procedures of language instruction. King did not hesitate to prophesy in favor of the ear method, the first in order of origin; the method which, as his own experiments with French and Spanish had convinced him, was far more profitable than the eye method, the system of grammatical analysis pursued in the schools. "The grammar of a language"—even the grammar of Greek and Latin, he insisted—"is a rather interesting thing to read over when you already know the language."

King ventured even further with the aural system he would substitute for the methods of the schools. "The people to teach languages," he declared,

are not university faculties, but home instructors, who, if they are required, would make children talk in Greek and Latin . . . fluently at the age of ten. . . . If the reader will chat in either of these tongues with a child so taught, and then attempt to hold similar discourse with a recent university graduate who attacked his foreign language as "optionals" at the age of twenty by the eye, he will promptly see that out of the mouths of babes and sucklings will come something facile, idiomatic, and free, while the collegian falters and wounds the patient atmosphere with the melancholy wreckage of his parts of speech.

Grounded as King suggested, a student of letters might arrive at his college prepared to follow programs of study that no longer lagged in vitality behind the technical curricula.

King's interest in education had long drawn him toward the academic life. The trustees of Columbia College were now transforming their school into a university, and there were plans to create, among other additions, chairs of geology and physical geography. Both Hewitt and Hamilton Fish endorsed King for appointment, at various times, and this appealed to him as a means to end the nomadism of his life as field geologist or mining engineer. But Seth Low, the president, may have been less impressed with King or with his conversational ease than Fish or Hewitt; or perhaps, as Fish suggested, the trustees may have been under some delusion about their financial policy. At any rate, King found the salary inadequate to maintain his two households. "I might have taken a college position," he later wrote, "and abandoned the family to sink. But whenever the moment came, I could not do it and struggled on my wavering way."

Many friends began to think that his "wavering way" had completely divorced King from pure science. But he had never really forsaken his plans to work out answers to some of the more profound dynamic problems of geology.

On returning from Europe he had written, "I came back with a keen appetite for geology and the intention of striking some smashing blow." But his business involvements had forced him to delay giving the absorbed attention necessary to frame satisfactory answers in his chosen field of research, and he "was peculiarly reluctant," as Emmons later remarked, "to publish any of his theories without verification." In a moment of levity he had offered to join Hay and Adams in publishing their "joint works under the title of 'The Impasse Series,' because they all ask questions that have no answers." Certainly, *Systematic Geology* had raised a most difficult poser, the question of subterranean fusion and the nature of the dynamics which had built the mountains and the continents.

King had first stated the problem in his address at Yale in 1877, when he had described geology as something more than "a science of ancient configuration. It is also," he had said, "a history of the varying rates and modes of action of terrestrial energy." A day would come, he held, when geologists would "translate the strata into a precise language of energy and time"; but not before the principles of geodynamics were thoroughly comprehended and explained. Geology had to be firmly grounded in physics.

He had offered his own hypothesis gingerly enough—a theory resting on Lord Kelvin's postulate of "secular refrigeration." Kelvin had assumed in an early publication that the temperature gradient of the earth, from surface to core, was the result of simple cooling from molten beginnings through geological time; that furthermore the earth, though solid, was still a very hot body in a comparatively early stage of refrigeration. Starting with these assumptions, King had reasoned that a critical shell—or *couche,* as he termed it—must exist at about forty or fifty miles below the surface of the globe. Below this point the temperature of fusion would exist, although the downward pressure from overlying materials would, in general, restrain the condition from developing beyond the latent state. In other words, compression kept the earth solid below the *couche*; the process of cooling had solidified it in the space above. The general configuration of this shell corresponded to the surface topography of the earth; it extended upward under the continents, and downward under the ocean basins.

"According to that view," as King had written in *Systematic Geology,*

under each continent, and especially under each lofty mountain region, this shell of the temperature of fusion must rise to its maximum radial distance from the centre of the earth. This thermal topography will, therefore, have its peaks under the centre of high mountain systems. As is obvious from all geological study, high mountain ranges are the centres of the most active and intense erosion. Maximum removal will, therefore, actually take place over the immediate top of the peaks of the thermal topography, and there the column of superincumbent matter, or as otherwise expressible, the actual superincumbent pressure, will be most suddenly and most remarkably varied during the history of erosion.

The effect of such reduction of pressure on matter along the temperature *couche* would depend, of course, on the rate of erosion. If, in some high mountain region, erosion took place faster than the underlying *couche* could recede through normal cooling, the result would be localized fusion, the creation of a molten lake of magma. So rapid a rate of denudation was inconceivable to the Uniformitarian. But King, the apostle of "modified Catastrophism," believed that his field work in the West had demonstrated the probability of such phenomena; at least he had found that a time of prodigious erosion had preceded each volcanic series during the Tertiary. The crux of his hypothesis lay in his speculation that the lakes of fused matter producing the Tertiary eruptions must have been a direct result of preceding erosion.

That would explain why continents reduced by erosion could, nevertheless, continue to rise; the expansion of magma melting along the *couche* would tend to elevate the surface level, sometimes even faster than the rate of denudation. It would also explain why ocean beds could keep on sinking in spite of collecting sediments; the pressure of accumulating detritus washed down from adjacent continents would cause magma, in a molten state below, to solidify with a considerable loss of volume.

King believed, however, that this process must reverse itself in time. When the beds of magma growing underneath the continents approached too near the surface, thermal induction gradually chilled them into solidity, and a course of slow subsidence would be set in motion—a sinking matched by a rising of the sea floors as a result of heat conducted from the interior of the earth. This process might go on until the continents and the oceans changed positions; or indeed until they began the cycle again, another link in a long procession, fusion alternating with solidification, upheaval with subsidence. King suspected that much of the continent building observed in the geological record could be thus explained.

He did not insist that his theory *was* the explanation. As Emmons later remarked,

A broad toleration of other ideas besides those in which he was immediately interested was one of King's marked characteristics. He himself entertained a number of views relating to upheaval and subsidence, each of which he hoped to put to the test in its turn. Among these, however, his earliest hypothesis seems to have retained preference. Though he was fully aware of the difficulties which it encountered, he insisted on having it either proved or disproved before [asserting or] abandoning it.

That could hardly be done until a great deal of empirical data had been determined and systematized. The latent heats of fusion for volcanic rocks would have to be established, as well as the difference in specific gravity between the liquid and the solid states of igneous materials. King had made these and other desired facts the object of research in the geophysical laboratory which he had established before resigning as director of the Geological Survey. Carl Barus had begun the investigations at rooms in the American Museum of Natural History, using the instruments which King had ordered at his own expense from Europe. King had retained general supervision of the work on leaving his post as director of the survey, and reserved the privilege of making a theoretical application of results in his projected treatise on upheaval and subsidence.

The laboratory was soon removed to a house in New Haven, and Barus settled down, with the help of William Hallock, on a program of high temperature research, pioneer work in the field of pyrometrics. He had made a good beginning by the date of King's return from Europe. But, pressed by politicians, Major Powell was soon obliged to order the laboratory dismantled, and the equipment brought to Washington. Barus and Hallock established themselves in rooms at the National Museum, and for the next eight years they conducted an imposing series of experiments. King kept in touch with them, and followed their investigations on the viscosity of solids, the measurement of high temperatures and high pressures, the thermodynamics of liquids, and the thermal conductivity of rocks. And he arranged with the Standard Oil Company for Hallock to make a series of temperature observations in a dry well at Wheeling, West Virginia—a shaft 4,500 feet deep, offering an extraordinary chance to sound the topic of isogeotherms.

The relevance of Barus and Hallock's data to the problems of dynamic geology was now becoming self-evident, and King hoped to write out a brief caveat on his chosen subject, staking out the ground he planned to cover. He went to Washington in December 1891, intending to give ten days to the task, while staying at Adams's lonely house. *
But on striking a snag in the final experiments, he began to wonder about the validity of his own hypothesis. "He has torn to pieces every known theory of upheaval, his own included," Hay reported to Adams,

and is now squirming under the ruins of the temple he has demolished. He has got to go to work all over at the volumetric structure of the molecule considered specifically, and its behavior under physico-chemical stresses. This will require a trifle of two or three years before he can see any result.

Unfortunately, a political hurricane was to rock the Geological Survey before Barus and Hallock could complete the work on which King was basing his own computations.

*On another such trip, earlier in the year, King had gone with Clara Hay to Rock Creek Cemetery to see the bronze statue by Augustus Saint-Gaudens that marked the grave of Clover Adams. To the serene though not quite human figure suggested by the Oriental goddess Kwannon the sculptor had sought to impart "a strong impression of mystery" and had succeeded in his aim. As King gazed at the cowl-shaded face, he was moved to exclaim: "It is the most important work yet done on our side,—the best of St. Gaudens or anybody else" (Hay, *Letters of John Hay,* II, p. 222).

A prior storm had struck as early as December 1884, when Congress had launched a probe of the several scientific bureaus of the government. Disaffection on Capitol Hill over Powell's growing emphasis on general geology at the expense of more practical work in economic geology had brought him under fire, and as the hearings of the Allison Commission progressed, they had concentrated more and more on the affairs of the Geological Survey. Powell was called to testify before the commission on sixteen different occasions, and he endured heavy pressures for nearly two years. But in time he reconsidered his tentative decision to resign, and in consequence of the eminent good sense of his testimony the Geological Survey emerged from the Allison Commission hearings stronger than before. The Coast and Geodetic Survey, on the other hand, did not fare so well. The drubbing it took culminated in the dismissal of Superintendent Hilgard and the resignation of other key personnel, and their going left a serious breach in the bulwarks of official science. Alexander Agassiz declined appointment as superintendent on the grounds of precarious health and lack of expertise in geodesy, and the head of the Treasury investigating team that had uncovered "irregularities" in the conduct of the Coast Survey was placed in temporary charge. It was crucial, in King's analysis of the situation in December 1886, that the right man should lead the bureau at this critical time, and the man he considered right was not the choice of Agassiz.

No one in or out of office had questioned the propriety of the government's involvement with scientific work more sharply than Agassiz, motivated as he was by his dream of making the Museum of Comparative Zoology at Harvard a preeminent center of scientific research, while at the same time fearing that the growth of government science might undercut that dream. At strategic moments he had raised his voice with telling effect against the government sponsorship of science. "It has killed all individuality in geology," he complained, "the Professors of Geology in the United States being, with few exceptions, the satellites of the Director of the Geological Survey." His censure was only slightly qualified by his close association with the Coast and Geodetic Survey and the fact that he had sailed on its schooners in pursuit of his personal researches in marine biology. His attitude would be characterized by a present-day historian as "the quintessence of laissez faire—the Government should in no way do any scientific work that could be done by [private] individuals except when it provides aid to my work."

King's strained relations with Agassiz over mining matters were not the reason for his taking a different stand in the contest over who should lead the Coast Survey in 1887. King threw his influence behind the candidacy of a friend named James P. Kimball, who had served as superintendent of the mint. Kimball's scientific training was excellent; he was a Ph.D. from the University of Göttingen, with post-doctoral studies at Freiberg; but better still, in King's opinion, he would listen to Marsh and himself "more than to Agassiz and the pure and abstract mathematicians." King had come to favor a highly integrated scientific program for the government, with the several scientific bureaus brought together in one executive department—perhaps the Department of Science advocated by the National Academy—and in connection with that idea he suggested to Marsh that, "with Kimball and Powell in, you and I could be the power behind the throne." He conferred on Kimball's behalf with the secretary of the treasury, Daniel Manning, and Manning arranged an interview for him at the White House. King may have known Grover Cleveland from banquets of the Round Table Club, but his influence with the president did not match his favor in Blaine's eyes, and Kimball failed to receive the appointment.

By 1890 a new crisis had assailed the Geological Survey, portended by a savage flare-up of the Battle of the Bones which had exercized Cope and Marsh for twenty years. Cope had never forgiven Marsh his victory in 1879 or Powell's naming him later as the principal pale-ontologist of the Geological Survey. But Cope's fury had burst all bounds at an order from the secretary of the interior, on prompting from Powell, that Cope's vast collection of fossil bones be sent to the National Museum according to law, without a just distinction drawn between the specimens Cope assembled through his own means and those gathered by Hayden at government expense. In such develop-ments Cope could see the sinister hand of Marsh at work, but Powell and the survey were also targets of his hatred.

In its exploitation of this feud the *New York Herald* observed on January 12, 1890, that

for some time past a volcano has been slumbering under the Geological Survey, and of late there has been indications that the time for an eruption was not far distant. Now it has arrived and the long pent-up forces have gained their freedom with a rush and a roar which, if it does not indeed carry the present management of the survey to official destruction, will certainly disturb the entire scientific world of America and bring in its train a series of charges and countercharges, recriminations and reproaches which will ring from one end of the land to the other.

In a paranoid prosecution of the feud Cope had insinuated King's name into the virulent paper sent to the *Herald*, "using it in such a way," claimed Arnold Hague, "as to imply that King agreed with the other side." In King's absence Hague consulted with Charles Nordhoff, editor of the *Herald* and a mutual friend, and prevailed on him to strike King's name from the offending copy—a matter for congratulations, since in its sensational treatment of the embroglio, the *Herald* handled the principals—Cope and Marsh and Powell—as if they were the likes of Sullivan and Kilrain.

The fracus turned a spotlight on congressional dissatisfaction over the survey's failure to produce immediate practical results. Especially bitter was the Western bloc's resentment over the slow progress of the Irrigation Survey, now nearly two years old, provoking vast anger by its suspension of settlement in the lands classified as "irrigable." The Cope-Marsh battle still raged when Powell was called to Capitol Hill to answer an array of questions about irrigation, the beginning of a series of appearances before the committees on irrigation of both chambers. The trouble grew formidable when the House Appropriations Committee scheduled hearings in June, followed by still more before the Senate Appropriations Committee in July. The unpent forces noted by the *Herald* had been marshaled by such implacable enemies as Hilary Herbert in the House and "Big Bill" Stewart in the Senate, and they were ready with searching questions. These the major parried adroitly, and in the end the hearings led to a startling mixture of results. Congress voted a bumper appropriation for the Geological Survey proper, but counterbalanced it by the nearly total elimination of funds for the Irrigation Survey. As that was a cherished program of Powell's, the implementation of his long-matured solution to a central problem of the West, its virtual destruction proved a devastating blow. In the words of Wallace Stegner, it "was the major defeat of [Powell's] life and the beginning of the end of his public career."

Two years later deep slashes in his budget forced him to drop sixteen members from his staff, cut the salaries of those who remained and make drastic retrenchments in general geology, paleontology, chemistry, and physics. It was clearer than ever that at the heart of the drive in Congress to curtail the survey's work in pure science and restore economic geology as its paramount mission was the aim to force Powell's resignation. Charles D. Walcott, the major's durable chief assistant, wrote of "a powerful party in both the House and . . . the Senate who appear to be determined that there shall be a change in the Directorship." He added that "the western mining men who are fighting Powell have confidence in King." Indeed, they had sounded King out as to his availability for reappointment as director, and as Powell had confessed his willingness to drop the reins in order to concentrate on anthropology, King's reply had been yes, provided the matter could be arranged without particular ado. Walcott felt sure that Powell would choose King as his successor. At the same time he thought it "a curious state of affairs that the Senators who are attacking the Major desire that King shall be appointed in his place, and that King should be in accord with them and also with the Major." But in the course of events Powell decided not to resign at this particular time. Instead, he took an extended leave of absence and Walcott assumed interim charge of the survey.

Meanwhile the men whom budget cuts had obliged Powell to drop included Barus and Hallock. The physical laboratory was closed, and its equipment was classified as "old junk." Fortunately much of it belonged to King, and he allowed Barus to take it with him when he moved to the Weather Bureau, where he served as physicist and occupied a laboratory lent by Alexander Graham Bell.

Under these circumstances, King could not be sure when the rest of the data for his treatise on upheaval would be ready. He decided, however, to release an introductory paper in which he sought to carry Lord Kelvin's calculations on the age of the earth to "a new precision." Kelvin's estimate had allowed the globe from 20 million to 400 million years as a solidified body suitable to sustain life. He had hesitated to settle on a more exact figure until more was known about the specific heats and conductivities of the rocks which composed the interior of the planet.

The findings of Barus, in King's opinion, now filled that gap. King accepted diabase as an average rock inside the earth, and took as a basis for his calculations the data Barus had ascertained for it—its latent heats of fusion, its specific heats, its volume expansion between liquid and solid states, under various pressures up to two thousand atmospheres. Assuming that the earth's crust had never floated on a molten layer of inferior density, he concluded: "We have no warrant for extending the earth's age beyond 24,000,000 years." Dana published the paper under the title "The Age of the Earth" in the *American Journal of*

Science for January 1893, and the Smithsonian Institution reprinted it later in the year. King continued at intervals to review the problem in the light of further considerations, and three years later he prepared another paper ("an appalling bit of physics," Hay remarked) which aimed to reach an even more precise conclusion. On this occasion, he computed that 20 million years had passed since the earth had assumed solid form, but he decided against printing another fragmentary piece of work. He still believed, nevertheless—or so he assured Hay—that he would "write the *Magnum Opus*" as soon as he could make sufficient money to devote three years to intensive research.

That day was never to come, and King could only face the problem with the stoicism he had suggested in another connection. "The human organism," he had declared in the *Forum*,

has rarely been subjected to a severer test than the study of scientific problems, nor is there a truer hero than an investigator who never loses heart in a life-long grapple with the powers of the universe. It requires courage of the highest order to stand for years face to face with one of the enigmas of nature; to interrogate patiently, and hear no answers, to try all known methods and weapons of attack, and yet see the lips of the sphinx compressed in stony immobility; to invoke the uttermost powers of imagination; to fuse the very soul in the fire of effort, and still press the listening ear against the wall of silence. It is easier to die in the breach.

It pleased King that Lord Kelvin accepted his estimate of the earth's age as one of the most authoritative statements that had yet been made on the subject, and twice commended it in public.* In Germany Helmholtz was also impressed. But King was spared the disillusionment that his hypothesis could never have led him to a more accurate conclusion about the planet's age. He did not realize, any more than Kelvin did at the time, that their approach had left out of consideration a fundamental fact of nature and that their basic assumptions would fail the test of new discovery.

*The first accolade occurred in a letter of 1895 to *Nature*, in which Lord Kelvin claimed that he was "not led to differ much from [Clarence King's] estimate of 24 million years." Then on June 2, 1897, Kelvin addressed the Victoria Institute on "The Age of the Earth as an Abode Fitted for Life." On this occasion his respectful acknowledgment of King's conclusion preceded a formulation that narrowed Kelvin's own estimate to something between 20 and 40 million years. Like King, he had based his new calculations in large measure on the findings of Carl Barus and William Hallock. See Sylvanus Thompson, *The Life of William Thomson, Baron Kelvin of Largs*, II, 943, 997.

Madame Curie would announce her physical bombshell in 1898, but even then King would still be unaware of the vast sources of thermal energy which his calculations had failed to take into account—sources that further work in atomic physics was to unveil in such an embarrassing plethora that most of the geophysics based on Kelvin's postulate of "secular refrigeration" must be relegated to the ashheap. Awareness of radioactive sources would, in time, undermine all solid foundation for computing the age of the earth from its temperature gradient. Indeed, measurements based on the rate of decay in radioactive matter were to roll back the birth of the globe two hundredfold beyond the span of King's estimate. Geophysicists ninety years later would commonly cite the age of the planet as about 4.5 billion years.

And yet not all of King's speculation was faulted ingenuity foundering on an insufficient base. Much of it was sound, conforming generally with the equilibrium theory formulated by the geodeticists G. B. Airy and J. H. Pratt and named "isostacy" by King's colleague C. E. Dutton—a principle that would be rigorously and extensively tested by the Coast and Geodetic Survey. King was able to bring his work on upheaval and subsidence to "an advanced stage of completion," according to Emmons, and geology would suffer some loss when he failed to publish it, even along the lines he had conceived as Kelvin's disciple. No manuscript would survive King, and any influence stemming from his geophysical thought would exert itself only in devious ways. *

---

* Any attempt to weigh the effects produced by this abortive phase of King's work leads to intangibles hard to assess. King's influence can be recognized, but it was the influence of a personality who impressed thought upon colleagues by word of mouth more than by the printed page. To this peculiarity several people have testified, including the third director of the U.S. Geological Survey. In his Annual Report for 1902 Charles D. Walcott wrote that "none could talk with [King] on any geological or general topic without receiving valuable suggestions"; the effects of which convinced Walcott that King would "continue indefinitely to exert a profound and beneficial influence." A similar opinion came to me from Charles H. Behre, Jr., Professor of Geology at Columbia University, in a letter of March 31, 1957:

King himself had many ideas about earth history and cosmogony with which relatively few people are familiar, largely, I believe, because he put little of this aspect of his thinking down on paper. . . . [As to his] cosmogonic theories, [his] ideas of earth heat, and the fundamental factors in megatectonics, I believe that King contributed mostly through his discussions with his contemporaries, such as S. F. Emmons, Barus, and others. He was . . . responsible for the establishment of a laboratory in Washington which led to the founding of the present-day very distinguished Geophysical Laboratory of the Carnegie Institution. Thus indirectly he did far more than he accomplished as a scientific writer.

Meanwhile, he dissipated his energies without restraint in the economic maelstrom in which he was entrapped; he rushed here or there, sometimes for thousands of miles, in the interest of one scheme or another, and lost hope with only the greatest reluctance that some of his enterprises would bring him wealth. "King had followed the ambitious course," wrote Adams. "He had played for many millions. He had more than once come close to great success, but the result was still in doubt." Suspense, however, would not continue long; a major disaster had struck in 1889 when the Santa Rosa Mill at Somrerete had failed to meet King's expectations, and he discovered his favorite hope of wealth fading like a dream.

Preliminary tests had proved misleading. King found too late that the average run of ore contained more lead than his new machinery could manage efficiently. The capacity of the rolls proved disappointing; the furnace failed to chloridize properly, and as a consequence the extraction of silver remained too low for a reasonable profit. The mine still held abundant ore, but it was rebellious ore, and the crucial problem remained, as always, how to reduce it cheaply enough to turn a profit. The task grew more perplexing with each new sag in the silver market. Had the former prices prevailed, the Santa Rosa Mill might have proved successful, notwithstanding all its difficulties. But now, unless further changes could increase efficiency, King knew that failure lay around the corner.

Continued experimentation failed to solve the problems, and then lack of capital blocked him further. The fiasco completed the alienation of his backers. The Billings syndicate turned away emphatically, and then both Billings and Astor died. As for the Boston trio, they seemed more hostile than ever, contemptuous of what they called "King's wretched talk of prospects." Quincy Shaw told him flatly "to prove that he had a mine that would run"—at a profit, of course.

King kept the mine in operation as long as possible; until in fact he had no alternative to conceding defeat. He resigned as president in May 1890 in hope that his friends in Boston might relent at a change in management, but they failed to respond. The closing of the mine then brought serious repercussions in Sombrerete, where native blackmailers used the denouncement law to extort large sums. At this vexing point King turned to capitalists in England and was on the point of closing a deal when the patience of his Boston friends gave out completely. They sold the mine abruptly and at a grievous loss to the Mexican Metallurgical Company, controlled by the empire-builder Robert A. Towne. Ultimately the Towne interests would succeed at Sombrerete, shipping the ore to their smelter in San Luis Potosí. They had no place for King, however, and he retired as director in August 1891, while receiving assurances from Henry Adams off in Samoa "that the South Seas can always shelter him though Sombreretes fall."

King now found that troubles did not come singly; shortly thereafter his ties with Prietas would also come to an end. Ore there had so plummeted in grade that the mill could make expenses only by working the accumulated tailings. Then sometime in 1891 a fire destroyed much of the timbering. But with ore so poor, the Trio refused to advance funds for restoration, and thus crippled, the mine was worked only enough to protect its title. Then "on the representation of a rascally mining captain," according to the son of Agassiz, Prietas was sold to the Creston-Colorado Company of Cleveland, whose subsequent management would turn it into what King had futilely dreamed of—"a most successful mine." In 1894 a judicious crosscut would strike a bonanza that King's explorations had missed through either poor luck or faulty judgment—a bonanza that would yield several million dollars worth of gold and silver before the vein played out.

"Every struggle [King] makes in his world of finance," Hay wrote, "gets him deeper in the mire, costs him something of life as well as of money." "If he would stop struggling," Hay added, "he would get on well enough. He owes nobody but those who will never bother him. But he *patauges* [wades about] in the mire as if his life depended on his getting out—and gets deeper in all the time." Hay lectured him like a Dutch uncle. But King felt driven by pressures that only increased with time, and his crony went on: "I am in despair about him. I cannot make him do what he ought, even though I offer to stand the racket." Concern for Ada and her babies had begun, no doubt, to shape King's life in ways that baffled even those who knew him best. In a moment of doubt or foreboding he wrote to her:

"My first duty now in these hard times is to make money enough for your expenses, and on that I use all my strength."

His travels had included several trips to El Paso in connection with his bank there. He had gone, too, to Tennessee and southern Arkansas to investigate holdings of pine forest for Eastern millionaires, and there had been side trips to local hot springs for his rheumatism; then trips to

Colorado, where he had examined a rich coal field and sought, as commission man, to sell it to the Union Pacific.

He had negotiated this affair with Charles Francis Adams, Jr., president of the railroad; he had also formed plans with Adams for building a branch line through northern California. Adams had asked him to explore the possibilities of placing bonds for $15 million in New York City; "and to my surprise," King wrote, "I found I could." He had hoped, once the line could be started, to organize another bank in the upper Sacramento Valley, as an "engine" for operations in real estate. He had found Adams "alive to the chance of making a fortune," but a sudden clash with Henry Villard and the Northern Pacific had caused them to defer the project, and before they could revive it Jay Gould had contrived the overthrow of Adams, and had him ousted as president of the Union Pacific, a revolution that also toppled King's deal in coal—that "provision" (as Hay described it) "for his declining years." But there were other projects; King was fertile with them, and Hay recorded, "He thinks, or says, that things are going his way yet."

There had been trips to examine phosphate lands in Florida, where a new industry was springing up, and then early in 1890 he had gone to Cuba to examine iron and manganese deposits; a trip which allowed him to know the people of Cuba well. Especially at Santiago de Cuba where, as Henry Adams would testify, "the charming little plaza is the evening resort of five hundred exquisite females, lovely as mulatto lilies and graceful as the palm trees whose height—of a hundred feet—they rival."

King had sold a field of coking coal to the owners of a Cuban railroad, and he now prepared to deal with them for an iron mine in the Santiago district. And yet no business matter could distract him entirely from his admiration of mulatto lilies; he carried home an enthusiasm which Howells could never forget. The novelist found that "it was measurably to imagine Cuba to hear him tell of his Cuban cousins and acquaintances, who flashed and glistened and darkled in his talk as they must have done in life." Especially the tawny-skinned young women who made cigars by rolling the leaves of tobacco up and down their bare thighs. The delight he took in the dusky women of Cuba was equalled only by his satisfaction at reports that arrived from Adams of old-gold beauty in Samoa. As Hay would advise their mutual crony, King's soul was "filled with measureless content because you have yielded to the charm of the Polynesian girl at last." The salient difference was that the enchantment of Henry Adams would not endure. In fact, he came to regard the Polynesian woman as much a failure as the New York woman, and John La Farge his fellow traveler was inclined to agree. The disclosure, however, did not seem to bother King. "I love primal woman so madly," he confessed to Hay, "that I would have ached with jealousy had they discovered her."

Soon King was off to Idaho with J. D. Hague to examine a silver mine which a Dutch sea captain—Joseph Delamar—had developed near Silver City; a mine which had paid so well in the past two years that the press was calling Delamar the "Monte Cristo of the West." The captain overflowed with energy; his gestures were those of a circus buffoon, but he knew the value of his mine. He wanted $2 million for its control. The bonanza impressed both King and Hague, and they undertook to sell it on commission.

King carried the proposition in his valise when he sailed that June for England, a voyage which caused him to miss the exercise at Brown which honored him with an LL.D. A summons had called him to testify against Sedgwick, his former agent in the Yedras promotion, who was pressing fraudulent claims against the Anglo-Mexican Mining Company. Hay had heralded King's arrival to Henry James, now in his self-styled period of "sawdust and orange peel," his tag for the stage. It turned out that James was now in Bavaria to attend the *Passion Play* at Oberammergau, but in reply to Hay's letter he declared: "I would stay a season in London for [King]—for he would make me feel as if it were *not* the season. And I would stay an autumn—for he would make me feel as [if] it *were* the season." There were other friendships for King to renew in London, but he did not permit socializing there to interfere with business. He lost no time in placing the Delamar matter before a British syndicate, shrewd men in the ways of mines; they were interested, but they dallied.

So King went on to Paris, with Abram Hewitt, and laid the proposition before a group of French financiers. They were interested too, but they also dallied, and time slipped by in a tour of museums and galleries, through which King guided Hewitt's son Edward. "Then," as Edward later recalled, "he went with me to Berlin, where he introduced me to some of the notables [including Baron von Richthofen, in the throes still of writing his five-volume tome on China and his travels there] and [King]," Edward added, "arranged for my matriculation in Berlin University." Hewitt himself had fallen ill, and King now lent his colored valet to help him back to England. Rail officials paid them great respect at the Paris station, placing them in a special carriage, and Alexander was relieved of all concern about the luggage. Somewhere along the way he learned that he had been taken for an Oriental potentate traveling incognito with an elderly British servant.

King followed, only to find the London syndicate still in a dilatory mood. He therefore had time for an outing with the convalescing Hewitt, and to watch the regatta at Maidenhead he hired a skiff at Oxford and rowed his friend down the Thames, the current doing most of the work. Eventually the syndicate agreed to buy the mine for around $1,700,000, but the delays in dealing with King had so exasperated "Monte Cristo" that, before the sale took place, he declined to extend King's option, in effect depriving him of a large commission. The devil of ill luck continued to stalk King, and Hay informed Adams off in the South Seas that five men had died in 1890, each ruining King by his untimely taking off, the last two in their death throes kicking over buckets of milk "which King had been a year in drawing."

Not that these melancholy events were the extent of King's misfortunes. His business reverses coincided with a mournful train of personal and family perplexities, and he was himself in acute torment from a polyp on the spine, arising from an old injury—one incurred perhaps in the buffalo mishap of 1863, or in the later attack by a Colorado mule. "This illness," he had written as early as the end of 1887, ". . . is the most serious of my life"; and when after long suffering an operation became imperative, he submitted in secret, lest it cause his mother distress, ailing as she herself was. Indeed in the grip of progressive paralysis she had come near dying in 1889, and during her long ordeal King had spent weeks within earshot of her sickroom. Her agonized suffering had disturbed him so profoundly that, on one occasion, he actually prayed for her release. It was "one of those family situations which with frightful certainty avalanche themselves down upon me," he explained to Adams—from which, he added, "the grave is my only escape." Eventually the condition of his mother improved. But how determined her possessiveness remained in spite of all infirmity! King feared her heart would break over his sister's marriage to an army officer in 1891, and he gave up much of another winter to be with her and give her consolation in her Newport house.

She worried over so many things, including his half-brother George Howland, a rather unstable young man, whose moods fluctuated from enthusiasm to the depths of depression. When a student of art at Yale, he had left before he had earned a degree; but since he could settle upon no other profession King at last sent him to train in private studios in Paris. Mrs. Howland worried more than ever on hearing, in 1892, that cholera raged in Europe, and nothing could ease her fears till King had cabled George to go to the Scottish highlands, far from the scourge.

But death soon struck at home. It ended a long period of semi-invalidism when it carried off Mrs. Little, King's aged grandmother, the large-hearted philanthropist whom he had dearly loved.* Still another blow had fallen in Brooklyn—hardly the least of those which rained on King in these years of sorrow—the death of his first-born child, Leroy.

King had always valued children; he had been a second father, virtually, to George and Marian; and sons and daughters of his friends regarded him as a kindly uncle. The children of J. D. Hague had reveled in his stories, in the games he played with them, the Indian games which he remembered from the plains, or in the excitement he had shown them; the Wild West Show, for instance, which Buffalo Bill had brought to the "Gardens" of Stanford White, the spectacle which they had watched from seats so close to the arena that a fat chief on a pinto pony had noticed King and, knowing him from earlier days, had pulled the horse up fast, and raised one hand and uttered a single, short, impressive "How!" to the delight of King's young comrades. How it pleased him to watch their happiness!

But he had taken special joy in Ada's brown-skinned babies—she had given him two daughters after Leroy. He had named the first one Grace, in memory of the sister he had lost in childhood, and he called the second Ada. He made plans for their education, including music, and his pockets were never empty of presents when he returned from his journeys. He could never see too much of his colored family. Yet he resisted temptation to go to Skillman Street as often as he wanted, even

* Of Mrs. Little's final days King wrote: "Early in May [1887], despite her ninetieth year, she fled in the gray of the morning from Newport, and went to visit one of her benevolent institutions in Providence, where she is in the habit of enjoying the annual celebration with a pack of Magdalens, who, from her own account, are distinctly the most charming and worthy specimens of their sex. Everybody fell on her neck, and almost everything [else, including] a gallon of boiling coffee, scalding her most dreadfully, burning her arm and side in the most fearful manner. She lay at the point of death for weeks, and was at last taken back to Newport and, by good nursing and good surgery, has made a quasi-recovery" (King to Hay, July 28, 1887, A37865[30](7), Hay Papers [Brown University Library]). The recovery was never complete, and invalidism was Mrs. Little's lot for the last six years of her life.

at night; and as his fortunes crumbled, his anxieties for their future grew.

"Darling," he wrote to Ada, after a trip to Brooklyn on which he thought it wiser not to see her,

. . . I got your love letter. My darling, I know all your feelings. I know just how you love me and how you miss me and how you long for the days and nights to come again when we can lie together and let our love flow out to each other and full hearts have their way. Your letter gave me true joy. I read it over and over and felt like a new man.

The reason I did not come to the house was that I thought there were more boarders and, darling, it will not do to have too many people see me. The most important thing to us of all others is that the property which will one day come to me shall not be torn away from us by some foolish, idle person talking about us and some word getting to my old aunt. For the sake of your darling babies we must keep this secret of our love and our lives from the world.

The need to live half his life in secrecy and the consequent strain did nothing to temper King's bias against the fashionable women of his set. They continued, he wrote "[to] accomplish the paradoxical feat of being simultaneously flat and sharp. I have become a sinless Jack-the-Ripper and go to all the funerals of women I can find. That's how I get even with the sex for the way they place me at dinner." He might jest, but life was grim and grew even grimmer with each new plunge of hope for mending his fortunes.

The latest failure involved the moves King had made to launch "a pearl shell company," a venture that languished when Democratic victory in November, 1892, caused prospective investors to hold back till they could see how tariff reform would affect the pearl industries. The pall of failure was somewhat tempered by the cheerful goodfellowship of Tati Salmon, the four-hundred-pound half-English Polynesian chief whom Henry Adams had met in Tahiti, and into whose sunny company the pearl negotiations had thrown King during Salmon's visit to New York. From the huge Tahitian emanated a soothing influence, "his repose of nerve and low, broad head" suggesting "such absence of competition, such ancestral sleep o'nights, such intellectual animality" that all the others whom King met seemed "like wire-hung jumping jacks, dancing an insane dance." King took the scantest stock in the Summerland of spiritualists, but it ensured an evening free of care to watch Theodore Roosevelt, relaxing from his Civil Service reforms, draw Tati out on ghosts. "Tati came out handsomely," King reported to Adams, "and chased the spirits of his ancestors all over the islands and up cocoanut trees and had them denounced and damned *sicundum artem.*" King added that "Teddy, not to be outdone, brought in a Mobile ghost belonging to his family and made him go through some creditable Hoo-Doo tricks with gore and knives a-plenty." King found the spirits almost as diverting as Tati's reports on Polynesian reactions to Adams and La Farge. But in the end not even the chief's rare equanimity could calm the tension building in King's nerves.

The fact was King had reached a crisis. Conflicting forces pulled him in all directions, and he felt no longer strong enough to bear the stress. It did not help that most of the country seemed to fare no better. The frontier had disappeared, that natural buffer against the emergencies of the nation, and as a young professor from Wisconsin pointed out, the first era of American history was drawing to a close. It seemed more like the end of the world to many in 1893.

Panic had broken loose in the wake of Cleveland's second inauguration, and the following summer wore on—as Brooks Adams, the brother of Henry, would recall—"amidst an excitement verging on revolution." "Men died like flies under the strain," wrote Henry himself, "and Boston grew suddenly old, haggard, and thin." This was the most profound collapse in the history of the country; and utterly helpless, King watched every possibility slip away for salvaging the wreckage of his fortunes. He had not been able to sleep for weeks, except in fitful snatches, and at the panic's height, in a torrid July, his spinal affliction struck again, more acute than ever.

"I cannot understand," he later wrote, "how I ever lived through the merciless agony which crazed and nearly killed me. It seems as if the human organism could not survive such suffering."

His doctor could help him but little, especially after the *coup de grâce* had struck from Texas. King learned that his bank in El Paso had closed its doors, a blow that grew in bitterness when word arrived that dubious practice on the part of Bronson, whom he had installed as president, had precipitated the failure. Bronson and the bank's cashier had diverted money to their own purposes, securing the loans with collateral on which little cash could be raised in the pinch. The comptroller of the currency dispatched an examiner to investigate the troubles, and he assumed charge of the bank until a receiver could be appointed. King requested delays, in the hope that he might raise sufficient funds for the bank to reopen. But where could one find money when hordes of frantic men were crying for capital to save their hides? King failed, the bank tottered into receivership, and Bronson and the cashier were indicted by a Federal grand jury for "willful misapplication of National Bank funds." It would make no difference in King's lot that they were eventually acquitted.

"I have lost everything," King said in despair. In the midst of the ruin his chief concern seemed to be in keeping knowledge of the wreckage from his mother, for she had seen family means swept away four times in the past and was now, King felt, incapable of standing another great shock in life. He himself was thousands of dollars in debt and saw no hope of recovery. The business way of life had ended in disaster for him—a disaster that posed a baffling moral to Henry Adams, who had wondered twenty years before if anyone in their generation was as "likely [as Clarence King] to leave so deep a trail."

Of all their contemporaries, King had seemed the best qualified to succeed in an age of competitive individualism. Actually, John Hay, of their close circle, would ultimately win the greatest measure of public success; but Adams found the contrast between Hay's achievement and King's misfortunes "quite superstitious. . . . King had more *suite*," he believed, "more chances of luck, more foresight, and vastly more initiative and energy." Why, then, had the Bird of Paradise failed? Adams could not account for it, except as a question simply of finances. "The result of twenty years' effort," he concluded, "proved that the theory of scientific education failed where most theory fails—for want of money."

But King's judgment had not been faultless; he had failed to make realistic allowances for the immense difficulties at the mines, for the labor and transportation problems there, and most of all for the perplexing conundrums in the extraction processes stemming from the rebellious character of the ores. King's frequent poor health had been another factor militating against success, too often balking his efforts at critical junctures; and he had been casual, even slipshod in his business management. But above all he had lacked the capital to endure—for Adams's diagnosis was correct—and all King's technical resources had, at crucial moments, been canceled out by a want of working funds. "The failure of the scientific scheme, without money to back it, was flagrant," Adams insisted; "in practice science was helpless without money. The weak holder was . . . sure to be frozen out."

Not only had King's science failed him as a business asset, but also he was inclined to hold it, along with his entire intellectual propensity, as the prime reason for his business debacle. "I ought to have made abundant money," he wrote in wistful self-analysis. "But I fear I stayed too long in pure science and got a bent for the philosophical and ideal side of life too strong for any adaptation to commercial affairs." Hay considered the matter in a different light, however. What King lacked as a businessman, in his opinion, was sufficient avarice, sufficient industry of the more plodding sort, and a sufficient run of ordinary luck. "A touch of avarice would have made him a Vanderbilt—a touch of plodding industry would have made him anything he chose"—a judgment to which Hay later added: "With talents immeasurably beyond any of his contemporaries [King had] everything in his favor but blind luck."

Though now in constant pain, he resorted to his profession to support his family. He spent a month at the Rossland mines in British Columbia, but the work there sapped his reserves and set his spine on fire, and in late October he returned in a state that shocked his friends. All pride in his appearance was gone. His hair was shaggy around the ears. His grizzled beard was badly in need of a trim, and his linen was dirty. He had lost much weight and spoke of bizarre lapses of memory. According to John La Farge, he would find himself "walking in certain streets without any notion of how he came there." He inferred some connection with a minor sunstroke he had suffered the year before, with a subsequent odd sensation in the right lobe of his brain.

On Sunday, October 29, 1893, he found himself in the lion house of Central Park. A throng of visitors milled about. What happened then is not clear. King claimed that bystanders "jostled" him against a Negro butler from a house on Madison Avenue. Whatever the actual facts, two detectives arrested him for "acting in a disorderly manner in the presence of a large crowd." They booked him at the Yorkville jail, but the next day his lawyer called the arrest a case of persecution "owing to King's well-known opposition to the candidacy of Mr. Maynard." The judge must have taken a mild view of the matter, although he found King guilty of "disorderly conduct." The fine was ten dollars.

Reporters besieged King at the Union League Club, his home at the time, causing him deep anxiety. He knew that his wits were sound enough nine-tenths of the time, but he lived in dread of what might happen in one of his lapses—something to make his marriage public knowledge? Or something even worse? Forebodings of further disaster overwhelmed him.

But friends, too, had grown concerned over his strange behavior,

and three of them, including John Cadwalader, urged him to be examined by his personal physician, Dr. Rufus Lincoln, in consultation with
a specialist in nervous diseases. On seeing him, the doctors certified
that King was mentally disturbed, that inflammation of the spine had
led to a state of acute depression, which at times stimulated melan-
cholia. They prescribed complete rest, with proper nursing, and King
agreed with a sense of profound relief. He consented to go before a
justice of the State Supreme Court, who signed the papers committing
him to Bloomingdale Asylum. It was Halloween. *

* When Henry James learned of King's breakdown, he said: "[King] was in his way a
fascinator. It's miserable to think one may never again see him as he delightfully was."
Then came an afterthought that sounded not a little like certain wry remarks of Henry
Adams: "In truth I never thought there was no madness at all in his sanity—and I feel
indeed as if there may be some sanity in his madness" (quoted in Edel, *Henry James: The
Treacherous Years*, p. 238).

20

Ebb Tide

Indian summer slipped by, and King rested body and spirit at the brownstone asylum on the battle site of Harlem Heights, the future campus of Columbia University. Spacious grounds enclosed the buildings there, in view of Grant's tomb, and there were walks and gardens and groves of evergreens, where one could idle in the open air, safe from the pressures of the city. Friends like J. D. Hague or John La Farge came to see King frequently, and Gardiner paid him almost daily visits. "If anything can drive him to sanity," Henry Adams wrote, "I think Gardiner can do it; he would drive me to a much further region."

The spinal inflammation waned slowly. Now and then it racked King with a sleepless night. But there was no return, as Hague reported, "of anything like mental derangement since the first week of his going to Bloomingdale. He has in fact no brain disease at all"—outside of an anemic condition in one lobe that distorted images from the left eye and made compensatory glasses necessary for a while. Certain of King's friends regretted that he had gone into a sanatarium for the insane, and some suggested that he place himself in the care of his fellow Centurian S. Weir Mitchell. Gardiner, in fact, went to Philadelphia late in November to talk with Mitchell in his consultation room ("the ghoul-haunted woodland of Weir," as some wag had called it). But the novelist-doctor, who considered nervous fatigue the national malady, suspected that nothing ailed King that rest and relaxation could not cure. He advised leaving the patient at Bloomingdale. He saw King within a week and could assure him that his mental lapses had been purely functional in origin; they had not come from any organic lesion of the brain. Continued rest was Mitchell's prescription—medicine which seemed to work.

"My rate of improvement is singularly regular," King soon wrote; "so much so that they have fixed a sort of time table for the various steps of complete recovery." At first, his doctors set October 1894 as the date for "good as new." But as King's condition continued to improve, they shortened their estimate of his convalescence, predicting total recovery by May. King planned, meanwhile, to head south on leaving Bloomingdale and pass the rest of the winter at some tropical haven where he might "lie in the shade of palms and continue the practice of patience and rest till the fire goes out of my poor nerves, and then if a month or two hence I feel the vigor I expect, I should like nothing so well as to 'do' an island."

His earlier work in Cuba had aroused his interest in the economic future of the West Indies. Plans for a private geologic survey of the islands had begun to simmer in his mind. He had broached the scheme to Becker in Washington, proposing that they undertake the work together, dividing the archipelago between them. King thought of taking islands beyond the Windward Passage as his sphere, leaving Cuba for Becker; and so he now made plans for a voyage to Haiti and then the Windward Islands, especially Dominica. "I have long known," he wrote, "that Dominica was the finest of all the islands on the testimony of everybody from the early English admirals who fought the French all over those seas, to Froude and Charles Kingsley."

He had invited Henry Adams, on the last day of 1893, to become his comrade on the voyage. "*South* I must go," he wrote,

and next week is to be my last in this house of madness. I shant like it so well a few months hence when Columbia College moves in here and displaces these open, frank lunatics with Seth Low and his faculty of incurables, so I better go now. What do you say to taking the island trip with me?

He promised not to bore his friend in case the temperature of his back shot up to the fusion point of diabase and "moral viscosity" set in.

"For my own part," Adams confessed long afterward, "I would always have joined him, whether in an asylum or out of it, rather than anyone else, and to that effect I must have written him."

King remained with friends in New York for a fortnight after "graduating" from his "institution of learning," and then entrained for Florida with his valet. They idled away another week in Tampa, waiting for Adams to tear "himself from the arms of—South Carolina."* As soon

---

* A bantering allusion to Elizabeth Cameron, with whom Adams was infatuated—the hostess of a picturesque retreat at St. Helena By-the-Sea on an island off the coast of South Carolina. King called her the "Dona," a pun on her role as the wife of "Senator Don" Cameron. Though he had been slow in warming to her, he claimed she was one

as Henry appeared, on February 3, 1894, they embarked for Cuba on a pleasant voyage with clear skies and tranquil water. King discovered, on reaching Havana, that Haiti and the Windward islands were inaccessible unless one trusted oneself to a crotchety little freighter that wallowed about in choppy seas for fourteen days, but that, he decided, was not too much to pay for a windward voyage.

"If I am able to resume work where I began four years since," he wrote to Becker, reversing the terms of his earlier proposal, "I shall lay my plans to do the geology of Cuba as part of my area if we make the Survey of the Antilles. This will leave the island of Hayti-Santo Domingo for you." He suggested that Becker arrange to meet the respective ministers in Washington and fan their interest.

If they understand that we are quite independent of the U.S. government and that serious economical benefits may accrue to their miserable little ring governments I am inclined to think they will co-operate with you. In beginning Cuba myself I know that I am facing a large contract with plenty of work and plenty of glory if I do well.

The natural bounty of that island had made a deep impression on King. He had found Cuba "rich beyond description, beautiful as Eden"; hardly more than a tenth of its area had been occupied, and he rejoiced over the opportunities that a survey would open for American enterprise. He tramped for a week about the Havana countryside, absorbed in geology, in spite of the sun which Adams considered torrid enough to melt the two of them into jellyfish.

The uplifted reef that fringed the coast had piqued King's curiosity, and he was hard at work on the problem of its contact with the marine tertiaries underneath. His observations filled him with excitement. "Agassiz is all wrong!" he exulted to Becker. But King was eager to reach the eastern end of the island, and on February 12 the travelers started for Batabanó on the south coast, two hours down from Havana.

There they boarded a coasting steamer in company with a diminutive matador from Spain, a popular idol who remained drunk when not seasick. The vessel picked its course through a maze of mangrove isles,

---

of the few women who had ever brought him "a rag of joy"; she had charmed him by her playful prophecy that he would one day marry his cook. Yet he could not help but feel a little resentful at the influence she wielded over Adams, a sentiment that seems to have been mutual.

then slashed into a screaming windstorm off Cape Cruz, "which King liked as little as I," wrote Adams, although they both defied the gale long enough for King to demonstrate the unsurpassed grandeur of the moonlit coast. The steamer reached Santiago harbor before dawn, after four days on the water, and the passengers hurried ashore to look for lodgings in the dark. King and Adams, wryly uncertain which of them was Don Quixote and which was Sancho Panza, drove from door to door, until at last they found quarters in an inn which rivaled Castile for its filth and smells and blatant confusion.

"I was rather disturbed at the situation," Adams wrote, "for Cuba had done King no visible good . . . Staying in Santiago was impossible. My only chance was to hire a house in the suburbs."

King then remembered F. W. Ramsden, the British consul, with whom he had dealt on his previous visit—a man of the world, whose collection of rare and beautiful butterflies reposed in the British Museum. The consul had also collected a sympathetic wife, and when the travelers dined with them she suggested a happy solution to the dilemma. Let them take, at Dos Bocas, the country home of Ramsden's business partner, another Englishman whose name was Brooks.

The matter was promptly arranged, and on riding a comic-opera railroad into the mountains King and Adams settled down in what they chose to label paradise. The square one-storied house was perched in a narrow canyon, lush with grass and forest which gave way to groves of palms and mangoes, oranges and bananas, all beneath the intense blue skies. There was plenty of scenery for Adams to paint, and plenty of mountains for King to climb, and both were content to while away a month there. King would later acknowledge the kind and healing gentleness with which Adams, "that pessimistic Angel," handled him during this period. "He was . . . genial and tropical in his warmth [and as] active as a chamois; and as for his talk, there was only bitter[ness] enough to give a cocktail effect to his high-proof spirit."

As soon as rest had restored King's dash, he attacked the surrounding geology with a vigor that impressed his crony as "fits of untimely energy." He would rise at six in the morning to climb the neighboring mountains with his field glasses and barometer, or to comb the railroad cuttings with a pickax and a basket. The region withheld its geological secrets, though, and King longed for fossils to unlock the riddles. And when his enthusiasm showed signs of flagging, Adams developed a fiercely contentious zeal for science, refuting every notion that King advanced. That drove him on to prove his opinions, until at last Adams made the slip of calling a chunk of coral a recent lava. For King, then, even argument lost its charm.

But there were other matters to absorb his interest, not merely the cockfights which amiable *vecinos* staged in the courtyard at Dos Bocas, and certainly not obsessive letter-writing like that which engrossed Adams. Before King realized it, he and his friend had drifted into the vortex of what Adams could only call "an ocean of mischief." It had taken King just ten days, as Adams figured, to make the acquaintance of every ancient black in the region; and it would be said that "listening to the croonings of a turbaned black grandmother . . . for some hint of Voodoo mysteries" was one of his most cherished experiences. He wormed from the Negroes nightly welcomes to their dances, weird and unconstrained orgies full of African sorcery and insinuations of conspiracy. Soon the innuendo turned to open disclosure, and King perceived Santiago as "the very *nidus* of revolution." He drank in tales of the *mambís'* dedicated struggle against the power of Spain during the Ten-Years' Revolt, and was reconciled to the rebellion in the offing.

And when the violence flared a year later, he could write:

I learned of the present Insurrection, long before it occurred, from the Cubans who knew my fervent sympathy for their cause. I have the personal acquaintance of many leaders and have travelled the island widely. . . . I succeeded in getting a pass from the military authorities at Santiago to visit in his prison my old friend Guillermon, the black lion whom the Spanish had arrested and cast into a cell for safe keeping. When the sentinel paced into the dungeon toward us, Guillermon talked in ordinary tones of a recent coal discovery, but when the soldier . . . strode out of the room and across a wide corridor, the old fighter's eyes blazed and his lips poured into my ears the secret of the coming war.

Adams compared the whole adventure to a novel by Frank Stockton, an olla podrida of the most conflicting ingredients; but the perils were real enough, as when a celebrated brigand—one José Daniele—met King's party while they were out to study coal seams. The bandit, however, had done no more than swill hot coffee and predict the coming insurrection. What had prevented him from estimating King's value in ransom or from acting on whatever notions he had gained thereby remained a mystery to Adams, unless they enjoyed protection from some influential personage in the area. Nothing so insubstantial abashed King, however. He continued to come and go among his

Cuban acquaintances, and his sympathies for their plight would later prompt him to agitate in the United States for the cause of Free Cuba.

Lest trouble explode about their ears sooner than anyone expected, Adams encouraged an early departure; yet not before they made one last geological excursion—a trip to the Gran Piedra, which Ramsden had arranged. The consul rode out with them in a small locomotive along the edge of the ocean and under cliffs of coral rock; and King would stop the engine whenever anything special caught his eye. A country priest, a guitar player, and men from the rural guard joined the party in the evening, and there were rum and singing under the stars. A private of the guard "danced the Bull-fight and the *Culebra*," Adams wrote,

with as much spirit as my Samoan friends used to put into their dances. . . . The *Cura* danced less well, but took his rum like a Saint, and applauded a variety of the very least spiritual songs I ever heard. They would have gone on all night, if at twelve o'clock, our host had not sent us to bed, for we had to get up at five.

Then they were off again, and they spent the second night on top of the mountain, where bright-eyed blue-and-green lizards crept up their legs and backs under their clothing.

King was content to wander on to any windward haunt of the ideal colored woman. Puerto Rico was their next stop, and then St. Thomas, where a smallpox quarantine ensured them two weeks of thorough rest. They delighted then in Martinique, which Lafcadio Hearn had so piquantly sketched; but St. Lucia, St. Kitts, Antigua, Monserrat, and St. Vincent seemed to them as dreary as Aberdeen. The travelers paused also at Trinidad and Barbadoes before sailing up to Nassau, where they found blacks aplenty. "King managed to amuse himself with the habits and manners of the Bahama niggers, who are a peculiar type," wrote Adams, "but I care not for that kind of archaican, or for conches"; so that after two weeks he coaxed King back to Florida, where phosphate matters claimed his attention.

Adams informed Hay:

Whatever else our trip has been, it has certainly been good for King. We are both as mad as Moses, and [King] has always been one of the maddest. You had the benefit of it when you were abroad with him and I have it now; but I think he is more sane now than he was then, and if he could be obliged to stay quiet for half an hour, I think he might be quite reasonable.

Another week brought the pair back to Washington, and King remained in Adams's house for the rest of April, his fifth vertebra all but well again, although he would complain of feeling a bit tired whenever they stayed up to talk all night.

There was little to please one now in Washington, where Coxey's Army had begun to straggle in and where, even more distressing to King, Major Powell's troubles seemed to have reached a climax. King left the capital about May 1, 1894, shortly before Powell finally announced his resignation, hounded by enemies and tortured by regenerated nerves in the stump of his shattered arm. The ostensible reason for the resignation was the major's need for surgery on the stump. The real reason was the relentless pressure of the opposition, which had alone practically driven him from office. The indignities heaped upon him included a thousand-dollar slash in salary, a device sometimes employed by the administration to humiliate an unpopular civil servant into bowing out. Powell's treatment troubled King, and he was happy to join a group who wished to honor the major in his somberest hour. Among King's first concerns on reaching New York City was Gardiner Hubbard's proposal to give Powell "a small farm by the sea on the island of Martha's Vineyard"; and hard pressed as King himself was, he pledged two hundred dollars to help build a summer cottage there. He also urged mutual friends to support the project.

The best thing he could see in Powell's retirement was the choice of successor. Charles D. Walcott had been no satellite of King's, but King understood the wisdom of his appointment. For one thing, it promised to reverse Powell's sustained retreat from economic geology and to reestablish the survey's earlier alliance with the mineral industries. "I think . . . Walcott is a man of remarkable executive ability," King announced in public later that year, "and the mining interests may rest assured that he appreciates the national importance of the Geological Survey and will use his best efforts to carry out the work to the advantage of all the mining communities in the country." Walcott did not wait to signal his intention of doing exactly that, while at the same time he broadened the mission of the survey to aid any other industry— indeed any practical endeavor—that could benefit from a knowledge of geology. It would be his enduring accomplishment, in the words of a later historian, "to combine the best of the King and Powell administrations into an organization that fulfilled the promise of 1879."

As King regained his vigor, he returned to the economic battleground, determined to keep his black family in a measure of comfort. Sometime during this period, he installed Ada and her children in an eleven-room house on North Prince Street, in a Flushing tract once known as Prince's Gardens. As this had been an extensive nursery, trees were its legacy—rows of Chinese cypress, dwarf horsechestnut, Japanese maple, cedar and gingko trees; which made it a place of cool, green shades in the spring or the summer, or of reds and gold in the fall. Here was a quietly beautiful spot in which to raise the family, and Ada, as time went on, increased its number by two more boys, christened Sidney and Wallace. In turn, King added servants to the household—a cook, a nurse, a laundress, and a gardener, even a music teacher for his daughters; all of which demanded money; but, as Hay observed, King was full of schemes again, "all of them brilliant, not to say irridescent, in promise." How like his old self he seemed, able to tell his friends: "There has been no return of the blasting pain which crazed me."

But Adams had serious reservations about New York's effects on King, and so he laid plans for new distractions—first a summer trip to the Yellowstone and the Teton country, to include Hay as well as King, and then another jaunt to the West Indies as soon as fall should come. "If I were in King's place," he had said to Hewitt, "I would keep as far from it"—New York—"as my credit would permit. He had better geologize the negro with me in eastern Cuba."

King received the suggestion with enthusiasm, but unable to commit himself conclusively to Adams's plans, he was evasive in his response. "I think he must have joined some oath-bound order," Hay complained, "which pledged him, under fearful sanctions, never to tell anybody anything." But King did give them a tentative promise to join the Yellowstone party if time permitted. Then off he pushed to examine a sick mine near Colville, Washington, in a landscape he described as "the Arctic-granite-and-pine-tree kind, with relentless skies of Calvinistic blue and the coldest stars in space." The work occupied him for weeks, after which he made a second trip to the Rossland district of British Columbia. That was when the Pullman strike developed, tying up trains and putting both Yellowstone and the Tetons out of the question.

King came east by way of Chicago, where he happened on Theodore

Roosevelt, straight from his badlands ranch and feeling "as rugged as a bull moose." King had no way of knowing how famous that phrase was destined to be, for now it merely echoed the way in which, just weeks before, he had underscored his own resurging health. "I am as strong as a Caribou," he had assured Hay, "and go up hill like an Elk." Likely enough on the train to New York King and Roosevelt talked outdoor matters suitable for the Boone and Crocket Club. Possibly, too, their conversation turned to the Caribbean, so interesting to both. Fate would take Roosevelt to the West Indies first, but King now thought of spending October and November on some exotic isle like Martinique or Trinidad, with a spell in eastern Cuba. Adams waited in Washington, all primed to go with him; but when the hour of departure arrived, King found that his many responsibilities forbade the trip, and he could only surmise what adventures he must miss.

Adams, who replaced King with a senator's son for traveling companion, found "Cuba totally ruined . . . more discontented than ever." Depression in the cane industry, with its train of miseries, made an explosion imminent, and King expected to hear at any moment that the insurgents had finally "launched the shout." He kept in touch with Cuban sympathizers in New York, and talked of Cuban affairs with many friends, especially friends at the Century Club, where he appeared at the Twelfth Night revels in the silver-spangled matador's suit he had bought in Spain. But mining commitments had drawn him west again for a study of the Old Dominion Mine, not far from Spokane, when the news broke that Cuban patriots had once again unfurled their five-bar flag with the single star. The press played the conflict up, especially after the Spanish fired on the American steamer *Alliança,* making her way through the Windward Passage; and King gave the reports his concentrated attention. "From that hour," he would declare, "I have watched the unfolding of the drama,—both the military movements on the Island, and the slow masterly spinning of the diplomatic cobwebs by the Spanish minister in this country around the executive arm of the United States Government."

He felt an extravagant sympathy for the *mambís,* desperate patriots ready with razor-sharp machetes to split the skull or slash the throat of every Spanish soldier sent against them. They had no delusions about the difficulties of their cause; and moved by their reckless courage, King could write:

In rushing to arms again, they act in full consciousness of what they are doing. . . . They enter this war as bravely as before, but with eyes open and with memory loaded down with visions of agony and blood. Of that adoration of liberty which is the only sure foundation of modern representative government, this insurrection is as pure and lofty an example as the course of human history can show.

With never a doubt as to the justice and integrity of *Cuba Libre*, King exulted in reports that the Insurgents had more than held their own in Oriente, even against Spain's most illustrious soldier, General Campos. The Spanish threw fortified trochas across the island to keep the war confined to the east. But rebel generals—Gomez and Maceo—pierced the lines almost at will, seized the initiative, and to King's delight outmarshalled the Spanish at every move.

It was the plan of General Gomez to beat the Spanish forces not by ordinary tactics but by bringing the economic life of the island to a standstill—by scorching the earth, burning the cane fields, destroying all basic industry; in short, by making Cuba worthless to the Spanish Crown, and much too expensive to hold. The Cubans could wage such a war of attrition as long, but only as long, as aid arrived from sympathizers in the United States. They depended on a stream of supplies from American ports, supplies which President Cleveland regarded as contraband, in deference to Spain; and as the American government instituted measures to halt the flow of munitions, only one course remained for the Insurgents. They must secure recognition, at least of their belligerency, and to that end the Cuban Junta launched a feverish propaganda drive.

King volunteered his help. Though still insolvent, he obstinately refused to take money for "new stories or old Turners"* from either Hay or Adams, who offered to pay him well. But to write something for the Cubans was another matter. He dashed an article off ("Shall Cuba Be Free?"), an appeal coruscating with brimstone and bias, as incendiary as he could make it; and the *Forum* published it in September 1895.

"Let us not deceive ourselves!" he argued.

Spain alone cannot conquer Cuba; she proved that in ten years of miserable failure. If we prevent the sending of munitions to Cuba, and continue to allow

---

*Nevertheless, sometime in 1896 King sold to Henry Adams the luminous oil by Turner called *The Whaler*, one of the finest paintings in his collection.

Spain to buy ships and arms and amunition here, it is we who will conquer Cuba, not Spain. It is we who will crush liberty!

He did not advocate American intervention in the war; on the contrary, the United States had only to take one step, in his opinion, to guarantee the triumph of the Insurrection. Let Grover Cleveland recognize Cuban belligerency; the Cubans themselves would do the rest.

"King's Cuban outbreak"—Adams's reference to the article—caused a momentary stir. The *Literary Digest* reprinted the gist of it; offprints were circulated as propaganda, and for his service as pamphleteer for *Cuba Libre,* the Junta listed King with public spirits like Governor Matthews of Indiana and John R. Dos Passos, father of the later novelist. On reading the piece in London, Adams thought it sane enough for Bloomingdale all over again, and he hoped that it would not move skittish friends to shut King up. King was still neck-deep in Cuban intrigue when Adams crossed the Atlantic a few weeks later. They spent two carefree days together in New York City, and after the "anarchy" of romps with John La Farge and Edward Hooper, Clover's brother, they talked Cuba together for hours on end, with King defending the fiery maneuvers of Gomez and Maceo. Adams feared that the odds were far too great for any hope of success, and he told King so. But King was prepared for any argument, and in the end his fervor converted Adams—as Adams would himself claim—"into the patient ally of the most uneasy and persistent conspirator [the Century] Club ever nourished in its bosom." Adams was so thoroughly converted that, on reaching Washington, he opened his house to agents of the Junta, turning it into a hotbed of intrigue, and launched a campaign to needle the President into a change of policy.

Friends of Cuba called public meetings in halls like Cooper Union to heighten general awareness of the island's plight, but like Adams, King worked best in private, exerting his personal force on individual men. "White-hot," he buttonholed friends, dropped gracious yet inciting words in influential parlors—as when Henry Cabot Lodge invited him to dine in Washington and placed him at the side of Richard Olney, secretary of state. Not that King's remarks left any discernable trace on the secretary's course of action; perhaps, indeed, King came to think, like Adams, that Olney was incapable of framing a policy adequate for the Cuban crisis. On that assumption Adams was quietly furnishing Don Cameron, of the Senate Foreign Relations Committee, with capitoline thunder against the administration's stand. Adams had drafted the minority report which Senator Cameron had sponsored in February, a call for the President to mediate with Spain for the recognition of Cuban independence. That was a more extreme step than even King had preached in the *Forum*, but it was a step which Insurgent successes seemed to warrant.

General Campos reeled before the "invasion" of the western provinces, the campaign led by Gomez and Maceo, and Spain finally called her "greatest soldier" home. The Cuban advance moved King to write another article for the *Forum*, a spirited chronicle of events woven from facts he had gathered from Insurgent sources; from the diary, first, of General Miro (Maceo's chief of staff), which he had read in manuscript; and then from long conversations with officers invalided from the field.

"Fire and Sword in Cuba," as he named the piece, appeared in September 1896, a tribute to the Rebel leaders, who became Homeric heroes under his pen. The most spectacular of them all was General Antonio Maceo, whom King regarded as a personal friend. So great was his admiration for this valiant mulatto, scarred with more than twenty battle wounds, that he requested Tiffany's to fill a special chest with silverware in Maceo's honor. The gleaming tribute arrived in December 1896. But before the presentation could be made, King learned that his hero had fallen in a minor skirmish. It was news that stunned; news that angered, too, as later reports (for who could tell they were fabrications?) depicted Maceo as the victim of a cowardly ruse. Spanish cravens had shot him down in cold blood, the story ran, as he had honored a flag of truce. And what a carnival day it provided the Cuban propagandists!

Adams had, meanwhile, brewed a second report for "Senator Don," a resolution for him to push through Congress. The Senate reported it out on December 21 while anger over Maceo's "murder" still ran high, and the newspapers were full of it, to wit: "That the independence of the Republic of Cuba be, and the same is hereby, acknowledged by the United States of America"; a policy which, if forced upon the President, could have meant immediate war. Cleveland refused to be stampeded.

King had neither desired nor advocated war with Spain, much as he wanted his Cubans free; nor did he believe, even during the martial frenzies of 1897, that war was inevitable. That he considered it possible was another matter, and when his friend George Dewey had assumed command of the Asiatic Squadron, he surprised a drawing room in Washington by predicting what the commodore would do in case hostilities did break out. He would "go into Manila harbor," King declared, "and sink the whole Spanish fleet!" Perhaps King had scented the plan which friends of his—Henry Cabot Lodge and the young Bull Moose who was now assistant secretary of the navy—had secretly spun for the Philippine Islands. If so, he declined to reveal it when, later, he gave the reasons behind his remark. He had known Dewey well, he said. "I knew where he was and that he could not stay there after a declaration of war; if he had to go somewhere, he would be sure to go where the Spanish fleet was; and if he found it he would sink it. You see, the argument was complete."

Economic barometers had reached dead ebb in 1897. King had passed much of these depression years in the netherworld of Western mines, having "evaded into space," as his friends complained, and there he would stay "to escape New York," bound always on some "quest for El Dorado." He had scarcely made expenses, after months of toil in Oregon and Washington; but the prospects of a mine not far from Spokane—the Old Dominion on which he had run a study—had quickened his spirits. The vein had yielded upward of a million dollars since its discovery, and the best production promised yet to come. King had proposed a large plant to handle the ores that were now packed out on mules for shipment to Tacoma. The bonanza fury had seized him again; a confirmed bimetallist, he was convinced that the silver industry would soon revive and bring prosperity.

King, however, had little faith in the panaceas of the Silverites, and once, while stopping at the Brown Palace, he had told the mining men of Denver: "I look not to the clamors of your Populists to start up your silver industry in its former brilliant activity, but to the genuine conviction of England, who to-day holds her restraining hand on the lever of your silver hoisting engine." English wealth depended on profits from trade more than on interest from investments, and trade requirements were now urging Great Britain to shift from a single gold standard to a bimetallic basis. King was sure the change would come, and with it a mining boom. He looked to the future with impatience, while, in the meantime, he pursued his profession with a drive so reckless that friends like Adams and Hay despaired as they watched him from a distance, a spectacle of exertion seemingly for the sake of motion alone. "Of course it will come to nothing," John Hay sighed.

King's wanderings led, at one time or another, to "most of the leading districts of Utah, Colorado and part of Dakota, parts of New

Mexico, practically the whole of California and Arizona." Even his interest in Mexico had revived. He became a consultant for the San Cristobal Mine in Zacatecas, where he invited Adams to go with him in the spring of 1897, on horseback and in leather suits, to carve their way with sharp machetes. "Come along," he begged, "and I will in the secrecy of the primeval woods admit the truth of all your geological criticism of me; and I will even execute in advance an assignment of half the brown girls we meet. Moreover I will be a second La Farge and never tell."

But Adams failed him now, just as the San Cristobal Mine would fail him after first arousing hope. Worse yet, his confidence in his magnum opus had all but sputtered out. He still fancied a strong resemblance between his temperament and that of Cervantes, but he now had grave doubts that his "petty misery" had left him force enough "to write [his own] Don Quixote." That did not deter him, however, from working out fresh fiction in his mind, and as late as August 1900 he would arrive at Sunapee "with a new book all ready to print"—that is, "all done but the writing," or so John Hay would inform Adams. "It is awfully good literature," added Hay, "to hear [King] talk about it." But each realized as clearly as the other that the book was only a dream, and would never be written down.

Adams knew moreover that by 1897 the whole game was up for King, "that henceforward his energies were to be thrown away, that the particular stake for which he had played was lost, by no fault of his, but by those strokes of financial bad luck which broke down fully half of the strongest men of our time." King had more than an inkling of this bleak truth, but he refused to sidestep his struggles, even when earnestly cautioned by his doctors against the hypertrophy of his heart. He collapsed in the summer of 1897 from a mild heart failure in Telluride, Colorado, where he represented the North American Exploration Company. He finished his report while flat in bed at a mountain hotel, but he was not to be stopped by merely an ailing heart. Calling on his great powers of recuperation, he seized his hammers again and hurried off for another job in Mexico. Work followed in the copper districts of Arizona, and there were journeys to California and New York. Friends reported that King remained as busy as ever, though he no longer seemed as sanguine as in former years, notwithstanding a welcome upturn in the economy.

In 1898 the war with Spain had achieved what neither Cleveland nor McKinley had been able to do. It made the business machine of

America hum once more, and returning prosperity brought the illusion of change in King's luck. At Telluride the Nellie Mine, in which he had taken stock for his services, entered a stage of remarkable productivity; and King was also prospering with copper promotions in Arizona. There were also coal deposits, in Colorado, which he hoped to "place," and finally a vast scheme for irrigating lands along the Colorado below the Mexican border. This project pleased him as much as his plans for a survey of the West Indies, which the troubles in Cuba had shelved indefinitely; and with his "valued anachronism"—Don Horacio Cutter—he planned to colonize the tract with Japanese farmers to raise cotton in the rich soil.

On the strength of King's prospects, his brother George married Virginia Stackpole, a "tall and stately" debutante from Beacon Street and carried her off to Paris, for he was still a student there, with King's indulgent blessing. King himself left for British Columbia after the wedding, and another round of travel began, such as always caused his friends to wonder where he would turn up next. He spent a month at Rossland, making daily examinations underground to ferret out the geology in the struggle between two rival mines, the Centre Star and the Iron Mask—a type of work King regarded as a necessity rather than a predilection. Dashes to Oregon, California, Mexico, and Colorado intervened. Then in April 1899 he testified for the Centre Star before the Supreme Court of British Columbia, where his chief adversary was his old friend Rossiter Raymond, whose study of mining law had lately gained him admittance to the New York bar. King had informed J. D. Hague that Rossiter's presence "does not add to my comfort." But King's evidence clinched the case, which involved a vein of enormous wealth. Such performances brought him generous fees. But never in such service would he allow himself to be bought—never would he allow his opinion to be twisted to meet a client's demands. As Emmons put the matter, "[King] was never willing to accept a retainer . . . until he had satisfied himself by personal examination that the contention of the side that desired his services was in accord with his reading of the geological structure and such as he could conscientiously subscribe to."

King remained in demand as an expert witness, recognized as he was as one of the master geologists of America; and his own solid grasp of mining law, the object of special study on his part as early as 1874, buttressed his scientific competence. Few attorneys could hope to shake his testimony. It surprised no one, then, that his services should be sought for the most spectacular mining lawsuit of the day, the War of the Copper Kings having opened in Butte, Montana. The long, irregular ridge that gave the city its name was commonly called "the richest hill in the world," and its wealth was in constant dispute at the federal courthouse there. And now the feud between Marcus Daly, of Anaconda, and former Senator William A. Clark—the feud which had rocked the whole state—had come to a head in litigation between Anaconda's Neversweat and the Colusa-Parrot, which Clark controlled. Each magnate assumed that his honor was at stake. "There's no strings on ye," Daly had thundered at D. W. Brunton, his consulting engineer; which meant, Don't count the cost. Brunton had set about preparing the case long before it came to trial, and King's name headed the list of experts he retained.

King arrived in Butte in February 1900 and began to make his customary thorough investigation. A young lawyer in Daly's employ was assigned to pilot him underground—Cornelius Kelley, who would later rise to the chairmanship of Anaconda Copper. But King was determined to get at the facts for himself, Kelley discovered. He would elude the party and wander off alone through the underground workings, candle in hand, to find independent answers. He studied the Neversweat, level by level, and made penciled notes on diagrams which company draftsmen had supplied him. He also went carefully through the Colusa-Parrot workings, and then through other local mines for a comprehensive understanding of the lode.

King remained a dandy to the end. He had brought his valet to Butte, and every evening Alexander brushed his overalls, scraped the candle drippings from the cloth, and pressed sharp creases back into the trouser legs; and he would send King out of a morning, the most dapper scientist Kelley would ever remember working at the mines. But Alexander was more than the ordinary valet; he did not merely specialize in looking after King's clothes. He took a serious interest in King's professional duties, and over the years, according to Rossiter Raymond, he had become "an invaluable assistant in geological underground work, observing with great acuteness, although without scientific knowledge, indications which more learned men might have overlooked." He, too, went down the shafts to help King in his quest for the facts of Butte geology.

Then of an evening King would join his fellow experts at the McDermott Hotel; they would gather around a special table and season their meals with wit and anecdote. "King made himself lovable to all," wrote Louis Janin, with stories perhaps like his recollection of the guide who had fairly oozed "Hugh-Millerty" before the open landscape, and who had chattered on and on as they rode toward the prospect King had agreed to examine. "When I look about me, Mr. King," he was saying, "and reflect on what geological formations mean, it strikes me ever anew how wonderful are the works of—" Just then his horse stepped into a prairie-dog hole, and the fellow hit the ground hard. Gasping for breath, he managed to mutter "God!" But whether to finish his sentence properly or to relieve his feelings King could never decide.

Even the knowledge of Alexander provided the nub for a blackface anecdote, a travesty of the valet's irreproachable English, illustrating King's relaxed regard for the truth when coining a story. This one turned on the fact that Louis Janin also employed a Negro servant. One day King noticed Alexander doubled over with laughter.

"What's the joke?" he asked.

"Say, Mistah King," came Alexander's reply, in minstrel-show accents, "you know Mistah Janin's nigger? Well, dat nigger is the most ignorantist nigger I ever see: yessah, he don't know nuffin. Wy dat nigger—ho, ho, ho, ho—dat nigger, Mistah King, he so ignorant he don't even know what hawnblende andesite am!"

The trial opened on March 20, while a scourge of pneumonia raged in Butte, killing half its victims. King had taken precautions against chills, but he now came down with a hoarseness which he could not shake in the palls of smoke that smothered the city. He gave his testimony, and then his doctor sent him to bed. He took no further part in the trial, and thoughts of Ada must have besieged him during his days of enforced idleness: "Ah, my darling," he wrote from Montana, "I lie in the lonely hours of night and long to feel your warm and loving arms about me and your breath on my face and the dear pressure of your lips against mine. My dearest, I love you with all the depth and warmth of my whole heart and will till I die."

The trial ended before King was released from the sickroom. But the court had found in favor of his principals, the Anaconda Company, the case having turned on questions of geological structure. King's testimony had been crucial.

Calling on his vaunted powers of recuperation, King felt well enough by June 1900 to plan a journey to the gold fields of Alaska and the Klondike. Friends cautioned against the trip, fearing for his health; but careless as ever of his strength, he smiled at their warnings and packed his satchel. Once again he proved that "his life was distinguished for remarkable physical vigor and energy." "Even up to the time of his last illness," Emmons wrote, "he was in the habit of enduring fatigues that would have worn out men of half his years." There was no exception to this fact in his impetuous tour of the gold regions, after he had shipped north from Seattle. If he followed his planned schedule, he remained at Dawson for about four days, but nowhere else sufficiently long for mail to reach him. It was his aim to visit Nome, where the rush had reached its crest at wild reports "of a sand-beach forty miles long . . . where the sand [was] gold, and every shovelful worth a dollar." The whirlwind journey, whatever his final itinerary, lasted most of the summer, but early September found him back in Seattle, where a friend wrote: "He returned from Alaska simply bubbling over with pleasure and stories of his trip, which he declared to have been the most interesting he had ever taken; 'but now,' he said, 'I am going to have a quiet week's visit here with you before taking up my work again.'"

The Yukon country seemed to have agreed with King (notwithstanding subsequent claims that the seeds of tuberculosis had been sown there), for his friend, who was a physician, added:

One morning, when I went to his room, he was just out of his tub and using his towel, and I exclaimed, ". . . *do* let me examine that splendid chest." And I thumped and pounded and listened, and he made droll remarks while really pleased with my verdict—for after a long experience, I had never found more perfect thoractic contents. The heart was a trifle large, but with the calm quietude of perfect strength; and a superb lung capacity and resonance everywhere—so that I said to him: "There is not a cleaner or more perfectly healthy man on foot today, and you ought to live to be at least a hundred."

And yet before the year was over, King had come down with whooping cough after investigating copper mines near Prescott, Arizona. "I have been desperately ill for ten days trying not to get pneumonia," he wrote just after Christmas, "and I am generally used up and worn out. This is not good preparation for severe work in Missouri."

He had committed himself to an appraisal of lead deposits at Flat River, south of St. Louis, the Exploration Company of London having purchased the property subject to his approval. King felt honor bound to make the investigation, and he kept his bargain, even though a doctor in Chicago had found that a tubercular patch of thumbnail size affected one of his lungs. Long before, in *Mountaineering*, he had wondered if difficulties of the chest "might inferentially be symptoms of original sin." In King's case, they had come with the failure of his aspirations. He had exhausted himself, and unrelenting worries had done the rest to undermine resistance.

The doctor cautioned him against exposing himself for the ten days allotted to the job at Flat River. Accidents prolonged the work for a month, through disagreeable weather; and on his return to Chicago, King learned that the lesion was now as large as his hand. So he yielded to his yearning for the tropics, going first to Florida in hope of relief, then on to the West Indies. "Sick as I was," he told a friend, "I embraced the divine palm trees, and swore a new allegiance to the tropical seas."

But the sun brought King no cure; his disease made galloping progress so that in April he renounced the islands. He returned to Washington in time to help vote Becker into the National Academy of Sciences and to see Alexander Agassiz chosen president. He seemed "fairly gay," wrote Adams, "even in paroxysms of coughing." Perhaps even then Adams and Hay sensed the irony of his quest. "The sunshine of life had not been so dazzling of late," Adams observed of their parting, "but that a share of it flickered out for [him] and Hay when King disappeared from their lives."*

Next, King made a cheerless trip to Newport to see his mother, in spite of fears that his wasted look might send her to the grave. Then he returned to Flushing to tell Ada of his arrangements for the future. She must take the children to Canada, where feelings against the colored were less intense. Toronto was his suggestion for a home. It would be hard, he knew, for her to uproot herself from Prince Street; but, "I cannot express to you," he wrote later, "what relief it is to me to have you get away from the place where you have lived so long and so comfortably, but where so many people felt curiosity about you and me." He added, "Whenever anyone asks about your husband tell them that you and [he] have agreed to separate and that you do not like to

* For Gore Vidal's touching fictional re-creation of King's last meeting with Henry Adams and the Hays see *Empire* (New York, 1987), pp. 272–78. "Although King was dying," Vidal writes, "he was determined to go in a great display of mind and wit and energy." In the scene that follows the novelist artfully invokes the warm goodfellowship of the four remaining Hearts. At the same time he is at pains to remind the reader that, "now that his life was near its end, [King] had managed to fail in the grandest manner." All that would remain would be "the memory that the Hearts all had of a glorious companion who could sit up till dawn speaking on the origins of life," or they could go view the grand peak named Clarence King in the Sierra Nevada. "A mountain and a memory were not much," Hay reflects, "but then what a life King had had."

discuss your family matters." He would try hard to live, he promised her, because of the children and his plans for their education. Meanwhile, she must enroll them at the Logan School, which he understood was the finest school in Toronto. He made her promise, also, not to worry about finances; whatever happened, she would be provided for. He could not tell her about his art collection, but it was worth far more than the chattel mortgages that Hay held against it, and friends like Hay and Gardiner would see that his wishes were carried out in case of his death. One of King's chief concerns was to quiet Ada's apprehensions as he prepared to leave her. He kissed her goodbye at the railroad station on May 9, 1901.

At first he tried the crisp air of Prescott, Arizona. But an all-day fever consumed his strength, and his heart faltered. The local doctor then sent him to California for the regimen of a Pasadena specialist. During a temporary rally he got condolences off to John Hay on the deaths of his son and his close friend Nicolay—a letter which Hay found "heartbreaking in grace and tenderness—the old King manner." But the fever smoldered on, and by the last of August King had lost forty pounds. Sometimes he fell into a dreamlike state, in which he relived the past, running the Fortieth Parallel Survey and climbing the peaks of his youth. Or, when his head cleared up, he would make compulsive attempts at self-analysis to probe the springs of his failure. He knew that his life as a field geologist was finished, his hammer forever laid away, whatever the gods might grant. "But I am fuller of geological ideas than ever," he declared, "and I shall mass and publish them if I get a reprieve." That, he sensed, might redeem the gravest error of his life, his virtual abandonment of science for the lure of business.

Meanwhile, he allowed himself to hope that his youthful achievements might be remembered, that Yale might honor him at her bicentennial celebration. But even that, though several friends worked hard on the university authorities, proved only a vain dream. A no more favorable outcome would meet the effort of Howells to secure King's election to the National Institute of Arts and Letters, now in its fourth year, membership in which was considered paramount recognition of creative achievement in America. Howells served as president, and the founding members—nearly 150 strong—included other bosom friends of King, so that his cause had staunch support, Hay calling membership for him "a felt want." There were vacancies caused by death, including that of Charles Dudley Warner, the institute's first president. But Quincy Ward, whose name was proposed at the same time as King's, would not gain membership till 1902. It would seem, therefore, that Howells had moved too late to win for King this urbane honor before his death would intervene.

The Pasadena doctor failed, and in the fall King moved to Phoenix, where he settled down in a new brick cottage, "as clean as a fresh shaving." Dr. Craig, the local physician, seemed more optimistic than King himself, who burned with fever. King had no fear of death for himself, but he grieved about his mother, * and worried over what the future held for Ada and the children.

Unable to tell his attendants that mail would come for him addressed to "James Todd," he felt obliged to confess his true identity to Ada, for incredibly she had not yet learned his real name. He asked her to record it in her Bible, so that she could refer to it in case it slipped her memory. He vowed to her that it was his "strongest desire" to legalize their union, if the opportunity should come; and, "You may want to take my name," he suggested, ". . . and have the children's name changed in the New York State Court at Albany. . . . I have studied it all out and consulted a good lawyer about it, and my only wish before God and for you is to do the very best thing for us all, and I am perfectly sure that what I have advised you is the best." Meanwhile, he kept Gardiner posted about his condition, so that his old friend might be prepared to handle his affairs in case he lost the fight. Two weeks in autumn were then cheered by a visit of Emmons and by their whimsical talk about Don Quixote.

Then one day in December, during a fit of coughing, King noticed blood on his handkerchief. Foreseeing a hemorrhage, he asked his servant to call the doctor. Then he knotted towels around the top of each arm and leg to stem the return flow of blood—precautions that saved him from immediate death. The doctor arrived, and King seemed to rally. He wanted no relative to see him now, least of all his mother; but Captain Clarence Townsley, his brother-in-law, heard of the crisis and rushed to Arizona as fast as the train could bring him.

The end was near, a matter (as King had put it) of "simply waiting till nature and the foe have done their struggle," but his sense of humor did not fail him. During a lucid moment in his delirium he heard the doctor say that the heroin must have gone to his head. Many a heroine, King

---

* After King's death Mrs. Howland wrote, "My one bitter and inconsolable regret is that I was not with him in those final months as I would have been had I known half the truth. But he wrote hopefully and said he would be home in April" (letter to Charles Webb Howard, January 17, 1902, J. D. Hague Collection).

replied, had gone to better heads than his was now. Perhaps it was his last pun; he died peacefully in his sleep the day before Christmas, 1901, at two in the morning. He had told the physician of Ada, and Dr. Craig telegraphed her at Toronto, and later wrote her more at length; and on preparing the death certificate he placed an M in the space for marital status.

"Yes, I knew Clarence King . . ." wrote Stedman in New York. "There was no one else like him. He has not left his fellow in wit, humor, zest, charm, and all that goes to make a man the life of the best company, and, as a loyal friend, one to inspire a love passing the love of women."

Captain Townsley brought the body back to Manhattan. From the White House came Theodore Roosevelt's wire of condolence, while King's coffin lay on a bank of flowers at the Brick Presbyterian Church, which John La Farge had decorated years before. (It was in the same church that Mark Twain would lie in state within the decade.) On New Year's morning, 1902, a day of arctic cold, the poet-minister Henry van Dyke read from the Bible and said a prayer instead of a sermon. The choir sang "Peace, Perfect Peace"; and amidst a fifty-man delegation from the Century Club, William Dean Howells could sense King's "smiling presence." Then Henry Adams, just home from Europe, helped to bear the casket out into the freezing wind, in company with Emmons, Gardiner, the two Hagues, Edward Cary, and Albert Bierstadt, the latter's own death just weeks away.

The next day a dozen mourners followed the hearse through Newport streets to an open grave in the Island Cemetery, near the burial spots of King's two infant sisters. Space was reserved beside the new grave for the final resting place of Mrs. Howland. Then soon a white marble headstone read:

"I am the Resurrection
and the Life," saith the Lord.

Epilogue

Ada did not remain long in Canada. After King's death she returned to New York City, where she made contact with Gardiner by means of an advertisement she placed in the daily *Herald,* among the personals on the front page. At once Gardiner's secretary installed her and the children in a small house on Kalmia Street, in Flushing, for which John Hay furnished the purchase money. There she lived with her family on sixty-five dollars a month, later reduced to fifty, which she thought derived from a trust fund that King had authorized.

In time the children, except the dead Leroy, grew to undistinguished maturity. Grace married a white policeman named James Burns and bore him a daughter whom they called Thelma and a son named Clarence. The younger Ada married a white soldier, Virgil Hite, but she soon divorced him and resumed the name of King. Later she figured as a material witness in a Bayside murder case. Her ex-husband was suspected of having shot a married junk dealer who was dating Ada in a local lovers' lane, but the police could never find him, and the crime was left unsolved. Wallace became a frequently unemployed musician, while Sidney was a construction worker who broke down after service in the First World War and was confined as an incompetent schizophrenic in the Kings Park State Hospital on Long Island.

In later years Ada the elder grew enormously fat. She also grew greedy for the principal of King's alleged trust fund—eighty thousand dollars, she believed. The payments she had received over the years had in reality come from the largesse of John Hay, then of his widow, and then still later of their son-in-law Payne Whitney, and finally of Mrs. Helen Hay Whitney after her husband's death. All of these benefactors had remained anonymous—quiet well-wishers whose chief concern had been to protect the sensibilities of King's white family and to ensure that his black family always had food on the table. Their contributions were transmitted through the office of the Legal Aid Society.

Then in 1931, after moves by Ada to put her claim into the hands of a lawyer, Mrs. Whitney stopped the monthly payments, leaving Ada dependent on her sporadic wages as a houseworker and on Sidney's meager V.A. check. Thereupon Ada and the children sued the trustees and the heirs of the Gardiner estate for possession of the presumed trust fund. The case dragged on for nearly three years, with the plaintiffs' lone witness discredited for undue imagination about the details of Ada's wedding ceremony and for having identified a photograph of President Garfield as that of King himself. The last resulted from a clever ploy by the defense attorneys, for there was at least a moderate facial resemblance between King and Garfield.

In November 1933 the New York State Supreme Court ruled that King had died insolvent, owing to the chattel mortgages John Hay had held on his art collection; that the proceeds from the sale in 1903 of this collection had, through the generosity of Hay, gone to support Mrs. Howland until her death in 1911; and that no trust fund had ever been established in favor of Ada or her children. They had merely been the objects of charity. In addition, the court denied the legality of Ada's ceremony in 1888, though it found that she and King had lived together "as Mr. and Mrs. James Todd." Thus their union could be properly styled a common-law marriage. Ada received title to the house on Kalmia Street, and presumably she continued to live there until her death over four decades after that of Clarence King.

Selected Bibliography

Federal Archives Consulted

National Archives, Washington, D.C.

Record Group 27. Records of the Weather Bureau. In this R.G. are filed the Matthew Maury Logs (transcripts).

Record Group 29. Records of the Bureau of the Census.

Record Group 48. General Records of the Department of the Interior.

Record Group 57. Records of the U.S. Geological Survey. In addition to U.S.G.S. records proper, this R. G. contains the files of predecessor organizations, including:

Records of the Hayden Survey (U.S. Geological and Geographical Survey of the Territories).

Records of the King Survey (U.S. Geological Exploration of the Fortieth Parallel), comprising one Letter Book of King's communications with General A. A. Humphreys and a file of Letters Received.

Records of the Powell Survey (U.S. Geographical and Geological Survey of the Rocky Mountain Region).

Records of the Wheeler Survey (U.S. Geographical Surveys West of the One Hundredth Meridian), comprising only a small fraction of Wheeler's files.

Record Group 59. General Records of the Department of State. In this R.G. is filed the correspondence of King, John Hay, and others with Secretary William M. Evarts concerning the appointment of Bret Harte to the Consular Service.

Record Group 77. Records of the Office of the Chief of Engineers. In this R.G. are filed originals of King letters and reports to General A. A. Humphreys. This R.G. also holds the bulk of the Wheeler archives in federal custody. Other Wheeler materials are found in the Western Americana Collection at Yale.

Record Group 101. Records of the Bureau of the Comptroller of the Currency. This R.G. holds a file on the failure and receivership of the El Paso National Bank in 1893 (No. 246).

Miscellaneous materials in the National Archives:
> Cartographic Records Branch. The holdings of this branch include cartographic materials of the King Survey and of King and Gardiner's reconnaissance in Arizona during the winter of 1865–66 under the command of General Irvin McDowell.
> Still Pictures Section. In the holdings of this section are the Timothy O'Sullivan photographs for the King Survey. They are supplemented by O'Sullivan photographs at the Bancroft Lib., the Lib. of Congress, the M.I.T. Lib., and the U.S. Geological Survey (Denver) among other places.

Smithsonian Institution, Washington, D.C. Accessions File and Letters Received.

N.B. My examination of federal records while researching for the first edition of this book involved original documents. Most of these records have since become available on microfilm.

Other Manuscript Collections Consulted

Adams (Charles Francis, Jr.) Papers, Massachusetts Historical Society, Boston.

The Adams Family Papers, Massachusetts Historical Society (Microfilm Reels 589–600).

Adams (Henry) Papers, Massachusetts Historical Society, Boston (microfilm).

American Museum of Natural History Letter Files, Museum Library, New York City.

Ashburner (William) Letters to William H. Brewer (C-B 504), Bancroft Lib., Berkeley.

Bailey (William Whitney) Papers.
> Brown Univ. Lib., Providence.
> Henry E. Huntington Lib., San Marino, Calif.
> New York Botanical Gardens Lib., The Bronx.

Bancroft Scraps, Bancroft Lib., Univ. of California, Berkeley.

Barlow (S. L. M.) Coll., Henry E. Huntington Lib., San Marino.

Becker (George F.) Papers, Lib. of Congress, Washington, D.C.

Boston News Service Clipping File, Baker Lib., Harvard Univ., Cambridge.

Brewer (William H.) Diaries, 1860–1864 (C-B 332); Notebooks and Field Books, 1860–1864 (C-B 224), Bancroft Lib., Univ. of California, Berkeley.

Brewer (William H.) Papers, Mss. and Archives, Yale Lib., New Haven.

Brewer (William H.) and J. D. Whitney Correspondence (C-B 312), Bancroft Lib., Univ. of California, Berkeley.

Brush (George J.) Papers, Mss. and Archives, Yale Lib., New Haven.

Cater (Harold Dean) transcripts of Clarence King letters, Cater Coll., Massachusetts Historical Society, Boston. There are some original King-to-Adams letters in the Cater Coll., but none not represented among the transcripts. The originals of the King-to-Hay letters are in Hay Papers at the John Hay Lib. at Brown Univ.

Connecticut State Census, Connecticut State Lib., Hartford.

Cooper-Hewitt Papers.

    Cooper Union Lib., New York City.

    Lib. of Congress, Washington, D.C.

    New-York Historical Society, New York City.

Crawford (F. L.) Notes, State Historical Society of North Dakota, Bismarck.

Cushing (Caleb) Papers, Lib. of Congress, Washington, D.C.

Dall (William H.) Papers, Record Unit 7073, Smithsonian Institution Archives, Washington, D.C.

Darrah (William C.) Coll. of Powell Materials, Gettysburg, Pa.

Davis (N. R.) Account Books and related papers, Philip Ashton Rollins Coll., Princeton Univ. Lib., Princeton.

Draper (Henry) Papers, New York Public Lib., New York City.

Dwight (Theodore F.) Coll., Massachusetts Historical Society, Boston.

Emmons (S. F.) Papers, Lib. of Congress, Washington, D. C. (Certain other Emmons materials are held in R.G. 57, the National Archives.)

Farquhar (Francis P.) Coll. of materials relating to Clarence King (Film C-B 542), Bancroft Lib., Univ. of California, Berkeley. These papers were still in Farquhar's possession when I was allowed to transcribe them. Originals of a number of the filmed items are now in the Huntington Lib.

Farquhar (Francis P.) Correspondence and Papers (C-B 517), Bancroft Lib., Berkeley.

Fields (James T.) Papers, Henry E. Huntington Lib., San Marino, Calif.

Frewen (Moreton) Papers, Lib. of Congress (microfilm examined at Columbia Univ. Lib.).

Gardiner (James T.) Papers (GL 11835), in the William C. Doane Coll., New York State Lib., Albany.

Gilman (Daniel Coit) Papers, The Johns Hopkins Univ. Lib., Baltimore.

Gray (Asa) Letter Files, Gray Herbarium, Harvard Univ., Cambridge.

Hague (Arnold) Letter Books and Papers—though largely a personal collection, these papers are held in R.G. 57, the National Archives.

Hague (James D.) Coll., Henry E. Huntington Lib., San Marino, Calif.

Hay (John) Papers.

    John Hay Lib., Brown Univ. Lib., Providence.

    Lib. of Congress, Washington, D.C.

    New York Public Lib. (scrapbooks and clippings), New York City.

Hayes (Rutherford B.) Presidential Coll., Rutherford B. Hayes Presidential Center, Fremont, Ohio.

Heard Family Commercial Papers, Baker Lib., Harvard Univ., Cambridge.

Higginson (Henry L.) Business Papers, Baker Lib., Harvard Univ., Cambridge.

Higginson (Thomas Wentworth) Diaries, Houghton Lib., Harvard Univ., Cambridge.

Hoffmann (Charles F.) Letters to J. D. Whitney and William H. Brewer (C-B 505), Bancroft Lib., Univ. of California, Berkeley.

Howells (William Dean) Papers, Houghton Lib., Harvard Univ., Cambridge.

King (Clarence) Papers, Henry E. Huntington Lib., San Marino (approximately 750 items, including personal papers of King and numerous items assembled by J. D. Hague in connection with Clarence King Memoirs; the collection is supplemented by miscellaneous materials of the King Survey held by the American Museum of Natural History and by a few King manuscripts at the Century Club, New York City).

King (Clarence) will, file no. 682-94 (Mar. 17, 1902), Records of the Surrogate Court of New York County, New York County Clerk's Office, New York City.

King (Sidney) incompetency case, file no. 12586-1921, Records of New York State Supreme Court, Kings County Clerk's Office, Brooklyn.

King vs. Peabody et al., file no. 76821-1931, Records of the New York State Supreme Court, New York County Clerk's Office, New York City.

Lowell (James Russell) Papers, Houghton Lib., Harvard Univ., Cambridge.

Marsh (O. C.) Papers, Peabody Museum Lib., Yale (supplemented by Marsh materials in Mss. and Archives, Yale Univ. Lib.), New Haven.

Meek (F. B.) Papers, Record Unit 7062, Smithsonian Institution Archives, Washington, D.C.

Merrill (George P.) Coll., Lib. of Congress, Washington, D.C.

Morrison, George A. "The King Families of New England" (unpublished manuscript), Vol. I, New York Public Lib., New York City.

Nebraska Writers Project. "First Herds and Ranches in Nebraska" (History of Grazing, LC-AC DR A512), Lib. of Congress, Washington, D.C.

Nelson, Clifford M. Biographical compilation on Clarence King. Office of Scientific Publications, U.S. Geological Survey, Reston, Va.

Newcomb (Simon) Papers, Lib. of Congress, Washington, D.C.

Newton (Benjamin) Shipping Papers, Baker Lib., Harvard Univ., Cambridge.

New York State Census, New York State Lib., Albany.

New York State Corporation Records, Department of State, Albany.

Olmsted (Frederick Law) Papers, Lib. of Congress, Washington, D.C. (microfilm).

Overland Monthly Account Book (1869–1875) and Letter Book, Univ. of California Lib., Berkeley.

Pumpelly (Raphael) Papers, Huntington Lib., San Marino, Calif.

Redman, J. T. "Reminiscences and Experiences on My Trip across the Plains to California Sixty-One Years Ago When I Drove Four Mules to a Covered

Wagon," Marshall, Mo., June 17, 1924, HM 20462, Henry E. Huntington Lib. Without question this account was based on a diary of the trip; another copy is found in the Ayer Coll., Newberry Lib., Chicago.

Rogers (William B.) Papers (MC 1), M.I.T. Lib., Cambridge, Mass.

Schurz (Carl) Papers, Lib. of Congress, Washington, D.C. (microfilm).

Sheffield Scientific School Archives, Mss. and Archives, Yale Univ. Lib., New Haven.

Sombrerete Mining Company Minutes Book, Sombrerete Mining Co., New York City.

Stedman (Edmund Clarence) Papers, Special Colls., Columbia Univ. Lib., New York City.

Suydam (Mary Ludwig) Papers, Historical Society of Pennsylvania, Philadelphia.

The United States vs. Edgar Beecher Bronson (1893), Files 823 and 989, Records of the U.S. District Court, El Paso.

Walcott (Charles D.) Papers, Record Unit 7004, Smithsonian Institution Archives, Washington, D.C.

Walker (Francis A.) Papers, M.I.T. Lib., Cambridge, Mass.

Watson (Sereno) Letter Files and Field Books, Gray Herbarium, Harvard Univ., Cambridge.

Weston Papers, Boston Public Lib., Boston.

W. D. Whitney Coll. of Whitney Family Papers, Mss. and Archives, Yale Univ. Lib., New Haven.

Willis (Bailey) Papers, Huntington Lib., San Marino.

Wyoming Stock Growers Association Archives, Univ. of Wyoming Lib., Laramie.

Yale College Class of 1862 Scrapbook, Yale Memorabilia Room, New Haven.

Published Works Consulted

Congressional Documents

35th Cong., 2nd Sess., S. Ex. Doc. 22 (Serial 982), ". . . Correspondence of Messrs. McLane and Parker, Late Commissioners to China." Washington, 1859.

36th Cong., 1st Sess., S. Ex. Doc. 30 (Serial 1032), ". . . the Instruction to, and Dispatches from, the Late and Present Ministers to China." Washington, 1860.

43rd Cong., 1st Sess., House Report 612 (Serial 1626), "Geographical and Geological Surveys West of the Mississippi." Washington, 1874.

44th Cong., 1st Sess., House Report 579 (Serial 1711), "The Emma Mine Investigation." Washington, 1876.

45th Cong., 2nd Sess., House Ex. Doc. 80 (Serial 1809), "Geological and Geographical Surveys . . . Report of Professor Powell." Washington, 1878.

45th Cong., 2nd Sess., House Ex. Doc. 81 (Serial 1809), "Geological and Geographical Surveys . . . Report of Professor Hayden." Washington, 1878.

45th Cong., 3rd Sess., House Ex. Doc. 72 (Serial 1858), "Cost of Geographical Surveys." Washington, 1879.

45th Cong., 3rd Sess., House Misc. Doc. 5 (Serial 1861), "A Report [of the National Academy of Sciences] on the Surveys of the Territories." Washington, 1879.

46th Cong., 2nd Sess., House Ex. Doc. 46 (Serial 1923), "Report of the Public Lands Commission, Created by the Act of Mar. 3, 1879." Washington, 1880.

48th Cong., 2nd Sess., House Ex. Doc. 267 (Serial 2304), "[The Nimo Report on] . . . Range and Cattle Traffic in the Western States and Territories." Washington, 1885.

49th Cong., 1st Sess., S. Misc. Doc. 82 (Serial 2345), "Testimony before the Joint Commission to consider the present organization of the Signal Service, Geological Survey, Coast and Geodetic Survey, and the Hydrographic Office of the Navy Department." Washington, 1886.

54th Cong., 1st Sess., S. Report 141 (Serial 3362), "Hostilities in Cuba." Washington, 1896.

54th Cong., 2nd Sess., S. Report 1160 (Serial 3474), "Recognition of Cuban Independence." Washington, 1897.

The Works of Clarence King

"Active Glaciers Within the United States," Atlantic Mo., XXVII (March 1871), 371–77.

"The Age of the Earth," American Journal of Science, XLV (Jan. 1893), 1–20. Reprinted in Smithsonian Institution, Annual Report, 1893 (Washington, 1894), pp. 335–52.

Annual Reports (1871–1878), U.S. Geological Exploration of the Fortieth Parallel:

[Report of Clarence King, Geologist in Charge, for 1871], in Report of the Secretary of War, Report of the Chief of Engineers: 42nd Cong., 2nd Sess., House Ex. Doc. 1, Part 2, Vol. 2 (Serial 1504), Appendix Z, pp. 1027–30.

"Geological Exploration of the 40th Parallel, from the Sierra Nevada to the Eastern Slope of the Rocky Mountains [1872], in Report of the Secretary of War, Report of the Chief of Engineers: 42nd Cong., 3rd Sess., House Ex. Doc. 1, Part 2, Vol. 2 (Serial 1559), pp. 101–2.

"Report of Mr. Clarence King, Geologist . . . [1873]," in Report of the Secretary of War, Report of the Chief of Engineers: 43rd Cong., 1st Sess., House Ex. Doc. 1, Part 2, Vol. 2 (Serial 1598), Appendix DD, pp. 1203–10.

"Annual Report of Mr. Clarence King, Geologist, for the Fiscal Year

Ending June 30, 1874," in *Report of the Secretary of War, Report of the Chief of Engineers*: 43rd Cong., 2nd Sess., House Ex. Doc. 1, Part 2, Vol. 2, Part 2 (Serial 1637), Appendix EE, pp. 477–80.

"Annual Report of Mr. Clarence King, Geologist, for the Fiscal Year Ending June 30, 1875," in *Report of the Secretary of War, Report of the Chief of Engineers*: 44th Cong., 1st Sess., House Ex. Doc. 1, Part 2, Vol. 2 (Serial 1676), Appendix KK, pp. 919–920.

"Annual Report of Mr. Clarence King, Geologist, for the Fiscal Year Ending June 30, 1876," in *Report of the Secretary of War, Report of the Chief of Engineers*: 44th Cong., 2nd Sess., House Ex. Doc. 1, Part 2, Vol. 2, Part 3 (Serial 1745), Appendix II, pp. 217–218.

"Annual Report of Mr. Clarence King, Geologist, for the Fiscal Year Ending June 30, 1877," in *Report of the Secretary of War, Report of the Chief of Engineers*: 45th Cong., 2nd Sess., House Ex. Doc. 1, Part 2, Vol. 2, Part 2 (Serial 1796), Appendix MM, p. 1207.

"Annual Report of Mr. Clarence King, Geologist, for the Fiscal Year Ending June 30, 1878," in *Report of the Secretary of War, Report of the Chief of Engineers*: 45th Cong., 3rd Sess., House Ex. Doc. 1, Part 2, Vol. 2, Part 3 (Serial 1846), Appendix MM, p. 1419.

"Artium Magister," *North American Rev.*, CXLVII (Oct. 1888), 369–84.

"The Ascent of Mount Tyndall," *Atlantic Mo.*, XXVIII (July 1871), 64–76.

"Bancroft's Native Races of the Pacific States," *Atlantic Mo.*, XXXV (Feb. 1875), 163–73.

"The Biographers of Lincoln," *Century Mag.*, XXXII (Oct. 1886), 861–69.

"Catastrophism and Evolution," *American Naturalist*, XI (1877), 449–70. Delivered at the 31st anniversary of the Sheffield Scientific School, on June 26, 1877, under the title of "Catastrophism and the Evolution of Environment," and published the following day in New York *Daily Tribune* under the same title. It was also issued under this title as a pamphlet of 37 pages.

"Copy of the Official Letter Addressed November 11th, 1872, to the Board of Directors of the San Francisco and New York Mining and Commercial Company by Clarence King, Geologist in Charge, Discovering the New Diamond Fields to be a Fraud." [San Francisco], n.d. The letter was also published in the *Mining and Scientific Press*, XXV (1872), 344, and in the *Engineering and Mining Journal*, XIV (1872), 379–80.

"The Descent of Mount Tyndall," *Atlantic Mo.*, XXVIII (Aug. 1871), 207–215.

"A Desert Sport." *Century Mag.*, LXXVI (June 1908), 286–92. (Signed by Edgar Beecher Bronson, but the body of the piece comprises what seems to be a literal transcript of an oral yarn by King. Bronson was expert at shorthand.)

"The Education of the Future," *Forum*, XIII (Mar. 1892), 20–33.

"The Falls of the Shoshone," *Overland Mo.*, V (Oct. 1870), 379–85.

"Fire and Sword in Cuba," *Forum*, XXII (Sept. 1896), 31–52.

First Annual Report of the United States Geological Survey, Washington, 1880.

"A General View of the Prescott Region . . . ," in *Report of J. Ross Browne on Mineral Resources of the States and Territories West of the Rocky Mountains*, pp. 467–74. Washington, 1868. Reprinted in the *Arizona Miner*, Jan. 23, 1869.

"A Great Mining Area [Cordilleran region]," *Mining and Scientific Press*, LXXX (April 26, 1900), 577–78. Derived from testimony that King gave at Rossland, B.C., in 1899.

"The Helmet of Mambrino," *Century Mag.*, XXXII (May 1886), 154–59. Reprinted in *Clarence King Memoirs* (New York, 1904), pp. 5–36; also as a separate booklet by the Book Club of California (San Francisco, 1938), with an introduction by Francis P. Farquhar. The Century Club of New York City now holds the original manuscript.

"Introductory Remarks," pp. vii–xiv, of *Statistics and Technology of the Precious Metals*, prepared under the direction of Clarence King, Special Agent, by S. F. Emmons and G. F. Becker, Washington, 1885 (Report of the U.S. [10th] Census, Vol. XIII).

"John Hay" (unsigned), *Scribner's Mo.*, VII (April 1874), 736–39. F. L. Pattee in *History of American Literature Since 1870*, p. 88, attributes this sketch to King; Tyler Dennett, biographer of Hay, accepts the attribution.

"Kaweah's Run," *Atlantic Mo.*, XXVIII (Oct. 1871), 396–405.

"Map of the Yosemite Valley from Surveys made by order of the Commissioners to manage the Yosemite Valley and Mariposa Big Tree Grove by C. King and J. T. Gardner 1865." New York, n.d. The map also accompanies *The Yosemite Book* (New York, 1868) and *The Yosemite Guide-Book* (Cambridge, 1869 and 1870).

Mining Industry (by James D. Hague, with geological contributions by Clarence King), Vol. III of the *Report of the U.S. Geological Exploration of the Fortieth Parallel.* Washington, 1870. King's contributions are "Mining Districts," pp. 1–9; "The Comstock Lode," pp. 11–96; "The Green River Coal Basin," pp. 451–73.

Mountaineering in the Sierra Nevada. 1st ed., Boston, 1872.

Mountaineering in the Sierra Nevada. 4th ed., with additions including maps, a preface dated March 1874, and seventeen new pages in the chapter on Mount Whitney. Boston, 1874.

Mountaineering in the Sierra Nevada. New ed., with minor textual changes "indicated" by King and with the 1874 preface. New York, 1902.

Mountaineering in the Sierra Nevada. Edited, with a preface and notes by Francis P. Farquhar. New York, 1935. There have been a number of reprints of *Mountaineering*, but only the editions here listed have been used for these researches.

"Note on the Uinta and Wahsatch Ranges," *American Journal of Science*, 3rd ser., XI (1876), 494.

Notes on Observed Glacial Phenomena and the Terminal Moraine of the N.E. Glacier, *Proceedings of the Boston Society of Natural History*, XIX (1876), 60–63.

"On the Discovery of Actual Glaciers in the Mountains of the Pacific Slope," *American Journal of Science*, 3rd ser., I (Mar. 1871), 157–67.

"Paleozoic Subdivisions of the Fortieth Parallel," *American Journal of Science*, 3rd ser., XI (1876), 475–82.

"Production of the Precious Metals in the United States," in the *Second Annual Report of the United States Geological Survey*, pp. 331–401, with plates xlviii–liii. Washington, 1881.

"The Range," *Atlantic Mo.*, XXVII (May 1871), 602–13.

Report of climb to Mount Tyndall, in J. D. Whitney, State Geologist, California State Geological Survey, *Geology*, I (Philadelphia, 1865), 384–87.

"Report of Mr. Clarence King," in the *Second Annual Report of the United States Geological Survey*, pp. 44–46. Washington, 1881.

"Report of Mr. Clarence King [on the] Physical Constants of Rocks," in the *Third Annual Report of the United States Geological Survey*, pp. 3–9. Washington, 1883. Actually prepared by a colleague at King's request.

Reviews (unsigned) of *The Andes and the Amazon; or, Across the Continent of South America* (New York, 1870), by James Orton; of *The Mississippi Valley: Its Physical Geography* (Chicago, 1869), by G. W. Foster; and of *Sketches of Creation* (New York, 1870), by Alexander Winchell. *Overland Mo.*, V (Dec. 1870), 578–83.

"Shall Cuba Be Free?" *Forum*, XX (Sept. 1895), 50–65.

"Shasta," *Atlantic Mo.*, XXVIII (Dec. 1871), 710–20.

Statistics of the Production of the Precious Metals in the United States. Washington, 1881.

"Style and the Monument" (unsigned), *North American Rev.*, CXLI (Nov. 1885), 443–53.

Systematic Geology, Vol. I of *Report of the U. S. Geological Exploration of the Fortieth Parallel.* Washington, 1878.

"Testimony on Rossland Veins and Minerals," *Mining* (Mar. 1900), 99–105.

The Three Lakes: Marian, Lall, Jan, and How They Were Named. [San Francisco], Christmas 1870. Copy (said to be one of three) consulted in Rare Book Room, New York Public Lib. Reprinted with an introduction by Francis P. Farquhar in *Sierra Club Bulletin*, XXIV (1939), No. 3; issued also as a pamphlet offprint.

"Through the Forest," *Atlantic Mo.*, XXVII (June 1871), 704–14.

U.S. Mining Laws and Regulations Thereunder and State and Territorial Mining Laws to which are appended Local Mining Rules, Compiled under the Direction of Hon. Clarence King, Special Agent, Tenth Census. Washington, 1885. (Report of U.S. [10th] Census, Vol. XIV).

"Wayside Pikes," *Atlantic Mo.*, XXVIII (Nov. 1871), 564–76.

Other Books and Articles, including Government Publications
Adams, Charles Francis, Jr. *Charles Francis Adams: An Autobiography.* Boston, 1916.
Adams, Henry. Editorial comments on the King Survey, *North American Rev.*, CXIII, No. 233 (July 1871), 204.
————. *The Degradation of the Democratic Dogma.* New York, 1919. Edited with a long introductory essay by Brooks Adams.
[————.] *Democracy: an American Novel.* New York, 1880.
————. *The Education of Henry Adams: An Autobiography.* Boston, 1918.
[————,] *Esther, A Novel,* by Francis Snow Compton. Scholars' Facsimiles and Reprints ed., New York, 1938.
————. *Henry Adams and His Friends: A Collection of His Unpublished Letters,* ed. with a long biographical introduction by Harold Dean Cater. Boston, 1947.
————. *Letters of Henry Adams,* ed. Worthington C. Ford. 2 vols. (1858–1891 and 1892–1918). Boston and New York, 1930–1938.
————. *The Letters of Henry Adams,* ed. J. C. Levenson *et. al.* Vols. I–III (1858–1868; 1868–1885; 1886–1892). Cambridge, Mass., 1982.
————. *Letters to a Niece and Prayer to the Virgin of Chartres,* with a Niece's Memories, by Mabel La Farge. Boston, 1920.
[————.] Note on Clarence King, *Nation,* XXV (Aug. 30, 1877), 137.
[————.] Review of *Mountaineering, North American Rev.*, CXIV (April 1872), 445–48.
[————.] Review of *Systematic Geology, Nation,* XXVIII (Jan. 23, 1879), 73–74.
Adams, James Truslow, *The Adams Family.* Boston, 1930.
————. *Henry Adams,* New York, 1933.
Adams, Marian Hooper. *The Letters of Mrs. Henry Adams, 1865–1883,* ed. Ward Thoron. Boston, 1936.
Agassiz, George R. *Letters and Recollections of Alexander Agassiz.* Boston, 1913.
American Art Galleries. *Catalogue of the Art and Literary Property Collected by the Late Clarence King.* New York, 1903.
————. *Catalogue of Valuable Paintings and Water Colors . . . of the Late Clarence King.* New York, 1903.
American Board of Commissioners for Foreign Missions. *Report 1838.*
Anderson (Navarro), Mary. *A Few Memories.* New York, 1896.
Armstrong, David Maitland. *Day Before Yesterday: Reminiscences of a Varied Life.* New York, 1920.
Arnold, Matthew. *Letters of Matthew Arnold, 1848–1888,* ed. George W. E. Russell. New York, 1900.
Asbury, Herbert. "Great Diamond Swindle," *American Mercury,* XXVI (May 1932), 41–49.

Asplund, Karl. *Anders Zorn: His Life and Work*. London, 1921.

Atherton, Gertrude. *California: An Intimate History.* New York, 1914.

Badè, William F. *The Life and Letters of John Muir.* 2 vols. Boston, 1923–1924.

Bailey, William Whitman. "Decisive Moments," *Brown University Alumni Mo.,* Jan. 1913, pp. 142–43.

————. "Recollections of the West Humboldt Mountains," *Appalachia,* IV (July 1885), 151–54.

[————.] "Scenery of Nevada," *Appleton's Journal,* V (May 1871), 616–18.

Balch, William R. *The Mines, Miners, and Mining Interests of the United States.* Philadelphia, 1882.

Bancroft, H. H. *The History of Mexico,* Vol. VI. San Francisco, 1888.

————. *Literary Industries.* New York, 1891.

Bartlett, Richard A. "Clarence King's Fortieth Parallel Survey," *Utah Historical Quart.,* XXIV (1956), 131–47.

————. *Great Surveys of the American West.* Norman, Okla., 1962. See Part II, pp. 123–215, for Bartlett's treatment of King and the King Survey.

Becker, George F. "Antiquities from under Tuolumne Table Mountain," *Bulletin of the Geological Society of America,* II (1891), 189–98.

————. "Biographical Notice of Samuel Franklin Emmons," *Transactions of the American Institute of Mining Engineers,* XLII (1911), 643–61.

————. *The Geology of the Comstock Lode and the Washoe District.* U.S.G.S. Monograph No. III. Washington, 1882.

Bell, P. L., and H. Bentley MacKenzie. *Mexican West Coast and Lower California.* Washington, D.C., 1923.

Benjamin, Marcus. "The Cosmos Club and its Relation to Men of Letters." Pamphlet. [Washington, 1928.]

Besant, Walter. *The Autobiography of Walter Besant.* New York, 1902.

Bishop, Isabella (Bird). *The Hawaiian Archipelago.* London, 1875.

Bishop, Joseph Bucklin. *Notes and Anecdotes of Many Years.* New York, 1925.

Blackmur, R. P. *Henry Adams,* ed. Veronica Makowsky. New York, 1980.

Boethius, Gerda. *Zorn.* Stockholm, 1949. Figure 32 in Boethius is a reproduction of Zorn's watercolor portrait of King.

Brace, Charles Loring. *The New West; or, California in 1867 and '68.* New York, 1869.

Brewer, William H. "John Wesley Powell," *American Journal of Science,* 4th ser., XIV (1902), 377–82.

————. Remarks before the Appalachian Club, March 5, 1886, *Appalachia,* IV (1886), 367–69.

————. ". . . Sereno Watson, 1820–1892," National Academy of Sciences, *Biographical Memoirs,* V (1905), 267–90.

[————.] "Two 'Bubbles'—How They Differed," *Nation,* XV (Dec. 19, 1872), 406–7.

————. *Up and Down California in 1860–1864: the Journal of William H. Brewer, Professor of Agriculture in the Sheffield Scientific School from 1864 to 1903*, ed. Francis P. Farquhar. New Haven, 1930.

Brewster, Edwin Tenney. *Life and Letters of Josiah Dwight Whitney.* Boston and New York, 1909.

Bronson, Edgar Beecher. *Cowboy Life on the Western Plains: Reminiscences of a Ranchman.* New York, 1910.

————. "A Man of East and West: Clarence King, Geologist, Savant, Wit," *Century Mag.*, LXXX, 376–82. Reprinted in *Cowboy Life on the Western Plains.*

————. *The Red-Blooded Heroes of the Frontier.* New York, 1910.

————. *Reminiscences of a Ranchman.* New York, 1908.

Brookings Institution (Institute for Government Research). *The U. S. Geological Survey: Its History, Activities and Organization.* New York, 1918.

Brooks, Bryant. *Memoirs of Bryant B. Brooks, Cowboy, Trapper, Lumberman, Stockman, Oilman, Banker, and Governor of Wyoming.* Glendale, Calif., privately printed, 1939.

Brooks, Paul. "Yosemite: The Seeing Eye and the Written Word," in Ansel Adams, *Yosemite and the Range of Light*, pp. 17–28. Boston, 1979.

Brooks, Van Wyck. *Howells: His Life and World.* New York, 1959.

————. *New England: Indian Summer, 1865–1915.* New York, 1940.

————. *The Times of Melville and Whitman.* New York, 1947.

Brown Univ. *The Historical Catalogue of Brown University, 1924.* Providence, 1924.

Browne, Charles Farrar. *Artemus Ward: His Works, Complete.* New York, 1875.

Browne, J. Ross. *The Mariposa Estate: Its Past, Present and Future.* New York, 1868.

————. *Report . . . on Mineral Resources of the States and Territories West of the Rocky Mountains.* Washington, 1868.

Bryant, Harold Child. *Outdoor Heritage.* San Francisco, Los Angeles and Chicago, 1929.

Burroughs, John Rolfe. *Guardian of the Grasslands: The First Hundred Years of the Wyoming Stock Growers Association.* Cheyenne, 1971.

Butler, Nicholas Murray. *Across the Busy Years: Recollections and Reflections.* 2 vols. New York, 1939.

Century Association. *The Century, 1847–1946.* New York, 1947.

————. *Century Memorials 1939.* [New York, 1939.]

Chapman, John Jay. *Memories and Milestones.* New York, 1915.

Chittenden, Russell H. *History of the Sheffield Scientific School of Yale University.* 2 vols. New Haven, 1928.

————. ". . . William Henry Brewer, 1828–1910," National Academy of Sciences, *Biographical Memoirs*, XII (1929), 287–323.

Clarke, John S. *The Life and Letters of John Fiske.* 2 vols. Boston, 1917.

Clarke, John M. *James Hall of Albany, Geologist and Paleontologist, 1811–1898.* Albany, 1921.

Clay, John. *My Life on the Range.* Chicago, privately printed [1924].

Clemens, Samuel L. *Mark Twain's Travels with Mr. Brown,* ed. Franklin Walker and George Ezra Dane. New York, 1940.

——. *Roughing It.* 2 vols. Hartford, 1872.

Condor, John J. *A Formula of His Own: Henry Adams's Literary Experiment.* Chicago, 1970.

Cortissoz, Royal. *John La Farge, A Memoir and a Study.* Boston and New York, 1911.

——. *The Life of Whitelaw Reid.* 2 vols. New York, 1921.

Cosmos Club. *The Twenty-Fifth Anniversary of the Founding of the Cosmos Club.* Washington, 1904.

Crosby, Harry H. "The Great Diamond Fraud," *American Heritage,* VII (Feb. 1956), 58–63, 100. Reprinted in the *American Heritage Book of Great Adventures of the Old West* (New York, n.d.), pp. 297–309.

Curti, Merle. *The Growth of American Thought.* New York and London, 1943.

Curtis, J. S. *The Silver-Lead Deposits of Eureka, Nevada.* U.S.G.S. Monograph No. VII. Washington, 1884.

Dahlgren, Charles B. *Handbook to the "Historic Mines of Mexico."* Trenton, 1886.

——. *Minas Historicas de la Republica Mexicana.* Mexico City, 1887.

Dall, W. H. *Spencer Fullerton Baird.* Philadelphia, 1915.

Dana, E. S., ed. *A Century of Science in America.* New Haven, 1918.

Dana, Julian. *The Man Who Built San Francisco: A Study of Ralston's Journey with Banners.* New York, 1936.

Darrah, William Culp. *Powell of the Colorado.* Princeton, 1951.

Davis, W. M. ". . . Grove Karl Gilbert, 1843–1918," National Academy of Sciences, *Biographical Memoirs,* XXI (1926), 5th memoir.

Dawson, Thomas F. *The Life and Character of Edward Oliver Wolcott.* New York, 1911.

Dennett, Tyler. *Americans in Eastern Asia.* New York, 1941.

——. "The Five of Hearts," *Scholastic,* XXVII (March 14, 1931), 6–7, 13.

——. *John Hay, from Poetry to Politics.* New York, 1933.

De Voto, Bernard. *Mark Twain's America.* Boston, 1932.

——. *Year of Decision.* Boston, 1943.

"Diamond Bubble and Its Bursting," *Nation,* XV (Dec. 12, 1872), 379–80.

Dickason, David H. "Clarence King—Scientist and Art Amateur," *Art in America,* XXXII (Jan. 1944), 41–51.

——. "Clarence King's First Western Journey," *Huntington Lib. Quart.,* VII (Nov. 1943), 71–87.

——. *The Daring Young Men: The Story of the American Pre-Raphaelites.* Bloomington, 1953.

———. "Henry Adams and Clarence King, The Record of a Friendship," *New England Quart.*, XVII (1944), 229–54.

Dingus, Rick. *The Photographic Artifacts of Timothy O'Sullivan.* Albuquerque, 1982.

Dodge, H. Augusta, ed. *Gail Hamilton's Life in Letters.* 2 vols. Boston, 1901.

Donaldson, Thomas. *Idaho of Yesterday.* Caldwell, Idaho, 1941.

———. *The Public Domain: Its History with Statistics.* Washington, D.C., 1884.

Dunham, Harold H. *Government Handout: A Study in the Administration of the Public Lands, 1875–1891.* New York, 1941.

Dunlap, William. *History of the Rise and Progress of the Arts of Design in the United States.* New York, 1834.

Dupree, A. Hunter. *Science in the Federal Government.* Cambridge, Mass., 1957.

Dusinberre, William. *Henry Adams: The Myth of Failure.* Charlottesville, 1980.

Dutton, Clarence E. . . . *Geology of the High Plateaus of Utah.* Washington, 1880.

———. *Tertiary History of the Grand Canyon District.* U.S.G.S. Monograph No. II. Washington, 1882.

Earnest, Ernest. *S. Weir Mitchell: Novelist and Physician.* Philadelphia, 1950.

Edel, Leon. *Henry James: The Middle Years* (1882–1895). Philadelphia and New York, 1962.

———. *Henry James: The Treacherous Years* (1895–1901). Philadelphia and New York, 1969.

Eliot, Ellsworth. *Yale in the Civil War.* New Haven, 1932.

Ellery, Harrison. "The Vernon Family and Arms," *New England Historical and Genealogical Register,* XXXIII (July 1879), 312 ff; also in *Rhode Island Historical Tracts,* No. 13, pp. 117–40.

Elliott, Maud H. "Some Recollections of Newport Artists," *Bulletin of the Newport Historical Society,* Jan. 1921.

———. *This Was My Newport.* Cambridge, Mass., 1944.

Emerson, Ralph Waldo. *Journals* (Boston and New York, 1909–1914), Vol. X.

Emmons, Samuel Franklin. "Biographical Memoir of Clarence King, 1842–1901," National Academy of Sciences, *Biographical Memoirs,* VI (1909), 25–55.

———. "Clarence King," *American Journal of Science,* 4th ser., XIII (Mar. 1902), 224–237.

———. "Clarence King—A Memorial," *Engineering and Mining Journal,* LXXIII (Dec. 28, 1901), 3–5.

———. *Geology and Mining Industry of Leadville, Colorado.* U.S.G.S. Monograph No. XII. Washington, 1886.

———. "The Geology of Government Explorations" (presidential address before the Geological Society of Washington, Dec. 1896), *Science*, new ser., V (1897), 1–15, 42–51.

————. "The Mining Work of the U.S. Geological Survey," *Transactions of the American Institute of Mining Engineers*, X (1882), 412–24.

————. "The Volcanoes of the U.S. Pacific Coast," *Journal of the American Geographical Society*, IX (1876–77), 44–65.

———— and George F. Becker. *Statistics and Technology of the Precious Metals.* Washington, 1885 (Report of the U.S. [10th] Census, Vol. XIII).

Eureka Consolidated Mining Company vs. Richmond Mining Company, of Eureka, Nevada. *Testimony of Clarence King . . . at the March Term of the Sixth Judicial District Court, 1873.* Eureka, *Eureka Sentinel*, 1873.

Fairchild, Herman LeRoy, *The Geological Society of America, 1888–1930: A Chapter in Earth Science History.* New York, 1932.

Farish, Thomas E. *Gold Hunters of California.* Chicago, 1904.

Farquhar, Francis P. *Exploration of the Sierra Nevada.* San Francisco, 1925.

————. *First Ascents in the United States, 1642–1900.* Pamphlet. Berkeley, privately printed, 1948.

————. *History of the Sierra Nevada.* Berkeley and Los Angeles, 1965.

————, ed. *Letters of Western Authors*, No. 10, Oct. 1935, "Clarence King," published for its members by the Book Club of California.

————. *Place Names of the High Sierra.* San Francisco, 1926.

————. "The Story of Mount Whitney," *Sierra Club Bulletin*, XIV (Feb. 1929), No. 1, 39–52.

————. "The Whitney Survey on Mount Shasta, 1862: A Letter from William H. Brewer to Professor Brush," *California Historical Society Quart.*, VII (1928), 121–31.

————. *Yosemite, the Big Trees, and the High Sierra.* Berkeley and Los Angeles, 1948.

Farquhar, Peter. "Site of the Diamond Swindle of 1872," *California Historical Society Quart.*, XLII (Mar. 1963), 49–53.

Faul, Henry. "Century-Old Diamond Hoax Reëxamined," *Geotimes*, XVII (Oct. 1972), 23–25.

Fenton, Carroll, and Mildred Fenton. *Giants of Geology.* New York, 1952.

Fiske, John. *The Letters of John Fiske*, ed. Ethel F. Fiske. New York, 1940.

Flippin, John R. *Sketches from the Mountains of Mexico.* Cincinnati, 1889.

Foerster, Norman. *Nature in American Literature: Studies in the Modern View of Nature.* New York, 1923.

Foote, Mary Hallock. Letters to Thomas F. Dawson, in L. J. Davidson, "Letters from Authors," *Colorado Mag.*, XIX (1942), 122–26.

————. *A Victorian Gentlewoman in the Far West: The Reminiscences of Mary Hallock Foote*, ed. Rodman W. Paul. San Marino, 1972.

Ford, James L. *Forty-Odd Years in the Literary Shop.* New York [1921].

Franklin, Fabian. *Life of Daniel Coit Gilman.* New York, 1910.

Frewen, Moreton. *Melton Mowbray, and Other Memories.* London, 1926.

Friedrich, Otto. *Clover* [Biography of Marian Hooper Adams]. New York, 1979.

Frink, Maurice. *Cow Country Cavalcade.* Denver, 1954.

Fussell, Edwin. *Frontier: American Literature and the American West.* Princeton, 1965.

Gabriel, Ralph H. *The Course of American Democratic Thought,* 2nd ed. New York, 1956.

Garcia, Trinidad. *Los Mineros Mexicanos.* 3rd ed. Mexico City, 1970.

Gaunt, William. *The Aesthetic Adventure.* New York, 1945.

————. *The Pre-Raphaelite Tragedy.* New York, 1942.

Geological Society of America. *Fiftieth Anniversary Volume, Geology 1888–1938.* New York, 1941.

Gilbert Munger, Landscape Artist, 1836–1903. New York, n.d.

Gilbert, G. K. "John Wesley Powell," *Science,* new ser., XVI (1902), 561–67.

————, ed. *John Wesley Powell: A Memorial to an American Explorer and Scholar.* Chicago, 1903.

————. *Lake Bonneville.* U.S.G.S. Monograph No. I. Washington, 1890.

Gilman, Daniel Coit. *Life of James Dwight Dana, Scientific Explorer, Mineralogist, Geologist, Zoologist.* New York, 1899.

Godkin, E. L. *The Gilded Age Letters of E. L. Godkin,* ed. William M. Armstrong. Albany, 1974.

Goetzmann, William H. *Exploration and Empire: The Explorer and the Scientist in the Winning of the American West.* New York, 1966.

Goodwin, C. C. *As I Remember Them.* Salt Lake City, 1913.

Goodyear, William A. "On the Situation and Altitude of Mount Whitney," *Proceedings of the California Academy of Sciences,* V (Aug. 4, 1873), 139–44; reprinted in *Mining and Scientific Press,* XXVII (1873), 97.

Gosse, Edmund. *Aspects and Impressions.* London, 1922.

Gressley, Gene M. *Bankers and Cattlemen.* New York, 1966.

Grinnell, George B., ed. *Brief History of the Boone and Crockett Club.* New York, 1910.

Hague, Arnold. ". . . Samuel Franklin Emmons, 1841–1911," National Academy of Sciences, *Biographical Memoirs,* VII (1913), 307–34.

Hague, James D. "Mount Whitney," *Overland Mo.,* XI (Nov. 1873), 460–64.

———— to Editor, *Overland Mo.,* new ser., XL, 335–36.

Hall, Frank. *History of the State of Colorado.* Vol. II. Chicago, 1890.

Hammond, John Hays. *Autobiography.* 2 vols. in one. New York, 1935.

Harpending, Asbury. *The Great Diamond Hoax and Other Stirring Incidents in the Life of Asbury Harpending,* ed. James H. Wilkins. San Francisco, 1913.

Harris, Harry. *Robert Ridgway* (reprinted from Jan.-Feb. 1928 issue of *The Condor*). Los Angeles, 1928.

Harris, Townsend. *The Complete Journal of Townsend Harris, First American Consul General and Minister to Japan.* New York, 1930.

Harte, Bret. *Tales of the Argonauts.* Boston and New York, 1907.

Harte, Geoffrey Bret, ed. *The Letters of Bret Harte.* Boston and New York, 1926.

Hay, John. *Addresses of John Hay.* New York, 1906.

———. *The Complete Poetical Works of John Hay.* Boston and New York, 1916.

———. *Letters of John Hay and Extracts from Diary.* 3 vols. Washington, 1908. Printed but not published (c. Clara S. Hay; selected by Henry Adams).

Hay, John, and W. D. Howells. *John Hay-Howells Letters: The Correspondence of John Hay and William Dean Howells, 1861–1905,* ed. George Monteiro and Brenda Murphy. Boston, 1981.

Hazen, Charles D., ed. *The Letters of William Roscoe Thayer.* Boston and New York, 1926.

Hewitt, Abram S. *The Selected Writings of Abram Hewitt,* ed. Allan Nevins. New York, 1937.

Hewitt, Edward R. *Ringwood Manor, the Home of the Hewitts.* Trenton, 1946.

———. *Those Were the Days.* New York, 1943.

Hibbard, B. H. *A History of the Public Land Policies.* New York, 1924.

Higginson, Thomas Wentworth. *Letters and Journals of Thomas Wentworth Higginson,* ed. Mary Thacher Higginson. Boston and New York, 1921.

———. *Oldport Days.* Boston, 1873.

Hitchcock, Charles H. *Hawaii and Its Volcanoes.* Honolulu, 1909.

Hittell, John S. *History of the City of San Francisco.* San Francisco, 1878.

Holt, Henry. *Garrulities of an Octogenarian Editor.* Boston and New York, 1923.

Horan, James D. *Timothy O'Sullivan: American's Forgotten Photographer.* Garden City, 1966.

Howe, M. A. De Wolfe, ed. *John Jay Chapman and His Letters.* Boston, 1937.

Howells, William Dean. "Editor's Easy Chair," Section 3, *Harpers Mo.,* CIV (1902), 836–37.

———. "Editor's Easy Chair," *Harper's Mo.,* CVIII (Dec. 1903), 153–59.

———. "John Hay in Literature," *North American Rev.,* CLXXXI (Sept. 1905), 343–51.

———. *Life in Letters of William Dean Howells,* ed. Mildred Howells. 2 vols. New York, 1928.

———. *Literary Friends and Acquaintances.* New York and London, 1902.

———. "Recollections of an Atlantic Editorship," *Atlantic Mo.,* C (Nov. 1907), 594–606.

[———.] Review of *Mountaineering, Atlantic Mo.,* XXIX (April 1872), 500–501.

Howland, Franklyn. *A Brief Genealogical and Biographical History of Arthur,*

Henry, and John Howland, and Their Descendants, of the United States and Canada. 2 vols. New Bedford, 1885.

Humboldt, Alexander. *Selections from the Works of the Baron de Humboldt Relating to the Climate, Inhabitants, Productions, and Mines of Mexico.* London, 1824.

Hunter, William C. *Bits of Old China.* London, 1885.

Hutchings, James M. *In the Heart of the Sierras.* Oakland, 1886.

————. *Scenes of Wonder and Curiosity in California.* New York and San Francisco, 1870.

Hutton, Laurence. *Talks in a Library with Laurence Hutton, Recorded by Isabel Moore.* New York and London, 1905.

Huxley, Leonard, ed. *Life and Letters of Thomas Henry Huxley.* 2 vols. New York, 1900.

Iddings, J. P. ". . . Arnold Hague, 1840–1917," National Academy of Sciences, *Biographical Memoirs,* IX (1919), 19–38. Expanded from memoir in *Bulletin of the Geological Society of America,* XXIX (1918), 35–48.

The Iron Mask Gold Mining Company vs. the Centre Star Mining and Smelting Company. . . . *Evidence by Clarence King, Waldemar Lindgren and Rossiter Raymond, Taken at Trial at Rossland, Commencing April 17th, 1899.* N.p., 1899. Copy consulted at American Engineering Societies Lib., New York City.

Irving, R. L. G. *The Romance of Mountaineering.* New York, 1935.

Jaffe, Bernard. *Men of Science in America: The Role of Science in the Growth of Our Country.* New York, 1944.

James, George Wharton. "Clarence King," *Overland Mo.,* new ser., LXXXI (Oct. 1923), 31–36.

————. *Heroes of California.* Boston, 1910. Contains a chapter on King that retells the Mount Tyndall story.

————. *Through Ramona's Country.* Boston, 1909.

James, Henry. *Henry James: Autobiography,* ed. F. W. Dupee. Garden City, N.Y., 1956.

————. *Henry James Letters,* ed. Leon Edel. Vols. II (1875–1883) and III (1883–1895). Cambridge, Mass., 1975 and 1980.

————. *Notes of a Son and Brother.* New York, 1914.

————. *Portraits of Places.* Boston, 1883.

————. *William Wetmore Story and His Friends.* Boston, 1903.

———— and John Hay. *Henry James and John Hay: The Record of a Friendship,* ed. George Monteiro. Providence, 1965.

Janin, Henry. "A Brief Statement of My Part in the Unfortunate Diamond Affair." Pamphlet. San Francisco, 1873.

Johnson, Robert Underwood. *Remembered Yesterdays.* Boston, 1923.

Jones, Idwal. *Ark of Empire.* [A book about the Montgomery Block, San Francisco.] Garden City, N.Y., 1951.

Jordy, William H. *Henry Adams, Scientific Historian.* New Haven, 1952.

Josephson, Matthew. *Portrait of the Artist as American.* New York, 1930.

Kaledin, Eugenia. *The Education of Mrs. Henry Adams.* Philadelphia, 1981.

Kemp, James F. *Ore Deposits of the United States.* New York, 1893.

King, Charles William. *The Claims of Japan and Malaysia upon Christendom.* Vol. I. New York, 1839.

King, Clarence, Memorial Committee of the Century Association. *Clarence King Memoirs: The Helmet of Mambrino,* ed. James D. Hague *et al.* New York, 1904.

King, Grace. *Memories of a Southern Woman of Letters.* New York, 1932.

King, Rufus. *Pedigree of King, of Lynn, Essex County, Mass., 1602–1891.* Genealogical chart, n.p., n.d. (c. 1891).

Kirkland, Edward C. *Charles Francis Adams, Jr., 1835–1915: The Patrician at Bay.* Cambridge, Mass., 1965.

Kramer, Howard D. "The Scientist in the West, 1870–1880," *Pacific Historical Rev.,* XII (Sept. 1943), 239–51.

La Farge, John. *An Artist's Letters from Japan.* New York, 1897.

———. *Reminiscences of the South Seas.* Garden City, N.Y., 1912.

Lee, Robert E. *From West to East: Studies in the Literature of the American West.* Urbana, 1966.

Leland, Charles Godfrey. *Memoirs.* New York, 1893.

Levenson, J. C. *The Mind and Art of Henry Adams.* Boston, 1957.

Lewis, Oscar. "The Launching of Bancroft's 'Native Races,' " *Colophon,* new ser., I, 323–32.

Liebling, A. J. "The American Golconda," *The New Yorker,* XVI (Nov. 16, 1940), 49–62.

Lindsay, R. B. ". . . Carl Barus, 1856–1935," National Academy of Sciences, *Biographical Memoirs,* XXII (1943), 171–213.

Little, George T. *Descendants of George Little [of] Newbury, Massachusetts.* Auburn, Maine, 1882.

Little, Sophia. *The Branded Hand, A Dramatic Sketch, Commemorative of the Tragedies of the South in the Winter of 1844–45!* Pawtucket, R.I., 1845.

———. *Christ in Prison.* N.p., 1883.

———. *Thrice Through the Furnace: A Tale of the Times of the Iron Hoof.* Pawtucket, 1852.

[Lloyd, Caroline.] *A Memorial of Lt. Daniel Perkins Dewey of the Twenty-Fifth Regiment Connecticut Volunteers.* Privately printed, Hartford, 1864.

Lord, Eliot. *Comstock Mining and Miners.* U.S.G.S. Monograph No. IV. Washington, 1883.

Lucas, E. V. *Edwin Austin Abbey, Royal Academician.* 2 vols. London and New York, 1921.

Ludlow, Fitz Hugh. *The Heart of the Continent.* New York, 1870.

Luhan, Mabel Dodge. *Intimate Memories* (New York, 1933–1936), Vol. III.

Lyman, George D. *Ralston's Ring.* New York, 1937.

McCornack, Ellen Condon. *Thomas Condon: Pioneer Geologist of Oregon.* Eugene, 1928.

Mack, Edward C. *Peter Cooper.* New York, 1949.

Mack, Effie Mona. *Mark Twain in Nevada.* New York, 1947.

Mane, Robert. *Henry Adams on the Road to Chartres.* Cambridge, Mass., 1971.

Manning, Thomas G. *Government in Science: The U.S. Geological Survey, 1867–1894.* Lexington, Ky., 1967.

————. "The Influence of Clarence King and John Wesley Powell on the Early History of the United States Geological Survey," *Interim Proceedings of the Geological Society of America,* part 2 (May 1947), 23–29.

Matthes, François. *The Geologic History of the Yosemite Valley.* Washington, 1930.

M[atthews], B[rander]. *The Roster of the Round Table Dining Club, with a Prefatory Note by the Fourth Secretary of the Club.* New York, 1926.

————. *These Many Years.* New York, 1917.

Maurice, Arthur Bartlett. *Fifth Avenue.* New York, 1918.

Merrill, George P. *Contributions to a History of American State Geological and Natural History Surveys.* U.S. National Museum Bulletin 109, Washington, 1920.

————. *The First One Hundred Years of American Geology.* New Haven, 1924.

Monger, J. W. H., and G. A. Davis. "Evolving Concepts of the Tectonics of the North American Cordillera," in Pacific Division/American Association for the Advancement of Science, *Frontiers of Geological Exploration of Western North America,* pp. 215–48. San Francisco, 1982.

Morris, Lloyd. *Postscript to Yesterday.* New York, 1947.

Morrison, George A. "The King Heraldry," *New York Genealogical and Biographical Record,* XLI (1910), 263–75, and XLII (1911), 7–26.

Muir, John. "Exploration in the Great Tuolumne Canyon," *Overland Mo.,* XI (Aug. 1873), 139–47.

————. *The Mountains of California.* New York, 1911.

————. "Studies in the Sierra II," *Overland Mo.,* XII (June 1874), 489–500.

Munroe, James P. *A Life of Francis Amasa Walker.* New York, 1923.

Muzzey, David S. *James G. Blaine, a Political Idol of Other Days.* New York, 1934.

National Academy of Sciences. *A History of the First Half Century of the National Academy of Sciences, 1863–1913.* Washington, 1913.

Nelson, Clifford M., and Mary C. Rabbitt. "The Role of Clarence King in the Advancement of Geology in the Public Service, 1867–1881," in Pacific Division/American Association for the Advancement of Science, *Frontiers of Geological Exploration of Western North America,* pp. 19–35. San Francisco, 1982.

Nelson, Clifford M., Mary Rabbitt, and Fritiof M. Fryxell. "Ferdinand Vandeveer Hayden: The U.S. Geological Survey Years, 1879–1886," *Proceedings of the American Philosophical Society,* CXXV, No. 3 (June 1981), 238–43.

Nevins, Allan. *Abram S. Hewitt, with Some Account of Peter Cooper.* New York, 1935.

The New Path, the Journal of the Society for the Advancement of Truth in Art, Vol. I (1863–1865).

Newberry, J. S. "Geological Survey of the Fortieth Parallel," *Popular Science Mo.,* XV (1879): 302–17.

Newcomb, Simon. *The Reminiscences of an Astronomer.* Boston, 1903.

Newhall, Beaumont, and Nancy Newhall. *T. H. O'Sullivan, Photographer.* Rochester, 1966.

Odell, Ruth. *Helen Hunt Jackson (H. H.).* New York, 1939.

Osgood, E. S. *The Day of the Cattleman.* Minneapolis, 1929.

Park, Roswell. *Pantology: or, A Systematic Survey of Human Knowledge.* Philadelphia, 1841.

Parsons, Julia. *Scattered Memories.* Boston [1938].

Paul, Rodman W. *Mining Frontiers of the Far West, 1848–1880.* New York, 1963.

Pearl, Roger H. "The Shiftless Belligerant Pike: An Early Western Emigrant Type as described by Clarence King," *California Historical Society Quart.,* XXXVIII (June 1959), 113–29.

Peirce, Charles S. *Collected Papers,* Vol. I (*Principles of Philosophy*) and Vol. VI (*Scientific Metaphysics*), ed. Hartshorne and Weiss. Cambridge, 1931–1935.

Pelzer, Louis. *The Cattleman's Frontier.* Glendale, Calif., 1936.

Pemberton, T. E. *The Life of Bret Harte.* New York, 1903.

Pennell, Elizabeth R. *Charles Godfrey Leland: A Biography.* 2 vols. Boston, 1906.

———. *The Life of James McNeill Whistler.* Philadelphia, 1908.

Perry, Bliss. *Life and Letters of Henry Lee Higginson.* Boston, 1921.

Powell, John Wesley. *Report on the Lands of the Arid Region of the United States, with a more detailed Account of the Lands of Utah.* Washington, 1878.

———. *Report on the Methods of Surveying the Public Domain.* Washington, 1878.

Powell, Lawrence Clark. *California Classics: The Creative Literature of the Golden State.* Los Angeles, 1971. Contains a chapter on King's *Mountaineering.*

Pumpelly, Raphael. *My Reminiscences.* 2 vols. New York, 1918.

———. *Report on the Mining Industry of the United States (Exclusive of the Precious Metals).* Report of the Tenth U.S. Census, Vol. XV. Washington, 1886.

Pyne, Stephen J. *Grove Karl Gilbert: A Great Engine of Research.* Austin and London, 1980.

Rabbitt, Mary C. *A Brief History of the U.S. Geological Survey.* Pamphlet. Washington, [1979].

———. *Minerals, Lands, and Geology for the Common Defense and General Welfare.* Vol. I, Before 1879; Vol. II, 1879–1904. Washington, 1979 and 1980.

Rabelais Club. *Recreations of the Rabelais Club,* II (1882–1885), with membership lists. N.p., n.d.

Rainsford, William S. *Story of a Varied Life: An Autobiography.* New York, 1922.

Raymond, Rossiter W. "Biographical Notice of Clarence King," *Transactions of the American Institute of Mining Engineers,* XXXIII (1902), 619–50.

———. "Biographical Notice [Henry Janin]," *Bulletin of the American Institute of Mining Engineers,* liii (1911), 18–36.

———. "Biographical Notice of J. D. Hague," *Bulletin of the American Institute of Mining Engineers,* xxvi (1909), 109–17.

Reid, Weymyss. *William Black, Novelist.* New York and London, 1902.

Report of the Commissioners to Manage Yosemite Valley and the Mariposa Big Tree Grove. For the Years 1866–67. San Francisco, 1868.

Richards, Bartlett, Jr., with Ruth Van Ackeren. *Bartlett Richards: Nebraska Sandhills Cattleman.* Lincoln, 1980.

Rickard, Thomas A. "The Great Diamond Hoax: How a Great Colorado Desert Was Salted with Gems in 1872." *Engineering and Mining Journal-Press,* CXIX (May 30, 1925), 884–88.

———. *A History of American Mining.* New York and London, 1932.

———. *Rossiter Worthington Raymond, A Memorial.* New York, 1910.

Rideing, William H. *Many Celebrities and a Few Others: A Bundle of Reminiscences.* Garden City, N.Y., 1912.

———. "With Wheeler in the Sierras." *Appleton's Journal,* new ser., III, 289–97.

Rider, Fremont. *Rider's California.* New York, 1925.

Ridgway, Robert. "Song Birds of the West," *Harper's Mo.,* LVI (May 1878), 857–80.

Robbins, R. M. *Our Landed Heritage: The Public Domain, 1776–1936.* Princeton, 1946.

Rogers, E. S. *Life and Letters of William Barton Rogers.* 2 vols. Boston and New York, 1896.

Roosevelt, Theodore. "Big Game Disappearing from the West," *Forum,* XV (1893), 767–74.

———. *Selections from the Correspondence of Theodore Roosevelt and Henry Cabot Lodge.* 2 vols. New York, 1925.

———. *The Wilderness Hunter.* New York, 1926.

Roper, Laura Wood. *F. L. O.: A Biography of Frederick Law Olmsted.* Baltimore and London, 1973.

Rothschild, Mrs. James de [Dorothy de]. *The Rothschilds of Waddesdon Manor.* New York, Paris, and Lausanne, 1979.

Rubens, Horatio S. *Liberty: The Story of Cuba.* New York, 1932.

Ruskin, John. *Fors Clavigera,* VII. Sunnyside, Orpington, Kent, 1877.

Samson, John. "Photographs from the High Rockies," *Harper's New Mo. Mag.,* XXXIX (Sept. 1869), 465–75.

Samuels, Ernest. *Henry Adams: The Major Phase.* Cambridge, Mass., 1964.

———. *Henry Adams: The Middle Years.* Cambridge, Mass., 1958.

———. *The Young Henry Adams.* Cambridge, Mass., 1948.

Sandoz, Mari. *Cheyenne Autumn.* New York, Toronto, and London, 1953.

Sargent, Shirley. *Galen Clark, Yosemite Guardian.* San Francisco, 1964.

Scheyer, Ernst. *The Circle of Henry Adams: Art & Artists.* Detroit, 1970.

Schmeckebier, Laurence F. *Catalogue and Index of the Publications of the Hayden, King, Powell, and Wheeler Surveys.* U.S.G.S. Bulletin 222. Washington, 1904.

Schuchert, Charles, and C. M. LeVene. *O. C. Marsh: Pioneer in Paleontology.* New Haven, 1940.

Scott, W. B. *Some Memories of a Paleontologist.* Princeton, 1939.

Sellerier, Carlos. *Data Referring to Mexican Mining.* Mexico City, 1901.

Shaler, Nathaniel S. *Autobiography of Nathaniel Southgate Shaler.* Boston, 1909.

Shebl, James M. "Introduction," pp. vii–xiii, to facsimile reprint of 1872 edition of King's *Mountaineering.* Lincoln and London, 1970.

———. *King, of the Mountains.* Stockton, 1974.

Simonds, Katharine. "The Tragedy of Mrs. Henry Adams," *New England Quart.,* IX (Dec. 1936), 564–82.

Smith, Henry Nash. "Clarence King, John Wesley Powell, and the Establishment of the United States Geological Survey," *Mississippi Valley Historical Rev.,* XXXIV (June 1947), 37–58.

———. *Virgin Land: The American West as Symbol and Myth.* Cambridge, Mass., 1950.

Snyder, Joel. *American Frontiers: The Photographs of Timothy O'Sullivan, 1867–1874.* Millerton, N.Y., 1981.

Sophia Little Home. *Annual Report 1894.*

Southworth, J. R. *El Estado de Sonora.* Nogales, 1897.

———. *Las Minas de Mexico: The Mines of Mexico.* Mexico City, 1905.

Spence, Clark C. *Mining Engineers & the American West: The Lace-Boot Brigade, 1849–1933.* New Haven, 1970.

Spring, Agnes Wright. *Seventy Years, A Panoramic History of the Wyoming Stock Growers Association.* [Chicago], 1942.

Starr, Kevin. *Americans and the California Dream, 1850–1915.* New York, 1973.

Stedman, Laura, and George Gould. *Life and Letters of Edmund Clarence Stedman*. 2 vols. New York, 1910.

Stegner, Wallace. *Beyond the Hundredth Meridian: John Wesley Powell and the Second Opening of the West*. Boston, 1954.

————. "Western Record and Romance," in *Literary History of the United States*, ed. Robert Spiller *et al.*, (New York, 1946), II, 862–77.

Stein, Roger B. *John Ruskin and Aesthetic Thought in America*. Cambridge, Mass., 1967. See pp. 168–85 for Stein's discussion of King.

Stevenson, Elizabeth. *Henry Adams: A Biography*. New York, 1955.

Stewart, George R. *Bret Harte: Argonaut and Exile*. Boston and New York, 1931.

Stoddard, Charles Warren. *Exits and Entrances*. Boston, 1903.

————. *The Island of Tranquil Delights*. Boston, 1904.

Stokes, Anson Phelps. *Memorials of Eminent Yale Men*. Vols. I-II. New Haven, 1914.

Taft, Robert. *Photography and the American Scene*. New York, 1938.

Taylor, Bayard. *At Home and Abroad*. 2nd ser. New York, 1862.

Taylor, Fitch W. *A Voyage Around the World*. 2 vols. 2nd. ed. New Haven and New York, 1842.

Taylor, Henry O. *A Layman's View of History*. New York, 1935.

Tehan, Arline Boucher. *Henry Adams in Love: The Pursuit of Elizabeth Sherman Cameron*. New York, 1983.

Thayer, William Roscoe. *The Life and Letters of John Hay*. 2 vols. Boston, 1915.

Thompson, Sylvanus. *The Life of William Thomson, Baron Kelvin of Largs*. 2 vols. London, 1910.

Thurman, Kelly. *John Hay as a Man of Letters*. Reseda, Calif., 1974.

Thurston, William. "Establishment of the U.S. Geological Survey." *Washington Academy of Sciences Journal*, LXI (1971), 7–12.

Turner, Stephen P. "The Survey in Nineteenth-Century American Geology: The Evolution of a Form of Patronage," *Minerva* XXV (Autumn 1987), 282–330.

Twitchell, J. H., ed. *Memorial of Samuel Mills Capron*. Hartford, 1874.

U. S. Geographical and Geological Survey of the Rocky Mountain Region, John Wesley Powell in charge. Reports. See Schmeckebier for listing.

U. S. Geographical Surveys West of the 100th Meridian, Lt. George M. Wheeler in charge. Especially *Geographical Report*, Vol. I (Washington, 1889). See Schmeckebier for listing.

U. S. Geological and Geographical Survey of the Territories, Ferdinand V. Hayden in charge. Reports and Bulletins, 1867 *et seq.* See Schmeckebier.

U.S. Geological Exploration of the Fortieth Parallel, Clarence King, U.S. Geologist, in charge. Report published as Professional Papers of the Engineer Department, U.S. Army, No. 18. 7 vols., plus atlas. Washington, 1870–1880.

I.   *Systematic Geology,* by Clarence King, 1878.
II. *Descriptive Geology,* by Arnold Hague and Samuel Franklin Emmons, 1877.
III. *Mining Industry,* by James D. Hague, with geological contributions by Clarence King, 1870.
IV. Part I, *Paleontology,* by Fielding B. Meek; Part II, *Paleontology,* by James Hall, and R. P. Whitfield; Part III, *Ornithology,* by Robert Ridgway, 1877.
V.   *Botany,* by Sereno Watson, aided by D. C. Eaton and others, 1871.
VI. *Microscopical Petrography,* by Ferdinand Zirkel, 1876.
VII. *Odontornithes: A Monograph on the Extinct Toothed Birds of North America,* by O. C. Marsh, 1880.

U.S. Geological Survey. Annual Reports, 1880 et seq.

van Dyke, Henry. "A Book of Charm by a Man of Science," *The Lamp,* XXVI (May 1903), 299–301.

Van Wyck, Frederick. *Recollections of an Old New Yorker.* New York, 1932.

Wagner, Vern. *The Suspension of Henry Adams: A Study of Manner and Matter.* Detroit, 1969.

Walcott, Charles D. "John Wesley Powell," *24th Annual Report . . . U.S. Geological Survey* (1903), pp. 271–87.

——— et al. "Necrology: Clarence King," *23rd Annual Report . . . U.S. Geological Survey* (1902), pp. 198–206.

Walker, George. "The Census of 1880," *North American Rev.,* CXXVIII (April 1879), 393–404.

Ward, H. G. *Mexico in 1827.* 2 vols. London, 1828.

Webb, Walter P. *The Great Plains.* Boston, 1931.

Wecter, Dixon. *Literary Lodestone: One Hundred Years of California Writing.* Pamphlet. Stanford, 1950.

Whipple, T. K. *Spokesmen: Modern Writers and American Life.* New York, 1928.

White, A. F. *Report of the State Mineralogist of Nevada for the years 1867 and 1868.* Carson City, 1869.

White, C. A. ". . . Ferdinand Vandiveer [sic] Hayden, 1839 [sic]–1887," National Academy of Sciences, *Biographical Memoirs,* III (1895), 395–413.

Whitney, Josiah D. *Climatic Changes of Later Geological Times.* Cambridge, Mass., 1882.

———. "Geographical and Geological Surveys," *North American Rev.,* CXXI, No. 248 (July 1875), 37–85; No. 249 (Oct. 1875), 270–314.

———, State Geologist, Geological Survey of California. *Geology,* Vol. I: *Report of Progress and Synopsis of Field Work from 1860 to 1864.* Philadelphia, 1865.

[———.] Review of *Mining Industry, North American Rev.,* CXIII (July 1871), 203–10.

———, State Geologist, Geological Survey of California. *The Yosemite Book:*

A Description of the Yosemite Valley and the Adjacent Region of the Sierra Nevada, and the Big Trees of California. New York, 1868.

———. *The Yosemite Guide-Book* [with same subtitle]. [Cambridge], 1870.

———. [Same title.] Revised pocket edition. [Cambridge], 1874.

Wild, Peter. *Clarence King.* Boise, 1981. Western Writers Series pamphlet No. 48.

Wilkins, Thurman. "Introduction," pp. v–xiv, to facsimile reprint of the 1872 edition of King's *Mountaineering.* Philadelphia and New York, 1963.

Williams, Henry T., ed. *The Pacific Tourist: Illustrated Trans-Continental Guide of Travel from the Atlantic to the Pacific Ocean.* New York, 1876. The name Clarence King appears on the title page in a list of "special contributors."

Willis, Bailey. *A Yanqui in Patagonia.* Stanford, 1947.

Wilson, A. D. "The Great California Diamond Mines, A True Story," *Overland Mo.,* new ser., XLIII (April 1904), 291–96.

Wisan, Joseph E. *The Cuban Crisis as Reflected in the New York Press.* New York, 1934.

Wolfe, Linnie Marsh. *Son of the Wilderness: The Life of John Muir.* New York, 1945.

Wood, William M. *Fankwei; or, The San Jacinto in the Seas of India, China, and Japan.* New York, 1859.

Woodard, Bruce A. *Diamonds in the Salt.* Boulder, 1967. The most complete study of the Diamond Fraud.

Wright, George F. *The Ice Age in North America and Its Bearings upon the Antiquity of Man.* New York, 1896.

———. "Some Remarkable Gravel Ridges in the Merrimack Valley," *Proceedings of Boston Society of Natural History,* XIX (Dec. 1876), 47–63. The last three pages are devoted to a direct quotation from Clarence King.

Wright, John K. *Geography in the Making: The American Geographical Society, 1851–1951.* New York, 1952.

Wright, William [Dan de Quille]. *The Big Bonanza.* New York, 1947.

Wyoming Stock Growers Association. *Wyoming Stock Growers Association Brandbook.* N.p., 1882.

Yale University. *Berzelius Society Catalogue 1874.*

———. *Catalogue 1860–61.*

———. *Obituary Records of Graduates . . . 1911–1912.*

Young, Bob and Jan. *Frontier Scientist: Clarence King.* New York, 1968. Highly suitable for young adult readers.

Dissertations

Crosby, Harry H. "So Deep a Trail: A Biography of Clarence King." Ph.D. diss., Stanford Univ., 1953. University Microfilms No. 5791.

Fielding, Lavinia. "Attitudes Toward Experience in Western Travel Narratives." Especially Chapter V, "Clarence King: Scientist with Sensibilities," pp. 129–61. Ph.D. diss., Univ. of Washington, 1975. University Microfilms No. 76-17465.

Hardwick, Bonnie Skell. "Science and Art: The Travel Writings of the Great Surveys of the American West after the Civil War." Ph.D. diss., Univ. of Pennsylvania, 1977. University Microfilms No. 78-06593.

Long, Barbara Ann Messner. "An Edition of *Mountaineering in the Sierra Nevada* by Clarence King." Ph.D. diss., Univ. of Pennsylvania, 1973. University Microfilms No. 73-24177. See Appendix I, pp. 562–691, for a critical collation of the several editions of *Mountaineering*.

Wilson, Richard B. "American Vision and Landscape: The Western Images of Clarence King and Timothy O'Sullivan." Ph.D. diss., Univ. of New Mexico, 1979. University Microfilms No. 80-03093.

Notes

To spare the reader the distraction of index figures in the text I have arranged the following notes by reference to the relevant page and to catch-words in the text. Most of the notes document quoted material; some however, refer to indirect quotations or to statements of fact. For catchwords in the case of direct quotations I have used, within quotation marks, the last words of each passage to be documented, while for indirect quotations or statements of fact I have adopted proper names or key words without quotation marks.

Preface to the Second Edition

Page

ix "as we do." Henry Adams to S. F. Emmons, 17 March [190–], Box 30, Emmons Papers.

    "to deprecate." *Harper's Mo.*, CIV (Apr. 1902), 837.

x "era of our history." Review of *Clarence King: A Biography*, *New England Quart.*, XXXI (1958), 538.

1

2 swipe of its paw. Roosevelt, *The Wilderness Hunter*, p. 218.

3 "his own den." E. B. Bronson, *Cowboy Life on the Western Plains*, p. 351.

    campfire story. MS sources for the grizzly bear episode include "C.K.'s notes for [J. D. Hague's] biographical notice of him for Appleton's [*Cyclopaedia of American Biography*]," undated MS, King Papers; S. F. Emmons's notes on King for R. W. Raymond, *ibid.*; Emmons diary 1871, entry for Oct. 28, Emmons Papers. See also *Clarence King Memoirs*, pp. 340–43.

    "not easily scared." "C.K.'s notes for [Hague's] biographical notice of him."

    "had met him." Gilder to J. D. Hague, Aug. 5, 1905, King Papers.

    "every roadside." *New York Tribune*, May 12, 1904, p. 8, col. 1 (unsigned but acknowledged by Cortissoz).

    "blithe blue." *Clarence King Memoirs*, p. 136.

    hazel. King to George F. Becker, Jan. 1 [1894], Merrill Coll.

4 "of the West." Goodwin, *As I Remember Them*, p. 172.

    "of his personality." *Clarence King Memoirs*, p. 125.

    "desert island." Cortissoz, *John La Farge: A Memoir and a Study*, p. 26.

    "incandescent." Morris, *Postscript to Yesterday*, p. 389.

"American generation." Brooks, *New England: Indian Summer, 1865–1915*, p. 188.

"not mentioned." De Voto, *Year of Decision*, p. 348.

"hardly possible." *The Education of Henry Adams*, p. 312.

5   "an avatar." *Ibid.*, pp. 311–12.

"existed in the world." *Ibid.*, p. 311.

"genius of his day." *Ibid.*, p. 313.

6   "made only one." *Clarence King Memoirs*, pp. 131–32; also, *Addresses of John Hay*, pp. 352–53.

Plantagenets; "crosslet, *or.*" George A. Morrison, "The King Heraldry," *New York Genealogical and Biographical Record*, XLI, 270–73.

"one thousand poundes." George A. Morrison, "The King Families of New England" (unpublished MS, New York Pub. Lib.), I, 52.

"shall thinke fitt." *Ibid.*, p. 53.

7   "mathematical instruments." *Ibid.*, p. 103.

"dividing line." *Ibid.*

Richard de Vernon. Harrison Ellery, "The Vernon Family and Arms," *New England Historical and Genealogical Register*, XXXIII (July, 1879), 319.

9   "hearts and souls." Sophia Little to Maria Weston, Sept. 26, 1840, Weston Papers.

"to the subject." Florence K. Howland to S. F. Emmons, Feb. 24, 1903, Emmons Papers.

"Zion's Corner." William C. Hunter, *Bits of Old China*, p. 166.

expedition of the *Morrison*. C. W. King, *Claims of Japan and Malaysia upon Christendom*, I, *passim*; American Board of Commissioners for Foreign Missions, Annual Report for 1838, p. 103; Tyler Dennett, *Americans in Eastern Asia*, p. 246.

Charles William King. *Chinese Repository*, VI (April, 1839), 637; VII (June, 1839), 76; XV (1846), 345.

10 "needless travails." Florence K. Howland to S. F. Emmons, Jan. 17 [1902], Box 29, Emmons Papers.

"on my heart." *Ibid.*

"affectionate sympathy." *Clarence King Memoirs*, p. 406.

"antique shabbiness." James, *Portraits of Places*, p. 345.

11 "larger cheer." *Mountaineering in the Sierra Nevada* (Boston, 1872), p. 242. Unless otherwise specified, all further citations of *Mountaineering* refer to this (the first) edition.

"heroine . . . native females." Fitch W. Taylor, *A Voyage Around the World*, II, 93.

"at Canton." Asher Robbins to Caleb Cushing, June 9, 1843, Cushing Papers.

12 "in the world." Taylor, *Voyage*, II, 188.

"nice fellows." John Heard, Jr., to parents, Mar. 13, 1844, Heard Papers.

"to the States." Benjamin Newton to parents, Mar. 18, 1844, Newton Shipping Papers.

"and a garden." The Chart of John Robbins. The death of Asher Robbins was noticed in the *Newport Mercury*, Mar. 1, 1845.

13 "relishing cuisine." *Mountaineering*, p. 215.

14 premonition. Eleanor Hague (interview), Pasadena, Calif., July 31, 1950; con-

firmed by Marian Hague, New York City, Mar. 16, 1953. Both recalled hearing the story from King.

"father's death." Florence K. Howland to S. F. Emmons, Jan. 17 [1902], Box 29, Emmons Papers. See *Newport Mercury*, Sept. 16, 1848, for death notices of both father and daughter.

"camphor pack." S. F. Emmons, "Clarence King Memoranda" (MS notes), Box 31, Emmons Papers.

"morally strongest." Bronson, *Cowboy Life*, pp. 333–34.

2

15 Christ Church Hall. "Clarence King Memoranda," Emmons Papers, Box 31; Florence K. Howland to S. F. Emmons, Feb. 24, 1903, *ibid.*

boardinghouse [of] a Mrs. Allen. Connecticut State Census records, 1850; Federal Census records, 1850 (R.G. 29, National Archives).

16 "down on the floor." Quoted in Pennell, *The Life of James McNeill Whistler*, I, 28.

17 "man with the rod." [King], Review of *Sketches of Creation* by Alexander Winchell, *Overland Mo.*, V (Dec. 1870), 582.

"my ignorance." Mrs. Howland to Emmons, Feb. 24, 1903, Emmons Papers.

"a veritable museum." *Ibid.*

"omnipotent Author." *Pantology; or, A Systematic Survey of Human Knowledge*, p. 401.

18 "in his career." "C.K.'s notes for [Hague's] biographical notice of him," King Papers.

"intellectual gifts." Emmons, quoted in "Necrology: Clarence King," 23rd Annual Report, U.S.G.S., p. 200.

"best possible." J. T. Gardiner, Notes on King for R. W. Raymond, King Papers.

"mind and soul." Florence K. Howland to J. D. Hague, July 27 [1904], King Papers.

19 Robbins Little; *Wild Pigeon*. Yale Univ., *Obituary Records of Graduates . . . 1911–1912*, p. 178. For abstracts of the voyage of the *Wild Pigeon*, Capt. Putnam, from New York to Canton, 1852–53, see Matthew Maury Logs, XLIV (R.G. 27, National Archives).

20 King and Co. "Clarence King Memoranda," pp. 50–51, Box 31, Emmons Papers; Morrison, "The King Families," I, 122, 129. For David O. King's activities in Siam see Townsend Harris, *The Complete Journal of Townsend Harris*, pp. 102n–103; also, William M. Wood, *Fankwei*, p. 106.

Judge John M. Niles. *Hartford Courant*, Review of E. T. Brewster's *Life and Letters of Josiah Dwight Whitney*, undated clipping in W. D. Whitney Coll.

"elementary studies." Hartford Public High School, *Catalogue . . . 1859–60*, p. 20.

"Classical II Division." Thomas J. Quirk, Principal of Hartford High School, Nov. 8 and Dec. 23, 1949 (information from school archives).

"Hartford Grammar School Master." Hartford High School, *Catalogue . . . 1941: Tercentenary ed., 1638–1938*, p. 109. See also J. H. Twitchell, ed., *Memorial of Samuel Miles Capron*.

21   "body of an idea?" "Artium Magister," *North American Rev.*, CXLVII (Oct. 1888), 179.

"did not dream of." Introduction to *Gail Hamilton's Life in Letters*, ed. H. Augusta Dodge, I, x.

"natural womanhood." King to John Hay, Aug. 12 [1888?], A37865[35](2), Hay Papers (Brown Univ. Lib.).

22   "noble vessel." *Thrice Through the Furnace: A Tale of the Times of the Iron Hoof*, p. 3.

"Christian civilization." *Ibid.*, p. 4.

"Marian shall be mine." *Ibid.*, p. 25.

"than thou art?" *Ibid.*, p. 31.

"enthusiastic abolitionist." Gardiner, Notes on King for R. W. Raymond, King Papers.

23   predicted clash . . . clash between the North and the South. *Ibid.*

"most brothers." 43rd Cong., 1st Sess., House Report 612 (ser. 1626), ". . . Surveys West of the Mississippi," p. 70.

Jonathan and David. [Caroline Lloyd], *A Memorial of Lt. Daniel Perkins Dewey, of the Twenty-Fifth Regiment Connecticut Volunteers*, p. 23.

"of saying love." King to Gardiner, Sat. Eve., otherwise undated [1860?], (HM 27814, Huntington Lib.).

24   "write beautifully." Gardiner, Notes for Raymond, King Papers.

"happy boyhood together." Dewey to King, quoted in [Lloyd], *Memorial*, p. 25.

"than conventional." Bronson, *Cowboy Life*, p. 330.

"we rambled." *Clarence King Memoirs*, p. 307.

"complete realization." *Ibid.*, p. 218. See p. 307 for Gardiner's reference to King's photographic memory. See also Emmons, National Academy of Sciences, *Biographical Memoirs*, VI (1909), p. 30.

"from the world." [Lloyd], *Memorial*, p. 25.

25   "in Christ." See letters of Mrs. Little, in *Christ in Prison*, pp. 60ff.

disaster of King and Co. 36th Cong., 1st Sess., S. Ex. Doc. 30 (ser. 1032), pp. 108, 114, 526.

opium. 35th Cong., 2nd Sess., S. Ex. Doc. Doc. 22, Pt. 2 (ser. 982), pp. 1353–55, 1366, 1420.

James Bowles. J. D. Whitney, Sr., to W. D. Whitney, Oct. 26, 1866, W. D. Whitney Coll.

26   "because of illness." Letter from Thomas J. Quirk, Principal, Nov. 8, 1949 (information from school records).

27   "real humility." King to Gardiner, Oct. 2, 1859, (HM 27809, Huntington Lib.).

"govern myself." *Ibid.*

"I have." King to Gardiner, Jan. 4, 1860, (HM 27810, Huntington Lib.).

28   "mighty inflaming." *Ibid.*

"Mother's announcement." King pocket diary 1860, entry for Apr. 13, King Papers.

"say *something*." King to Gardiner, Apr. 26, 1860, (HM 27812, Huntington Lib.).

"as thankful." King to Gardiner, May 20 [1860], (HM 27813, Huntington Lib.).

3

30 "Christian era." "The Education of the Future," *Forum*, XIII (Mar. 1892), 24.
    "future tense." *Ibid.*, p. 20.
    "for centuries." *Garrulities of an Octogenarian Editor*, p. 34.
    "half man." *Forum*, XIII, 29.
31 "half his brain unborn." *Ibid.*, pp. 28–29.
    "badgering grammarians." "Artium Magister," *North American Rev.*, CXLVII
        (Oct. 1888), 377–78.
    registered. *Yale Banner*, XVII (1860), No. 1, p. 2; Yale Univ., *Catalogue 1860–61*,
        p. 10.
32 "boat and fence." *North American Rev.*, CXLVII (Oct. 1888), 370.
    "test tubes." A. D. White, in Fabian Franklin, *Life of Daniel Coit Gilman*, p. 324.
    "none in America." *American Journal of Science*, 2nd ser., XXX (1860), 308.
33 "sermons in stones." *The University Quarterly*, I (1860), 212–13.
    "in the country." *American Journal of Science*, 2nd ser., XXX (1860), 308.
    "in my studies." King to Gardiner, Oct. 10, 1861 (HM 27821, Huntington Lib.).
        See also *idem*, Mar. 18, 1862, (HM 27824, Huntington Lib.).
    "philanthropic radicals." King to Gardiner, Mar. 28 [1860], (HM 27811, Hunt-
        ington Lib.).
34 "the institution." *Ibid.*
35 "keep in trim." Dewey to King, n.d., quoted in [Lloyd], *Memorial*, p. 28.
    "my soul in two." King to Gardiner, Mar. 18, 1862, (HM 27824, Huntington
        Lib.).
36 "in my way I do." *Ibid.*
    "training theories." King to Gardiner, Jan. 30, 1862, (HM 27823, Huntington
        Lib.).
    "'if found out.'" *Clarence King Memoirs*, pp. 377–78.
    "greatest graduate." Quoted in A. Phelps Stokes, *Memorials of Eminent Yale Men*,
        II, 82.
37 "his travels." Gardiner to his mother, June 14, 1862, Gardiner Papers.
    "in Switzerland." King to Gardiner, Oct. 10, 1861 (HM 27821, Huntington
        Lib.).
38 "with honor." Letter signed by eleven Yale professors to President Hayes, Jan. 10,
        1879, Hayes Coll.
    "plenty of fun." King to Gardiner, Jan. 30, 1862, (HM 27823, Huntington Lib.).
    cruise to Canada. "Clarence King Memoranda," p. 45, Box 31, Emmons Papers;
        Gardiner to his mother, Aug. 9, 1862, Gardiner papers. King had sketched
        plans for the trip in his letter to Gardiner of Oct. 10, 1861.
    "apprehended and detained." [Lloyd], *Memorial*, p. 32.
39 "exempt from draft." Gardiner to his mother, Aug. 14, 1862, Gardiner Papers.
    "their country." *New York Evening Post*, Aug. 9, 1862, p. 2, col. 2.
    "sneaking cowards." Quoted, *ibid.*
    back to New York State. "Clarence King Memoranda," p. 45, Emmons Papers.
    Dewey . . . 25th Regiment. [Lloyd], *Memorial*, pp. 32–33.

4

40   "by that light." Brewer to Brush, Oct. 1, 1862, ed. F. P. Farquhar, *California Historical Society Quart.*, VII (1928), 125.
     "sea of smoke." *Ibid.*, p. 129.
     "settles it." *Ibid.*, p. 121. *Cf. Clarence King Memoirs*, p. 315.
41   "that direction." King to Brush, Jan. 30, 1863, Brush Papers.
     "perhaps harder." Gardiner to his mother, Oct. 26, 1862, Gardiner Papers.
     "little den." *Ibid.*
     "near New York." *Mountaineering*, p. 209.
     "modern thought." *Mountaineering* (4th ed., 1874), p. 296.
42   "to a pebble." Quoted in Gabriel, *The Course of American Democratic Thought* (2nd ed., 1956), pp. 170–71.
     "a literal Bible." King to Gardiner, Sat. eve., otherwise undated, (HM 27814, Huntington Lib.).
     "still vital." "Journal of Trip to Northern Sierras" (D23), entry for Sept. 20, 1863, King Papers.
     "good as sunshine." Gardiner to his mother, Jan. 31, 1863, Gardiner Papers.
     "of the city." *Ibid.* For information about the American Pre-Raphaelites see David Dickason, *The Daring Young Men.*
43   "with themselves." *The New Path*, I (Jan. 1864), 114.
     "true art in America." *Ibid.*, I (May 1863), 11.
     "capable of." Private Notes, 1863 (A2), King Papers.
     "for Yale." King to George J. Brush, Jan. 30, 1863, Brush Papers.
     "across the plains." Notes on King for Raymond, King Papers.
44   "a great man." Quoted in [Lloyd], *Memorial*, p. 24.
     "rocky road." J. T. Redman, "Reminiscences and Experiences on My Trip across the Plains to California Sixty-One Years Ago When I Drove Four Mules to a Covered Wagon," Marshall, Mo., June 17, 1924 (HM 20462, Huntington Lib.). Hereafter cited as Redman MS.
45   "Missouri emigrant." Notes on King for Raymond, King Papers.
     Troy [Kansas, episode]. Redman MS (HM 20426, Huntington Lib.).
     luminous snake. *Ibid.*
46   "limits given." Roosevelt, *The Wilderness Hunter*, p. 195. Other sources for the buffalo chase and King's accident include the Redman MS; *Clarence King Memoirs*, pp. 378–81; Roosevelt, "Big Game Disappearing from the West," *Forum*, XV (1893), 769. David Dickason retells the story in "Clarence King's First Western Journey," *Huntington Lib. Quart.*, VII (Nov. 1943), pp. 75–76.
47   Miss Amanda. Redman MS (HM 20426, Huntington Lib.).
     Indian camp. "Clarence King Memoranda," p. 44, Box 31, Emmons Papers.
     "Caucasian prejudices." *Mountaineering*, p. 38.
48   "instructive history." Gardiner, "Proposed Discovery of New York by the State Survey," Address before the Yale Alumni Society, Gardiner Papers.
     aroused Shoshones. Redman MS; *cf.* 38th Cong., 1st Sess., House Ex. Doc. 1, pp. 514–16.
     "natural outgrowth." *Clarence King Memoirs*, p. 334. See also S. F. Emmons, "The Geology of Government Explorations," *Science*, new ser., V (1897), 43.

"sundried brick"; "of granite." Redman MS (HM 20462, Huntington Lib.).
49 Brigham Young. *Ibid.*
    "every canyon." Ludlow, *The Heart of the Continent,* p. 282.
    "same road." Gardiner to his mother, Sept. 11, 1863, Farquhar Coll.
    "dark green pines." *Mining Industry,* p. 12.
50 "so many nights." "Journal of Trip in northern Sierras" (D23), entry for Sept. 6,
    1863, King Papers.
    fire [at the Pioneer Foundry]. *San Francisco Evening Bulletin,* Aug. 7, 1863, p. 2,
    col. 3; Gardiner to his mother, Sept. 17, 1863, Farquhar Coll.; William
    Ashburner to George J. Brush, Sept. 22, 1863, Brush Papers.
    Placerville Road. Gardiner to his mother, Aug. 25, 1863, Farquhar Coll.; and
    Mar. 10, 1864, *ibid.*
51 "life and luxury." *Mountaineering,* p. 210.
    "wolves' clothing." Bronson, *Cowboy Life,* p. 341.
    "fascinating individual." Quoted by F. P. Farquhar, ed., *Up and Down California
    in 1860–1864: The Journal of William H. Brewer,* p. 469n.
52 "evening together." Farquhar, ed., *loc. cit.; cf. Clarence King Memoirs,* pp. 311–
    12.
    "to vulgarity." *Mountaineering* (4th ed.), p. 303; *cf.* 1st ed., p. 287: ". . . from
    barbarism to regularity."
    "at my hotel." *Cf.* Brewer, *Up and Down California,* p. 469.
53 "than Agassiz." Gardiner to his mother, Mar. 10, 1864, Farquhar Coll.
    "ever made." Charles W. Eliot to President Hayes, Feb. 28, 1879, Hayes Coll.
    "sons of Thor." *Century Mag.,* XXXII (Oct. 1886), 861.
54 "complete wretchedness." *Mountaineering,* p. 288.
    "miserable hole." *Up and Down California,* p. 455.
    "of all kinds." "Journal" (D23), entry for Sept. 12, 1863, King Papers.
    "I'm omnivorous." *Ibid.,* entry for Sept. 15, 1863.
    "well posted." Brewer to Brush, June 22, 1864, Brush Papers.
55 "had seen *this!*" *Clarence King Memoirs,* p. 319.
    "moonlit distance." "Journal" (D23), entry for Sept. 29, 1863, King Papers.
    "of admiration." *Clarence King Memoirs,* p. 321.
    "of my life." *Ibid.,* p. 320, Confirmation appears in Brewer's Notebook, Sept.-
    Oct., 1863 (C-B 224, Bancroft Lib.).
    "splendid!" "Journal" (D23), entry for Sept. 29, 1863, King Papers. See also
    Brewer, *Up and Down California,* p. 465.
56 "channel or gallery." *Up and Down California,* p. 473.
    "muffled explosion." *Mountaineering,* p. 262.

5

57 "it jolly." Charles Farrar Browne, *Artemus Ward: His Works, Complete,* p. 195.
    "Sunday mountain." *Mountaineering,* p. 182.
58 "unpleasant work." Brewer to Brush, Jan. 1864, quoted in Stokes, *Memorials of
    Eminent Yale Men,* II, 90.
    "of his stories." Ashburner to Brewer, Jan. 22, 1865, Ashburner Letters.

"tons of rock." Hoffmann to J. D. Whitney, Feb. 8, 1864, Hoffmann Letters.

"gummed together." *Mountaineering*, p. 179.

"plump pampered belemnites." *Ibid.* (1874 ed.). In 1872 King had employed the term "cephalopoda," the class to which belemnites belong.

"by Mr. King." *Geology*, I, 224.

59   Humboldt Mountains. King, Field notes 1864 (A2), entries for April 19–22, King Papers; Brewer diary 1864, entry for May 13 (C-B 332, Bancroft Lib.).

"Nevada Territory." *American Journal of Science*, 2nd ser., XXXVIII (1864), 260; also Whitney to Brewer, July 10, 1864 (C-B 312: 100, Bancroft Lib.).

60   "small party." *Geology*, I (1865), 365.

"new Alps." *Mountaineering*, p. 25.

"cropped hair." *Up and Down California*, p. 505.

"meets the eye." Quoted in Farquhar, *History of the Sierra Nevada*, p. 134.

61   "variously combined." Whitney, *Geology*, I, 365.

difficult crossing. Brewer supplies many details in *Up and Down California*, pp. 508–12; see also Whitney, *Geology*, I, 366–67.

62   "congratulating us." "Proposed Discovery of New York by the State Survey," Gardiner Papers.

"King of the Mountains." King, *Mountaineering*, p. 41; Brewer, *Up and Down California*, pp. 514–15.

"apple-green." *Mountaineering*, p. 41.

"climb for him." "Field notes . . . 1864" (B1), King Papers.

63   "'to tell of.'" Letter dated June 22, 1864, Brewer File, Asa Gray Papers.

Buck. King uses this name in *Mountaineering*, pp. 36–40, but *Bullock* in his notes (D12), King Papers.

"States pants." Notes (D12), King Papers.

64   "possibly hostile." Brewer, *Up and Down California*, p. 519.

"be the first." *Mountaineering*, p. 46.

65   "ornamental finish." *Ibid.*, p. 48.

"highest points of California." *Ibid.*, p. 50.

"inaccessible." Brewer to A. F. Meyer, Jan. 11, 1873 (HM 27835, Huntington Lib.).

"top of California." *Mountaineering*, p. 51.

"specimen of health." *Up and Down California*, p. 525.

66   "our minds to try." King to Whitney (draft in Notebook D4, "California Survey, 1864"), King Papers.

"confronted them." *History of the Sierra Nevada*, p. 145.

"of the cliff." Quoted in Whitney, *Geology*, I, 385.

67   "of roping down." Farquhar, *History of the Sierra Nevada*, p. 154.

"serious sky." *Mountaineering*, pp. 78–79.

"calmness of space." *Ibid.*, p. 80.

"MOUNT TYNDALL." *Ibid.*, p. 75.

"but inaccessible." *Ibid.*, p. 76.

68   "early cathedrals." *Ibid.*, p. 80.

"gave myself up." Quoted in Whitney, *Geology*, I, 387.

"to inform you." *Mountaineering*, p. 92.

"on the Survey." *Up and Down California*, p. 527.

"for his pluck." Whitney to Brewer, Aug. 10, 1864 (C-B 312: 101, Bancroft Lib.).

69   "the 'Hog ranch.'" "Field Notes . . . summer of 1864" (B1), King Papers.

"in the Sierras." *Mountaineering*, p. 109.

"better land." "Journal of Trip in Northern Sierras" (D23), entry for Oct. 13, 1863, King Papers.

"by the wayside." *Mountaineering*, p. 105.

the Newtys of Pike. See *ibid.*, pp. 94–111.

70   "darkness of future." *Ibid.*, p. 110.

71   "to attain." *Geology*, I, 390.

"wrong routes." *History of the Sierra Nevada*, p. 148.

"where to go." Remarks before the Appalachian Club, Mar. 5, 1886, *Appalachia*, IV (1886), 369.

"debris slopes." "Field Notes . . . summer of 1864" (B1), King Papers.

"flitted about." *Mountaineering*, p. 112.

72   "smiles of the señoritas." Bronson, *Cowboy Life*, p. 326.

"quiet revery." *Mountaineering*, p. 115.

"brutal lines." *Ibid.*, 113.

"Ka-we-ah." King to James T. Fields, Mar. 9 [1871] (FI 3160, Huntington Lib.).

73   "and sympathy." *Mountaineering*, p. 126.

"streaming light." *Ibid.*, p. 127.

"party came in." Notes on Mount Whitney trip, July 1864 (in B1), King Papers.

"professor of belles-lettres." Quoted in Laura W. Roper, *F.L.O.: A Biography of Frederick Law Olmsted*, p. 226.

"stories of his adventures." *Ibid.*

Mount Clarence King. Whitney, *Geology*, I, 392.

74   "as Switzerland." E. T. Brewster, *Life and Letters of Josiah Dwight Whitney*, p. 238.

"of the survey." "C.K.'s notes for [Hague's] biographical notice of him," King Papers.

6

75   "and limits." *Report of the Commissioners to Manage Yosemite Valley . . . for the Years 1866–67*, p. 3.

76   "its history." "Field Notes and Observations on the Yosemite Valley and Surrounding Country, Oct.-Nov., 1864" (B2), King Papers.

77   pristine fault. *Ibid.*; *Mountaineering*, p. 7.

"owe our lives." "Field Notes . . . Yosemite . . . 1864" (B2), King Papers.

"closing triangles." *Ibid.* See also *Mountaineering*, p. 149 (*n.b.* King's discrepancy in chronology).

78   "and escape." *Mountaineering*, p. 169.

"to a tempest." *Ibid.*, p. 171.

Moses Taylor. San Francisco *Alta California*, Dec. 11, 1864.

"black-and-tan sister." *Mountaineering*, p. 176.

79   "wind-swayed hammock." Unsigned review, *Overland Mo.*, V (Dec. 1870), 578–79.

"toward the sea." "Bancroft's Native Races," *Atlantic Mo.*, XXXV (Feb. 1875), 172.

"and uphold." J. D. Whitney to Brewer, Aug. 10, 1864 (C-B 312: 101, Bancroft Lib.).

"C. R. KING, SUPT." Yosemite Notebook, 1864, back flap, King Papers.

80   "see him." W. D. Whitney to J. D. Whitney, Feb. 26, 1865, W. D. Whitney Coll.

"good work." J. D. Whitney to W. D. Whitney, Mar. 1, 1865, *ibid.*

"suspended life." "The Biographers of Lincoln," *Century Mag.*, XXXII (Oct. 1886), 864.

"complete sham." Quoted in Farquhar, *Yosemite, the Big Trees, and the High Sierra*, p. 34.

"went his way." *Century Mag.*, XXXII (Oct. 1886), 864.

81   "for the winter." J. D. Whitney to Brewer, Dec. 8, 1865 (C-B 312: 182, Bancroft Lib.).

"parts of Arizona." King, Report on Arizona Reconnaissance, 1866 (B11), King Papers.

"their scalps." J. D. Whitney to W. D. Whitney, Dec. 24, 1865, W. D. Whitney Coll.

Bella Union Hotel. *Los Angeles Semi-Weekly News*, Dec. 29, 1865.

82   the road. The itinerary of King and Gardiner is reconstructed from entries in Notebooks D5 and D6, King Papers.

83   "and himself." R. W. Raymond, in *Clarence King Memoirs*, p. 332. Raymond had heard of this close escape from King himself. Other accounts include Gardiner, "The Trail Between the Cedar Bushes," Gardiner Papers; Emmons, "Clarence King Memoranda," p. 46 (verso), Box 31, Emmons Papers; *idem* in National Academy of Sciences, *Biographical Memoirs*, VI (1909), 35.

"for a pastime." "Bancroft's Native Races," *Atlantic Mo.*, XXXV, 170.

"had been killed." Brewer to Whitney, May 8, 1866 (C-B 312: 212, Bancroft Lib.).

84   "their packs." "Reconnaissance in Arizona, Winter of 1865 and 1866" (B5), King Papers.

"northern Arizona." "Notes on the Map of a Portion of Arizona Surveyed by C. King and J. T. Gard[i]ner" (Cartographic Records Branch, National Archives).

85   "never be travelled." "Reconnaissance in Arizona" (B5), King Papers.

"mining feet." J. D. Whitney to Brewer, Apr. 25, 1866 (C-B 312: 208, Bancroft Lib.).

"of the dead." *Mountaineering*, p. 21.

"results however." J. D. Whitney to Brewer, Apr. 25, 1866 (C-B 312: 208, Bancroft Lib.).

"no competitors." J. D. Whitney to Brewer, May 6, 1866 (C-B 312: 209, Bancroft Lib.).

86   "beryl sky." *Mountaineering*, p. 22.

"of the place." *Ibid.*, p. 183.

"out of Moses." Quoted in George R. Stewart, *Bret Harte: Argonaut and Exile*, p. 143.

"bony fide find." J. D. Whitney to W. D. Whitney, July 18, 1866, W. D. Whitney Coll. For a contemporary account of the find see *American Journal of Science*, 2nd ser., XLIII (1867), 265–66.

"on this coast." Quoted in Stewart, *Harte*, p. 142.

87   "old Missouri!" *Californian*, July 28, 1866.

Tertiary age of man. For King's attitude see *Atlantic Mo.*, XXXV, 169; also *American Naturalist*, XI (1877), 452, 459. See also G. F. Becker, in *Bulletin of the Geological Society of America*, II (1891), for notice of the discovery by King of the relic which seemed, in his opinion, to support Whitney's hypothesis.

"other summit." *Mountaineering*, p. 198.

Minarets. [King], Report to Whitney, 1866 (K1), J. D. Hague Coll. See also Whitney, *Yosemite Guide-Book* (1870), pp. 109–10; Farquhar, *History of the Sierra Nevada*, p. 151.

88   "glacier dragon." Report to Whitney, 1866 (K1), J. D. Hague Coll.

Mount Ritter. *Ibid.*; J. D. Whitney to Brewer, Oct. 5, 1866 (C-B 312: 234, Bancroft Lib.); Whitney, *Yosemite Guide-Book* (1870), p. 109; Farquhar, *History of the Sierra Nevada*, p. 151.

regions beyond Mount Hoffmann. Notebook D7, King Papers, indicates the itinerary of the trip east of Yosemite Valley, 1866.

"without wings." Quoted in Fremont Rider, *Rider's California*, p. 369. See also Whitney, *Yosemite Guide-Book* (1870), p. 99.

89   Grand Canyon of the Tuolumne. *Mining and Scientific Press*, XIII (Oct. 6, 1866), 223.

"some uneasiness." King, Note on the Mount Conness climb, 1866, Farquhar transcript, present whereabouts unknown.

"John Conness." *Mountaineering*, p. 267.

"on me alone." King to Henry Adams, Sept. 25, 1889 (Emmons transcript), Emmons Papers.

90   "and geographical exploration." Quoted in Bartlett, *Great Surveys of the American West*, p. 143.

7

99   "in its favor." *The Education of Henry Adams*, pp. 234–35.

100   "a good fellow." "New Haven Memoranda" (A2), King Papers.

"Fortieth Parallel Survey." Notes on King for Raymond, King Papers.

101   "sublime." Brewer, Data for E. T. Brewster's biography of J. D. Whitney (Farquhar transcript), Farquhar Papers. A draft of Brewer's letter is preserved in King, "New Haven Memoranda" (A2), King Papers.

"national domain." Quoted by R. W. Raymond, *Transactions of the American Institute of Mining Engineers*, XXXIII (1902), 631.

"and country." Humphreys to Stanton, Jan. 21, 1867, in 43rd Cong., 1st Sess., House Report 612 (ser. 1626), p. 84.

"white-hot." *Clarence King Memoirs*, p. 411.

102   "Sierra Nevada." Sec. 3 (last added item), Appropriations Bill for Legislative, Executive and Judicial Expenses, 39th Cong., 2nd Sess., approved Mar. 2, 1867. See *U. S. Statutes at Large*, XIV, 457.

"act of legislature." *The Education of Henry Adams*, p. 312.

"of this generation." *The New West: Or, California in 1867 and '68*, pp. 14–15.

"your place." *Clarence King Memoirs*, p. 385.

"satisfy me." King to Spencer Baird, Mar. 28, 1867, Smithsonian Institution Letters Rec'd 1867.

"natural resources." Humphreys to King, Mar. 21, 1867, King Survey Letters Rec'd (R.G. 57, National Archives).

103   "with pleasure." King to Humphreys, Mar. 28, 1867, King Survey Letter Book of letters and reports to chief of Engineers (R.G. 57, National Archives).

"enveloped it." "Memorial of Arnold Hague," *Bulletin of the Geological Society of America*, XXIX (1918), 38.

"love of ease." Gardiner to his mother, June 7, 1867, Farquhar Coll.

104   "to suit me." *Cf.* Arnold Hague, "Samuel Franklin Emmons," in National Academy of Sciences, *Biographical Memoirs*, VII (1913), 316.

"as anybody." W. W. Bailey, "Clarence King," *Providence Journal*, Dec. 29, 1901.

"pertinent questions." *Ibid.*

"American geology." G. P. Merrill, *The First One Hundred Years of American Geology*, p. 531.

105   "of the century." *The Education of Henry Adams*, p. 312.

"scientific man." Brewster, *Josiah Dwight Whitney*, p. 257.

"and organization." "C.K.'s notes for [Hague's] biographical notice of him," King Papers.

"only charm." Bailey to his brother, May 20, 1867 (HM 27837, Huntington Lib.).

the baby. For this episode see *Clarence King Memoirs*, pp. 386–90; also W. W. Bailey, "To California with Clarence King" (HM 39965, Huntington Lib.).

106   "social or literary." Bailey, "To California." (HM 39965, Huntington Lib.).

107   "restore him." Gardiner to his mother, June 7, 1867, Farquhar Coll.

"a performer." J. D. Whitney to W. D. Whitney, June 8, 1867, W. D. Whitney Coll.

"ask advice." *Ibid.*

108   "caper sauce." W. W. Bailey, "Itinerary, U.S. Geological Exploration of the 40th Parallel" (New York Botanical Garden Lib.).

109   "necessary institutions." Bailey, "Itinerary," entries for July 5 and 9, 1867.

110   "geological work." Quoted in "Necrology: Clarence King," 23rd Annual Report, U.S.G.S. (1902), p. 198.

to make an atlas. King to Humphreys, Dec. 18, 1867, King Survey Letter Book. See *Systematic Geology*, Appendix, pp. 763–69, for Gardiner's statement "Geodetical and Topographic Methods . . ."

111   "than the Indians." Bailey to his brother, Dec. 7, 1867 (HM 27848, Huntington Lib.).

112   *"at least the squaw."* See E. B. Bronson, *Reminiscences of a Ranchman*, pp. 3–22. John Samson includes a description of the same captious type in "Photographs from the High Rockies," *Harper's New Mo. Mag.*, XXXIX (Sept. 1869), 469–70.

113   "the sandhills." King to Humphreys, June 4, 1868, King Survey Letter Book.

"and cheerful." Bailey to his brother, Jan. 6, 1868 (HM 27850, Huntington Lib.).

"and Hell." Quoted in Goetzmann, *Exploration and Empire*, p. 440.

mosquitoes. Ridgway, *Ornithology*, p. 353.

114   " 'git up and get.' " Bailey to his brother, Sept. 2, 1867 (HM 27842, Huntington Lib.).

115   "love to linger." Bailey to editor, *Providence Journal*, Oct. 12, 1867 (published in Supplement, Nov. 11, 1867).

"two or three." Bailey to William B. Rogers, Dec. 29, 1867 (HM 39973, Huntington Lib.).

"severely shocked." King to Humphreys, Dec. 18, 1867. *Cf.* Bailey, "Itinerary," entry for Sept. 18, 1867; and Bailey to editor, *Providence Journal*, Oct. 12, 1867 (published Nov. 11, 1867).

116   "gathered there." McCornack, *Thomas Condon: Pioneer Geologist of Oregon*, p. 43. See also Charles Schuchert and C. M. LeVene, *O. C. Marsh: Pioneer in Paleontology*, pp. 180–81.

117   "in their hands." Bailey, "Itinerary," entry for Dec. 2, 1867.

"on the continent." King to Humphreys, Dec. 18, 1867, King Survey Letter Book.

"complete success." King to Humphreys, Dec. 18, 1867 (second letter of this date), King Survey Letter Book (R.G. 57, National Archives).

118   "of the country." *First Annual Report of the United States Geological Survey*, p. 4.

"in their pockets." Bartlett, *Great Surveys of the American West*, p. 133.

"quartz mill." King to George J. Brush, Dec. 30, 1867, Brush Papers.

"them either." *Ibid.*

8

119   "our meals." Bailey to editor, *Providence Journal*, Jan. 26, 1868 (published Feb. 28, 1868, p. 1, col. 8).

"in the street." *San Francisco Evening Bulletin*, June 13, 1867, p. 1, col. 5.

120   "for Mrs. Baldwin." "Virginia City, Nev. 1868" (D16), entry for Jan. 2, King Papers.

"cansou fichus." Quoted in Mack, *Mark Twain in Nevada*, p. 238.

"of all praise." Emmons diary 1868, entry for Jan. 10, Emmons Papers.

"and marriageable." *Gold Hill Daily News*, Jan. 9, 1868, p. 3, col. 2.

121   "ever collected." King to Brush, Nov. 2 [1868], quoted in Stokes, *Memorials of Eminent Yale Men*, II, 82.

"got tyght." Diary 1868, entry for Jan. 31, Emmons Papers.

"progressive companionship." "Private Notes," 1867–68 (D12), King Papers.

engagement. Emmons diary 1868, entry for Apr. 13, Emmons Papers.

122   "to please King." Notes on King for R. W. Raymond, King Papers.

John Henry Hill. King to Humphreys, July 10, 1868, King Survey Letter Book; Harry Harris, *Robert Ridgway*, p. 25; Va. City *Territorial Enterprise*, May 12, 1868; Dickason, *The Daring Young Men*, pp. 259–67.

123   "field for study." W. W. B[ailey], in *Providence Journal*, July 25, 1868, p. 2.

"intent to kill." Quoted in Harry Harris, *Robert Ridgway*, pp. 22–23.

124   "in the world." King to Humphreys, July 10, 1868, King Survey Letter Book.

"in depth." *Mining Industry*, p. 95.

"becoming festivities." W. W. B[ailey], *Providence Journal*, July 25, 1868, p. 2, col. 2.

125 " 'hell on grass.' " "Clarence King's Celery Story," Arnold Hague Papers.

"like a bloodhound." "C.K.'s notes for [Hague's] biographical notice of him."

"to obedience." *Ibid.* See also "Deserter Arrested," *Daily Reese River Reveille*, July 23, 1868.

126 "bright in color." *Mining Industry*, p. 12.

"from sight." John Samson, *Harper's New Mo. Mag.*, XXXIX, 471.

"Chippy." Ridgway, *Ornithology*, pp. 528–31.

127 "the name." *The Three Lakes: Marian, Lall, Jan, and How They Were Named*, no page number.

"sheet of foam." *Mountaineering*, pp. 188–89. King's notes for the falls description occur in a notebook labeled "Memoranda" (D9), King Papers.

"tertiary volcanic." King to Humphreys, Nov. 14, 1868, King Survey Letter Book (R.G. 57, National Archives).

twenty-five dollars. Account Book of the *Overland Mo.*, 1869–1875 (Univ. of California Lib., Berkeley).

128 "landscape painting." *San Francisco Evening Bulletin*, Sept. 24, 1870, p. 1, col. 3.

"in the desert." J. D. Whitney to Brewer, Nov. 26, 1868 (C-B 312: 330, Bancroft Lib.).

Lake Lahonton. *Systematic Geology*, p. 13.

130 "of investigation." *Lake Bonneville*, p. 17.

131 "indeed superb." J. D. Whitney to Brewer, Nov. 19, 1868 (C-B 312: 327, Bancroft Lib.).

"Silliman's friendship." Whitney to Brewer, Nov. 22, 1868 (C-B 312: 329, Bancroft Lib.).

Benjamin Butler. *Clarence King Memoirs*, p. 384.

132 "good purpose." *Engineering and Mining Journal*, LXXVII (May 26, 1904), 849.

"Engineer Department." Humphreys to the secretary of war, Mar. 8, 1869, King Survey Letters Rec'd (R.G. 57, National Archives).

"as a barbarian." King to Brush, Apr. 7, 1869, Brush Papers.

"I go West." *Ibid.*

133 "Pacific Ocean." *Systematic Geology*, p. 492.

Gilbert's elucidation. See *ibid.*, pp. 490–92.

"in the world." *Ibid.*, p. 11.

134 "with this work." King to Humphreys, June 17, 1869, King Survey Letter Book (R.G. 57, National Archives).

"Parleys Park." King to Gardiner, June 22, 1869, (HM 27826, Huntington Lib.).

"fallen condition." King to Brush, June 17, 1869, Brush Papers.

"flare up at it." *Ibid.*

"unremittingly yours." King to J. D. Hague, June 17, 1869, J. D. Hague Coll.

135 "to social life." Becker, *Transactions of the American Institute of Mining Engineers*, XLII (1911), 644–45.

"without a wrinkle." *Clarence King Memoirs*, p. 345.

"he returned." *Ibid.*, pp. 401–2.

"four-foot canvases." King to Gardiner, June 22, 1869, (HM 27826, Huntington Lib.).

"speed in plants." King to Brush, June 17, 1869, Brush Papers.
136 "past my bed." *The Three Lakes*, no pagination.
     "supply of coal." *Mining Industry*, p. 457.
137 "scientific hatred." J. D. Hague, in *Overland Mo.*, 2nd ser., XL (1902), 335f.
     "sympathetic side." "Miscellaneous Notes, 1869" (D17), King Papers.
     "next October." King to J. D. Hague, Apr. 6 [1869], J. D. Hague Coll.
138 "good thing." King to N. R. Davis, Apr. 9, 1880, "Cattle" Letter-Press Book
     (C7), King Papers.
     "the woman." King to Adams, Sept. 25, 1889, Emmons transcript, Emmons
     Papers.
     "come to grief." *Clarence King Memoirs*, p. 413.

9

139 "boarding school of girls." *The Education of Henry Adams*, p. 271.
     "Philistines." King to Brush, Apr. 7, 1869, Brush Papers.
140 "falling behind." King to Humphreys, Feb. 3, 1870, King Survey Letter Book
     (R.G. 57, National Archives).
141 "this child's lot." King, "Miscellaneous Notes . . . 1870" (D19), King Papers.
     F. A. Clark's topographical Notebook 1870 (55–091 K, American Museum of
     Natural History) contains another copy with minor variations.
     Marryatt. See *Clarence King Memoirs*, pp. 393–96.
     "Jim's mother." Emmons diary 1870, entry for Aug. 16, Emmons Papers.
     "resourcefulness." Speech at 25th Anniversary of U.S.G.S., Apr. 1904, Em-
     mons Papers.
142 "in America." King to Humphreys, Sept. 2, 1870, King Survey Letter Book
     (R.G. 57, National Archives).
     "Starr King's knob." Emmons diary 1870, entry for Aug. 19, Emmons Papers.
     "half whim." "The Ghost That Jim Saw," *The Poetical Works of Bret Harte*
     (Boston, 1883), pp. 173–75.
     "an orchard." *Mountaineering*, p. 1.
     "enamelled with ice." *Ibid.*, p. 228.
     "in one sweep." *Ibid.*, p. 229.
143 "for one's thoughts." *Ibid.*, p. 238.
     "of blue blocks." King, *Atlantic Mo.*, XXVII (1871), 373.
     "steep *névé.*" *Ibid.*
     "startling discovery." King to Humphreys, Oct. 10, 1870, King Survey Letter
     Book (R.G. 57, National Archives).
144 "see a glacier." King, *American Journal of Science*, 3d ser., I (1871), 159.
     "hundred feet deep." Quoted in Wright, *Proceedings of the Boston Society of
     Natural History*, XIX (1876), 61.
145 "rottin' timber." "Miscellaneous Notes . . . 1870" (D19), King Papers.
     "'Heathen Chinee.'" [King], "John Hay," *Scribner's Mo.*, VII (Apr. 1874), 737.
146 "write them [down]." Inscription in copy of *Mountaineering* presented to Mrs.
     J. D. Hague, May 22, 1872 (courtesy of Miss Marian Hague). The volume is
     now in the custody of the Huntington Lib.

"from his pen." *Clarence King Memoirs*, p. 291.

James T. Fields. Emmons diary 1869, entries for Feb. 9 and Mar. 18. Howells mentions the "sporting articles" in *Life in Letters of William Dean Howells*, I, 148.

147 "American geology." King to Humphreys, Jan. 23, 1871, King Survey Letter Book.

148 "all over Boston." *Memories and Milestones*, pp. 241–42. See also M. A. DeWolfe Howe, ed., *John Jay Chapman and His Letters*, pp. 121–22.

"Adamses came." T. K. Whipple, *Spokesmen*, p. 29; Henry O. Taylor, *A Layman's View of History*, p. 67.

149 "of consultation." *New York Times*, Jan. 4, 1902, Supplement ("Saturday Review of Books and Arts"), p. 8.

"heavy ballast." Quoted in Farquhar's Preface to *Mountaineering* (1935), p. 11.

150 "before breakfast." Quoted in Forester, *Nature in American Literature*, pp. 244f.

"Which?" King to Fields, Mar. 9 [1871] (FI 3160, Huntington Lib.).

"chronic emigrants." Field Notes . . . summer of 1864 (B1), King Papers.

"into semi-barbarism." *At Home and Abroad*, 2nd ser., p. 51.

"over the West." *Mountaineering*, p. 105.

"our literature." "Western Record and Romance" in *Literary History of the United States*, ed. Spiller *et al.*, II, 873.

Yank Clement [or Clements]. William Rideing, "With Wheeler in the Sierras," *Appleton's Journal*, new ser., III, 293.

151 " 'Bonheur.' " *Mountaineering*, p. 210.

"out of him." *Clarence King Memoirs*, p. 148.

"by glimpses." *Atlantic Mo.*, XXIX (Apr. 1872), 500.

"adventures." Data for Brewster's life of Whitney (Farquhar transcript in Farquhar Papers), p. 94.

"of fiction." Quoted by J. D. Hague, *Overland Mo.*, 2nd ser., XL (1902), 336.

"understanding." *Clarence King Memoirs*, p. 410.

152 "well told." Jan. 23, 1875—clipping, D. C. Gilman Coll.

"into science." King to Fields, Mar. 24, 1871 (FI 3161, Huntington Lib.).

"Western geology." King, *Atlantic Mo.*, XXVII (Mar. 1871), 372.

153 "the cream." King to Humphreys, Jan. 23, 1871, King Survey Letter Book (R.G. 57, National Archives).

"Western United States." "On the Discovery of Actual Glaciers," *American Journal of Science*, 3rd ser., I, 167.

live glaciers. Brewer to Whitney, Mar. 14, 1871 (C-B 312: 437, Bancroft Lib.). For a full bibliographical note on this controversy see Farquhar, *Yosemite, the Big Trees, and the High Sierra*, p. 51.

"appropriation." Humphreys to King, Mar. 28, 1871, King Survey Letters Rec'd (R.G. 57, National Archives).

154 "indigo hue." *Mountaineering*, p. 274.

"difficult route." Farquhar in his Preface to *Mountaineering* (1935), p. 17.

"our feet." *Mountaineering*, p. 277.

"been mistaken." *Mountaineering* (4th ed., 1874), p. 281.

155 "magnifying glass." Goodyear to Brush, Oct. 1873, Brush Papers.

"September, 1873." *Mountaineering* (4th ed., 1874), pp. 281–82.

"Mount Whitney." *Visalia Weekly Delta,* Sept. 11, 1873, p. 3, col. 1.

"the summit." *Mountaineering* (4th ed., 1874), p. 292.

"before me." Quoted in W. F. Badè, *Life and Letters of John Muir,* I, 396.

156   "and spire." *Mountaineering* (4th ed.), p. 295.

Bret Harte. Thomas Donaldson, *Idaho of Yesterday,* pp. 356–58.

157   "reading the proofs." *Clarence King Memoirs,* p. 136.

"my associations." *Ibid.,* p. 139.

"classed him." *Ibid.* See also Howells, "Recollections of an Atlantic Editorship," *Atlantic Mo.,* C (Nov. 1907), 604.

158   Parker, the Indian agent. Private Notes, 1867 (D12), King Papers.

"an hour ago." *Mountaineering,* pp. 284–86.

"of travel." "C.K.'s notes for [Hague's] biographical notice of him," King Papers.

"that fits it." *Clarence King Memoirs,* p. 224.

159   "the heading 'Fiction.'" R.L.G. Irving, *Romance of Mountaineering,* p. 224.

"mountaineering literature." Preface, King's *Mountaineering* (1935), p. 15.

160   "of the age." *Exploration and Empire,* p. 377.

"impeccable classic." *California,* p. x.

162   "commissariat mule." Adams, *The Education of Henry Adams,* p. 311.

"for guests"; "or doubt." *Ibid.*

had met before. Emmons diary 1870, entry for May 2, Emmons Papers. For the meeting at Cheyenne in 1871 see *Letters of Henry Adams,* ed. Ford, I (1858–1891), 212–13.

"in Siberia." *Letters of Henry Adams,* ed. Ford, I, 211.

"toward dawn." *The Education of Henry Adams,* p. 311.

163   "in the running." *Ibid.,* p. 346.

"of his day." *Ibid.,* p. 313.

"of our lives." *Clarence King Memoirs,* pp. 159–60.

"Kings were one." *The Education of Henry Adams,* p. 313.

"or Alexander." *Ibid.,* p. 311.

"American type." *North American Rev.,* CXIV (Apr. 1872), 445.

164   "tired of us." *Clarence King Memoirs,* p. 161.

WIND PILLS. Notes by O. C. Marsh, Arnold Hague Papers (R.G. 57, National Archives).

"constant trouble." King to Humphreys, Oct. 8, 1871, King Survey Letter Book (R.G. 57, National Archives).

165   "on any map." King to Humphreys, Dec. 16, 1871, *ibid.*

"outdone by Powell." King to Humphreys, Dec. 18, 1871, *ibid.*

166   "more provisions." King to Humphreys, Dec. 16, 1871, *ibid.*

"of the age!" J. D. Whitney to Brewer, Nov. 18, 1871 (C-B 312: 447, Bancroft Lib.).

10

167   "his employ." *Congressional Globe,* XLV[1] (Jan. 26, 1873), 631.

"very badly." O. L. Palmer to Humphreys, Nov. 30, 1871, King Survey Letter Book (R.G. 57, National Archives).

168 "they're gone." Notebook 1872 (D43), King Papers.

"old-gold girls." *Letters to Henry Adams*, ed. Ford, I, 410.

"of a screen." *The Island of Tranquil Delights*, p. 260.

"of celibacy." King to W. D. Howells, Dec. 17, 1871 (Houghton Lib. MS Am 800.20 [11091]).

"skeptics at home." Adams, *Letters*, ed. Levenson *et al.*, III, 331.

169 "blue green pool." *Reminiscences of the South Seas*, pp. 209–210.

"satisfaction." Adams, *Henry Adams and His Friends*, ed. Harold D. Cater, p. 218.

"Kalakauan fête." Bronson, *Cowboy Life*, p. 326.

"of them all." *Ibid.*

Princess Keelikolani. For a description of the princess and her house see Bishop, *The Hawaiian Archipelago*, p. 65.

"the Princess." King to George F. Becker, Dec. 31 [1893], Merrill Coll.

170 "then congealed." *Systematic Geology*, p. 716; quoted in Hitchcock, *Hawaii and Its Volcanoes*, p. 213, where King's visit to the crater is dated.

"other oceans." Adams, *Henry Adams and His Friends*, ed. Cater, p. 163.

172 "diamond discovery." King to Humphreys, Nov. 27, 1872, King Survey Letter Book (R.G. 57, National Archives).

"to report on." "The Diamond Discovery of 1872" (typescript), Box 32, Emmons Papers. Another copy of this account exists in the Emmons material held with the records of the U.S. Geological Survey (R.G. 57, National Archives).

"a month!" San Francisco *Alta California*, Aug. 1, 1872, p. 1, col. 2.

"confidence rests." *Ibid.*: quoted in Harpending, *The Great Diamond Hoax and Other Stirring Incidents in the Life of Asbury Harpending*, p. 225.

"attractive one." Henry Janin, Report to Gen. S. L. M. Barlow, *Engineering and Mining Journal*, XIV (Sept. 3, 1872), 156.

173 "careful study." King to Humphreys, Nov. 27, 1872, King Survey Letter Book.

174 "Ruskin calls for." *Mountaineering*, p. 210.

175 "and suspicion." San Francisco *Bulletin*, Oct. 7, 1872; Harpending, *The Great Diamond Hoax*, p. 228.

"Fortieth Parallel Survey." King, Deposition in the case of Rubery vs. Grant and Sampson, London *Times*, Dec. 24, 1874; reprinted in the *San Francisco Call*, Jan. 21, 1875, p. 1.

"the spot was." King to Humphreys, Nov. 27, 1872, King Survey Letter Book. See also the *Nation*, XV (Dec. 12, 1872), 379.

176 "ordinary individual." A. D. Wilson, *Overland Mo.*, new ser., XLIII (Apr. 1904), 292.

"to go there." King Deposition, London *Times*, Dec. 24, 1874.

"carboniferous fossils." Emmons, "The Diamond Discovery of 1872." Entries in Emmon's diary for 1872 bear out this account.

"[the] investigation." Quoted in "Necrology: Clarence King," 23rd Annual Report, U.S.G.S. (1902), p. 204.

177 "rude castenets." Emmons, "The Diamond Discovery of 1872," Box 32, Emmons Papers.

"Green River Canyon." King to Humphreys, Nov. 27, 1872.

November 3. Emmons diary 1872, entry for Nov. 3. N.B. conflict with King's subsequent statements (e.g., Deposition) that they had reached the "diamond fields" on November 2.

"of the stream." King, Deposition, London *Times*, Dec. 24, 1874.

"the spot." "The Diamond Discovery of 1872," Box 32, Emmons Papers.

"be gathered." *Ibid.*

178   "natural gravels." King, Deposition, London *Times*, Dec. 24, 1874.

"suspicious look." "The Diamond Discovery of 1872," Box 32, Emmons Papers.

"dislodged it." King, Deposition, London *Times*, Dec. 24, 1874.

179   "find rubies." "The Diamond Discovery of 1872," Box 32, Emmons Papers.

"ant hills." *Ibid.*

"of a man." King, Deposition, London *Times*, Dec. 24, 1874.

a swindle. See King's letter of Nov. 11, 1872, to the Directors of the San Francisco and New York Mining and Commercial Company (*Mining and Scientific Press*, XXV, 344) for an itemized statement of "ten links of proof" indicating fraud.

180   "as it is." "The Diamond Discovery of 1872."

"stars as guides." Wilson, *Overland Mo.*, new ser., XLIII, 296.

"unparalleled fraud." King, *Mining and Scientific Press*, XXV, 344.

181   "grace from you." "The Diamond Discovery of 1872." See also Merrill, *The First One Hundred Years of American Geology*, p. 539; Bronson, *Cowboy Life*, p. 351.

"in [its] bottle." "The Diamond Discovery of 1872."

183   "Bunker Hill Monument." David Colton, Report, *San Francisco Evening Bulletin*, Nov. 25, 1872.

"would be." Nov. 26, 1872, p. 1, col. 1.

"financial calamity." Editorial, Nov. 28, 1872.

"upon the market." "Potted Diamonds" (ed.), *San Francisco Morning Bulletin*, Nov. 27, 1872.

"isn't he trumps?" J. D. Whitney to Brewer, Dec. 5, 1872 (C-B 312: 482, Bancroft Lib.).

184   "as his success." *San Francisco Morning Bulletin*, Nov. 27, 1872.

"own operations." Humphreys to King, Jan. 10, 1873, King Survey Letters Rec'd.

"*of the land.*" *Overland Mo.*, X (Jan. 1873), 96.

184   "[entire] survey." Vol. XV (Dec. 12, 1872), 380.

$600,000. Bartlett, *Great Surveys*, p. 212n. N.B. the discrepancy with the figure cited by Powell ($387,000 for the King Survey) in *Report on the Methods of Surveying the Public Domain*, p. 11.

"Grand Canyon." Goetzmann, *Exploration and Empire*, p. 458.

11

186   "claim me." *Mountaineering* (4th ed.), p. iv.

"or wilderness." *Exits and Entrances*, p. 239.

"progresses well." King to Humphreys, Feb. 11, 1873, King Survey Letter Book.

"scientist in America." *Literary Industries*, p. 178.

187   "atmosphere of romance." *Engineering and Mining Jour.*, LXXVII (May 24, 1904), 849.

"fell dead." King to George F. Becker, Apr. 4, 1881, "Census" Letter-Press Book (C5), King Papers.

"new, hopeful." King to Gardiner, Feb. 15, 1873, Gardiner Papers.

"desertion." Vol. XVIII (June 4, 1874), 361.

"*of the intellect.*" King to Gardiner, Feb. 15, 1873, Gardiner Papers.

188 "of the science." *A Yanqui in Patagonia,* p. 31.

189 "with diamonds." J. D. Whitney to Brewer, Jan. 5, 1873, Farquhar transcript, present whereabouts unknown.

"slippery pathway." J. D. Whitney to Brewer, June 14, 1873 (C-B 312: 498, Bancroft Lib.).

Sierra Iron Company. King and J. D. Hague, "Report on the Property of the Sierra Iron Company situated in Sierra and Plumas Counties, California," Feb. 1873, A56106, Brown Univ. Lib.

"stay bought." *Cf.* remark of Zinc Barnes in De Voto, *Mark Twain's America,* p. 129.

"mining expert." *Mining and Scientific Press,* XXVII (July 12, 1873), 26.

190 "in New York." J. D. Hague to King, July 28, 1873 (draft), J. D. Hague Coll.

"integrity." *As I Remember Them,* p. 172.

"honest partisan." *Clarence King Memoirs,* p. 360.

"to cross-examiners." *Ibid.,* pp. 361–62.

191 "geological chance." Quoted in 44th Cong., 1st Sess., House Report 579 (ser. 1711), p. 634.

"auction sale." Hewitt, *The Selected Writings of Abram S. Hewitt,* p. 148.

192 "soap-bubbles." Adams, *Letters,* ed. Ford, I, 255.

"Mount Whitney." *San Francisco Bulletin,* Sept. 27, 1873, p. 2, col. 2.

193 "geological empire." *Mountaineering* (4th ed.), pp. 295–97.

194 "continental growth." King to Humphreys, Dec. 17, 1873, King Survey Letter Book (R.G. 57, National Archives).

"of exhaustion." *Ibid.*

"surely undermined." Vol. CXIV (Apr. 1872), 446.

195 "thing forever." J. D. Hague to King, Aug. 4, 1874 (draft), J. D. Hague Coll.

[King's] deposition. London *Times,* Dec. 24, 1874.

"expect to know." Bronson, *Reminiscences of a Ranchman,* p. 3.

"book and owl." *Clarence King Memoirs,* pp. 92–3.

196 "our omelet." *Century Mag.,* XXXII (May 1886), 154; *Clarence King Memoirs,* pp. 5–7.

"or macaroni." *Clarence King Memoirs,* p. 44.

"my eccentricities." *Ibid.,* p. 71.

"for promotion." *Ibid.,* p. 48.

197 "estate in the world." *Ibid.,* p. 61.

"in *great* capitals." J. D. Hague to King, July 22, 1873 (draft), J. D. Hague Coll.

198 "suffered intensely." *Clarence King Memoirs,* p. 293.

"but rest." King to George J. Brush, June 4, 1874, Brush Papers.

"at Washington." King to Brush, Apr. 7, 1874, Brush Papers.

"modern life." *Mountaineering* (4th ed.), p. 283.

199 "painful illness." King to Humphreys, Apr. 22, 1874, King Survey Letter Book.

"in Mining Cases." Hoffmann to Whitney, May 13, 1874, Hoffmann Letters.

"advanced condition." King to Humphreys, Feb. 25, 1874, King Survey Letter Book (R.G. 57, National Archives).

"American investigators." *Ibid.*

200 "of the rocks." *Bulletin of the Geological Society of America,* XXIX (1918), 40.

201 "elder Agassiz." National Academy of Sciences, *Biographical Memoirs,* VI (1909), 43.

"ploughing erosion." *Systematic Geology,* p. 483.

"whole subject." (1870), pp. 83–84; (pocket ed., 1874), p. 117.

202 "nerve and skill." Muir, "Exploring in the Great Tuolumne Canyon," *Overland Mo.,* XI (Aug. 1871), 140–41.

"hopeless floundering." *Systematic Geology,* p. 478n.

203 "had enjoyed." *As I Remember Them,* p. 172.

"ambitious bidding." *Literary Industries,* p. 178.

"Digger Indians." *The Education of Henry Adams,* p. 87.

204 "a disgrace." *Henry Adams and His Friends,* ed. Cater, p. 70.

"unalloyed praise." Quoted in Bancroft, *Literary Industries,* p. 180.

"of development." Quoted, *ibid.,* pp. 180–81.

Pelican-Dives struggle. See Dawson, *The Life and Character of Edward Oliver Wolcott,* pp. 94–95.

205 "Colorado mule." King to Adams, Mar. 9, 1882, Dwight Coll. See also *Letters of Henry Adams,* ed. Levenson *et al.,* II, 454.

"half the time." King to Humphreys, Aug. 22, 1875, King Survey Letter Book (R.G. 57, National Archives).

"relinquish work." King to Humphreys, Jan. 11, 1875, King Survey Letter Book (R.G. 57, National Archives).

"scientific autocrats." King to Humphreys, Aug. 22, 1875, *ibid.*

12

206 "its thoughts." Mabel Dodge Luhan, *Intimate Memories,* III, 3.

"three people." *Clarence King Memoirs,* p. 140.

207 "hotfoot home." Bronson, *Century Mag.,* LXXX, 381–82.

"high society." E. R. Hewitt, *Ringwood Manor, the Home of the Hewitts,* p. 107.

"my judgment." Quoted in Nevins, *Abram S. Hewitt,* p. 544.

"said a word." Holt, *Garrulities,* p. 136.

208 "of Lincoln." *Century Mag.,* XXXII (Oct. 1886), 864.

"afternoon of life." *Ibid.,* p. 866.

"ready to dine." B[rander] M[atthews], *The Roster of the Round Table Dining Club, with a Prefatory Note by the Fourth Secretary of the Club,* p. 10.

209 "oysters and ale." *The Letters of John Fiske,* p. 193.

"United States, perhaps." *Mark Twain's Travels with Mr. Brown,* ed. Franklin Walker and G. Ezra Dane, p. 88.

"in our country." *Clarence King Memoirs,* pp. 234–35.

"readier wit." Amstrong, *Day Before Yesterday: Reminiscences of a Varied Life,* p. 320.

"brilliantly clever." Rainsford, *Story of a Varied Life: An Autobiography,* p. 316; *cf.* p. 344.

"subtlest philosophy." *Clarence King Memoirs,* p. 235.

"the original." *Appleton's Annual Cyclopaedia,* XLI, 441.

"in his presence." *Clarence King Memoirs,* p. 218.

210   "his material." Ford, *Forty-Odd Years in the Literary Shop*, pp. 243–44.
      "face of man." *Remembered Yesterdays*, p. 226.
      "and persiflage." *Clarence King Memoirs*, pp. 125–26.
      "down about us." Quoted in *The Century, 1847–1946*, p. 39.
      "and learning." *Story of a Varied Life*, p. 316.
      "about Clarence King." Butler, *Across the Busy Years*, II, 436.
211   "Western life." *Clarence King Memoirs*, p. 196.
      "a multitude." *Ibid.*, p. 355.
      "are made of." *Ibid.*, pp. 126–27.
      "a great writer." *Ibid.*, p. 126.
      "constructive imagination." Bronson, *Cowboy Life*, p. 328.
      "publish it?" King to James R. Osgood, Jan 22 [1878], Betts Coll., Manuscripts
         and Archives, Yale Univ. Lib.
212   "fancy finishing." *Clarence King Memoirs*, pp. 141–42.
      "upon the peel." King to Howells, undated (MS Am 800.20 [1180], Houghton
         Lib.).
      "semitropical type." H. C. Lay to J. D. Hague, Dec. 18, 1903, King Papers.
      "of the Caribbean." King, Draft for the beginning of a novel, King Papers.
      "above the water." "Miscellaneous Notes" (D17), King Papers.
213   "none ever got." *Cowboy Life*, pp. 357–58.
      "had been penwork." *Clarence King Memoirs*, p. 355.
214   "had time to." Rideing, *Many Celebrities and a Few Others: a Bundle of Reminis-
         cences*, p. 93.
      "the corpse in." *Tales of the Argonauts*, p. xxvi.
      "*impenitent mule.*" *Mountaineering*, p. 215.
      "paid for." Donaldson, *Idaho of Yesterday*, p. 358.
215   "passed there." Quoted in Stewart, *Bret Harte: Argonaut and Exile*, p. 243.
      "country's literature." Samuel Wilkeson to the Hon. Wm. M. Evarts, Apr. 10,
         1879, State Dept. Records (R.G. 59, National Archives).
      "soon arranged." G. Bret Harte, ed., *The Letters of Bret Harte*, p. 170.
      "active days." King to Gardiner, Sept. 29, 1875, Gardiner Papers.
      "of California." Florence K. Howland to D. C. Gilman, June 6, 1875, Gilman
         Coll.
216   "their enemies." *The Education of Henry Adams*, p. 321.
      "public service." King to James Emott, Esq., June 7, 1876, in the *New York
         Tribune*, June 15, 1876, p. 2, col. 3.
217   "the campaign." *Ibid.*
      "his friends." *Clarence King Memoirs*, p. 149.
      "other ideals." *The Education of Henry Adams*, p. 321.
      "Far East." Bronson, *Reminiscences of a Ranchman*, p. 5.
218   "Puritan mother." Laura Stedman and George Gould, *Life and Letters of Edmund
         Clarence Stedman*, II, 474.
219   "every page." *Letters and Journals of Thomas Wentworth Higginson*, p. 274.
      "the Atlantic." John S. Clark, *The Life and Letters of John Fiske*, II, 88.
      "of Egypt." *New York Tribune*, Aug. 26, 1876, p. 12, col. 1.
      "ever saw." Leonard Huxley, ed., *Life and Letters of Thomas Henry Huxley*, I, 496.
      "a rib." "Jokes on O. C. M. by C. King," Arnold Hague Papers.

220   "one volume." King to Humphreys, Dec. 18, 1876, King Survey Letter Book.
       "without delay." *Huxley,* ed. Leonard Huxley, I, 497.
       "last twenty years." Quoted in Bernard Jaffe, *Men of Science in America,* p. 291.
       "American continent." *American Naturalist,* XI (1877), 464.
       "theory of science." [Henry Adams], *Nation,* XXV (Aug. 30, 1877), 137.
       "fan vigorously." George F. Becker to Henry Draper, July 2, 1877, Draper Papers.
221   "the two ideas." *American Naturalist,* XI (1877), 463.
       "of the biologists." *American Naturalist,* XI, 464–465.
222   "water catastrophe." *Ibid.,* p. 461.
       "points of catastrophe." *Ibid.,* p. 469.
       "of salvation." *Ibid.*
       "into being." *Ibid.,* p. 470.
223   "at several points." Quoted in W. M. Davis, National Academy of Sciences,
          Biographical Memoirs, XXI (1926), 111.
       "in fallacy." King to Dr. Suydam, undated, Mary Ludwig Suydam Papers.
       "most efficient." Peirce, *Collected Papers,* Vol. I (*Principles of Philosophy*), p. 42.
          See also Vol. VI (*Scientific Metaphysics*), p. 17.
224   "is safe." King to S. F. Baird, Dec. 18, 1878, Smithsonian Inst. Letters Rec'd.
       "my own." King to Humphreys, Mar. 1878, King Survey Letter Book; *Systematic
          Geology,* p. xi. For a brief summary of *Systematic Geology* see Merrill, *The First
          One Hundred Years of American Geology,* pp. 533–37.
       "geological history." *Systematic Geology,* p. 3.
       "epitome of geological history." *Ibid.*
225   "nonconformable strata." *Ibid.,* p. 532.
       "lime-formation." *Ibid.,* pp. 535–36.
226   "Cordilleran history." *Ibid.,* p. 540.
227   "physical conjecture." *Ibid.,* p. 747.
       "ragged edge." King to James R. Osgood, Jan. 22 [1878], Betts Coll., Manuscripts
          and Archives, Yale Univ. Lib.
       "than Genesis." Goetzmann, *Exploration and Empire,* p. 464.
       "better advantage." New ser., XVII, No. 97 (Jan. 1879), 63.
       "greater credit." Gilbert to President Hayes, Mar. 5, 1879, Hayes Coll.
228   "seen it." Vol. XXVIII (Jan. 23, 1879), 74.
       "in the country." James Hall to President Hayes, Jan. 4, 1879, Hayes Coll.
       "of the continent." *Clarence King Memoirs,* pp. 240–41.
       "Lyell's *Principles.*" Quoted in "Necrology: Clarence King," 23rd Annual Report,
          U.S.G.S. (1902), p. 202.
       "history of geology." Fairchild, *The Geological Society of America, 1888–1930,* p.
          47.
       "ever been written." G. P. M[errill], "King, Clarence," *Dictionary of American
          Biography.*

13

230   "namely beef." Quoted by Raymond, *Transactions of the American Institute of
          Mining Engineers,* XXXIII (1902), 631.
       "grow rich." Quoted in Osgood, *The Day of the Cattleman,* pp. 85–86.

231   "cattle kings." *Cheyenne Sun*, Oct. 24, 1877.
      "Rocky Mountain summer." King to D. C. Gilman, Nov. 11 [1877], Gilman Papers.
      Stonehenge. Details about the ND ranch come from Bronson, *Reminiscences of a Ranchman*, pp. 28–30.
232   "[ESG] herd." *Cheyenne Sun*, Aug. 24, 1877 (citing the *Greeley Tribune*).
      "was executed." Gardiner to Henry L. Higginson, Apr. 29, 1879, Higginson Papers.
      "Weld County." *Cheyenne Sun*, Aug. 24, 1877.
233   "in the business." Quoted in Burroughs, *Guardian of the Grasslands*, p. 99.
      "to Cheyenne." *Reminiscences*, p. 5.
      "winter feed." John Clay, *My Life on the Range*, p. 91.
234   "the bunch." *Reminiscences*, pp. 80–81.
      "Niobrara River." King to Humphreys, Nov. 6, 1877, King Survey Letter Book.
      "on the Niobrara." King to Humphreys, Apr. 24, 1878, King Survey Letter Book (R.G. 57, National Archives).
      "juicy buffalo grass." *Reminiscences*, p. 131. See also p. 307.
235   "Ogallala Sioux." *Ibid.*, p. 130.
      "a hell-hole." *The Red-Blooded Heroes of the Frontier*, p. 79.
      "special talent." King to A. S. Hewitt, Jan. 3, 1881 [*sic* for 1882], "Cattle" Letter-Press Book (C7), King Papers.
236   "should offer." "Extracts from a letter [Bronson to King] dated Fort Robinson, Jan. 19 [1879]," Schurz Papers, Vol. XLVIII.
      "[my man]." King to Carl Schurz [Feb. 1879], *ibid.*
      Lakota Company, Ltd. Report of Commissioners and Certificate of Incorporation, Lakota Co., Ltd., New York State Corporation Records, Act of 1875, Vol. 5C: 35 (Dept. of State, New York State).
237   "irresistible current." *North American Rev.*, CXLVII, 383–84.
      "extravagance." Gardiner to his mother, Apr. 12, 1879, Gardiner Papers.
      range to eastern Oregon. Facts about King and Davis's purchases there are found in *Report on the Productions of Agriculture* (Vol. III, U.S. Tenth Census), p. 1080; N. R. Davis Cash Book 1878–83, Rollins Coll.; *Cheyenne Sun*, Feb. 7 and Apr. 17, 1879; *Portland Oregonian*, May 2, 1879; Winnemucca *Silver State*, Apr. 9 and May 16, 1879.
238   "march for Colorado." King to Adams, May 14, 1879, Dwight Coll.
      "annual scare." King to Davis, Apr. 9, 1880, "Cattle" Letter-Press Book (C7), King Papers.
      "in the gulches." *Carbon County Journal*, Mar. 13, 1880, quoted by Agnes W. Spring, *Seventy Years, a Panoramic History of the Wyoming Stock Growers Association*, p. 51.
      cattle along Snake River and the Bear. Facts about the trail drive of 1880 come from the N. R. Davis Cash Book 1878–83; Brooks, *Memoirs of Bryant B. Brooks*, p. 94.
      "Laramie road." King to N. R. Davis, Apr. 15, 1880, "Cattle" Letter-Press Book (C7), King Papers.
      Circle Bar Ranch. *Cheyenne Sun*, May 2, 1880; *Cheyenne Daily Leader*, May 2, 1880; King to Davis, May 6 and May 20, 1880, "Cattle" Letter-Press Book (C7); Bryant Brooks, *Memoirs*, p. 97.

239   "Rocky Mountains." O. C. Marsh's Notes on King, Arnold Hague Papers.
       "my fun." King to Davis, Apr. 9, 1880, "Cattle" Letter-Press Book (C7), King
           Papers.
       Rocky Mountain Cattle Company. Report of Commissioners and Certificate of
           Incorporation, Rocky Mountain Cattle Co., New York State Corporation
           Records, Act of 1875, Vol. 6C: 91 (Dept. of State, New York State).
240   "until he collapsed." Roper, F. L. O., p. 389.
       "good start." King to A. S. Hewitt, Jan. 3 188[2], C7, King Papers.
       "of division." King to Davis, Jan. 3, 1881 [sic for 1882], ibid.
241   "sub-Arctic winter." Osgood, Day of the Cattleman, p. 101.
       [sale of] the Lakota holdings. A. S. Hewitt to Sir John Pender, Oct. 24 and Nov.
           27, 1882, Cooper-Hewitt Papers (Cooper Union); Bronson, Reminiscences,
           pp. 306–307.
242   Dakota Stock and Grazing Company. N. R. Davis Cash Book 1878–83; Memo-
           randum of Association, Dakota Stock and Grazing Co., London Registrar of
           Companies (Microfilm at State Historical Society of Colorado); Cheyenne
           Daily Leader, May 15, 1883, p. 3, col. 3.
       "with a smile." King to Davis, Jan. 3, 1881 [sic for 1882]. "Cattle" Letter-Press
           Book (C7), King Papers.
       "able to move." Osgood, Day of the Cattleman, p. 221.
       "in America." King to Emmons, Aug. 29 [1901], Box 30, Emmons Papers.

14

253   "at its height." "C.K.'s notes for [Hague's] biographical notice of him," King
           Papers.
       "civilian survey." New York Tribune, Apr. 25, 1874, p. 2, col. 4.
254   "hazardous experiment." Agassiz to Newcomb, Apr. 22, 1878, Newcomb Papers.
       "ever known." Address at the 25th Anniversary of the U.S. Geological Survey,
           Apr. 1904, Emmons Papers.
255   "head and hands." King to Gardiner, Feb. 15, 1873, Gardiner Papers.
256   "movement in Washington." "C.K.'s notes for [Hague's] biographical notice of
           him," King Papers. See Willis, A Yanqui in Patagonia, p. 30, for a mention of
           King as the leader of the movement.
       "in the consolidation struggle"; "that of Powell." Exploration and Empire, pp.
           588–89.
       "leaving no trail." Wilson, "American Vision and Landscape: The Western
           Images of Clarence King and Timothy O'Sullivan," unpublished Ph.D. disser-
           tation, University of New Mexico, 1979, p. 207.
       "crisis was averted." Clarence King Memoirs, p. 272.
       "man in Washington." The Education of Henry Adams, pp. 294–95.
       "of King's suggestion." Idaho of Yesterday, p. 356.
257   "relationship with Hewitt." Goetzmann, Exploration and Empire, p. 583n.
       Rabbitt's conclusion. Minerals, Lands, and Geology, I, p. 264.
       choice of committeemen. National Academy of Sciences, Proceedings, I, 150.
258   "scientific work." Powell, Report on the Methods of Surveying the Public Domain,
           p. 6.

"of the country"; "his expeditions"; "political effect." Newberry to Hewitt, Jan. 20, 1877, Cooper-Hewitt Papers (Lib. of Congress); quoted in full in Darrah, *Powell of the Colorado,* pp. 240–41.

"the alphabet." *Forum,* XIII (Mar. 1892), 27.

259   "out of that." E. R. Hewitt, *Those Were the Days,* pp. 53–54. Edward C. Mack also mentions the telephone scheme in *Peter Cooper,* pp. 308–9.

"influence for me." King to J. D. Whitney, Jan. 16, 1879, W. D. Whitney Coll.

"*thought of.*" King to Brewer, Jan. 15, 1879, (HM 27832, Huntington Lib.).

"lively manner." King to Newcomb, Friday eve [undated], Newcomb Papers.

260   "laid down by [King]." *Clarence King Memoirs,* p. 272.

"public domain." For the report and recommendations of the National Academy see National Academy of Sciences, *Proceedings,* I, pp. 141–46; also 45th Cong., 3rd Sess., House Misc. Doc. 5 (Ser. 1861).

261   "of hara-kiri." Newcomb to Marsh, Nov. 22, 1878, Marsh Papers.

"King personally." Hilgard to Marsh, Nov. 28, 1878, Marsh Papers.

"great friendship." *Ibid.*

"report before him." Marsh to W. B. Rogers, Nov. 19, 1878, quoted in Schuchert and LeVene, *O. C. Marsh,* p. 254.

"with great fulness." King to W. B. Rogers, Feb. 25, 1880, Box 6, Rogers Papers.

"without delay." Newcomb to Marsh, Dec. 7, 1878, Marsh Papers.

262   "great scientist." *Life in Letters of William Dean Howells,* I, pp. 261–62.

"the country." Elinor N. Howells to Lucy Hayes [Jan. 4, 1879], Hayes Coll.

"the fight." King to D. C. Gilman, Jan. 15, 1879, Gilman Papers.

"thoroughly with [him]." Nevins, ed., *Selected Writings of Abram Hewitt,* p. 209.

"field of action"; "National Domain." King to W. B. Rogers, Feb. 25, 1880, Box 6, Rogers Papers.

"distracted state." King to Marsh, Jan. 18 [1879], Marsh Papers.

"landed interests." *Cong. Record* (45th Cong., 3rd Sess.), VIII, Appendix, p. 217.

"[were] rampant." King to Marsh, Jan. 18 [1879], Marsh Papers. See also Darrah, *Powell of the Colorado,* pp. 249–50.

"powerful lobby." King to A. S. Bickmore, Feb. 2 [1879] (Files, American Museum of Natural History).

263   "all work." King to Marsh, Jan. 2 [1879], Marsh Papers.

"with Congress." King to George J. Brush [Jan. 26, 1879], Brush Papers.

"white-hot." *Clarence King Memoirs,* p. 411.

"liked it or not." *The Education of Henry Adams,* p. 317.

"the President." *Pandora,* in *The Novels and Tales of Henry James* (New York, 1909), XVIII, p. 131.

"ever evolved." James Truslow Adams, *The Adams Family,* p. 327.

"prop and stay." *The Letters of Mrs. Henry Adams, 1865–1883,* p. 274.

264   "angry monkeys." Adams, *Henry Adams and His Friends,* ed. Cater, p. 89.

"the surveys." King to Carl Schurz, Feb. 1879, Schurz Papers.

"capitalists." *Cong. Record* (45th Cong., 3rd Sess.), VIII, Part 2 (Feb. 11, 1879), p. 1203. Nevins includes Hewitt's speech in *The Selected Writings of Abram Hewitt,* pp. 209–26.

"national domain." King, *First Annual Report of the United States Geological Survey* (1880), pp. 3–4.

265   "opponent." A. S. Packard to Hayden, Jan. 14, 1879, Hayden Survey, Personal
        Letters Rec'd (R.G. 57, National Archives).
266   "seeking the man." Donaldson, *Idaho of Yesterday,* p. 356.
        "President's support." King to Marsh, Jan. 2 [1879], Marsh Papers.
        "scientific man." Newcomb, *The Reminiscences of an Astronomer,* pp. 257–58.
        "mutual aid." 45th Cong., 2nd Sess., House Ex. Doc. 80 (Ser. 1809), p. 13.
        "appreciate his work." Powell to Garfield, Mar. 7, 1879, Powell Survey Letters
        Sent (R.G. 57, National Archives).
267   "be crushed." "C.K.'s notes for [Hague's] biographical notice of him," King
        Papers.
        "inside track." King to Marsh, Jan. 2 [1879], Marsh Papers.
        "strictly right." Quoted in Brewster, *Josiah Dwight Whitney,* p. 339.
        recommendations. More than three dozen recommendations of King are filed in
        the Hayes Coll.
        "best thing." F. A. Walker to A. S. Bickmore, Apr. 9, 1879 (Files, American
        Museum of Natural History).
268   "in continental geology." *Engineering and Mining Journal,* XXVII (Mar. 8, 1879),
        159.
        "be fired." *The Reminiscences of an Astronomer,* p. 259.
        "Government Printing Office." Powell to Garfield, Mar. 7, 1879, Powell Survey
        Letters Sent (R.G. 57, National Archives).
        "weight indeed." *The Reminiscences of an Astronomer,* pp. 259–60.
269   "in detail." Brewer, Data for Brewster's life of Whitney (transcript, pp. 21–22),
        Farquhar Papers.
        "and unpromising." Charles W. Eliot to President Hayes, Feb. 28, 1879, Hayes
        Coll.
        "own corps." "C.K.'s notes for [Hague's] biographical notice of him," King
        Papers.
        "the Government." *New York Tribune,* Apr. 4, 1879, p. 1, col. 2.
        "was crushing." *Letters of Henry Adams,* ed. Levenson *et al.,* II, 355.
270   "will have." King to Brewer, Jan. 15, 1879, (HM 27832, Huntington Lib.).
        "want him." Adams to Marsh, Apr. 9, 1879, Marsh Papers.

15

271   "early policy." The Iron Mask Gold Mining Company vs. the Centre Star Mining
        and Smelting Co., . . . *Evidence of Clarence King . . . ,* p. 5.
        "being hung." King to Powell, June 2 [1879], Powell Survey Letters Rec'd (R.G.
        57, National Archives).
272   "national wealth." King to Hon. H. G. Davis, Dec. 15, 1879, U.S.G.S. Letters
        Sent (R.G. 57, National Archives); *New York Tribune,* Mar. 6, 1880, p. 1,
        col. 2.
        "enlightenment and education." *Ibid.*
273   "national necessity." *Ibid.*
        "old states." King to Schurz, May 14 [1879], Schurz Papers.
        "not parted title." Rabbitt, *Minerals, Lands, and Geology,* II, p. 20.
        "into the States." Concerning House Resolution 116 see *Cong. Record* (46th

Cong., 1st Sess.), IX, Part 2, pp. 2420–24; also, *First Annual Report of the United States Geological Survey,* pp. 77ff.

274   "mahogany desks." George F. Becker to his mother, Jan. 20, 1880, Box 5, Becker Papers.

"topographical work." King to Capt. George M. Wheeler, Sept. 13, 1879, "U.S.G.S." Letter-Press Book (C1), King Papers.

275   "mining industry." *New York Tribune,* Apr. 26, 1880, p. 1, col. 1.

"popularize the Survey." King to Schurz, May 14 [1879], Schurz Papers.

"and mineral oils." Pumpelly, *My Reminiscences,* II, 618.

276   "old Vernon house." *Ibid.,* p. 619.

"chemical analysis." *Ibid.,* p. 618.

"irrigable lands." King to Schurz, May 14 [1879], Schurz Papers.

"any one else." King to Schurz, May 29, 1879, Schurz Papers.

"to my taste." King to Powell, June 2 [1879], Powell Survey Letters Rec'd (R.G. 57, National Archives).

277   "United States." *First Annual Report of the United States Geological Survey,* p. 5.

278   "special value." 46th Cong., 2nd Sess., House Ex. Doc. 46 (Ser. 1923), "Report of the Public Lands Commission," p. vii.

"London tailor." Foote, *A Victorian Gentlewoman in the Far West,* p. 180.

"Eureka, Nevada." King to Schurz, May 14 [1879], Schurz Papers.

"stone fireplace." *Colorado Mag.,* XIX (1942), 123. See also Foote, *A Victorian Gentlewoman in the Far West,* pp. 181–82.

279   "snow-line." *John Bodewin's Testimony* (Boston, 1886), p. 38.

280   "foreign sinners." Donaldson, *Idaho,* p. 363.

"Mormon women." *Ibid.,* p. 363.

"I'm poisoned." *Ibid.,* p. 366.

281   "everywhere." King to Schurz, Nov. 7, 1879, Schurz Papers.

283   "on that point." King to Emmons, Oct. 2, 1880, U.S.G.S., General Correspondence (R.G. 57, National Archives).

"be introduced." *New York Tribune,* Apr. 26, 1880, p. 1, col. 1.

"agreeably thorough." *Transactions of the American Institute of Mining Engineers,* XLII, 647–48.

"bachelor Castle"; "cold potato." Hay to Howells, May 10 [1880], Howells Papers. See also James P. Munroe, *A Life of Francis Amasa Walker,* p. 209. Also *John Hay-Howells Letters,* p. 42.

"that room." *Transactions of the American Institute of Mining Engineers,* XLII, 648.

284   "replied King." Becker to his mother, Jan. 25, 1880, Box 5, Becker Papers.

"postage free." See Pumpelly, *My Reminiscences,* II, 619 and *n.*

285   "hundredth meridian." *Report of the Secretary of the Interior,* for 1879–80, p. 50.

"extravagant humbug." *The Letters of Mrs. Henry Adams,* p. 271.

286   "feet below." *Cong. Record* (46th Cong., 2nd Sess.), X, Part 4, 3160.

"midsummer." King to N. R. Davis, Apr. 9, 1880, "Cattle" Letter-Press Book (C7), King Papers.

"like mine." King to Davis, May 20, 1880, *ibid.*

287   "as 'din.'" Howells in *Clarence King Memoirs,* p. 141.

"china vases." "A few mild and wifely suggestions to Dr. George Ferdinand Becker . . . 1880," Box 15, Becker Papers.

"of the country." Quoted in Rabbitt, *Minerals, Lands, and Geology,* II, 42.

"was irksome." Willis, *A Yanqui in Patagonia,* p. 31.

288 "full activity." "C.K.'s notes for [Hague's] biographical notice of him," King Papers. See also Emmons in National Academy of Science, *Biographical Memoirs,* VI, 44.

289 "wholly successful." King to the U.S. Geological Survey (telegram), Feb. 16, 1880, U.S.G.S. Letters Rec'd (R.G. 57, National Archives).

290 "Our Byron." Quoted in Samuels, *Henry Adams: The Middle Years,* p. 31.

"in America." Josephson, *Portrait of the Artist as American,* p. 169.

Five of Hearts. See Dennett in *Scholastic,* XXVIII (1931), 6–7, 13.

"realize it." King to Hay, May 30, 1885, A37865[20](2), Hay Papers (Brown Univ. Lib.).

"no one else does." Arnold Hague to Emmons, Feb. 16, 1881, U.S.G.S. General Correspondence (R.G. 57, National Archives).

"of service." Powell to Emmons, Mar. 24, 1881, Emmons Papers.

291 "Geological Survey." *New York Tribune,* Mar. 16, 1881, p. 1, col. 4; *Second Annual Report of the United States Geological Survey,* p. xi.

"graceful regret." "C.K.'s notes for [Hague's] biographical notice of him," King Papers. See Rabbitt, *Minerals, Lands, and Geology,* II, p. 54, for a verbatim quotation of the letters of King and the president in their interchange.

"my knowledge." Quoted in Schuchert and LeVene, *O. C. Marsh,* p. 266.

"the Survey." *Mining and Scientific Press,* XLII (Mar. 26, 1881), 200.

"heroic figure." *Minerals, Lands, and Geology,* II, v–vi.

292 "cannot be separated." *Ibid.*

16

293 "the throne." King to Becker (telegram), Mar. 17, 1881, Box 15, Becker Papers.

"United States." See Powell, *Fourth Annual Report of the United States Geological Survey,* for 1882–83, p. xiii; also, *Science,* I (Mar. 23, 1883), 185.

294 "of labours." King to Emmons, July 1, 1881, U.S.G.S. General Correspondence (R.G. 57, National Archives).

295 "of his own." *Nation,* XXV (Aug. 30, 1877), 137.

of Continents. Carl Barus to M. K. Jessup, July 30, 1882 (Files, American Museum of Natural History).

"me personally." King to Gen. Walker, Oct. 2 [1882], "Census" Letter-Press Book (C5), King Papers.

296 "any information." King to Walker, Apr. 21, 1882, *ibid.*

"entirely to him." Becker to G. W. Seaton, Supt. of the Census, Feb. 8, 1883, Census Bureau Records (R.G. 29, National Archives).

"the industry." King to Powell, Dec. 12, 1881, U.S.G.S. Letters Rec'd (R.G. 57, National Archives).

"mining engineer." *Mining and Scientific Press,* XLII (Mar. 26, 1881), 200.

297 "Philistine vulgarity." *Forum,* XIII (Mar. 1892), 20.

"going on." Bronson, *Cowboy Life,* p. 329.

"such a people?" *North American Rev.,* CXLI (Nov. 1885), 446.

"his generation." Quoted in *The Education of Henry Adams*, p. 416.

"wrought-iron derrick." *Forum*, XIII (Mar. 1892), 29.

"its practice." *Clarence King Memoirs*, p. 215.

"think of it there." *Ibid.*, p. 414.

298   "for beautiful things." *Ibid.*, pp. 196–97.

Prietas. For the history of this vein see *Mining and Scientific Press*, LVI (Jan. 28, 1888), 50; Bell and MacKenzie, *Mexican West Coast*, pp. 223–24.

299   Minas Prietas Mining Company. The Minas Prietas Mining Company certificate of incorporation, New York State Corporation Records, Act of 1848, Vol. LXI: 114 (Dept. of State, New York State).

Harshaw. Clippings re the Harshaw, Boston News Service Clipping File (Baker Lib., Harvard); King to A. Agassiz and Q. Shaw, Sept. 15, 1880, "Misc. Mining" Letter-Press Book (C9), King Papers.

300   The Rosario Mine. Flippin, *Sketches from the Mountains of Mexico*, pp. 53–57.

"a fiasco." King to S. L. M. Barlow, Jan. 22, 1880, "Misc. Mining" Letter-Press Book (C9), King Papers. The S. L. M. Barlow Coll. contains several letters between King and Barlow concerning the Rosario Mine.

"for twenty-seven hours." *My Reminiscences*, II, 649–50; King to Pumpelly (telegram), July 21, 1880, "Yedras" Letter-Press Book (C3), King Papers.

Yedras Mining Company. Yedras Mining Company certificate of incorporation, New York State Corporation Records, Act of 1848, Vol. LXIII: 221½ (Dept. of State, New York State).

301   "good people." King to J. J. Higginson, Apr. 20, 1880, King Papers.

"the outcrop." King to J. J. Higginson, July 24, 1880, "Yedras" Letter-Press Book (C3), King Papers.

"than none." *Mountaineering*, p. 271.

"the mines." *Clarence King Memoirs*, pp. 123–24.

302   "charming city." King to J. J. Higginson, Oct. 4, 1880, "Prietas" Letter-Press Book (C4), King Papers.

"experience again." King to W. N. Olmsted, Sept. 16, 1880, "Yedras" Letter-Press Book (C3), King Papers.

"water level." King to J. J. Higginson, Oct. 4, 1880, C4, King Papers.

"livery stable." *Clarence King Memoirs*, pp. 403–4.

303   "ore in sight." King to J. D. Hague, July 15, 1880, J. D. Hague Coll.

"had suffered." King to Agassiz and Shaw, Sept. 15, 1880, C9, King Papers.

"[vein's] condition." *Ibid.*

"shall get it." *Ibid.*

"quartz mining." *John Brent* (Boston, 1862), p. 6.

304   Chinese cook. For this anecdote see John Hays Hammond, *Autobiography*, I, 181.

"down gallantly." King to J. J. Higginson, Oct. 5, 1880, "Yedras" Letter-Press Book (C3), King Papers.

"the mine." *Ibid.*

"out of pocket." *The Letters of Mrs. Henry Adams*, p. 248.

"and respect." Becker to Emmons, Feb. 19, 1881, U.S.G.S. General Correspondence (R.G. 57, National Archives).

305   [developments at] Yedras. King to J. J. Higginson, Sept. 16, 1880, "Yedras" Letter-Press Book (C3), King Papers.

"in the shafts." *The Letters of Mrs. Henry Adams*, pp. 259–60.

"feel uneasy." *Ibid.*, p. 248.

306 "cavalier servant's." Becker to Emmons, Feb. 19, 1881.

"for woman." *Atlantic Mo.*, XXXV (Feb. 1875), 172.

"Godmother." Becker to Emmons, Feb. 19, 1881.

"Corn Stack." King to George Tew, Mar 8, 1882, King Papers.

"two hemispheres." *Selections from the Works of the Baron de Humboldt Relating to the Climate, Inhabitants, Productions, and Mines of Mexico*, p. 252. For the history of Sombrerete see also the *Mining Record*, XIV (July 21, 1883), 51; *Engineering and Mining Journal*, LIII (Apr. 30, 1892), 483, and LIV (Dec. 24, 1892), 604; H. G. Ward, *Mexico in 1827*, II, 534–48; Charles B. Dahlgren, *Handbook to the "Historic Mines of Mexico,"* p. 12; Dahlgren, *Minas Históricas de la República Mexicana*, pp. 58–60; Trinidad Garcia, *Los Mineros Mexicanos*, 143–52.

307 "of expression." *Cowboy Life*, p. 357.

308 Sombrerete Mining Company. Certificate of incorporation (May 11, 1882), New York State Corporation Records, Act of 1848, Vol. LXVIII: 49. For data from the Minutes Book of this company I am indebted to Mr. John H. Nicholls, Secretary, Sombrerete Mining Co. (Nicholls to writer, Mar. 30, 1953).

"child's play." *Mining Record*, XIV, 51.

"the mines drained." Hoffmann to Brewer, Nov. 18, 1884, Hoffmann Letters.

"approved methods." *Mining Record*, XIV, 51. See also *Engineering and Mining Journal*, XL (Aug. 1, 1885), 82.

309 "probable failure." King to Gilson, Dec. 10, 1881, "Prietas" Letter-Press Book (C4), King Papers.

"and nursed." *Henry Adams and His Friends*, ed. Cater, p. 114.

310 "work before." King to Gilson, Dec. 10, 1881, C4, King Papers.

"saddle and all." King to Adams, Mar. 9, 1882, Dwight Coll.; see also *Letters of Henry Adams*, ed. Levenson *et al.*, II, 454.

"aether and knife." King to John Hay, Feb. 13 [1882], A37865[6], Hay Papers (Brown Univ. Library).

"in Clarence King." *Letters and Recollections of Alexander Agassiz*, ed. G. R. Agassiz, p. 193.

311 "the question." *Ibid.*, p. 204.

"Pacific coast." Pumpelly, *My Reminiscences*, II, 654.

Britannic; Henry Janin. *New York Tribune*, May 6, 1882, p. 4, col. 5.

"green in advance." King to Henry Adams, May 5, 1882, Dwight Coll.

17

312 "his delight." *Clarence King Memoirs*, pp. 203–5.

"safer investments." *Statistics and Technology of the Precious Metals*, p. viii.

George S. Sedgwick. Details about Sedgwick are from King's "Observations on Sedgwick's Bill of Particulars," Mar. 7, 1888, H. L. Higginson Papers.

313 "as toastmaster." *Clarence King Memoirs*, p. 207.

"sapphire sky." *Century Mag.*, XXXII (Oct. 1886), 864–65.

"is Morton?" *The Letters of Mrs. Henry Adams*, p. 271.

"a barmaid." *Ibid.*, p. 375.

"in France." *Clarence King Memoirs*, p. 207.

"placid consistency." *Henry James: Autobiography*, ed. F. W. Dupee, pp. 155–56.

"perfect ease." *Clarence King Memoirs*, p. 124.

314 "Don Quixote." *Ibid.*, p. 8.

"Spanish inn." *Ibid.*, p. 167.

"fairly groans." *Century Mag.*, XXXII (Oct. 1886), 866.

"to be pleased." *The Alhambra* (New York, 1852), p. 20.

"Lima, Señor?" *Clarence King Memoirs*, p. 33.

315 "love and garlic." *Ibid.*, p. 24.

"golden helmet." *Ibid.*, p. 13.

"disc of green." *Ibid.*, p. 23.

316 "it is yours." *Ibid.*, pp. 26–28.

"[to] one side." *Ibid.*, p. 3.

"and blundered." King to Hay, Friday [May 1886], A37865[21], Hay Papers (Brown Univ. Lib.).

"literature"; "English language"; "in America." *New York Tribune*, May 12, 1904, p. 8, col. 1; and Dec. 29, 1901, Sunday Supplement (acknowledged by Cortissoz).

317 "rather English, life." F. H. Mason to Hay, Sept. 1 [1883], A39958[19](2), Hay Papers (Brown Univ. Lib.).

"its stratification." *Clarence King Memoirs*, p. 143.

"blush like a virgin." F. H. Mason to Hay, June 12 [1882], A39958[17](2), Hay Papers (Brown Univ. Lib.).

318 "I ever saw." King to Hay, [no month] 27, 1882, A37865[3], Hay Papers (Brown Univ. Lib.).

"London society." *Aspects and Impressions*, p. 27.

"in cheese." *The Education of Henry Adams*, p. 197.

"and frivolity." Moreton Frewen, *Melton Mowbray*, p. 97.

[Osgood's banquet.] Weber, *James Ripley Osgood*, pp. 198–200. The Houghton Lib., Harvard, holds a menu for this dinner dated Sept. 7, 1882, and signed by Hay, Howells, James, Harte, King, Aldrich, Warner, and others who were present.

319 "munificence." *Clarence King Memoirs*, p. 146.

Beethoven; Schiller. *New York Tribune*, Oct. 10, 1882, p. 4, col. 5.

"the part." Howells, *Harper's Mo.*, CVIII (Dec. 1903), 157.

320 "too good for it." *Ibid.*, p. 157.

"of London life." F. H. Mason to Hay, Sept. 1 [1883], A39958[19](2), Hay Papers (Brown Univ. Lib.).

"parts of town"; "violence befell him." King, quoted in Edel, *Henry James: The Treacherous Years*, p. 237. See p. 238 for indication of James's company in London slums.

"in *Oliver Twist*." F. H. Mason to Hay, Sept. 1 [1883], A39958[19](2), Hay Papers (Brown Univ. Lib.).

321 "Elizabethan sovereign." Miss Marian Hague (interview), New York City, Mar. 16, 1953.

"permit themselves." *Clarence King Memoirs*, p. 146.

"live with him." *Life in Letters of William Dean Howells*, I, 337.

"live without [King]." Quoted in Edel, *Henry James: The Treacherous Years*, p. 237.

"blood-brotherhood." *Clarence King Memoirs*, p. 208.

322 "well enough together." *Ibid.*, p. 406.

"and condolences." *Ibid.*, pp. 143–44.

[picnic with Crosse & Blackwell girls.] *Ibid.*, p. 369.

Lady Dalhousie. See Frewen, *Melton Mowbray*, pp. 106, 108, 110.

Circle Bar Ranch. Memorandum of Association, Dakota Stock & Grazing Co., London Registrar of Companies (microfilm at State Historical Society of Colorado); Maurice Frink to writer, Nov. 9, 1955.

Moreton Frewen. See *Melton Mowbray, passim.*

323 "Irish store cattle." Osgood, *Day of the Cattleman*, p. 111.

"of hearts." *Clarence King Memoirs*, p. 123.

"nobody resents it." Quoted in James and Hay, *Henry James and John Hay*, p. 168n.

" 'nobility and gentry.' " *Clarence King Memoirs*, p. 124.

"morals and statesmanship." King to Hay, Aug. 15, 1882, A37865[7](2), Hay Papers (Brown Univ. Lib.).

324 "about *Aristoc*"; "getting at it." King to Hay [Dec. 1882], A37865[6](2), Hay Papers (Brown Univ. Lib.).

"for the dukes." Miss Eleanor Hague (interview), July 31, 1950; confirmed by Miss Marian Hague, Mar. 16, 1953.

"am fatigued." King to Hay, [Dec. 1883], A37865[6](2), Hay Papers (Brown Univ. Lib.).

"get at him." F. H. Mason to Hay, Sept. 1 [1883], A39958[19](2). Hay Papers (Brown Univ. Lib.).

"for that man!" Mason to Hay, Nov. 10 [1883], A39958[22](2), *ibid.*

"a little, English." King to Hay, Aug. 24 [1882], A37865[8](2), *ibid.*

"Irish peeress." *Letters of Henry Adams*, ed. Ford, I (1858–1891), 347.

"certainly is." *Ibid.*, p. 348.

"nothing about him." *Letters of Henry Adams*, ed. Levenson et al., II, 488.

325 [Paris negotiations re Yedras]. King's "Observations on Sedgwick's Bill of Particulars," Mar. 7, 1888, Higginson Papers.

"by the millions"; "out of the shops." Quoted in Edel, *Henry James: The Middle Years*, p. 55; *Henry James Letters*, ed. Edel, II, 387, 392.

"lover of character." Edel, *Henry James: The Treacherous Years*, p. 237.

"man in the world." Quoted, *ibid.*

"magic spells"; "fairy-godmother." James and Hay, *Henry James and John Hay*, p. 92.

"unsatisfactory creature"; "as he [was] delightful." Quoted, Edel, *Henry James: The Treacherous Years*, p. 237.

" 'my real home.' " Quoted in James, *Henry James Letters*, ed. Edel, III, 551.

326 "as a London company." King to Hay, Jan. 26, 1883, A37865[10], Hay Papers (Brown Univ. Lib.).

Anglo-Mexican Mining Company. *Engineering and Mining Journal*, XXXVI (Sept. 22, 1883), 187, and XXXVII (Feb. 9, 1884), 97; *Mining Journal*, LIII,

Part 2 (Sept. 8, 1883), Supplement, p. 1054; and LVII, Part 2 (Dec. 24, 1887), p. 1554; King's "Observations on Sedgwick's Bill of Particulars," Mar. 7, 1888, Higginson Papers.

"finest in the world." *Mining Journal*, LIV (Jan. 12, 1884), 45.

"and abundant yield." *Ibid.*

"art-loving mind." *North American Rev.*, CXLI (Nov. 1885), 445.

327   "unflinching extravagance." Quoted by Cortissoz, *The Life of Whitelaw Reid*, II, 86.

King house in Newport. Bronson, *Cowboy Life*, p. 332.

328   "a fool of himself." See Hay, *Complete Poetical Works of John Hay*, pp. 99–106.

impecunious *doña.* Miss Eleanor Hague (interview), July 31, 1950; confirmed by Miss Marian Hague, Mar. 16, 1953, the piece then being in her possession.

Sedgwick. Miss Marian Hague (interview), Mar. 22, 1953.

329   Gilbert Munger. Bronson, *Cowboy Life*, p. 354; *Gilbert Munger, Landscape Artist, 1836–1903*; *New York Commercial Advertiser*, Jan. 5, 1904.

Zorn. Arnold Hague to J. D. Hague, Apr. 26 and May 3, 1902, King Papers; Karl Asplund, *Anders Zorn: His Life and Work*, pp. 6–7. Zorn's portrait of King is reproduced in *Zorn* by Gerda Boethius.

"but life-like." King to Hay, [Mar. 1883], A37865[14]; see also *idem*, Mar. 8 [1883], A37865[11](3), Hay Papers (Brown Univ. Lib.).

"Mesdag and Israels." *Clarence King Memoirs*, p. 129.

330   "of the Apaches." *Ibid.*

"nothing recognized." *Mountaineering*, p. 92.

"were evident." *Clarence King Memoirs*, p. 191.

"all over him." Hay to Howells, July 27, 1883, in *Letters of John Hay and Extracts from Diary*, II, 80.

331   "deserves another." *Clarence King Memoirs*, p. 130.

"an old song." E. V. Lucas, *Edwin Austin Abbey, Royal Academician*, I, 143–45. A reproduction of the picture faces p. 145 in Lucas (I). It was also published in *Book of the Tile Club*.

Black's house in the Strand. Lucas, *Abbey*, I, 139–40; Wemyss Reid, *William Black, Novelist*, pp. 193, 250.

"[his essay on] Emerson." Arnold, *Letters of Matthew Arnold, 1848–1888*, ed. G. W. E. Russell, II, 254.

332   "your door or not." King to Hay, Oct. 1883, A37865[17], Hay Papers (Brown Univ. Lib.).

[Hay and Arnold's lecture.] Thayer, *John Hay*, II, 70.

"or Clarence King." Matthews, *These Many Years*, p. 275.

Kinsmen. *Ibid.*, pp. 232–33; Laurence Hutton, *Talks in a Library with Laurence Hutton, Recorded by Isobel Moore*, p. 328; *The Critic*, X (new ser. VII), 154.

333   "fulminate and bang." Quoted in E. R. Pennell, *Charles Godfrey Leland*, II, 59. For more about the Rabelais Club see Matthews, *These Many Years*, pp. 281–285; Walter Besant, *Autobiography*, pp. 240–41; Rabelais Club, *Recreations of the Rabelais Club*, II (1882–1885), including membership lists.

"of the day." *New York Tribune*, Apr. 25, 1880, p. 8, col. 4.

"dream in life." King to J. D. Hague, June 27, 1884, King Papers.

Krakatoa's stagy legacy. See Mary Anderson, *A Few Memories*, p. 139.

334 "back this summer." S. F. Emmons to G. F. Becker, June 13, 1884, Becker
       Papers.
     "only two years." King to J. D. Hague, June 27, 1884, King Papers.
335 "forever & ever." F. H. Mason to Hay, Sept. 1 [1883], A39958[19](2), Hay
       Papers (Brown Univ. Lib.).
     "happy England." *North American Rev.*, CXLI (Nov. 1885), 449.
     "in mourning." Hay to Howells, Sept. 16, 1884, Howells Papers.

18

336 "than English." *North American Rev.*, CXLI (Nov. 1885), 450.
     "our pride." *Ibid.*
     "nervous disease." Quoted in Bronson, *Cowboy Life*, p. 329.
337 "the right thing." *Clarence King Memoirs*, p. 149.
     "after marriage." *Letters of Henry Adams*, ed. W. C. Ford, I, 360.
     "and Rebellion." See D. G. Farrelly, " 'Rum, Romanism and Rebellion' Resur-
       rected," *Western Political Quart.*, VIII (June 1955), 262–70.
338 "sun has set!" King to Hay, Nov. 5 [1884], A37865[16], Hay Papers (Brown
       Univ. Lib.).
     "without hesitation." King to D. C. Gilman, Feb. 27, 1885, Gilman Papers.
     "mercy in gray." *North American Rev.*, CXLI (Nov. 1885), 450.
     Great American Sedative. See Josephson, *Portrait of the Artist as American*,
       p. xxii.
     "balls in New York." Adams, *Letters*, ed. Levenson *et al.*, II, 573.
     "like a vagrant." *Ibid.*, III, 115.
339 La Farge. Cortissoz, *John La Farge, A Memoir and a Study*, pp. 12–13.
     "10th Street den." King to Hay, May 30, 1885, A37865[20](2), Hay Papers
       (Brown Univ. Lib.).
     "somewhere here." *Clarence King Memoirs*, p. 192.
340 "American race." *North American Rev.*, CXLI, 443–444. For an earlier statement
       by King on a future American race see *Overland Mo.*, V (Dec. 1870), 581.
     "Roman works." *North American Rev.*, CXLI, 450.
     "Romanesque style." *Ibid.*, p. 453.
     "over with [La Farge]." *John La Farge*, 198.
341 "as the land." *Clarence King Memoirs*, pp. 194–95.
     "in Hoboken." *North American Rev.*, CXLI, 448.
     "in New York!" *Ibid.*, p. 445.
     "stained glass." *Clarence King Memoirs*, p. 193.
342 "my little treasures." King to J. D. Hague, June 7, 1887, King Papers. See also
       J. D. Hague, "Memorandum of articles belonging to Clarence King now in my
       possession [1885]," L9; 7, J. D. Hague Coll.
     "Earth-dwellers." *Clarence King Memoirs*, p. 201.
     "desperate failure." *My Reminiscences*, II, 653.
343 "the difficulties." *Engineering and Mining Journal*, XLV (Mar. 10, 1888), 179.
     "us all rich." George Tew to King, Jan. 2, 1883, King Papers. Concerning work at
       Sombrerete see the *Mining Record*, XIV (July 21, 1883), 51, and (Aug. 4,

1883), 92; *Engineering and Mining Journal*, XL (Aug. 1, 1885), 82, and LIV (Dec. 24, 1892), 604.

"Sombrerete ever saw." Tew to W. N. Olmsted, Feb. 22, 1883 (telegram), King Papers.

"state of things." Hoffmann to Whitney, Feb. 29, 1884, Hoffmann Letters.

344   "in the sky." *Life and Letters of Henry Lee Higginson*, pp. 411–12.

"can recommend." Tew to King, Jan. 2, 1883, King Papers.

"no efficiency here." Mahlon Sands to H. L. Higginson, Nov. 3, 1886, H. L. Higginson Papers.

blamed King for the muddle. See *Letters and Recollections of Alexander Agassiz*, p. 192.

345   compromise. Q. A. Shaw to King, Jan. 5, 1886, Higginson Papers; *Mining Journal*, LVII (Dec. 17, 1887), Part 2, 1515.

"there may be." Shaw to H. L. Higginson, Nov. 22, 1886, Higginson Papers.

"and money"; "infernal sink." Agassiz to H. L. Higginson, Feb. 24, 1887, Higginson Papers.

"in Mexico." *Letters and Recollections of Alexander Agassiz*, pp. 224–25.

"common sense [in] King." Letter dated Jan. 13, 1887, Higginson Papers.

King's resignation as managing director. *Mining Journal*, LVII (Dec. 17, 1887), Part 2, 1515; *ibid.*, (Dec. 24, 1887), 1554; also LIX (May 4, 1889), 506; W. N. Olmsted to H. L. Higginson, Jan. 13, 1887, Higginson Papers.

346   "spells of depression." Arnold Hague to J. D. Hague, Feb. 18 [188–], J. D. Hague Coll.

"in front of me." *Clarence King Memoirs*, pp. 86–87.

"sore and unsuccessful." King to Hay, [Dec. 1897], A35451[792], Hay Papers (Brown Univ. Lib.).

"—all gone." King to Hay, Century Club, [Nov.] 30, [1885], A37865[19], *ibid.*

347   "enjoy their ease." *Clarence King Memoirs*, p. 151–52.

"our national cakewalk." *A Traveler from Altruria* (New York, 1894), p. 209.

348   "with you at the last." *Letters of John Hay*, II, 98.

349   "little *Esther.*" *Letters of Henry Adams*, ed. W. C. Ford, I, 377.

"of helplessness." *Esther, a Novel*, pp. 149–50.

350   "suggest it." King to Hay, July 4 [1886], A37865[23](3), Hay Papers (Brown Univ. Lib.).

"let it die." *Letters of Henry Adams*, ed. W. C. Ford, I, 377.

"badly made monkeys." *Ibid.*, pp. 377–78.

351   "I am one." King to John Hay [Jan. 1887?], Hay Papers (Lib. of Congress).

"such is Hay." *Century Mag.*, XXXII (Oct. 1886), 868.

"in life." King to D. C. Gilman, Feb. 27, 1885, Gilman Papers.

352   "delicate and pretty." *Letters of Henry Adams*, ed. Levenson *et al.*, II, 592.

"he is there." *Letters of John Hay*, II, 112–113.

"or their clank." King to Adams, Sept. 10, 1887, Emmons transcript, Emmons Papers; *idem*, Cater transcript.

"nothing about it." *Letters of John Hay*, II, 112.

353   "morning to night." King to Hay, Apr. 27, 1887, A37865[28](7), Hay Papers (Brown Univ. Lib.).

"a great success." King to Hay, July 28, 1887, A37865[30](7), *ibid.*

"a remarkable book." King to Hay, May 30, 1885, A37865[20](2), *ibid.*

"to be changed." *Ibid.*

354 "to have slept." King to Hay, July 28, 1887, A37865[30](7), Hay Papers (Brown Univ. Lib.).

"and Penates"; "the next morning." *Ibid.*

"well, *Locksley Hall.*" *Ibid.*

"I ever shall." *Ibid.*

"throes of printing." King to Hay, Oct. 2 [1889], A37865[40], Hay Papers (Brown Univ. Lib.).

"delight he had." *Clarence King Memoirs,* p. 141.

355 "art put together." King to Hay, July 18 [1888], A37865[36](2), Hay Papers (Brown Univ. Lib.).

"scene in America." King to Hay, July 28, 1877, A37865[30](7), *ibid.*

" 'burn this.' " King to Barlow, June 18, 1887, Barlow Coll.

356 "her welfare." *Ibid.*

"would be best." *Ibid.*

"restaurants in New Orleans." King to Hay, July 28, 1887, A37865[30](7), Hay Papers (Brown Univ. Lib.).

357 "well-cooked rice." Grace King, *Memories of a Southern Woman of Letters,* pp. 195–96.

"sure not to find." King to Adams, Sept. 10, 1887, Emmons transcript.

"out of Concord." King to D. C. Gilman, July 21, 1886, Gilman Papers.

358 "of Matthew Arnold." *Ibid.*

"summer colony." *Ibid.*

"of the lake." King to Clara Hay, Mar. 7 [1888], A37865[33], Hay Papers (Brown Univ. Lib.).

"his novel now." *Letters of John Hay,* II, 131.

"into *Harper's,* Alas!" King to Hay, Jan. 11, 1887, Hay Papers (Lib. of Congress).

"our minds." *Letters of John Hay,* II, 147.

"kinship with Omar." Dennett, *John Hay,* p. 87.

359 "of unfair women." *Henry Adams and His Friends,* ed. Cater, pp. 310–11.

"of Mexico." Emmons to Becker, Feb. 27, 1881, Box 15, Becker Papers.

"and negroes." *Clarence King Memoirs,* p. 172.

"American woman." *The Education of Henry Adams,* p. 313.

"paralyzes me for a week." King to Henry Adams, Sept. 17 [1888], Cater transcript.

"dictionary of a mind." *North American Rev.,* CXLI (Nov. 1885), 448.

"sugary insipidity." *Mountaineering,* p. 225.

360 "both sides or none." Quoted in Bronson, *Cowboy Life,* p. 355.

"perfect woman." *North American Rev.,* CXLVII (Oct. 1888), 383.

"types more robust." *The Education of Henry Adams,* p. 313.

"and the crystals." *Clarence King Memoirs,* p. 172.

"primeval woman." King to Hay, July 28, 1887, A37865[30](7), Hay Papers (Brown Univ. Lib.).

"of his own." *Clarence King Memoirs,* p. 172.

361 "do the rest." Quoted in Samuels, *Henry Adams: The Major Phase,* p. 14.

"African type." Quoted in Henry James, *William Wetmore Story and His Friends,*

p. 71. *Cf.* King's remarks on Story's "Lybian Sibyl" in *Overland Mo.*, V (1870), 578.

362   "of the white race." Quoted in R. U. Johnson, *Remembered Yesterdays*, p. 226.
"Y-A-S." *New York Herald-Tribune*, Nov. 22, 1933.
"assume command." *Mountaineering*, p. 246.
"comparative gynecology." *Letters of John Hay*, II, 131.
"yours forever." Quoted in *New York Daily Mirror*, Nov. 22, 1933, p. 9, col. 3.
"aristocratic in belief." "C.K.'s notes for [Hague's] biographical notice of him," King Papers.

363   James Todd. Plaintiffs' Trial Memorandum (pp. 164, 167), King vs. Peabody *et al.*, File No. 26821-1931, Records of the New York State Supreme Court (New York County Clerk's Office).
wedding ceremony. *Ibid.*; *New York American*, Nov. 21, 1933; *New York Daily Mirror*, Nov. 21, 1933, p. 8, col. 1; *New York Daily News*, Nov. 21, 1933, p. 3, col. 1; *Long Island Daily Star*, Nov. 21, 1933.
"religious trappings." New York *Amsterdam News*, Nov. 22, 1933.
"chocolate and all kinds." *Long Island Press*, Nov. 21, 1933, p. 2, col. 2; *New York Daily Mirror*, Nov. 21, 1933, p. 8, col. 3.
"my only one." Quoted in Plaintiffs' Trial Memorandum (p. 163), King vs. Peabody *et al.*; *New York Daily Mirror*, Nov. 22, 1933, p. 9.

364   "own individual lives?" King to W. D. Howells, undated (MS Am 800.20 [1108], Houghton Lib.).
"mostly lost." *The Education of Henry Adams*, p. 328.

19

365   "prince-with-the-tarts." *Life and Letters of Edmund Clarence Stedman*, II, 376.
"hat-rack on a mule." *Clarence King Memoirs*, p. 344.

366   "marry a woman." King to Hay, [Mar.? 1893], A37865[74], Hay Papers (Brown Univ. Lib.).
"nonproductiveness." *Clarence King Memoirs*, p. 87.
"intellectual climate." King to John Hay, undated, Hay Papers (Lib. of Congress).
"historical works." *Letters of John Hay*, II, 113.
"had I the chance." King to Adams, Sept. 25, 1889, Emmons transcript, Emmons Papers.

367   "and exalts grammar." Vol. CXLVII (Oct. 1888), 379.
"upon their petals." *Ibid.*, p. 370.
"of American character." *Ibid.*, p. 384.
"or high art." *Ibid.*, p. 377.
"old treadmillers." King to D. C. Gilman, Oct. 1888 (fragment), Gilman Papers.
"with his hind hoofs." T. A. Rickard, ed., *Rossiter Worthington Raymond, A Memorial*, p. 63.

368   "practical account." *Forum*, XIII (Mar. 1892), p. 25.
"of the stars." *Ibid.*, p. 28.
"age of biology." *Ibid.*, p. 27.
"know the language." *Ibid.*, p. 32.

"parts of speech." *Ibid.*

369 "my wavering way." King to Hay, Aug. 22, 1901, quoted in Dennett, *John Hay*, p. 161.

"some smashing blow." King to George J. Brush, September 14 [1884], Brush Papers.

"without verification." Lecture concerning King's views "on certain problems of geological physics," Box 32, Emmons Papers.

"have no answers." *Letters of Henry Adams*, ed. W. C. Ford, I, 383.

"terrestrial energy." *American Naturalist*, XI, 464.

"secular refrigeration." *Systematic Geology*, p. 701. King continued, for the rest of his life, to agree with Kelvin's basic assumption. *Cf.* his remarks in the Iron Mask Gold Mining Company vs. the Centre Star Mining and Smelting Company, . . . *Evidence of Clarence King* . . . *1899*, pp. 14–15.

370 "history of erosion." *Systematic Geology*, p. 703.

[King's] theory. In addition to material from *Systematic Geology* (pp. 701–5, 727–29), this outline of King's hypothesis draws from his papers "Catastrophism and Evolution" and "The Age of the Earth," from remarks in the Iron Mask Gold Mining Company vs. the Centre Star Mining and Smelting Company, . . . *Evidence of Clarence King* . . . *1899* (pp. 7, 14–15), and from Emmons's lecture concerning King's views "on certain problems of geological physics" (Emmons Papers). See also Emmons, *Geology and Mining Industry of Leadville*, pp. 299–300.

371 "abandoning it." Emmons, Lecture concerning King's views, Box 32, Emmons Papers.

372 "any result." *Letters of John Hay*, II, 234. Hay paraphrased passage in King to Hay [Jan. 1892] A37865[43](2), Hay Papers (Brown Univ. Lib.).

373 "of the Geological Survey." Agassiz to Huxley, Oct. 16, 1877, in *Letters and Recollections of Alexander Agassiz*, p. 231.

"aid to my work." Rabbitt, *Minerals, Lands, and Geology*, II, 118.

374 "pure abstract mathematicians." King to Marsh, Jan. 8, 1887, Marsh Papers.

"behind the throne." *Ibid.*

375 "land to the other." *New York Herald*, Jan. 12, 1887, p. 10, col. 1.

"with the other side." A. Hague to George B. Grinnell, Jan. 16, 1890, Arnold Hague Papers.

"his public career." *Beyond the Hundredth Meridian*, p. 337.

376 "change in the Directorship." Quoted in Rabbitt, *Minerals, Lands, and Geology*, II, 213.

"confidence in King." Quoted *ibid.*

"with the Major." Quoted *ibid.*

"old junk." "Carl Barus," *Proceedings of the American Academy of Arts and Science*, LXXI, 485.

"24,000,000 years." *American Journal of Science*, 3rd ser., XLV (Jan. 1893), 15.

377 "bit of physics." *Letters of John Hay*, II, 355; Thayer, *John Hay*, II, 121.

20,000,000 years. *Mining and Scientific Press*, LXXII (Feb. 15, 1896), 128.

"*Magnum Opus.*" *Letters of John Hay*, II, 355.

"in the breach." *Forum*, XIII (Mar. 1892), 26.

378 "stage of completion." *Clarence King Memoirs*, p. 290.

379   "still in doubt." *The Education of Henry Adams*, p. 328.

"talk of prospects." Q. A. Shaw to H. L. Higginson, June 24, 1891, Higginson Papers.

"that would run." Shaw to Higginson, Nov. 14, 1889, *ibid.*

380   "though Sombreretes fall." *Henry Adams and His Friends*, ed. Cater, p. 213.

"mining captain"; "successful mine." Agassiz, *Letters and Recollections of Alexander Agassiz*, p. 192. See also Bell and MacKenzie, *West Coast of Mexico*, p. 223; Southworth, *Las Minas de Mexico*, pp. 219–20; idem, *El Estado de Sonora*, pp. 49, 53.

"as of money." *Letters of John Hay*, II, 208.

"all the time"; "stand the racket." *Ibid.*, II, 234.

"all my strength." King to Ada Todd, undated, as quoted in Plaintiffs' Trial Memorandum (p. 170), *King vs. Peabody et al.*

381   "found I could." King to G. F. Becker, Nov. 10 [1889], Merrill Coll.

"making a fortune." *Ibid.*

"declining years." *Letters of John Hay*, II, 203. See C. F. Adams, Jr., . . . *An Autobiography*, pp. 197–98.

"his way yet." *Letters of John Hay*, II, 201.

"they rival." *Henry Adams and His Friends*, ed. Cater, p. 309.

"have done in life." *Clarence King Memoirs*, pp. 148–49.

"Polynesian girl at last." Quoted in Samuels, *Henry Adams: The Major Phase*, p. 13.

382   "had they discovered her." King to Hay, undated [1891], A37865[53] (2), Hay Papers (Brown Univ. Lib.).

"*were* the season." James to Hay, June 23, 1890, A37835[15](3), *ibid.*

"in Berlin University." *Those Were the Days*, p. 154.

383   Alexander taken for an Oriental potentate. *Clarence King Memoirs*, pp. 348n–349n.

"year in drawing." *Letters of John Hay*, II, 203.

"serious of my life." King to Clara Hay, Dec. 30, 1887, A37865[31], Hay Papers (Brown Univ. Lib.).

"my only escape." King to Adams, Sept. 25, 1889, Emmons transcript, Emmons Papers.

384   Wild West Show; Buffalo Bill. Miss Eleanor Hague (interview), July 31, 1950; confirmed by Miss Marian Hague, Mar. 16, 1953.

385   "from the world." King to Ada Todd, undated, quoted in the *New York Daily Mirror*, Nov. 22, 1933, p. 9, cols. 2–3; *New York Daily News*, Nov. 22, 1933, p. 3, col. 2.

"place me at dinner." King to Adams, undated [1892?], Cater transcript.

"insane dance." King to Adams, Nov. 12 [1892], Cater transcript.

386   "knives a-plenty." *Ibid.*

"verging on revolution." *The Degradation of the Democratic Dogma*, p. 94.

"old, haggard, and thin." *The Education of Henry Adams*, p. 338.

"such suffering." *Henry Adams and His Friends*, ed. Cater, 306n.

387   "National Bank funds." *The United States vs. E. B. Bronson* (1893), Dockets 823 & 989, U.S. District Court, El Paso, Texas.

"lost everything." King to Horace Cutter, paraphrased in Louis Janin to J. D. Hague, Nov. 5, 1893, King Papers.

"so deep a trail." *The Education of Henry Adams*, p. 312.

"initiative and energy." *Letters of Henry Adams*, ed. W. C. Ford, II, 456.

"want of money." *The Education of Henry Adams*, p. 346.

"to be frozen out." *Ibid.*, p. 347.

388 "to commercial affairs." King to John Hay, Aug. 22 [1901], Hay Papers (Lib. of Congress); Dennett, *John Hay*, p. 161.

"anything he chose." Hay to Howells, Jan. 30 [1890], *John Hay-Howells Letters*, p. 97.

"but blind luck." Quoted in Adams, *The Education of Henry Adams*, p. 416.

"he came there." La Farge to Adams, Nov. 7 [1893], A37431[28](2), Hay Papers (Brown Univ. Lib.).

"disorderly conduct." *New York World*, Oct. 31, 1893, p. 8, col. 4.

389 Bloomingdale Asylum. *New York Tribune*, Nov. 1, 1893, p. 7, and Nov. 4, 1893, p. 7, col. 1; *New York Sun*, Nov. 3, 1893, p. 1, col. 5; Adams, *Henry Adams and His Friends*, ed. Cater, pp. 294–95; *Letters of Henry Adams*, ed. W. C. Ford, II, 34.

20

390 "further region." *Henry Adams and His Friends*, ed. Cater, p. 298.

"disease at all." J. D. Hague to E. B. Bronson, Dec. 4, 1893, J. D. Hague Coll. S. Weir Mitchell. *Ibid.*; J. D. Hague to Hay, Nov. 24, 1893, A40157 [1566], Hay Papers (Brown Univ. Lib.).

"woodland of Weir." Earnest, *S. Weir Mitchell*, p. 152.

"complete recovery." King to G. F. Becker [Dec. 1893], Merrill Coll.

391 " 'do' an island." King to Becker, Dec. 31 [1893], *ibid.*

"and Charles Kingsley." *Ibid.*

"island trip with me." *Clarence King Memoirs*, pp. 162–63.

"have written him." *Ibid.*, p. 165.

392 "Hayti-Santo Domingo for you." King to Becker, Feb. 8 [1894], Merrill Coll.

"if I do well." *Ibid.*

"beautiful as Eden." *Forum*, XX (1895), 57.

"all wrong!" King to Becker, Feb. 8 [1894], Merrill Coll.

393 "as little as I." *Clarence King Memoirs*, p. 166.

"in the suburbs." *Henry Adams and His Friends*, ed. Cater, p. 310.

"high-proof spirit." King to Hay, May 16 [1894]. A37865[70](2), Hay Papers (Brown Univ. Lib.).

"untimely energy." *Letters of Henry Adams*, ed. Ford, II, 39.

394 "ocean of mischief." *The Education of Henry Adams*, p. 349.

"of Voodoo mysteries." Bronson, *Cowboy Life*, p. 326.

"of revolution." *Forum*, XXII (1896), 32.

"coming war." *Ibid.*, pp. 31–32.

395 "get up at five." *Letters of Henry Adams*, ed. Ford, II, 41. See pp. 42–43 for further details about the trip to the Gran Piedra.

"or for conches." *Henry Adams and His Friends*, ed. Cater, p. 316.

396 "be quite reasonable." *Ibid.*, pp. 315–16.

"Martha's Vineyard." King to Becker, Sunday [May 1894], Merrill Coll.

"in the country." *Denver Republican*, Sept. 14, 1894 (copy courtesy of the Denver Public Library).

397   "promise of 1879." Rabbitt, *Minerals, Lands, and Geology . . . Vol. 2*, p. 239.

house on North Prince Street. Testimony of Ada King and Henrietta Williams, and Plaintiffs' Trial Memorandum, King vs. Peabody *et al.*; *New York Daily Mirror*, Nov. 21, 1933, p. 8, col. 1.

"iridescent in promise." Quoted in Thayer, *John Hay*, II, 119.

"which crazed me." King to Hay, June 4 [1894], A37865[72], Hay Papers (Brown Univ. Lib.).

"in eastern Cuba." *Henry Adams and His Friends*, ed. Cater, p. 321; quoted in Nevins, *Hewitt*, p. 549.

"anybody anything." *Letters of John Hay*, II, 299.

"stars in space." King to Adams, Jan. 4 [1894], Cater transcript.

398   "as a bull moose." Roosevelt, *Selections from the Correspondence of Theodore Roosevelt and Henry Cabot Lodge*, I, 134.

"like an Elk." King to Hay, Sept. 2 [1895], A35451[781]. Hay Papers (Brown Univ. Lib.).

"discontented than ever." Adams, *Henry Adams and His Friends*, ed. Cater, p. 336.

"United States Government." *Forum*, XXII (1896), 32.

399   "history can show." *Forum*, XX (1895), 61.

Gomez and Maceo. See Rubens, *Liberty: The Story of Cuba*, p. 243, for an indication of King's reaction to their campaign. Cf. King in *Forum*, XXII (1896), 42 ff.

400   "crush liberty!" *Forum*, XX (1895), 64.

"King's Cuban outbreak." *Henry Adams and His Friends*, ed. Cater, p. 350.

"in its bosom." *Clarence King Memoirs*, p. 181.

401   [Tiffany's] silverware in Maceo's honor. American Art Galleries, *Catalogue of the Art and Literary Property Collected by the Late Clarence King*, item 228.

"United States of America." See 54th Cong., 2nd Sess., S. Report 1160 (Ser. 3474), "Recognition of Cuban Independence," (1896), pp. 1–25.

402   "whole Spanish fleet!" *Clarence King Memoirs*, p. 356.

"argument was complete." *ibid.*

"evaded into space." Quoted in Thayer, *John Hay*, II, 125.

"to escape New York." Adams, *Letters of Henry Adams*, ed. Ford, II, 120.

"for El Dorado." Hay, *Letters of John Hay*, III, 4.

"hoisting engine." *Denver Republican*, Sept. 15, 1894.

"come to nothing." Quoted in Thayer, *John Hay*, II, 118.

403   "California and Arizona." The Iron Mask Gold Mining Company vs. the Centre Star Mining and Smelting Company, . . . *Evidence of Clarence King . . . 1899*, p. 5.

"and never tell." *Clarence King Memoirs*, p. 183.

"[his own] Don Quixote." King to Hay, Nov. 14 [1895], A37865[75]. Hay Papers (Brown Univ. Lib.).

"talk about it." Hay to Adams, Aug. 22, 1900, Henry Adams Papers (reel 16).

"men of our time." *Clarence King Memoirs*, pp. 184–85.

404   "to my comfort." King to J. D. Hague, Feb. 3, 1899, J. D. Hague Coll., Box 12.

"conscientiously subscribe to." Quoted in "Necrology: Clarence King," 23rd Annual Report, U.S.G.S. (1902), p. 204.

405   "no strings on ye." D. W. Brunton, "Technical Reminiscences" (reprinted from *Mining and Scientific Press*), p. 16.

a young lawyer in Daly's employ. Cornelius Kelley (interview), Mar. 12, 1952.

"might have overlooked." *Clarence King Memoirs*, p. 347.

"lovable to all." Louis Janin to J. D. Hague, Jan. 16, 1903, J. D. Hague Coll.

406   to mutter "God!" *New York Tribune*, Mar. 16, 1901, p. 7, col. 5.

"what hawnblende andesite am." Quoted in Spence, *Mining Engineers & the American West*, pp. 341–42.

"till I die." Quoted in *New York Daily Mirror*, Nov. 22, 1933, p. 9, cols. 3–5.

Alaska and the Klondike. J. D. Hague to Arnold Hague, May 17, 1900 (draft), J. D. Hague Coll.; J. D. Hague to Horace Cutter, June 27, 1900 (draft), *ibid.*; *Mining and Scientific Press*, LXXX (1900), 497.

407   "vigor and energy"; "half his years." Quoted in "Necrology: Clarence King," 23rd Annual Report, U.S.G.S. (1902), p. 200.

"worth a dollar." Adams, *Letters*, ed. Ford, II, 261–262.

" 'my work again.' " Alexander R. Becker to S. F. Emmons, June 23, 1902, Box 28, Emmons Papers.

"at least a hundred." *Ibid.*

"work in Missouri." King to Emmons, Dec. 28, 1900, Box 28, Emmons Papers.

408   "of original sin." *Mountaineering*, p. 291.

"the tropical seas." King to H. M. Adkinson, Apr. 26, 1901. King Papers.

"paroxysms of coughing." *Letters of Henry Adams*, ed. Ford, II, 327.

"from their lives." *The Education of Henry Adams*, p. 396.

"about you and me." King to Ada Todd, Oct. 1901, quoted in Plaintiffs' Trial Memorandum (p. 166), King vs. Peabody *et al.*

409   "family matters." *Ibid.*

"old King manner." Quoted by Adams in *The Education*, p. 416.

"get a reprieve." King to Emmons, Aug. 29 [1901], Emmons Papers.

[Yale bicentennial.] King to Emmons, Aug. 29 [1901], Box 30, Emmons Papers; President Hadley to C. D. Walcott, Sept. 25, 1901, Box 28, *ibid.*; A. Hague to Emmons, Sept. 27 [1901], Box 29, *ibid.* The Emmons Papers contain several other letters in re efforts to secure an LL.D. for King from Yale.

National Institute of Arts and Letters. Howells to Hay, Feb. 25, 1901, A35451[595], Hay Papers (Brown Univ. Lib.).

"a felt want." Handwritten postscript at top of Hay to R. U. Johnson, Mar. 9, 1901, Hay folder, files of the American Academy and Institute of Arts and Letters.

410   "fresh shaving." King to John Hay, Nov. 3 [1901], Hay Papers (Lib. of Congress).

"is the best." King to Ada Todd, Oct. 1901, quoted in Plaintiffs' Trial Memorandum (p. 166), King vs. Peabody *et al.*

hemorrhage. Emmons, Notes for R. W. Raymond, King Papers; Hay to Emmons, Dec. 13, 1901, Box 18, Emmons Papers; Gardiner to Emmons, Dec. 13, 14, and 15, 1901, Boxes 27, 28, and 30, *ibid.*

"have done their struggle." Quoted by Adams in *The Education*, p. 416.

411   M for marital status. Death certificate of Clarence King (Division of Vital

Statistics, Arizona State Department of Health, Phoenix).

"love of women." *New York Tribune,* Dec. 27, 1901, p. 7, col. 1.

[funeral.] *New York Tribune,* Jan. 2, 1902; *New York Times,* Jan. 2, 1902; Emmons diary 1902, entries for Jan. 1 and 2, Emmons Papers; *Clarence King Memoirs,* pp. 152–53; Adams, *The Education,* p. 416.

Epilogue

412   Sources include the New York Census Records for 1915; file no. 12586-1921 in re Sidney King's incompetency (Kings County Clerk's Office); King vs. Peabody *et al.* file no. 26821-1931, Records of the New York State Supreme Court (New York County Clerk's Office); *New York Herald,* Nov. 19, 1902, p. 1; *New York Times,* Nov. 21, 1933, and Jan. 24, 1934; *New York Herald-Tribune,* Nov. 22, 1933, and Jan. 24, 1934; *New York Daily News,* Nov. 21, 1933, and Jan. 24, 1934; *New York Daily Mirror,* Nov. 21 and 22, 1933; New York *Amsterdam News,* Nov. 22, 29, 1933, and Jan. 24, 1934.

Index

Abbey, Edwin A., 331, 332: "The Old Song," 331, 342

Abraham Lincoln: A History (Hay and Nicolay), 351

Adams, Brooks, 386

Adams, Charles Francis, Jr., 381

Adams, Clover. *See* Adams, Mrs. Henry

Adams, Henry, 287, 319, 356, 369, 389n; friendship of, with King, 4–5, 5n, 23n, 89, 62–64, 263–64, 270, 290, 309–10, 352, 366, 372, 391–96, 397, 398, 400, 402, 403, 408 & n; appraisal of King by, 5, 162–3, 387; *The Education of Henry Adams*, 5, 6, 162, 222, 252n; friendship of, with Hay, 5 & n, 23n, 290, 310, 352; "love" of King by, 23n: models George Strong on King, 26n, 350 & n; *Esther: A Novel*, 26n, 349–50, 349n, 350n; quoted, 99, 139, 380, 391; characterizes legislation for King Survey, 102; characterizes King Survey, 105; King to, on marriage, 138; on King's life and work, 145n, 161n, 169, 203, 212n, 216, 359, 216–17, 169, 270, 295, 314, 324, 338, 359, 360, 364, 379, 387, 403, 395–96, 397; "Prayer to the Virgin of Chartres," 145n; on King's *Mountaineering*, 161n; meets King, 162 & n; and Emmons, 162, 164, 230; visits Green River Canyon, 164; visits Hilo, Hawaii, 168; on Fortieth Parallel Corps, 181; in Newport, 191–92; on health hazards of survey work, 194; for a "party of the centre," 216; disapproves of Blaine, 217; reviews King's "Catastrophism and Evolution," 222; on *Systematic Geology*, 227–28; told of King's cattle drive,

237–38; *Life of Albert Gallatin*, 263; salon of, 263; *Democracy*, 264, 319, 337, 346, 349n; gives King introduction to Lowell, 313; on Americans in London, 318; on Bret Harte, 320; Hay to, on King, 323; on 1884 presidential campaign, 337; and La Farge, 339, 350 & n, 382, 386; effect of wife's death on, 348–49, 350; as Francis Snow Compton, 349; *History of the United States . . .* , 349; goes to Japan, 350; King to, on his hard lot, 352, 357, 383; *A Letter to American Teachers of History*, 367; Hay to, on King's researches, 372; and Tati Salmon, 385–86; on Panic of 1893, 386; on Gardiner, 390; infatuated with Mrs. Cameron, 391n; with King in Cuba, 392–95; on conditions in Cuba, 393, 394, 395, 398; buys Turner's *The Whaler*, 399 & n; works for *Cuba Libre*, 400–401; King's last meeting with, 408 & n; at King's funeral, 411

Adams, Mrs. Henry, 309, 310, 350; death of, 4, 348, 352n; meets King, 191–92; salon of, 263; and King's puns, 290n; as model for Esther Dudley, 349; grave of, 372n

Adams, Marian Hooper. *See* Adams, Mrs. Henry

Adams, Mount, 153

Adams salon, 263–64

Agassiz, Alexander, 99, 324., 374, 392; King meets, 131; Adams cites preeminence of, 163; at Castle Hill, Newport, 218; in cattle business, 236; on King's honesty, 254; supports King for director, U.S. Geological Survey, 267; mining ventures of, 299, 303,

Agassiz, Alexander (*continued*)
308, 343; cancels Mexican trip with
King, 310–11; ousts King from
Yedras management, 345; opposes
government sponsorship of science,
373; elected president of National
Academy of Sciences, 408
Agassiz, Louis, 53, 152, 201; on age of
earth, 42; recommends King, 100;
and Mount Shasta, 143; illness of,
147; H. Adams's admiration for, 162
Agassiz, Mount: King climbs and
names, 136; on Farquhar's list of
King's first ascents, 155n
"Age of the Earth, The" (King), 376
"Age of the Earth as an Abode Fitted
for Life, The" (Kelvin), 377n
Airy, G. B., 378
Alaska, 143, 156; Cotter in, 107;
King's trip to, 406–407
Aldrich, Thomas Bailey, 318, 319, 332
Allison Commission, 373
Allston, Washington, 7
Alps, 41, 68, 136
Alta, Calif., 109
America, postbellum, 99; King's ap-
praisal of, 336–37
American Academy of Arts and Sci-
ences, 216
American Association for the Advance-
ment of Science, 36, 216
American Geographical Society, 198,
216
American Institute of Mining Engi-
neers, 199, 216
American Journal of Science, 18, 129,
167, 275n; King contributes to, 147,
376–77; in re *Systematic Geology*,
227. See also *Silliman's Journal*
American Museum of Natural History,
267, 294–95, 371
American Naturalist, King contributes
to, 222
American Philosophical Society, 215–
16
American Pre-Raphaelites, 42, 122
American Telephone and Telegraph
Co., 259n
Amsterdam, Netherlands, 182, 184
Anaconda Copper Co., 405, 406
Anaconda Mine, Butte Mont., 308

Anaho Island, Nev., 111, 123
Angel's Camp, Calif., 86
Angle of Repose (Stegner), 279n
Anglo-Mexican Mining Co., 326, 333,
344, 345 & n, 382
Apache Indians, 81, 83 & n, 203, 298,
301, 330
Apalachian districts, 286
Archean Era, 224–25
Archil, 197
Argenta, Nev., 137
Aristocracy (King's projected novel),
323–24
Arizona, 355, 410; King and Gardiner's
exploration of, 81, 84–85; Gardiner
and King's map of, 84; Hualapais in,
111; diamond fields reputed in, 171;
ruled out as diamond site, 175, 176;
King's mining affairs in, 289;
Harshaw Mine in, 302–303; King in,
403; King and Doré plan trip to, 330
Armstrong, Maitland, 209
Army. *See* U.S. Army
Army Engineers. *See* U.S. Army Engi-
neers
Arnold, Matthew, 324, 331–32, 358
Arnold, Philip, 182, 184
"Around Yosemite Walls" (King), 158
"Artium Magister" (King), 367
Ashburner, William, 37, 57; disparages
King, 58; visits Wawona, 73; serves
on Yosemite Commission, 75; praises
King, 166
Astor, John Jacob, II, 344, 379
Atherton, Gertrude, 160–61
Atkins, John D. C., 261, 267, 273;
supports King for director, U.S.
Geological Survey, 268
Atlantic Monthly, 146, 148, 150, 203,
208, 261, 280n, 306, 319; King con-
tributes to, 147, 148, 150, 103–204,
306; Bret Harte's contract with, 156
Auburn, Calif., 109
Aurora, Calif., 193
Austin, Nev., 122; as mining center,
124; as scene of King's "celery story,"
124–25
Azoic Age, 224

Bahamas, King in, 395

Bailey, William Whitman 104 & n,
105, 106, 108, 111, 114, 115–16,
119, 122–23

Baird, Spencer F., 140, 253, 261, 291;
endorses King, 101; recommends R.
Ridgway, 104; backs King in 1869,
131; chosen Secretary of Smithsonian, 254

Baker, Mount, 153

Bancroft, George, 218, 287, 313

Bancroft, H. H., 186, 203, 218; and
King, 203–204; *Native Races of the
Pacific States*, 203, 204, 218; *Wild
Tribes*, 204

Bank of California, 171, 180, 181; suspension of, 185

Barlow, Samuel L. M., 171, 294, 355–
56

Barnard, Mrs. F. A. P., 207

Bart, Black. *See* Black Bart (highwayman)

Barus, Carl, 318, 372, 376, 377, 378n;
work of, in geophysics, 289, 295,
371–72

Battle of the Bones (Marsh-Cope feud),
260, 374

Bear River, 136; Big Bend of, 238

Bear River (Yampa), 165, 175 & n

Bear Valley, Calif., 57, 73, 86

Becker, George F., 333, 391, 392; with
U.S. Geological Survey, 281, 282,
283–84, 287, 288–89, 293, 295–96,
311; census work of, 282, 283–84,
295–96, 311; King's correspondence
with, 392; elected to National Academy of Sciences, 408

Behre, Charles H., Jr., 378n

Bell, Alexander Graham, 258, 259n,
376

Belle Fourche River, 239, 240

Berry, J. P. 179–80

Berzelius Society, King elected to, 36

Bible, 31, 42, 53, 410, 411

Bierstadt, Albert, 28, 45n, 160, 175,
329; with King in the Sierra, 173–
74; King buys paintings of, 174n; at
King's funeral, 411

Big Bend: of the Truckee, 110, 111,
112; of the Humboldt, 122; of the
Bear, 238

Big Bonanza (Comstock Lode), 124,285

Big Meadows (near Lassens's Peak), 54;
(near South Kings), 63–64, 68

Bill Williams Fork, Ariz., 84–85

Billings, Frederick, 344, 352, 357, 379

"Biographers of Lincoln, The" (King),
351

Biological evolution, King on, 30, 368;
T. H. Huxley on, 219

Bishop Creek, Calif., 174

Black Buttes Station, Wyo, 1, 180

Black Hills, 233, 239

Black Mountain, Calif., King and Gardiner climb, 87–88

Black Rock country (Desert), Nev.,
116, 117

Black's Fork, Wyo., 153

Blaine, James G. 355, 374; backs King
in 1879, 131; King on, 217, 337–38;
King asks support of, 266; offended
by *Democracy*, 285–86; presidential
nomination of, 334; defeated by
Cleveland, 337

Bland-Allison Act, 272

Blitzen Valley, Ore, 237

Bloody Canyon, Calif., 89

Bloomingdale Asylum, 389,390–91,400

Bolles, James. *See* Bowles, James

Bonneville Lake, 136, 274, 281, 285,
288; described by G. K. Gilbert, 130;
King searches for outlet of, 133;
Gilbert names, 227

Boone and Crockett Club, 365, 398

Boston, Mass., 6, 8, 12, 17, 79, 99,
167, 299, 324, 334; King visits
Whitney at, 80; King's disparagement
of, 132; King speaks at Thursday
Club in, 146; King visits Saturday
Club at, 147; King's quip about, 148;
meets New York in Newport, 217;
King takes Ada Todd to, 363; in
Panic of 1893, 386

Boston Society of Natural History, 216

Bowles (Bolles), James, 25, 27

Brace, Charles Loring, 207; quoted on
King, 102; as King's fellow traveler to
California, 102n; *The New West*,
102n

Branded Hand, The (Little), 13

Bread-Winners, The (Hay), 319, 351

Brevoort House, N.Y.C., 294, 310,
337, 338, 346

Brewer, William H., 55, 64, 80, 85, 130, 151n, 259, 270; as second in charge of California Geological Survey, 37; and Mount Shasta, 40, 55–56, 143; meets King and Gardiner, 51–53; to Forest Hill, Calif., 53; reconnaissance by, of northern California mountains, 53–56; re Pluto's Cave, 56; on King's distaste for unpleasant work, 58; re J. Ross Browne, 60; leads High Sierra exploration, 60–65, 68–69, 73–74; re a hollow sequoia, 62–63; and Mount Brewer, 65 & n; commends King, 68; quoted on mountain climbing, 71; to Yosemite and upper Tuolumne, 75; measures drop of Yosemite Falls, 76; recommends King to Sec. Stanton, 99–100, 101; credits Whitney with idea of King Survey, 107n; and Tison the squatter, 112; on King's pioneer use of new ideas, 143n; on King's mountaineering sketches, 151; names Mount Clarence King, 174; names Mount Whitney, 192; memorializes Congress on forest conservation, 199; re King's views on catastrophism and evolution, 223; signs Yale letter in support of King, 267; confers with Pres. Hayes, 269

Brewer, Mount: first ascent of, 65; named for W. H. Brewer, 65n; elevation of, 65n

Brick Presbyterian Church, N.Y.C., King's funeral at, 411

Bridger Basin, 164

Brinley, Charles A., 81, 84, 86

Bristow, Benjamin, 217

British Columbia, 388, 397, 404; Supreme Court of, 404

Britton, A. T., 277, 279, 280, 282, 283

Bronson, Edgar Beecher, 206, 211, 213 & n, 360, 386–87; in cattle business, 233–36, 240–41; describes range in Nebraska, 234; on Dull Knife's outbreak, 235–36; *Reminiscences of a Ranchman,* 236n; on King's fluency, 307

Brooklyn, N.Y., 26, 385; King lives in, 27; King settles Ada Todd in, 363; Leroy Todd dies in, 384

Brooks, Phillips, 99, 350n

Brooks, Van Wyck: on Clarence King, 4; on King's *Mountaineering,* 161n

Brown University, 8, 207; grants King LL.D., 382

Browne, J. Ross, 83, 150, 197; draws caracature of 1864 exploring party, 60; publishes King on Prescott region, 85, 146; "A Dangerous Journey," 151n; *Crusoe's Island,* 151n

Brownell, William Crary, 24, 158, 209, 210, 297

Browns Park (Hole), Colo., 165, 175, 176, 177

Brunswick Hotel, N.Y.C., 339, 346, 348, 363

Brush, George Jarvis, 33, 41, 54, 134, 198, 200; praises King, 36; W. H. Brewer and, 37, 40, 58; King promises to collect for, 43; King renews ties with, 80; impressed by King's Comstock data, 130

Bryant, William Cullen, 17, 207, 209

Buena Vista Canyon, Nev., 115

Buffalo Bill. *See* Cody, William F.

Bullion, Mount, 57, 60

Bullion City, Nev., 173

Burns, Clarence (King's grandson), 412

Burns, James, 412

Burns, Thelma (King's granddaughter), 412

Bureau of [American] Ethnology, 265, 282, 291

Butler, Benjamin F., 44, 171, 184, 197, 218; sponsors King Survey, 131–32

Butte, Mont., 281, 405, 406

Cable, George Washington, 355, 361

Cache Valley, 133

Calaveras Skull, 86–87, 137

Calef, Master, 17

California, 2, 19, 37, 100, 102, 150, 195, 202, 269; gold rush to, 15; J. D. Dana in, 37; King's first arrival in, 50–51; map of, 60, 74; drought in, 60–61, 61n, 241; King in, 81, 403, 404; King Survey borders on, 110, 117; legislature of, 131; Hispanic settlement of, 196; King spends leave in, 199 N. R. Davis buys horses in, 237; Public Lands Commission in, 281; King returns from, 309; British swells in, 329; King seeks bank site in, 353, 355; King's last illness in, 409

California, Bank of. *See* Bank of California

California Geological Survey, 40, 43, 55n, 58n, 151; launched in 1860, 37; financial condition of, 52, 78, 81; office of, 52; Charles W. Eliot's assessment of, 53; King serves with, 53–78, 80, 85–90; Central Pacific Railroad and, 59; report (*Geology*) of, 60, 81, 146, 201; explores High Sierra, 60–74; publicizes ("discovers") sequoias, 62; proposes Yosemite as state park, 75; training furnished by, 79; disaster of, in state legislature, 131

Cambrian Period, 225

Cambridge, Mass., 42, 87, 259; King shows Comstock charts at, 131; King in, 157

Cameron, Sen. James Donald ("Senator Don") 285n, 391n, 400–401

Cameron, Elizabeth (Mrs. James Donald Cameron), 285n, 350n, 391n

Campos, Arsenio. *See* Martinez Campos, Arsenio

Camulos Rancho, Calif., 353–54

Canoe and the Saddle, The (Winthrop), 41

Canton, China, 8, 9, 10, 11, 12, 14, 19, 25

Capitol Hill, 131, 273, 373, 375

Capron, Samuel, 20, 22

Captain Bonneville, Adventures of (Irving), 160, 161n

Carnegie Institution, Geophysical Laboratory of, 378n

Carson City, Nev., 49, 118, 119, 122, 154

Cary, Edward, 209, 210, 228; on King's *Mountaineering*, 161n; at King's funeral, 411

Cascade Mountains, 41, 141, 201

Cataclysmic geology, King's, 295

"Catastrophism, modified," 221, 370

"Catastrophism and Evolution" (King), 222–23

"Catastrophism and the Evolution of Environment" (King), 220

Cavallier, promoter, 314, 325

Cenozoic Era, 224

Census of gold and silver mining. *See* Precious metals, census of

Central Pacific Railroad, 51, 59, 108, 109, 173

Central Park, N.Y.C., 27n, 57, 295; King arrested in, 388

Central Valley, Calif., 60–61, 61n, 86

Century Association, 365. *See also* Century Club

Century Club, 5, 209, 316n, 366, 398, 400, 411

Century Magazine, King contributes to, 316, 346n, 351; serializes Hay and Nicolay's *Abraham Lincoln,* 351

Cervantes, Miguel de, 196, 314, 316, 330, 403

Chapman, John Jay, 148 & n

Charles Scribner's Sons, 160n

Cheyenne, Wyo, 162, 170, 231; King forms cattle company at, 164; Loving-Goodnight trail ends at, 230; cattle shipped east from, 232; E. B. Bronson ticketed for, 233; as a cattle capital, 235; snowed under in 1880, 238; King in, 277; Emmons in, 278; Public Lands Commission in, 279; Frewen brothers and, 323

Cheyenne Indians, 216, 233, 235–36, 236n

Cheyenne River, 238–39

Chicago, Ill., 232, 240, 397, 407–408

Chihuahua, Mexico, 298, 300, 310

China, 9, 10, 11, 12, 13, 313

China Sea, 8, 14

China trade, 7, 12, 13

Chippy I (kingbird), 126, 135; II (kingbird), 135

Christ Church Hall, Pomfret, 15–16

Churchill, Lord Randolph, 322, 323

Circle Bar Ranch, Wyo, 238, 322; range of, 239

Civil War, 57n, 99, 208, 296, 297; draft records of, 39n

Clarence King, Mount, Calif., 58n, 73, 408n; named by Brewer, 174

Clarence King, Mount, Colo., renamed Mount Copeland, 165n

Clarence King Memoirs, 5, 16n, 31n, 38n, 161n, 196n, 316n, 322n

Clark, Frederick A.: joins King Survey, 103; with King when lightning

Clark, Frederick A. (*continued*)
strikes, 115; joins 1870 campaign,
141; explores flanks of Shasta, 144;
with U.S. Geological Survey, 281
Clark, Galen, 69, 73, 75, 78
Clark, Mount, 107n, 158; King re-
names the Obelisk, 77; King and
Gardiner make first ascent of, 87; on
Farquhar's list of King's first ascents,
155n
Clarke, Rev. James Freeman, 207
Clark's Ranch (Station), 69, 73, 78,
86, 88
Clemens, Samuel Langhorne, *See*
Twain, Mark
Clement(s), Yank, 150–51 & n
Cleveland, Grover, 337, 374, 386, 399,
400, 401, 403
Coal Measures, Upper, 225
Coast and Geodetic Survey, 261, 274,
281, 286, 373, 378. *See Also* Coast
Survey
Coast and Interior Survey, 260, 264
Coast Survey, 110, 253. *See also* Coast
and Geodetic Survey
Colorado (state), 99, 170, 172, 193,
200; Hayden works in, 129; Powell
works in, 129; mines of, 137; gold
fields of, 140; too civilized for
Adams, 164; salted diamond fields in,
177; Paleozoic sediments in, 225;
Loving-Goodnight trail crosses, 230;
King's cattle drive to, 237–38; Hay-
den and Wheeler clash in, 254; Pub-
lic Lands Commission in, 279; coal
deposits in, 381, 404; King in, 402,
404
Colorado River, 82, 404; descended by
Powell, 129, 140; Powell lectures on,
162
Colorado [River] Division, U.S.
Geological Survey, 274, 280
Colton, Gen. David, 181, 182, 183,
187
Columbia College, 116, 207, 260, 257,
267, 332, 369, 391. *See also* Colum-
bia University
Columbia University, 210, 390. *See also*
Columbia College
Comstock Lode, 116, 171, 286, 313;
King's first visit to, 50; King and
Whitney at, 59; King examines, 118,

119, 123–24, 138; King's chapter on,
124, 132, 139; King on future of,
124; King's charts of, 130, 167; Big
Bonanza at, 124 285; litigation over,
189; Becker studies, 288; miners at,
308
Congress. *See* U.S. Congress
Conness, John: introduces Yosemite
bill, 75; King names Mount Conness
for, 89; Whitney recommends King
to, 90; advocates plan for King Sur-
vey, 102; backs King in 1869, 131
Conness, Mount, 89, 102; on Far-
quhar's list of King's first ascents,
155n
Conservation of energy, King on, 30,
367–68
Consolidated Eureka Mine, 189
Continental Divide, 134, 153. *See also*
Great Divide
Continental ice sheet, 200, 227
Cook, Rev. Mr., 363
Cook, Clarence, 42–43
Cooper, Edward, 236, 259
Cooper, Peter, 207, 233, 259
Cooper Union, 198, 400
Cope, Edward Drinker, 260, 261, 267,
374, 375
Copeland, Mount, once named Mount
Clarence King, 165n
Cordilleras, 152, 201, 221, 225, 228;
orographical movements in, 226; tec-
tonic studies of, 229n
Cortissoz, Royal, 3, 4, 316, 339, 340
Cosmos Club, 268
Cotter, Dick, 47, 50, 63, 64; joins
1864 exploring party, 60; climbs
mount Tyndall, 65–68; nearly loses
life, 68, 78, 107; joins Yosemite sur-
vey, 75; attempts to climb Mount
Clark, 77; rescued by King in snow-
storm, 78; Alaskan ordeal of, 107;
joins King Survey, 107
Craig, Dr. R. W., 410, 411
Creston-Colorado Co., 380
Creston Mine, Mexico, 309
Cretaceous Period, 226
Crusoe's Island (Browne), 151n
Cuba, 315, 381, 391, 392, 397, 398,
400, 404; King in, 381, 392–95; insurrection in, 394, 398–401; King
agitates for freedom of, 395, 399–40

Cuban Junta, 399, 400
Culiacán, Sinaloa, Mexico, 300, 304, 305
Custer, Henry, 103, 105, 111, 116, 117 122
"Cut-off Copples's" (King), 157n
Cutter, Horace F. (Don Horacio), 195–96, 197, 315, 316 & n, 404; J. D. Hague's sketch of, 196n; Lower California land scheme of, 197

Dakota, 239, 274, 402
Dakota Stock and Grazing Company, 242
Dalhousie, Lady, 322
Dall, William H., 265n
Dalles, The, Ore, 41, 116
Daly, Marcus, 405
Dana, James Dwight, 36–37, 80, 147, 152, 257, 275n, 376; Manual of Geology, 41, 227; recommends King, 100; recommends J. D. Hague, 103; prints King's contributions, 129; and the glacial question, 143; and Mount Shasta, 144; Archean system of, 193; declines to back King, 267
Dana, Mount, 89
Dangerous Angel, The (Kelland), 179n
"Dangerous Journey, A" (Browne), 151n
Darrah, William Culp, 229n
Darwin, Charles, 30, 170, 223; theory of evolution, 116; The Descent of Man, 219; on Marsh's Odontornithes, 220
Davidson, Mount, 50, 118, 123, 286
Davis, G. A., 229n
Davis, N. R., 231, 235, 322; conducts survey of Great Salt Lake, 133, 135; and King form cattle company, 164; in cattle business, 230–33, 237–39, 240–42; teaches Bronson cattle business, 233; Oregon cattle drive of, 237–38; operates horse ranch, 242
Dawes, Sen. Henry L., 285
Dawson, Canada, 407
D. C. Murray (ship), 167
Dead Man Creek, Neb., 235, 236
Deadman Ranch, Neb., 235, 241
Dean, Miss ("Deany"), 120–21, 212; announces engagement with King, 121; King breaks engagement with, 137; and Mrs. Howland, 137n

DeForest, John W., 319
Delamar, Joseph, 382
Delamar Mine, Idaho, 382
Delano, Alonzo (Old Block), 150
Delmonico's, N.Y.C., 108, 156, 310, 337, 363
del Valle family, 353–54
Democratic Party, 34, 337
Democracy (Adams), 264, 319, 323–24, 337, 346, 349n; King rumored as author of, 285–86
Denver, Colo., 161, 274, 277, 402
De Quincey, Thomas, 327
Derby, George H. (John Phoenix), 150
Derby Day, 313, 322n
Descent of Man, The (Darwin), 219
Descriptive Geology (Emmons and Hague), Volume II of Fortieth Parallel Report, 224
Desert Land Act, 238
Devil's Gate, 47
De Voto, Bernard, on King, 4
Dewey, Daniel, 23, 28; friendship of, with King, 23–24, 28; quoted, 24; writes to King, 35; on Canadian cruise, 38–39; enlists in Connecticut volunteers, 39; death of, 44
Dewey, Adm. George, 401–402
Diamond Mesa, 178n, 181
Diamond Swindle of 1872, 171–185; King gives deposition on, 195
Diaz, Porfirio, 298
Dickason, David, on King as art amateur, 339n
Dickens, Charles, 320, 323, 331; Oliver Twist, 320
Dickinson, Emily, 218
Diehl, Israel S., 153n
Digger Indians, 63, 161n, 203; King's literary treatment of, 159
Dinocerata (Marsh), 285
Dives Company, 203
Dives Mine, 204–205
Dodge, Mary A. (Gail Hamilton), 21, 286
Dolbear, Amos, 258
Dominica, 391
Donaldson, Thomas, 256, 277, 278, 279 & n, 280; gives King's views on Harte, 156n
Doré, Gustav, 329–30; King's deprecation of, 330

Dos Bocas, Cuba, King and Adams at, 393–94
Douglas, Stephen, 34
Downtown Club, N.Y.C., 366
"Dream of Bric-à-Brac (C. K. *Loquitur*)" (Hay), 327
Dred Scott case, 34
Drought, Great, in California, 60–61, 61n, 241
Drum Barracks, Calif., 81
Drumlins, King's explanation of, 144 & n
Dudley, Esther (character), 349–50
Dull Knife (Cheyenne chief), 235–36
Dunlap, William, 7
Dunraven, Earl of, 241
Dupree, A. Hunter, 229n
Dutton, Clarence E., 229n, 274, 277, 285; on King as organizer, 287; with U.S. Geological Survey, 288; names theory of "isostacy," 378

East Humboldt Mountains (Ruby Mountains), Nev., 126n
East India Co., 8
East Range (Paiute Range), Nev., 115n
Eaton, Danield Cady, 134, 135; herbarium of, 156
Echo Canyon, Utah, 48, 136
Eckart, W. R., 285; mill rolls developed by, 352
Edel, Leon, 325
Edison, Thomas, 258
"Education of the Future, The" (King), 367
Education of Henry Adams, The (Adams), 5, 6, 162, 222, 352n
Edward, Prince of Wales, 106, 321–22, 323. *See also* Edward VII
Edward VII, 322n. *See also* Edward, Prince of Wales
82 85 brand, 239, 240
El Capitan, Yosemite, 76
El Paso, Texas, 353, 355, 380, 386; National Bank of, 353, 386–87
Eldredge-Gould model of "punctuated equilibria," 221n
Eliot, Charles William, 53 & n, 269
Elizabeth (barmaid), King tips, 320–21
Elizabeth Island Group, 200
Elk Mountain, Wyo., 238, 239, 240, 242, 279
Emerson, Ralph Waldo, 147, 331

Emigrant Trail, 127
Emma Mine, Utah, 190–191; scandal concerning, 191
Emmons, Samuel Franklin, 31n, 38n, 49n, 83n, 162n, 257, 279n, 378n; quoted, 104, 121, 334, 369, 378; on King's life and work, 49n, 122, 131, 141, 146, 198, 228, 256, 359, 371, 409, 406–7; with Fortieth Parallel Survey, 104, 108, 114, 116, 117, 118, 122, 126, 129, 133, 136, 140, 141, 144, 162, 164, 170, 172–73, 175–80, 186, 191, 198, 199, 200, 224, 230, 254; on Miss Dean, 120; notes King's despondency, 131; works in Boston, 132; and Brigham Young, 132; contribution of, to *Mining Industry*, 139–40; friendship of, with King, 140; and Mount Rainier, 144, 147; discovers Mount Rainier glacier, 147; and H. Adams, 162, 164, 230; on Henry Janin, 172; Diamond Swindle and, 175–76, 177, 178, 179, 180, 181; examines Emma Mine, 191; with King in White Mountains, 191; sent to Europe, 200; on advances in glaciology, 201; finishes *Descriptive Geology*, 224; in cattle business, 231–32, 232n; King predicts national survey to, 254; with U.S. Geological Survey, 270, 274, 282–84, 288, 311, 348; census work of, 282, 283–84, 295, 311; King to, on his illness, 294; meets King for last time, 410; at King's funeral, 411
Empire (Vidal), 23n, 27n, 408n
Energy, King on conservation of, 30, 367–68
Engineer Bureau, 259n. *See also* U.S. Army Engineers
Engineer Corps. *See* U.S. Army Engineers
Engineer Department, 132. *See also* U.S. Army Engineers
Engineering and Mining Journal, 267
England, 13, 331, 332, 334–35, 345, 353, 402; King in, 67n, 312–13, 379, 382, 383; King sells N. R. Davis & Co. in, 241; M. Frewen brings cattle to, 323; estheticism in, 326; Oriental art furor in, 327; economic frosts in, 333. *See also* London; *see also* Scotland

Eocene, 226, 285
Escalante Range, 165
ESG herd, 232
Esther (Adams), 26n, 349 & n; as roman à clef, 350n
Estheticism, 326–27
Eureka, Calif. (mining camp), 53
Eureka, Nev., 189, 191, 194, 278, 281, 295
Eureka (boat), 133, 135–36
Europe: King's wish to study surveys in, 271; King in, 312–35, 382–83. *See also* England; London; Paris; Scotland; Spain
Evans, Griff, 162
Evarts, William Maxwell, 210, 215, 287, 319
Evolution Group, Calif., 174
Exploration and Empire (Goetzmann), 256
Exploration Co. of London, 407
Exploration of the Colorado River of the West (Powell), 160

Fagoago, House of, 307
Fairchild, Herman, LeRoy, 228
"Falls of the Shoshone, The" (King), 127–28, 147, 156, 158
Fan Kuei, 8
Farquhar, Francis P., 151n; on King's Mount Tyndall climb, 66, 68n; on King's "genius" for wrong routes, 71; reprints King's Three Lakes, 146n; lists King's first ascents, 155n; re King's Mount Tyndal account, 159
Farrer, Thomas, 43
Feather River, Calif., 54
Fells, the (Hay's Sunapee retreat), 358
Fenton, Carroll, 228n
Fenton, Mildred, 228n
Fields, James T., 146–47, 148–49, 152, 157, 208, 211
"Fire and Sword in Cuba" (King), 401
Fish, Hamilton, 369
Fisherman's Peak, pushed as name for Mount Whitney, 155, 192
Fiske, John, 209, 219
"Five of Hearts," 290, 310, 350, 351. *See also* "Four of Hearts"
Flat River, Mo., 407–408
Florida, 381, 391, 395, 408
Flushing, N.Y., 408; Ada Todd moves to, 397, 412

Foote, Arthur, 278, 279n
Foote, Mary Hallock, 104n, 278–79 & n; *The Led-Horse Claim,* 278; on a survey party at Leadville, 279: "Reminiscences," 279n
Ford, James L., 209–10
Ford, Paul Leicester, 209
Forest conservation, 199
Forest Hill, Calif., 52, 53
Fort Bridger, Wyo., 48, 153, 166, 176, 179
Fort Fred Steele, Wyo., 234
Fort Hall, Idaho, 48, 238
Fort Kearney, Neb., 46, 47
Fort Mohave, Calif., 82, 83
Fort Whipple, Ariz., 83
Fortieth Parallel Corps: King chooses, 103–104; H. G. Parker a favorite of, 111n; did not name Kings Peak, 165n
Fortieth Parallel Survey (U.S. Geological Exploration of the Fortieth Parallel) 104n, 107n, 134, 138, 223, 230, 253, 260, 409; King conceives idea of, 59, 79, 89, 107n; Gardiner on creation of, 100; King named head of, 102; King chooses staff of, 103–104; 1867 field work of, 107–118; mapping procedures of, 110; geological procedures of, 110; collections of, 117, 130, 199–200, 295; 1868 field work of, 122–28; loses literary priority re Lake Bonneville, 130; compared by King with competing surveys, 130n; Gen. Grant writes commendation of, 131; 1869 field work of, 132–37; reports of, 139–40, 165n, 167, 200, 205, 211, 219, 220, 223–28, 228n–29n; 1870 field work of, 141–45, 147; glaciers discovered by, 143, 147; makes pioneer use of photography in field, 143n; 1871 field work of, 153–56, 163–66; *Mining industry* establishes practicality of, 167; 1872 field work of, 170–81, 183; salted diamond fields in area surveyed by, 175; cost of, 185; achievement of, 105, 185
Fortuny y Carbo, Mariano, 314, 317 & n, 319, 329
Forty Mile Desert, Nev., 114
Forum, King contributes to, 297, 377, 399, 401

"Four of Hearts," 351, 352, 408n. *See also* "Five of Hearts"
France, 313–14, 326. *See also* Paris
Franklin, Benjamin, 7
Franklin Lake, Nev., 126
Freiberg School of Mines, Germany, 43, 79, 103, 374
Frémont, John Charles, 22–23, 41, 57, 100, 123, 177; "discovers" South Pass, 48; names Great Basin, 128; Mount Shasta and, 143, 144
French, Peter, 237
French Revolution, The (Carlyle), 346
Frewen, Moreton, 241, 242n, 322–23
Frewen, Richard, 241, 242n, 322
Friedrich, Otto: *Clover*, 350n
Fry, E. M., 181
Fryxell, Fritiof M., 275n
Fugitive Slave Law, 22

Gabb, William, 58
Galápagos Islands, 170
Galena Hill, Calif., 53
Gallatin, Albert, 263
Gardiner (Gardner), James Terry, 137n; meets King, 23; intamacy of, with King, 23 & n; spelling of surname by, 23n; on King's nature study, 24; King's correspondence with, 27, 28, 33, 34, 35–36; transfers to Sheffield, 33, 36; on J. D. Dana, 37; Canadian cruise of, 38–39; quoted, 38–39, 49, 62, 237; studies law, 41; lives with King in N.Y.C., 42; ill health of, 43; re first trip west, 43, 44–52; regarding King's sociability, 44–45; arrival of, in California, 51; and Brewer, 51, 52; employed by Army Engineers, 53; with California Geological Survey, 60, 65, 80, 85–86, 87–89; Mount Gardiner named for, 73; and King survey Yosemite, 75–78; in San Francisco, 78, 106; in Nicaragua, 78–79; and King explore Arizona Territory, 81, 84–85; captured by Indians, 82–83; reported killed, 83; "The Trail Between the Cedar Bushes" (MS), 83n; on his map of Arizona, 84; and King climb Mount Clark, 87 & n; and King climb Mount Dana, 89; and King climb Mount Conness, 89; on King's pursuasiveness, 100; and map of Central Sierra, 100, 107;

with Fortieth Parallel Survey, 103, 108, 109, 110, 111, 115, 117, 121, 131, 132, 133, 136, 140, 141, 170, 175 & n, 176; on Cotter's mental condition, 107; and Josephine Rogers, 121, 128; Diamond Swindle and, 175 & n, 176; leaves King Survey, 187; joins Hayden Survey, 187; re King's resolve to abandon survey work, 188n; H. H. Bancroft and, 203; in cattle business, 231–32, 236, 241; defection of, from military control, 255; supports King for director, U.S. Geological Survey, 267; topographical methods of, 269; mining ventures of, 300, 302–303, 345; visits King at asylum, 390; to handle King's posthumous affairs, 409, 410, 412; at King's funeral, 411; and Ada Todd, 412
Gard[i]ner, Mount, 73
Garfield, James A., 258, 264, 266, 289, 291, 313, 413
Garrison, William Lloyd, 21, 33
Geike, Archibold, 275n, 287
Gemstone Swindle. *See* Diamond Swindle of 1872
General Grant Grove, 62; Tree, 62
General Land Office, 257, 260, 276; grid surveys of, 129; administers Hayden Survey, 129; criticized by Major Powell, 258
"General View of the Prescott Region, A" (King), 85
Genesee Creek, Calif., 58
Genesee Valley, Calif., 54
Geographical and Geological Survey of the Rocky Mountain Region, 130. *See also* Powell Survey
Geographical Surveys West of the One Hundredth Meridian, 130, 260, 265. *See also* Wheeler Survey
Geological and Geographical Survey of the Territories, 129. *See also* Hayden Survey
Geological Exploration of the Fortieth Parallel. *See* Fortieth Parallel Survey
Geological Society of America, 216
Geological Society of London, 216
Geology (Whitney, Report of the California Geological Survey), 81, 146, 201; quoted re High Sierra exploration, 60

Geophysics, 289, 295, 369–72, 376; work by Barus in, 289, 295, 371–72, 377n; King's involvement in, 369–72, 376–78, 377n, 378n
George, Henry, 347
Gérôme, Jean Léon, 79; "Red Flamingoes," 329
Germany, 326; Emmons secures microscopes in, 200
Gifford, R. Swain, 207, 329
Gilbert, Grove Karl, 229n, 285; anticipates King on Lake Bonneville, 130; locates Bonneville outlet, 133; on King's "Catastrophism and Evolution," 223; on achievement of *Systematic Geology;* 227; with U.S. Geological Survey, 270, 274, 281, 288
Gilbert Peak, 165n
Gilder, Richard Watson, 316
Gilder, Rodman, 3
Gilman, Daniel Coit, 19, 31n, 38n, 219, 338, 358, 367; founds the Johns Hopkins University, 215
Glacial Age, King's studies of, 200–201
Glaciers: Fortieth Parallel Survey's discovery of, 143, 147; King's study of, 144, 144n, 152
Glaciology, taught by L. Agassiz, 42; studied by King, 42
Glasgow, Scotland, 215, 317, 319
Glendale Crossing, Nev., 109, 116, 117
Godkin, Edwin Lawrence, 207, 222, 263, 264; founds Round Table Club, 208
Goetzmann, William H., 229n; on King's *Mountaineering,* 160; *Exploration and Empire,* 256; on importance of King's consolidation role, 256
Gold and silver census. See Precious metals, census of
Gold Hill, Nev., 44, 50, 51, 120
Gold Rush, 15, 37, 48
Golden Era, 120
Goldsmith, Oliver, *She Stoops to Conquor,* illustrated by Abbey, 342
Gomez, José Miguel, 399, 400, 401
Goodwin, C. C., on King's explorations, 4; on King's integrity, 190; on King and Muir, 202–203
Goodyear, William A., 154–55, 179n, 202
Goshute Indians, 49

Gosse, Edmund, 318, 332
Göttingen, University of, 103, 374
Gould, Jay, 337, 381
Gould, Stephen Jay, 221n
Gould & Curry Mine, Nev., 119
Grabhorn Press, 151n
Gran Piedra, Cuba, 395
Grand Canyon, 185, 274, 280, 285
Grand Canyon of the Tuolumne. See Tuolumne, Grand Canyon of; see also Great Tuolumne Canyon
Granite Peak, Ariz., 84
Grant, Ulysses S., 104n, 255, 339–40; King confers with, 131; tomb of, 340–41, 390
Grant administration, 139
Gray, Asa, 62; recommends Bailey, 104
Gray, Elisha, 258
Great American Desert, 100
Great Basin, 89, 101, 122, 194, 201, 226, 281; King and Gardiner cross, 49; Whitney projects geological section across, 59; named by Frémont, 128; Watson's collection of flora of, 130; lava flows in, 141; Watson's book on flora of, 156; Gilbert's operations in, 274; Becker's operations in, 284
Great Basin Division, U.S. Geological Survey, 274, 280–81
Great Bethel, Va., 35n
Great Divide, 133. See also Continental Divide
Great Freeze of 1886–1887, 242 & n
Great Plains, 100, 230; at end of Pliocene, 227; replaces inland sea, 226
Great Salt Desert, 49, 125
Great Salt Lake, 48, 128, 129, 136; surveyed by King Survey, 133; preceded by Lake Bonneville, 227
Great Tuolumne Canyon, 202. See also Tuolumne, Grand Canyon of
Greeley, Horace, 43, 182, 183
Greeley, Colo., 161–62
Greeley Tribune, 232
Green Park, London, 318
Green River, 48, 164, 165, 175, 176, 184; descended by Powell, 129, 140; at Ladore, 226; King's cattle drown in, 238
Green River Canyon, 177
Green River City, Wyo., 128, 153

Green River Coal Basin, King's chapter on, 139
Green River Divide, 136
Green River Station, Wyo., 176
Greytown, Nicaragua, 80, 212
Grizzley Flats, Calif., 303–304, 310
Guaymas, Mexico, 301–302
Guillermon (the "black lion"), 394
Gulf of California, 310
Gulf of Mexico, 276
Gunnison, John, 100

Haddon Hall, England, Vernons of, 7
Hadrian (Roman emperor), King's lost work on, 346 & n
Haggin, James Ben Ali, 187
Hague, Arnold, 164, 375; with Fortieth Parallel Survey, 103, 108, 118, 129, 130, 139–40, 141, 142, 162, 163, 164, 170, 172–73, 177, 200, 224; and chemistry of Washoe process, 130, 139; contributes to Mining Industry, 139–40; and Mount Hood, 142, 147; with King in Hawaiian Islands, 167–70; Diamond Swindle and, 177; finishes Descriptive Geology, 224; in cattle business, 241; with U.S. Geological Survey, 270, 274, 281, 285, 348; at King's funeral, 411
Hague, Eleanor, 314n
Hague, James Duncan, 137, 192, 278, 279n, 314n, 342, 384; Clarence King Memoirs and, 5, 316n, 322n; King to, 16n, 68n, 134, 138, 334, 362, 404; on King's life and work, 36, 135, 151, 361n; meets King, 36, 103; with Fortieth Parallel Survey, 103, 108, 109, 116, 118, 132, 134, 135, 137, 146, 167; Mining Industry, 132, 137, 139–40, 167; with King in Idaho, 146, 382; with King in Oregon, 146; as mining consultant, 167, 188–89, 382; Diamond Swindle and, 176; mining ventures of, 194–95, 303–304, 382; and H. F. Cutter, 196 & n, 197, 316n; visits King at asylum, 390; at King's funeral, 411
Hague, Mrs. James D., 146, 337
Hague-King Co., 167, 169
Haiti, 391, 392
Hale, Joseph P., 197
Hall, Anne, 7

Hall, James, 224, 280
Hallock, William, 318, 372, 376, 377n
Hamilton, Alexander, 217
Hamilton, Gail. See Dodge, Mary A.
Hamilton, Nev., 194
Hangtown (Placerville), Calif., 51
Hanna, Mark, 99
Hannibal, Mo. 44
Harlem Heights, N.Y.C., 390
Harpending, Asbury, 178n–179n
Harpignies, Henri, 329
Harshaw Mine, Ariz., 299–300, 302–303
Hart, William, 28
Harte, Bret, 127, 137, 150, 156–57, 156n, 161n, 181, 279n, 361; on Calaveras Skull, 86–87; and King, 137, 142, 147, 151, 156–57, 156n, 214–15, 319–20; verse of, 145; and John Hay, 208n 215, 318–20; "Chiquita," 208n; "The Heathen Chinee," 208n; as lecturer, 214; borrows details from Mountaineering, 214 & n; "Morning on the Avenue," 214; in London, 319–20, 331, 332, 333; The Luck of Roaring Camp (play), 320
Hartford, Conn., 20, 21, 22, 23, 26, 35, 39, 57, 113, 148; High School, 20–21, 367
Hartford Press, 23
Hartington, Marquis of, 324
Harvard College, 17, 42, 53, 103, 133, 162, 309; King breaks news of glaciers at, 147; C. S. Peirce at, 223; H. Adams resigns from, 263; Whitney blocks support for King at, 267
Hat Creek, Wyo, 238, 239; Ranch, 242
Havana, Cuba, King and Adams at, 392
Havillah Mountains (Sonoma Range), Nev., King captures deserter in, 125
Hawaii, island of, 168, 169
Hawaiian Hotel, Honolulu, 168
Hawaiian (Sandwich) Islands, King visits, 167–70
Hawley, Joseph R., 318
Hawthorne, Julian, 332
Hawthorne, Nathaniel: The Scarlet Letter, 212, 278
Hay, Adelbert Stone (Del), 409

Hay, Clara Stone. *See* Hay, Mrs. John
Hay, John, 321n, 362, 369, 399; friendship of, with Adams, 5 & n, 23n, 290, 352 & n; friendship of, with King, 5n, 23n, 209, 283, 290, 310, 325, 327, 352 & n, 366, 409; appraisal of King by, 4, 6, 7, 211, 297, 322n, 323, 372, 380, 383, 388; as statesman, 99; gift of, for friendship, 207; and Lincoln, 207–208; 351; *Castilian Days*, 208; King on, 208 & n; "Little Breeches," 208 & n; and Bret Harte, 208n, 215, 319–20; privy to authorship of *Democracy,* 264; as assistant secretary of state, 283, 290; edits *New York Tribune,* 294; mining ventures of, 300, 345; on King's foreign languages, 301, 313; receives "Helmet of Mambrino" MS, 316; Henry James to, 317n; *The Bread-Winners,* 319, 351; and Howells, 319; King to, 324, 326, 346, 360, 382, 398; "A Dream of Bric-à-Brac (C. K. *Loquitur*)," 327; satirizes King's collecting of Oriental art, 327–28; and Zorn's portrait of King, 329; with King at Doré's atelier, 330; and Matthew Arnold, 331–32; in London, 331, 332, 333; and Rabelais Club, 333; on King's departure from England, 335; as supporter of Blaine, 337; quoted, 348, 358, 366, 377, 381, 402, 403; learns authorship of *Esther,* 349n; *Abraham Lincoln: A History,* 351; King's appraisal of, 351 success of, 351, 387; and Sunapee, N.H., 357–58; Adams to, on King's mental state, 395–96; King's last meeting with, 408 & n; on a King letter, 409; and King's estate and heirs, 413
Hay, Mrs. John (née Clara Stone), 351; privy to authorship of *Democracy,* 264; friendship of, with King and Adams, 290, 310, 352; and the Matthew Arnolds, 332; and Sunapee Lake, 358; with King at Mrs. Adams' grave, 372n; King's last meeting with, 408n; and King's black family, 412
Hayden, Ferdinand V., 137, 152, 257, 261, 262, 266, 374; surveys Nebraska, 129; surveys parts of Wyoming and Colorado, 129; transferred to Interior Department, 129; and F. B. Meek, 140; Gardiner joins, 187; N. R. Davis winters *mulada* of, 231; corps of, 253; clashes with Wheeler in Colorado, 254; J. S. Newberry's opinion of, 258; as sponsor of E. D. Cope, 260; in contest for directorship, U.S. Geological Survey, 265; Powell's efforts to block, 267; Whitney supports candidacy of, 267; beaten for geological directorship, 267; condemned by Powell, 268; disparaged by Eliot of Harvard, 269; with U.S. Geological Survey, 274–75, 275n, 291
Hayden Survey, 260, 265; discontinued, 265; publications of, 275. *See also* Geological and Geographical Survey of the Territories
Hayes, Rutherford B., 227, 261, 263, 266, 267, 274–75; King's supporters confer with, 268–69; nomination of King by, 269; Howells introduces King to, 287; presses King to remain in office, 288
Hayes, Mrs. Rutherford B. (Lucy), 262, 287
Hearn, Lafcadio, 356, 395
Hearst, George, King's quip about, 187
"Heathen Chinee" (Harte), 145, 208n
Hecla Copper Mine, 299
Heine, Heinrich, 321
Hell's Hollow, Calif., 58
Helmholtz, Hermann W. Ludwig, 377
"Helmet of Mambrino, The" (King), 316
Henry, Joseph, 131, 253, 254
Henry Chauncey (steamship), 80, 105
Henry's Fork, Green River, 164
Hereford Gardens, England, 322
Hermosillo, Mexico, 302
Hewitt, Abram S., 273, 338, 397; on his admiration of King, 207; eloquence of, 209; in cattle business, 235–36, 239–40, 241; refers survey problem to National Academy of Sciences, 256; leads consolidation movement in Congress, 257, 259, 261, 262, 264, 265; and King's telephone scheme, 259; and Rossiter

Hewitt, Abram S. (*continued*)
  Raymond, 267; supports King for director, U.S. Geological Survey, 268; as mayor, N.Y.C., 347–48; recommends King for Columbia professorship, 369; with King in Europe, 382–83
Hewitt, Edward Ringwood, 258–59, 382
Higginson, Henry Lee, 99, 299, 325
Higginson, James J., 299, 300
Higginson, Thomas Wentworth, 218–19
High Plains, 230, 233
High Sierra, 64, 75, 153, 192; California Geological Survey explores, 60–74, 149; King studies ancient glacier system of, 170, 174
High Uintas, 164, 230
Hilgard, Julius, 110, 253, 261; dismissal of, 373
Hill, John Henry, 122–23, 127; on scenery of Nevada, 123; exhibits in Manhattan, 132
Hilo, Hawaii, 168
History of the United States . . . (Adams), 349
Hitchcock, Mr., of the *Sun*, 210
Hitchcock, Edward, *Geology*, 17
Hite, Virgil, 412
Hite Mine, Calif., 198
Hockanum River, Conn., 24
Hockett Trail, Calif., 69, 155
Hoesch, Jan, 53, 60
Hoffmann, Charles F., 57, 58, 60, 65, 73, 74, 75, 80, 89, 154, 199, 308, 343
Hoffmann, Mount, 76–77, 88
"Hog ranch," 69
Holland, 326
Holmes, Oliver Wendell (1809–1894), 86, 147–48
Holt, Henry, 149n, 212n, 285, 290n, 349, 358; on Yale College, 30; on King and Hay, 207; privy to authorship of *Democracy*, 264
Holy Kings, River of the, 58n
Homer, Winslow, 339n
Honey Lake, Calif., 54
Hong Kong, China, 19, 345n
Honolulu, 168
Honton, Baron de la, 128
Hood, Mount, 142, 147

Hooper, Edward, 400
Hooper, Dr. Robert, 348, 349n
Hopkins, Sarah Winnemucca, 123; *Life Among the Piutes*, 123
Hopkins Grammar School, Hartford, 20
Horseshoe Gorge, Green River, 165
Hot Springs Mountains, 111; King goes blind in, 114
Houghton, Lord (Richard Moncton Milnes), 333
Hoqua (hong merchant), 12
Howe, Julia Ward, 218, 323
Howells, William Dean, 99, 213, 279n, 325, 330, 358, 363; quoted, 151, 319, 321, 354, 381; and King, 157, 217, 280n, 287, 317, 319, 320, 337; on *Mountaineering*, 159, 161n; on King's review of Bancroft's *Native Races*, 204; on scope of King's sympathies, 207; and John Hay, 208, 283; on King's aim to write novel, 211–12; recommends King to President Hayes, 261–62; in London, 318, 332, 333; in New York, 347; backs King for National Institute of Arts and Letters, 409–10; at King's funeral, 411
Howells, Mrs. William Dean, 262, 287
Howland, George Snowdon (King's stepfather), 25–26, 27, 80; marries Florence King, 29; family of, 41; death of, 89; losses of, 99
Howland, Mrs. George Snowdon (King's mother, formerly Mrs. James Rivers King, née Caroline Florence Little), 8, 9, 10, 12, 23, 211, 362, 387, 410; background of, 8–9; baptized a Moravian, 9; marries James Rivers King, 9; gives birth to Clarence King, 10; considers going to China, 11; gives birth to Florence and Grace Vernon King, 13; premonition of, 14; close ties of, with King, 14, 17, 18 & n, 19n, 28, 132, 137–38, 359, 362, 410n; joins United Congregationalists, 16; and King's education, 17, 18, 20; as abolitionist, 21; decides to remarry, 25–26; moves to Brooklyn, 27; marries Howland, 28–29; on stepson "Snoddy," 29n; gives birth to daughter Marian, 41; concerned over Sioux uprisings, 44; gives birth to son

George, Jr., 80; and King's engagement, 132, 137n; in California, 186;
indicts West, 215; King visits, 217,
338; and Matthew Arnold, 331; with
King at Sunapee, 358; near death,
383; anxieties of, 384; King's last
visit with, 408; grave site of, 411;
the Hays' support of, 413
Howland, George Snowdon, Jr. (King's
half-brother), 338, 358, 383, 384;
birth of, 80; marriage of, 404
Howland, John Snowdon (King's step-
brother "Snoddy"), 29 & n
Howland, Marian (King's half-sister,
Mrs. Clarence P. Townsley), 126,
145–46, 311, 329, 358, 384; birth
of, 41; visits the John Hays, 352;
marriage of, 383
Hualapais Indians, 82, 83 & n, 111
Hubbard, Gardiner, 396
Hudson River, 41, 42
Hudson River School, 43
Huerfano (stallion), 242
Humboldt, Alexander von, 41, 62, 306
Humboldt Marshes, Nev., 114
Humboldt Mountains, 59
Humboldt Mountains, East (Ruby
Range), 126n
Humboldt Mountains, West, 59, 114,
115–16
Humboldt Palisades. Nev., 173
Humboldt River, 49n, 114, 170; Big
Bend of, 122
Humboldt route, 137
Humboldt Sink, Nev., 113
Humboldt Valley, Nev., 116
Humboldt Wells, 127
Humphreys, Gen. Andrew A., 103,
257; reports pro King Survey, 101;
sends King his orders, 102; King re-
ports to, 117, 134, 140, 143, 152,
175, 193, 199, 223, 234; King con-
fers with, 131, 191; orders King west
in 1870, 140–41; rejects King's plan
for volcano study, 153; rejects King's
plan for boat expedition, 165; dis-
pleasure of, re diamond exposé, 184;
agrees on publishing Marsh's Odontornithes, 220; resigns from National
Academy of Sciences, 261; relieves
King as U.S. geologist, 263
Humphreys, Mount, 170, 171, 174
Hunt, Helen. See Jackson, Helen Hunt

Huntress (ship), 11, 12
Huronian horizon, 225
Hutchings, James M., 76, 153n
Hutchings House, Yosemite, 77
Hutchinson, W. H., on King's Moun-
taineering, 161n
Hutton, Laurence, 318, 332
Huxley, Thomas Henry, 219, 317, 324;
King on, 220; on importance of
Marsh's fossils, 220; and genealogy of
the horse, 222
Hyde, Mr. (William Hyde's father), 50
Hyde, William, 44, 45, 78; joins
Yosemite survey, 75; and the
Yosemite map, 80

Ice Age, 221
"Ice Dragon's Nest, The" (King), 145
& n
Ice Slough, 47
Idaho, 116, 127, 146, 382; King's trail
herds in, 238
Iddings, J. P., 103, 200
Iliff, J. W., cattle of, 231
Illilouette River, Yosemite, 77
Illinois, 34, 80; colleges in, support
Powell, 129; and the Pike, 150
Independence, Calif., 174
Independence Rock, 47
Independent Party, 217
Indian Pass, Ariz., 84
Inheritance of acquired characteristics,
223
In Memoriam (Tennyson), 23 & n
Innis, George, 339n
Interior, U.S. Department of, 257,
260, 274, 294; takes jurisdiction over
Hayden Survey, 129; versus the
Army Engineers, 255
Inyo Mountains, Calif., 192
Ireland, 312
Iritaba (Mohave chief), 83n
Iron Mask Mine, Rossland, B.C., 404
Irrigation Survey, 375
Irving, Henry, 332–33
Irving, R. D., 285
Irving, Washington, 314; The Sketch
Book, 41, 159; Astoria, 161n; Adven-
tures of Captain Bonneville, 160, 161n
Irvington, N.Y., 41, 79, 80, 173
Island Cemetery, Newport, King's burial
at, 411
Isostacy, theory of, 378

Israels, Josef, 329
Italy, 326

Jackson, Helen Hunt, 218, 279n, 353–
54; *Ramona*, 218, 353
Jack-the-Ripper, 385
Jamaica, 109
James, Henry, 99, 213n, 317, 335, 336,
338; on Newport, R.I., 10; and
Charlotte King, 39n, 313; and John
Tyndall, 149; on Clover Adams, 263;
Pandora, 263; and King, 317n, 320,
325; Bolton Street flat of, 318: *The
Princess Casamassima*, 320; quoted,
321, 382; *A Little Tour in France*,
325; and Rabelais Club, 333; re
King's nervous breakdown, 389n
James, William, 346
James family, 15
Janin, Henry, 279n; Diamond Swindle
and, 172, 174, 175 & n, 177, 178,
180, 181, 182–83; in cattle business,
241; and Prietas Mine, 298; and
Harshaw Mine, 299; and Mount
Pleasant Mine, 303; with King in
Mexico, 305; with King to England,
311–12
Janin, Louis, 196, 405–406
Japan, 9, 327, 328, 350
Jay, John, 217
Jefferson, Thomas, 33
Jerome sisters, 242n
*Joaquin Murieta: The Brigand Chief of
California*, 151n
Job's Peak, Nev., King struck by light-
ning on, 115
John Brent (Winthrop), 41, 212
John Day Basin, 116, 219
Johns Hopkins University, The, 215,
267, 367
Johnson, Professor (at Sheffield), 33, 80
Johnson, Eastman, 207, 210
Johnson, Ricardo, 299
Johnson, Robert Underwood, 361–62;
on King's smile, 210
Jones, Dr. (of Murphy's), 86
Jones' Wood, N.Y.C., 341
Julesburg, Colo., 47
Jurassic Period, 58, 225, 226

Kaibab Plateau, 288

Kalakaua, 169
Kames, King's explanation of, 144 & n
Kanab region, Ariz., 280
Kanakas, 168, 304
Kansas, 45, 226, 277; in the days of
John Brown, 218
Kansas-Nebraska troubles, 22
Kaweah (King's horse), 61, 72
Kaweah River, Calif., 58, 63, 69
"Kaweah's Run" (King), 72, 146, 151
& n, 161n
Kearsarge Pass, Calif., 74, 174
Keelikolani, Princess, 169
Kelland, Clarence Buddington: fic-
tionalizes Diamond Swindle, 179n;
The Dangerous Angel, 179n
Kelley, Cornelius, 405
Kelvin, Lord, 317, 377 & n; "secular
refrigeration" postulate of, 369–70,
378; estimate by, of earth's age, 376,
377n; "The Age of the Earth as an
Abode Fitted for Life," 377n. *See also*
Thomson, Sir William
Kentucky, 34, 184
Kern Canyon, Calif., 66, 71
Kern County, Calif., 281
Kern plateau, 155
Kern River, 66, 70
Kern Sierra, 69; King determines main
features of, 71; King's plat of, 80
Kilauea, King examines crater of, 169–
70
Kilauea (paddlewheeler), 168
Kimball, James P., 374
King, Ada (wife): sues Gardiner heirs,
413. *See also* Todd, Ada (the elder,
King's wife)
King Ada (daughter), 412. *See also*
Todd, Ada (the younger, King's
daughter)
King, Benjamin, 7, 8
King, Caroline (aunt), 10
King, Charles William (uncle), 8, 9–
10, 313; on *Morrison* expedition, 11;
death of, 12
King, Charlotte (Mrs. Charles William
King, aunt), 11, 39n, 313
King, Clarence Rivers: appearance of,
1, 3, 44, 120, 135, 157, 188, 314,
317; rheumatism (arthritis) of, 1,
139, 140, 198, 287–88; shoots grizzly
in lair, 3, 166; personal qualities of,

3, 44–45, 58, 74, 105, 122, 135, 143n, 163, 187, 209–11, 297–98, 322n, 323; founds U.S. Geological Survey, 4; death of, 4, 5, 411; as symbol of his generation, 4; bust of, 4; ancestry of, 6–9; birth of, 10; childhood of, 10–11, 15–17, 18–19; Negro nurse of, 10, 22, 361; regard of, for Negroes, 10, 22, 102n, 216 & n, 359, 361–62, 361n; in Newport, 10–11, 102, 132, 217–19; *Systematic Geology*, 11, 127n, 149n, 170, 205, 206, 211, 213n, 219, 220, 224–28, 228n–229n, 231, 234, 369, 370; with father at home, 12–13; love of, for Oriental things, 13, 327–28; close ties of, with mother, 14, 17, 18 & n, 19n, 28, 132, 137–38, 359, 408, 410 & n; in Pomfret, Conn., 15–17; at Christ Church Hall, 15–17; schooling of, 15–17, 20–22, 26, 31–38, 42, 80; religious training of, 16–17; finds first fossil, 17; nature study of, 17, 18, 24; in Boston, 17, 79, 132, 147–48; taught by mother, 18; in New Haven, Conn., 18–19, 31–38, 40, 80, 99–100, 140, 147; adolescence of, 20–29; at Hartford High School, 20–21, 26; and abolition, 22, 22n, 33–34; sexual orientation of, 23n; photographic memory of, 24, 159; early pietism of, 24; melancholy of, 26, 28, 131, 186, 346; unspecified illness of, 26, 166, 167, 194, 199, 215, 294, 296, 304; religious views of, 26n–27n; as model for George Strong, 26n, 350 & n; in New York City, 27–28, 42–43, 103, 198–99, 206–207, 208–209, 271, 294–95, 310, 336–42; on conservation of energy, 30, 367–68; on biological evolution, 30, 368; on classical education, 30–31, 367; at Sheffield (Yale) Scientific School, 31–38, 80; Civil War's effect on, 35–36, 38–39, 39n; as campus athlete, 36, 74; elected to Berzelius Society, 36; receives Ph.B. degree, 38 & n; on Canadian cruise, 38–39; decides to become geologist, 41; studies glaciology, 42; American Pre-Raphaelites and, 42–43; first trip

West, 44–52; in San Francisco, 52, 57, 58, 75, 78, 106–7, 121, 137, 170, 171, 172, 173, 175, 186–87, 195, 288–89, 303, 306, 353; with California Geological Survey, 53–78, 80, 85–89; notebooks of, 53, 54, 63, 69, 79, 87, 121, 128, 137, 146, 150, 212–13, 280n, 321n; climbs Lassen's Peak, 54–55; "Shasta's Flanks," 56; examines Mariposa Estate, 57–59; geographical features named for, 58n, 73, 164, 164n–65n, 174, 408n; examines West Humboldt Mountains, 59; conceives idea of Fortieth Parallel Survey, 59, 79, 89, 107n; explores the High Sierra, 60–71, 74; climbs Mount Tyndall, 65–68; meets John Tyndall, 67n, 317; Mount Whitney and, 69, 71, 153–55, 179n, 192–93; and Newty family, 69–70; as raconteur, 72, 106, 112, 124–25, 146, 148–49, 149n, 151, 156n, 209–11, 233, 361n, 405–406; "Kaweah's Run," 72, 146, 151 & n; reaction of, against science, 72–73, 137, 187–88, 297; attracted by dark skin tones, 73, 138, 306, 354–55, 359 & n; meets Galen Clark, 73; surveys Yosemite, 75–78; "A Sierra Storm," 77, 78, 158; rescues Cotter in snowstorm, 78; in Nicaragua, 78–79; malaria of, 79, 80, 114, 171, 198, 287–88, 302, 310; Yosemite mapping errors of, 80; Kern Sierra plats of, 80; explores Arizona Territory, 81, 84–85; captured by Indians, 82–83; "A General View of the Prescott Region," 85; "The Range," 85, 149 & n, 226; explores Merced Group, 87–88; climbs Black Mountain, 87–88; Grand Canyon of the Tuolumne and, 88–89; resigns from Whitney Survey, 89; proposes Fortieth Parallel Survey, 100–101; in Washington, D.C., 100–02, 131–32, 261–69, 271, 274, 281, 282–84, 285–88, 289–91, 372 & n, 396, 408; as head of Fortieth Parallel Survey, 102–228 passim, 228n–229n, 263; chooses Fortieth Parallel staff, 103–104; Gardiner as chief assistant to, 103, 108, 109, 110, 111, 115, 117, 131, 132, 133, 136, 140, 141,

King, Clarence Rivers (*continued*)
170, 175 & n, 176; assisted by Arnold Hague on King Survey, 103,
108, 118, 129, 130, 139–40, 141,
142, 162, 163, 164, 167–70, 172–
73, 177, 200, 224; assisted by J. D.
Hague on Fortieth Parallel Survey,
103, 108, 109, 116, 118, 132, 134,
135, 137, 146, 167; assisted by S. F.
Emmons on King Survey, 104, 114,
116–17, 118, 131, 133, 136, 140,
141, 144, 147, 167, 170, 172–73,
175–80, 186, 191, 198, 200–201,
224, 230, 254; in Panama, 105–106;
Prince of Wales and, 106, 321–22 &
n, 323; "Merced Ramblings," 107n,
158; *Mountaineering in the Sierra Nevada*, 107n, 148–52, 151n, 157–61,
160n, 161n, 168, 195, 201, 203,
211, 214, 218, 278, 316, 330, 355,
407; studies the Comstock Lode,
118, 119, 123–24, 138; liking of, for
Indians, 123, 203, 216, 236, 304,
306, 354–55, 358, 359; contributes
to *Overland Mo.*, 127–28, 147; "The
Falls of the Shoshone," 127–28; Bret
Harte and, 127, 137, 142, 147, 151,
156–57, 156n, 214–15, 319–20;
charts the Comstock, 130; sponsored
by Benjamin F. Butler, 131–32; confers with U. S. Grant, 131; climbs
and names Mount Agassiz, 136; studies coal measures along Union Pacific, 136; inner conflicts of, 137,
296–97, 346–47, 366; chapter by, on
Comstock geology, 139; verses of,
140–41, 145 & n; Pacific Coast volcano study of, 141–43, 153, 198;
hires Carleton E. Watkins, 141–42,
145; climbs Mount Shasta, 142–43;
discovers Mount Shasta's glaciers,
143; names Whitney Glacier, 143;
glacier studies of, 144 & n, 152–53,
170, 174, 200–201; "The Stone
Giant's Bowl," 145; "The Ice
Dragon's Nest," 145 & n; as author,
145–47, 145n, 148–52, 151n, 157–
61 & n, 160n, 316–17, 323–24,
367–68, 376–77, 399, 401; meets
Oliver Wendell Holmes, 147–48;
contributes to *American Journal of Science*, 147, 376–77; contributes to the
Atlantic Mo., 147, 148, 150, 203–
204, 306; "Through the Forest," 149;
"Wayside Pikes," 150, 157n; sup-
presses *Mountaineering in the Sierra
Nevada*, 151n, 160n; "Shasta," 152;
"Cut-off Copples's," 157n; "The
Newtys of Pike," 157n; "Around
Yosemite Walls," 158; meets Henry
Adams, 162 & n; as cattleman, 164,
230–242, 297, 322–23; defends
Comstock charts, 167; visits
Hawaiian Islands, 167–70; "old-gold
girls" and, 168–69 & n, 170, 309,
359; love of, for archaic woman,
169, 360, 382; Diamond Swindle
and, 171–85, 195; desire of, for
wealth, 188, 297–98; as mine consultant, 188–91, 382, 388, 397, 398,
402–404; as expert witness, 190,
203–204, 404–406; investigates
Emma Mine, 190–91; reviews Utah
geology, 191; studies White and Inyo
Mountains, 192–93; Murphy Mine
and, 194–95; slumming by, 206–207,
320, 321n; joins social clubs, 208–
10, 235, 268, 338, 365–66; Century
Club and, 209–10; as writer *manqué*,
211–13 & n, 317, 320, 321n, 323–
24, 346, 353–54, 355, 403; joins
professional societies, 215–16; as Republican, 216–17; "Catastrophism
and the Evolution of Environment,"
220; theorizes on catastrophism and
evolution, 220–23; "Catastrophism
and Evolution," 222; contributes to
the *American Naturalist*, 222; considered for secretary of Smithsonian,
253–54; predicts a national geological survey, 254; leads movement to
consolidate surveys, 256–57; interest
of, in telephone, 258–59; as candidate for directorship of U.S. Geological Survey, 258, 261–69; drafts
"enabling clause" for U.S. Geological
Survey, 262; as director of U.S.
Geological Survey, 269–70, 271–92;
assisted by S. F. Emmons on U.S.
Geological Survey, 270, 274, 278,
282–84, 288, 295, 311; assisted by
Arnold Hague on U.S. Geological
Survey, 270, 274, 281, 285; serves
on Public Lands Commission, 276–
82; plans publications program of
U.S. Geological Survey, 284–85;

rumored as author of *Democracy*, 285–86; and Washington society, 285–87; in Mexico, 289, 301–302, 304–306, 342–43, 344, 352–53; compiles first annual report of U.S. Geological Survey, 289 & n; resigns as director of U.S. Geological Survey, 290–91; tenure as geological director assessed, 291–92; retains connections with U.S. Geological Survey, 294; scientific library of, 295; cataclysmic theories of, 295; *The Upheaval and Subsidence of Continents* (projected book), 295; geophysical laboratory and, 295, 371–72, 376, 377n, 378n; compiles precious metals reports, 295–96; *Statistics of the Production of the Precious Metals in the United States*, 296; *The Precious Metals* (projected book), 296; retires from public service, 296; attitude of, toward American plutocracy, 296–97; contributes to *Forum*, 297, 377, 399, 401; fantasizes on becoming art patron, 298, 334, 342; Mexican mining ventures of, 298–302, 304–309, 310–11, 313, 314, 325–26, 333–34, 342–45, 345n, 352–53, 357, 379–80; in Europe, 312–35, 382–83; in London, 312–13, 317, 318–21, 322, 323–24, 325–26, 328–29, 331–35, 382, 383; in Paris, 313–14, 316, 317, 325, 330, 382; tours Spain, 314–16; in Morocco, 315; "The Helmet of Mambrino," 316; visits Sir John Clark, 317; in Scotland, 317–18; as collector, 317, 325, 326–31, 339 & n; *Aristocracy* (projected novel), 323–24; Anders Zorn's portrait of, 329; America appraised by, 336–37; suggestions of, for Grant's tomb, 339–41; "Style and the Monument," 340; plans house, 341–42; "The Biographers of Lincoln," 351; El Paso National Bank and, 353, 386–87; on *Ramona*, 353; "Santa Rita" (projected novel), 353, 354, 355; at Rancho Camulos, 353–54; Luciana (Indian woman) and, 354, 355, 358, 359; arranges affairs of aged quadroon, 355–56; at Sunapee Lake, 357–58; dual life of, 358, 362–64, 365, 380, 384–85, 397; aversion

of, for Nordic women, 359–60, 359n; opinion of, on women, 359–61; marriage of, 363, 365; children of, 363, 380, 384–85, 397, 412–13; "Artium Magister," 367; contributes to *North American Review*, 367; "The Education of the Future," 367; appraises American teaching methods, 367–68; geophysics and, 369–72, 376–78, 377n, 378n; subterranean hypothesis of, 369–72; consults with Grover Cleveland, 374; availability of, for reappointment as geological director, 376; on age of earth, 376–77; influence of, 378 & n; concern of, for black family, 380, 384–85, 408–409; in Florida, 381, 391, 395, 408; visits Cuba, 381, 392–95; spinal trouble of, 383, 386, 388, 389; reasons for failure of, 387–88; nervous breakdown of, 388–89, 390–91; and Bloomingdale Asylum, 389; visits Windward Islands, 395; visits Nassau, 395; "Shall Cuba be Free?," 399; works for *Cuba Libre*, 399–401; "Fire and Sword in Cuba," 401; visits Alaska and the Klondike, 406–407; tuberculosis of, 407–10; funeral of, 411; burial of, 411; Gardiner manages posthumous affairs of, 412. *See also* Todd, James

King, Mrs. Clarence Rivers. *See* Todd, Ada (the elder, King's wife); King, Ada (wife)

King, Clarence, Mount. *See* Clarence King, Mount

King, David O. (uncle), 12, 19, 20, 25

King, Florence (sister), birth of, 13; death of, 13; grave of, 411

King Frederick (uncle), 8, 12, disappearance of, 19–20

King, Grace (author), 356–57

King, Grace (daughter): marries James Burns, 412; gives birth to Thelma and Clarence Burns, 412. *See also* Todd, Grace (King's daughter)

King, Grace Vernon (sister): birth of, 13; death of, 14; grave of, 411

King, James Rivers (father), 8, 13, 19; marriage of, to Florence Little, 9; in China Trade, 11; helps Dr. Peter Parker, 12; makes visit home, 12–13; death of, 14; heirs of, 20, 25

King, Mrs. James Rivers (née Caroline Florence Little). *See* Howland, Mrs. George Snowdon

King, Leroy (son), 412. *See also* Todd, Leroy (King's son)

King, Malcolm, 176

King, Samuel, 7

King, Mrs. Samuel (née Amey Vernon), 7

King, Samuel, Jr., 7, 8

King, Mrs. Samuel, Jr. (née Harriet Vernon), 8

King, Sidney (son), 413; incompetence of, 412. *See also* Todd, Sidney (King's son)

King, Thomas Starr, 75

King, Vernon (cousin), 39n

King, Wallace (son), 412. *See also* Todd, Wallace (King's son)

King & Co., 19; failure of, 25

King & Talbot Co., 8

King Crest on Grand Canyon Rim, Ariz., 165n

King-Davis brand (ND), 232n

King family, coat of arms of, 6

King house, Newport, 7, 11, 102, 217, 327

King Lake, Calif., 165n

"King of the Mountains" (Big Tree), 62

King Peak, Anarctica, 165n

King Survey: *See* Fortieth Parallel Survey

Kingdom of the Yellow Robe (Siam), 20

Kinge, Daniel, 6, 7

Kinge, Daniel, Jr., 6

Kinge, Ralphe, 6

Kings Park State Hospital, Long Island, 412

Kings Peak: named for Clarence King, 164, 164n–165n; elevation of, 165n; U.S. Board on Geographic Names on, 165n

Kings River, 58 & n, 62, 66; South Fork of, 58n, 63, 73; gorge of, 174

Kingsley, Charles, 79, 391

Kinsmen, the, 332–33

Klamath River, 40, 56

Klondike, the, King's trip to, 406–407

Knickerbocker Club, 208–209, 366

Knollys, Lord (Edward VII's secretary), 322n

Krakatoa, 333

Ladore, Green River, 165, 226

La Farge, John, 99, 347, 400, 403; *Reminiscences of the South Seas*, 169n; on King's life and work, 210–11, 298, 340–41, 388; and King at Studio Building, 339; with Adams in Japan, 350; as model for Wharton in *Esther*, 350n; with Adams in Polynesia, 382, 386; visits King in asylum, 390; Brick Presbyterian Church decorated by, 411

Lafayette Square, Washington, D.C., 352

Laffan, William ("Polyphemus"), 318, 332

Lahonton, Lake, 128, 129; King names, 227

Lakota Co., Ltd., 236, 241

La Mancha, province of, Spain, 196, 315

Lamarck, Jean Baptiste, 223

Lancaster, Alexander, 361, 382–83, 405; King's anecdote about, 406

Lander Cut-off, 237

Lang, Andrew, 332, 333

Langley, Samuel Pierpont, 154n

Langley, Mount, 154n; King mistakes and climbs as Mount Whitney, 154; on F. P. Farquhar's list of King's first ascents, 155n. *See also* Sheep Rock

Langtry, Lillie, 324

Laramie, Wyo., 177

Laramie Hills (Mountains), 234

Laramie Plain, 230, 234, 239

Las Prietas, village of, Sonora, Mexico, 302

Lassen, Mount. *See* Lassen's Peak (Butte)

Lassen's Peak (Butte), 40, 54–55, 59, 147; elevation of, 55n; on F. P. Farquhar's list of King's first ascents, 155n

Latter Day Saints, 280. *See also* Mormons; Mormonism

Laurentian horizon, 225

Lawrence, Mrs. Bigelow, 287

Lawton's Valley, R.I., 218

Lazy D brand, 237

Leadville, Colo., 278, 279n, 284, 285, 288; boom at, 279

Led-Horse Claim, The (Foote), 278
Lee, Madeleine (character), 264, 287, 323
Lehi, Utah, 280
Leidy, Joseph, 219
Leipsig, Germany, 200
Leland, Charles Godfrey, 333
Lent, William M., 171
Letter to American Teachers of History, A (Adams), 367
Leutze, Emanuel, "Washington Crossing the Delaware," 339
Library of Congress: catalogues *Democracy* under King's name, 286
Liebig, Baron Justus von, 36
Life Among the Piutes (Sarah Winnemucca Hopkins), 123
Life and Adventures of Joaquin Murieta, The (Ridge), 151n
Life of Albert Gallatin (Adams), 263
Lincoln, Abraham, 33–34, 35, 39, 171; John Hay the protégé of, 5, 207–208; signs Yosemite bill, 75; death of, 80; King on Hay and, 208; Hay and Nicolay's biography of, 351
Lincoln, Dr. Rufus, 389
Literary Digest, 400
Little, Robbins (King's uncle), 18, 19; practices law, 42; as guest of King Survey, 132; as director of Astor Library, 199
Little, Sophia (King's grandmother, née Sophia Louise Robbins), 9, 10, 148n, 338; *The Branded Hand*, 13; as abolitionist, 21–22, 22n; *Thrice Through the Furnace*, 22; as the "prisoner's friend," 25; Moravian faith of, 39n; death of, 384; last days of, 384n
Little, William (King's grandfather), 8, 37
Little, Mrs. William. *See* Little, Sophia
"Little Breeches" (Hay), 208
Little Snake River, 165–66, 175
Little Tour in France, A (James), 325
Little Yosemite, 77, 88
Liverpool, England, 109, 312
Locksley Hall (Tennyson), 354, 359n
Lodge, Henry Cabot, 216, 239, 263, 361, 400, 402
Logan School, Toronto, 409
London, 184, 219, 311, 325, 328; King in, 312–13, 317, 318–21, 322, 323–24, 325–26, 328–29, 331–35, 382, 383; King's slumming in, 320; Gilbert Munger in, 329; Peter the Great in, 331; King on, 338; Henry Adams in, 400
London *Times. See Times* (London)
Lone Pine, Calif., 154, 155
Long Island, 28, 412
Longfellow, Henry Wadsworth, 86, 147–48; *Evangeline,* 145n; *Hanging of the Crane,* 278: *The Skeleton in Armor,* 278
Longs Peak, Colo., 162, 164, 165n
Lord, Eliot, 278, 285
Lorillard, Pierre, 344, 365
Los Angeles, Calif., 81, 85, 353
Loving-Goodnight trail, 230
Low, Gov. Frederick, 75, 108
Low, Seth, 207, 369, 391
Lowell, James Russell, 145, 313, 322, 333, 334
Lower California, 197
Luciana (Indian woman), King's romantic interest in, 354, 355, 358, 359
Luck of Roaring Camp, The (Harte play), 320
Ludlow, Fitz Hugh, 45n, 58
"Lybian, Sibyl" (Story), 79, 361
Lyceum Theater, London, 333
Lyell, Charles, 221n; *Principles of Geology,* 228; system of, 295
Lyman, Chester S., 80
Lynn, Mass., 6

McAllister, Ward, 217
Macao, China, 8, 11
McClellan, George B., 38, 171
McCosh, James, 223
McDowell, Irvin, 81, 83, 85
Maceo, Antonio, 399, 400; death of, 401
Mackay, Mrs. John W., 313
McKinley, William, 99, 403
Madelin Plain, Calif., 147
Madison Square Gardens, N.Y.C., 384
Madrid, Spain, 208, 314
Magdalena Bay, Baja Calif., 197
Maidenhead, England, 383
Maine, 131, 337
Màlaga, Spain, 314
Malbone, Edward, 7
Mammoth Cave, Ky., 119n

Manhattan, 27–28, 41, 198, 411; John Henry Hill exhibits in, 132
Manila, P.I., 12, 402
Manitou Springs, Colo., 231
Manning, Daniel, 374
Manual of Geology (Dana), 41, 227
Marian, Lake (Overland Lake), 142; King names, 127
Mariposa, Calif., 65, 73, 77
Mariposa Estate, 57, 59
Mariposa Grove of Big Trees, 75
Mariposa Mining Co., 57, 75
Mariposa Trail, 75, 77
Marryatt, Mrs. (Jim Marryatt's mother), 141
Marryatt, Jim, 112, 118; joins King Survey, 109; with King at Lake Marian, 126–27; becomes King's general helper, 128; sensitivity of, to the occult, 139, 141, 142; reunion of, with mother, 141
Marsailles, France, 329
Marsh, Dr. John, 75, 199
Marsh, Othniel Charles, 152, 270, 375; alerted by King to Oregon fossils, 116; fossil collection of, 219; King's jokes about, 219; *Odontornithes*, 220; hears King on catastrophism and evolution, 220–21; and genealogy of horse, 222; guided by Buffalo Bill, 234; jokes about King, 239; as acting president of National Academy of Sciences, 254, 257–58, 259, 260–61; signs Yale letter supporting King, 267; confers with President Hayes, 269; *Dinocerata*, 285; named paleontologist for U.S. Geological Survey, 374
Martha's Vineyard, 201, 396
Martin, Homer, 210
Martinez Campos, Arsenio, 399, 401
Martinique, 395, 398
Marysville, Calif., 281
Mason, General, 83, 84, 85
Massachusetts, 6, 7, 74, 131, 148
Matson, James, 86
Matthews, Gov. (of Indiana), 400
Matthews, Brander, 332, 338
Mauna Loa, King visits, 169–70
Maury, Matthew F., 19
Mayflower, 8, 26
Maynard, Mr. (politician), 388

Mazatlán, Sinaloa, Mexico, 300, 304
Mead, George G., 104n
Medici, Lorenzo de, 334
Medicine Bow, Wyo., 238, 239, 279
Medicine Bow Peak, 225, 238
Meek, Fielding Bradford, 140, 224
Melville, Herman, 347
Merced Canyon, Calif., 173, 198
Merced Group, Calif., 87
"Merced Ramblings" (King), 107n, 158
Merced River, Calif., 76, 78, 170
Meredith, George, 333
Merrill, George P., on *Systematic Geology*, 228
Mesdag, Hendrik Willem, 329
Mesozoic Era, 225
Metropolitan Club, 366
Mexican Central Railroad, 343
Mexican Indians, 304
Mexican Metallurgical Co., 379–80
Mexican War, 13
Mexico, 13, 106, 288; King in 289, 304, 306, 313, 403, 404; as rich mining country, 298; King's mining ventures in, 298–302, 304–309, 310–11, 342–45, 345n, 352–53, 357, 379–80
Mexico City, Mexico, 310
Michigan, 299
Middle Feather River, Calif., 54
Middle San Joaquin River, Calif., 74
Millais, John, 329
Millbrae, home of D. O. Mills, 187
Miller, Henry, 237
Miller, Hugh, 406
Millerton, Calif., 73, 151; Road, 72, 151 & n
Millet, Frank, 332
Millet, Jean François, 339
Mills, Darius Ogden, 187
Mills, Enos, 165n
Millwood (Thomas sawmill), Calif., 62
Milnes, Richard Moncton. *See* Houghton, Lord
Minarets, Merced Group, King names, 87
Minas Prietas, Sonora, Mexico, history of, 298–99
Minas Prietas Mining Co., 299
Mineral Hill, Nev., 173
Mining Industry (Hague), 132, 137, 139–40; reception of, 167

Miocene, 221, 226
Miro, General, 401
Mission Indians, Calif., 353
Mississippi Bubble, 183
Mississippi delta, 101
Mississippi River, 37n, 275n
Mississippi Valley, 286
Missouri, 45, 150, 407
Missouri River, 45, 129, 135
M.I.T. (Massachusetts Institute of
    Technology), 103, 228, 257
Mitchell, Maria, 218
Mitchell, Dr. S. Weir, 209, 218; on
    King's nervous breakdown, 390
Modern Painters (Ruskin), 41, 159, 330
Mohave Indians, 83n
Mojave River, 82
Mommsen, Theodor, 336
Monarchy (King's projected novel, also
    called Aristocracy), 323
Monger, J. W. H., 229n
Mono Lake, Calif., 89
Mono Pass, Calif., 89
Monserrat (island), 395
Montana, 242n, 323, 406
Montez, Lola, 333
Montgomery Block, San Francisco: Cal-
    ifornia Geological Survey office at,
    52, 107; King Survey office at, 170,
    171, 173, 175, 186; Joseph P. Hale
    at, 197
Montreal, 39
Mooney, Ralph, 259n
Moore, Charles H., 43
Moran, Thomas, 160
Moravian Brotherhood, 9
Morgan, Lewis Henry, sociologist, 204
Morgan, J. Pierpont, 99, 366
Mormon Tabernacle, Salt Lake City, 48
Mormonism, 280 & n. *See also* Latter
    Day Saints; Mormons
Mormons, 48, 49, 165, 280n. *See also*
    Latter Day Saints; Mormonism
"Mornings on the Avenue" (Harte),
    214
Morocco, King in, 315
Morris, Lloyd, on King, 4
Morrison (ship), 9, 11
Morton, Levi P., 313, 329
Moses Tayler (steamship), 78
Mosquito Mountains, Colo., 278
Mother Lode, Calif., 57, 158, 160

Moulton, Louise Chandler. *See*
    Chandler, Louise (Mrs. Moulton)
Mount Pleasant Mine, Calif., 303–304,
    310
Mount Pleasant Mining Co., 303
Mountaineering in the Sierra Nevada
    (King), 27n, 107n, 148, 155n, 157n,
    195, 201, 203, 211, 278, 316, 407;
    King suppresses, 151n, 160n; discus-
    sion of, 157–61; King's disparage-
    ment of, 158; publication of, 158,
    168; Harte borrows details from, 214;
    T. W. Higginson on, 218–19; Doré
    criticized in, 330; realism pioneered
    by, 355
Muir, John, 39n, 155, 161n, 202n;
    finds his first glacier, 87; discovers
    Mount Ritter glaciers, 88; climbs
    Mount Ritter, 88; King and, 150,
    201–203; "Studies in the Sierra,"
    201; on origin of Yosemite, 201–202
Mulligan letters, 337
Munger, Gilbert, 135, 142, 145, 329;
    paintings of, illustrate *Systematic
    Geology*, 227
Murphy Mine, Nev., 194–95
Murphy's, Calif., 86
Murrieta, Joaquin, 151 & n
Museum of Comparative Zoology, Har-
    vard, 373
Mustang Colt (Frémont), 22–23
Muybridge, Eadweard, 142n, 355

Nanking, China, 13; Treaty of, 13
Nassau, Bahamas, 395
Nation, 43, 185, 187, 207, 295; Adams
    reviews King's "Catastrophism and
    Evolution" in, 222; Adams reviews
    Systematic Geology in, 227–28
National Academy of Sciences, 216,
    253, 254, 256, 260, 261, 374, 408
National Bank of El Paso. *See* El Paso
    National Bank
National Era, 21
National Institute of Arts and Letters,
    409
National Museum, 4, 108, 123, 228,
    265, 361, 372, 374
Native Races of the Pacific States (Ban-
    croft), 203, 204, 218
Natural Selection, 223
Natural Theology (Paley), 42

Nature, 275n, 377n
Naushon Island, Mass., 200
Navarro, Mary Anderson. *See* Anderson, Mary
ND herds, 236
ND ranch, 231
Nebraska, 45, 277; surveyed by Hayden, 129; Bronson describes rangeland in, 234; Bartlett Richards becomes largest cattle grazer in, 241
Nelson, Clifford M., 165n, 275n
Nevada, 50, 85, 111, 112–13, 113n, 147, 172, 195; King's field work of 1864 in, 59; map work in, 110; state minerologist of, 122; Austin as a mining center of, 124; Pleistocene lake in, 128; plateau of, 129; mining litigation in, 189; King reviews geology of, 194; Paleozoic continent west of, 225; George Strong in, 350n
Nevada Basin, 129
Neversweat Mine, Butte, Mont., 405
New England, 20, 23, 164, 200, 212, 357
New Hampshire, King in, 191, 357–58
New Haven, Conn., 18–19, 33, 35, 36, 40–41, 148, 153, 156; William Ashburner visits, 37; King does graduate study at, 80; Brewer in, 99; King ill at, 104; King Survey headquarters at, 140; Gardiner in charge of survey office at, 141; Marsh's fossils at, 219; geophysical laboratory at, 372
New Mexico, 175, 402–3; Public Lands Commission in, 279
New Orleans, La., 355, 356, 361
New Path, 43, 122
New York City, 5, 8, 41, 120, 171, 334, 400; King lives with Gardiner in, 42; King in, 103, 191, 199, 271, 294, 338, 348, 357, 358, 391, 396, 398; King's corps sails from, 104; King sails from, 105, 311; Julius Bien in, 156; King Survey headquarters in, 198; King's slumming in, 206–7, 320; Bret Harte on his last years in, 214–15; Republican Reform Club of, 216; meets Boston in Newport, 217; *Systematic Geology* completed in, 234; King's business address in, 299; Five of Hearts in, 310; Bret Harte in,

147, 319; King's opinion of, 336, 338; Howells in, 347; King arranges double life in, 363; Ada Todd returns to, 412
New York Herald, 374, 375, 412
New York Public Library, 146n
New York State, 39, 239, 403; Blaine loses, 337; interracial marriage legal in, 362
New York State Supreme Court, 389, 410, 413
New York Sun, 210, 214, 259
New York Times, 182n, 259
New York Tribune, 43, 201, 206, 207, 222, 283, 294, 320
New York World, 259
Newberry, John Strong, 116, 257, 268–69; on Hayden, 258
Newcomb, Simon, 151n, 253, 257, 259, 261, 266; supports King for geological director, 268
Newport, R.I., 7, 8, 9, 10–11, 15, 21, 120, 148, 331, 342; King in, 102, 132, 338, 408; Miss Dean at, 137n; Bret Harte in, 156; King meets Clover Adams at, 191–92; society in, 217–18; Pumpelly's headquarters at, 276; King takes Ada Todd to, 363; King buried at, 411
Newty family, 69–70, 150, 161n
"Newtys of Pike, The" (King), 70, 157n
New West, The (Brace), 102n
Nicaragua, 78
Nicaragua, Lake, 78
Nicolay, John George, 409; *Abraham Lincoln: A History,* 351
Niles, John M., 20, 23, 25
Niobrara River, 234–35, 239
Nordhoff, Charles, 375
North American Exploration Co., 403
North American Review, 167, 263, 340, 367
North Dome, Yosemite, 76
Northern Pacific Railroad, 344, 381
N. R. Davis & Co., 230, 231, 236, 238; King sells, 241

Oakland, Calif., 59, 60, 170, 186
Obelisk, the (Mount Clark), 77, 87; King renames, 77
Odontornithes (Marsh), 220

Old Block. *See* Delano, Alonzo
Old Dominion Mine, Wash., 398, 402
"Old-gold girls": King's penchant for, 168–69, 169n, 170, 309; Charles W. Stoddard on, 168; John La Farge on, 168–69: La Farge paints, 169 & n
Old Jules (Sandoz), 240
"Old Song, The" (Abbey), 331, 342
Old Winnemucca. *See* Winnemucca, Old (Paiute chief)
Olmsted, Frederick Law, 57 & n, 132, 207, 239; camps at Wawona, 73; with Brewer at Yosemite, 75; as chairman of Yosemite Park Commission, 75; receives King and Gardiner's plats and notes, 78
Olmsted, John, 240; as guest of King Survey, 132
Olmsted, Owen, 239–40; death of, 240
Olmsted, William N., 345
Olney, Richard, 400
Olyphant, D. W. C., 19
Olyphant, David, 9
Olyphant & Co., 9, 19
Olyphant, King & Co., 19
Olyphant, Talbot & Co., 8
On the Origin of Species (Darwin), 30
Oregon, 56, 69, 195, 402, 404; emigrants bound for, 48; King and J. D. Hague in, 116, 146; King-Davis cattle drive from, 237–38, 270; Station, 238
Oregon Trail, The (Parkman), 160, 161n
Oriente, province of, Cuba, 399
Ornithology (Ridgway), Part III of volume IV of Fortieth Parallel Report, 224
Osgood, James R., 148, 211, 258, 318 & n, 332
O'Sullivan, Timothy H., 111, 115, 146; joins King Survey, 104; readies mobile darkroom, 108; photographs mine interiors, 119 & n; photographs Uintas, 136; on expedition to Panama, 141; returns to King Survey, 170; photographs of, illustrate *Systematic Geology*, 227
Ouida. *See* Ramée, Marie de la
Overland Lake (Lake Marian), 127
Overland Monthly, 127, 142, 145, 147, 184, 192, 214; King publishes in, 127–28, 147; Muir publishes in, 201

Overland Road, 49, 124
Overland stage, 47
Owens Lake, Calif., 67
Owens River, 74
Owens Valley, 74, 173, 174, 192
Owl Creek, Colo., 231, 237, 239, 240, 242, 286
Owyhee district, Idaho, 116
Owyhee River, 237
Oxford, Robert, Bishop of, 6

Pacheco Pass, Calif., 60, 85
Pacific Division, U.S. Geological Survey, 274, 281
Pacific Mail Steamship Co., 80
Pacific Railroad Surveys, 101
Pacific Union Club. *See* Union Club, San Francisco
Page, Horace, 264
Pagoda Hill (J. Ross Browne's home), 60
Paiute Indians, 112, 117, 123, 126, 169, 173; place names of, 189
Paiute Range (East Range), Nev., 115
Palace Hotel, San Francisco, 281, 298
Paleozoic Era, 193, 224–25
Paley, William: *Natural Theology*, 42; *View of the Evidences*, 42
Palisades (in Sierra Nevada), 73
Panama, 170, 204; baby episode in, 105–106; O'Sullivan in, 141
Panama City, Panama, 106, 141
Pandora (James), 263
Panic of 1857, 25
Panic of 1873, 197, 230, 232, 255, 333
Panic of 1893, 386–87
Pantology (Park), 16, 17
Paris, 208, 311, 319, 328, 404; King in, 313–14, 316, 317, 325, 330, 382; George Howland trains in, 384
Park, Rev. Roswell, 15–17, 42; *Pantology*, 16, 17
Parker, H, G., Indian agent, 117, 158; lends sailboat *Nettie*, 111; prepares specimens for Ridgway's collection, 111n
Parker, Dr. Peter, 12
Parker House, Boston, 147
Parkman, Francis, 236; *The Oregon Trail*, 160, 161n
Parleys Park, Utah, 136; King's base at, 134–35

Parliament, 322, 326
Parsons, Alfred, 332
Parsons, Sam, 42; on Canadian cruise, 38–39
Passion Play, 382
Patagonian Range, Ariz., 299
Patterson, Carlisle, 261
Patterson, Thomas N., 262
Pavy, F., 325
P brand (Peter French), 237
Pearl River, China, 11
Peavine Mountain, 109, 111
Pecos Valley, Texas, 241
Peirce, C. S., 223 & n
Pelican-Dives controversy, 204
Pelican Mine, 203, 204–205
Pennsylvania, University of, 15, 267
Peru, 105
Peter the Great, 331
Petrography, 199–200
Philadelphia, 327, 333; Centennial Exhibition at, 318, 327
Philippine Islands, 402
Phillips, Wendell, 33, 35
Phoenix, John. *See* Derby, George H.
Phoenix, Ariz., 410
Piccadilly, London, 318
Pike, the: Bayard Taylor on, 150; as a literary type, 150, 208 & n; King's handling of, 150, 159–60
Pike County, Mo., 150
Pike County ballads (Hay), 208
Pikes Peak, Colo., 44
Pinyon Mountains, Nev., 173
Pioche, Nev., 194
Pioneer Foundry, Gold Hill, Nev., fire at, 50
Pit River, Calif., 55
Pit River Indians, 117, 123
Placerville, Calif., 51, 59, 303
Placerville Road, 50, 152
"Plain Language from Truthful James" (Harte), 145
Platte River, 46, 47
Players Club, 365
Pleistocene, 128, 129, 130, 227
Pliocene, 86, 221, 226, 227
Pluto's Cave, Calif., 56
Plymouth Rock, 42
Poker Flat, Calif., 54
Polk, James K., 13, 15
Pomfret, Conn., 15–17
Pony Express, 49

Populists, 402
Porter, Noah, 267
Portland, Ore, 116
Potawatomi Indians, 45
Potomac River, 352
Potosi, Calif., 54
Powder River, 239, 322
Powder River Cattle Co., 241
Powell, John Wesley, 165, 229n, 274, 280, 374; on King, 110; descends Green and Colorado rivers, 129, 140; exchanges data with King, 140; *Exploration of the Colorado River of the West,* 160; lectures on Colorado River, 162; descent of Grand Canyon by, 185; views of, on Uinta geology, 226; corps of, 253; and movement to consolidate surveys, 256, 257, 259, 261, 262; *Report on the Lands of the Arid Region,* 257; on General Land Office, 258; and Bureau of Ethnology, 265, 291; praises King's grasp of survey problems, 266; supports King for geological director, 268; on F. V. Hayden, 268; King to, 271; with Public Lands Commission, 276, 282; presses King to remain as geological director, 290; as director of U.S. Geological Survey, 291–92, 293–94, 295, 372; reshapes program of U.S. Geological Survey, 293–94; attacks on, in Congress, 348; before Allison Commission, 373; involved in Marsh-Cope feud, 375; drive to force resignation of, 375–76; resignation of, 396
Powell, Lawrence Clark, 213, 363n
Powell Survey, 260; discontinued, 265. *See also* Geographical and Geological Survey of the Rocky Mountain Region
Prado Gallery, Madrid, 314
Prager, Conrad (character), 279n
Pratt, J. H., 378
"Prayer to the Virgin of Chartres, The" (Adams), 145n
Pre-Cambrian Era, 225
Precious Metals, The, 296
Precious metals, census of, 271, 275, 276, 282–84, 295–96, 311
Precious metals industry, 282–84; King reports on, 295–96
Pre-Raphaelite Brotherhood, 42

Prescott, Ariz., 81, 83, 84–85, 146, 407, 409
Presidio, the, San Francisco, 85, 141
Prietas Mine, Sonora, Mexico, 300–302, 308–309, 310, 311, 342, 380; history of, 298–99
Prince's Gardens, Flushing, N.Y., 397
Princess Casamassima, The (James), 320
Princess Sarah. *See* Hopkins, Sarah Winnemucca
Principles of Geology (Lyell), 228
Promontory Point, Utah, 132
Prussia, 20
Pteraspis, 4
Public Lands Commission, 264, 276, 278, 279 & n, 282; Thomas Donaldson serves on, 256; composition of, 276–77; Western tour of, 277–81
Puerto Rico, 395
Puget Sound, 41
Pullman strike, 397
Pumpelly, Raphael, 263, 282, 300, 342, 357; in cattle business, 236; joins U.S. Geological Survey, 270; census work of, 275–76, 284, 285
Pumpkin Buttes, Wyo., 239–40
Punch, 331, 332
"Punctuated equilibria," Eldredge-Gould model of, 221n
Purnell, Annie, 363
Putnam, Israel, 16
Pyramid Lake, 109, 111, 122, 158, 169
Pyrometrics, 372

Quarternary, 227
Quebec (city), 39
Quincy, Mass., 5

Rabelais Club, 332, 333
Rabbitt, Mary C., 257, 275n, 291–92
Rachel, French actress, 212
Racine College, 17
Rainier, Mount, 144, 147
Rainsford, William, 209, 210
Ralston, William, 171, 177, 180, 181, 182; death of; 185; takes option on Emma Mine, 190
Ramée, Marie de la, 322
Ramsden, F. William, 393, 395
Ramona (Jackson), 218, 353
Rancho Sanchez, 167, 170

Rancho Valgame Dios, Yedras, Mexico, 304
"Range, The" (King), 85, 149 & n, 226
Ratcliffe, Silas (character), 285
Raymond, Rossiter, 83n, 198, 213, 279n, 367, 404; describes King in camp, 135; on King as expert witness, 190; on choosing the right geological director, 267–68; re Alexander Lancaster, 405
Red Canyon, Green River, 165
"Red Flamingoes, The" (Gérôme), 329
Red Rock Pass, 133
Red Sea, 12
Reed, John, 206
Reese River, Nev., 125
Reform clubs, 217
Reid, Whitelaw, 99, 206, 210, 222, 294
"Reminiscences" (Foote, MS), 279n
Reminiscences of a Ranchman (Bronson), dedicated to King's memory, 236n
Reminiscences of the South Seas (La Farge), 169n
Report on the Lands of the Arid Region (Powell), 257
"Report on the Surveys of the Territories" (National Academy of Sciences), 260
Republican Party, 22, 23, 337, 351; King's affiliation with, 216–17
Republican Reform Club of New York, 216
Republicanism, 338
Revelations, Book of, 42
Revenue Stamp (Digger Indian), 63
"Rex" (King's dog), 286
Rhine River, 37
Rhode Island, 7, 9. *See also* Newport, R.I.
Richards, Bartlett, 240, 241
Richardson, Henry Hobson, 99, 207, 352
Richelieu River, 39
Richmond, Va., 35n, 39n
Richmond Mine, Eureka, Nev., 189, 194
Richthofen, Baron Ferdinand von, 107, 226, 382
Rickard, Thomas A.: and King's exposé of Diamond Swindle, 178n
Ridge, John Rollin (Yellow Bird), 151n

Ridgway, Robert, 108, joins King Survey, 104; collecting of, 111 & n; 115–16, 123, 126; at Pyramid Lake, 122–23; on Pit River Indian depredation, 123; and Chippy I and Chippy II, 126, 135; and *Ornithology*, 139
Rigveda, 41
Ringwood Manor, 207, 338
Rio Tinto, Spain, copper district of, 315
Ritter, Mount, 202; King fails to gain top of, 88; John Muir climbs, 88; Muir finds glaciers on, 88
Ritter Group, 87
Roaring River, 64
Robbins, Asher, 9, 10, 11, 12
Robert, Bishop of Oxford, 6
Roberts, George D., 174, 176, 178, 182; expedition of, 176; dies same day as King, 182n
Rock Creek Cemetery, 348, 372n
Rockwell, Porter, 128
Rocky Mountain Cattle Co., 239, 241
Rocky Mountain Division, U.S. Geological Survey, 274, 278
Rocky Mountain Ranch, 240
Rocky Mountains, 85, 89, 101, 102, 129, 146, 164, 201, 205, 212, 274, 284, 331, Whitney maps, 133; Marsh calls King "owner" of, 239
Rogers, Josephine, 121
Rogers, William B. (of MIT), 228, 257
Roosevelt, Theodore, 2; fame of, 37n; on King's buffalo hunt, 46, 47n; and Republican Reform Club, 217; defeated by Hewitt for mayor, N.Y.C., 347; founds Boone and Crockett Club, 365; and a family ghost, 385–86; with King to New York, 397–98; as assistant secretary of Navy, 402; wires condolence on King's death, 411
Rosario Mine, Chihuahua, Mexico, 300
Rosebud Indian Agency, 240
Rossetti, Dante Gabriel, 218, 327
Rossland, B.C., 397, 404
Rossland mines, 388
Rothschild, Baron Ferdinand James de, 321, 322, 329
Roughing It (Twain), 160, 161n, 279n
Round Table Club, 208, 374
Rouses Point, N.Y., 38
Ruby Gulch, 178, 181, 183

Ruby Hill, Nev., 189, 190
Ruby Range (East Humboldt Mountains), 126, 155n, 173
Ruby Valley, Nev., 126, 129
"Rum, Romanism, and Rebellion," 337
Ruskin, John, 42, 43, 55, 68, 174; *Modern Painters*, 41, 159, 330; and King, 330–31
Russell process of lixiviation, 301
Ryder, Albert Pinkham, 339n, 347

Sacramento, Calif., 51, 53, 59, 81, 116; Speers train in, 50; King Survey camp at, 107–108; King's corps contracts malaria at, 114
Sacramento plain, 142
Sacramento River, 40
Sacramento Valley, 381
Saguenay River, 39
St. Charles Hotel, New Orleans, 355, 356
Saint-Gaudens, Augustus, 372n
St. Helens By-the-Sea, S.C., 391n
St. Helens, Mount, 153
St. James, Court of, 313
St. John's Wood, London, 320
St. Joseph, Mo., 44
St. Kitts (island), 395
St. Lawrence River, 39
St. Louis, Mo., 44, 407
St. Lucia (island), 395
St. Peter, Lake, 39
St. Thomas, Virgin Islands, 395
St. Vincent (island), 395
Salem, Mass., 8
Salido Mine, Chihuahua, Mexico, 310
Salmon, Tati, 385–86
Salt Lake City, Utah, 128, 132, 134, 135, 191, 274, 288; description of, 48; Public Lands Commission in, 279–80
Salt Valley, Nev., 115
Sambourne, Linley, 332
Samoa, 381
San Cristobal Mine, Zacatecas, Mexico, 403
San Diego, Calif., 355
San Francisco, Calif., 52, 141, 175, 183; King in, 57–58, 78, 85, 106, 121, 153, 154, 171, 180, 186, 288–89, 303, 306, 353, 355; King takes Hoffmann to, 75; Calaveras Skull arrives in, 86; Harte's reputation in,

156; King ill in, 166, 171; Diamond Swindle in, 172, 173–74, 176, 183; King gives Diamond Swindle deposition at, 195; Public Lands Commission in, 281, 298; Yedras bullion shipped to, 305; King imports sawmill from, 305; supplies works for Sombrerete, 308

San Francisco *Alta California,* 172, 183

San Francisco and New York Mining and Commercial Co., 171

San Francisco Bay, 57, 85, 119, 141, 147, 173, 174, 175, 185, 186, 205

San Francisco Bulletin, 152, 174, 183, 192

San Francisco Chronicle, 183

San Francisco Mountain, 153, 288

San Gabriel Mission, Calif., 82

San Gabriel Mountains: named by California Geological Survey, 82n

San Joaquin basin, 88

San Joaquin River, 88

San José, Calif., 60

San Juan del Sur, Nicaragua, 78

San Juan North, Calif., 53

San Juan River, Nicaragua, 79

San Luis, Potosí, Mexico, 380

Sandoz, Mari: *Old Jules,* 240

Sandwich Islands, 167–70

Santa Barbara, Calif., 353

Santa Clara Valley, Calif., 353

Santa Maria River, 84

"Santa Rita" (King's projected novel), 212n, 353, 354, 355

Santa Rosa Mill, Sombrerete, Mexico, 352, 357, 379

Santiago de Cuba, King in, 381, 393, 394

Santo Domingo, 392

Sarah, Princess. *See* Hopkins, Sarah Winnemucca

Saintsbury, George, 333

Sargent, A. A., 167, 172, 184, 185

Saturday Club, Boston, 148, 209; King attends, 147

Savage Mine, Virginia City, Nev., 119

Savile Club, London, 324, 333

Scarlet Letter, The (Hawthorne), 212, 278

Schiller, Friedrich von, 319

Schmidt, "lapidary," 178n

Schofield, J. M., 141

Schurz, Carl, 217, 282, 285, 287, 289,

290; and "party of the centre," 216; told of Dull Knife's outbreak, 236; approves survey consolidation plan, 261; King and, 262, 264, 271; opposes Hayden for geological director, 266; supports King for geological director, 267, 269; and term *national domain,* 273; King reports to, 276, 278, 281, 288; plays Chopin, 287

Schuyler, Eugene, 42

Schuyler, Philip, 207, 294

Scotland, 357; King in, 317–18

Scribner's. *See* Charles Scribner's Sons

Scribner's Monthly, 208n, 218

Seattle, Wash., 407

Secret Valley, Nev., 127

"Secular refrigeration," Lord Kelvin's postulate of, 369, 378

Sedgwick, Anne Douglas (Nannie), 329

Sedgwick, George S., 312–13, 314, 325, 328–29, 333, 382

Sedgwick, Mrs. George S., 329

Senate. *See* U.S. Senate

Sequoias, 75; King visits, 62

Serra, Junipero, 196

Seven Dials, London, 320, 321n, 323

76 brand (Frewen brothers), 323; herd, 323

Seville, Spain, 315

Shakespeare, William, 31, 184; *Hamlet,* 276

"Shall Cuba Be Free?" (King), 399

Shanghai, China, 25; King & Co. branch at, 19

Shasta, Mount, 55, 56, 58, 144, 147, 153 & n, 156, 158, 200; Brewer and Whitney climb, 40; Brewer denies glaciers on, 56; painted by John Henry Hill, 132; King climbs 142–44; glaciers of, 143–44; King's verses on, 145

"Shasta" (King), 152

"Shasta's Flanks" (King), 56

Shastina, 142–43

Shaw, Quincy A.: in cattle business, 236, 239; mining ventures of, 299, 303, 308, 345, 379

Sheep Rock (Mount Langley), Calif., 71, climbed by King as Mount Whitney, 154; as bogus Mount Whitney, 154, 155. *See also* Mount Langley

Sheffield, Joseph, 32

Sheffield Hall, Yale, 35, 37, 38
Sheffield Scientific School, 31n, 32, 41, 54, 207; King reads paper at, 26n, 220–22; program at, 33; King graduates from, 38; King studies astronomy at, 80; King relocates corps at, 140. *See also* Yale Scientific School; Yale College (University)
Sheldon, F. H., 231–32
Sherman, John, 261, 287
She Stoops to Conquer (Goldsmith), 342
Shiloh, Tenn., 140
Ship Wheel Ranch, Wyo., 240
Shoshone Falls, Snake River, 127, 142, 146, 147; King's vignette on, 127–28, 147, 156, 158
Shoshone Indians, 48
Shoshone Mountains, 110, 125
Siam, 20
Siberia, 107, 164
Sickles, Daniel, 208
Sidney, Neb., 235
Sierra Iron Co., 189
Sierra Madre Mountains (San Gabriel Mountains), Calif., 82
Sierra Madre, Mexico, 296, 305, 344; Occidental, 310
Sierra Nevada, 49, 65, 66, 69, 102, 129, 146, 195, 201, 408n; King's first trip across, 50; Brewer's rapid reconnaissance of, 52; King and Whitney cross, 59; southern extension of, explored by California Survey, 60–74; earliest record of "roping down" in, 66–67; Gardiner's map of central part of, 100, 103, 107: Sereno Watson crosses, 113: King and J. D. Hague cross, 116; lava flows of, 141, 149n; King's descriptions of, 151; "color-glory" of, 159; King's *Mountaineering* first "real literature" about, 161n; King's glacier studies in, 170, 174; A. Bierstadt's company in, 174; at end of Pliocene, 227
Sierra Prieta, Ariz., 84
"Sierra Storm, A" (King), 77, 78, 158
Sierra Tramps, 128
Silliman, Benjamin, Jr., 130–31, 189; puffs Emma Mine, 190–91
Silliman's *Journal*, 32. See also *American Journal of Science*
Siluria, 4

Silurian Period, 194
Silver City, Idaho, 116, 382
Silver City, Nevada, 120
Silver Plume, Colo., 203, 205
Silverites, King on, 402
Simpson, James H., 49, 100, 129
Simpson route, 49n
Sinaloa, Mexico, 289, 298, 300, 304, 325
Singapore, 12
Sioux Indians, 47, 216, 233, 234, 240
Siskiyou Mountains, 40, 56
Sisson, J. H., 142
Skeleton in Armor, The (Longfellow), 278
Sketch Book, The (Irving), 41, 159
Sketch Club, 209
Skull Valley, Ariz., 84
Slack, John, 182, 184
Slavery, 13, 21; King's attitude toward, 33–34
Smalley, George, 320
Smith, F. Hopkinson, 210
Smith, Hank G. (character), 150, 173
Smithsonian Institution, 101, 116, 140, 253, 261, 265 & n, 377; takes jurisdiction of Powell Survey, 130; backs King in 1869, 131
Snake River, 127, 128, 133, 238; basin of, 127, 237; valley of, 133
Social Register, 366
Society for the Advancement of Truth in Art, 43
Socrates, 195
Soda Springs, Yosemite, 88, 89
Soho, London, 317
Soldiers Pass, 193
Solomons, Theodore, on King's *Mountaineering*, 161n
Sombrerete, Zacatecas, Mexico, 306, 343, 379
Sombrerete Mine, 306, 310, 342, 344, 352–53, 357, 379; King's plans for, 307–308; King's development of, 308
Sombrerete Mining Co., 308
Sombrerete mines, Zacatecas, history of, 306–307
Sonoma Range (Havillah Mountains), 125n
Sonora, Mexico, 289, 298, 301, 303
Sonora Pass, Calif., 89
Sou, Captain (Paiute chief), 117

South Carolina: secession of, 34; Henry Adams in, 391
South China Sea, 20
South Humboldt River, 173
South Kings River, 63
South Pass, 48; "discovered" by Frémont, 62
South Seas, 37, 103, 309, 383
Spain, 306, 318 & n, 326, 329, 392, 399, 401; King's tour of, 314–16; war with, 401–402, 403
Spanish-American War, 401–402
Speers, Mr. (mule trader), 44, 45, 49–50
Speers, Mrs. (mule trader's wife), 44
Speers train, 47
Spofford, Harriet Prescott, 21
Spokane, Wash., 398, 402
Stackpole, Virginia, married to George Howland, 404
Standard Oil Co., 372
Stanford, Leland, 108
Stanislaus River, 89, 137
Stanley, Lady, 321n
Stansbury, Howard, 100, 135
Stanton, Edwin McMasters, 38, 101, 102, 104n; Brewer recommends King to, 100, 101
Star Peak, Nev., King climbs, 59
Starr King, Mount, 142
State, U.S. Department of, 290
Staten Island, N.Y., 200
Statistics of the production of the Precious Metals in the United States (King), 296
Stearns, Robert E. C., 202n
Stedman, Edmund Clarence, 312, 313, 321, 322n, 331, 342, 365; regarding King, 411
Steens Mountains, 237
Stegner, Wallace, 150, 164n, 229n, 375; regarding King's *Mountaineering*, 161n; *Angle of Repose*, 279n
Stein's Mountains. *See* Steens Mountains
Stevenson, Robert Louis, 169, 317, 365; *New Arabian Nights*, 312
Stewart, Parson, 124
Stewart, William ("Big Bill"), 120, 375
Stiles, Ezra, 7
Stillwater Mountains, 115
Stockton, Calif., 50

Stockton, Frank, 394
Stoddard, Charles Warren Stoddard, 142, 186; on "old-gold girls," 168; *Poems*, 168n
Stoddard, Richard Henry, 207
"Stone Giant's Bowl, The" (King), 145
Stonehenge (ND ranch), 231
Story, William Wetmore, "Lybian Sibyl," 79, 361
Stowe, Harriet Beecher: *Uncle Tom's Cabin*, 22
Stratford, England, 331
Strong, George (character modeled on King), 26n, 350 & n
Stuart, Gilbert, 7
"Studies in the Sierra" (Muir), 201
Studio Building, N.Y.C., 338–39
Sturgis, Russell, Jr., 43
Sturgis, Thomas, 232
Sturgis, Lane & Goodall, 232
"Style and the Monument" (King), 340
Summit Tunnel, Calif., 109
Sumner, William Graham, 209
Sundry Civil Appropriations Bill, 256
Sundry Civil Expenses Bill, 265
Sunapee Lake, N.H., 357, 403
Sunapee Mountain, N.H., 358
Sunnyside (Irving's home), 41
Superior, Lake, 285
Surveys, U.S. Government, consolidation of, 253–270
Swann, Alex, 233–34
Sweetwater River, 237
Switzerland, 37, 56, 74, 326, 329
Systematic Geology (King), 11, 127n, 149n, 170, 205, 211, 213n, 220, 231, 369, 370; preparation of, 206, 219; synopsis of, 224–27; publication of, 227; reception of, 227–28; reputation of, 228, 228n–29n; completion of, 234

Tacoma, Wash., 402
Taft, Robert, 119n
Tahiti, 385
Tahoe, Lake, 59, 150; move to change name of, 192
Taiping Rebellion, 13
Talbot & Olyphant, 11
Tammany Hall, 348
Tampa, Fla., King in, 391
Tangier, Morocco, King in, 315

Taylor, Rev. Mr., 121
Taylor, Bayard, 150, 207
Tayopa Mine, Sonora, Mexico, 298
Tejon, Calif., 52
Telephone, King's interest in, 258–59
Teller, Henry M., 204
Teller, Walter Magnus, 359n
Telluride, Colo., 403, 404
Ten Years' Revolt, Cuba, 394
Tenaya, Lake, Yosemite, 76
Tenaya Canyon, Yosemite, 77
Tennessee, 380
Tennyson, Alfred, Lord: In Memoriam,
    23 & n; Locksley Hall, 354, 359n
Tenth Census. See U.S. Bureau of the
    Census, Tenth Census
Terry, David S., 182
Tertiary, 136, 149n
Tertiary age of man, J. D. Whitney's
    theory of, 87
Teton country, Wyo., 397
Tew, George., 300, 343–44, 352
Texas, 237, 386; Davis buys cattle
    from, 231; Bronson moves to, 241;
    King's bank in, 353, 386–87
Thames River, 324, 329, 383
Theocritus, 209
Thiel Mountains, Anarctica, 165n
Thomas sawmill (Millwood), Calif., 62
Thomson, Sir William, 317. See also
    Kelvin, Lord
Thousand Spring Valley, 127
Three Brothers, Yosemite, 76
Three Crows (brand), 234, 235; herd,
    235, 236
Three Lakes, The: Marian, Lall, Jan,
    And How They Were Named (King),
    146n
Thrice Through the Furnace (Little), 22
"Through the Forest" (King), 149
Thursday Club of Boston, 146
Ticonderoga, N.Y., 38
Tiffany, Charles, 182, 184
Tiffany's, N.Y.C., 401
Times (London), 195
Todd, Ada (the elder, King's wife),
    358–59, 406; life with King, 362–
    64, 384–85; marries King, 363–64;
    babies of, 363, 384, 397; King's con-
    cern for, 380; moves to Flushing,
    397; King's final meeting with, 408–
    409; learns King's true identity, 410;
    notified of King's death, 411; returns

from Canada, 412. See also King,
    Ada (wife)
Todd, Ada (the younger, King's daugh-
    ter), 384. See also King, Ada (daugh-
    ter)
Todd, Grace (King's daughter), 384. See
    also King, Grace (daughter)
Todd, James (King's assumed name),
    363, 410, 413
Todd, Mrs. James, 413. See also Todd,
    Ada (the elder, King's wife); King,
    Ada (wife)
Todd, Leroy (King's son), 363, 412;
    death of, 384.
Todd, Sidney (King's son), 397. See also
    King, Sidney (son)
Todd, Wallace (King's son), 397. See
    also King, Wallace (son)
Toiyabe Mountains, Nev., 122, 194
Tolstoy, Leo, 347
Toronto, Canada: King to send family
    to, 408–409; Logan School at, 409;
    Ada Todd at, 411
Town and Country Club, 218
Towne, Robert A., 380
Townsley, Clarence Page, 410; brings
    King's body east, 411
"Trail Between the Cedar Bushes, The"
    (Gardiner, MS), 83n
Train, George Francis, 136–37
Treasury, U.S. Department of, 261;
    Daniel Manning secretary of, 374
Triassic Period, 226
Trilling, Lionel, 23n
Trinidad, 395, 398
Trinity Church, Newport, R.I., 9
Trinity College, Hartford, Conn., 35
Trowbridge, William P., 257
Troy, Kans., 45
Troy, N.Y., 33
Truckee, Captain (Paiute chief), 123
Truckee Meadows, Nev., 109, 117
Truckee Mountains, Nev., 109, 111
Truckee River, Nev., 109, 111, 122;
    Big Bend of, 110, 111, 112
Tuckerman, Henry: Book of the Artists,
    written at Studio Building, N.Y.C.,
    339
Tucson, Ariz., 301
Tulare plain, Calif., 72
Tuolumne, Grand Canyon of the, 88–
    89. See also Great Tuolumne Canyon
Tuolumne, upper, 77, 88, 173

Tuolumne Meadows, 88
Tuolumne River, 75
Tuolumne Table Mountain, 87
Turf Club, London, 324
Turkey, 328
Turner, Frederick Jackson, 386
Turner, Joseph Mallord William, 330–
31, 339, 399; *The Whaler*, 399n
Tuxedo Club, 365
Tuxedo Park, 359n, 365
Twain, Mark (Samuel Langhorne
Clemens), 4, 37n, 60, 113n, 115,
161n, 315, 318, 332, 411; lampoons
Mrs. "Sandy" Baldwin, 120; casts as-
persions on Bret Harte, 156n; *Rough-
ing It*, 160, 161n, 279n; on Century
Club, 209; *The Gilded Age*, 318
XX Club, 338
Twenty-fifth Regiment, Connecticut
Volunteers, 39
Twin River Mining Co., 194
Two Years Before the Mast (Dana), 160,
161n
Tyndall, John, 41, 55, 65, 149, King
meets, 67n; 317
Tyndall, Mount, 67, 90, 149, 154; first
ascent of, by King and Cotter, 65–
68; King's descent of, 68; King's report on, 68; John Muir climbs, 150;
on F. P. Farquhar's list of King's first
ascents, 155n; King's exaggerations in
sketches on, 159

Uinkaret Plateau, 280, 288
Uinta Mountains, 1, 136, 164–65,
164n; elevation of, in late Cre-
taceous Period, 226
Uncle Tom's Cabin (Stowe), 22
Undine (gig), 38, 39
Unicorn, the, Yosemite, 88
Uniformitarianism, and catastrophism,
220–22, 221n
Union, 34, 38, 39
Union Army, 38, 104n
Union Club, San Francisco (Pacific
Union Club), 106, 137, 195, 196
Union Iron Works, San Francisco, 353
Union League Club, N.Y.C., 338, 342,
365, 366, 388
Union Pacific Railroad, 128, 129, 136,
137, 381
Unionville, Nev., 115, 122
United Congregationalists, 16

United States, Powell inaugurates
geologic map of, 293
U.S. Agriculture Department. *See* Agriculture, U.S. Department of
U.S. Army, 81, 101; appropriations
bill, 131
U.S. Army Engineers, 53, 90, 131,
133, 153, 184, 187, 253, 257, 261;
administers Wheeler Survey, 130;
versus the Interior Department, 255;
opposes survey consolidation plan,
262; Wheeler Survey continues in,
265
U.S. Board on Geographic Names,
154n; on naming of Kings Peak,
164n–65n
U.S. Bureau of [American] Ethnology.
See Bureau of [American] Ethnology
U.S. Census Bureau (Census Office),
275, 294, 296; Tenth Census of,
271, 275–76, 281, 282–84, 295–96,
366
U.S. Coast and Geodetic Survey. *See*
Coast and Geodetic Survey; Coast
Survey
U.S. Coast Survey. *See* Coast Survey;
Coast and Geodetic Survey
U.S. Congress, 15, 59, 76, 89, 188,
259, 260, 262, 286, 401; grants
Yosemite to California, 75; King lobbies, 101; King's success with, 107,
256; authorizes survey of Nebraska,
129; grants aid to J. W. Powell, 129;
W. H. Brewer memorializes, 199;
Western surveys and, 253, 254; economy moves in, 255; survey consolidation plan submitted to, 261; opinion
of, splits over survey consolidation,
264; Western bloc in, 264; consolidation measure enacted by, 265; R.
Raymond follows consolidation battle
in, 267; and term *national domain*,
273; and Tenth Census, 275; intention of, re land classification, 277;
rejects bill of Public Lands Commission, 282; publishes T. Donaldson's
report, 282; extends U.S. Geological
Survey over entire country, 293;
moves in, to transfer U.S. Geological
Survey to Agriculture Department,
294; attacks on J. W. Powell in, 348;
Allison Commission of, 373; slashes
funds for Irrigation Survey, 375

U.S. Exploring Expedition, 37
U.S. General Land Office. *See* General Land Office
U.S. Geological Explorations of the Fortieth Parallel. *See* Fortieth Parallel Survey
U.S. Geological Survey, 260, 281, 372, 378n; founded by King, 4; on Mount Lassen's elevation, 55n; on Mount Brewer's elevation, 65n; on Mount Whitney's elevation, 155n; map of, makes first mention of Kings Peak, 165n; as result of King's suggestion, 256; bill authorizing, 264, 265; King sworn in as director of, 271; census work of, 271, 275–76, 281, 282–84, 295–96, 366; organization of, 273–74; field divisions of, 274; land classification policy of, 277; publications program of, 284–85, 289 & n, 296; new districts proposed for, 286; appropriations for, 287; first annual report of, 289 & n; King resigns from, 291; significance of King's tenure at, 291–92; Powell's program for, 293–94; King's unofficial connection with, 294–96; geophysical laboratory of, 295, 371–72, 376, 378n; attacks on Powell's conduct of, 348; probed by Congress, 373, 375; Irrigation Survey in, 375; King's availability to resume direction of, 376; Powell resigns from, 396
U.S. House of Representatives, 265; Public Lands Committee of, 198, 254, 255, 264; Appropriations Committee of, 256, 261, 273, 375
U.S. Interior Department. *See* Interior, U.S. Department of
U.S. Public Lands Commission. *See* Public Lands Commission
U.S. Sanitary Commission, 57n
U.S. Senate, 167, 261, 286, 291, 401; Public Lands Committee of, 269; Appropriations Committee of, 286, 375; Foreign Relations Committee of, 400
U.S. State Department. *See* State, U.S. Department of
U.S. Supreme Court, 34, 190
U.S. Treasury Department. *See* Treasury, U.S. Department of

U.S. War Department. *See* War, U.S. Department of
U.S. Weather Bureau, 376
Upheaval and Subsidence of Continents, The (King), 295
Utah, 402; Lake Bonneville located in, 130; highest point in, 164n; King's review of geology of, 191; cattle drives from, 234
Utah Basin, 129, 133

Valgame Dios Rancho, Yedras, Mexico, 304
Van Buren, Martin, 20
Vanderbilt, Cornelius ("Commodore"), 78
Van de Velde, Madame, 319–20
van Dyke, Henry, 161n; officiates at King's funeral, 411
Vassar College, 79
Vaux, Calvert, 207
Vedder, Elihu, 332
Valasquez, Diego Rodriguez de Silva, 314
Venice, Italy, 329
Venus of Milo, 355
Verde Mine, Sonora, Mexico, 309
Vermillion Basin, Colo., 175, 226
Vermillion Canyon, Colo., 177
Vermont, 131, 150
Verne, Jules, 137, 152
Vernon, Amey (Mrs. Samuel King), 7
Vernon, Harriet (Mrs. Samuel King, Jr.), 8
Vernon, Richard de, 7
Vernon House, Newport, R.I., 276
Vernons of Haddon Hall, 7
Victoria, Queen, 322
Victoria Institute, 377n
Victorian Gentlewoman in the Far West, A (Foote), 279n
Victorio (Apache chief), 301
Vidal, Gore, *Empire*, 23n, 27n, 408n; on Henry Adams "love" for King, 23n; on King's last meeting with Adams and the Hays, 408n
Vienna, Austria, 208
View of the Evidences (Paley), 42
Villard, Henry, 381
Vinton, Rev. Francis, 9
Virgin of Chartres, 361
Virgin River, 129

Virginia, 38
Virginia City, Nev., 50, 118, 119, 122, 212, 343; King as dandy in, 120; King's engagement announced at, 121; Gardiner married at, 128; painted by John Henry Hill, 132
Virginia City *Territorial Enterprise*, 121
Virginia Mountains, Nev., 109, 111
Virginian, The (Wister), 323
Virgin's Tears, Yosemite, 76
Visalia, Calif., 61, 64, 68, 69, 71–72, 175
Volcano House, Mauna Loa, 170
Vulcanism, King's interest in, 143, 170

Waddesdon Manor, Buckinghamshire, England, 321, 322, 324
Wadsworth, Nev., 111
Walcott, Charles D., 280, 291–92; quoted, 376; on King's influence, 378n; succeeds Powell as geological director, 396; King on, 396
Walker, Francis A., 207, 304; as superintendent of Census, 275, 276, 283, 284, 295; on Carl Schurz, 267; King's working agreement with, 271
Walker, Franklin, on King's *Mountaineering*, 161n
Walker House, Salt Lake City, 279–80
Wall Street, N.Y.C., 99, 192
War, U.S. Department of, 101, 107, 135, 167, 176, 184, 255
War of the Copper Kings, 404–405
Ward, Artemus (Charles Farrar Browne), 57
Ward, Oliver (character), 279n
Ward, Quincy A., 207, 210, 409–10; recommends King to Century Club, 209
Ward, Richard, 7
Ward, Samuel ("Uncle Sam"), 323
Ward, Susan Burling (character), 279n
Waring, George, 207, 218
Warner, Charles Dudley, 318 & n, 321, 353–54, 356, 358, 409; *The Gilded Age*, 318
Warren, G. K., atlas of, 100
Warren and Guiterman, 238
Wasatch Mountains, 48, 128; surveyed by King Survey, 133, 134; Emma mine located in, 190; King studies orographical problems along, 191;

Paleozoic ocean breaking around, 225; Paleozoic sediments in, 225; elevation of, in late Cretaceous Period, 226; at end of Pliocene, 227
Washington, D.C., 4, 5, 6, 13, 20, 100, 134, 198, 282, 283, 287; Yosemite legislation at, 75; King lobbies at, for King Survey, 100–101; King Survey remittance from, 108; King ships collections to, 130; King removes headquarters from, 140; Powell lectures on Colorado River at, 162; defense of *Mining Industry* at, 167; Gardiner in, 187; King on his accomplishments in, 242; movement in, to consolidate surveys, 256; A. S. Hewitt most useful public man in, 256; Madelein Lee investigates power in, 264; King supporters consult president at, 269; headquarters of U.S. Geological Survey at, 274; Public Lands Commission meets in, 281–82; King's "bachelor castle" in, 283–84; social rounds in, 286–87; Powell favors centralizing U.S. Geological Survey in, 293; reason for King's leaving, 296; King expected in, 305; the Adamses at, 263, 310; King in, 261, 271, 352, 396, 408; King takes Ada Todd to, 363; geophysical laboratory in, 372; Adams awaits King in, 398; Adams intrigues for free Cuba in, 400, 401
"Washington Crossing the Delaware" (Leutze), 339
Washington Square, N.Y.C., 41, 42
Washington (state), 402; (territory), 144
Watford, England, 6
Watkins, Carleton E., 141–42 & n, 145
Watson, Sereno, 135; joins Fortieth Parallel Survey, 113; replaces W. W. Bailey, 122; collection by, on Great Basin flora, 126, 130; submits botanical report, 156
Wawona, Calif., 73, 74, 78
"Wayside Pikes" (King), 150, 157n
Weather Bureau. *See* U.S. Weather Bureau
Weber Quartzites, 225
Weber Valley, Utah, 48

Wecter, Dixon, on King's *Mountaineering*, 161n
Weld County, Colo., 232
Wells Fargo, 72
West Humboldt Mountains, 59, 114, 115–16
West Indies, 6, 391, 397, 398, 404, 408
West Point (U.S. Military Academy), 257
Western surveys, rivalry among, 253, 255
Western Union, 49, 351
Weston, Maria, 148n
Whaler, The (Turner), 399n
Whampoa, China, 19
Wheeler, George M., 170, 192, 274; launches Wheeler Survey, 130; under command of chief of engineers, 130; clashes with Hayden in Colorado, 254; eliminated for geological directorship, 258; as sponsor of E. D. Cope, 260
Wheeler Survey (Geological Surveys West of the One Hundredth Meridian), 130, 260, 265
Wheeling, W. Va., King arranges temperature observations in, 372
Whistler, James McNeill, 327, 339 & n; caned by Roswell Park, 16
Whiskey Diggings, Calif., 54
Whiskey Ring, 216
White, Andrew D., 139
White, Stanford, 348, 366, 384
"White Cloud Peak" (Ruby Range), on F. P. Farquhar's list of King's first ascents, 155n
White House, Carson City, Nev., 119
White House, Washington, D.C., 25, 140, 208, 217, 266, 268, 287, 289, 291, 337, 351, 374, 411
White Mountains, Calif., 192, 193
White Mountains, N.H, 191
White Pine Mountains, Nev., 194
White River, 234
White Star line, 312
Whitechapel, London, 317
Whitehall, N.Y., 38
Whitfield, Robert Parr, 224
Whitman, Walt, 347
Whitney, Helen Hay, 412, 413

Whitney Josiah Dwight, 57, 137, 197, 202, 343; directs California Geological Survey, 37, 40, 43, 52–90 *passim;* and Mount Shasta, 40, 143, 144; and King, 53, 58, 59, 68, 69, 73, 80, 85, 89, 105, 107 & n, 131, 152, 183, 188–89, 259, 267; authorizes High Sierra exploration, 60; on King's first try at Mount Whitney, 71; serves on Yosemite Commission, 75; subsidence theory of, to explain Yosemite, 77, 201–202; in East, 78, 79; *Geology,* 81, 146, 201; on King and Gardiner in Arizona, 81; Calaveras Skull and, 86–87; *The Yosemite Book,* 107n: opinion of, on Comstock Lode, 124; feud of, with B. Silliman, Jr., 131; Rocky Mountain expedition of, 133–34; publishes King's Mount Tyndall report, 146, 149; robbed by highwayman, 152; praises *Mining Industry,* 167; condemns Emma Mine, 190; attempt to remove name of, from Mount Whitney, 192; rejects glaciation as creator of Yosemite, 201; *Yosemite Guide-Book,* 201; recommended by Charles W. Eliot, 269
Whitney, Payne, 412
Whitney, William C., 99, 209
Whitney, William Dwight, 37, 80
Whitney, Mount, 153, 156, 193; naming of, 67, 69; King's first attempt to climb, 69, 71, 174; King climbs Sheep Rock instead of, 154, 179n; as site of S. P. Langley's solar observations, 154n; King climbs, 155, 192; elevation of, 155n; move to change name of, 192; Muir scales east face of, 202
Whitney Glacier, named by King, 143
Whitney Survey. *See* California Geological Survey
Wight, Peter B., 43
Wild Pigeon (ship), 19
Wild Tribes (Bancroft), 204
Wild West Show (Buffalo Bill's), 384
Wilde, Oscar, 310, 314, 326; *The Duchess of Padua,* 331
Wilkes, Charles, 37 & n; reports of, 135
Willett, promoter, 314

William Brown & Co. *See* Brown & Co.
Williams, Roger, 7
Williamson, James A., 257, 276–77
Williamson, R. S., 101, 106; Mount Williamson named for, 67, 90; recommends King, 90
Willis, Bailey, 287; on King's attitude toward geology, 188
Willis, William, 172, 182
Wilson, Allen D., 141; Diamond Swindle and, 175, 176, 178, 180; with U.S. Geological Survey, 278
Wilson, Richard B., 256
Wind River Mountains, 48
Windsor Park, England, 322
Windward Islands, 391, 392
Windward Passage, 391, 398
Winnemucca, Old (Paiute chief), 117, 123, 189
Winnemucca, Sarah. *See* Hopkins, Sarah Winnemucca
Winnemucca, Nev., 170
Winnemucca Lake, 109
Winthrop, Gov. John, 35n
Winthrop, Theodore, 35, 44, 116, 150, 303; *Cecil Dreeme*, 41; *John Brent*, 41, 212; *The Canoe and the Saddle*, 41
Wisconsin, University of, 201
Wister, Owen: *The Virginian*, 323
Wolcott, Edward Oliver, 204
Woods Hole, Mass., 140, 145
Woolsey, Theodore Dwight, 18
Wormley's Hotel, Washington, D.C., 262, 263, 264, 268, 283, 289
World War I, 412
Wright, George Frederick, 144 & n, 201
Wright's Canyon, Nev., 114
Wyoming, 1, 153, 170, 172, 176, 277; Paleozoic sediments in, 225; ND cattle drive across, 239: cattle in, for shipment to England, 323
Wyoming Stock Growers Association, 232, 235

Yale College (University), 18, 19, 31, 32, 33, 34, 35, 36, 38, 39, 43, 74, 134; status of, in 1869, 30; standard

reading at, 42; gives King's corps farewell dinner, 104; laboratories at, 140; King breaks news of glaciers at, 147; King Survey's geological collections transferred from, 199; King at, 201; O. C. Marsh's expedition from, 234; letter from, supporting King, 267; King reads paper at, 369; George Howland at, 383–84; declines to grant King LL.D., 409. *See also* Sheffield Scientific School; Yale Scientific School
Yale Banner, 31n
Yale Scientific School, 31, 52. *See also* Sheffield Scientific School; Yale College (University)
Yampa River (Bear River), 165, 175n
Yaqui Indians, 302, 343
Yavapais Indians, 82
Yedras (village), Sinaloa, Mexico, 304
Yedras Mine, Sinaloa, Mexico, 301, 305, 308, 310–11; Pumpelly examines, 300; developments at, 304–305; promotion of, 312, 314, 324, 382; sale of, 325–26; labor problems at, 342–43, 345n, 347; King reassesses, 344; King ousted from management of, 345, 352; production at, 345n; King's failure at, 347
Yedras Mining Co., 300, 301, 311, 326, 345
Yellowstone country, 397
Yosemite, 73, 88–89, 146, 207; King's first visit to, 59; 1864 survey of, 75–78, 152, 158; King and Gardiner's map of, 80; King at, in 1865, 86; F. A. Clark chains in, 103; Muybridge and Watkin's photograph, 142n; Whitney's subsidence theory of, 201–202; glaciation as creator of, 201–202; Muir's views on origin of, 202; Munger's paintings of, 329
Yosemite Book, The (Whitney), 107n; Whitney rejects King's notes for, 80
Yosemite Creek, 77
Yosemite Falls, 76; total drop of, 76 & n
Yosemite Guide-Book (Whitney), 201
Yosemite National Park, 362
Yosemite State Park, 75, 199
Yosemite Valley, 75, 77

Young, Brigham, 49, 132; attends King Survey sale, 136
Yuba River, upper, 189
Yucatán, Mexico, 310
Yukon country, 407
Yuma Indians, 82

Zacatecas, Mexico, 357, 403

Ziem, Felix, 329
"Zion's Corner" (Olyphant & Co.), 9, 13
Zirkel, Ferdinand, 200; completes memoir on King Survey rocks, 223
Zirkel, Mount, 200
Zorn, Anders, 329